Inferential Statistics Selection Guide

Number of Samples	Nature of Variable		
	Unordered Qualitative Variable	Ordered Qualitative Variable	Quantitative Variable
One sample	z test for p, 12.2* z interval for p, 12.2 χ^2 test for goodness of fit, 17.3 χ^2 test for independence, 17.4	z test for p, 12.2 z interval for p, 12.2 χ^2 test for goodness of fit, 17.3 χ^2 test for independence, 17.4	t test for μ, 10.2 t interval for μ, 11.2 t test for ρ, 12.3 z interval for ρ, 12.3
Two independent samples	z test for $p_1 - p_2$, 14.4 z interval for $p_1 - p_2$, 14.4	z test for $p_1 - p_2$, 14.4 z interval for $p_1 - p_2$, 14.4 Mann-Whitney U test, 18.3	t test for $\mu_1 - \mu_2$, 13.2 t interval for $\mu_1 - \mu_2$, 13.2 F test for σ_1^2 / σ_2^2, 14.2 F interval for σ_1^2 / σ_2^2, 14.2
Two dependent samples	z test for $p_1 - p_2$, 14.5 z interval for $p_1 - p_2$, 14.5	z test for $p_1 - p_2$, 14.5 z interval for $p_1 - p_2$, 14.5 Wilcoxon T test, 18.4	t test for $\mu_1 - \mu_2$, 13.4 t interval for $\mu_1 - \mu_2$, 13.4 t test for σ_1^2/σ_2^2, 14.3 t interval for σ_1^2/σ_2^2, 14.3
Multiple independent samples	χ^2 test for equality of p's, 17.5 χ^2 test for homogeneity of p's, 17.5	χ^2 test for equality of p's, 17.5 χ^2 test for homogeneity of p's, 17.5	Completely randomized ANOVA design, 15.5 Fisher-Hayter test for μ's, 15.6, 16.4 Scheffé's test for μ's, 15.6, 16.4 Completely randomized factorial ANOVA design, 16.4
Multiple dependent samples			Randomized block ANOVA design, 16.3 Fisher-Hayter test for μ's, 16.3 Scheffé's test for μ's, 16.3

*Section where statistic is described.

STATISTICS
An Introduction

FIFTH EDITION

STATISTICS
An Introduction

Roger E. Kirk
Baylor University

THOMSON

WADSWORTH

Australia • Canada • Mexico • Singapore • Spain
United Kingdom • United States

THOMSON

WADSWORTH

Statistics
Roger E. Kirk

Publisher: Michele Sordi
Assistant Editor: Gina Kessler
Editorial Assistant: Christina Ganim
Technology Project Manager: Lauren Keyes
Marketing Manager: Karin Sandberg
Marketing Assistant: Natasha Coats
Senior Marketing Communications Manager: Linda Yip
Content Project Manager: Karol Jurado
Creative Director: Rob Hugel
Senior Art Director: Vernon Boes
Print Buyer: Doreen Suruki

Permissions Editor: Sarah D'Stair
Production Service: Pre-Press Company, Inc.
Text Designer: John Edeen
Copy Editor: Karen Carriere
Illustrator: Pre-Press Company, Inc.
Cover Designer: Brenda Duke Design
Cover Image: Hoberman Collection (from Photonica)
Cover Printer: RR Donnelley Crawfordsville
Compositor: Pre-Press Company, Inc.
Printer: RR Donnelley Crawfordsville

Printed in the United States of America
1 2 3 4 5 6 7 11 10 09 08 07

Library of Congress Control Number: 2006933545

ISBN-13: 978-0-534-56478-0
ISBN-10: 0-534-56478-X

Thomson Higher Education
10 Davis Drive
Belmont, CA 94002–3098
USA

For more information about our products, contact us at:
Thomson Learning Academic Resource Center
1–800–423–0563

For permission to use material from this text or product, submit a request online at
http://www.thomsonrights.com.
Any additional questions about permissions can be submitted by e-mail to **thomsonrights@thomson.com.**
ExamView® and ExamView Pro® are registered trademarks of FSCreations, Inc. Windows is a registered trademark of the Microsoft Corporation used herein under license. Macintosh and Power Macintosh are registered trademarks of Apple Computer, Inc. Used herein under license.

Preface

Statistics: An Introduction was written for students in the behavioral sciences, health sciences, and education who are taking their first course in statistics. Its goals are twofold: to provide a sound introduction to descriptive and inferential statistics and to help students read and understand statistical presentations in their field.

The fifth edition of *Statistics* reflects more than four decades of experience teaching introductory statistics to almost 5,000 students. During this time I have seen the profound impact that advances in technology—computers, calculators, the Internet, and multimedia classrooms—have had on the way I teach statistics and the way my students learn statistics. The time-honored approach of teaching students to mechanically follow cookbook formulas is no longer appropriate. Computers and calculators have taken the drudgery out of statistics and broadened the students' statistical horizons. Now students can compute the most complex statistics in a matter of seconds. As a result, students need to understand the assumptions and limitations of the procedures they use, they need guidelines to help them decide when to use various procedures, and they need to understand the logic of the procedures. In addition, they need a foundation for understanding statistical presentations in their field. *Statistics* was written to meet these needs.

The fifth edition has been extensively revised in response to recommendations in the 2001 *Publication Manual of the American Psychological Association* (APA). The manual recommends that researchers provide sufficient descriptive statistics—sample sizes, means, standard deviations, and correlations—so that readers can understand the results being reported. The manual also recommends reporting confidence intervals and measures of effect size. In keeping with this recommendation, confidence intervals and measures of effect size are presented alongside traditional null hypothesis significance tests. Because students do statistics on computers and calculators, the focus throughout the text is on definitional formulas.

Other changes include (1) a greater emphasis on visual approaches to understanding data such as box plots and graphs of confidence intervals and (2) numerous examples, interspersed throughout the text, of the way statistical results are presented in scientific publications. The examples follow APA publication guidelines. In response to reviewers' comments, I have simplified the discussion of probability and selected advanced topics.

Students will find this edition easier to read. Feedback from students has enabled me to identify and simplify the hard places. I remain convinced that clarity and readability can be achieved without sacrificing accuracy and depth of coverage. In this edition, I continue to rely on verbal rather than mathematical explanations. To be sure, the student will encounter the usual formulas, but the level of mathematics is very elementary. A familiarity with high school algebra is sufficient for understanding the text. For those whose mathematical skills are rusty, Appendix A reviews elementary mathematics. Students can use the Test of Mathematical Skills in Appendix A to identify those procedures that they need to review.

Statistics contains many features that should make learning statistics easier. These features include (1) an overview of each chapter called "Looking Ahead: What Is This Chapter About?" that includes a list of learning objectives, (2) an expanded discussion in Chapter 1 of how to study statistics, (3) the use of color and boldface type to emphasize new terms and definitions, (4) an extensive glossary of statistical symbols (Appendix B), (5) "Check Your Understanding" exercises interspersed throughout each chapter, (6) a review at the end of each chapter called "Looking Back: What You Have Learned?" that highlights the most important ideas in the chapter, and (7) comprehensive review exercises at the end of each chapter. The exercises indicate which concepts and procedures are most important, present interesting real-life examples from journal articles of the way statistics are used, and provide practice in applying what has been learned. Answers are given in Appendix C for all of the "Check Your Understanding" exercises.

The student database in Appendix E provides additional sources of exercises. The database enables students to gain experience drawing random samples and computing statistics using real data. Students will find that selecting an appropriate statistic is easier with the help of the Selection Guide for descriptive and inferential statistics on the front endpaper. The back endpaper provides a quick reference for important formulas.

Students and professors will appreciate the Power Point transparencies and SPSS programs that are available on the companion website at

http://www.thomsonedu.com/psychology/kirk

The transparencies provide an outline of my lectures and the computational examples that I use in my teaching. The website also contains learning objectives; guides to new symbols, equations, and statistical tests; key terms; and more. An Instructor's Manual with Test Bank (available in paperback, as a download, or in the ExamView computerized test bank format) provides sources of supplementary teaching materials, multiple choice and essay questions for exams, and answers to all chapter review exercises in the text. For instructors, electronic transparencies provide most of the book's figures and tables in PowerPoint® slides, and JoinIn on Turning Point makes lectures interactive with in-class quizzing and polling.

It is a pleasure to express my appreciation to Dana Nelson, University of Washington; Charles Halcomb, Wichita State University; David Horner, California State Polytechnic University; Ron Salazar, San Juan College; Joan Michael, North Carolina State University; Russell Uyeno, TIM School, University of Hawaii; Thomas Nygren, Ohio State University; Jason Nier, Connecticut College; Mark Durn, Athens State University for reading the manuscript and for their thoughtful comments. Marcus Boggs, Erik Evans, Gina Kessler, Christina Ganim, Karin Sandberg, Linda Yip, Vernon Boes, and Karol Jurado of Thomson Wadsworth and Crystal

Parenteau of Pre-Press Company also deserve special recognition for their efforts in making this book a reality.

I am grateful to the literary executor of the late Sir Ronald A. Fisher, F. R. S., to Frank Yates, F. R. S., and to Longman Group Ltd., London, for permission to reprint Tables D.1, D.2, D.3, D.6, and D.7 from their book *Statistical Tables for Biological, Agricultural and Medical Research*, sixth edition (1974).

I am also grateful to E. S. Pearson and H. O. Hartley, editors of *Biometrika Tables for Statisticians*, Volume 1, and to the *Biometrika* trustees for permission to reprint Tables D.5 and D.9.

I want to express my appreciation to my statistics classes for what I trust has been a mutually rewarding learning experience. Comments about this edition and suggestions for future editions are most welcome. My web page

www.baylor.edu/~Psychology/Roger_Kirk/kirk.html

contains a list of typographical errors that is updated as they are discovered.

Roger E. Kirk

Roger_Kirk@baylor.edu

About the Author

Roger E. Kirk received his Ph.D. in experimental psychology from the Ohio State University and did postdoctoral study in mathematical psychology at the University of Michigan. He is a Distinguished Professor of Psychology and Statistics at Baylor University. He founded and, for 25 years, directed Baylor's Behavioral Statistics Ph.D. program and the Institute of Statistics, now the Department of Statistical Science. He has published extensively in the areas of statistics, psychoacoustics, and human engineering and is the author of five statistics books. His first book, *Experimental Design*: *Procedures for the Behavioral Sciences*, has been identified by the Institute for Scientific Information as one of the most frequently cited books in its field. Dr. Kirk is a fellow of the American Psychological Association (Divisions 1, 2, 5, and 13) and the American Psychological Society. He is a past president of the Society for Applied Multivariate Research, Division 5 of the American Psychological Association, and the Southwestern Psychological Association. In recognition of his teaching effectiveness, he was named the Outstanding Tenured Teacher in the College of Arts and Sciences and designated a Master Teacher, Baylor University's highest teaching honor. He is the 2005 recipient of the Jacob Cohen Award for Distinguished Contributions to Teaching and Mentoring from Division 5 of the American Psychological Association.

Contents

1 Introduction to Statistics 1

1.1 Introduction   2
1.2 Studying Statistics   4
1.3 Basic Concepts   6
1.4 Describing Characteristics by Numbers   11
1.5 Historical Development of Statistics   22
1.6 Looking Back: What Have You Learned?   24

2 Frequency Distributions and Graphs 29

2.1 Introduction   30
2.2 Frequency Distributions   30
2.3 Introduction to Graphs   41
2.4 Graphs for Qualitative Variables   41
2.5 Graphs for Quantitative Variables   44
2.6 Shapes of Distributions   48
2.7 Misleading Graphs   52
2.8 Looking Back: What Have You Learned?   54

3 Measures of Central Tendency 61

3.1 Introduction   62
3.2 Mode   62
3.3 Mean   64
3.4 Median   68
3.5 Relative Merits of the Mean,
      Median, and Mode   73
3.6 Location of the Mean, Median,
      and Mode in a Distribution   77
3.7 Mean of Two or More Means   78
3.8 More about the Summation Operator   79
3.9 Looking Back: What Have You Learned?   83

4 Measures of Dispersion, Skewness, and Kurtosis   89

4.1 Introduction   90
4.2 Four Measures of Dispersion   91
4.3 Relative Merits of the Measures of Dispersion   105
4.4 Dispersion and the Normal Distribution   109
4.5 Detecting Outliers   109
4.6 Skewness and Kurtosis   112
4.7 Looking Back: What Have You Learned?   115

5 Correlation   123

5.1 Introduction to Correlation   124
5.2 A Numerical Index of Correlation   127
5.3 Pearson Product-Moment Correlation Coefficient   129
5.4 Interpretation of Correlation Coefficient: Explained and Unexplained Variation   135
5.5 Some Common Errors in Interpreting a Correlation Coefficient   138
5.6 Factors That Affect the Size of a Correlation Coefficient   140
5.7 Spearman Rank Correlation   147
5.8 Other Kinds of Correlation Coefficients   151
5.9 Looking Back: What Have You Learned?   151

6 Regression   159

6.1 Introduction to Regression   160
6.2 Criterion for the Line of Best Fit   161
6.3 Another Measure of Ability to Predict: The Standard Error of Estimate   169
6.4 Assumptions Associated with Regression and the Standard Error of Estimate   172
6.5 Multiple Regression and Multiple Correlation   173
6.6 Looking Back: What Have You Learned?   178

7 Probability   183

7.1 Introduction to Probability   184
7.2 Basic Concepts   187

7.3 Probability of Combined Events   190
7.4 Counting Simple Events   198
7.5 Looking Back: What Have You Learned?   202

8 Random Variables and Probability Distributions   207

8.1 Introduction   208
8.2 Random Sampling   208
8.3 Random Variables and Their Distributions   212
8.4 Binomial Distribution   219
8.5 Looking Back: What Have You Learned?   224

9 Normal Distribution and Sampling Distributions   229

9.1 Introduction   230
9.2 The Normal Distribution   230
9.3 Interpreting Scores in Terms of z Scores and Percentile Ranks   238
9.4 Sampling Distributions   242
9.5 Looking Back: What Have You Learned?   250
9.6 Supplementary Notes   253

10 Statistical Inference: One-Sample Hypothesis Test   257

10.1 Introduction to Hypothesis Testing   258
10.2 Hypothesis Testing   263
10.3 One-Sample t Test for a Mean   271
10.4 More about Hypothesis Testing   274
10.5 Looking Back: What Have You Learned?   285

11 Statistical Inference: One-Sample Confidence Interval   291

11.1 Introduction   292
11.2 Confidence Interval for μ 293
11.3 Practical Significance   299
11.4 Looking Back: What Have You Learned?   302

12 Statistical Inference: Other One-Sample Test Statistics 307

12.1 Introduction to Other One-Sample Test Statistics 308
12.2 One-Sample z Test and Confidence Interval for a Proportion 308
12.3 One-Sample t Test and z Confidence Interval for a Correlation 315
12.4 Looking Back: What Have You Learned? 318

13 Statistical Inference: Two Samples 323

13.1 Introduction to Hypothesis Tests for Two Samples 324
13.2 Two-Sample t Test and Confidence Interval for $\mu_1 - \mu_2$ Using Independent Samples 324
13.3 Two Randomization Strategies: Random Sampling and Random Assignment 337
13.4 Two-Sample t Test and Confidence Interval for $\mu_1 - \mu_2$ Using Dependent Samples 341
13.5 Looking Back: What Have You Learned? 351

14 Statistical Inference: Other Two-Sample Test Statistics 361

14.1 Introduction 362
14.2 Two-Sample F Test and Confidence Interval for Variances Using Independent Samples 362
14.3 Two-Sample t Test and Confidence Interval for Variances Using Dependent Samples 370
14.4 Two-Sample z Test and Confidence Interval for Proportions Using Independent Samples 374
14.5 Two-Sample z Test and Confidence Interval for Proportions Using Dependent Samples 379
14.6 Looking Back: What Have You Learned? 383

15 Introduction to the Analysis of Variance 391

15.1 Introduction 392
15.2 Purpose of Analysis of Variance 392
15.3 Basic Concepts in ANOVA 394
15.4 Completely Randomized Design 403
15.5 Assumptions Associated with a CR-p Design 410
15.6 Multiple Comparison Procedures 412

15.7 Practical Significance   419
15.8 Looking Back: What Have You Learned?   422

16 Other Analysis of Variance Designs   429

16.1 Introduction   430
16.2 Basic Experimental Design Concepts   430
16.3 Randomized Block Design   435
16.4 Completely Randomized Factorial Design   446
16.5 Looking Back: What Have You Learned?   461

17 Statistical Inference for Frequency Data   467

17.1 Introduction   468
17.2 Three Applications of Pearson's Chi-Square Statistic   468
17.3 Testing Goodness of Fit   470
17.4 Testing Independence   477
17.5 Testing Equality of $c \geq 2$ Proportions   485
17.6 Looking Back: What Have You Learned?   490
17.7 Supplementary Note   496

18 Statistical Inference for Ranked Data   499

18.1 Introduction   500
18.2 Assumption-Freer Tests   500
18.3 Mann-Whitney U Test for Two Independent Samples   502
18.4 Wilcoxon T Test for Dependent Samples   507
18.5 Comparison of Parametric Tests and Assumption-Freer Tests for Ranked Data   512
18.6 Looking Back: What Have You Learned?   514

Appendixes   519

Appendix A: Review of Basic Mathematics   519
Appendix B: Glossary of Symbols   533
Appendix C: Answers to Check Your Understanding Exercises   541
Appendix D: Tables   599
Appendix E: Student Database   627
References   641
Index   645

STATISTICS

An Introduction

1

Introduction to Statistics

1.1 Introduction
Looking Ahead: What Is
  This Chapter About?
Some Misconceptions
What Is Statistics?
Why Study Statistics?
Kinds of Statisticians

1.2 Studying Statistics
Develop Effective Study
  Techniques
Plan to Read More Slowly
Don't Worry if You
  Weren't an Ace
  in Math
Resolve to Review Often
Master Foundation
  Concepts before Going
  on to New Material
Strive for Understanding

1.3 Basic Concepts
Population and Sample
  Defined
Descriptive and Inferential
  Statistics
Random Sampling
Check Your
  Understanding of
  Sections 1.1 to 1.3

**1.4 Describing
Characteristics
by Numbers**
Variables and Constants
Perspectives on Numbers
Classification of Variables
  in Mathematics
Measuring Operations in
  the Behavioral Sciences,
  Health Sciences, and
  Education
Nominal Measurement
Ordinal Measurement
Interval Measurement
Ratio Measurement
Implications of the Two
  Ways of Thinking about
  Numbers
Some Subtle Problems in
  Interpreting Numbers
Check Your Understanding
  of Section 1.4

**1.5 Historical Development
of Statistics**
National Statistics
Probability Theory
Experimental Statistics
Check Your
  Understanding
  of Section 1.5

**1.6 Looking Back: What
Have You Learned?**
Review Exercises for
  Chapter 1

1.1 INTRODUCTION

Looking Ahead: What Is This Chapter About?

When a student came to me recently for help with statistics, I posed the question, "What is the chapter about?" The student's answer, "About 36 pages," was not what I had hoped to hear. To give you a heads up, I provide a brief overview at the beginning of each chapter.

This chapter begins with a discussion of what statistics is and why you should study it. I then share tips for studying statistics and define some basic concepts: population, sample, and random sample. You will learn that there are two broad categories of statistics: descriptive statistics and inferential statistics. The chapter continues with a discussion of the way mathematicians classify variables and the rules psychologists and others use to assign numbers to characteristics of people. For history buffs, I end the chapter with a brief description of the origins of statistics.

After reading the chapter, you should know the following:

- What statistics is
- Why you should study it (although you might prefer almost any other form of torture)
- How to study statistics
- The meaning of basic concepts such as population, sample, and random sample
- The two broad categories of statistics
- The way mathematicians classify variables and the way psychologists measure characteristics
- The origins of statistics

Some Misconceptions

It is widely believed that statistics can be used to prove anything—which implies, of course, that it can prove nothing. Furthermore, the word *statistics* conjures up visions of numbers piled upon numbers, uninterpretable charts, and computers cranking out gloomy predictions. To the ordinary person, besieged from all sides by advertising claims, statistics is hocus-pocus with numbers. It was Benjamin Disraeli who said, "There are three kinds of lies—lies, damned lies, and statistics."[1] In primitive cultures, exaggeration was common. One writer, with tongue in cheek, reasoned that because primitive people did not have a science of statistics, they were forced to rely on exaggeration, which is a less effective form of deception. Another writer remarked, "If all the statisticians in the world were laid end to end—it would be a good thing." Whatever its public image, statistics endures as a required course, and my students continue to refer to it, affectionately no doubt, as Sadistics 2402.

---

[1] Three books indicate that Disraeli's view of statistics is still with us: *How to Tell the Liars from the Statisticians* by Hooke and Liles, *Misused Statistics: Straight Talk for Twisted Numbers* by Jaffe and Spirer, and *Statistical Deception at Work* by Mauro.

What Is Statistics?

In spite of frequent misuse, statistics can be a powerful tool for making decisions in the face of uncertainty. The word *statistics* comes from the Latin *status*, which is also the root for our modern term *state* or political unit. Statistics was a necessary tool of the state, because to levy a tax or to wage war a ruler had to know the number of subjects in the state and the amount of their wealth. Gradually the meaning of the term expanded to include any type of data.

> Today the word **statistics** has four distinct meanings. Depending on the context, it can mean (1) data; (2) functions of data, such as the mean and range; (3) techniques for collecting, analyzing, and interpreting data for subsequent decision making; and (4) the science of creating and applying such techniques.

Why Study Statistics?

A knowledge of statistics yields more than the obvious benefits. For example, it generates new ways of thinking about questions and effective tools for answering them. It takes only a cursory examination of the professional literature in your field to see the inroads made by statistical techniques and ways of thinking. Statistics helps researchers make sense of data and is an indispensable research tool, but its usefulness is not limited to research. In many fields, it is virtually impossible to read research articles and keep up with new developments without an understanding of elementary statistics. Also, statistics is an interesting subject—some people even find it fascinating.

In all likelihood, you are reading this book because it was assigned in your required statistics course. You have been told that the study of statistics is necessary, and there is a strong implication that it will be good for you. At this point you may be skeptical. Just what can you expect to learn by studying statistics? A quick scan of this book will give you an idea. You will acquire a new vocabulary, because in many ways learning statistics is like learning a foreign language, and you will learn to manipulate numbers according to symbolic instructions. But more important, you will learn when and how to apply statistics to research problems in the behavioral sciences, health sciences, and education. Your study of statistics should enable you to read the literature in your field with greater understanding and make you a more critical consumer of statistical presentations in the mass media. And you should gain a greater appreciation of the probabilistic nature of scientific knowledge. Statistics involves a special way of thinking that can be used not only in research but also in one's daily life. I hope that you will add this way of thinking to your conceptual arsenal.

Kinds of Statisticians

> Users of statistics fall into four categories: (1) those who must be able to read and understand statistical presentations in their field; (2) those who select, apply, and interpret statistical procedures in their work; (3) applied statisticians; and (4) mathematical statisticians.

This book addresses those in the first two categories, including psychologists, educators, speech therapists, biologists, nurses, medical researchers, and physical therapists, to mention only a few. In each case the person's primary interest is in his or her own field, be it counseling or physical therapy; he or she is interested in statistics because it is a useful tool for answering questions in that field. These people are both consumers and users of statistics. Their knowledge of statistics can range from meager to expert.

The applied statistician helps professionals in substantive areas to use statistics effectively. He or she may work for industry or a government agency, engage in a private consulting practice, or teach in a university. Unlike individuals in the first two categories, an applied statistician usually has advanced degrees in statistics.

The mathematical statistician is primarily interested in pure (mathematical) statistics and probability theory rather than in the application of statistics to substantive areas. Most likely this statistician teaches in a university and makes contributions to the theoretical foundations of statistics that may ultimately be used by those with applied interests.

1.2 STUDYING STATISTICS

Develop Effective Study Techniques

Psychologists say that learning is easier when you can integrate new information into an existing knowledge base. Unfortunately, as you begin your study of statistics, your statistical knowledge base is minimal. Building a knowledge base is easier if you use effective study techniques. For example, always survey your reading material by thumbing through the assigned pages and noting topic headings and boldface terms. Try to get a sense of what the material is about. Your survey will provide a general orientation to the material and help you fit facts together as you develop your statistical knowledge base.

Before you begin reading a section in the text, turn the section heading into a question. The question for this section might be, "What are some effective study techniques?" After you have formed your question, look for the answer as you read the section. Research on learning tells us that an active, searching attitude on the part of the reader promotes better learning than does a passive attitude. After reading a section, try to recall the main points of the section by reciting out loud. All of us have had the experience of reading a paragraph and having no idea of what we have just read. Knowing that we will attempt to recall what we are reading develops a mental set to select and retain important facts.

Most forgetting takes place within the first 24 to 48 hours after learning. You can minimize the forgetting process by reviewing your assignment a day or so after reading it. Look at the major headings and boldface terms and see whether you can recite the main points that were covered in the section and define each boldface term. If the contents of some sections are hazy, reread these sections and see whether you can then recall the main points.[2]

---

[2] These study suggestions are based on the famous SQ3R study method developed by Francis P. Robinson (1946). The letters SQ3R stand for *Survey, Question, Read, Recite,* and *Review.*

Plan to Read More Slowly

Statistics cannot be read like assignments in history, English, or political science. Ideas and computational procedures in statistics are presented in a highly symbolic form and use a specialized vocabulary that you must learn. Consequently, a 30-page assignment may take three or four times as long to read as a comparable assignment in history. You will understand many sections of this book on a first reading; others will require two or more readings, lots of concentration, and perhaps some time between readings for the ideas to sink in.

Don't Worry If You Weren't an Ace in Math

If you're concerned about the level of mathematics required to understand statistics, stop worrying. Most statistical procedures in this book involve nothing more complicated than addition, subtraction, multiplication, and division. Although this book makes some use of high school algebra, the level is very elementary. For those whose skills are rusty, the essential arithmetic and algebra are reviewed in Appendix A.

Appendix A also contains a diagnostic math test that you can take to assess your math skills and see if you have forgotten anything. I encourage you to check out your skill level by taking the test and grading your performance. I have provided a table of norms based on the scores of my students over the past 10 years.

But don't get too hung up on mathematics. Treat this course less like a math course and more like a course in logic. You should focus on the concepts and the logic underlying statistical procedures. Leave the mathematics and computations to calculators and computers.

Resolve to Review Often

Unless you frequently review this material, it will slip away. Don't skip the *Check Your Understanding* exercises at the end of each section and the end-of-chapter *Review Exercises*. They (1) provide feedback about what you know and what you don't, (2) indicate which concepts and computational procedures are the most important, (3) offer numerous examples of how statistics are used, and (4) give you practice in applying what you are learning. Answers to all of the *Check Your Understanding* exercises are given in Appendix C. The "Looking Back: What Have You Learned?" section at the end of each chapter also is useful for reviewing because it showcases the most important concepts and places the topics in perspective.

The best way to learn statistics is to *do* statistics. By doing the *Check Your Understanding* exercises "by hand" with the aid of a calculator you will gradually learn how to follow the sequence of mathematical operations represented by a formula. Computing a statistic by hand helps to develop an intuitive understanding of the statistic. Once you have an intuitive understanding, it is time to let a computer do the work.

Master Foundation Concepts before Going on to New Material

In statistics, as in mathematics or a foreign language, the material presented first is the foundation for what follows. It is best to master each chapter before you go on to the next. Fight the temptation to cram. Cramming can be effective for some subjects, at least as far as tests are concerned. But in statistics, it inevitably results in a superficial understanding of basic concepts and subsequent learning problems. Periodic reviews require discipline, but they pay off.

Strive for Understanding

This book contains hundreds of formulas. I have not memorized all of them, and neither should you. Some, such as the one for the arithmetic mean, $\overline{X} = \sum X/n$, appear so often that you really can't help learning them; the others aren't worth the effort. I decided a long time ago, when faced with my inability to remember telephone numbers and addresses, that books are better repositories than my head for such things. In all likelihood you will do most of your statistical calculations with computers and calculators. These tools have phenomenal memories for formulas and can spew out statistics at the press of a key.

Instead of memorizing formulas, strive to understand the logic underlying the statistical procedures that you are learning, and think about ways that each new statistic can be applied. In what situations is the statistic useful? How is the statistic interpreted? What assumptions must be fulfilled to interpret the statistic? When you read about an experiment in your field, consider how you would have designed it and how you would have analyzed the data. And check out your ideas by talking about them with your professor and other students. There is no better way to deepen your understanding of a new concept than to explain it to a classmate.

1.3 BASIC CONCEPTS

Population and Sample Defined

Many statistical terms are a legacy from the time when statistics was concerned only with the condition of the state. *Population*, for example, originally meant, and still means, the total number of inhabitants of a state. Its meaning in statistics is broader.

> A **population** is the collection of all people, objects, or events having one or more specified characteristics.

The population is identified when you specify its common characteristics. All the people listed in a telephone directory constitute a population, as does the number of heads and tails obtained in tossing a coin for eternity.

> A single person, object, or event is called an **element** of the population.

The population of telephone book listees contains a **finite** number of elements; the population resulting from tossing the coin contains an **infinite** number.

A population is either concrete or conceptual. For example, the population of telephone book listees is **concrete**—given sufficient time you could contact each person because the number of elements is finite and the population is well defined.

The population of heads and tails is **conceptual**—try as you may, you cannot record all the results of tossing a coin for eternity. This population exists as an idea rather than as a material object.

A population could consist of all the students in a university (people), their cars (objects), or their pep rallies (events).

> The number or label used to represent an element of the population is called an **observation** or **datum.**

It is a measurable characteristic of the elements. The observation for students in a university might be their GPAs, their cars' gas mileage, or the number attending pep rallies. If 362 students attended the second pep rally, the observation for this event is 362 students. The selection of an appropriate population for an experiment is determined by the nature of the research questions that a researcher wants to answer as well as by such practical matters as the availability of population elements.

> A **sample** is a proper subset of a population.

That is, a sample can contain a single element or all but one of the population elements. For practical reasons—such as limited resources and time or because the population is infinite in size—most research is carried out with samples rather than with populations. It is assumed that the study of a sample will reveal something about the population. This leap of faith often appears to be justified, as when a laboratory technician analyzes a sample of a patient's blood or when an automobile manufacturer crash-tests a sample of bumpers. Occasionally, however, samples lead us astray. Later you'll see how and why.

Descriptive and Inferential Statistics

It is useful to divide statistical techniques into two broad categories: descriptive and inferential.

> **Descriptive statistics** are tools for depicting or summarizing data so that they can be more readily comprehended.

When we say that a player's lifetime batting average is .420 or when we determine that 51% of voters favor a presidential candidate, we are using descriptive statistics. A computer printout listing the Scholastic Aptitude Test (SAT) scores of all college students in California would boggle our minds; however, a statement that their mean SAT score is 1094 would not. Large masses of data are difficult to comprehend. Descriptive statistics reduce data to some form, usually a number, that one can easily comprehend. I discuss a variety of descriptive statistics in the first half of this book.

It is usually impossible for researchers to observe all the elements in a population. Instead they observe a sample of elements and generalize from the sample to all the elements—a process called **induction** in which the researcher reasons from the particular facts or cases to draw general conclusions.

> Researchers are aided in this process by **inferential statistics,** which are tools for inferring the properties of one or more populations by inspecting samples drawn from the populations.

Inferential statistics were developed to improve decision making in cases where successive observations exhibit some degree of variation although they are obtained under conditions that appear to be identical. The variation may be due to (1) the inherent variability in the phenomenon being observed or differences among participants, (2) errors of measurement, (3) undetected changes in conditions, or (4) a combination of these factors. In the behavioral sciences, health sciences, and education, differences in the past experiences and heredities of participants are the major stumbling blocks to inferring the properties of populations from observing samples.

Inferential statistics are useful for answering questions such as the following. A medical researcher wants to know whether a new drug will arrest the development of cancer in humans. It is impossible to administer the drug to the population of all cancer patients, but it is possible to administer the drug to a sample. The medical researcher would probably attempt to control attitudinal and other extraneous factors by administering an inert druglike substance, a *placebo*, to half the sample and the new drug to the other half. Consider two possible outcomes of the experiment. In one outcome, the remission of cancer occurs in 100% of the sample receiving the new drug and in only 8% of those receiving the placebo. The difference, 100% versus 8%, between the drug and placebo samples is dramatic. The medical researcher would probably conclude without the benefit of inferential statistics that if the drug had been administered to the population of all cancer victims, the remission rate would have been much higher than if the population had received the placebo. Consider now a different outcome. What if the remission rate were only 12% for the new drug and 8% for the placebo? Is the drug really more effective than the placebo? I know from years of conducting experiments that chance factors can produce a difference between two samples even though the samples are taken from the same population and receive identical treatments. Is the difference, 12% versus 8%, greater than would be expected by chance? Stated another way, if the experiment were repeated many, many times, could the medical researcher predict with confidence that over the long run the difference would favor the sample receiving the drug? This is the kind of question that can be answered using inferential statistics. I describe procedures for answering such questions in the second half of the book.

Random Sampling

Some samples provide a sound basis for drawing conclusions about populations; others do not. The difference lies in the method by which the samples are selected.

> The method of drawing samples from a population such that every possible sample of a particular size has an equal chance of being selected is called **random sampling,** and the resulting samples are **random samples.**

People, when left to their own devices, find it virtually impossible to produce random samples. Consider the following experiment. One hundred people are asked to write down a random sample of four numbers from the first 20 positive integers. According to our definition of random sampling, samples containing the elements 1, 2, 3, 4 or 14, 16, 18, or 20, for example, should occur as frequently as any other sample of size four. It turns out that such samples are rarely produced. People avoid writing down samples with consecutive or equally spaced integers and attempt to produce samples that span the range from 1 to 20.

Sampling methods based on haphazard or purposeless choices, such as soliciting volunteers, using students enrolled in introductory psychology, or selecting every 10th person in an alphabetical listing of names, produce **nonrandom samples.** Such samples, unlike random samples, do not provide a sound basis for deducing the properties of populations. Hence, in this book, sampling refers to random sampling. A detailed discussion of random sampling in Chapter 8 must await the development of other basic concepts. At this point, I will simply illustrate several characteristics of random samples.

Consider a box containing 300 balls, each identified by a number stamped on its surface. Of the balls, 200 are red (R) and 100 are black (B). If you did not know the ratio of red to black balls, which is two to one (denoted by 2:1), you could estimate the ratio by drawing a random sample of balls from the box. You close your eyes, shake the box vigorously, reach in, withdraw a ball, note its color and number, and replace it. You do this six times and obtain the following sample: R_{102}, R_{75}, B_{39}, R_{62} B_{37}, R_{50}. The subscripts, 102, 75, and so on denote the numbers stamped on the balls. From this sample you would infer that the box contains more red than black balls—in fact, twice as many red balls. Suppose you drew four more samples, each time replacing the balls drawn, and obtained the following:

Sample 2	R_{154}, B_{62}, R_{35}, R_{143}, R_4, R_{29}
Sample 3	R_{104}, B_{41}, B_{21}, R_{50}, R_{192}, R_{67}
Sample 4	B_{28}, B_{41}, R_{150}, B_{61}, R_{88}, R_{148}
Sample 5	R_{152}, R_{120}, B_{88}, R_{33}, R_{36}, B_5

The results of the five random samples are summarized in Table 1.3-1.

This simple experiment illustrates several points about random samples. First, the elements obtained (and the ratio of red to black balls) differ from sample to sample. This is referred to as **sampling fluctuation** or **chance variability.** Second, the

TABLE 1.3-1   Outcomes of Drawing Five Random Samples

	Sample				
Color of Balls	*1*	*2*	*3*	*4*	*5*
Number of red balls	4	5	4	3	4
Number of black balls	2	1	2	3	2
Ratio of red to black	2:1	5:1	2:1	1:1	2:1

characteristics of a sample do not necessarily correspond to those in the population. It turns out, however, that the larger a random sample, the more likely it is to resemble closely the population. Hence, researchers prefer to work with large samples if it is economically feasible. Although there is no guarantee that large random samples will resemble the population, in the long run they are more likely to do so than small ones.

CHECK YOUR UNDERSTANDING OF SECTIONS 1.1 TO 1.3[3]

1. Users of statistics fall into four categories.
   a. List the categories.
   b. Considering your vocational goals, into which category do you fall? Why?
2. For each of the following statements, indicate (a) the population, (b) the element, and (c) the observation to be recorded.
   a. At least 50% of white women students in this university are ambivalent about having a career.
   b. Tequila Tech students are involved in more automobile accidents than other drivers in their age group.
   c. At least 23% of the homes in Chickasha, Oklahoma, have high-definition televisions.
   d. Students at Ginebra University who hold outside jobs have higher grade point averages than those who do not hold outside jobs.
   e. According to a recent Centers for Disease Control report, 1 of every 92 American men between the ages of 27 and 39 has the AIDS virus.
   f. According to the U.S. Department of Education, 49.5% of female high school students have performed a community service during the past two years.
3. What are the lower and upper limits on the size of a sample?
4. Indicate whether each of the following procedures would produce a random sample (R) or a nonrandom sample (NR) of students in an introductory psychology class.
   a. Write each student's name on a slip of paper, place the slips in a hat, shake the hat thoroughly, and draw out 10 names.
   b. Place the blindfolded instructor in the middle of a circle made up of all the class members. Have the instructor point to 10 people around the circle. The student nearest to where the instructor points becomes an element of the sample.
   c. For each student, flip a fair coin. If the coin lands heads, the student is in the sample.
   d. Line up the students from the tallest to the shortest. The 3rd, 5th, 7th, . . . , 21st students become members of the sample.

---

[3] Answers to the *Check Your Understanding* exercises are given in Appendix C. These exercises often contain multiple questions about a particular concept. If you have a good grasp of the concept, answering three or four questions about it may not be an efficient use of your time. If, however, your answer to a question is incorrect, reviewing the concept in the text and then answering several more questions dealing with the concept is advisable. One of the purposes of these exercises is to provide feedback about what you know and what you don't know.

5. Terms to remember:
   a. Statistics
   b. Population
   c. Element
   d. Observation (datum)
   e. Sample
   f. Descriptive statistics
   g. Induction
   h. Inferential statistics
   i. Random sample
   j. Nonrandom sample
   k. Sampling fluctuation (chance variability)

1.4 DESCRIBING CHARACTERISTICS BY NUMBERS

People, objects, and events have many distinguishable characteristics. Early in the design of an experiment, the researcher must make two key decisions: What characteristics should I measure? And how should I measure them? The answer to the first question is determined by the researcher's interests. Suppose a researcher is interested in comparing the SAT scores of men and women college students. College students differ in many ways: gender, age, SAT scores, major, hair color, family income, and so forth, but only two characteristics are of interest in this example: gender and SAT score. The researcher will measure these characteristics and ignore the others. The second question, concerning how the characteristics should be measured, is less straightforward. The issue here is how to assign numbers to people, objects, or events so that the numbers accurately reflect the characteristic you want to measure. In the process of examining this issue, I will discuss variables and constants and see how mathematicians classify variables.

Variables and Constants

A **variable** is a characteristic that can take on different values. A variable also is a symbol, often a letter toward the end of the alphabet, such as X or Y, that is used to stand for an unspecified element of a set.

The set of elements for which the variable stands is called the **range** of the variable, and each element of the range is called a **value.** When I assign to a variable one of the elements in its range, I say that the variable "takes" this value. For example, the variable of gender might take the value "women."

A **constant** is a characteristic that does not vary. A constant also is a symbol, often a letter toward the beginning of the alphabet, such as a, b, or c, whose range consists of a single element.

The ratio of the circumference of a circle to its diameter, denoted by π, is a constant because its range consists of the single value 3.1415926536 . . . .

Perspectives on Numbers

I noted that the selection of the characteristics to be measured is relatively straight-forward and is determined by the researcher's interests. The second key decision—deciding how the characteristics should be measured or classified—is not as simple. For example, you could measure or classify the scholastic aptitude of seniors at Linden McKinley High by (1) assigning each student a label such as average, high average, or superior, based on his or her SAT score; (2) ranking or ordering students' SAT scores from highest to lowest and assigning each student the number of his or her rank; or (3) assigning each student her or his actual SAT score. Depending on the measuring scheme adopted, Jonathan Whiz would be designated, respectively, superior, 3, or 1480. The variable of political preference can be classified by assigning a unique symbol such as D or 1 to Democrats, I or 2 to independents, and R or 3 to Republicans.

The assignment of numbers or labels to characteristics of people, objects, or events and the accuracy of the representation are central concerns of researchers. This is not true for mathematicians. Mathematicians often manipulate symbols that are totally devoid of empirical meaning. They are interested in the formal properties of the systems they create; applications in the real world are often left to other specialists. Mathematicians and mathematical statisticians have laid the foundation for a vast collection of statistical tools. The researcher who uses these tools must decide whether a particular tool is appropriate for his or her research application and whether the numbers assigned to variables accurately represent the characteristics of interest. This division of interest between the developers and the users of statistics has led to two ways of thinking about numbers.

Classification of Variables in Mathematics

Mathematicians classify variables as qualitative or quantitative.

> A **qualitative variable** is a symbol whose range consists of attributes or nonquantitative characteristics of people, objects, or events. For example, the letter X could represent gender (men, women), Y could represent race (Caucasian, African American, Asian, other), and Z could represent the grade in a course (A, B, C, D, or F).

The categories of a qualitative variable are (1) mutually exclusive (nonoverlapping), which implies that an element cannot be in more than one category, and (2) exhaustive, which implies that an element must be in one of the categories. The categories may or may not suggest an order or rank. For example, grades in a course—A, B, C, D, or F—clearly order academic achievement from highest to lowest, but no order is suggested by the categories for gender, race, religious preference, or blood type. Course grade is an example of an **ordered qualitative variable.** Gender, race, religious preference, and blood type are examples of **unordered qualitative variables.**

> A **quantitative variable** is a symbol whose range consists of a count or a numerical measurement of a characteristic.

Quantitative variables can be discrete or continuous. A variable is **discrete** if its range can assume only a finite number of values or an infinite number of values that is countable. That is, the infinite number of values can be placed in a one-to-one correspondence with the counting or natural numbers. Family size is an example of a variable with a finite range. It can assume values 1, 2, 3, 4, and so on, but not 200, 8000, or any noninteger value such as 0.5 and 4.3. The rational numbers—numbers that can be expressed as the ratio of two integers, for example, 2/2, −2/3, or 7/4— illustrate countably infinite numbers. There is no largest number and no smallest number, and between, say, 1 and 2, an infinite number of rationals can be inserted, for example, 3/2, 4/3, 5/4. . . . Other examples of discrete quantitative variables are the number of parking tickets received, the number of trials required to learn a list of nonsense syllables, and one's score on a standardized achievement test. In each of these examples, the value assigned to the variable is obtained by counting, and the counting units—family members, parking tickets, learning trials, or achievement test items—are equivalent in arriving at the total count.

By contrast, a variable is **continuous** if its range is uncountably infinite. Such a range can be likened to points on a line that have no interruptions or intervening spaces between them. Examples of continuous variables are temperature in Bangor, Maine, during January, length of fish caught off the Florida Keys, and speed of cars on the New Jersey Turnpike. Although a variable is continuous, our measurement of it is by necessity discrete because of limitations in the measuring instrument. For example, the thermometer is usually calibrated in 1° steps, the ruler in 1/16 inch, and the speedometer in 1 mile per hour. Consequently, our measurement of continuous variables is always approximate. Discrete variables, on the other hand, can be measured exactly. A husband and wife with two children are a family of exactly four, but a temperature of 80°F can be any temperature between 79.5° and 80.5°F.

The classification scheme for variables is summarized in Table 1.4-1. It is useful to mathematicians and statisticians because the nature of the variable determines which mathematical tools can be used to solve problems and do derivations and proofs. Hence, the classification scheme is a convenience; it was not devised to mirror characteristics in the real world. When you use statistical methods to answer real-world questions, you must remember that the methods were developed to analyze numbers as

TABLE 1.4-1 Mathematicians' Classification of Variables

Type of Variable	Characteristics
Qualitative variable	Range consists of nonoverlapping and exhaustive categories that represent attributes or nonquantitative characteristics.
Unordered	Categories do not suggest an order or rank.
Ordered	Categories suggest an order or rank.
Quantitative variable	Range consists of a count or a numerical measurement of a characteristic.
Discrete	Range consists of only a finite number of values or an infinite number of values that is countable.
Continuous	Range consists of an uncountably infinite number of values.

numbers. If the numbers analyzed bear no relation to the characteristics in which you are interested, the statistical methods will yield answers that are meaningless.

Measuring Operations in the Behavioral Sciences, Health Sciences, and Education

Numbers are used for a variety of purposes, three of which are of particular interest to behavioral scientists, health scientists, and educators: (1) to serve as labels, (2) to indicate rank in a series, and (3) to represent quantity. For example, a football player is identified by the number 10 on his uniform, a team is ranked number two in the UPI poll, and the winning touchdown play covered 20 yards. Without thinking, you treat these numbers differently. It doesn't take a football fan to know that player 30 is not three times player 10 and that the number two team is not necessarily twice as good as the number four team, but a 20-yard touchdown play did indeed move the ball twice as far down the field as a 10-yard play. You intuitively treat the numbers differently because they involve different levels of measurement.

> **Measurement** is the process of assigning numbers or labels to characteristics of people, objects, or events according to a set of rules.

You will see that the rules used to assign the numbers or labels determine the level of measurement. S. S. Stevens (1946), a behavioral scientist, identified four levels of measurement: nominal, ordinal, interval, and ratio.

Nominal Measurement

> **Nominal measurement** is the simplest of the four levels. It consists of assigning elements to mutually exclusive and exhaustive *equivalence classes* so that those in the same class are considered to be equivalent to one another, whereas those in different classes are not equivalent. The classes are then denoted by a set of distinct labels. The set of labels constitutes a **nominal scale.**

The assignment of men to one equivalence class called "men" and women to the other called "women" is nominal measurement. The set of labels, "men" and "women," constitutes a nominal scale. Numbers can be used instead of words to identify the two classes, for example, 1 for women and 2 for men. Numbers used in this way are simply alternative labels for the equivalence classes. You could just as well have assigned the numbers 9 and 6, respectively, to women and men. The substitution of the number 9 for 1 and the number 6 for 2 is an example of a **one-to-one transformation.**[4] The numbers 9 and 6 are as useful for distinguishing between the equivalence classes as any other one-to-one transformation. The numbers in a

---

[4] A one-to-one transformation associates with each element in one set one and only one element in a second set and vice versa. For example, if one set is men's names {Jim, Chuck, Keith} and the second set is numbers {5, 12, 3}, each name can be paired with one and only one number. A one-to-one transformation could result in substituting 12 for Jim, 3 for Chuck, and 5 for Keith.

nominal scale could be added, subtracted, averaged, and so on, but the resulting numbers would tell us nothing about the equivalence classes represented by the numbers. For example, $1 + 2 = 3$ and $9 + 6 = 15$, but neither 3 nor 15 corresponds to any characteristic of men or women. This follows because we did not utilize the properties of size and order of numbers when we assigned them to the classes. The only property of numbers that we utilized is that 1 is distinct (different) from 2, 3. . . .Thus, the labels assigned to equivalence classes in nominal measurement have the property only of *distinctness.*

There are many examples of nominal scales in psychology and education, for example, Eysenck's four personality types (stable-extrovert, stable-introvert, unstable-extrovert, unstable-introvert), the primary taste qualities (sweet, sour, salty, bitter), and categories of psychoses (organic, functional). There is a correspondence between a nominal scale and the range of one of the mathematician's types of variables. The nominal scale corresponds to the range of an unordered qualitative variable.

Ordinal Measurement

Ordinal measurement consists of assigning elements to mutually exclusive and exhaustive equivalence classes that are ranked or ordered with respect to one another. The classes are then denoted by numbers or other ordered symbols, such as letters of the alphabet, that reflect the rank of the classes. The labels assigned to equivalence classes in ordinal measurement have the properties of *distinctness* and *order*. The set of labels constitutes an **ordinal scale.**

The labels used in ordinal measurement contain more information than those in nominal scales: both distinctness and order.

The ranking of political candidates with respect to voter appeal is an example of ordinal measurement. If candidate Jane is judged to have the greatest appeal, followed by Keith, Lewis, and then Marvin, I could assign Jane the number 1; Keith, 2; Lewis, 3; and Marvin, 4. I have no reason to believe that Keith, ranked second, is half as appealing to voters as Jane, or that the difference in appeal between Jane and Keith, 1 versus 2, is the same as the difference between Keith and Lewis, 2 versus 3. The numbers indicate rank order but not magnitude or difference in magnitude between classes. The numbers assigned to the equivalence classes can be subjected to any strictly increasing monotonic transformation. A **strictly increasing monotonic transformation** permits one to replace the original set of numbers with new numbers as long as the new numbers have the same order as the original numbers. For example, the set of ordered numbers 2, 16, 39, 40 would serve just as well as 1, 2, 3, 4 to rank the four candidates, because only the order and not the distance between any two numbers is important. Alternatively, I could assign the ordered letters of the alphabet to the candidates: *A* to Jane, *B* to Keith, *C* to Lewis, and *D* to Marvin. The transformations that can be applied to ordinal scales are more restrictive than those that can be applied to nominal scales. This follows because the labels in ordinal scales contain more information that needs to be preserved—both distinctness and order—than do the labels in nominal scales.

Some characteristics, such as people's heights, can be measured in several ways, for example, ranking from tallest to shortest or recording actual feet and inches. The latter procedure assigns numbers that represent the magnitudes of the equivalence classes and therefore has several advantages over ordinal measurement, as you shall see later. For the moment, simply note that ordinal measurement is most often used when it is difficult or impossible to apply more refined measuring procedures. For example, it is difficult to precisely measure the tastiness of three pizzas or the leadership qualities of four political candidates. However, it is not too difficult to rank-order pizzas with respect to tastiness or candidates with respect to leadership qualities.

Numerous examples of ordinal scales can be found in the behavioral sciences, health sciences, and education, for example, classification of mentally subnormal children (borderline, educable, trainable, profoundly retarded) and professorial rank (instructor, assistant professor, associate professor, professor). Such ordinal scales correspond, in the language of the mathematician, to the range of an ordered qualitative variable.

Interval Measurement

The numbers assigned in interval measurement contain much more information than the labels used in nominal and ordinal measurement.

> In **interval measurement,** the numbers assigned to equivalence classes have the properties of distinctness and order; in addition, equal differences between numbers reflect equal magnitude differences between the corresponding classes. The measurement procedure consists of defining a unit of measurement, such as a calendar year or 1°F, and determining the number of units required to represent the difference between equivalence classes. The set of numbers assigned to the equivalence classes constitutes an **interval scale.**

In our measurement of calendar time, the same amount of time elapsed between 1970 and 1971 as between 1971 and 1972, and, similarly, the temperature difference between 70° and 75°F is the same as that between 80° and 85°F. A given numerical interval, say 1 year or 5°F, represents the same difference in the characteristic measured, irrespective of the location of that interval along the measurement scale. In other words, numerically equal distances along the measurement continuum represent empirically equal differences among the corresponding equivalence classes— that is, the measured characteristic.

Because the units of measurement along interval scales are empirically equal, it is meaningful to perform most arithmetic operations on the numbers. For example, I can say that the difference between 80° and 60°F is twice as great as that between 60° and 50°F. That is, the ratio of intervals $(80° - 60°F)/(60° - 50°F) = 2$ has meaning with respect to temperature. However, not all arithmetic operations are permissible because the starting point or origin of an interval scale is always arbitrarily defined and does not correspond to an absence of the measured characteristic. In the case of the Fahrenheit scale, 0°F corresponds to the temperature produced by mixing equal quantities by weight of snow and salt. This 0 does not indicate an absence of molecular action and hence an absence of heat. Therefore, although 80°F/40°F = 2, I cannot say that 80°F is twice as hot as 40°F. The ratio 80°F/40°F = 2 is uninterpretable because the zero point on the scale, 0°F, does not correspond to the absence of temperature. The same interpretation problem occurs for calendar time, which is measured from the birth of Christ, and altitude, which is measured from sea level.

The numbers in an interval scale can be subjected to any positive linear transformation. A **positive linear transformation** of a variable, say X, consists of multiplying X by a positive constant b and adding a constant a to the product. That is, a transformed value, X', is given by $X' = a + bX$. For example, degrees Fahrenheit, F, can be transformed into degrees Celsius, C, by means of the positive linear transformation

$$X' = a + bX$$

$$C = \frac{5}{9}(-32) + \frac{5}{9}F,$$

where $X' = C$, $a = \frac{5}{9}(-32)$, $b = \frac{5}{9}$, and $X = F$. Although the variable represented by an interval scale may be continuous, our measurement of it is always discrete because measuring instruments are calibrated in discrete steps. Thus, in practice an interval scale corresponds to the range of a discrete quantitative variable.

Ratio Measurement

The numbers assigned in ratio measurement contain the most information.

> In **ratio measurement,** the numbers assigned to equivalence classes have the properties of distinctness, order, and equivalence of intervals; in addition, the origin of the scale represents the absence of the measured characteristic. The set of numbers assigned to the equivalence classes constitutes a **ratio scale.**

Ratio scales have all the properties of interval scales plus an absolute zero. Most scales in the physical sciences are ratio scales—height in inches, weight in pounds, temperature on the Kelvin scale, and elapsed time such as the age of an object.

Not only is the difference between 5 and 6 inches the same distance as that between 10 and 11 inches, but also an object that is 10 inches long is twice as long as an object that is 5 inches long. Ratio scales permit you to make meaningful statements about the ratio of the numbers assigned to the two objects, for example, 10 inches/5 inches = 2; hence 10 inches is twice as long as 5 inches. The properties of a ratio scale mentioned in the previous paragraph permit you to perform all arithmetic operations on the numbers. However, the only transformation of a ratio scale that preserves these properties is **multiplication by a positive constant:** $bX = X'$, where b is a positive number, X is the original value, and X' is the transformed value. For example, I can transform inches into centimeters by multiplying inches by the constant $b = 2.54$: 10 inches is equal to

$$(2.54)(10 \text{ in.}) = 25.4 \text{ cm}$$

and 5 inches is equal to

$$(2.54)(5 \text{ in.}) = 12.7 \text{ cm}$$

Ten inches is twice as long as 5 inches and, similarly, 25.4 centimeters is twice as long as 12.7 centimeters. As I move from measurement in which the labels contain the least information (nominal scales) to those containing more information (ordinal, interval, and ratio scales), more and more constraints are placed on the transformations that can be meaningfully applied. This occurs because the numbers in ordinal, interval, and ratio scales contain more information that can be altered or destroyed by a transformation. In practice, a ratio scale, like the interval scale, corresponds to the range of a discrete quantitative variable. The major characteristics of the four scales are summarized in Table 1.4-2.

TABLE 1.4-2   Overview of Levels of Measurement

Level of Measurement	*Characteristics*
Nominal	Symbols serve as labels for mutually exclusive and exhaustive equivalence classes. The symbols have the property of distinctness. *Appropriate transformation*: any one-to-one substitution. *Corresponds to*: range of an unordered qualitative variable. *Examples*: gender, eye color, racial origin, personality types, and primary taste qualities.
Ordinal	Ordered symbols, usually numbers, indicate rank order of equivalence classes. The symbols have the properties of distinctness and order. The size of differences between ordered symbols provides no information about differences between equivalence classes. *Appropriate transformation*: monotonic. *Corresponds to*: range of an ordered qualitative variable. *Examples*: military rank, classification of mentally retarded children, rank in high school, and a supervisor's ranking of employees.
Interval[a]	Equal differences among numbers reflect equal magnitude differences among equivalence classes, but the origin or starting point of the scale is arbitrarily determined. Numbers have the properties of distinctness, order, and equivalence of intervals. *Appropriate transformation*: positive linear. *Corresponds to*: range of a discrete quantitative variable. *Examples*: Fahrenheit and Celsius temperature scales, calendar time, and altitude.
Ratio[a]	All the properties of interval scales apply, and, the origin of the scale reflects the absence of the measured characteristic. *Appropriate transformation*: multiplication by a positive constant. *Corresponds to*: range of a discrete quantitative variable. *Examples*: height, weight, Kelvin temperature scale, and measures of elapsed time.

 [a] These two levels are sometimes referred to collectively as **metric measurement** or **numerical measurement**.

Implications of the Two Ways of Thinking about Numbers

This chapter has described two ways of thinking about numbers: one reflects the concerns of mathematicians, and the other reflects the concerns of behavioral scientists, health scientists, and educators. We have developed statistical methods for analyzing numbers as numbers, whether or not the numbers are true measures of some characteristic. If the assumptions associated with the statistical methods are fulfilled, they will produce answers that are formally correct as numbers. This is true regardless of the degree of correspondence between the numbers and the characteristic they represent. The problem comes in translating statistical results into statements about the real world. If numbers representing a nominal scale are manipulated arithmetically, the result will be numbers that are numerically correct but uninterpretable. If nonsense is put into the equation, nonsense indeed will come out.

Most researchers are very sensitive to the potential pitfalls associated with interpreting numbers produced by statistical procedures—and rightfully so. Some authors have even gone so far as to prescribe the statistical procedures that can be used with each measurement scale.[5] Except in the physical sciences, few scales have equal intervals, so the number of statistical techniques on the approved list is relatively small. However, this position fails to recognize that the measurement of many variables in the behavioral sciences and education lies somewhere between the ordinal and interval levels. The IQ scale is a good example. Most psychologists and educators agree that the 10-point difference between IQs of 100 and 110 represents a slightly smaller intellectual difference than the 10-point difference between IQs of 130 and 140. Although the 10-point differences do not represent identical intellectual differences, the intellectual differences are believed to be similar. Hence, IQ scores contain more information than ordinal scales but less than interval scales.

Another example of a measurement scale that is between the ordinal and interval levels is the attitude rating scale: strongly disagree $= -2$, disagree $= -1$, neutral $= 0$, agree $= 1$, strongly agree $= 2$. The numbers $-2, -1, 0, 1, 2$ contain ordinal information. However, it is unlikely that the actual difference in attitudes between 0 and 1, for example, is identical to the difference between 1 and 2. But the difference in attitudes between 0 and 1 is probably similar to the difference between 1 and 2. Thus, the five numbers along the attitude scale do contain some information about the magnitude differences in attitudes.

Should we avoid performing arithmetic operations on scores when the measurement is between the ordinal and interval levels? Researchers have heatedly debated this question. We cannot look to mathematicians and statisticians for answers because the question is outside their province. The answer must come from users of statistics who are acquainted with the problems of translating numerical answers into statements about the real world. An examination of the professional literature reveals that most experts in the behavioral sciences, health sciences, and education do apply arithmetic operations to numbers even though the measurement is somewhere between the ordinal and interval levels. Further, they interpret

---

[5] Examples can be found in Senders (1958), Siegel (1956), and Stevens (1946, 1951).

the results as if the size of a difference between the numbers reflects something about the size of a difference in the measured characteristics. Apparently, experts prefer to utilize whatever magnitude information the numbers contain, even though differences among the numbers only approximate the true magnitude differences.

If a researcher believes that any transformation of a set of numbers that preserves the order of the original numbers adequately represents the equivalence classes, the numbers contain no magnitude information, and they should not be treated as though they do. In the final analysis, it is the researcher, the person most familiar with the data, who must decide how much information the numbers contain.

Some Subtle Problems in Interpreting Numbers

The preceding discussion has emphasized the importance of avoiding interpretation errors by being sensitive to the degree of correspondence between a set of numbers and the characteristic they represent. Consider now some not-so-obvious interpretation problems that occur when a test has an arbitrary zero point. Suppose that on a standardized arithmetic-achievement test, Mortimer received a score of 0; Dude, a score of 30; and Reginald, a score of 60. Can you conclude that Mortimer knows nothing about arithmetic? Obviously not; a score of 0 means that he couldn't answer any questions on the test, but easier questions may exist that he could answer. Achievement tests, as well as many other tests, have arbitrary rather than absolute zero points and therefore fall short of ratio measurement. It follows that although Reginald's score of 60 is twice as high as Dude's 30, Reginald's arithmetic achievement isn't necessarily twice Dude's.

The interpretation problem that results from a lack of equal intervals is subtler. Suppose I compare the effectiveness of two methods of teaching arithmetic. Students in a class using method A gained an average of 10 points; those in a class using method B gained an average of 7 points. The results seem straightforward—on the average, students using method A gained more points than those using method B. But suppose that at the beginning of the experiment the two classes were not equal in arithmetic achievement. Let the average score for class A be 50 and the average score for class B be 80. Is it possible that a 7-point change from 80 to 87 represents more improvement in arithmetic achievement than a 10-point change from 50 to 60? Unless I know that, say, a 10-point change anywhere on the measurement scale represents the same empirical change, the interpretation of the experiment is equivocal. The greater the difference between the classes' initial average achievement scores, the greater the interpretation problem.

Consider finally the interpretation problem that occurs when a test does not have enough difficult items to adequately differentiate among high-scoring participants. Suppose that two individuals make the top score of 60. For one participant, this may represent maximum capability, but the other person may be capable of a much higher performance. The measuring instrument is simply incapable of showing it. Because of the limitations of the measuring instrument, it would be incorrect to conclude that the two individuals are equal in the characteristic measured.

Because numbers do not always mean what they appear to mean, they must be carefully scrutinized. The key principle that runs throughout this section is that a researcher must be guided by two sets of rules. When the tools of statistics are used, the mathematician's and statistician's rules must be followed. When the numbers are interpreted as statements about the real world, the behavioral scientist's measurement rules must be followed.

CHECK YOUR UNDERSTANDING OF SECTION 1.4

6. Ignoring for the moment the limitations of measuring instruments, classify measures of the following according to the mathematician's scheme (unordered qualitative, U; ordered qualitative, O; discrete quantitative, D; continuous quantitative, C).
   a. Size of family
   b. Race
   c. Paper and pencil test of marital compatibility
   d. Seeding of tennis players in a tournament

7. Because of the limitations of measuring instruments, measurement of some variables is of necessity approximate. Classify the variables in Exercise 6 according to whether our measurement is exact (E) or approximate (A).

8. Reclassify the variables in Exercise 6 according to the mathematician's scheme, taking into account limitations in our ability to measure some of the variables.

9. Classify the variables in Exercise 6 with respect to the level of measurement, taking into account limitations in our ability to measure some of the variables.

10. For each level of measurement, indicate the appropriate transformation that can be performed on the numbers.

11. Four kinds of transformations are described in this section. For each level of measurement, list all of the kinds of transformations that can be performed without altering the information contained in the original measurements.

12. What level of measurement is most often achieved (a) in the physical sciences and (b) in the behavioral sciences and education?

13. A score of 0 on an achievement test does not necessarily mean that the individual knows nothing about the subject. Explain.

14. Suppose that achievement test scores for a control group increased from 62 to 65, and those for the experimental group increased from 68 to 74. What must be true to conclude unequivocally that the experimental group improved twice as much as the control group?

15. Terms to remember:
    a. Variable
    b. Range of variable
    c. Value of variable
    d. Constant
    e. Qualitative variable
    f. Quantitative variable
    g. Discrete variable
    h. Continuous variable
    i. Measurement
    j. Nominal scale
    k. One-to-one transformation
    l. Ordinal scale
    m. Monotonic transformation
    n. Interval scale
    o. Positive linear transformation
    p. Ratio scale

1.5 HISTORICAL DEVELOPMENT OF STATISTICS

National Statistics

The science of statistics grew out of an attempt to solve practical problems associated with raising taxes, producing insurance tables, and determining the odds in games of chance. Its subject matter was shaped by three lines of development: national statistics, probability theory, and experimental statistics. The oldest of these three is **national statistics,** which was enumerative and descriptive in character; national statistics can be traced to the beginning of recorded history. David numbered his people, and the Egyptians and Romans kept detailed records of taxes and other state resources. Caesar Augustus simplified the enumerative process by ordering all citizens to report to the nearest statistician, better known as the tax collector. The descriptive use of statistics came of age in the work of English army captain John Graunt (1620–1674), who in 1662 published a small book of birth and death statistics for London that covered the years from 1604 to 1661. Unlike earlier works, such as William the Conqueror's *Domesday Book*, which simply contained data compiled for purposes of taxation and military service, Graunt's book summarized and interpreted the data. His was the first work to shed light on the regularity of social phenomena. It marked the beginning of a theory of annuities and led to the founding of insurance societies.

Probability Theory

A second and independent line of development in statistics is **probability theory.** The earliest traces of probability, found in the Orient around 200 B.C., concerned whether an expected child would be a boy or girl. However, the real impetus for the development of probability came not from prospective parents but from gamblers who wanted to know the odds of winning at various games of chance. Leading mathematicians and scientists of the day—Pierre de Fermat (1601–1665), Blaise Pascal (1623–1662), Christianus Huygens (1629–1695), and James Bernoulli (1654–1705)—responded to the problem. Gradually they chiseled out the foundation of a theory of probability. A milestone in this development was the discovery of the normal curve of errors by Abraham de Moivre (1667–1754), a mathematics tutor who supplemented a meager income by calculating odds for gamblers at the coffeehouses he frequented. Apparently, de Moivre did not appreciate the significance of his discovery; it was published in 1733 only obscurely as a supplement written in Latin to a limited reprinting of a book he had published three years earlier. Therefore, it remained for others to demonstrate the pervasiveness of the *normal distribution.* For more than a century it was attributed to a later discoverer, Carl Friedrich Gauss (1777–1855), one of the greatest mathematicians of all time. It also was discovered independently by Pierre-Simon de Laplace (1749–1827), who forsook a cleric's robe for his lifework in celestial mechanics and probability. Both Laplace and Gauss used the normal distribution in investigating errors of observation in astronomy. Lambert Adolphe Jacques Quetelet (1796–1874), who is considered the father of social science, saw that the normal distribution and probability theory could be applied to all observational sciences: astronomy, anthropology, physics, the census, and the statistics of mental and moral traits. He used the normal curve, for example, to predict the number and type of crimes committed. His work integrated national statistics and probability theory and paved the way for the third line of development—experimental statistics.

Experimental Statistics

The emerging interest in the sciences in the early 1800s created a need for new statistical procedures and principles to guide the design of experiments. The result was **experimental statistics.** Its development was dominated by intellectual giants such as Sir Francis Galton (1822–1911). Lewis Terman, the developer of the Stanford-Binet intelligence test, estimated Galton's IQ at about 200. Galton, more than anyone before, used statistics in investigating problems of people and nature. His major statistical contributions were regression and correlation procedures (see Chapters 5 and 6), which he used to unravel mysteries of heredity. Karl Pearson (1857–1936) refined the mathematical theory of regression and made an astonishing number of additional contributions to statistical theory and practice. Perhaps his greatest contribution was the development in 1900 of the chi-square test for goodness of fit (see Chapter 17), which is used to test the significance of differences between observed data and those expected on the basis of some hypothesis.

The modern era in experimental statistics was ushered in by William Sealey Gosset (1876–1937), who derived the t distribution (see Chapter 10) in 1908. Thus began the development of exact inductive procedures appropriate for both large and small samples. Heretofore researchers had relied on large-sample statistical procedures. Gosset, who published under the pseudonym "Student," was a brewer for Messrs. Guinness. His discovery, like others in statistics, resulted from a practical need—in this case, the need for inductive procedures appropriate for small samples. He was involved in brewing research, where variable materials and susceptibility to temperature changes precluded the use of large samples.

The modern era matured in the work of Sir Ronald A. Fisher (1890–1962), whose contributions to statistics are legion. He is best remembered for his derivation of the F distribution, contributions to the design and analysis of experiments, and heated exchanges about statistical theory with Jerzy Neyman (1894–1981) and Egon Pearson (1895–1981). Fisher's work was a unique blend of the rigor of the mathematician with a commonsense approach; the latter was undoubtedly due to his applied work in agriculture, biology, and genetics.

Neyman and Pearson carefully consolidated the work of Fisher and others while developing their own theory of statistical inference. The bulk of the statistical arsenal of today's researcher can be traced to Fisher, Neyman, and Pearson. But in response to changing research needs, there have been many new developments. The computer has made possible the solution of problems that were heretofore intractable and has sparked new lines of inquiry. It seems unlikely, however, that a new era could be dominated to the extent that Fisher, Neyman, and Pearson dominated the one from 1920 to the present.

16. What three lines of development shaped the subject matter of contemporary statistics?
17. Briefly summarize the major characteristics of the three lines of development that shaped the subject matter of contemporary statistics.
18. What distinguishes the modern era in experimental statistics from the previous period?
19. Terms to remember:
    a. National statistics
    b. Probability theory
    c. Experimental statistics

1.6 LOOKING BACK: WHAT HAVE YOU LEARNED?

Statistics is an indispensable tool for making sense out of data and for communicating the results of research. The word *statistics* has several meanings. For example, it can refer to characteristics of data such as the mean and range and to techniques for collecting, analyzing, and interpreting data. Your study of statistics will help you to (1) read the professional literature in your field and keep up with new developments, (2) design and analyze simple experiments, and (3) detect statistical fallacies in the mass media and research reports. In addition, you should learn new, more critical and analytical ways of thinking.

Research questions usually concern characteristics of populations. For example, what do people of voting age think about an issue? Is one teaching approach for fifth graders more effective than another? Do 21-year-old women prefer smaller families than men of the same age? The populations are, respectively, the attitudes of voters on the issue, the achievement scores of fifth graders, and the preferred family sizes of 21-year-old women and men. The term *population* generally refers to all the inhabitants of a city, state, or country. In statistics it refers to the collection of all people, objects, or events having one or more specified characteristics. It is rarely possible to observe all the elements of a population, either for practical reasons or because the population is infinite in size. Instead, we conduct research on a sample of elements. A sample can contain a single element or all but one of the population elements. If every sample of a particular size has an equal chance of being selected from the population, the sampling process is said to be random.

Statistics can be applied to data from samples or from populations to obtain a clearer understanding of their characteristics. If you obtained a random sample of 21-year-old women and men, you might find that on the average they prefer, respectively, 2.2 and 2.4 children. In addition, you might learn that the range for women was 0 to 9 and that for men was 0 to 7. The numbers 2.2 and 2.4 and the ranges 0 to 9 and 0 to 7 are descriptive statistics; they summarize characteristics of the two samples. Description is one important application of statistics. A second important application is inferring characteristics of a population by observing a sample. The sample statistics for preferred family size, for example, provide our best guess about the corresponding population values. Furthermore, inferential statistics can be used to decide whether the populations from which the samples of women and men were obtained differ in preferred family size. These two uses of statistics—description and inference—are discussed in the first and second halves of this book.

Once a researcher has identified the population of interest and the characteristic to be observed, he or she must decide how the characteristic should be measured. Mathematicians and statisticians have historically classified variables as qualitative (unordered or ordered) or quantitative (discrete or continuous). This scheme evolved because different mathematical tools are used in derivations and proofs for the two kinds of variables.

Behavioral scientists, on the other hand, developed a classification scheme that reflected their concern with the degree to which numbers mirror the characteristics they represent. A four-level classification of measurement resulted: nominal, ordinal, interval, and ratio. Today we recognize that the measurement of many variables in the behavioral sciences and education lies somewhere between the ordinal and interval levels.

Modern statistics is the culmination of three historical lines of development: national statistics, probability theory, and experimental statistics. The origins of statistics are in antiquity, yet most of the material in this book is the product of the 20th century. You can expect to see an acceleration in the development of new statistical tools and theory—an acceleration made possible, in part, by the advent of the computer with its phenomenal capacity for information processing and storage.

REVIEW EXERCISES FOR CHAPTER 1[6]

1. The word *statistics* has four distinct meanings. List them.
2. The chapter mentions several benefits of studying statistics. List at least three benefits.
3. How does the original meaning of the term *population* differ from today's statistical definition?
4. For each of the following statements, indicate (a) the population, (b) the element, and (c) the observation to be recorded.
   a. In the previous presidential election, 36% of 18- to 24-year-olds voted.
   b. Approximately 16% of all children under 18 are members of families whose incomes are below the poverty level.
   c. Approximately 42% of all prison inmates are 21 to 26 years old.
   d. Approximately 32% of all high school graduates 18 to 24 years old are enrolled in college.
   e. Four out of 10 Americans are under 25 years old.
   f. According to a recent Centers for Disease Control report, one of every 1,667 American white women between the ages of 27 and 39 has the AIDS virus.
   g. According to the U.S. Department of Education, 38.4% of male high school students have performed a community service during the past two years.

[6] Answers to the *Review Exercises* are given in the *Instructor's Manual*.

5. (a) Why is most research conducted on samples rather than populations? (b) How is sample size related to the resemblance between a random sample and the population?

6. Distinguish between descriptive and inferential statistics.

7. Mathematicians and behavioral scientists have somewhat different interests in numbers. Discuss these differences.

8. Ignoring for the moment the limitations of measuring instruments, classify measures of the following variables according to the mathematician's scheme (unordered qualitative, U; ordered qualitative, O; discrete quantitative, D; continuous quantitative, C).
   a. Employee production on an assembly line
   b. Paper-and-pencil test of creativity
   c. Political party affiliation
   d. Final standing of football teams in the Big 12 Conference
   e. Weight loss after jogging 3 miles
   f. Number of reported suicides in 2003
   g. Major in college
   h. Religious preference
   i. Grading scale in school (A, B, C, D, F)
   j. Amount of rainfall
   k. Sexual orientation (heterosexual, lesbian, gay man, bisexual woman or man)

9. Because of the limitations of measuring instruments, the measurement of some variables is of necessity approximate. Classify the variables in Exercise 8 according to whether our measurement is exact (E) or approximate (A).

10. Reclassify the variables in Exercise 8 according to the mathematician's scheme, taking into account limitations in our ability to measure some of the variables.

11. (a) In what three ways do behavioral scientists use numbers in measurement? (b) Give three examples of each use.

12. Classify the variables in Exercise 8 with respect to level of measurement, taking into account limitations in our ability to measure some of the variables.

13. For each level of measurement, list the properties that characterize the numbers assigned to the equivalence classes.

14. Who is in the best position to determine the degree of correspondence between a set of numbers and the corresponding equivalence classes and hence to determine the arithmetic operations that can meaningfully be applied?

15. What does a score of 0 on an achievement test mean?

16. Suppose that a group of inner-city students improved their arithmetic achievement test scores by an average of 8 points, whereas a group of students from an affluent neighborhood improved their scores only by an average of 6 points. Explain how it is possible that the 6-point increase might actually represent a greater increase in arithmetic achievement than the 8-point increase.

17. List at least one major contribution that each of the following men made to statistics.
    a. Abraham de Moivre (1667–1754)
    b. Lambert Adolphe Jacques Quetelet (1796–1874)
    c. Francis Galton (1822–1911)
    d. Karl Pearson (1857–1936)
    e. William Sealey Gosset (1876–1937)
    f. Ronald A. Fisher (1890–1962)
    g. Jerzy Neyman (1894–1981)
    h. Egon Pearson (1895–1981)

2

Frequency Distributions and Graphs

2.1 Introduction
Looking Ahead: What Is
This Chapter About?
Need to Depict and
Summarize Data

2.2 Frequency Distributions
Ungrouped Frequency
Distribution for
Quantitative Variables
Grouped Frequency
Distribution for
Quantitative Variables
Determining the Number
and Size of Class
Intervals for a
Quantitative Variable
The Pros and Cons of
Grouping Data
Relative Frequency
Distributions
Cumulative Frequency
Distributions
Frequency Distributions
for Qualitative Variables
Check Your Understanding
of Section 2.2

2.3 Introduction to Graphs

**2.4 Graphs for Qualitative
Variables**
Bar Graph
Pie Chart
Check Your Understanding
of Section 2.4

**2.5 Graphs for Quantitative
Variables**
Histogram
Frequency Polygon
Cumulative Polygon
Stem-and-Leaf Display
Check Your Understanding
of Section 2.5

2.6 Shapes of Distributions
Bell-Shaped Distributions
Skewed Distributions
Bimodal Distributions
J, U, and Rectangular
Distributions
Check Your Understanding
of Section 2.6

2.7 Misleading Graphs
Check Your Understanding
of Section 2.7

**2.8 Looking Back: What
Have You Learned?**
Review Exercises for
Chapter 2

2.1 INTRODUCTION

Looking Ahead: What Is This Chapter About?

This chapter describes two kinds of procedures for depicting and summarizing data: frequency distributions and graphs. The procedures for constructing frequency distributions for quantitative variables differ slightly from those used to construct frequency distributions for qualitative variables. Also, different kinds of graphs are used to depict the two kinds of variables. The chapter ends with a description of some commonly encountered distributions and some ways that graphs can mislead you.

After reading the chapter, you should know the following:

- How to construct frequency distributions for quantitative and qualitative variables
- The merits of relative frequency distributions and cumulative frequency distributions
- How to construct bar graphs and pie charts for qualitative variables
- How to construct histograms, frequency polygons, cumulative polygons, and stem-and-leaf displays for quantitative variables
- The names of commonly encountered distributions and four important properties of distributions
- How you can be mislead by graphs

Need to Depict and Summarize Data

No two people respond exactly the same way in a situation. Even responses that have been overlearned exhibit some variability from time to time. On occasion, quarterbacks fumble the exchange from center, pianists play wrong notes, and actors muff their lines. It seems that variation in the behavior of people is inevitable. This lack of consistency is more troublesome in the behavioral sciences, health sciences, and education than in the physical sciences. A chemist can be confident that different samples of H_2O will react with another substance the same way under controlled tests. But this kind of consistency where people are involved is rare. The variability problem is usually handled by observing many people or by making many observations of the same people. The presumption is that if the researcher observes enough people or observes the same person enough times, errors due to variability will average out. This research strategy produces mountains of data and calls for procedures for depicting and summarizing the data so that they can be more readily comprehended. Two kinds of descriptive tools are used for this purpose: graphical methods and numerical methods. This chapter is devoted to graphical methods; numerical methods are described in Chapters 3 through 6.

2.2 FREQUENCY DISTRIBUTIONS

The first step in summarizing data is to construct a frequency distribution. This involves defining two or more equivalence classes and counting the number of observations in each class.

An **equivalence class** can be (1) a single score value (for example, Yale students with a 4-point GPA), (2) a collection of score values (Yale students with from five to nine traffic tickets), (3) or a qualitative category (Yale students with blue eyes). A table showing the equivalence classes and the frequency with which their score values occur is called a **frequency distribution.**

The equivalence classes of a frequency distribution are called **class intervals.** If each of the class intervals is a single score value, the frequency distribution is said to be **ungrouped.** If each class interval spans two or more score values, for example, Yale students with five to nine traffic tickets, the frequency distribution is **grouped.**

Ungrouped Frequency Distribution for Quantitative Variables

Suppose you administered a test of leadership aptitude to all high school football coaches in Punt County, Iowa. Their test scores are shown in Table 2.2-1. If you examine the table carefully, you see that the smallest score is 30 and the largest is 68 and that most of the scores are in the high 40s and low 50s. You can extract the same information more easily from the ungrouped frequency distribution in Table 2.2-2, which associates with each score value, X, the frequency of its occurrence, f. In constructing the frequency distribution, I followed the convention of putting the largest score at the upper left of the table. In addition, each number between the largest and the smallest scores is listed in the distribution so that every possible score can be tallied and the gaps between scores easily detected.

The frequency distribution is an effective organizing device, but some information is lost. I cannot tell from Table 2.2-2 which coach made the highest score, which coach made the lowest score, or that one of the coaches is a woman. I must refer to the original data for this information.

TABLE 2.2-1   Leadership Aptitude Scores

Coach	Score	Coach	Score	Coach	Score
John Granados	55	Tom Pennington	39	Frank Sanford	45
Jamie Brooks	46	David Lilley	68	Dave Abbott	33
Gary Tsang	52	Bill Reynolds	52	William Scott	50
Charlie Keele	51	William Tubbs	54	Ron Smith	51
Jim Bohannon	48	Tom May	48	Charles Dilday	54
John Mills	50	Mike Bratcher	46	James Lamb	59
Ed Massey	30	John Achor	47	William Tobin	49
David Weaver	53	Joseph Vardaman	44	Roger Sloan	42
Jack Patton	57	Alden Daniel	49	Robert Frish	56
Jane Benedict	62	Robert Stanford	50	Michael Rowatt	53

TABLE 2.2-2   Ungrouped Frequency Distribution for Leadership Aptitude Scores from Table 2.2-1

Score X	Frequency f	Score X	Frequency f	Score X	Frequency f	Score X	Frequency f
68	I	58	0	48	II	38	0
67	0	57	I	47	I	37	0
66	0	56	I	46	II	36	0
65	0	55	I	45	I	35	0
64	0	54	II	44	I	34	0
63	0	53	II	43	0	33	I
62	I	52	II	42	I	32	0
61	0	51	II	41	0	31	0
60	0	50	III	40	0	30	I
59	I	49	II	39	I		

TABLE 2.2-3   Grouped Frequency Distribution for Leadership Aptitude Scores from Table 2.2-1

Class Interval	Frequency, f
66–68	1
63–65	0
60–62	1
57–59	2
54–56	4
51–53	6
48–50	7
45–47	4
42–44	2
39–41	1
36–38	0
33–35	1
30–32	1
	$n^a = 30$

[a] n denotes the total number of scores in the frequency distribution.

Grouped Frequency Distribution for Quantitative Variables

If the spread of scores for a quantitative variable is large, as in Table 2.2-2, it is useful to construct a **grouped frequency distribution** in which each class interval spans two or more score values. A grouped frequency distribution for the leadership aptitude data is shown in Table 2.2-3. This table is much easier to interpret than the ungrouped frequency distribution in Table 2.2-2.

Class intervals for a quantitative variable have a **nominal lower limit** and a **nominal upper limit;** for the class interval 66–68 they are, respectively, 66 and 68. However, the interval 66–68 actually includes any number *equal to or greater than* 65.5 and *less than* 68.5. The numbers 65.5 and 68.5 are called the **real limits** of the interval. They extend 0.5 below the nominal lower limit and approximately 0.5 above the nominal upper limit.[1] The nominal limits are used to represent each class interval. The real limits show that there are no gaps between the class intervals. For example, there is no gap between the class intervals 63–65 and 66–68 because

63–65 includes any number ≥ 62.5 and < 65.5
66–68 includes any number ≥ 65.5 and < 68.5.

The real limits are used to compute the **class interval size.** The size of a class interval, denoted by i, is given by

✻ i = Real upper limit − Real lower limit.

For example, the size of the class interval 66–68, where the real lower limit = 65.5 and the real upper limit $\cong 68.5$, is

$$i = 68.5 - 65.5 = 3,$$

as illustrated in the following figure:[2]

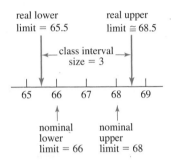

The concepts of real limits and class interval size also apply to the class intervals in ungrouped frequency distributions such as the one in Table 2.2-2. For the class interval 68, for example, the real limits are 67.5 and 68.5.[3] The class interval size is

$$i = 68.5 - 67.5 = 1,$$

as illustrated in the following figure:

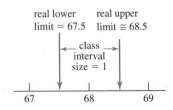

---

[1] If my measurements were accurate to the nearest tenth, so that I had class intervals such as 6.6–6.8, the class interval nominal limits would be 6.6 and 6.8 and the real limits would be 6.55 and 6.85. These values are obtained by adding and subtracting 0.05 instead of 0.5 from the nominal limits. Similarly, if the class interval were 0.66–0.68 and my measurements were accurate to the nearest hundredth, the nominal limits would be 0.66 and 0.68 and the real limits would be 0.655 and 0.685, which differ from the nominal limits by ± 0.005.

✻ [2] The symbol $\cong$ means "approximately equal."

[3] Some variables do not follow this convention. A common example is age. If a person is 21, this means that the 21st birthday has passed but the 22nd has not. The real limits for the age 21 are 21.0 and 21.999.

Several conventions are followed in constructing a frequency distribution. They are not inviolate rules; instead, think of them as guidelines for constructing easily interpreted tables.

1. The class intervals should be mutually exclusive—that is, the class intervals should be chosen so that a score belongs in one and only one interval.
2. For quantitative variables, there should be no gaps between the class intervals. For completeness, class intervals whose frequencies equal zero are included in the distribution (see class intervals 36–38 and 63–65 in Table 2.2-3).
3. All quantitative class intervals should have the same width or size.[4]
4. The distribution should have 10 to 20 class intervals unless the number of scores is very small, in which case it may be desirable to use fewer class intervals. For qualitative variables, the number of class intervals is usually dictated by the nature of the variable. For example, if the variable is gender, there may be three class intervals: men, women, and unknown.
5. For quantitative variables, one of the preferred class interval sizes should be used; these class intervals are 1, 2, 3, 5, 10, 15, 20, 25. . . .
6. The nominal lower limit of each quantitative class interval should be equal to the size of the class interval multiplied by an integer. For such cases, the nominal lower limit of a class interval is said to be an integer multiple of the class interval size. In Table 2.2-3, for example, the nominal lower limit of the class interval 30–32 is 30 and is equal to 3×10, where 3 is the class interval size and 10 is the integer multiplier. If the smallest score had been 31 instead of 30, the class interval still would be 30–32 and not 31–33 because 31 is not an integer multiple of 10.
7. For quantitative variables, opinion is divided as to whether the class interval containing the largest score should be at the top (top left) of the table or at the bottom (bottom left) of the table. My own preference is to put the class interval containing the largest score value at the top left as in Table 2.2-2 and at the top as in Table 2.2-3. However, many computer statistical packages put the class interval containing the largest score value at the bottom of the table. For qualitative variables, the order of the class intervals should reflect the order inherent in the variable. If the variable is unordered and logic does not suggest an order, the class intervals can be ordered alphabetically.

Determining the Number and Size of Class Intervals for a Quantitative Variable

The conventions for constructing a grouped frequency distribution provide general guidelines for the number and size of class intervals. You know that there should be 10 to 20 class intervals (unless there are only a few scores) and that one of the

[4] Sometimes this is not possible or desirable. Suppose that one participant was unable to learn a list of nonsense syllables in the usual number of trials, 6 to 10, required by most participants. After the 20th trial, the participant was still unable to meet the learning criterion and gave up. This participant cannot be given an exact score; he or she falls into the top class interval "20 or more." This interval is open because its real upper limit can not be specified. Or suppose that the class intervals represent family income. It might be desirable to make the bottom and top class intervals open to include the few families with extremely small or extremely large incomes.

preferred class interval sizes, 1, 2, 3, 5, 10, 15, 20, 25, . . . , should be used. With these guidelines in mind, you can estimate the number and the size of class intervals in a trial-and-error fashion using the following formula:

$$\frac{\text{Range}}{\text{Preferred } i} = \text{A number between 10 to 20 class intervals}$$

where the range is equal to the real upper limit of the largest score minus the real lower limit of the smallest score. A preferred class interval size ($i = 1$ or 2 or 3 or . . .) is selected by trial and error so that the formula yields between 10 and 20 class intervals. To illustrate, the largest and smallest scores in Table 2.2-1 are 68 and 30. The range is $68.5 - 29.5 = 39$. If a class interval size of 2 is tried in the formula, there will be $39/2 \cong 20$ class intervals. Because there are only 30 scores, a smaller number of class intervals would be preferable. If a class interval size of 3 is tried, the formula yields $39/3 = 13$ class intervals, the number used in Table 2.2-3. A class interval size of 5 should not be used because it would give only $39/5 \cong 8$ class intervals. For most sets of data, there will be no more than two class interval sizes that give the desired 10 to 20 class intervals. As a general rule, when the number of scores is small, use fewer than 15 class intervals; when the number is large, use 15 to 20 class intervals.

Suppose that I have administered a test of reading readiness to 26 children enrolled in the first grade. The largest and smallest scores on the test are 132 and 73; the range is $132.5 - 72.5 = 60$. How many class intervals should the frequency distribution have and what should their size be? By trial and error and the formula

$$\frac{\text{Range}}{\text{Preferred } i} = \text{A number between 10 to 20 class intervals}$$

I see that two grouping schemes are possible: the class interval size, i, can be either 3 or 5 because both class interval sizes yield between 10 and 20 class intervals

$$\frac{60}{3} = 20 \qquad \text{and} \qquad \frac{60}{5} = 12$$

The one in which $i = 5$ is preferred because there are only 26 scores. The smallest class interval, following convention 6 given earlier, would be 70–74 because 70 is an integer multiple of $i = 5$—that is, $5 \times 14 = 70$. The largest class interval would be 130–134 because 130 is an integer multiple of $i = 5$—that is, $5 \times 26 = 130$. This grouping scheme actually results in 13 instead of 12 class intervals. The formula for estimating the number of class intervals has underestimated the required number because the smallest score (73) does not fall at or close to the real lower limit of its class interval (69.5) nor does the largest score (132) fall at or close to the real upper limit of its class interval (134.5). If the extreme scores had been 134 and 70 instead of 132 and 73, the formula for estimating the number of class intervals would have given 13 intervals—the number actually used.

Suppose that I had tested 221 children instead of 26 in the example given earlier. In this case, I would have used a class interval size of 3. The smallest and largest class intervals would be 72–74 and 132–134 because 72 and 132 are integer multiples of $i = 3$: $3 \times 24 = 72$ and $3 \times 44 = 132$. Even though the use of $i = 3$ results in 21 class intervals, it is preferred to $i = 5$ because of the large number of scores. The purpose of graphical methods is to make data easier to comprehend, and sometimes the best way to do this is to depart from the conventions.

The Pros and Cons of Grouping Data

Grouping scores into class intervals where $i > 1$ results in the loss of some information. For example, I know from Table 2.2-3 that four scores occur in the class interval 54–56, but I do not know their individual values. One must weigh this disadvantage against the simplicity achieved by grouping. If the spread of scores is large, a grouped frequency distribution is more easily interpreted.

Relative Frequency Distributions

To help users interpret a frequency distribution, it is often beneficial to express each frequency as either a proportion or a percentage of the total number of scores. The formulas for **proportionate frequency** ($Prop\ f$) and **percentage frequency** ($\%f$) are

$$Prop\ f = \frac{f}{n} \quad \text{and} \quad \%f = \frac{f}{n} \times 100$$

where f is the frequency of a class interval, and n is the total number of scores.

A distribution that shows the $Prop\ f$ or $\%f$ for each class interval is called a **relative frequency distribution.**

The frequency associated with each class interval also can be shown along with either $Prop\ f$ or $\%f$. For purposes of illustration, a relative frequency distribution that includes f, $Prop\ f$, and $\%f$ is shown in Table 2.2-4.

TABLE 2.2-4   Relative Frequency Distributions for Leadership Aptitude Scores from Table 2.2-1

Class Interval	f	Prop f	% f
66–68	1	.03	3
63–65	0	0	0
60–62	1	.03	3
57–59	2	.07	7
54–56	4	.13	13
51–53	6	.20	20
48–50	7	.23	23
45–47	4	.13	13
42–44	2	.07	7
39–41	1	.03	3
36–38	0	0	0
33–35	1	.03	3
30–32	1	.03	3
	$n = 30$	Sum = .98[a]	Sum = 98[a]

[a] Due to errors introduced by rounding numbers, the sums do not equal 1.00 and 100.

TABLE 2.2-5 History Achievement Scores for Classes Taught by Different Methods

Achievement Scores	Method A		Method B	
	f	%f	f	%f
150–154	1	1	1	3
145–149	0	0	2	6
140–144	2	3	2	6
135–139	4	5	4	12
130–134	6	8	6	19
125–129	8	11	8	25
120–124	9	12	5	16
115–119	10	14	2	6
110–114	8	11	1	3
105–109	8	11	0	0
100–104	6	8	1	3
95–99	5	7	0	0
90–94	3	4	0	0
85–89	2	3	0	0
80–84	1	1	0	0
	$n = 73$	Sum = 99[a]	$n = 32$	Sum = 99[a]

[a] Due to errors introduced by rounding numbers, the sums do not equal 100.

The transformation (conversion) of frequencies into *Prop f*'s or *% f*'s converts each frequency into a relative frequency in which the possible range of values is, respectively, 0 to 1 or 0 to 100. Relative frequencies indicate whether a frequency is "relatively large" rather than whether it is "absolutely large." For example, the class interval 48–50 in Table 2.2-4 contains only seven scores, but this is a relatively large proportion (*Prop f* = .23, almost one-fourth) of the total number of scores. Relative frequencies are particularly useful in comparing two frequency distributions with different n's. Consider the history achievement scores shown in Table 2.2-5 for high school students taught by two methods. Because of the great difference in n's, a comparison of percentage frequencies is more meaningful than a comparison of frequencies. You can see from the two %f columns that method B resulted in a higher percentage of high achievement scores than method A. The superiority of method B is not obvious from an inspection of the two f columns.

Cumulative Frequency Distributions

A **cumulative frequency distribution** shows the number, proportion, or percentage of scores that occur below the real upper limit of each class interval.

Such a distribution helps in answering the following kinds of questions. If Susan's score is 62, how many students did better and how many did worse? Or, what score divides the bottom 25% of students from the remainder of the class?

TABLE 2.2-6   Cumulative Frequency Distributions for Leadership Aptitude Scores from Table 2.2-1

(1) Class Interval	(2) f	(3) Cum f	(4)[a] Cum Prop f	(5)[b] Cum % f
66–68	1	1 + 29 = 30	1.00	100
63–65	0	0 + 29 = 29	.97	97
60–62	1	1 + 28 = 29	.97	97
57–59	2	2 + 26 = 28	.93	93
54–56	4	4 + 22 = 26	.87	87
51–53	6	6 + 16 = 22	.73	73
48–50	7	7 + 9 = 16	.53	53
45–47	4	4 + 5 = 9	.30	30
42–44	2	2 + 3 = 5	.17	17
39–41	1	1 + 2 = 3	.10	10
36–38	0	0 + 2 = 2	.07	7
33–35	1	1 + 1 = 2	.07	7
30–32	1	1 + 0 = 1	.03	3
	$n = 30$			

[a] Column 4 is obtained by dividing each *Cum f* in column 3 by $n = 30$.
[b] Column 5 is obtained by multiplying column 4 by 100.

To construct a cumulative frequency distribution, you begin with a frequency distribution like the one in columns 1 and 2 of Table 2.2-6. A given cumulative frequency, denoted by *Cum f*, is obtained by adding the frequency in column 2 for the class interval to the cumulative frequency recorded in column 3 for the class interval below it. For example, in the class interval 30–32, $f = 1$, and there are no scores below, so the *Cum f* for that class interval is $1 + 0 = 1$. For the class interval 33–35, $f = 1$, which, added to the *Cum f* below, yields a *Cum f* of $1 + 1 = 2$. The cumulative frequency recorded for the top class interval should equal the total number of scores, n.

Cumulative frequencies can be transformed into *Cum Prop f* and *Cum % f* by the formulas

$$Cum\ Prop\ f = (Cum\ f)/n$$

and

$$Cum\ \%\ f = [(Cum\ f/n)] \times 100$$

These relative frequencies are shown in columns 4 and 5 of Table 2.2-6.

Frequency Distributions for Qualitative Variables

Constructing frequency distributions for qualitative variables is simple because no decisions about size and number of class intervals have to be made—the equivalence classes of the variable become the class intervals. Consider the unordered qualitative variable of political party affiliation: Democrat, Independent, Republican, and unspecified or other. If I obtained a random sample of college students at Ohio State University and determined their political affiliation, I could construct a frequency

TABLE 2.2-7   Political Affiliation of Students at Ohio State University

(1) Political Affiliation	(2) f	(3)[a] Prop f	(4)[b] % f
Democrat	92	.42	42
Independent	33	.15	15
Republican	85	.38	38
Unspecified or other	11	.05	5
	n = 221	Sum = 1.00	Sum = 100

[a] Column 3 is obtained by dividing each f in column 2 by n = 221.
[b] Column 4 is obtained by multiplying column 3 by 100.

distribution like the one in columns 1 and 2 of Table 2.2-7. The equivalence classes are ordered alphabetically for lack of a more logical sequence. For ordered qualitative variables, class intervals should preserve the order inherent in the original equivalence classes.

The frequencies in column 2 of Table 2.2-7 are converted to *Prop f* in column 3 and *% f* in column 4. Cumulative frequencies are not shown; they are not meaningful because the order of the class intervals was arbitrarily determined.

CHECK YOUR UNDERSTANDING OF SECTION 2.2

1. A marriage counselor asked his clients to keep a record of the number of arguments they had during the week. The following data for 23 couples were obtained. Construct an ungrouped frequency distribution for these data.

```
2   5   4   9   6
4   3   3   5  10
5   0  13   4   2
1   7   6   3
4   5   4   4
```

2. Assembly-line workers were asked to complete a job-satisfaction questionnaire. Construct an ungrouped frequency distribution for the following scores, where large scores correspond to high satisfaction.

```
7   8   4  25   9   8   4  15  11   9
6   9   7   7  10  17   5  10   5   8
3   7  11   8  13  22   7   8   7   6
10   6   7   9   4   8   6   6   8  11
15  21   5  11   6   9   5  12  10   8
```

3. List the guidelines for constructing an ungrouped frequency distribution.
4. For the following nominal class intervals, give the real limits and the class interval size.
   a. 50–54   b. 74   c. 18.0–19.9

5. For each of the following, give (a) the number of class intervals, (b) the size of the class interval, and (c) the nominal limits of the class interval containing the smallest score.

	Largest Score	Smallest Score	Number of Scores
a.	68	22	53
b.	260	106	21
c.	254	92	91

6. A test of mechanical aptitude was given to seniors at Middlecenter High School. Construct a grouped frequency distribution for the following data.

80	73	51	81	46	85	84
75	44	84	87	95	48	88
50	35	52	93	43	59	63
47	66	55	58	62	51	75
86	82	89	34	77	73	59

7. In a traffic safety project, the reaction time of 27 participants to the onset of a light was measured in milliseconds. For the following data, (a) construct two grouped frequency distributions having different i's, and (b) discuss the relative merits of the two grouping schemes.

186	187	211	185	196	193
184	185	191	188	192	190
188	190	202	199	189	
193	186	180	205	187	
189	195	184	198	202	

8. For the data in Exercise 6, construct a relative frequency distribution using *Prop f.*

9. Thirty-two college students participated in a paired-associates learning experiment in which they were shown 12 nouns written in hiragana (a Japanese writing system) and asked to learn the corresponding English words. The number of trials each participant needed to be able to correctly anticipate the 12 English words on two consecutive trials is shown here. Construct a cumulative frequency distribution for the data.

10	9	11	12	6	14	10	12
11	10	12	10	9	11	16	8
9	7	8	11	10	8	12	12
13	10	10	9	11	13	7	11

10. For the data in Exercise 1, construct a cumulative proportionate frequency distribution.

11. Researchers asked a random sample of 29 students from each of the following classifications—freshman, sophomore, junior, senior, and graduate student—whether they believed in extrasensory perception (ESP). The classifications of students who believed in ESP are listed here. Construct a frequency distribution for these data.

junior	senior	junior	sophomore	junior
freshman	junior	freshman	junior	sophomore

sophomore	senior	senior	senior	junior
graduate	sophomore	junior	freshman	senior
freshman	junior	junior	senior	sophomore
junior	senior	sophomore	senior	

12. Under what condition is it meaningless to construct a cumulative frequency distribution for a qualitative variable?

13. Terms to remember:

a. Equivalence class	b. Frequency distribution
c. Class interval	d. Ungrouped frequency distribution
e. Grouped frequency distribution	f. Nominal limits
d. Real limits	e. Class interval size
f. Proportionate frequency	g. Percentage frequency
h. Relative frequency distribution	i. Cumulative frequency distribution

2.3 INTRODUCTION TO GRAPHS

Frequency distributions present the main features of data succinctly, but they are still abstract numerical representations and require effort to interpret. Graphs can impart the same information and speak to us more directly. Their ease of interpretation makes them particularly useful when you want to present data to the general public.

There are many ways to graph data. In fact, whole books have been devoted to the subject.[5] My presentation is limited to the six most common graphs: bar graphs, pie charts, histograms, frequency polygons, cumulative polygons, and stem-and-leaf displays. Qualitative variables are usually represented by bar graphs and pie charts. Quantitative variables are usually represented by histograms, frequency polygons, cumulative polygons, and stem-and-leaf displays.

2.4 GRAPHS FOR QUALITATIVE VARIABLES

Bar Graph

Once a frequency distribution has been made, most of the work of constructing a **bar graph** has been done. The only step remaining is to represent the data in a two-dimensional figure, as illustrated in Figure 2.4-1 for the data in Table. 2.2-7. Class intervals are represented along the horizontal axis (**abscissa, or X axis**), and frequencies are represented along the vertical axis (**ordinate, or Y axis**). The zero point or origin of the vertical axis is located at the X and Y **intercept**—the point where the two axes cross. A vertical bar is erected over each class interval such that its height corresponds to the number of scores in the interval. The bars can be any width, but they should not touch. A space between the bars emphasizes the discrete, qualitative character of the class intervals. By convention, the height of the graph should be 66% to 75% of its width. This results in a rectangular figure whose proportions according to the ancient Greeks are the most aesthetically pleasing. Also, the X and

[5] Several examples are Arken and Colton (1938), Cleveland (1985), and Tufte (1983).

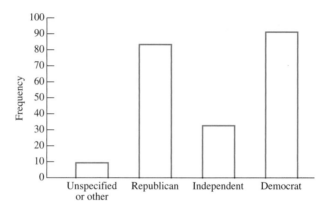

Figure 2.4-1. Political affiliation of a random sample of $n = 221$ students at Ohio State University. (Data from Table 2.2-7.)

Y axes of the graph should be labeled and a figure caption provided to help the reader interpret the graph.

The Y axis also can be used to represent proportionate frequency or percentage frequency, depending on the questions of interest to the researcher. You saw in Section 2.2 that these transformations are useful in determining whether a frequency is large in a relative rather than an absolute sense and in comparing frequency distributions with different total numbers of scores.

Pie Chart

Perhaps the most easily interpreted graph is a **pie chart,** which is merely a circle divided into sectors representing the proportionate frequency or percentage frequency of the class intervals.

A pie chart is illustrated in Figure 2.4-2 for the data in Table 2.2-7. To construct a pie chart, think of the pie chart as a circle that has 60 minutes like the face of a clock. To determine the size of a pie sector corresponding to one of the class intervals, convert its *Prop f* or *% f* into minutes. This is accomplished using the following formulas:

$$Prop\ f \times 60 \quad \text{or} \quad (\%\ f/100) \times 60$$

For Figure 2.4-2, the minutes corresponding to the four percentage frequencies are as follows:

Democrat	(42%/100) 60 = 25.2 min
Independent	(15%/100) 60 = 9.0 min
Republican	(38%/100) 60 = 22.8 min
Unspecified or other	(5%/100) 60 = 3.0 min

Thus, 42% corresponds to 25.2 minutes after 12 o'clock; the next 15% corresponds to 25.2 + 9.0 = 34.2 minutes after 12 o'clock; the next 38% corresponds to

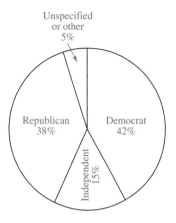

Figure 2.4-2. Political affiliation in percentage frequency of a random sample of $n = 221$ students at Ohio State University. (Data from Table 2.2-7.)

$25.2 + 9.0 + 22.8 = 57$ minutes; and the final 5% corresponds to $25.2 + 9.0 + 22.8 + 3.0 = 60$ minutes or 12 o'clock. By visualizing the face of a clock, you can mark off the four pie sectors on the pie chart. The last steps in constructing the pie chart are to label the sectors and provide an appropriate figure caption.

CHECK YOUR UNDERSTANDING OF SECTION 2.4

14. College students were asked to name their favorite leisure-time activity. The five most commonly mentioned activities were rapping with friends (RF), reading (R), watching television (TV), participating in a sport (PS), and drinking (D). Construct a bar graph for the following data.

RF	PS	D	RF	R	TV	RF	D	PS
RF	RF	R	TV	RF	D	TV	RF	TV
D	TV	RF	RF	D	RF	R	R	RF
R	R	TV	D	TV	D	D	RF	TV
TV	RF	PS	TV	RF	TV	TV	D	
D	D	TV	RF	PS	RF	RF	D	

15. A study was conducted in an Arizona nursing school to determine whether students would have a positive attitude toward research after conducting a research project of their own. After completing a required research course and project, students were asked to indicate which one of four statements best represented their attitude. Of the 230 student nurses who responded, 31 checked the statement that said they would like to be involved in research after graduation. Seventy-three checked the statement that said nurses should understand research as a part of their professional responsibility. Sixty checked the statement that said they felt confident in their ability to evaluate research in nursing. Sixty-six checked the statement that said the required project was responsible

for their improved understanding of the research process. Construct a bar graph for these data. (Suggested by Van Bree, Nancee S. [1981]. Undergraduate research. *Nursing Outlook, 29,* 39–41.)

16. Construct a pie chart for the data in Exercise 14.
17. Construct a pie chart for the data in Exercise 15.
18. Terms to remember:
    a. Bar graph   b. Abscissa   c. *X* axis
    d. Ordinate   e. *Y* axis   f. Intercept
    g. Pie chart

2.5 GRAPHS FOR QUANTITATIVE VARIABLES

Histogram

> A **histogram** is similar in appearance and construction to a bar graph, but it is used for quantitative variables rather than qualitative variables. It is constructed by erecting vertical bars over the *real limits* of each class interval, with the height of each bar corresponding to the number of scores in the interval. The bars of adjacent class intervals should touch, leaving no space between the bars; this emphasizes the continuous, quantitative character of the class intervals.

Except for these differences, histograms and bar graphs are constructed in the same manner: (1) The class intervals are represented along the horizontal axis, and frequency is represented along the vertical axis; (2) the zero point or origin of each axis is located at the *X* and *Y* intercept; (3) the height of the graph is 66% to 75% of its width; and (4) the two axes are labeled appropriately, and a figure caption is given to help the reader interpret the graph.

A histogram for the data in Table 2.2-3 is shown in Figure 2.5-1. Note that the sides of the bars are located at the real limits of the class intervals rather than at the

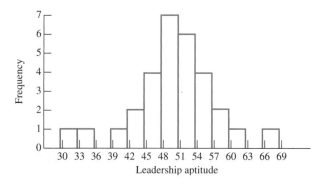

Figure 2.5-1. Histogram for leadership aptitude scores for *n* = 30 football coaches. (Data from Table 2.2-3.)

nominal limits, for example, 29.5–32.5 and not 30–32. Either frequency or relative frequency can be represented along the vertical axis. The transformation of frequencies to relative frequencies is discussed in Section 2.2.

Frequency Polygon

To construct a **frequency polygon** from a frequency distribution, you begin as though you were making a histogram. The horizontal axis is marked off into class intervals, and the vertical axis is marked off into numbers representing frequencies. However, the frequency of a class interval is not represented by a vertical bar but by a dot placed at the proper height over the midpoint of the class interval. The **midpoint of a class interval** is given by

$$\text{Midpoint} = \frac{\text{Upper limit of class interval} + \text{Lower limit of class interval}}{2}$$

For example, the midpoint of the class interval 30–32 is $(32 + 30)/2 = 31$. Finally, adjacent dots are joined by straight lines. At each end of the graph, two additional class intervals containing no scores are identified and lines are dropped to their midpoints so as to anchor the graph to the horizontal axis. A frequency polygon for the data in Table 2.2-3 is shown in Figure 2.5-2. Frequency polygons and histograms impart the same information; the choice between them is largely a matter of personal preference. The histogram is probably a little easier for the general public to interpret, but the stepwise bars tend to obscure the shape of the distribution. The frequency polygon is preferred when two or more sets of data are represented in the same graph because superimposed histograms often overlap and obscure one another.

Cumulative Polygon

Section 2.2 showed that a cumulative frequency distribution could be used to show the number, proportion, or percentage of scores that lie below the real upper limit of each class interval. This same information can be presented graphically by a **cumulative polygon.** Instead of placing dots over the midpoints of class intervals,

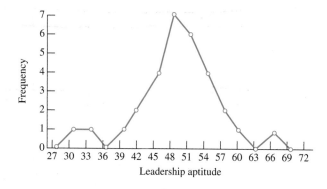

Figure 2.5-2. Frequency polygon for leadership aptitude scores for $n = 30$ football coaches. (Data from Table 2.2-3.)

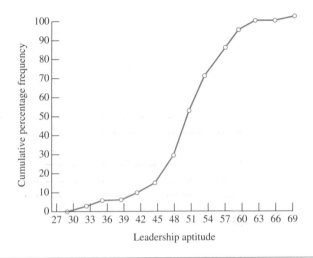

Figure 2.5-3. Cumulative percentage frequency polygon for leadership aptitude scores for $n = 30$ football coaches. (Data from Table 2.2-6.)

you place them over the real upper limits. The vertical axis can represent *Cum f*, *Cum Prop f*, or *Cum % f*. A cumulative percentage frequency polygon for the data in Table 2.2-6 is shown in Figure 2.5-3. As is usually the case in the behavioral sciences and education, the cumulative polygon has the characteristic S shape. The S shape occurs whenever there are more scores in the middle of the frequency distribution than at the extremes. Graphs that are S shaped are called **ogives** (pronounced "oh jives").

Stem-and-Leaf Display

Another useful graphic procedure is the **stem-and-leaf display**.[6] It resembles a histogram that has been turned on its side. A stem-and-leaf display is illustrated in Table 2.5-1 for the data in Table 2.2-1. The first step in constructing the display is to specify class intervals following the procedures in Section 2.2. The class intervals become the *stems* of the display. A score is represented by its class interval, the stem, and by its trailing digit, the *leaf*. For example, the score 30 in Table 2.2-1 falls in the class interval 30–32, and its trailing digit is 0. This score of 30 is represented in Table 2.5-1 by the leaf 0 on the stem 30–32. The appearance of the display can be improved by ordering the leaves on a stem from the smallest to the largest. It is customary to put the smallest class interval at the top of the display and the largest class interval at the bottom and to place a vertical line between the leaves and stems, as shown in Table 2.5-1. If these conventions are followed and the display is rotated 90° counterclockwise, the display looks like a histogram in which the vertical bars have been replaced by columns of numbers.

An important advantage of a stem-and-leaf display over a histogram is that the stem-and-leaf display provides all of the information that is contained in a histogram *and* preserves the value of the individual scores. For example, in Table 2.5-1, you

---

[6] The procedure was popularized by John Tukey (1977).

TABLE 2.5-1 Stem-and-Leaf Display for Data from Table 2.2-1

(1) Stem (Class Interval)	(2) Leaf (Trailing Digit)	(3) Frequency (f)
30–32	0	1
33–35	3	1
36–38		0
39–41	9	1
42–44	2 4	2
45–47	5 6 6 7	4
48–50	8 8 9 9 0 0 0	7
51–53	1 1 2 2 3 3	6
54–56	4 4 5 6	4
57–59	7 9	2
60–62	2	1
63–65		0
66–68	8	1
		$n = 30$

TABLE 2.5-2 Stem-and-Leaf Display for Job Satisfaction of First-Line Supervisors and Assembly-Line Workers (Data from Exercise 2 in Section 2.2 and Exercise 4 in Review Exercises for Chapter 2)

Leaf First-Line Supervisors	Stem	Leaf Assembly-Line Workers
	2–3	3
	4–5	4 4 4 5 5 5 5
6	6–7	6 6 6 6 6 6 7 7 7 7 7 7 7
	8–9	8 8 8 8 8 8 8 9 9 9 9 9
	10–11	0 0 0 0 1 1 1 1
2	12–13	2 3
4 5	14–15	5 5
6 7	16–17	7
8 8 9	18–19	
0 0 1 1	20–21	1
2 3	22–23	2
4 5	24–25	5

know the value of the four scores in the class interval 54–56. They are 54, 54, 55, and 56. If desired, the stem-and-leaf display can be supplemented with a frequency distribution, as in column 3 of Table 2.5-1. Also, two sets of data can be presented in the same table by placing one set on the left side of the stems and the other set on the right side, as in Table 2.5-2. This back-to-back stem-and-leaf display makes it easy to compare the two distributions.

A stem-and-leaf display can be simplified by using only the first or leading digit(s) of a stem (class interval). For example, the class interval 10–19 can be represented by the stem 1, the class interval 20–29 by the stem 2, the class interval 150–159 by the stem 15, and so on. Most statistical packages use this abbreviated representation of stems.

CHECK YOUR UNDERSTANDING OF SECTION 2.5

19. The following data represent the number of cigarettes smoked per day by mothers whose first babies were stillborn. Construct a histogram for these data.

27	25	31	22	3	16	15
21	32	29	30	12	14	26
9	27	25	27	30	28	31
30	18	0	23	20	21	19
28	16	10	19	13		

20. Rats were shown three illuminated symbols; their task was to press the lever below the symbol that differed from the other two. The dependent measure was the number of trials required before the rat could make eight consecutive correct responses. Construct a histogram for these data.

52	34	57	47	54	56	46
60	63	42	20	50	81	41
43	51	36	73	56	77	59
50	42	58	65	42	58	63
66	55	53	63	53	54	61

21. Determine the midpoints of the following class intervals.
    a. 20–24   b. 8–11   c. 132–133   d. 15–29
22. Construct a frequency polygon for the data in Exercise 19.
23. Construct a frequency polygon for the data in Exercise 20.
24. (a) Construct a cumulative polygon for the data in Exercise 19; plot *Cum % f* on the ordinate. (b) Estimate the score above which 50% of the cases fall.
25. How can you tell from a frequency distribution whether a cumulative polygon for the data would have an S shape?
26. Construct a stem-and-leaf display for the data in Exercise 19.
27. Terms to remember:
    a. Histogram   b. Frequency polygon
    c. Class interval midpoint   d. Cumulative polygon
    e. Ogive   f. Stem-and-leaf display

2.6 SHAPES OF DISTRIBUTIONS

Graphs come in many different shapes. Some shapes occur with enough regularity that they have been given special names. These shapes are shown in Figure 2.6-1.

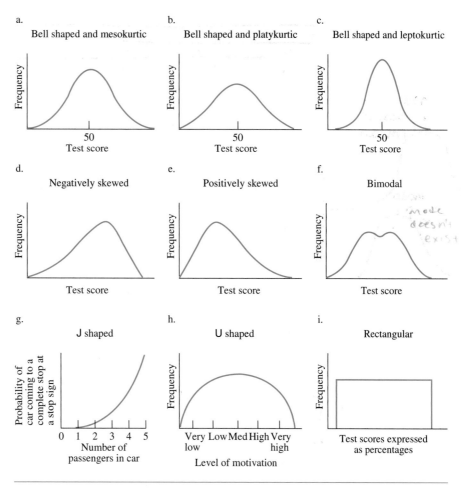

Figure 2.6-1. Common distributions in behavioral and educational research.

Bell-Shaped Distributions

Figure 2.6-1(a) approximates the shape of the **normal distribution**, which is discussed in Chapter 9. This important distribution is symmetrical—that is, the right half is the mirror image of the left half—and it has a particular degree of peakedness.

> The property of being peaked, flat, or somewhere in between is referred to as **kurtosis.**

The normal distribution is **mesokurtic**; *meso-* means intermediate. Distributions that are flatter than the normal distribution are called **platykurtic**; *platy-* means flat or broad. Those that are more peaked are called **leptokurtic**; *lepto-* meaning slender or narrow. Examples of these distributions are shown in Figure 2.6-1(b) and (c). These distributions and the one in (a) all center on the same test score, 50. The point on which a distribution centers is an important characteristic of the distribution and is referred to as its **central tendency.** Another important characteristic of a distribution is its **dispersion**—the extent to which scores are spread out around a central point. The scores in Figure 2.6-1(c), for example, have less dispersion or scatter than those in (a) and (b).

Skewed Distributions

Distributions are either symmetrical or asymmetrical.

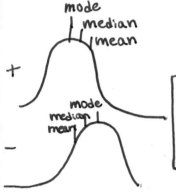

> If the right half of a distribution is the mirror image of the left half, the distribution is **symmetrical.** If the longer tail of an asymmetrical distribution extends toward the X and Y intercept, as in Figure 2.6-1(d), the distribution is **negatively skewed.** If the longer tail extends away from the intercept, as in Figure 2.6-1(e), the distribution is **positively skewed.**

A negatively skewed distribution results, for example, if the participants are given a very easy test. Because most of the participants score high and only a few score low, the longer tail trails off toward the X and Y intercept. A positively skewed distribution results if the test is very hard.

Bimodal Distributions

> A distribution is **bimodal** if it has two humps, each with the same maximum frequency.

Bimodal distributions often result when two distinct samples are represented on a single graph. For example, a graph like that shown in Figure 2.6-1(f) would result if you plotted the masculinity scores of 50 men and 50 women.

> A graph with three or more humps, each with the same maximum frequency, is **multimodal.**

Technically, a distribution is bimodal or multimodal only if its humps have the same frequency. Nevertheless, distributions with pronounced but slightly unequal humps are commonly described as bimodal or multimodal.

J, U, and Rectangular Distributions

> **J and U distributions** are so named because their shapes resemble those letters.

A J-shaped curve like the one in Figure 2.6-1(g) is obtained, for example, if the probability of coming to a complete stop at a stop sign is plotted on the vertical axis and the number of passengers in the car is plotted on the horizontal axis. A reversed J curve is obtained if the number of people arriving for church is plotted on the vertical axis and the number of minutes that they are late is plotted on the horizontal axis. Similar results are obtained in most studies of conforming social behavior—most people conform to social conventions and laws, so fewer and fewer people exhibit larger degrees of nonconformity.

An inverted U curve like the one in Figure 2.6-1(h) is obtained, for example, if performance on a difficult task is plotted on the vertical axis and level of motivation of the participants is plotted on the horizontal axis.

> A **rectangular** or **uniform** distribution is one in which each class interval has the same frequency.

A rectangular distribution is produced when test scores are converted to percentiles (see Section 4.2) and the number of scores in the class intervals 0–10th percentile, 10th–20th percentile, . . . , 90th–100th percentile is graphed. It follows that the resulting graph will be rectangular because each of the 10 class intervals by definition must contain 10% of the scores.

This section described some common distributions, and in the process introduced four important characteristics of distributions: (1) central tendency, (2) dispersion, (3) symmetry or lack of symmetry (skewness), and (4) kurtosis. In Chapters 3 and 4 you will learn how to compute numbers that represent each of these important characteristics.

CHECK YOUR UNDERSTANDING OF SECTION 2.6

28. Indicate whether the following statements are true or false.
    a. A normal distribution is symmetrical and mesokurtic.
    b. If the upper half of a distribution is not the mirror image of the lower half, the distribution is asymmetrical.
    c. A distribution that is more peaked than the normal distribution is called platykurtic.
    d. The tail of a positively skewed distribution extends away from the X and Y intercept.
    e. A distribution with two maximum humps, each with the same frequency, is said to be multimodal.

29. Draw the shape of a frequency polygon that would occur in each of the following experiments. Identify each distribution.
    a. Miss America contestants take a masculinity test.
    b. An intelligence test is given to a large sample of sixth-grade children.
    c. Students at Curtis Institute of Music take a test of musical aptitude.
    d. Students are surprised with a pop quiz immediately after the Christmas vacation.

30. Terms to remember:
    a. Normal distribution
    b. Kurtosis
    c. Mesokurtic
    d. Platykurtic

e. Leptokurtic   f. Central tendency
g. Dispersion   h. Symmetrical distribution
i. Skewness (negative and positive)   j. Bimodal
k. Multimodal   l. J distribution
m. U distribution   n. Rectangular (uniform) distribution

2.7 MISLEADING GRAPHS

Graphs should be constructed so that they accurately portray the essential character-istics of data. Not all graphs do this—some even defy correct interpretation. Two graphs of the same data can convey entirely different impressions, as shown in Figures 2.7-1(a) and (b), which report crime statistics for three similar neighbor-hoods. In neighborhood A, cruising patrol cars were eliminated during a three-month trial period; neighborhood B had five cruising cars during the period; and C was flooded with 15 cars. Your conclusions about the effects of patrol cars would probably depend on which graph you saw. Figure 2.7-1(a) gives the impression that the presence or absence of patrol cars is associated with a dramatic difference in crime rate. Note, however, that the largest difference—1000 versus 970—is only 3%. Such a small difference could just as easily be attributed to chance factors or to differences in crime reporting procedures. The graph is misleading because it vio-lates the 66% to 75% height-width rule mentioned in Section 2.4 and because the Y axis begins with a frequency of 960 crimes instead of 0 crimes.[7] The use of such misleading graphing procedures is contrary to the aim of statistics, which is to help the user make sense out of data.

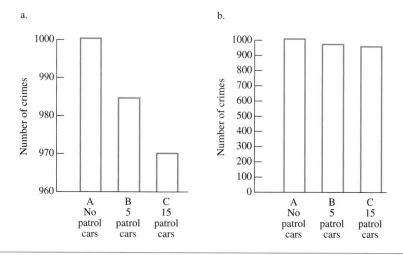

Figure 2.7-1. Number of reported crimes in three similar neighborhoods during a three-month test period. Note how graph (a) gives the false impression of a great difference in crime rate across the three conditions.

[7] Huff (1954) and Tufte (1983) illustrate other misleading techniques and provide examples of outstand-ing graphs.

a.
b.

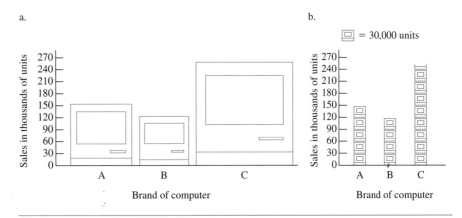

Figure 2.7-2. Pictograms representing sales of three popular computers. Pictogram (a) is misleading because our perception of sales is influenced by the heights of the pictures and by their areas, and area is an irrelevant dimension.

A more subtle form of misrepresentation can occur in pictograms.

A **pictogram** represents quantity by presenting pictures of the objects being compared.

Pictograms are often used in the mass media in place of bar graphs and histograms to enliven a presentation. Consider Figure 2.7-2, in which sales for three brands of computers are represented by two types of pictograms. Figure 2.7-2(a) is inherently misleading because our perception of the sales of the three brands is influenced not only by the heights of the pictures but also by their areas, and area is an irrelevant dimension. For example, sales for brand C are approximately twice those for brand B, but the area of brand C's picture is 4.3 times larger than that of brand B. The pictogram is Figure 2.7-2(b) provides a more realistic representation of sales.

CHECK YOUR UNDERSTANDING OF SECTION 2.7

31. Prepare two bar graphs for the following data. Design one to deliberately suggest that government spending has been stable, the other to suggest a dramatic increase in government spending.

Month	Spending	Month	Spending
June	$29,400,000	October	$29,500,000
July	29,200,000	November	29,600,000
August	29,300,000	December	29,800,000
September	29,600,000	January	30,200,000

32. Term to remember:
    a. Pictogram

2.8 LOOKING BACK: WHAT HAVE YOU LEARNED?

You have learned about two descriptive devices that make data easier to comprehend: frequency distributions and graphs. A frequency distribution is a first and sometimes final step in summarizing data. It organizes data into a number of equivalence classes called class intervals and shows the number of observations that fall into each class interval. The distribution is ungrouped if each class interval is a single score value; if the classes contain two or more score values, the distribution is grouped. Grouping simplifies the interpretation of data by assigning scores to a limited number of class intervals, usually between 10 and 20.

A graph is a pictorial representation of a frequency distribution and hence is easier to interpret. The most common graphs for qualitative variables are bar graphs and pie charts. Histograms, frequency polygons, cumulative polygons, and stem-and-leaf displays are used to represent quantitative variables.

A graph should present data accurately, unambiguously, and in such a way that its main characteristics can be seen at a glance. To achieve this end, certain conventions are followed: (1) frequency is plotted on the Y axis, and equivalence classes are plotted on the X axis; (2) the zero point (or origin) of the Y axis is placed at the X and Y intercept; (3) the height of the graph is 66% to 75% of its width; (4) the X and Y axes are labeled; and (5) a figure caption is provided.

REVIEW EXERCISES FOR CHAPTER 2

1. Construct an ungrouped frequency distribution for the ages of study-abroad candidates at their most recent birthday. The data are as follows.

18	20	19	20
20	19	19	19
23	18	20	21
17	20	18	20

2. For the following nominal class intervals, give the real limits and the class interval size.
   a. 16   b. 60–69   c. 18.00–19.99
   d. 12.0–14.9   e. 0–0.4   f. 1.50–1.74

3. For each of the following, give (i) the number of class intervals, (ii) the size of the class interval, and (iii) the nominal limits of the class interval containing the smallest score.

	Largest Score	Smallest Score	Number of Scores
a.	37	8	106
b.	62	23	273
c.	164	126	29
d.	52	0	22

4. First-line supervisors were asked to complete a job-satisfaction questionnaire. Construct a grouped frequency distribution for the following data.

25	23	18	24	14
21	17	12	19	
15	6	22	16	
20	20	21	18	

5. What are the advantages and disadvantages of grouped and ungrouped frequency distributions?

6. For the job-satisfaction data in Exercise 4, construct a relative frequency distribution using $\% f$.

7. Construct a relative frequency distribution for comparing the job satisfaction of assembly-line workers in Exercise 2 in "Check Your Understanding of Section 2.2" with that of first-line supervisors in Exercise 4.

8. Under what conditions is a relative frequency distribution more informative than an ordinary frequency distribution?

9. For the data in Exercise 6 in "Check Your Understanding of Section 2.2," construct a cumulative frequency distribution.

10. For the first-line supervisors' data in Exercise 4, construct a cumulative percentage frequency distribution.

11. a. Students enrolling in Introductory Sociology were randomly assigned to one of three classes: traditional lecture (TL), guided reading (GR), or lecture with multimedia supplements (LM). Following are the class assignments of the students who scored in the top 30 on the final examination; construct a frequency distribution for these data.

    b. What does your distribution tell you about the relative effectiveness of the classes?

LM	GR	LM	TL	GR	LM
LM	TL	GR	LM	LM	GR
TL	TL	TL	LM	LM	LM
GR	LM	LM	LM	TL	TL
LM	LM	TL	GR	LM	LM

12. Twenty-five physicians were asked what they felt was the main health threat to male executives. The most common responses were occupational stress (OS), obesity (OB), smoking (S), lack of exercise (LE), and other (O). Construct a frequency distribution for these data.

OB	OS	S	OB	LE
S	OB	OB	OS	O
LE	S	OS	S	OB
O	LE	O	LE	LE
OB	LE	O	O	OB

13. Toss a die 30 times and construct a frequency distribution showing the number of times each die face occurred.

14. Contrast the procedures for constructing frequency distributions for qualitative variables with those for quantitative variables.

15. Information from a biographical inventory was used to compute a socioeconomic index for students in a university marching band. Scores above 72 were classified as very high (VH); scores from 61 to 72, as high (H); scores from 43 to 60, as middle (M); and scores below 43, as low (L). Construct a bar graph for the following data.

H	H	H	H	M	VH	VH	H	M
M	L	H	M	VH	H	H	H	VH
H	M	M	H	H	VH	H	M	
VH	H	H	M	M	VH	M	L	
H	VH	VH	H	H	M	VH	M	
M	M	VH	L	M	H	H	VH	

16. The value of psychoeducational programs as a means of preventing and relieving problems of daily living is gaining acceptance in the medical community. A health maintenance organization used a questionnaire to survey the health needs of its members. The following table shows the number of respondents who selected one of nine popular programs as the one in which they were most interested. Construct a bar graph for these data. (Suggested by Burnell, George M., and Taylor, Peter H. [1982]. Psychoeducational programs for problems in living. *Health and Social Work, 7*(1), 7–13.)

Program	Number Indicating Primary Interest
Weight reduction	154
Fatigue	101
Marital and sex problems	92
Coping with physical problems	71
Stress	65
Heart disease prevention	61
Assertiveness	60
Stop smoking	48
Headaches	47

17. Research was conducted to investigate "citizen contacting," in which an individual approaches government officials or other powerful persons to obtain help for themselves and others. Among the countries surveyed were Austria, the Netherlands, and the United States. The citizens initiating the contacts during the preceding two years were classified according to level of educational achievement. (a) Construct a bar graph for each country for the following data. (b) What conclusions can you draw from your graphs? (Suggested by Zuckerman, A. S., and West, D. M. [1985]. The political bases of citizen contacting: A cross-national analysis. *The American Political Science Review, 79*, 117–131.)

Country	1 (low)	2	3	4	5	6 (high)
Austria	.03	.07	.07	.13	.12	.25
Netherlands	.04	.09	.11	.21	.25	.23
United States	.11	.15	.21	.30	.37	.51

Proportion Making Contact by Level of Education
Level of Education

18. Construct a bar graph for the Introductory Sociology data in Exercise 11.
19. Construct a bar graph for the physician data in Exercise 12; plot percentage frequency on the *Y* axis.
20. Describe the procedure for constructing a bar graph from a frequency distribution.
21. Construct a pie chart for the Introductory Sociology data in Exercise 11.
22. Construct a pie chart for the socioeconomic data in Exercise 15.
23. Describe the procedure for constructing a pie chart from a frequency distribution.
24. Construct a histogram for the first-line supervisors' data in Exercise 4. Plot percentage frequency on the ordinate.
25. Construct a histogram for the reaction-time data in Exercise 7 in "Check Your Understanding of Section 2.2." Plot proportionate frequency on the ordinate.
26. How does the construction of histograms and bar graphs differ?
27. Determine the midpoints of the following class intervals.
    a. 1.50–1.74   b. 100–104   c. 0–2   d. 60–69
28. A study was undertaken to determine how well psychological crises resulting from traumatic events are resolved over time. The participants included 15 female cancer patients who underwent breast surgery for the first time, 15 female patients who underwent less-serious surgery (gall bladder removal, hernia repair, and so forth), and 15 physically healthy (nonsurgery) women. Each patient took the Halpern Crisis Scale at intervals of 0, 3, 7, 11, and 15 weeks. The 0 interval represented the night before surgery. The sample of healthy control participants also took the scale at the same time intervals. The following data, based on the number of women with a Halpern Crisis Scale score over 72, were obtained. A score above 72 is considered a high crisis score. (Suggested by Gottesman, David, and Lewis, Marc S. [1982]. Differences in crisis reactions among cancer and surgery patients. *Journal of Consulting and Clinical Psychology, 50,* 381–388.)

Group	0	3	7	11	15
Cancer surgery	11	12	14	12	14
Other surgery	8	11	12	10	8
Nonsurgery	4	5	5	6	5

Week Number

(a) Construct a frequency polygon for these data. Plot the data for each group on the same graph; do not anchor the polygon to the horizontal axis. (b) Write a short paragraph giving your interpretation of these data.
29. Construct a frequency polygon for the first-line supervisors' data in Exercise 4. Plot percentage frequency on the ordinate.

30. What are the relative merits of histograms and frequency polygons?
31. Construct a cumulative polygon for the reaction-time data in Exercise 7 in "Check Your Understanding of Section 2.2."
32. (a) Construct a cumulative polygon for the data in Exercise 20 in Section 2.5; plot *Cum prop f* on the ordinate. (b) Estimate the score below which 50% of the cases fall and the score below which 20% of the cases fall.
33. Data on the prevalence of prostate carcinoma by age range were collected. (a) Construct a relative frequency polygon for the data listed in the following table. (b) Use your polygon to estimate the age at which 50% of men could be expected to have prostrate cancer. (c) One cannot construct a cumulative frequency polygon for these data. Explain. (Suggested by Stamey, T. A. [1982]. Cancer of the prostate: An analysis of some important contributions and dilemmas. *Monographs in Urology, 3,* 65–94.)

Age Group	Percent with Disease
90–99	61.3
80–89	38.0
70–79	29.8
60–69	20.5
50–59	11.8
40–49	6.9
30–39	2.1

34. Construct a stem-and-leaf display for the lever-pressing data in Exercise 20 in "Check Your Understanding of Section 2.5."
35. Indicate whether the following statements are true or false.
    a. A distribution that is flatter than the normal distribution is called mesokurtic.
    b. *Lepto* in *leptokurtic* means slender or narrow.
    c. The tail of a negatively skewed distribution extends away from the X and Y intercept.
    d. A distribution with three maximum humps, each with the same frequency, is bimodal.
36. Draw the shape of a frequency polygon that would occur in each of the following experiments. Identify each distribution.
    a. Students at Juilliard School of Music take a test of musical aptitude.
    b. Students are surprised with a pop quiz immediately after the Easter vacation.
    c. Participants attempt to solve 20 complex puzzles under five levels of motivation: very low, low, medium, high, and very high.
    d. Number of crimes per 1,000 inhabitants is determined for the population of five cities; it turns out that the cities have the same crime rate.
    e. The scores for 30 engineering majors and 30 business majors on a test of mechanical aptitude are plotted.
    f. Strength of grip is measured for 20 young boys, 20 men in their early 20s, and 20 men over age 65.
    g. Arrival time is recorded for people who are late for a concert.
    h. The number of persons contracting polio in the United States from 1940 to 1970 is determined from hospital records.

37. The following data are sales figures for vacuum cleaner salespeople. Prepare graphs that suggest that (a) all the salespeople are producing at a uniformly high level, (b) Chapman should be fired, and (c) they should all be fired.

Chapman	$66,000	Hillis	$68,200
Hays	$67,300	Schmeltekopf	$71,000
Daniel	$69,900	Lilley	$71,100

38. Use a statistical software package to obtain a histogram for the data on first-line supervisors in Exercise 4.
39. Use a statistical software package to obtain a bar graph for the data on physicians in Exercise 12.
40. Use a statistical software package to obtain a bar graph for the socioeconomic data in Exercise 15.
41. Use a statistical software package to obtain a histogram for the mechanical-aptitude data in Exercise 6 in "Check Your Understanding of Section 2.2."
42. Use a statistical software package to obtain a histogram for the reaction-time data in Exercise 7 in "Check Your Understanding of Section 2.2."
43. Use a statistical software package to obtain a stem-and-leaf display for the learning data in Exercise 9 in "Check Your Understanding of Section 2.2."
44. Use a statistical software package to obtain a stem-and-leaf display for the data on first-line supervisors in Exercise 4.

3

Measures of Central Tendency

3.1 Introduction
Looking Ahead: What Is
    This Chapter About?
Other Important
    Characteristics of Data

3.2 Mode
Check Your Understanding
    of Section 3.2

3.3 Mean
Summation Notation for
    the Mean
Computing the Mean
    from a Frequency
    Distribution
Check Your Understanding
    of Section 3.3

3.4 Median
Computing the Median
    from a Frequency
    Distribution
Check Your
    Understanding
    of Section 3.4

**3.5 Relative Merits of the
    Mean, Median, and
    Mode**
Merits of the Mean
Merits of the Median
Merits of the Mode
Summary of the Properties
    of the Mean, Median,
    and Mode
Check Your
    Understanding
    of Section 3.5

**3.6 Location of the Mean,
    Median, and Mode in a
    Distribution**
Check Your
    Understanding
    of Section 3.6

**3.7 Mean of Two or More
    Means**
Check Your
    Understanding
    of Section 3.7

**3.8 More about the
    Summation Operator**
Summation Rules
Proof That the Mean Is
    a Balance Point
Check Your
    Understanding
    of Section 3.8

**3.9 Looking Back: What
    Have You Learned?**
Review Exercises for
    Chapter 3

3.1 INTRODUCTION

Looking Ahead: What Is This Chapter About?

This chapter describes three statistics for summarizing data. In the previous chapter, you learned how to use frequency distributions and graphs to summarize data. Sometimes it is desirable to summarize further by using numbers to describe interesting properties of the data. The most important property of data is usually its **central tendency,** the score value on which a distribution centers. This value is popularly called the *average*; it connotes what is typical, usual, representative, or expected. Because of these different connotations, statisticians prefer to use the more precise terms of **mode, mean,** and **median** in referring to the central tendency of a distribution. As you will see, these terms refer to three distinct conceptions of central tendency.

After reading the chapter, you should know the following:

- How to compute and interpret the mode, mean, and median
- How to represent the sum of two or more numbers using the summation symbol, $\sum$ (Greek capital sigma)
- The advantages of the three measures of central tendency and when to use each
- The relative position of the mode, mean, and median in symmetrical and asymmetrical distributions
- How to compute the mean of several means

Other Important Characteristics of Data

Central tendency is arguably the most interesting and important characteristic of data. Close behind central tendency in importance is **dispersion,** which is the extent to which scores differ from one another—that is, their scatter or heterogeneity. Several ways of describing dispersion are discussed in Chapter 4. Chapter 4 also discusses two other important properties of data: **skewness** and **kurtosis.** Measures of skewness tell you whether a distribution is symmetrical or asymmetrical; measures of kurtosis tell you whether a distribution is peaked or flat. Numbers representing these four properties of data—central tendency, dispersion, skewness, and kurtosis—provide a relatively complete summary of the information contained in frequency distributions and graphs. In many cases, a knowledge of only two of these, central tendency and dispersion, is sufficient for your purposes.

3.2 MODE

The simplest of the three conceptions of central tendency is the mode, denoted by *Mo*.

> The **mode** is the score or qualitative category that occurs with the greatest frequency.

TABLE 3.2-1   Frequency Distribution of Family Size of College Professors

X	f
11	1
10	0
9	0
8	1
7	1
6	2
5	4
4	10
3	8
2	8
1	5
	$n = 40$

Consider the following scores that represent the number of times in September that 11 college students called their parents long distance:

$$0 \quad 0 \quad 0 \quad 1 \quad 1 \quad 1 \quad 1 \quad 2 \quad 2 \quad 3 \quad 9.$$

Note that 0 occurs three times; 1, four times; 2, twice; and 3 and 9, once. The mode is 1, because it occurs with the greatest frequency. If data are tabulated in an ungrouped frequency distribution (a distribution that has a class interval size of one), you can determine the mode at a glance. This can be seen for the distribution of family size of college professors shown in Table 3.2-1. The largest frequency, 10, is associated with a family size of 4; hence, the mode is 4. This tells you that the most *typical* family size for this sample is 4, an easy-to-understand concept. As these examples show, the mode is determined by inspection rather than by computation. The mode can be used to describe the central tendency of both qualitative and quantitative variables, but it is most often used for qualitative variables. You will see why this is true when I compare the relative merits of the three measures of central tendency in Section 3.5.

The mode should be computed from an ungrouped frequency distribution if possible. If only a grouped frequency distribution (a distribution that has a class interval size greater than one) is available, the midpoint of the class interval with the greatest frequency is designated as the mode. The mode in this case is imprecise because a different grouping scheme would give different class interval midpoints and hence a different mode.

As a measure of central tendency, the mode has a particularly serious limitation— it may not exist. You saw in Section 2.6 that a distribution can have two nonadjacent scores (or class intervals) with the same maximum frequency. Such distributions are called bimodal and cannot be described by a mode. It is customary in such cases to mention that the distribution is bimodal and to report the scores (or class interval midpoints) associated with the two maximum frequencies. A mode cannot be determined because there is no most typical score.

CHECK YOUR UNDERSTANDING OF SECTION 3.2

1. The behavior of members of the university wine-tasting club was rated following their biweekly learn-by-doing meeting. The following scale was used: N = no change in behavior, S = slight change in verbal or emotional expressions, M = marked change in verbal or emotional expressions, C = clumsiness in locomotion, and G = gross intoxication. (a) Determine the mode for the following data: $N, S, S, G, M, N, S, M, M, C, G, N, S, M, C, S, S, M, S, S.$ (b) What type of variable do the data represent?
2. The ruling structures of 11 emerging nations were classified as 1 = premobilized authoritarian, 2 = conservative authoritarian, and 3 = premobilized democratic. (a) Determine the mode for the following data: 1, 3, 1, 1, 2, 3, 1, 3, 3, 1, 3. (b) What type of variable do the data represent?
3. Why should the mode be computed from ungrouped rather than grouped data whenever possible?

3.3 MEAN

> The most widely used and familiar measure of central tendency is the **arithmetic mean**—the sum of scores divided by the number of scores.

The mean[1] is commonly known as the average. The usual symbol for a sample mean is $\overline{X}$ and is read "X bar."[2] The letter X identifies the variable that has been measured; the bar above X indicates the mean of the X variable. Other letters toward the end of the English alphabet—for example, Y and Z—also are used as symbols for variables, and the corresponding means are denoted by $\overline{Y}$ and $\overline{Z}$.

It is customary to denote characteristics of samples by English letters and characteristics of populations by lowercase Greek letters. As you have seen, the mean of a sample is usually denoted by $\overline{X}$. The mean of a population is denoted by μ, the Greek letter **mu,** and is pronounced "mew." When it is necessary to distinguish among several sample means or several population means, number or letter subscripts can be used, for example, $\overline{X}_1$ and $\overline{X}_2$, $\overline{X}_A$ and $\overline{X}_B$, and μ_1 and μ_2. The distinction between samples and populations appears in another way—a descriptive measure for a sample is called a **statistic;** a descriptive measure for a population is called a **parameter.** Thus, $\overline{X}$ is a statistic, but μ is a parameter.

Summation Notation for the Mean

The mean of a sample is obtained by dividing the sum of the scores by the number of scores. At this point, I will describe a useful notation for the sum of scores.

---

[1] There are several kinds of means, but this book discusses only the arithmetic mean.

[2] Research journals that follow the guidelines in the *Publication Manual* (2001) of the American Psychological Association denote the sample mean by M. The use of $\overline{X}$ to denote the mean is recommended by the American Statistical Association (Halperin, Hartley, & Hoel, 1965).

Suppose that I am interested in the frequency of movie attendance of college students. I can denote this variable by the capital letter X and individual values of the variable by X and a subscript: $X_1, X_2, \ldots, X_i, \ldots, X_n$. According to this notation, X_1 is the frequency of movie attendance for student 1, X_2 is the frequency for student 2, and X_n denotes the frequency for the nth or last student in the sample. I will let i be a general subscript that designates an unspecified one of the $i = 1, \ldots, n$ students (read "i equals one through n students"). The i in X_i can be replaced by any integer between 1 and n inclusive.[3] Suppose that we obtained the following values of X_i for frequency of movie attendance: $X_1 = 3$, $X_2 = 1$, $X_3 = 4$, and $X_4 = 2$. The mean of these $n = 4$ scores is given by

$$\overline{X} = \frac{X_1 + X_2 + X_3 + X_4}{n} = \frac{3 + 1 + 4 + 2}{4} = \frac{10}{4} = 2.5$$

When there is a large number of scores, this formula for $\overline{X}$ is tedious to write. In this case it is customary to write the formula using the **summation symbol** Σ, the Greek capital sigma. The symbol Σ, like $+$, indicates that you should perform the operation of addition. However, $+$ indicates the addition of only two numbers, whereas $\sum_{i=1}^{n}$, which is also written as $\sum_{i=1}^{n}$, means to perform addition until all $i = 1, \ldots, n$ numbers have been added.[4] The expression $\sum_{i=1}^{n} X_i$ is equivalent to $X_1 + X_2 + \cdots + X_n$. The expression $\sum_{i=1}^{n} X_i$ says to let the first value of X_i be X_1; add to this the second value, X_2; and continue until the X_nth value has been added. In the notation $\sum_{i=1}^{n}$, i is called the **index of summation, 1** is the **initial value** of i, and n is its **terminal value.** Using summation notation, the formula for the mean movie attendance of four students is written

$$\overline{X} = \frac{\sum_{i=1}^{4} X_i}{4}$$

which is equivalent to

$$\overline{X} = \frac{X_1 + X_2 + X_3 + X_4}{4}$$

The general formula for a sample mean is written as

$$\overline{X} = \frac{\sum_{i=1}^{n} X_i}{n}$$

where X_i denotes the variable of interest, $\sum_{i=1}^{n}$ says to sum over the $i = 1, \ldots, n$ scores, and n is the number of scores.

[3] The letter i also is used to denote the size of a class interval; this use is discussed in Section 2.2. Because there are only 26 letters in the alphabet, it is not surprising that a letter often has multiple meanings.

[4] Rules of summation are described in Section 3.8.

When the initial and terminal values for the summation are clearly understood, the formula can be simplified to

$$\overline{X} = \frac{\Sigma X_i}{n} \quad \text{or} \quad \overline{X} = \frac{\Sigma X}{n}$$

Computing the Mean from a Frequency Distribution

The formula $\overline{X} = \sum_{i=1}^{n} X_i / n$ is appropriate for data in their original unordered state.

If the data have been ordered in a frequency distribution, the mean can be computed from

$$\overline{X} = \frac{\sum_{j=1}^{k} f_j X_j}{n}$$

where X_j denotes the midpoint of the jth class interval, f_j is the frequency of scores in the jth class interval, $\sum_{j=1}^{k}$ says to sum over the $j = 1, \ldots, k$ class intervals, and n is the number of scores.

The use of this formula is illustrated in Table 3.3-1. The data are scores on the Wakefield Self-Assessment Depression Inventory for a sample of 20 men facing exploratory cancer surgery.

Two formulas for computing the mean have been described:

$$\overline{X} = \frac{\sum_{i=1}^{n} X_i}{n}$$

where $i = 1, \ldots, n$ (n is the number of scores) and

$$\overline{X} = \frac{\sum_{j=1}^{k} f_j X_j}{n}$$

where $j = 1, \ldots, k$ (k is the number of class intervals). In the first formula, X_i denotes the value of the ith score. To compute the mean, the scores are summed and then divided by n, the number of scores. In the second formula, X_j denotes the midpoint of the jth class interval, and f_j, the frequency of scores in that class interval. To compute the mean, you first obtain $f_j X_j$ for each class interval. Next you sum these products, and finally you divide the sum by n, the number of scores.

CHECK YOUR UNDERSTANDING OF SECTION 3.3

4. Identify the following.
   a. X_1 b. X_i c. μ_1 d. X_j

TABLE 3.3-1   Depression Scores of Males Facing Exploratory Cancer Surgery (A Score of 25 or above Indicates Extremely High Depression)

(i) Data (X_j denotes the value of the jth class interval, f_j is the frequency in the jth class interval, j = 1, ..., k, and n is the number of scores)

X_j	f_j	$f_j X_j$
28	1	(1) (28) = 28
27	0	(0) (27) = 0
26	1	(1) (26) = 26
25	2	(2) (25) = 50
24	3	(3) (24) = 72
23	4	(4) (23) = 92
22	3	(3) (22) = 66
21	0	(0) (21) = 0
20	1	(1) (20) = 20
19	2	(2) (19) = 38
18	1	(1) (18) = 18
17	0	(0) (17) = 0
16	1	(1) (16) = 16
15	0	(0) (15) = 0
14	1	(1) (14) = 14
$n = 20$		$\sum_{j=1}^{k} f_j X_j = 440$

(ii) Computation of $\overline{X}$ from an ungrouped frequency distribution

$$\overline{X} = \frac{\sum_{j=1}^{k} f_j X_j}{n} = \frac{440}{20} = 22$$

5. Write out the following, listing individual values of the variable.

   a. $\sum_{i=1}^{n} X_i$ b. $\sum_{j=1}^{k} f_j X_j / n$ c. $\sum_{\substack{i=1 \\ i \neq 3}}^{4} Z_i / n$

6. The socioeconomic level of white families in a predominantly black neighborhood was rated on the basis of income, educational attainment, physical condition of dwelling, and number of home appliances. Compute the mean using $\sum_{i=1}^{n} X_i / n$ for the following socioeconomic scores.

5	4	9	5	3	4
4	6	7	5	3	2
6	2	5	1	7	

7. The following data represent the number of suicides per 10,000 inhabitants in predominantly rural prefectures in Japan. Compute the mean using $\sum_{i=1}^{n} X_i/n$.

22	10	12	2	10	9	16	11	8
14	11	8	13	10	9	12	0	10
12	8	11	5	7	10	7	9	9
9	8	7	8	5	14	3	10	11

8. For the data in Exercise 6, construct an ungrouped frequency distribution and compute the mean using $\overline{X} = \sum_{j=1}^{k} f_j X_j/n$.

9. For the data in Exercise 7, construct an ungrouped frequency distribution and compute the mean using $\overline{X} = \sum_{j=1}^{k} f_j X_j/n$.

10. Terms to remember:
    a. Mu
    b. Statistic
    c. Parameter
    d. Summation symbol, Σ
    e. Index of summation
    f. Initial value of i
    g. Terminal value of i

3.4 MEDIAN

> The **median** is the point in a distribution that divides the data into two groups having equal frequency.

The median is denoted by *Mdn*. As its name suggests, the median is the middle score when scores have been arranged in order of size and n, the number of scores, is odd. When n is even, the median is the midway point between the two middle scores. The procedure for determining the median is slightly different, depending on whether n is odd or even and whether a frequency distribution has been constructed for the data. If the number of scores is small, the median can be determined by inspection. Consider the case in which n is odd, and the scores are 2, 3, 5, 8, 9, 11, 12. When the scores are ordered from smallest to largest along the number line, as in Figure 3.4-1, it is immediately apparent that the median is 8. This follows because there are three scores below the median of 8 and three scores above 8.

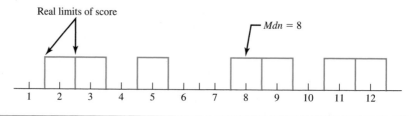

Figure 3.4-1. Determination of the median when n is odd.

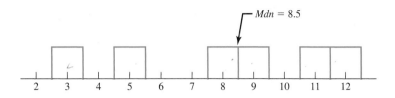

Figure 3.4-2. Determination of the median when *n* is even.

Rules for determining the median are as follows:

If *n* is odd

> *Mdn* is the $(n + 1)/2$th score from either end of the number line.

If *n* is even

> *Mdn* is the midway point between the $n/2$th score and the $(n/2) + 1$th score from either end of the number line.

Consider Figure 3.4-1 again. Because *n* is odd, the median is the $(n + 1)/2$th score from either end of the number line. For example, $(n + 1)/2 = (7 + 1)/2 = 4$; hence, the median is the fourth score counting from either end. Figure 3.4-2 illustrates the location of the median along the line when *n* is even and the scores are 3, 5, 8, 9, 11, 12. Any point along the number line larger than 8 and less than 9 would qualify as the median. By convention, the median is taken as the midway point between the $n/2$th score and the $(n/2) + 1$th score. For example, $6/2 = 3$ and $(6/2) + 1 = 4$. The midway point between the third score (8) and the fourth score (9), counting from the left, is $(8 + 9)/2 = 8.5$, which is the median.

Frequencies greater than 1 at the middle score value may present special problems. The median for Figure 3.4-3(a) is obviously 8, but what about Figure 3.4-3(b)? According to my definition, the median should be the $(n + 1)/2 = (7 + 1)/2 = 4$th score from either end. This score is 8, but below 8 there are three scores and above 8, only two scores. The problem is resolved by dividing the interval 7.5–8.5 into two smaller subintervals, 7.5–8 and 8–8.5. This is shown in the upper part of Figure 3.4-3(b). Going four scores from the lower end of the number line, I reach the score defined by 7.5–8, which has a midpoint at $(7.5 + 8)/2 = 7.75$; similarly, four scores from the upper end also is the score defined by 7.5–8. Thus, the median is 7.75, the midpoint of the score defined by the subinterval 7.5–8. Now consider the scores in Figure 3.4-4. Again I can subdivide the interval—assigning a third of the interval 7.5–8.5 to each score. This results in three smaller subintervals—7.500–7.833, 7.833–8.167, 8.167–8.500—as shown in the upper part of the figure. Because *n* is even, the median is the score value that is midway between the $n/2 = 4$th and the $(n/2) + 1 = 5$th scores. These scores are defined by the subintervals 7.500–7.833 and 7.833–8.167, respectively. The midpoints of these subintervals are 7.667 and 8.000; the median is $(7.667 + 8.000)/2 = 7.833$.

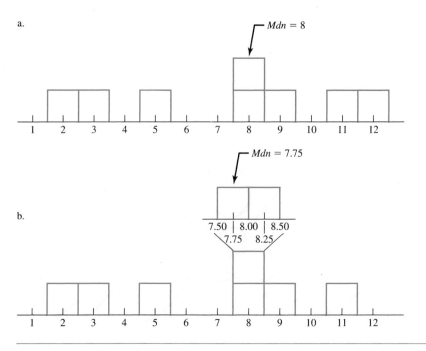

Figure 3.4-3. Determination of the median when the frequency of the middle score value is greater than 1.

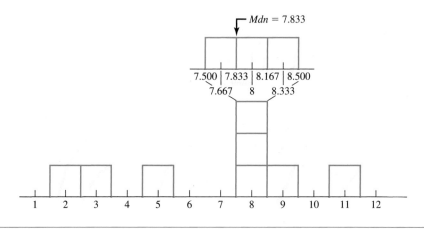

Figure 3.4-4. Determination of the median when the frequency of the middle score value is greater than 1.

Computing the Median from a Frequency Distribution

I determined the median in Figures 3.4-3 and 3.4-4 by **interpolating**—dividing the class interval containing the median into subintervals and finding the point that represented the $(n + 1)/2$th score or the point that was midway between the $n/2$th and $(n/2) + 1$th scores. When data have been ordered in a frequency distribution, the interpolation can be accomplished by means of a formula. The computation is illustrated in Table 3.4-1 for the data in Figure 3.4-4. The meaning of the terms in the formula as well as instructions for using the formula are given in parts (ii) and (iii), respectively, of Table 3.4-1.

TABLE 3.4-1   Procedure for Computing the Median from a Frequency Distribution

(i) Data and computational formula

X_j	f_j	$Cum\,f$ [a]	
11	1	8	
10	0	7	$Mdn = X_{ll} + i\left(\dfrac{n/2 - \Sigma f_b}{f_i}\right)$
9	1	7	
8	3	6	
7	0	3	$= 7.5 + 1\left(\dfrac{8/2 - 3}{3}\right)$
6	0	3	
5	1	3	
4	0	2	$= 7.5 + 1\left(\dfrac{4/2 - 3}{3}\right)$
3	1	2	
2	1	1	$= 7.5 + 0.33 = 7.83$
	$n = 8$		

(ii) Definition of terms

X_j = value of jth class interval

f_j = frequency of jth class interval

X_{ll} = real lower limit of class interval containing the median

i = class interval size

n = number of scores

Σf_b = number of scores below X_{ll}

f_i = number of scores in the class interval containing the median

(continued)

TABLE 3.4-1 *(continued)*

(iii) Computational sequence

1. Compute $n/2 = 8/2 = 4$.
2. Locate the class interval containing the $n/2 = $ 4th score in the *Cum f* column. The median will fall somewhere in this class interval. The fourth score occurs in the class interval 8. This class interval contains the fourth, fifth, and sixth scores; X_{ll} for this class interval is 7.5.
3. Compute i: $i = $ (Real upper limit of class interval – Real lower limit of class interval), for example, $i = 8.5 - 7.5 = 1$.
4. Determine Σf_b, the number of scores below $X_{ll} = 7.5$.
5. Determine f_i, the number of scores in the class interval containing the median.

[a] Cumulative frequency is discussed in Section 2.2.

CHECK YOUR UNDERSTANDING OF SECTION 3.4

11. Determine the median for the following scores.
    a. 9, 3, 16, 5, 21
    b. 16, 19, 17, 31
    c. 3, 1, 3, 4, 5
    d. 3, 4, 4, 2, 8
12. For the data in Exercise 7 in "Check Your Understanding of Section 3.3," construct an ungrouped frequency distribution and compute the median using

$$Mdn = X_{ll} + i\left(\frac{n/2 - \Sigma f_b}{f_i}\right)$$

13. The computational procedure for the median illustrated in Table 3.4-1 calculates the median from below—that is, by coming halfway through the scores, starting from the lowest class interval. Alternatively, the median can be computed by coming down halfway from above—that is, from the highest class interval. The computational formula is

$$Mdn = X_{ul} - i\left(\frac{n/2 - \Sigma f_a}{f_i}\right)$$

By analogy with the definitions in Table 3.4-1, define each of the symbols in the alternative formula.
14. For the data in Table 3.4-1, compute the median by coming down halfway from above—from the highest class interval. The computational formula is

$$Mdn = X_{ul} - i\left(\frac{n/2 - \Sigma f_a}{f_i}\right)$$

3.5 RELATIVE MERITS OF THE MEAN, MEDIAN, AND MODE

Computation of each of the measures of central tendency is fairly simple. Which one should a researcher use for a given problem? The choice should be based on (1) the shape of the distribution, (2) the intended uses of the statistic, (3) the nature of the variable, and (4) the mathematical properties and merits of the mean, median, and mode.

Although they all are measures of central tendency, the mean, median, and mode impart somewhat different information. Consider the scores in Figure 3.5-1. By inspection, you see that the mode is 3. The median is the $(n + 1)/2 = $ 3rd score from either end of the number line. This score falls in the interval with real limits 2.5–3.5. When the interval is divided in half, the real limits of the third score are 3–3.5 and its midpoint is 3.25; hence, the median is 3.25. The mean is $\overline{X} = (2 + 3 + \cdots + 8)/5 = 4$. These three numbers—3, 3.25, and 4—represent different conceptions of the point around which the scores cluster. For a unimodal set of data plotted as a histogram,

1. the *mode* is the score value with the largest frequency—the most typical score;
2. the *median* is the score point that divides the ordered scores into two samples of equal size;
3. the *mean* is the score point at which the distribution balances—its center of gravity.

If a distribution is asymmetrical, as in Figure 3.5-1, the mean and the median are unequal; the value of the mode may or may not differ from the values of those for the mean and the median. If a distribution is symmetrical, the mean and the median are equal; if, in addition, the distribution is unimodal, all three measures are equal.

Merits of the Mean

The mean has a number of mathematical properties that make it the preferred measure of central tendency for relatively symmetrical distributions and for

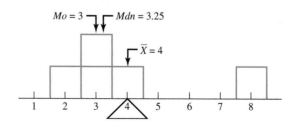

Figure 3.5-1. Comparison of the $\overline{X}$, *Mdn*, and *Mo* in a unimodal distribution. The number line can be thought of as a teeter-totter whose balance point is the mean.

quantitative variables. One of these properties is its sampling stability. Suppose that from an extremely large population I repeatedly drew random samples of size *n*. If I computed the mean for each sample, I would expect the means to be similar but not identical. Suppose that I also computed the median and the mode for each sample. The variability from sample to sample of these statistics would be greatest for the mode and least for the mean. The better **sampling stability** of the mean is an important advantage, especially when one uses inferential statistics to draw conclusions about the central tendency of a population by observing a single sample.

Another advantage of the mean is that it is amenable to arithmetic and algebraic manipulations in ways that the median and mode are not. In other words, the mean is **mathematically tractable.** Therefore, if further statistical computations are to be performed, the mean is usually the measure of choice. This property accounts for the appearance of the mean in the formulas for many important statistics.

The mean is the only one of the three measures that reflects the value of each score. Recall that the mean is computed from the sum of all the scores, $\sum X_i$. The median, on the other hand, is independent of the value of each score (other than the median value itself) as long as the *number* of scores above and below the median is not altered. If, for example, the score of 8 in Figure 3.5-1 is changed to 5, the values of the median and the mode are unchanged; the value of the mean, however, is changed from 4 to 3.4.

It is no accident that the balance point of the scores in Figure 3.5-1 coincides with the mean. This fulcrum property of the mean follows from the mathematical statement $\sum_{i=1}^{n}(X_i - \overline{X}) = 0$, the sum of the deviation of the mean from each score is equal to zero. In Figure 3.5-1, for example, $\sum_{i=1}^{n}(X_i - \overline{X}) = (2 - 4) + (3 - 4) + \cdots + (8 - 4) = 0$, and this will be true for any distribution. If you think of the deviation $(X_i - \overline{X})$ as a distance, the mean is the point from which the sum of the distances to all the scores is zero. For a proof of this property, see Section 3.8.

There are three situations in which the mean is not the preferred measure of central tendency: when the distribution is very skewed, when the data are qualitative in character, and when the distribution is **open-ended**—that is, when the values of extreme scores are unknown. I will discuss the first two situations here and the third in the following section on the median.

Suppose that the following data were obtained for the number of minutes required to solve math problems: 10.1, 10.3, 10.5, 10.6, 10.7, 10.9, 56.9. The mean is 120/7 = 17.1; the median is 10.6. Which number best represents the central tendency of the seven scores? Most readers would agree that it is 10.6, the median. The mean is unduly affected by the lone extreme score of 56.9. Any time a distribution is extremely asymmetrical, the mean is strongly affected by the extreme scores and, as a result, falls farther away from what would be considered the distribution's central area.

The mean cannot be computed when the data are qualitative in character. Suppose that the dependent variable is eye color and I collect the following data: blue, brown, brown, gray, blue, brown. There is no meaningful way to represent these data by a mean. I could, however, compute the mode and say that the most typical eye color is brown.

Merits of the Median

Although the mean is usually the preferred measure of central tendency, there are several situations in which the median is preferred. As I mentioned earlier, the median is not sensitive to the values of the scores above and below it—only to the number of such scores. Unlike the mean, it is not affected by extreme scores, and thus it is a more representative measure of central tendency for very skewed distributions. Also, it can be computed when the values of the extreme scores are unknown. Suppose, for example, that I recorded the number of trials required to learn a list of paired adjectives and Japanese kana (writing) symbols. The data are as follows: 12, 17, 17, 18, 21, 24, > 41. After the 41st trial, the poorest learner was still unable to learn the list and gave up; his score is some number greater than 41. The distribution is open-ended because the value of the extreme score is unknown. Although the exact value of one of the scores is unknown, the median can be computed for these data. Notice that three scores are above 18 (21, 24, > 41) and three are below (12, 17, 17); hence, the median is 18. The mean cannot be computed because the value of the extreme score is unknown.

The median has the added advantage of being easy to compute; when the number of scores is small, it can be determined by inspection.

The principal disadvantages of the median relative to the mean are (1) its poorer sampling stability and (2) its poorer mathematical tractability. For these and other reasons, the median is not used as frequently as the mean in advanced descriptive and inferential statistical procedures.

Merits of the Mode

The mode is the only measure of central tendency that can be used with unordered qualitative variables such as eye color, blood type, race, and political party affiliation. For quantitative variables that are inherently discrete, such as family size, it is sometimes a more meaningful measure of central tendency than the mean or the median. Who ever heard of an average family with 3.7 members? It makes more sense to say that the most typical family size is 3, the mode. Other than these two applications, the mode has little to recommend it except its ease of estimation.

Let us consider why the mode is called the most typical score. Because the mode is the score that occurs most frequently, the number of scores not equal to the mode is as small as it possibly can be. In Figure 3.5-1, for example, three scores differ from the mode; they are 2, 4, and 8. However, four scores differ from the mean (2, 3, 3, and 8), and five scores differ from the median (2, 3, 3, 4, and 8). Hence, the mode is the most typical score.

The mode has a number of limitations. Its sampling stability is much poorer than that of the mean and the median, and it also is less mathematically tractable. Therefore, it is rarely used in advanced descriptive and inferential statistics. However, the mode, like the median, can be computed for an open-ended distribution if the distribution is known to be unimodal and if the unknown scores do not have the greatest frequency. However, because of the median's superior mathematical properties, it is preferred for this application.

Consider another limitation of the mode. A mode may not exist for a set of data, as when the distribution is bi- or multimodal. In such cases, it is customary to report the two or more scores with the same maximum frequency. Because many variables in the behavioral sciences are approximately normally distributed, the existence of two scores with the same maximum frequency suggests the presence of two underlying distributions. This would occur if I administered a test of masculinity to a sample containing an equal number of men and women. To report a mean or a median for such data would be misleading without also reporting that the distribution is bimodal and the values of the maximum scores.

Summary of the Properties of the Mean, Median, and Mode

The mean is

1. the balance point of a distribution, the point for which $\sum_{i=1}^{n}(X_i - \overline{X}) = 0$;
2. the preferred measure for relatively symmetrical distributions and quantitative variables;
3. the measure with the best sampling stability;
4. widely used in advanced statistical procedures;
5. mathematically tractable;
6. the only measure whose value is dependent on the value of every core in the distribution;
7. more sensitive to extreme scores than the median and the mode and, hence, is not recommended for markedly skewed distributions;
8. not appropriate for qualitative data; and
9. not appropriate for open-ended distributions.

The median is

1. the point that divides the ordered scores into two samples of equal size;
2. second to the mean in usefulness;
3. widely used for markedly skewed distributions because it is sensitive only to the number rather than to the values of scores above and below it;
4. the most stable measure that can be used with open-ended distributions;
5. more subject to sampling fluctuation than the mean;
6. less mathematically tractable than the mean; and
7. less often used in advanced statistical procedures.

The mode is

1. the score that occurs most often and, therefore, the most typical value;
2. the only measure appropriate for unordered qualitative variables;
3. more appropriate than the mean or the median for quantitative variables that are inherently discrete;
4. the easiest measure to compute;
5. much more subject to sampling fluctuation than the mean and the median;
6. less mathematically tractable than the mean and the median;
7. not necessarily existent, as when a distribution has two or more scores with the same maximum frequency; and
8. rarely used in advanced statistical procedures.

CHECK YOUR UNDERSTANDING OF SECTION 3.5

15. For the following sets of data, what measures of central tendency would you compute? Justify your choices.
    a. 9, 6, 5, 7, 1, 6, 7, 8, 10, 6, 5, 4, 3, 6, 9, 7, 4, 5, 6, 8, 3, 2
    b. 6, 5, 9, 6, 7, 5, 6, 8, 3, 4, 5, 7, 5, 4, 8, 5
    c. 3, 5, 8, 5, 7, 9, 4, 2, 5, 6, 6, 23
16. Rank the three measures of central tendency with respect to the following characteristics; let 1 = most and 3 = least.
    a. Sampling stability
    b. Appropriateness for qualitative variables
17. Terms to remember:
    a. Sampling stability
    b. Mathematically tractable
    c. Open-ended distribution

3.6 LOCATION OF THE MEAN, MEDIAN, AND MODE IN A DISTRIBUTION

If a distribution is unimodal and symmetrical, the mean, median, and mode have the same value. If the distribution is unimodal but skewed, usually the three measures will be arranged in a predictable order. This order is illustrated in Figure 3.6-1. In both examples, the mean is on the side of the distribution that has the longest tail, and the median falls about one-third of the distance from the mean to the mode. To remember the order—mean, median, mode—note that it is alphabetical, starting from the longer tail. This order occurs because the mean is affected by the value of extreme scores. The median is affected by the presence of extreme scores but not by their value. The mode, however, is not affected by extreme scores unless they

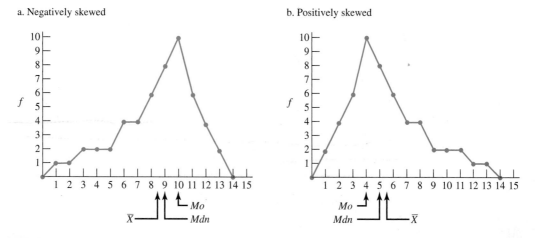

Figure 3.6-1. Location of the $\overline{X}$, *Mdn*, and *Mo* for skewed distributions.

happen to have the greatest frequency of occurrence. This ordering of the mean, median, and mode holds for most unimodal distributions.

The relative location of the mean and median can be used to determine whether a distribution is positively or negatively skewed. For negatively skewed distributions, it is virtually always true that $Mdn > \overline{X}$; for positively skewed distributions, $\overline{X} > Mdn$. If, for example, you know that the median is 25 and the mean is 20, you would strongly suspect that the distribution is negatively skewed. The greater the discrepancy between the two values, the greater the departure from symmetry.[5]

A knowledge of the relative location of the mean, median, and mode in asymmetrical distributions can be used to intentionally distort the interpretation of data and mislead consumers of statistics. If you were to graph the wages of workers in one of the construction industries, you would probably obtain a positively skewed distribution. If you were negotiating a new contract for the workers, you would want to report the modal salary, a lower figure than the median or mean, in defending your request for a wage increase. However, if you were on the other side of the negotiating table, you would cite the mean, a higher figure, in arguing against the need for an increase. Even though both the mean and the mode are correct as measures of central tendency, they are misleading when the distribution is markedly skewed. The more appropriate measure for such a distribution is the median. This example illustrates one of the classic ways in which statistics can be used to mislead the unwary.

CHECK YOUR UNDERSTANDING OF SECTION 3.6

18. Determine the shape—for example, symmetrical, positively skewed, and so on—of each distribution from the following measures of central tendency.
   a. $\overline{X} = 16, Mdn = 10$ b. $\overline{X} > Mdn$
   c. $\overline{X} = 34, Mdn = 34, Mo_1 = 28,$ d. $\overline{X} = 46, Mdn = 46, Mo = 46$
      $Mo_2 = 40$
   e. $Mo = 19, Mdn = 12$ f. $\overline{X} = 23, Mdn = 23, Mo_1 = 20,$
      $Mo_2 = 23, Mo_3 = 27$

3.7 MEAN OF TWO OR MORE MEANS

Suppose that two introductory sociology classes obtained the following mean scores on a departmental examination: 80 and 90. What is the mean of the two means? If each class had the same number of students, you could compute the mean of the means $\overline{X} = (\overline{X}_1 + \overline{X}_2)/2 = (80 + 90)/2 = 85$. If, as is more likely, the classes contain different numbers of students, you must weight the means proportional to their respective sample sizes. Assume that $\overline{X}_1 = 80$ and $n_1 = 20$ and that $\overline{X}_2 = 90$ and $n_2 = 40$. The **weighted mean,** $\overline{X}_W$, is given by

$$\overline{X} = \frac{n_1\overline{X}_1 + n_2\overline{X}_2 + \cdots + n_n\overline{X}_n}{n_1 + n_2 + \cdots + n_n} = \frac{20(80) + 40(90)}{20 + 40} = 86.7$$

[5] A more sophisticated measure of skewness is described in Section 4.6.

The weighted mean is closer to 90 than to 80; this reflects the larger n_2 associated with $\overline{X}_2 = 90$.

CHECK YOUR UNDERSTANDING OF SECTION 3.7

19. For the following data, compute weighted means.
    a. $\overline{X}_1 = 30$, $n_1 = 10$; $\overline{X}_2 = 50$, $n_2 = 20$
    b. $\overline{X}_1 = 20$, $n_1 = 10$; $\overline{X}_2 = 25$, $n_2 = 10$; $\overline{X}_3 = 30$, $n_3 = 20$
20. Term to remember:
    a. Weighted mean

3.8 MORE ABOUT THE SUMMATION OPERATOR

Section 3.3 introduced the summation operator, Σ. You learned that the symbol $\sum_{i=1}^{n}$ tells you to perform an operation, namely, add the terms corresponding to i equals 1 through n. Many proofs[6] in statistics involve rules for using the summation operator with variables and constants. This section describes four of these rules and illustrates their use in proving that the sum of the deviation of the mean from each score is equal to zero. Other proofs involving the summation operator are used in Exercise 23 of "Check Your Understanding of Section 3.8" and in Exercise 21 of the Review Exercises for Chapter 3.

Summation Rules

The following summation rules are widely used in statistical proofs and derivations. An understanding of these rules will go far toward taking derivations out of the realm of magic.

Rule 3.8-1. The Sum of a Constant Let c be a constant; the sum over $i = 1, \ldots, n$ of the constant can be written as the product of the upper limit of the summation, n, and c. That is,

$$\sum_{i=1}^{n} c = \overbrace{c + c + \cdots + c}^{n \text{ terms}} = nc$$

For example, let $c = 2$ and $i = 1, \ldots, 3$; then

$$\sum_{i=1}^{3} 2 = \overbrace{2 + 2 + 2}^{3 \text{ terms}} = 3(2) = 6$$

---

[6] A proof is a process that is used to show that a particular statement follows logically from other accepted statements. Once a statement has been proved, it becomes a theorem and can be used to prove other statements.

Thus, anytime you see $\sum_{i=1}^{n} c$, you can write it as nc. Similarly, $\sum_{j=1}^{k} c$ can be written as kc.

Rule 3.8-2.[7] The Sum of a Variable Let V_i be a variable with values $V_1, V_2, \ldots, V_n$; the sum over $i = 1, \ldots, n$ of the variable is

$$\sum_{i=1}^{n} V_i = V_1 + V_2 + \cdots + V_n$$

For example, let $V_1 = 2$, $V_2 = 3$, and $V_3 = 4$; then

$$\sum_{i=1}^{3} V_i = 2 + 3 + 4 = 9$$

Rule 3.8-3. The Sum of the Product of a Constant, c, and a Variable, V_i
The expression $\sum_{i=1}^{n} cV_i$ can be written as the product of the constant and the sum of the variable—that is,

$$\sum_{i=1}^{n} cV_i = c \sum_{i=1}^{n} V_i$$

For example, let $c = 2$, $V_1 = 2$, $V_2 = 3$, and $V_3 = 4$; then

$$\sum_{i=1}^{3} cV_i = 2(2) + 2(3) + 2(4) = 18$$

$$= c \sum_{i=1}^{n} V_i = 2(2 + 3 + 4) = 2(9) = 18$$

Similarly, the sum of a variable, V_i, divided by a constant, c,

$$\sum_{i=1}^{n} \frac{V_i}{c}$$

can be written as the reciprocal of the constant times the sum of the variable—that is,

$$\frac{1}{c} \sum_{i=1}^{n} V_i$$

For example, let $c = 2$, $V_1 = 2$, $V_2 = 3$, and $V_3 = 4$; then

$$\sum_{i=1}^{3} \frac{V_i}{c} = \frac{2}{2} + \frac{3}{2} + \frac{4}{2} = 4.5$$

$$= \frac{1}{c} \sum_{i=1}^{3} V_i = \frac{1}{2}(2 + 3 + 4) = \frac{1}{2}(9) = 4.5$$

Rule 3.8-4. Distribution of Summation If the only operation to be performed before summation is addition or subtraction, the summation sign can be distributed among the separate terms of the sum. Let V and W be two variables; then

[7] This rule was introduced in Section 3.3.

$$\sum_{i=1}^{n}(V_i + W_i) = \sum_{i=1}^{n} V_i + \sum_{i=1}^{n} W_i$$

For example, let $V_1 = 2$, $V_2 = 3$, $V_3 = 4$, $W_1 = 5$, $W_2 = 6$, and $W_3 = 7$; then

$$\sum_{i=1}^{3}(V_i + W_i) = (2 + 5) + (3 + 6) + (4 + 7) = 27$$

$$= \sum_{i=1}^{3} V_i + \sum_{i=1}^{3} W_i$$

$$= (2 + 3 + 4) + (5 + 6 + 7) = 27$$

This rule applies to any number of terms. For example, let V_i, W_i, and X_i be variables and a, b, and c be constants; then, according to Rules 3.8–1, 3.8–2, and 3.8–4,

$$\sum_{i=1}^{n}(V_i + W_i + X_i + a + b + c) = \sum_{i=1}^{n} V_i + \sum_{i=1}^{n} W_i + \sum_{i=1}^{n} X_i + na + nb + nc$$

Proof That the Mean Is a Balance Point

In Section 3.5 I said that the mean is the point such that $\sum_{i=1}^{n}(X_i - \overline{X}) = 0$. I can construct a simple proof of this assertion using Rules 3.8-1, 3.8-2, and 3.8-4. In the expression $\sum_{i=1}^{n}(X_i - \overline{X})$, X_i is a variable; but for any set of scores, $\overline{X}$ is a constant. Hence,

$$\sum_{i=1}^{n}(X_i - \overline{X}) = \sum_{i=1}^{n} X_i - \sum_{i=1}^{n} \overline{X} \quad \text{Rules 3.8-4 and 3.8-2}$$

$$= \sum_{i=1}^{n} X_i - n\overline{X} \quad \text{Rule 3.8-1 (Note that for any set of data, } \overline{X} \text{ is a constant.)}$$

By definition, $\overline{X} = \sum_{i=1}^{n} X_i / n$. It follows that $n\overline{X} = n(\sum_{i=1}^{n} X_i / n) = \sum_{i=1}^{n} X_i$. Substituting $\sum_{i=1}^{n} X_i$ for $n\overline{X}$ in $\sum_{i=1}^{n} X_i - n\overline{X}$ gives

$$\sum_{i=1}^{n} X_i - \sum_{i=1}^{n} X_i = 0$$

I have just shown that $\sum_{i=1}^{n}(X_i - \overline{X}) = 0$. Consider the following scores where $X_1 = 2$, $X_2 = 3$, $X_3 = 4$, and $\overline{X} = (2 + 3 + 4)/3 = 3$; then

$$\sum_{i=1}^{n}(X_i - \overline{X}) = (2 - 3) + (3 - 3) + (4 - 3)$$

$$= -1 + 0 + 1 = 0$$

CHECK YOUR UNDERSTANDING OF SECTION 3.8

21. Write the following expressions as the sum of individual values of the variables X and Y or the constant a; for example, $\sum_{i=1}^{n} X_i = X_1 + X_2 + \cdots + X_n$.

    a. $\displaystyle\sum_{i=1}^{3} X_i$ b. $\displaystyle\sum_{i=1}^{4} Y_i$ c. $\displaystyle\sum_{j=1}^{3} f_j X_j$

    d. $\displaystyle\sum_{j=1}^{k} f_j X_j$ e. $\displaystyle\sum_{i=1}^{3} aX_i$ f. $\displaystyle\sum_{i=1}^{n} (X_i + a)$

22. Let X and Y denote variables and let a and b denote constants. Assume that the values of the variables and the constants are as follows.

    $X_3 = 4 \qquad Y_4 = 9 \qquad a = 2$
    $X_2 = 3 \qquad Y_3 = 4 \qquad b = 3$
    $X_1 = 2 \qquad Y_2 = 2$
    $ Y_1 = 1$

    Determine the values of the following expressions.

    a. $\displaystyle\sum_{i=1}^{3} a$ b. $\displaystyle\sum_{i=1}^{4} b$ c. $\displaystyle\sum_{i=1}^{n} X_i$

    d. $\displaystyle\sum_{i=1}^{n} Y_i$ e. $\displaystyle\sum_{i=1}^{3} X_i$ f. $\displaystyle\sum_{i=1}^{n} aX_i$

    g. $\displaystyle\sum_{i=1}^{3} (X_i + a)$ h. $\displaystyle\sum_{i=1}^{4} (Y_i + a - b)$ i. $\displaystyle\sum_{i=1}^{2} (X_i + a)$

23. The following proofs show the effect on the mean of adding a constant to each score or multiplying each score by a constant. For each proof, identify the summation rules from Section 3.8 that were used.

    a. Let $\overline{X}_{X+c}$ be the mean of a distribution that has been altered by adding a constant c to each score—that is, $X_1 + c, X_2 + c, \ldots, X_n + c$. Then

    $$\overline{X}_{X+c} = \frac{\sum_{i=1}^{n} (X_i + c)}{n} = \frac{\sum_{i=1}^{n} X_i + \sum_{i=1}^{n} c}{n} = \frac{\sum_{i=1}^{n} X_i + nc}{n} = \frac{\sum_{i=1}^{n} X_i}{n} + c = \overline{X} + c$$

    Thus, the effect of adding a constant c to each score is to change $\overline{X}$, the mean of the original scores, to $\overline{X} + c$. Similarly, it can be shown that the effect of subtracting a constant from each score is to change $\overline{X}$ to $\overline{X} - c$.

    b. Let $\overline{X}_{cX}$ be the mean of a distribution that has been altered by multiplying each score by a constant c—that is, $cX_1, cX_2, \ldots, cX_n$. Then

    $$\overline{X}_{cX} = \frac{\sum_{i=1}^{n} (cX_i)}{n} = \frac{c\sum_{i=1}^{n} X_i}{n} = c\overline{X}$$

Thus, the effect of multiplying each score by a constant c is to change $\overline{X}$, the mean of the original scores, to $c\overline{X}$. Similarly, it can be shown that the effect of dividing each score by a constant is to change $\overline{X}$ to $\overline{X}/c$.

3.9 LOOKING BACK: WHAT HAVE YOU LEARNED?

Three measures of central tendency are described in this chapter: the mean, median, and mode. The different measures result from different ways of conceptualizing the point around which scores cluster. The mean is the point on which the distribution balances—its center of gravity; the median is the point that divides the ordered scores into two samples of equal size; and the mode is the score value with the greatest frequency—the most typical score.

The mean is the most widely used of the measures, partly because of its superior sampling stability and partly because many advanced statistical procedures are based on it. The median and the mode, by contrast, are **terminal statistics;** their usefulness in advanced descriptive and inferential procedures is limited.

There are three situations in which the mean is not the preferred measure of central tendency: when the distribution is markedly skewed, when the variable is qualitative in character, and when the distribution is open-ended. For markedly skewed distributions, the median is preferred because it is not as sensitive as the mean to the presence of extreme scores. For unordered qualitative variables, the mode is used because it is the only one of the three measures that can be computed. In addition, the mode may be more meaningful for inherently discrete ordered qualitative variables such as family size.

You learned how to use the operator symbol Σ to represent the sum of several scores. You also learned four rules involving the sum of a constant, sum of a variable, sum of the product of a constant and variable, and sum of terms in parentheses.

REVIEW EXERCISES FOR CHAPTER 3

1. In a paired-associates learning experiment, data representing the number of trials necessary to reach the criterion of three consecutive errorless trials were 10, 6, 11, 10, 9, 8, 10, 11, 14, 12, 10, 9, 11, 10, 12, 9, 8, 9. (a) Determine the mode. (b) What type of variable do the data represent?
2. The electoral systems of 11 emerging nations were classified as N = noncompetitive, P = partially competitive, and C = competitive. (a) Determine the mode for the following data: $N, P, N, C, N, P, P, N, N, C, N$. (b) What type of variable do the data represent?
3. The mode may not exist; explain why this is so.
4. Identify
   - a. $\overline{X}$
   - b. μ_Z
   - c. Y_2
   - d. $\overline{Y}$
   - e. Y_j
   - f. Z_k
   - g. Y_n
   - h. n
   - i. f_j
   - j. k
   - k. $\overline{Z}_3$

5. Write out the following, listing individual values of the variable.

   a. $\sum_{i=1}^{5} Y_i/n$ b. $\sum_{j=1}^{6} f_j Y_j/n$ c. $\sum_{\substack{j=1 \\ j \neq 2}}^{4} f_j Z_j$

   d. $\sum_{i=1}^{n} (n_i \overline{X}_i)/n_i$

6. The socioeconomic level of black families in a predominantly black neighbor-hood was rated on the basis of income, educational attainment, physical condi-tion of dwelling, and number of home appliances. Compute the mean using $\sum_{i=1}^{n} X_i/n$.

5	6	4	5	10	6	3	5	7	6
3	4	5	8	5	4	7	1	6	7

7. The following data represent the number of suicides per 10,000 inhabitants in predominantly urban prefectures in Japan. Compute the mean using $\overline{X} = \sum_{i=1}^{n} X_i/n$.

23	24	21	19	23	24	25	22	21	27
24	23	23	22	20	23	26	25	24	22
20	17	26	23	21	25	14	21	23	24
26	24	23	22	25	23	25	28		

8. For the socioeconomic data in Exercise 6, construct an ungrouped frequency distribution and compute the mean using $\overline{X} = \sum_{j=1}^{k} f_j X_j/n$.

9. For the suicide data in Exercise 7, construct an ungrouped frequency distribu-tion and compute the mean using $\overline{X} = \sum_{j=1}^{k} f_j X_j/n$.

10. For a small number of scores, how is the median determined when (a) n is odd and (b) n is even?

11. Determine the median for the following scores.

    a. 2, 8, 11, 19, 3, 26, 28
    b. 3, 1, 3, 4
    c. 3, 5, 5, 4, 8
    d. 3, 5, 5, 4, 8, 5

12. For the suicide data in Exercise 7, construct an ungrouped frequency distribu-tion and compute the median using

$$Mdn = X_{ll} + i\left(\frac{n/2 - \Sigma f_b}{f_i}\right)$$

13. For the suicide data in Exercise 7, construct an ungrouped frequency distribu-tion and compute the median by coming down halfway from above—from the highest class interval. The computational formula is

$$Mdn = X_{ul} - i\left(\frac{n/2 - \Sigma f_a}{f_i}\right)$$

The symbols X_{ul} and f_a denote, respectively, the real upper limit of the class in-terval containing the median and the number of scores above X_{ul}.

14. For the following sets of data, what measures of central tendency would you compute? Justify your choices.
    a. 4, 3, 7, 5, 4, 2, 12, 6, 5, 4, 3, 3, 2, 7, 1, 6, 4, 5, 3, 5
    b. Eye color: blue, brown, brown, blue, green, brown, gray, brown, blue
    c. 7, 8, 6, 7, 8, 9, 1, 6, 5, 3, 7, 8, 7, 6, 7, 8, 5, 7
    d. Family size: 4, 3, 5, 4, 1, 2, 4, 6, 5

15. Rank the three measures of central tendency with respect to the following characteristics; let 1 = most or hardest and 3 = least or easiest.
    a. Suitability for advanced applications
    b. Mathematical tractability
    c. Sensitivity to value of each score
    d. Ease of computation

16. For each of the following distributions, indicate on the X axis the approximate location of $\overline{X}$, *Mdn,* and *Mo.*

a.

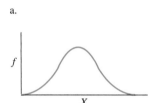

b.

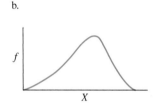

c.

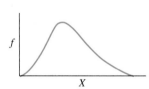

d.

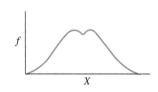

17. Determine the shape, for example, symmetrical, positively skewed, and so on, of each distribution from the following measures of central tendency. Assume a distribution similar to those in Exercise 16.
    a. $\overline{X} = 21$, *Mdn* = 21, *Mo* = 21   b. *Mdn* = 109, $\overline{X} = 116$
    c. $\overline{X} = 73$, *Mdn* = 84   d. $\overline{X}$ = *Mdn* = *Mo*
    e. $\overline{X}$ = *Mdn* ≠ *Mo*

18. For the following data, compute weighted means.
    a. $\overline{X}_1 = 50$, $n_1 = 20$; $\overline{X}_2 = 100$, $n_2 = 30$
    b. $\overline{X}_1 = 8$, $n_1 = 10$; $\overline{X}_2 = 12$, $n_2 = 30$; $\overline{X}_3 = 18$, $n_3 = 20$
    c. $\overline{X}_1 = 100$, $n_1 = 20$; $\overline{X}_2 = 200$, $n_2 = 20$

19. Write the following expressions as the sum of individual values of the variables X and Y or the constant a; for example, $\sum_{i=1}^{n} X_i = X_1 + X_2 + \cdots + X_n$.
    a. $\sum_{i=1}^{5} X_i$ b. $\sum_{j=1}^{4} f_j Y_j$ c. $\sum_{i=1}^{4} a Y_i$
    d. $\sum_{j=1}^{3} (Y_j - a)$

20. Let X and Y denote variables, and let a and b denote constants. Assume that the values of the variables and the constants are as follows:

$$X_3 = 4 \quad Y_4 = 9 \quad a = 2$$
$$X_2 = 3 \quad Y_3 = 4 \quad b = 3$$
$$X_1 = 2 \quad Y_2 = 2$$
$$ Y_1 = 1$$

Determine the values of the following expressions:

a. $\displaystyle\sum_{i=1}^{2} b$

b. $\displaystyle\sum_{i=1}^{2} a$

c. $\displaystyle\sum_{i=1}^{3} Y_i$

d. $\displaystyle\sum_{i=1}^{n} bY_i$

e. $\displaystyle\sum_{i=1}^{4} (Y_i - b)$

f. $\displaystyle\sum_{i=1}^{3} (X_i + Y_i)$

21. The following proofs show the effect on the mean of subtracting a constant from each score or dividing each score by a constant. For each proof, identify the summation rules from Section 3.8 that were used.

a. Let $\overline{X}_{X-c}$ be the mean of a distribution that has been altered by subtracting a constant c from each score—that is, $X_1 - c, X_2 - c, \ldots, X_n - c$. Then

$$\overline{X}_{X-c} = \frac{\displaystyle\sum_{i=1}^{n} (X_i - c)}{n} = \frac{\displaystyle\sum_{i=1}^{n} X_i - \sum_{i=1}^{n} c}{n} = \frac{\displaystyle\sum_{i=1}^{n} X_i - nc}{n}$$

$$= \frac{\displaystyle\sum_{i=1}^{n} X_i}{n} - c = \overline{X} - c$$

Thus, the effect of subtracting a constant c from each score is to change $\overline{X}$, the mean of the original scores, to $\overline{X} - c$.

b. Let $\overline{X}_{X/c}$ be the mean of a distribution that has been altered by dividing each score by a constant c—that is, $X_1/c, X_2/c, \ldots, X_n/c$. Then

$$\overline{X}_{X/c} = \frac{\displaystyle\sum_{i=1}^{n} (X_i/c)}{n} = \frac{\dfrac{1}{c}\displaystyle\sum_{i=1}^{n} X_i}{n}$$

$$= \frac{1}{c}\overline{X} = \overline{X}/c$$

Thus, the effect of dividing each score by a constant c is to change $\overline{X}$, the mean of the original scores, to $\overline{X}/c$.

22. Use a statistical software package to obtain a histogram and compute the mean and median for the socioeconomic data in Exercise 6.

23. Use a statistical software package to obtain a histogram and compute the mean and median for the suicide data for urban prefectures in Exercise 7.

24. Use a statistical software package to obtain a histogram and compute the mean and median for the socioeconomic data for white families in Exercise 6 in "Check Your Understanding of Section 3.3."

25. Use a statistical software package to obtain a histogram and compute the mean and median for the suicide data for rural prefectures in Exercise 7 in "Check Your Understanding of Section 3.3."

4

Measures of Dispersion, Skewness, and Kurtosis

4.1 Introduction
Looking Ahead: What Is This Chapter About?
What Measures of Dispersion Tell You

4.2 Four Measures of Dispersion
Range
Semi-Interquartile Range
Standard Deviation
Index of Dispersion
Check Your Understanding of Section 4.2

4.3 Relative Merits of the Measures of Dispersion
Standard Deviation
Semi-Interquartile Range
Range
Index of Dispersion
Summary of the Properties of the Measures of Dispersion
Check Your Understanding of Section 4.3

4.4 Dispersion and the Normal Distribution
Check Your Understanding of Section 4.4

4.5 Detecting Outliers
Detecting Outliers with a Box Plot
Check Your Understanding of Section 4.5

4.6 Skewness and Kurtosis
Skewness
Kurtosis
Check Your Understanding of Section 4.6

4.7 Looking Back: What Have You Learned?
Review Exercises for Chapter 4

4.1 INTRODUCTION

Looking Ahead: What Is This Chapter About?

In the previous chapter, you learned when and how to compute several measures of central tendency. This chapter explores three other important properties of data: dispersion, skewness, and kurtosis. Measures of dispersion represent the spread or scatter of scores around a central point or the distinguishability of scores. Four measures of this important property are described: range, semi-interquartile range, standard deviation, and index of dispersion. You will learn when and how to compute each of the measures.

Measures of skewness and kurtosis represent, respectively, the asymmetry and peakedness of data. Knowledge of these two characteristics, along with knowledge of central tendency and dispersion, provide a fairly complete description of one's data.

By now you have probably discovered how easy it is to enter wrong numbers in your calculator or transpose numbers when you read the calculator display. Such errors are a fact of life. Some errors are obvious; others are more difficult to detect. You will learn several statistical procedures for detecting scores that differ sufficiently from the main body of data as to raise questions about their accuracy.

After reading the chapter, you should know the following:

- How to compute and interpret the range, semi-interquartile range, standard deviation, and index of dispersion
- The advantages of the four measures of dispersion and when to use each
- How to detect scores whose accuracy is questionable
- How to compute and interpret a measure of skewness
- How to compute and interpret a measure of kurtosis

What Measures of Dispersion Tell You

Mr. Jacques and Mrs. Booker are taking a well-deserved break in the teachers' lounge. The conversation turns to Mrs. Booker's third-grade class. "I've got a bunch of little monsters this year. I can't seem to keep their interest for more than 10 minutes. I had to discipline Emerson twice this morning for flying paper airplanes during arithmetic, and Waldo is still picking fights. I just can't understand it; this class has the same average IQ as my class last year, and you remember how good those kids were." As Mrs. Booker contemplates her options—face the class for seven more months, resign and start a family, or go back to college and work on a master's degree in computer science—we wonder what makes one class a joy and the other a disaster. The frequency polygon in Figure 4.1-1 provides the answer. Although the two classes have almost identical mean IQs, this year's class is much more heterogeneous in learning aptitude. Last year, for example, there were no children with IQs below 90; this year there are two. That's Waldo in the class interval 75–79—moderately retarded. At the other end of the distribution in the 140–144 class interval is our paper-plane thrower—a potential genius. It is small wonder that this year's class, with its wide range of aptitude, is giving Mrs. Booker problems.

Information about central tendency is important, but central tendency tells only part of the story; the heterogeneity or dispersion of scores is often just as informative. The measures of central tendency described in Chapter 3 represent points on which a distribution centers. As you will see, the most widely used measures of dispersion

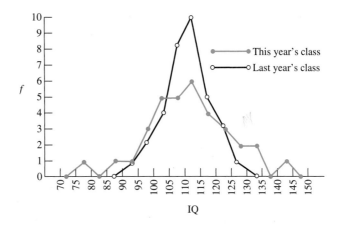

Figure 4.1-1. Frequency polygons for two third-grade classes with the same central tendency but different dispersions.

represent the spread or scatter of scores around a central point and are expressed in terms of distance along a distribution's horizontal, or *X,* axis. Many measures of dispersion have been proposed. I describe the four most useful measures in the behavioral sciences, health sciences, and education.

4.2 FOUR MEASURES OF DISPERSION

Range

Intuitively, the simplest measure of dispersion is the **range**—the distance between the largest and smallest scores. The range is denoted by *R* and is computed from the formula

inclusive

$$R = X_{ul\,(largest\;score)} - X_{ll\,(smallest\;score)}$$

where X_{ul} is the real upper limit of the largest score and X_{ll} is the real lower limit of the smallest score. Alternatively, the range can be computed from

noninclusive

$$R = X_{j(largest\;score)} - X_{j(smallest\;score)}$$

where $X_{j(largest\;score)}$ is the midpoint of the largest score and $X_{j(smallest\;score)}$ is the midpoint of the smallest score.

The first formula is sometimes called the **inclusive range;** I will use it throughout the book. The second formula for the **noninclusive range** is often used in computer packages.

Consider this year's class in Figure 4.1-1. If Emerson's 144 is the highest IQ and Waldo's 76 is the lowest, the range is $144.5 - 75.5 = 69$. The range of 69 IQ points is a distance along the *X* or horizontal axis that includes 100% of the scores. In general, the larger the range, the greater the spread or scatter of scores.

In spite of its simplicity, the range is not widely used. For one thing, its value is determined by the two most extreme scores, so its sampling stability—that is, its variability from one random sample to the next—is quite poor. Also, the range cannot be manipulated arithmetically and algebraically, which is another way of saying that it is not mathematically tractable. Furthermore, the range is not meaningful for unordered qualitative data. These and other disadvantages discussed in Section 4.3 limit its usefulness as a measure of dispersion.

As you will see, each measure of dispersion is typically reported with a particular measure of central tendency. For quantitative data, the range can be reported with the mode, thereby giving a more complete picture of data. However, because the mode often is used with unordered qualitative data, a different measure of dispersion is needed. The index of dispersion described later fills this need.

Semi-Interquartile Range

You have seen that the sampling stability of R is poor because it is computed from the two most extreme scores in a distribution. A second measure of dispersion, the semi-interquartile range, is based on two scores closer to the center of the distribution. Hence, it is considerably more stable than R.

> The **semi-interquartile range,** denoted by Q, is defined as one-half the distance between the first quartile point, Q_1, and the third quartile point, Q_3. These points and the median are shown in Figure 4.2-1. The formula for Q is
>
> $$Q = \frac{Q_3 - Q_1}{2}$$

The computation of Q_1 and Q_3 is similar to that for the median and is illustrated in Table 4.2-1. The data are IQ scores from Mrs. Booker's current class. The

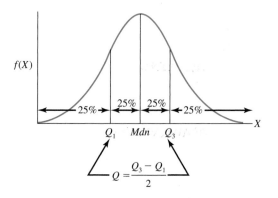

Figure 4.2-1. Q_1 is a point below which 25% of the scores fall and above which 75% fall; Q_3 is a point below which 75% fall and above which 25% fall. The median is sometimes referred to as Q_2, because it is a point that divides the distribution of scores into two equal size subsamples. The semi-interquartile range, Q, is half the distance from Q_1 to Q_3.

TABLE 4.2-1   Computational Procedures for Q_1, Q_3, and Q (Data from Figure 4.1-1, This Year's Class)

(i) Data and computational formulas

^aX_j	f_j	Cum f
144	1	
134	1	
131	1	
128	1	
125	1	
122	3	
118	1	26
117	3	25
111	6	22
109	2	16
105	3	14
101	5	11
99	2	6
96	1	4
94	1	3
87	1	2
76	1	1
	$n = 34$	

$$Q_1 = X_{ll} + i\left(\frac{n/4 - \Sigma f_b}{f_i}\right)$$

$$= 100.5 + 1\left(\frac{8.5 - 6}{5}\right)$$

$$= 100.5 + 0.5 = 101.0$$

$$Q_3 = X_{ll} + i\left(\frac{n3/4 - \Sigma f_b}{f_i}\right)$$

$$= 117.5 + 1\left(\frac{25.5 - 25}{1}\right)$$

$$= 117.5 + 0.5 = 118.0$$

$$Q = \frac{Q_3 - Q_1}{2}$$

$$= \frac{118.0 - 101.0}{2} = 8.5$$

(ii) Definition of terms

X_j = value of *j*th class interval

f_j = frequency of *j*th class interval

X_{ll} = real lower limit of class interval containing Q_1 or Q_3

i = class interval size

n = number of scores

Σf_b = number of scores below X_{ll}

f_i = number of scores in class interval containing Q_1 or Q_3

(continued)

TABLE 4.2-1   *(continued)*

(iii) Computational sequence illustrated for Q_1

1. Compute $n/4 = 34/4 = 8.5$.
2. Locate the class interval containing the $n/4 = 8.5$th score in the *Cum f* column; the 8.5th score occurs in the class interval 101. For this class interval, X_{ll} is 100.5.
3. Compute i: i = Real upper limit of class interval – Real lower limit of class interval = $101.5 - 100.5 = 1$.
4. Determine $\Sigma f_b = 6$.
5. Determine $f_i = 5$.

---

^a To conserve space, class intervals with $f_j = 0$ have been omitted.

semi-interquartile range for these data is 8.5. The larger the value of Q, the greater the distance between Q_1 and Q_3, and, in general, the greater the spread or scatter of scores.

The semi-interquartile range is often reported along with the median to give a more complete description of data. For a symmetrical distribution, the median plus or minus the semi-interquartile range, $Mdn \pm Q$, gives two points on the X or horizontal axis such that the interval between the points contains 50% of scores, as illustrated in Figure 4.2-1. For the data in Table 4.2-1, the *Mdn* plus or minus Q, 110.7 ± 8.5, gives the interval 102.2–119.2. The interval 102.2–119.2, however, does not contain exactly 50% of the scores because the distribution is not symmetrical.

The semi-interquartile range, like the median, is a terminal statistic; by this I mean that its usefulness in advanced descriptive and inferential procedures is very limited. The semi-interquartile range shares both the advantages and the disadvantages of the median because it is computed from "medianlike" descriptive statistics, Q_1 and Q_3. I will now digress for a moment to describe another medianlike statistic—the percentile.

> A **percentile point,** also called a **percentile** or **centile** and denoted by $P_\%$, is a point on the X or horizontal axis below which a specified percentage of scores falls. The term **percentile rank,** denoted by P_R, refers to the percentage of scores that falls below the percentile point.

Procedures for computing percentile points corresponding to the 25th, 50th, and 75th percentile ranks already have been described because these points correspond, respectively, to Q_1, *Mdn*, and Q_3. Percentiles corresponding to other percentile ranks can be computed using a modification of the Q_1 formula as follows:

$$P_\% = X_{ll} + i\left(\frac{n(P_R/100) - \Sigma f_b}{f_i}\right)$$

where $P_\%$ identifies a percentile point and P_R, a percentile rank. The other symbols—X_{ll}, i, n, Σf_b, and f_i—are defined in Table 4.2-1; replace Q_1 with $P_\%$.

Suppose that you wanted to determine the percentile point corresponding to the 60th percentile rank. To determine P_{60} for the data in Table 4.2-1, first compute $n(P_R/100) = 34(60/100) = 20.4$. By following the computational sequence illustrated in part (iii) of Table 4.2-1 and substituting $n(P_R/100) = 20.4$ for $n/4 = 8.5$, you obtain

$$P_{60} = 110.5 + 1\left(\frac{34(60/100) - 16}{6}\right) = 110.5 + 1\left(\frac{20.4 - 16}{6}\right)$$

$$= 110.5 + 0.7 = 111.2$$

This tells you that the IQ score of 111.2 represents a point below which 60% of the scores in this year's class fall.

Sometimes you have a score in mind and want to determine the percentile rank of the score. This situation is the reverse of that just described, where you had the 60th percentile rank in mind and wanted to determine the corresponding percentile point. Suppose that for the data in Table 4.2-1 you wanted to know the percentile rank of the IQ score of 105.3. The percentile rank of IQ = 105.3 can be determined by using the following formula:

$$P_R = \frac{100}{n}\left[\Sigma f_b + \frac{f_i(P_\% - X_{ll})}{i}\right]$$

$$P_R = \frac{100}{34}\left[11 + \frac{3(105.3 - 104.5)}{1}\right] = 39.4$$

The first step in computing the percentile rank is to locate the class interval in Table 4.2-1 that contains the IQ score 105.3. This score falls in the class interval 105; the real limits of this class interval are 104.5 and 105.5. Thus, the lower limit of the class interval containing the score 105.3 is $X_{ll} = 104.5$. Note that there are $f_i = 3$ scores in this class interval and that there are $\Sigma f_b = 11$ scores below this class interval. Inserting these values in the formula and solving for the percentile rank gives 39.4. You know from this result that 39.4% of the scores in this year's class fall below an IQ score of 105.3.

Percentiles and percentile ranks are widely used in reporting the performance of individuals on psychological tests. I will return to percentiles in Chapter 9.

Standard Deviation

The **standard deviation,** denoted by S for a sample and by σ for a population, is the most important and most widely used measure of dispersion. The formulas for S and σ are, respectively,

$$S = \sqrt{\frac{\sum\limits_{i=1}^{n}(X_i - \overline{X})^2}{n}} \quad \text{and} \quad \sigma = \sqrt{\frac{\sum\limits_{i=1}^{n}(X_i - \mu)^2}{n}}$$

where $\overline{X}$ and μ denote the sample and population means, respectively.[1]

You can develop an intuitive understanding of the standard deviation by examining the formula for S. First note that, unlike R and Q, S is computed from every score in a distribution; second, each score is expressed as a deviation from the mean, $(X_i - \overline{X})$; third, each deviation is squared; and fourth, the squared deviations are summed. What would happen if you did not square the deviations? You know from Chapter 3 that for any distribution,[2]

$$\sum(X_i - \overline{X}) = 0$$

so squaring or some other operation on the deviations is necessary for the sum to equal a value other than zero. Finally, note that the sum of the squared deviations is divided by n, which gives us the mean squared distance by which the scores deviate from the mean. To convert $\sum(X_i - \overline{X})^2/n$ back into deviations expressed in the original unit of measurement, you take its square root.[3]

To summarize, the standard deviation is a number that (1) is based on every score in a distribution and (2) represents the square root of the mean squared distance of scores from the mean. In general, the larger the value of S, the greater is the spread or scatter of scores. Because the standard deviation is based on every score in the distribution, its sampling stability is much better than that of other measures of dispersion. For this reason and because it is mathematically tractable, the standard deviation is widely used in advanced descriptive and inferential statistics.

---

[1] When the population standard deviation, σ, is estimated from sample data, a better estimator is given by

$$\hat{\sigma} = \sqrt{\frac{\sum\limits_{i=1}^{n}(X_i - \overline{X})^2}{n-1}}$$

and is denoted by $\hat{\sigma}$. This statistic is used with inferential statistics in Chapters 10 to 16 .

[2] For a proof, see Section 3.8.

[3] The square of standard deviations—S^2, σ^2, and $\hat{\sigma}^2$—is another measure of dispersion and is called *variance*. The formulas for the three variances are

$$S^2 = \sum(X_i - \overline{X})^2/n,$$

$$\sigma^2 = \sum(X_i - \mu)^2/n, \text{ and}$$

$$\hat{\sigma}^2 = \sum(X_i - \overline{X})^2/(n-1)$$

The measures S^2 and σ^2 are, respectively, the sample variance and the population variance. The measure $\hat{\sigma}^2$ is an estimator of the population variance and is widely used in inferential statistics. I will return to $\hat{\sigma}^2$ in Chapter 14 and in Chapters 15 and 16, when I discuss the analysis of variance.

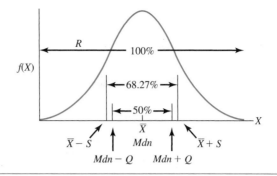

Figure 4.2-2. A region that contains 68.27% of the area of the normal distribution is marked off by $\overline{X} \pm S$; $Mdn \pm Q$ contains 50% of the area, and the R contains 100% of the area.

As you saw earlier, each measure of dispersion is typically reported with a particular measure of central tendency—R with Mo and Q with Mdn. The standard deviation is reported with the mean. One special type of distribution, called the *normal distribution*, is often approximated by behavioral science data such as IQs (see Section 2.6 and Chapter 9). For this distribution, the mean plus and minus the standard deviation ($\overline{X} \pm S$) is an interval that contains 68.27% of scores, as Figure 4.2-2 illustrates. The other two dispersion measures are shown in the figure for comparison.

Computation of the standard deviation is illustrated in Table 4.2-2. The data represent ratings of the socioeconomic level of white families in a predominantly black neighborhood. For these data, $\overline{X} = 5$ and $S = 2.3$. If you compute $\overline{X} \pm S$, you obtain 5 ± 2.3, or the interval 2.7–7.3. It can be shown,[4] using the formula for a percentile rank presented earlier, that the interval 2.7–7.3 contains only 63.34% of the scores. This percentage, 63.34%, is reasonably close to the 68.27% that would be obtained for a normal distribution. The slight discrepancy occurs because the data in Table 4.2-1 contain only 12 scores and the distribution deviates appreciably from the normal distribution.

The formula for S just illustrated is called the **deviation formula** because the formula involves computing deviations—$(X_i - \overline{X})$—and squaring the deviations. If $\overline{X}$ is not an integer, the rounding error in $\overline{X}$ can lead to a small error in the standard deviation. The problem can be avoided by carrying the computation of $\overline{X}$ to several more decimal places than the final answer for the standard deviation.[5] The simplest way to compute the standard deviation is to enter the scores in a calculator that has a standard

[4] To show that the interval $\overline{X} \pm S = 2.7$–7.3 contains only 63.34% of the socioeconomic level ratings of the white families, I can use the formula for the percentile rank to find the percentiles corresponding to 2.7 and 7.3. The corresponding percentiles are 18.33 and 81.67. Between these two percentiles are 63.34% of the scores (81.67 − 18.33 = 63.34).

[5] In the precomputer era, the standard deviation was often computed using a *raw score formula* that did not introduce a rounding error. Calculators and computers have virtually eliminated the need for raw score formulas.

TABLE 4.2-2   Computation of the Standard Deviation

(i) Data

(1) X_i	(2) $X_i - \overline{X}$	(3) $(X_i - \overline{X})^2$
5	5 − 5 = 0	0
9	9 − 5 = 4	16
2	2 − 5 = −3	9
8	8 − 5 = 3	9
6	6 − 5 = 1	1
5	5 − 5 = 0	0
4	4 − 5 = −1	1
7	7 − 5 = 2	4
4	4 − 5 = −1	1
3	3 − 5 = −2	4
1	1 − 5 = −4	16
6	6 − 5 = 1	1

$$\sum_{i=1}^{n} X_i = 60 \qquad\qquad \sum_{i=1}^{n} (X_i - \overline{X})^2 = 62$$

$$\overline{X} = \frac{\sum_{i=1}^{n} X_i}{n} = \frac{60}{12} = 5$$

(ii) Computation of S

$$S = \sqrt{\frac{\sum_{i=1}^{n}(X_i - \overline{X})^2}{n}} = \sqrt{\frac{62}{12}} = 2.3$$

deviation key. After all the scores have been entered, the standard deviation is obtained with the press of a key.[6]

The standard deviation also can be computed from an ungrouped frequency distribution, a distribution that has a class interval size of one. For this case, the formula for S is modified as follows:

$$S = \sqrt{\frac{\sum_{j=1}^{k} f_j (X_j - \overline{X})^2}{n}}$$

[6] Many statistical calculators have two keys for computing a standard deviation: one labeled σ_{n-1} and another labeled σ_n. The standard deviations produced by the two keys are defined by the formulas, respectively,

$$\hat{\sigma} = \sqrt{\frac{\Sigma(X_i - \overline{X})^2}{n-1}} \qquad \text{and} \qquad S = \sqrt{\frac{\Sigma(X_i - \overline{X})_2}{n}}$$

TABLE 4.2-3 Computation of the Standard Deviation for an Ungrouped Frequency Distribution (Data from Table 4.2-2)

(i) Data

(1) X_j	(2) f_j	(3) $f_j X_j$	(4) $f_j(X_j - \overline{X})^2$
9	1	$(1)(9) = 9$	$(1)(9-5)^2 = 16$
8	1	$(1)(8) = 8$	$(1)(8-5)^2 = 9$
7	1	$(1)(7) = 7$	$(1)(7-5)^2 = 4$
6	2	$(2)(6) = 12$	$(2)(6-5)^2 = 2$
5	2	$(2)(5) = 10$	$(2)(5-5)^2 = 0$
4	2	$(2)(4) = 8$	$(2)(4-5)^2 = 2$
3	1	$(1)(3) = 3$	$(1)(3-5)^2 = 4$
2	1	$(1)(2) = 2$	$(1)(2-5)^2 = 9$
1	1	$(1)(1) = 1$	$(1)(1-5)^2 = 16$
$n = 12$		$\sum_{j=1}^{k} f_j X_j = 60$	$\sum_{j=1}^{k} f_j(X_j - \overline{X})^2 = 62$

$$\overline{X} = \frac{\sum_{j=1}^{k} f_j X_i}{n} = \frac{60}{12} = 5$$

(ii) Computation of S

$$S = \sqrt{\frac{\sum_{j=1}^{k} f_j(X_j - \overline{X})^2}{n}} = \sqrt{\frac{62}{12}} = 2.3$$

where X_j is the value of the jth class interval, f_j is the frequency of scores in the jth class interval, and summation is performed over the $j = 1, \ldots, k$ class intervals. Computation of the standard deviation using this formula is illustrated in Table 4.2-3 for the socioeconomic data in Table 4.2-2. The results of the computation in Table 4-2-3 agree with those in Table 4.2-2.

Index of Dispersion

The three measures of dispersion discussed thus far—R, Q, and S—are distance measures and are commonly used with quantitative variables. If data do not contain distance information, as is the case for unordered qualitative variables such as gender and major in college, how can you describe dispersion? One approach is to think of dispersion as the distinguishability of observations—more precisely, as the number of pairs of observations actually distinguishable relative to the maximum possible number. Consider the example in Figure 4.2-3(a) in which there are two

a.   b.

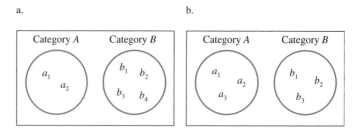

Figure 4.2-3. In figure a, elements are assigned to $c = 2$ qualitative categories such that those within a category are indistinguishable with respect to some characteristic. Figure b illustrates the case in which the number of distinguishable pairs $(a_1b_1, a_1b_2, \ldots, a_3b_3)$ is maximal. The maximum number of distinguishable pairs occurs when the elements are evenly divided among the categories, for example, three in category A and three in B.

qualitative categories called A and B that contain a total of six elements. Suppose that the elements in the A and B categories, denoted by a_i and b_j, represent men and women students in a coed dorm who slept through breakfast yesterday. The two elements in A are indistinguishable in the sense that they are both men who missed breakfast; likewise, the four elements in B (women who also missed breakfast) are indistinguishable. However, the elements in A can be distinguished from the elements in B. Thus, among the six elements there are eight distinguishable pairs of elements: $a_1b_1, a_1b_2, a_1b_3, a_1b_4, a_2b_1, a_2b_2, a_2b_3$, and a_2b_4. I denote the observed number of distinguishable pairs by DP. In this example, DP is equal to 8. The minimum value of DP, which represents minimum dispersion, is zero. A value of zero occurs when all the elements are in one category and hence are indistinguishable. The maximum possible number of distinguishable pairs is denoted by DP_{max} and occurs when the elements are evenly divided among the categories, as in Figure 4.2-3(b). It can be determined from Figure 4.2-3(b) that the maximum possible number of distinguishable pairs for $c = 2$ categories and $n = 6$ observations is nine ($DP_{max} = 9$): $a_1b_1, a_1b_2, a_1b_3, a_2b_1, a_2b_2, a_2b_3, a_3b_1, a_3b_2$, and a_3b_3.

The ratio DP/DP_{max}—the number of distinguishable pairs to the maximum possible number of distinguishable pairs—is called the **index of dispersion** and is denoted by D.[7]

For the data in Figure 4.2-3(a), you have seen that $DP = 8$ and that $DP_{max} = 9$. Hence,

$$D = \frac{DP}{DP_{max}} = \frac{8}{9} = .89$$

which means that the observed dispersion is .89 as large as its maximum possible value.

---

[7] This index also is called the index of qualitative variation.

To summarize, the minimum value of $D = DP/DP_{max}$ is 0 and occurs when $DP = 0$, which indicates that all the elements are in one category. The maximum value of D is 1 and occurs when $DP = DP_{max}$, which indicates that the elements are evenly divided among the c categories. Thus, D ranges over values 0–1; the larger D, the larger the observed number of distinguishable pairs of elements relative to the maximum number and, hence, the greater the dispersion.

When the number of observations n is large, it is tedious to determine DP and DP_{max} by enumerating or listing all of the possible a_ib_j pairs. A simple alternative formula for D that does not require an enumeration of the a_ib_j pairs is

$$D = \frac{c\left(n^2 - \sum_{j=1}^{c} n_j^2\right)}{n^2(c-1)}$$

where c is the number of categories, n is the number of observations, and n_j is the number of observations in each of the $j = 1, \ldots, c$ categories.[8] For the data in Figure 4.2-3(a),

$$D = \frac{2[(6)^2 - (2)^2 - (4)^2]}{(6)^2(2-1)} = .89$$

the same value obtained previously.

The index of dispersion is particularly useful for comparing the dispersions of several distributions based on the same set of c categories. Suppose that I have asked married women with either a high school or a college education to rate their marital happiness. The results of the survey along with the mode and the index of dispersion are shown in Table 4.2-4. Although the modes are identical, the dispersion of the college graduates' distribution ($D_{CG} = .88$) is smaller than that for the high school graduates ($D_{HG} = .96$). It is evident from Table 4.2-4 that college grads are more likely to rate their marriage as moderately happy and less likely to use other rating categories such as very unhappy.

For unordered qualitative data, the only appropriate measure of central tendency is the mode. For such data, the appropriate measure of dispersion to report with the mode is the index of dispersion. The index of dispersion has two disadvantages: ① it is a terminal statistic (its usefulness in advanced descriptive and inferential statistics is limited), and ② it is less familiar than R, Q, and S, which are based on the concept of distance rather than on the number of distinguishable pairs of observations.

CHECK YOUR UNDERSTANDING OF SECTION 4.2

1. Compute the range for the following sets of numbers.

   a. 11, 6, 5, 2, 9, 14, 17, 4   b. 7, 1, 6, 6, 6, 7, 7, 16

   c. 12, 8, 15, 9, 7, 6, 7   d. 11, –2, 3, 7, 6, 8

---

[8] The derivation of the formula is given by Kirk (1978, pp. 91–93).

TABLE 4.2-4   Marital Happiness Ratings of Women with Either a High School or a College Education

(i) Data

Rating	n_j, High School Graduate	n_j, College Graduate
Very happy	15	12
Moderately happy	28	39
Neutral	16	30
Unhappy	13	12
Very unhappy	8	3
	$n = 80$	$n = 96$
	$Mo =$ Moderately happy	$Mo =$ Moderately happy
	$D_{HG} = .96$	$D_{CG} = .88$

(ii) Computation of D

$$D = \frac{c\left(n^2 - \sum_{j=1}^{c} n_j^2\right)}{n^2(c-1)}$$

$$D_{HG} = \frac{5[(80)^2 - (15)^2 - (28)^2 - (16)^2 - (13)^2 - (8)^2]}{(80)^2(5-1)} = \frac{24{,}510}{25{,}600} = .96$$

$$D_{CG} = \frac{5[(96)^2 - (12)^2 - (39)^2 - (30)^2 - (12)^2 - (3)^2]}{(96)^2(5-1)} = \frac{32{,}490}{36{,}864} = .88$$

2. The ranges in Exercises 1a and 1b are identical, although the first set of numbers appears to be more heterogeneous than the second. Why doesn't the range reflect this difference?

3. Data representing the length of time required to notice the onset of a warning light during the performance of a simulated driving test are listed in the following table. (a) Compute the median and the semi-interquartile range for these data. (b) Compute P_{10} and P_{90}. (c) Construct a histogram.

X_j, Time (Seconds)	f_j	X_j, Time (Seconds)	f_j
32	1	26	3
31	1	25	2
30	2	24	1
29	3	23	0
28	4	22	0
27	6	21	1

4. For the data in Exercise 3, compute the percentile rank for $X = 30$. For these data, note that $i = 1$ and that the real limits of a score, say 27, are 26.5 and 27.5.

5. Preschool children, particularly those who are very intelligent, often create imaginary companions. The following data represent the number of companions created by 15 children.

4	2	5	3	1
3	2	1	2	3
2	4	3	2	0

(a) Compute the mean and the standard deviation using the formulas $\overline{X} = \sum_{i=1}^{n} X_i/n$ and $S = \sqrt{\sum_{i=1}^{n}(X_i - \overline{X})^2/n}$. (b) If you have a calculator with a standard deviation key, compute the standard deviation with your calculator.

6. The effects of a terrorist attack in the Middle East on attitudes about work were investigated for a large multinational manufacturer. Job satisfaction data for a small branch office in India are as follows.

46	54	65	43	54
53	64	46	56	44
45	43	57	61	32

(a) Compute the mean and the standard deviation using the formulas $\overline{X} = \sum_{j=1}^{k} f_j X_j/n$ and $S = \sqrt{\sum_{j=1}^{k} f_j(X_j - \overline{X})^2/n}$. (b) If you have a calculator with a standard deviation key, compute the standard deviation using your calculator.

7. Researchers surveyed the attitudes of a random sample of white women college students toward having a career. (a) For the data in the table, compute the mode and the index of dispersion. (b) Construct a bar graph.

Category	f
Strongly desire career	16
Moderately desire career	23
Undecided about career	19
Don't want career	10

8. The following proofs show the effect on the standard deviation of adding a constant to each score or multiplying each score by a constant. For each proof, identify the summation operations and the number of the summation rules from Section 3.8 that were used.

   a. Let S_{X+c} be the standard deviation of a distribution that has been altered by adding a constant c to each score X_i—that is, $X_1 + c, X_2 + c, \ldots, X_n + c$. To determine the effect on S of adding a constant, I replace X_i by $(X_i + c)$ and $\overline{X}$ by $\sum_{i=1}^{n}(X_i + c)/n$ in the formula $S = \sqrt{\sum_{i=1}^{n}(X_i - \overline{X})^2/n}$, as follows.

$$S_{X+c} = \sqrt{\frac{\sum_{i=1}^{n}\left[(X_i + c) - \sum_{i=1}^{n}(X_i + c)/n\right]^2}{n}}$$

$$= \sqrt{\dfrac{\displaystyle\sum_{i=1}^{n}\left(X_i + c - \sum_{i=1}^{n}X_i/n - nc/n\right)^2}{n}}$$

$$= \sqrt{\dfrac{\displaystyle\sum_{i=1}^{n}(X_i + c - \overline{X} - c)^2}{n}}$$

$$= \sqrt{\dfrac{\displaystyle\sum_{i=1}^{n}(X_i - \overline{X})^2}{n}}$$

$$= S$$

Because $S_{X+c} = S$, you know that adding a constant c to each score does not affect the value of the standard deviation. Similarly, it can be shown that subtracting a constant also does not affect the value of the standard deviation.

b. Let S_{cX} be the standard deviation of a distribution that has been altered by multiplying each score X by a positive constant c—that is, $cX_1, cX_2, \ldots, cX_n$. The effect of this alteration can be shown by replacing X_i by cX_i and $\overline{X}$ by $\sum_{i=1}^{n} cX_i/n$ in the formula $S = \sqrt{\sum_{i=1}^{n}(X_i - \overline{X})^2/n}$, as follows.

$$S_{cX} = \sqrt{\dfrac{\displaystyle\sum_{i=1}^{n}\left(cX_i - \sum_{i=1}^{n}cX_i/n\right)^2}{n}}$$

$$= \sqrt{\dfrac{\displaystyle\sum_{i=1}^{n}\left(cX_i - c\sum_{i=1}^{n}X_i/n\right)^2}{n}}$$

$$= \sqrt{\dfrac{\displaystyle\sum_{i=1}^{n}(cX_i - c\overline{X})^2}{n}}$$

$$= \sqrt{\dfrac{\displaystyle\sum_{i=1}^{n}c^2(X_i - \overline{X})^2}{n}}$$

$$= \sqrt{\dfrac{c^2\displaystyle\sum_{i=1}^{n}(X_i - \overline{X})^2}{n}}$$

$$= c\sqrt{\frac{\sum_{i=1}^{n}(X_i - \overline{X})^2}{n}}$$

$$= cS$$

Because $S_{CX} = cS$, you know that the effect of multiplying each score by a positive constant c is to change S, the standard deviation of the original scores, to cS. Similarly, it can be shown that the effect of dividing each score by a positive constant c is to change S to S/c.

If c is a negative constant, $S_{CX} = |c|S$. The use of $|c|$ ensures that $|c|S$ is positive and is consistent with the definition of the standard deviation as the positive square root of $\sum_{i=1}^{n}(X_i - \overline{X})^2/n$.

9. Interpret the following: (a) $\overline{X} = 100$, $S = 15$, and the distribution is approximately normal, (b) $Mdn = 70$, $Q = 12$, (c) $Mo = 16$, $R = 4$, (d) $Mo =$ Category of Pizza Inn pizza, $D = .25$.

10. Terms to remember:
    a. Inclusive range
    b. Noninclusive range
    c. Semi-interquartile range
    d. Percentile point
    e. Percentile rank
    f. Standard deviation
    g. Deviation formula for S
    h. Index of dispersion

4.3 RELATIVE MERITS OF THE MEASURES OF DISPERSION

Standard Deviation

The standard deviation, which is typically reported with the mean, is the most important and most widely used measure of dispersion for quantitative variables whose distributions are relatively symmetrical. Its popularity is due largely to its superior sampling stability and its mathematical tractability. There are two situations, however, in which the standard deviation is neither a preferred nor an appropriate measure of dispersion: when a distribution is very skewed and when the data are qualitative.

Consider the case of a skewed distribution. The value of the standard deviation is computed by squaring the deviation of each score from the mean. The squaring operation gives undue weight to extreme scores in the longer tail of the distribution and results in a much larger standard deviation than would have been obtained in the absence of extreme scores. This is a disadvantage. For example, suppose that you wished to compare the dispersion of two distributions that are similar except that one contains several very extreme scores in the longer tail. In spite of the similarity of the two distributions, their standard deviations would be quite different, and the comparison would be misleading. A few extreme scores exert an influence that is disproportionate to their number.

Consider next the case of a qualitative variable. If the variable is ordered, the magnitude of differences between numbers on the measurement scale does not contain meaningful information about the variable. If the variable is unordered, the magnitude of differences between numbers on the measurement scale contains no information about the variable. In either case, the standard deviation is not an appropriate measure of dispersion because the measuring scale does not contain useful distance information.

Semi-Interquartile Range

The semi-interquartile range, which is reported with the median, is computed from the medianlike statistics Q_1 and Q_3 and shares many of the median's advantages and disadvantages. For example, the semi-interquartile range is limited to descriptive applications with quantitative variables and is relatively intractable mathematically. Nevertheless, it is preferred over the standard deviation in two situations that I will now describe.

You learned in Section 3.5 that the median can be computed for open-ended distributions. This also is true of the semi-interquartile range if the unknown scores lie above Q_3 or below Q_1. Thus, the semi-interquartile range can be computed when the value of one or more extreme scores is unknown. The standard deviation also can be computed when there are unknown scores, but none of the procedures for doing so is entirely satisfactory.

The semi-interquartile range also is preferred over the standard deviation for skewed distributions. Recall that the semi-interquartile range is sensitive to the number but not to the value of scores lying above Q_3 and below Q_1. As a result, the semi-interquartile range is less influenced by the extreme scores in the longer tail of a distribution than is the standard deviation. In summary, there are only two situations in which the semi-interquartile range is preferred over the standard deviation: when a distribution is markedly skewed or when it is open-ended.

Range

The range is used for quantitative variables and may be reported with the mode. The great advantage of the range is its simplicity—it is easy to understand and to compute. As a result, it is used widely as a preliminary measure of dispersion. It also is used in deciding how to group data in a frequency distribution, an application that was described in Section 2.2.

The major deficiency of the range is its poor sampling stability. The value of the range is determined by only two scores (the largest and the smallest), which means that it is not sensitive to most of the score values.

Another deficiency is its dependency on sample size. If scores are randomly sampled from a population, the range will tend to be larger for larger samples because large samples are more likely to include extreme scores. These deficiencies, plus its poor mathematical tractability, limit the range to descriptive applications.

Index of Dispersion

The index of dispersion, which is reported with the mode, is the only measure of dispersion that is appropriate for unordered qualitative variables. Unlike other dispersion measures, it represents not distance but the number of distinguishable pairs of observations relative to the maximum possible number. The main disadvantages of the index of dispersion are that it is less familiar than the other measures of dispersion and that it is rarely used in advanced statistical procedures.

Summary of the Properties of the Measures of Dispersion

The standard deviation is

1. a distance measure—the square root of the squared distance by which scores deviate from the mean;
2. the preferred measure for quantitative variables whose distributions are relatively symmetrical;
3. often reported with the mean—for a normal distribution, $\overline{X} \pm S$ is an interval that contains 68.27% of scores;
4. the measure with the best sampling stability;
5. widely used, implicitly or explicitly, in advanced statistics;
6. mathematically tractable;
7. the only widely used measure of dispersion whose value is affected by the value of every score in the distribution;
8. fairly sensitive to extreme scores, so it is not recommended for markedly skewed distributions; and
9. not appropriate for qualitative variables.

The semi-interquartile range is

1. a distance measure—one-half the distance between the first and the third quartiles;
2. often reported with the median for quantitative variables;
3. closely related to the median, because both are defined in terms of quartile points;
4. sensitive only to the number and not to the value of scores above Q_3 and below Q_1; hence, it often is used for markedly skewed distributions;
5. the only relatively stable measure of dispersion that is appropriate for open-ended distributions;
6. more subject to sampling fluctuation than the standard deviation;
7. less mathematically tractable than the standard deviation; and
8. rarely used in advanced statistical procedures.

The range is

1. a distance measure—the distance between the largest and the smallest scores;
2. often reported with the mode for quantitative variables;
3. the simplest measure of dispersion to compute and interpret;
4. used in deciding how to group data in a frequency distribution;
5. much more subject to sampling fluctuation than the other measures of dispersion;
6. dependent on sample size—the larger the sample size, the larger, on the average, the range;
7. less mathematically tractable than the standard deviation; and
8. rarely used in advanced statistical procedures.

The index of dispersion is

1. a measure of the distinguishability of observations—that is, the number of distinguishable pairs of observations relative to the number possible. The index is 0 when all observations are in one qualitative category (minimum dispersion), and it has its maximum value of 1 when the observations are evenly distributed over the categories (maximum dispersion);
2. the only measure of dispersion appropriate for unordered qualitative variables;
3. reported with the mode;
4. rarely used in advanced statistical procedures; and
5. less familiar than the standard deviation, range, and semi-interquartile range, which are based on the concept of distance.

CHECK YOUR UNDERSTANDING OF SECTION 4.3

11. What measure of central tendency and dispersion would you compute for the following data? Defend your choice.

a.

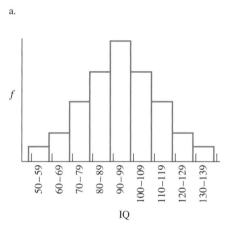

IQ

b.

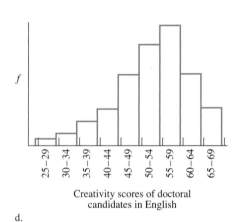

Creativity scores of doctoral candidates in English

c.

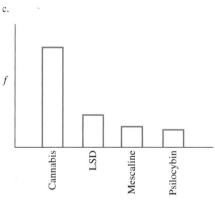

Frequency of drug use among teenagers

d.

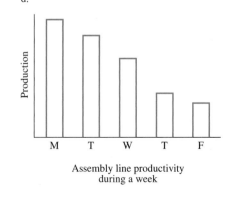

Assembly line productivity during a week

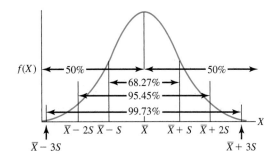

Figure 4.4-1. Percentage of scores contained in selected intervals around the mean for a normal distribution.

4.4 DISPERSION AND THE NORMAL DISTRIBUTION

The distribution of many variables in the behavioral sciences, health sciences, and education resembles the bell-shaped normal distribution. Because this distribution is so important, its properties have been studied extensively by mathematicians. You saw in Section 4.2 that for a normal distribution, the interval $\overline{X} \pm S$ includes 68.27% of scores. Suppose that you are interested in the interval $\overline{X} \pm 2S$ or $\overline{X} \pm 3S$. The percentage of scores included in these intervals is shown in Figure 4.4-1. It can be seen that an interval of six standard deviations includes almost all of the scores, 99.73%. Also, $\overline{X} \pm S$ gives the two scores that mark the **inflection points** of the normal distribution—that is, the points where the curve changes from convex to concave or the reverse.

CHECK YOUR UNDERSTANDING OF SECTION 4.4

12. For a normal distribution, what percentage of the scores falls (a) below $\overline{X} + S$? (b) between $\overline{X} - 3S$ and $\overline{X} + 3S$? (c) above $\overline{X} - 2S$? (d) below $\overline{X} - S$?
13. Term to remember:
    a. Inflection point

4.5 DETECTING OUTLIERS

In collecting data, there are many opportunities for mistakes to occur. People misread instruments, transpose numbers, record data in the wrong place, present the wrong experimental condition or instructions, and fail to notice that equipment has malfunctioned. Often these mistakes produce scores that are indistinguishable from correct data and go undetected. However, when you find that John's IQ is 1100 and Susan's height is 56 feet, you know that something is wrong.

> Scores that are unusually large or small relative to other scores are called **outliers**.

Outliers can seriously affect the integrity of data and result in biased or distorted sample statistics and faulty conclusions. Some outliers are obvious, such as an IQ of 1100 or a height of 56 feet, but not all outliers are so obvious. There are gray areas. A number of criteria have been suggested for identifying obvious and not-so-obvious outliers. According to one criterion, an outlier is any score that falls outside of the interval given by

$$Mdn \pm 2(Q_3 - Q_1)$$

Another criterion identifies an outlier as any score that falls outside of the interval

$$\overline{X} \pm 2.5S$$

For the IQ scores in Table 4.2-1, the two criteria give the following intervals:

$$Mdn \pm 2(Q_3 - Q_1) = 110.7 \pm 2(118.0 - 101.0) = 76.7 \text{ to } 144.7$$

and

$$\overline{X} \pm 2.5S = 110.35 \pm 2.5(13.53) = 76.5 \text{ to } 144.2$$

Both criteria identify one outlier—Waldo's score of 76. Of the two criteria, $Mdn \pm 2 (Q_3 - Q_1)$ is preferred because the Mdn, Q_3, and Q_1 are less influenced by extreme scores than are the $\overline{X}$ and S. A widely used rule for detecting outliers is based on a box plot, which is described in the next section.

Outliers should be carefully examined. Their presence suggests the possibility of some form of data contamination. Data that are obviously erroneous must be either corrected or discarded. For example, an examination of the records might reveal that John's IQ is 110 rather than 1100 and that Susan is only 5.6 feet tall, not 56 feet. However, school records might confirm that Waldo's score of 76 is correct. Outliers should be discarded if they are impossible—for example, an IQ of 1100—or if there is ample evidence that they have resulted from some form of data contamination— for example a participant recorded his answers in the wrong column of an answer sheet or the equipment malfunctioned.

Detecting Outliers with a Box Plot

Chapter 2 showed that graphs are effective ways to present data. John Tukey, who introduced the stem-and-leaf display, developed another innovative display called a **box-and-whiskers plot** or simply **box plot** (Tukey, 1977). A box plot presents important features of data and identifies outliers if they are present. There are several versions of this popular display; a simplified version for the IQ data in Table 4.2-1

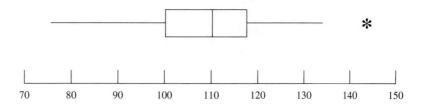

Figure 4.5-1. Box plot for the IQ data in Table 4.2-1. The vertical line in the center of the box denotes the median. The lower and upper ends of the box denote the first and third quartiles, respectively. The whiskers are lines that extend from each end of the box to the outermost data points that fall within the distances computed as $Q_1 - 1.5(Q_3 - Q_1) = 75.5$ and $Q_3 + 1.5(Q_3 - Q_1) = 143.5$. The outermost data points that fall within these distances are 76 and 134. Data points outside the whiskers are outliers and are represented by an *. One data point, 144, is identified as an outlier.

is shown in Figure 4.5-1. The box plot in Figure 4.5-1 provides the following information:

1. Median ($Mdn = 110.7$). This point is represented by the vertical line in the central area of the box.
2. First quartile ($Q_1 = 101.0$) and third quartile ($Q_3 = 118.0$). These two points are represented by the ends of the box.
3. Lines, called **whiskers.** The two whiskers extend from each end of the box to the outermost data points that fall within the distances computed as

$$Q_1 - 1.5(Q_3 - Q_1) = 101.0 - 1.5(118.0 - 101.0) = 75.5$$

and

$$Q_3 + 1.5(Q_3 - Q_1) = 118.0 + 1.5(118.0 - 101.0) = 143.5$$

The left whisker extends from $Q_1 = 101.0$ down to 76, the smallest score that is greater than or equal to $Q_1 - 1.5(Q_3 - Q_1) = 75.5$. The right whisker extends from $Q_3 = 118.0$ up to 134, the largest score that is less than or equal to $Q_3 + 1.5(Q_3 - Q_1) = 143.5$.
4. Outliers, which are represented by asterisks, are scores that fall outside the whiskers. One score, 144, falls above the right whisker.

The box plot identified one outlier, 144. Furthermore, it is evident that the distribution is negatively skewed because the left whisker is longer than the right whisker and the distance from Q_1 to the Mdn is greater than the distance from the Mdn to Q_3. The two criteria described earlier for detecting outliers identified a different outlier, 76. Because the distribution is skewed, the box plot rather than the other criteria should be used to identify outliers.

Box plots provide a lot of information at a glance. I will use them in later chapters to summarize the central tendency and dispersion of data and identify outliers. They are especially useful for comparing two or more sets of data. For this purpose, box plots are stacked, one above another, or turned 90° and placed side by side.

CHECK YOUR UNDERSTANDING OF SECTION 4.5

14. a. Use the criterion $Mdn \pm 2(Q_3 - Q_1)$ to determine whether there is reason to believe that outliers exist in the data presented in Table 4.2-2.
    b. Construct a box plot for these data. Compare the results with those obtained in (a).
15. a. Use the criterion $Mdn \pm 2(Q_3 - Q_1)$ to determine whether there is reason to believe that outliers exist in the reaction-time data presented in Exercise 3 in "Check Your Understanding of Section 4.2."
    b. Does the use of the criterion $\overline{X} \pm 2.5S$ lead to the same decision as $Mdn \pm 2(Q_3 - Q_1)$?
    c. Construct a box plot. Compare the results with those obtained in (a) and (b).
16. Terms to remember:
    a. Outlier   b. Box-and-whisker plot
    c. Whisker

4.6 SKEWNESS AND KURTOSIS

To complete my description of a distribution, I need two more statistics: indexes of skewness and kurtosis. You learned in Section 2.6 that skewness refers to the asymmetry of a distribution and kurtosis, to its peakedness or flatness.

Skewness

A number of indexes of skewness have been developed; the most widely used one is

$$Sk = \frac{\dfrac{\Sigma(X_i - \overline{X})^3}{n}}{S^3},$$

where S denotes the standard deviation (see Section 4.2).[9] If a distribution is **symmetrical,** $Sk = 0$; if it is **positively skewed,** $Sk > 0$; and if it is **negatively skewed,** $Sk < 0$.

Computation of Sk is illustrated in Table 4.6-1. For these data, $Sk = -0.7$, which indicates that the distribution is negatively skewed, as Figure 4.6-1 shows.

---

[9] This index, developed by Karl Pearson, is sometimes denoted by $\sqrt{\beta_1}$ and sometimes by g_1.

TABLE 4.6-1   Example Illustrating Computation of Measures of Skewness and Kurtosis

(i) Data

X_i	$(X_i - \overline{X})$	$(X_i - \overline{X})^2$	$(X_i - \overline{X})^3$	$(X_i - \overline{X})^4$
6	2	4	8	16
5	1	1	1	1
5	1	1	1	1
5	1	1	1	1
5	1	1	1	1
4	0	0	0	0
3	−1	1	−1	1
2	−2	4	−8	16
1	−3	9	−27	81

$$\sum_{i=1}^{n} X_i = 36 \quad \sum_{i=1}^{n}(X_i - \overline{X}) = 0 \quad \sum_{i=1}^{n}(X_i - \overline{X})^2 = 22 \quad \sum_{i=1}^{n}(X_i - \overline{X})^3 = -24 \quad \sum_{i=1}^{n}(X_i - \overline{X})^4 = 118$$

$$\overline{X} = \frac{\sum_{i=1}^{n} X_i}{n} = \frac{36}{9} = 4$$

(ii) Computation of Sk

$$S = \sqrt{\frac{\sum_{i=1}^{n}(X_i - \overline{X})^2}{n}} = \sqrt{\frac{22}{9}} = 1.563$$

$$Sk = \frac{\dfrac{\sum_{i=1}^{n}(X_i - \overline{X})^3}{n}}{S^3} = \frac{\dfrac{-24}{9}}{(1.563)^3} = \frac{-2.667}{3.818} = -0.7$$

(iii) Computation of Kur

$$Kur = \frac{\dfrac{\sum_{i=1}^{n}(X_i - \overline{X})^4}{n}}{S^4} - 3 = \frac{\dfrac{118}{9}}{(1.563)^4} - 3 = \frac{13.111}{5.968} - 3 = -0.8$$

The value of *Sk* can be used to compare the type and the degree of skewness of two distributions independent of any differences in central tendency and dispersion. However, in practice, *Sk* is rarely computed because it is easy to detect asymmetry by looking at a frequency distribution or a graph of the data.

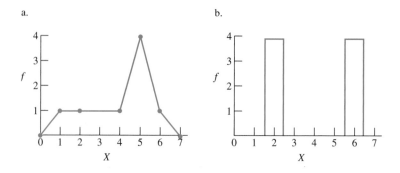

Figure 4.6-1.   (a) Frequency polygon for data in Table 4.6-1; $Sk = -0.7$ and $Kur = -0.8$. (b) Histogram for a perfectly symmetrical bimodal distribution; $Sk = 0$ and $Kur = -2$.

Kurtosis

The most common index of **kurtosis** is

$$Kur = \frac{\dfrac{\Sigma(X_i - \overline{X})^4}{n}}{S^4} - 3$$

where S is the standard deviation (see Section 4.2).[10] If a distribution is flatter (has a broader hump and thicker tails) than the normal distribution, it is called **platykurtic,** and $Kur < 0$. If its peakedness is the same as that of the normal distribution, it is **mesokurtic,** and $Kur = 0$. If it is more peaked (has a narrower hump and thinner tails) than the normal distribution, it is **leptokurtic,** and $Kur > 0$.

Computation of Kur is illustrated in Table 4.6-1.

A graph for these data and one for a perfectly symmetrical bimodal distribution are given in Figure 4.6-1. In Figure 4.6-1(a), $Kur = -0.8$, and in Figure 4.6-1(b), $Kur = -2$. Unfortunately, the interpretation of Kur is not as straightforward as that of Sk. It turns out that the value of Kur is dependent not only on the central peak of a distribution, but also on the fullness of its tails. Therefore, for distributions that deviate appreciably from the normal form, like those in Figure 4.6-1, the interpretation of Kur is ambiguous. For such distributions, it is doubtful whether any single statistic can adequately measure the quality of peakedness.

---

[10] This index is also denoted by g_2. As originally developed by Karl Pearson, the index was equal to $Kur + 3$ and was denoted by β_2.

CHECK YOUR UNDERSTANDING OF SECTION 4.6

17. Age at onset of Parkinson's disease, a degenerative brain disorder, was determined for a sample of adults between 60 and 70 years old. (a) Determine the type and degree of skewness for these data. (b) Construct a histogram. (c) Does the histogram support your decision based on *Sk?*

67	68	60	64	68	63
68	70	63	70	68	69
70	69	69	69	69	68
62	70	70	64	66	66
66	69	67	67	70	67

18. One theory predicts that the distribution of reaction times in a paired-associates learning task will be leptokurtic. (a) Do the following learning data support the prediction? (b) Determine the type and degree of skewness for these data.

28	28	27	29	29
29	31	32	28	30
27	28	30	31	25
24	27	28	25	27
28	24	32	27	28
29	28	27	28	29

19. Determine the type and the degree of kurtosis for the Parkinson's-disease data in Exercise 17.
20. Terms to remember:
    a. Symmetrical distribution
    b. Positively and negatively skewed
    c. Kurtosis
    d. Platykurtic
    e. Mesokurtic
    f. Leptokurtic

4.7 LOOKING BACK: WHAT HAVE YOU LEARNED?

Measures of dispersion summarize the extent to which scores differ from one another, either quantitatively in terms of the spread or scatter of scores or qualitatively in terms of their distinguishability.

Of the four measures of dispersion discussed in this chapter, three are based on the concept of distance and are appropriate for variables that contain distance information. They are the range, the semi-interquartile range, and the standard deviation. The most important and widely used of the three is the standard deviation, which is typically reported with the mean.

The index of dispersion, which is reported with the mode, describes the distinguishability of observations. Specifically, it indicates the number of distinguishable pairs of observations relative to the maximum possible number of distinguishable pairs. The lower bound of the index, 0, occurs when all observations are in one category; its upper bound, 1, occurs when the observations are evenly distributed over the categories. The index of dispersion is the only one of the dispersion measures that is appropriate for unordered qualitative variables.

Dispersion and central tendency are generally the most important characteristics of a distribution, and they completely describe a normal distribution, which is by definition symmetrical and mesokurtic. For nonnormal distributions, *Sk* and *Kur* provide interesting but somewhat less important information about skewness (asymmetry) and kurtosis (peakedness), respectively.

REVIEW EXERCISES FOR CHAPTER 4

1. Compute the range for the following sets of numbers.
   a. 3, 9, 5, 6, 5, 4, 5   b. 26, 18, 30, 24, 23, 24
   c. 52, 49, 34, 53, 69, 50, 62   d. 3, –4, 5, 2, 1, 2
2. For what kind of variable can you compute the mode but not the range?
3. Researchers measured the emotional stability of a random sample of encounter-group participants at Nelase Institute. (a) Compute the median and the semi-interquartile range for the emotional stability scores listed in the table. (b) Compute P_{20}. (c) Construct a histogram.

X_j, Emotional Stability	f_j	X_j, Emotional Stability	f_j
30	1	18	3
27	1	17	3
25	2	16	3
23	2	15	4
22	2	13	2
21	2	12	2
20	3	10	2
19	4	8	1

4. For the data in Exercise 3, compute the percentile rank for (a) $X = 13$, (b) $X = 19$, and (c) $X = 25$.
5. Describe the nature of the distance represented by the standard deviation.
6. Infants are not as passive and undiscriminating about stimulation as we once thought; they show distinct preferences when given an opportunity to control stimuli presented to them. The following data are the number of trials required for infants to learn to control visual stimuli by varying their sucking responses. (a) Compute the mean and the standard deviation for these data using the formulas $\overline{X} = \sum_{i=1}^{n} X_i/n$ and $S = \sqrt{\sum_{i=1}^{n}(X_i - \overline{X})^2/n}$. If you have a calculator with a standard deviation key, compute the standard deviation using your calculator. (b) Construct a frequency polygon.

81	73	75	72	76	74
77	72	71	74	72	73
73	70	78	73	71	69
75	74	68	70	69	73
72	70	66	71	75	72
76	74	73	77		

7. In a concept-learning experiment, chimpanzees were taught to recognize a triangle in different orientations. Compute the mean and the standard deviation for these data using the formulas $\overline{X} = \sum_{j=1}^{k} f_i X_j / n$ and $S = \sqrt{\sum_{j=1}^{k} f_j (X_j - \overline{X})^2 / n}$. If you have a calculator with a standard deviation key, compute the standard deviation using your calculator.

X_j, Number of Trials	f_j	X_j, Number of Trials	f_j
50	1	45	6
49	3	44	4
48	4	43	2
47	6	42	1
46	8	41	1

8. For the emotional-stability data in Exercise 3, (a) compute the mean and the standard deviation using the formulas $\overline{X} = \sum_{j=1}^{k} f_j X_j / n$ and $S = \sqrt{\sum_{j=1}^{k} f_j (X_j - \overline{X}) / n}$. If you have a calculator with a standard deviation key, compute the standard deviation using your calculator. (b) Construct a frequency polygon.

9. Researchers surveyed the attitudes of a random sample of black female high school students toward having a career. (a) For the data in the table, compute the mode and the index of dispersion. (b) Construct a bar graph.

Category	f
Strongly desire career	38
Moderately desire career	19
Undecided about career	5
Do not want career	17

10. More than a million college-bound high school seniors participated in the College Board's Admissions Testing Program for the 2003–2004 year. The responses of men and women to the question "What is the highest level of education you plan to complete beyond high school?" are as follows. (Suggested by *Profiles, College-Bound Seniors, 2004*. [2005]. New York: College Entrance Examination Board.)

Category	f_{men}	f_{women}
Two-year training program	13,510	15,609
Associate in arts degree	6,101	15,122
B.A. or B.S. degree	133,795	160,484
M.A. or M.S. degree	116,362	118,046
M.D., Ph.D., other professional degree	83,240	77,559
Undecided	82,805	100,973
	$n = 435{,}813$	$n = 487{,}793$

a. Compute the mode and the index of dispersion for the men and the women.
b. Is the magnitude of the dispersion of educational plans for men and women appreciably different?

11. The following proofs show the effect on the standard deviation of subtracting a constant from each score or dividing each score by a constant. For each proof, identify the summation operations from Section 3.8 that were used.

a. Let S_{X-c} be the standard deviation of a distribution that has been altered by subtracting a constant c from each score X_i—that is, $X_1 - c, X_2 - c, \ldots, X_n - c$. To determine the effect on S of subtracting a constant, I replace X_i by $(X_i - c)$ and $\overline{X}$ by $\sum_{i=1}^{n}(X_i - c)/n$ in the formula $S = \sqrt{\sum_{i=1}^{n}(X_i - \overline{X})^2/n}$, as follows.

$$S_{X-c} = \sqrt{\frac{\sum_{i=1}^{n}\left[(X_i - c) - \sum_{i=1}^{n}(X_i - c)/n\right]^2}{n}}$$

$$= \sqrt{\frac{\sum_{i=1}^{n}\left[X_i - c - \sum_{i=1}^{n}\frac{X_i}{n} + \sum_{i=1}^{n}\frac{c}{n}\right]^2}{n}}$$

$$= \sqrt{\frac{\sum_{i=1}^{n}\left[X_i - c - \sum_{i=1}^{n}\frac{X_i}{n} + \frac{nc}{n}\right]^2}{n}}$$

$$= \sqrt{\frac{\sum_{i=1}^{n}(X_i - c - \overline{X} + c)^2}{n}}$$

$$= \sqrt{\frac{\sum_{i=1}^{n}(X_i - \overline{X})^2}{n}}$$

$$= S$$

Because $S_{X-c} = S$, you know that subtracting a constant c from each score does not affect the value of the standard deviation. Similarly, it can be shown that adding a constant also does not affect the value of the standard deviation.

b. Let $S_{X/c}$ be the standard deviation of a distribution that has been altered by dividing each score X by a positive constant c—that is, $X_1/c, X_2/c, \ldots, X_n/c$. The effect of this alteration can be shown by replacing X_i by X_i/c and $\overline{X}$ by $\sum_{i=1}^{n}(X_i/c)/n$ in the formula $S = \sqrt{\sum_{i=1}^{n}(X_i - \overline{X})^2/n}$, as follows.

$$S_{X/c} = \sqrt{\frac{\sum_{i=1}^{n}\left(X_i/c - \sum_{i=1}^{n}(X_i/c)/n\right)^2}{n}}$$

$$= \sqrt{\frac{\sum_{i=1}^{n}\left[\frac{X_i}{c} - \sum_{i=1}^{n}\left(\frac{1}{c}X_i\right)/n\right]^2}{n}}$$

$$= \sqrt{\frac{\sum_{i=1}^{n}\left(\dfrac{X_i}{c} - \dfrac{1}{c}\sum_{i=1}^{n}\dfrac{X_i}{n}\right)^2}{n}}$$

$$= \sqrt{\frac{\sum_{i=1}^{n}\dfrac{1}{c^2}(X_i - \overline{X})^2}{n}}$$

$$= \sqrt{\frac{\dfrac{1}{c^2}\sum_{i=1}^{n}(X_i - \overline{X})^2}{n}}$$

$$= \frac{1}{c}\sqrt{\frac{\sum_{i=1}^{n}(X_i - \overline{X})^2}{n}}$$

$$= \frac{1}{c}S = S/c$$

Because $S_{X/c} = S/c$, you know that the effect of dividing each score by a positive constant c is to change S, the standard deviation of the original scores, to S/c. Similarly, it can be shown that the effect of multiplying each score by a positive constant c is to change S to cS. If c is a negative constant, $S_{X/c} = S/|c|$. The use of $|c|$ ensures that $S/|c|$ is positive and is consistent with the definition of the standard deviation as the positive square root of $\sum_{i=1}^{n}(X_i - \overline{X})^2/n$.

12. Interpret the following: (a) *Mdn* = 50, *Q* = 8, (b) *Mo* = 30, *R* = 5, (c) $\overline{X}$ = 70, *S* = 10, and the distribution is approximately normal, (d) *Mo* = Category of Ford cars, *D* = .20.

13. What measure of central tendency and dispersion would you compute for the following data? Defend your choice.

a.

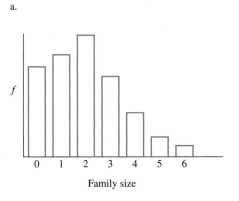

Family size

b.

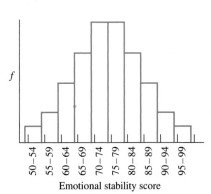

Emotional stability score

(graphs continued on following page)

c.   d.

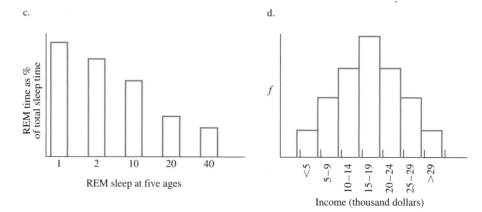

14. For a normal distribution, what percentage of the scores falls (a) above $\overline{X} - 3S$? (b) above $\overline{X} + 2S$? (c) between $\overline{X} - 2S$ and $\overline{X} + 2S$? (d) below $\overline{X} - S$?
15. a. Use the criterion $Mdn \pm 2(Q_3 - Q_1)$ to determine whether there is reason to believe that outliers exist in the emotional-stability data presented in Exercise 3.
    b. Construct a box plot for these data. Compare the results with those obtained in (a).
16. a. Use the criterion $Mdn \pm 2(Q_3 - Q_1)$ to determine whether there is reason to believe that outliers exist in the sucking-response data presented in Exercise 6.
    b. Does the use of the criterion $\overline{X} \pm 2.5S$ lead to the same decision as $Mdn \pm 2(Q_3 - Q_1)$?
    c. Construct a box plot. Compare the results with those obtained in (a) and (b).
17. Researchers measured the reading readiness of preschool children in two neighborhoods. (a) Determine the type and the degree of skewness for these data. (b) Which set of data has the greatest skewness? (c) Construct a histogram for each neighborhood. (d) Do the histograms support your decision based on *Sk?*

Neighborhood A						Neighborhood B				
30	33	32	31	35	33	29	32	28	29	29
32	29	33	30	32	28	30	31	26	30	28
31	31	29	31	26	30	28	29	29	34	30
32	30	33	32	27	32	29	27	30	31	35

18. Determine which set of data in Exercise 17 deviates most from the normal distribution in terms of kurtosis.
19. Why is *Kur* not an entirely satisfactory measure of peakedness?
20. Use a statistical software package to obtain a box plot and compute the mean and standard deviation for the emotional-stability data in Exercise 3. Determine whether the software package computed S or $\hat{\sigma}$.

21. Use a statistical software package to obtain a box plot and compute the mean and standard deviation for the sucking-response data in Exercise 6. Determine whether the software package computed S or $\hat{\sigma}$.

22. Use a statistical software package to obtain a box plot and compute the mean and standard deviation for the learning data in Exercise 7. Determine whether the software package computed S or $\hat{\sigma}$.

5

Correlation

5.1 Introduction to Correlation
Looking Ahead: What Is This Chapter About?
Correlation and Regression Distinguished
A Bit of History
Check Your Understanding of Section 5.1

5.2 A Numerical Index of Correlation
Check Your Understanding of Section 5.2

5.3 Pearson Product-Moment Correlation Coefficient
Information Contained in the Cross Product
Check Your Understanding of Section 5.3

5.4 Interpretation of a Correlation Coefficient: Explained and Unexplained Variation
Check Your Understanding of Section 5.4

5.5 Some Common Errors in Interpreting a Correlation Coefficient
Error: Interpreting r in Direct Proportion to Its Size
Error: Interpreting r in Terms of Arbitrary Descriptive Labels
Error: Inferring Causation from Correlation
Check Your Understanding of Section 5.5

5.6 Factors That Affect the Size of a Correlation Coefficient
Nature of the Relationship between X and Y
Truncated Range
Spurious Effects Due to Subgroups with Different Means or Standard Deviations
Non-normality and Heterogeneity of Array Variances
Check Your Understanding of Section 5.6

5.7 Spearman Rank Correlation
The Problem of Tied Ranks
Check Your Understanding of Section 5.7

5.8 Other Kinds of Correlation Coefficients

5.9 Looking Back: What Have You Learned?
Review Exercises for Chapter 5

5.1 INTRODUCTION TO CORRELATION

Looking Ahead: What Is This Chapter About?

Correlation, which is described in this chapter, and regression, which is described in the next, are procedures for examining the relationship between two variables. Both procedures involve two variables where the scores for one variable are paired with the scores for the other variable. The paired scores could represent salary and job satisfaction of college graduates, SAT scores and freshmen GPAs, and incidence of breast cancer and amount of radiation exposure from cell phones. In each case, you are interested in predicting a score for one variable from a score for the other variable or in knowing the strength of the relationship between the two variables.

After reading this chapter, you should know the following:

- The similarities and differences between correlation and regression
- How to compute and interpret the Pearson and Spearman correlation coefficients
- Common errors in interpreting correlation coefficients
- Factors that affect the size of correlation coefficients

Correlation and Regression Distinguished

It should be apparent that correlation and regression procedures have some features in common and as a result are often confused. Perhaps the simplest way to distinguish between them is by means of examples. The classic regression situation involves one dependent variable and one or more independent variables. The **independent variable** is the variable that is controlled or manipulated by a researcher so that its effect on a **dependent variable** can be determined. Suppose a researcher performs an experiment in which different dosages of amphetamine, the independent variable, denoted by X, are administered to children suffering from hyperkinesis, a behavioral disorder characterized by restlessness, inattention, and disruptive behavior. The children are randomly assigned to, say, seven dosage levels. Following administration of the drug, changes in frequency of hyperkinetic behavior, the dependent variable, denoted by Y, are recorded. For each child the researcher has paired X and Y scores representing, respectively, dosage and behavior change. The researcher is interested in knowing whether the two variables are related and, if so, in predicting Y from a knowledge of X. This information would enable the researcher to identify effective dosages of amphetamine. This experiment illustrates the key features of a problem in **regression.** First, there is a clearly defined independent variable—amount of amphetamine. Second, the children are randomly assigned to the preselected dosage levels of amphetamine. Third, the value of the dependent variable for a given dosage was not selected in advance—it is free to vary. This is in contrast to the independent variable, whose seven values were selected in advance. Finally, the researcher is interested in predicting Y from a knowledge of X.

Contrast this experiment with one in which tests of reading readiness and intelligence are administered to a sample of children, yielding paired X and Y scores, respectively, for each child. The researcher is interested in knowing whether reading readiness and intelligence are related and, if so, in the strength of the association. In addition, the researcher might want to predict either variable from a knowledge of the other. This experiment illustrates a classic **correlation** situation. How does it differ from the regression situation? First, there is no obvious independent variable. Second, because the researcher did not preselect the values of either X or Y in advance, both X and Y are free to vary. Finally, the researcher is interested in assessing the strength of the association between X and Y and possibly in predicting either variable from a knowledge of the other.

To summarize, both correlation and regression procedures are concerned with assessing the relationship between two variables where the scores for one variable are paired with the scores for the other variable. They differ with respect to (1) the nature of the variables (the presence or absence of an independent variable), (2) use of random assignment of participants to the experimental conditions, (3) the researcher's principle interest (predicting Y from X or assessing the strength of relationship), and, (4) to some extent, the kinds of conclusions that can be drawn. In practice, the distinction between regression and correlation situations often is not as clearly drawn as has been described. For example, it is common in a regression situation to assess the strength of the association between X and Y. However, it is important to be able to distinguish between the two situations because the assumptions underlying the use of regression and correlation procedures differ.

A Bit of History

The concepts of correlation and regression were developed by Sir Francis Galton during his investigations of the genetic transmission of natural characteristics. He was intrigued by the question "How is it possible for a whole population to remain alike in its features during many successive generations if the average produce of each couple resembles the parents? " Data from one of his studies on the inheritance of stature are reproduced in Table 5.1-1. Parents' height is plotted on the horizontal, or X, axis and offspring's height on the vertical, or Y, axis. It is customary in such presentations to make the lengths of the X and Y axes approximately equal. This representation of the joint frequency of two variables is called a **bivariate frequency distribution** or **scatterplot (scatter diagram, scattergram).** Consider the entry in the cell at the intersection of column 68.5 and row 69.2; the frequency is 48. This means that for parents whose height was 68–69 inches, there were 48 offspring whose height was 68.7–69.7 inches. The circles in Table 5.1-1 identify the class intervals containing the median of each column as calculated by Galton. We see, as did Galton, that the relationship between height of offspring and height of parents is approximately *linear*—that is, the set of circled numbers approximates a straight line. Galton developed a procedure for finding the "straight line of best fit," thereby laying the foundation for correlation and regression.

A straight line provides a reasonably good fit for many relationships found in behavioral, health, and educational research. Even relationships that are nonlinear are often approximately linear over some portion of their range. But let us return to the question that sparked Galton's interest. How is it that a population remains alike?

TABLE 5.1-1   Scatterplot of Midparent Height and Height of Adult Offspring[a] (Female Heights Multiplied by 1.08)

Height of Adult Offspring	<64	64.5	65.5	66.5	67.5	68.5	69.5	70.5	71.5	72.5	≥73
				Midparent Height (inches)[b]							
≥73.7							5	3	2	4	
73.2						3	4	3	2	2	(3)
72.2			1		4	4	11	4	9	(7)	1
71.2			2		11	18	20	7	4	2	
70.2			5	4	19	21	25	14	(10)	1	
69.2	1	2	7	13	38	48	(33)	(18)	5	2	
68.2	1		7	14	28	(34)	20	12	3	1	
67.2	2	5	(11)	(17)	(38)	31	27	3	4		
66.2	2	(5)	11	17	36	25	17	1	3		
65.2	(1)	1	7	2	15	16	4	1	1		
64.2	4	4	5	5	14	11	16				
63.2	2	4	9	3	5	7	1				
62.2		1		3	3						
<61.7	1	1	1			1		1			

[a] Galton (1889, p. 208). I am grateful to Edward W. Minium for bringing these data to my attention.

[b] A circle marks the class interval containing the median of each column.

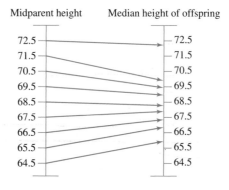

Figure 5.1-1. Arrows relate height (in inches) of parents to median height of offspring. Tall parents tend to have slightly shorter offspring, and short parents tend to have slightly taller offspring. Galton referred to this as reversion toward the mean.

The answer is in the trend represented by the circled numbers in Table 5.1-1. Galton saw that on the average, short parents have offspring who tend to be slightly taller than they are, whereas tall parents have offspring who tend to be slightly shorter than they. This is shown more clearly in Figure 5.1-1. Galton referred to this tendency as **regression** or **reversion toward the mean**; he called the best-fitting straight line in a scatterplot the **regression** or **reversion line.**

In the discussion that follows, I'll focus on variables like those in Table 5.1-1 that appear to be linearly related.[1] Many relationships of interest in the behavioral sciences, health sciences, and education fall into this category.

CHECK YOUR UNDERSTANDING OF SECTION 5.1

1. A speech therapist who was interested in the relationship between two tests of articulation disorders administered the tests to 26 children. (a) Construct a scatterplot like Table 5.1-1 for the data in the following table. (b) Does the relationship appear to be linear or nonlinear?

Participant	Test A	Test B	Participant	Test A	Test B
1	26	36	14	33	39
2	28	35	15	22	33
3	25	34	16	24	32
4	21	32	17	27	35
5	25	33	18	29	36
6	26	32	19	32	39
7	26	34	20	28	36
8	31	37	21	25	36
9	27	34	22	24	34
10	20	30	23	25	34
11	23	32	24	27	36
12	30	38	25	26	34
13	29	37	26	26	35

2. Discuss the meaning of the term *regression toward the mean.*
3. Terms to remember:
   a. Independent variable
   b. Dependent variable
   c. Regression
   d. Correlation
   e. Bivariate frequency distribution
   f. Scatterplot
   g. Linear relationship
   h. Regression line

5.2 A NUMERICAL INDEX OF CORRELATION

> The degree of association or strength of relationship between two variables is represented by a number called a **correlation coefficient.** The Pearson product-moment correlation coefficient is a measure of the linear relationship between two variables, X and Y, and is denoted by r_{XY} or simply r. The population correlation coefficient is denoted by the Greek letter ρ (rho).[2]

---

[1] The nonlinear case is treated in advanced texts such as Kirk (1995, pp. 197–198).

[2] The letter r from the word *reversion* was originally used by Sir Francis Galton to denote the slope of the best-fitting straight line. This line is defined in Section 6.2.

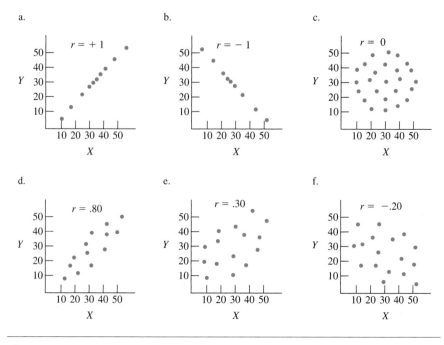

Figure 5.2-1. Scatterplots illustrating various degrees of correlation.

The value of a correlation coefficient can range from −1 to +1. A value of +1 denotes a perfect **positive relationship;** this is depicted in the scatterplot in Figure 5.2-1(a). For this case, all the data points fall on a straight line such that high scores on one variable are paired with high scores on the other, and low scores are paired with low scores. A coefficient of −1 denotes a perfect **negative or inverse relationship.** For this case, the data points also fall on a straight line, but high scores on one variable are paired with low scores on the other and vice versa, resulting in a line that slopes down instead of up. This is shown in Figure 5.2-1(b). If there is no linear association between the variables, r is equal to 0. In this case, the data points tend to fall in a circle, as shown in Figure 5.2-1(c). Intermediate degrees of association are represented by coefficients less than 0 ($-1 < r < 0$) or by coefficients greater than 0 ($0 < r < 1$). Some examples of intermediate degrees of association for normally distributed X and Y variables are depicted in Figures 5.2-1(d) through (f). As shown in the figures, the data points for intermediate values of r tend to form an ellipse; the lower the degree of association, the more the ellipse resembles a circle.

CHECK YOUR UNDERSTANDING OF SECTION 5.2

4. Match the r values 1, −1, 0, .4, and −.9 with the scatterplots shown here.

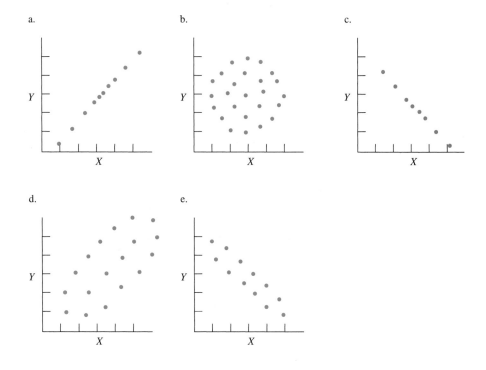

5. Would you expect the correlation between the following to be positive, negative, or essentially zero?
   a. Masculinity of fathers and sons
   b. Reaction time and number of lights in a visual discrimination task
   c. Mechanical aptitude and mother's height
   d. Verbal intelligence and percentage of words filled in on crossword puzzles
6. Terms to remember:
   a. Correlation coefficient   b. Positive relationship
   c. Negative relationship

5.3 PEARSON PRODUCT-MOMENT CORRELATION COEFFICIENT

The most widely used index of correlation is called the **Pearson product-moment correlation coefficient,** after Karl Pearson (1857–1936), who contributed so much to its development. The coefficient is appropriate for describing the linear relationship between two quantitative variables.

The deviation or definitional formula for Pearson's r is

$$r = \frac{\dfrac{\sum (X_i - \overline{X})(Y_i - \overline{Y})}{n}}{\sqrt{\left[\dfrac{\sum (X_i - \overline{X})^2}{n}\right]\left[\dfrac{\sum (Y_i - \overline{Y})^2}{n}\right]}}$$

TABLE 5.3-1 Computation of r for Fathers' and Sons' Authoritarianism Scores

(i) Data

Family	Father's Score, X_i	Son's Score, Y_i	$(X_i - \overline{X})^2$	$(Y_i - \overline{Y})^2$	$(X_i - \overline{X})(Y_i - \overline{Y})$
1	25	28	17.2225	0.5625	3.1125
2	32	31	8.1225	5.0625	6.4125
3	40	41	117.7225	150.0625	132.9125
4	29	33	0.0225	18.0625	−0.6375
5	31	25	3.4225	14.0625	−6.9375
6	16	18	172.9225	115.5625	141.3625
7	28	26	1.3225	7.5625	3.1625
8	36	38	46.9225	85.5625	63.3625
9	33	34	14.8225	27.5625	20.2125
10	29	36	0.0225	52.5625	−1.0875
11	23	20	37.8225	76.5625	53.8125
12	27	28	4.6225	0.5625	1.6125
13	37	30	61.6225	1.5625	9.8125
14	30	26	0.7225	7.5625	−2.3375
15	27	22	4.6225	45.5625	14.5125
16	20	23	83.7225	33.0625	52.6125
17	28	29	1.3225	0.0625	−0.2875
18	38	36	78.3225	52.5625	64.1625
19	35	32	34.2225	10.5625	19.0125
20	19	19	103.0225	95.0625	98.9625
	583	575	792.5500	799.7500	673.7500

$$\overline{X} = \frac{583}{20} = 29.1500 \qquad \overline{Y} = \frac{575}{20} = 28.7500$$

(ii) Computational procedure

$$\frac{\Sigma(X_i - \overline{X})(Y_i - \overline{Y})}{n} = \frac{673.7500}{20} = 33.6875$$

$$\frac{\Sigma(X_i - \overline{X})^2}{n} = \frac{792.7500}{20} = 39.6275 \qquad \frac{\Sigma(Y_i - \overline{Y})^2}{n} = \frac{799.7500}{20} = 39.9875$$

$$r = \frac{\dfrac{\Sigma(X_i - \overline{X})(Y_i - \overline{Y})}{n}}{\sqrt{\left[\dfrac{\Sigma(X_i - \overline{X})^2}{n}\right]\left[\dfrac{\Sigma(Y_i - \overline{Y})^2}{n}\right]}} = \frac{33.6875}{\sqrt{(39.6275)(39.9875)}} = .85$$

The calculation of r is illustrated in Table 5.3-1. The data are 20 paired scores of fathers and sons on a test of authoritarianism, which measures rigidity, dependency, and ethnocentrism. The coefficient is equal to .85. This tells you two things about the relationship: (1) its strength, represented by the extent to which the value of r differs from zero, and (2) the direction (positive or negative) of the relationship, represented by the sign of r. In the following discussion, you will see why r reflects this information. I will say more about interpreting r in Section 5.4.

Information Contained in the Cross Product

The formula for Pearson's r looks complicated. You are probably wondering how r reflects both the nature of the relationship between two variables and the strength of the relationship. As you will see, a careful examination of the formula provides the answer. In the formula for r, a person's scores on the two variables, X and Y, are expressed as deviations from their respective means as follows: $(X_i - \overline{X})$ and $(Y_i - \overline{Y})$. The product of the two deviations, $(X_i - \overline{X})(Y_i - \overline{Y})$, is called the **cross product.** If a person is above the mean on both variables, the algebraic sign of $(X_i - \overline{X})(Y_i - \overline{Y})$ is positive, and the associated data point falls in quadrant 1 of Figure 5.3-1(a). If a person is below the mean on both variables, the sign of $(X_i - \overline{X})(Y_i - \overline{Y})$ also is positive because it is the product of two negative numbers, but the corresponding data point falls in quadrant 3 of Figure 5.3-1(a). If a person is above the mean on one variable but below the mean on the other, the sign of $(X_i - \overline{X})(Y_i - \overline{Y})$ is negative, and the data point falls in either quadrant 2 or quadrant 4.

In Figure 5.3-1(a), most of the data points are in quadrants 1 and 3; hence the algebraic sign of the sum $\Sigma(X_i - \overline{X})(Y_i - \overline{Y})$ is positive. When this sum is positive, the two variables are said to be positively related—that is, an increase in one variable is accompanied by an increase in the other. If an inverse relationship exists between X and Y, most of the data points fall in quadrants 2 and 4, and the sign of

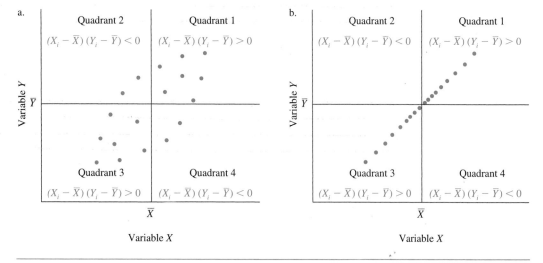

Figure 5.3-1. All cross products, $(X_i - \overline{X})(Y_i - \overline{Y})$; in quadrants 1 and 3 are positive; those in quadrants 2 and 4 are negative. For simplicity, examples (a) and (b) use data whose X and Y dispersions are equal. Such equality is rarely observed for real data.

$\Sigma (X_i - \overline{X})(Y_i - \overline{Y})$ is negative. From the foregoing discussion, it follows that the algebraic sign of $\Sigma(X_i - \overline{X})(Y_i - \overline{Y})$ in the numerator of

$$r = \frac{\dfrac{\Sigma(X_i - \overline{X})(Y_i - \overline{Y})}{n}}{\sqrt{\left[\dfrac{\Sigma(X_i - \overline{X})^2}{n}\right]\left[\dfrac{\Sigma(Y_i - \overline{Y})^2}{n}\right]}}$$

indicates whether X and Y are positively or inversely related—the nature of the relationship. As you will see next, the numerator also indicates the strength of the relationship.

The greater the strength of the relationship between X and Y, the larger is the absolute value of the sum of the cross products, $\Sigma(X_i - \overline{X})(Y_i - \overline{Y})$. Consider Figure 5.1-1(b) where $r = 1$. For this case, the sum of the cross products is as large as it can be because the largest $(X_i - \overline{X})$ is paired with the largest $(Y_i - \overline{Y})$, the second largest $(X_i - \overline{X})$ with the second largest $(Y_i - \overline{Y})$, and so on. A much smaller sum of cross products occurs when some large $(X_i - \overline{X})$'s are paired with small $(Y_i - \overline{Y})$'s and vice versa as in Figure 5.3-1(a) where $r = .65$. If the r in Figure 5.3-1(a) were equal to 0, the data points would fall within the area of a circle instead of an ellipse. In this case, positive $(X_i - \overline{X})$'s are as likely to be paired with negative $(Y_i - \overline{Y})$'s as with positive $(Y_i - \overline{Y})$'s, resulting in a sum of cross products that is equal to 0. In summary, the sign of $\Sigma(X_i - \overline{X})(Y_i - \overline{Y})$ indicates whether the relationship is positive or negative. The size of the absolute value of $\Sigma(X_i - \overline{X})(Y_i - \overline{Y})$ indicates the strength of the association.

On reflection, it also is apparent that the value of $\Sigma(X_i - \overline{X})(Y_i - \overline{Y})$ is affected by the number of paired X and Y scores: For correlations not equal to zero, the larger the number of pairs of scores, the larger the absolute value of $\Sigma(X_i - \overline{X})(Y_i - \overline{Y})$. To obtain a measure of strength of association that is independent of the number of pairs of scores, you compute the mean of the cross product sum:

$$S_{XY} = \frac{\Sigma(X_i - \overline{X})(Y_i - \overline{Y})}{n}$$

where n is the number of paired X and Y scores. This mean is called the **covariance** of X and Y and is denoted by S_{XY}. If you divide the covariance by the standard deviations of X and Y, S_X and S_Y, you obtain a measure of strength of association that also is independent of the size of the dispersions of the X and Y variables. The resulting statistic,

$$r = \frac{S_{XY}}{S_X S_Y} = \frac{\dfrac{\Sigma(X_i - \overline{X})(Y_i - \overline{Y})}{n}}{\sqrt{\left[\dfrac{\Sigma(X_i - \overline{X})^2}{n}\right]\left[\dfrac{\Sigma(Y_i - \overline{Y})^2}{n}\right]}}$$

was defined earlier as the Pearson product-moment correlation coefficient.

To summarize, the heart of the correlation formula is the cross product sum $\Sigma(X_i - \overline{X})(Y_i - \overline{Y})$. This sum reflects both the nature of the relationship between X and Y (positive versus inverse) and the magnitude of the relationship. The cross product sum is divided by n to free it of dependence on the number of paired X and Y scores; it is divided by $S_X S_Y$ to free it of dependence on the size of the dispersions of the X and Y variables. Because of these operations and because X and Y are expressed as deviations from their respective means, the r statistic is a dimensionless index of a linear relationship. This means that the value of r does not depend on the unit of measurement of either the X or Y variables or on the value that is designated as the zero point or origin of either measuring scale. To put it another way, multiplying X or Y by a positive constant or adding a constant (a positive linear transformation) does not affect the value of r. As stated earlier, r ranges over the interval -1 to $+1$.

The following section examines ways to interpret r, but first I will make one more comment about it. If the dispersion of either X or Y is equal to zero (S_X or $S_Y = 0$), the correlation coefficient is undefined. On reflection, this seems reasonable because $r = S_{XY}/S_X S_Y$ and division by $S_X S_Y = 0$ is undefined. In words, this means that the concept of strength of association is meaningless when X or Y is a constant.

CHECK YOUR UNDERSTANDING OF SECTION 5.3

7. Researchers administered a reading test and an intelligence test to a random sample of first-grade children and obtained the following data. Compute r using the deviation formula or a calculator with a correlation routine.

Child	Reading Readiness Score	IQ Score		Child	Reading Readiness Score	IQ Score
1	45	102		11	43	104
2	40	100		12	50	108
3	48	106		13	42	96
4	45	101		14	40	99
5	38	98		15	41	96
6	43	100		16	48	102
7	36	92		17	47	104
8	41	102		18	37	94
9	42	102		19	42	98
10	50	110		20	45	100

8. Studies have shown that music can affect mood, emotion, task performance, and cognition. It was hypothesized that the tempo of country-western music played in bars was related to the consumption of alcohol. Observers visited three bars featuring recorded country-western music on three Friday nights. They obtained permission to tape-record the music and to observe patrons at

selected tables. When the music began, the observers recorded the rate at which each patron sipped an alcoholic beverage. The investigators analyzed the music tapes for the tempo (beats per minute) of each song and determined the mean number of sips during each song. They obtained the following data. (Suggested by Bach, Paul J., and Schaefer, James M. [1979]. The tempo of country music and the rate of drinking in bars. *Journal of Studies on Alcohol, 40*, 1058–1059.)

Tempo	Mean Number of Sips	Tempo	Mean Number of Sips
35	1.150	80	0.900
38	1.150	85	0.725
44	0.400	91	0.725
48	1.075	93	0.875
51	0.950	100	0.525
64	0.975	102	0.800
68	0.950	108	0.775
68	0.925	112	0.750
72	0.875	118	0.625

   a. Construct a scatterplot for these data and decide whether the data appear to be linearly related.
   b. Compute r using the deviation formula or a calculator with a correlation routine.
   c. What does the r tell you about the relationship between tempo and sips per minute.

9. If you have a calculator with a correlation routine, use it to compute r for the data in "Check Your Understanding of Section 5.1," Exercise 1.

10. Calculate $\Sigma(X_i - \overline{X})(Y_i - \overline{Y})$ for the following data points. In which quadrants of Figure 5.3-1 would the majority of the data points fall? Are the variables related, and, if so, is the relationship positive or negative?

a.		b.		c.		d.	
X	Y	X	Y	X	Y	X	Y
9	14	9	14	9	13	6	12
11	17	11	14	10	18	9	16
13	17	11	16	12	9	14	15
7	12	9	16	9	20	11	17

11. For the data in Exercise 10, make figures like Figure 5.3-1.
12. For the data in Exercise 10, calculate r.
13. a. What does $\Sigma(X_i - \overline{X})(Y_i - \overline{Y})$ tell you about the relationship between X and Y?
    b. In computing r, why is $\Sigma(X_i - \overline{X})(Y_i - \overline{Y})$ divided by n?
14. For a set of data with $S_X = 6$ and $S_Y = 5$, what is the largest possible value that S_{XY} can be? (*Hint:* The maximum value of $r = +1$ and $r = S_{XY}/S_X S_Y$.)

15. a. If $n = 2$ and $S_X S_Y$ does not equal zero, what are the possible values of r? (*Hint:* Consider where the two data points for a linear relationship could fall in a scatterplot like Figure 5.3-1.)
    b. Make a scatterplot that supports your answer.

16. The correlation coefficient for the following data is undefined. Why is this statement true?

X	Y
8	4
8	6
8	3
8	7
8	5

17. Terms to remember:
    a. Pearson product-moment correlation coefficient   b. Cross product
    c. Covariance

5.4 INTERPRETATION OF CORRELATION COEFFICIENT: EXPLAINED AND UNEXPLAINED VARIATION

As you have seen, a Pearson product-moment correlation coefficient reflects the nature and the strength of the linear association between two variables. However, two other statistics, both functions of r, are more useful for getting an intuitive feel for the strength of association represented by r. These statistics are the **coefficient of determination, r^2,** which is equal to the square of the correlation coefficient, and the **coefficient of nondetermination, k^2,** which is equal to $1 - r^2$.

If you examine the authoritarianism scores in Table 5.3-1, you see that there is variation among the fathers' X scores and among the sons' Y scores. What accounts for this variability? One reason why the sons' Y scores differ is that their fathers' X scores differ. Because X and Y are correlated ($r = .85$), a father who has a high score is likely to have a son who also has a high score. Thus, because of the linear relationship between X and Y, some of the variation among the Y scores can be accounted for or explained by variation among the X scores. However, not all the variation can be explained in this way because some fathers who have the same authoritarianism score (X) have sons with different authoritarianism scores (Y). Consider, for example, families 4 and 10 where X denotes the father's scores and Y denotes the son's scores: $X_4 = X_{10} = 29$, but $Y_4 = 33$ and $Y_{10} = 36$.

For a given linear relationship between X and Y, you would like to know how much of the Y-score variability is accounted for by the X-score variability and how much is not accounted for. This information is given, respectively, by r^2 and k^2. I will denote the variability of the X and Y scores by S_X^2 and S_Y^2, respectively. Recall from Section 4.2 that S_X^2 and S_Y^2 are sample variances and that variance is measure of the dispersion of scores. If I divide S_X^2 by itself and S_Y^2 by itself, I change both variances into proportions with values equal to 1. Each of these proportions can be partitioned into two components, as follows:

$$\frac{S_X^2}{S_X^2} \quad = \quad r^2 \quad + \quad k^2$$

$$\begin{pmatrix} \text{Total } X \text{ variance} \\ \text{expressed as a} \\ \text{proportion} \end{pmatrix} = \begin{pmatrix} \text{Proportion of } X \\ \text{variance explained} \\ \text{by } Y \text{ variance} \end{pmatrix} + \begin{pmatrix} \text{Proportion of } X \\ \text{variance not explained} \\ \text{by } Y \text{ variance} \end{pmatrix}.$$

$$\frac{S_Y^2}{S_Y^2} \quad = \quad r^2 \quad + \quad k^2$$

$$\begin{pmatrix} \text{Total } Y \text{ variance} \\ \text{expressed as a} \\ \text{proportion} \end{pmatrix} = \begin{pmatrix} \text{Proportion of } Y \\ \text{variance explained} \\ \text{by } X \text{ variance} \end{pmatrix} + \begin{pmatrix} \text{Proportion of } Y \\ \text{variance not explained} \\ \text{by } X \text{ variance} \end{pmatrix}.$$

Thus, the total variance expressed as a proportion is equal to the coefficient of determination, r^2, plus the coefficient of nondetermination, k^2. To compute r^2 you square the correlation coefficient; k^2 is computed from $k^2 = 1 - r^2$.

For the authoritarianism data in Table 5.3-1, $r^2 = (.85)^2 = .72$ and $k^2 = 1 - .72 = .28$. This means that .72 (or $.72 \times 100 = 72\%$) of the variance of the Y scores can be explained by the linear relationship with the X scores, but .28 of the variance of the Y scores is not explained. The converse also is true; for example, 72% of the variance of the X scores can be explained by the linear relationship with the Y scores. The linear relationship between the fathers' and sons' scores enables me to account for much of the variance in the sons' or the fathers' authoritarianism scores (72%); however, 28% of the variance is not accounted for. In all likelihood I could find other variables, such as the sons' or fathers' levels of education, that would enable me to reduce the percentage of unaccounted-for variance. The index k^2 is a measure of how much of the variance remains to be accounted for.

A visual representation of the proportion of explained and unexplained variance is shown in Figure 5.4-1, where the proportions $S_Y^2/S_Y^2 = 1$ and $S_X^2/S_X^2 = 1$ are represented by the areas of circles. The area in which the circles overlap corresponds to r^2; the nonoverlap areas correspond to k^2. If r is equal to $+1$ or -1, the circles completely overlap, as shown in Figure 5.4-1(c), and all the variance of one variable is explained by that of the other variable. If r is equal to 0, the circles do not overlap, as shown in Figure 5.4-1(d), and none of the variance of either variable is explained by that of the other variable.

Most variables of interest to behavioral scientists, health scientists, and educators are affected by a multiplicity of factors. School performance, for example, is affected by academic aptitude, scholastic motivation, health, and parental support for achievement, to name only a few. A correlation between performance and academic aptitude of .30, for example, tells you that you have accounted for $(.30)^2 = .09$

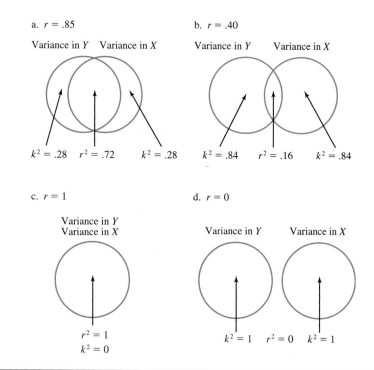

Figure 5.4-1. Visual representation of r^2, the proportion of variance of one variable that is explained by the variance of the other variable, and k^2, the proportion that is not explained by the variance of the other variable.

of performance variance and that you have to look to other variables to account for the remaining $1 - .09 = .91$ of the variance. Note that because $r^2 \leq |r|$, values of $|r|$ close to 1 are required to account for an appreciable proportion of variance. Not until $r = .71$ does $r^2 = .50$.

CHECK YOUR UNDERSTANDING OF SECTION 5.4

18. For the following experiments, compute r^2 and k^2 and interpret them verbally and by means of diagrams like those in Figure 5.4-1.
    a. The correlation between freshman English grades and grades in a physical education bowling class was .22.
    b. The correlation between a self-report instrument measuring family cohesion and men's marital satisfaction was .56.
    c. The correlation between the last two digits of students' Social Security numbers and total fiber (vegetable, fruit, and cereal) consumed per week was .03.
19. Terms to remember:
    a. Coefficient of determination   b. Coefficient of nondetermination

5.5 SOME COMMON ERRORS IN INTERPRETING A CORRELATION COEFFICIENT

Error: Interpreting *r* in Direct Proportion to Its Size

Correlation coefficients are often incorrectly interpreted. A common error is to interpret *r* as the percentage of association between two variables. For example, it is incorrect to say that an *r* of .60 means that there is a 60% association between the variables. Such a statement is meaningless. Does it mean that 60% of the elements are associated? The value of *r* does not indicate the percentage of association but rather is a measure of strength of association on a scale of -1 to $+1$.

A related error is concluding, for example, that an *r* of .80 represents twice the relationship indicated by an *r* of .40 or that an increase in correlation from .10 to .20 represents the same increase as that from .60 to .70. The error in such interpretations becomes apparent when you consider that an *r* equal to .80 accounts for 64% of the variance, whereas an *r* equal to .40 accounts for only 16% of the variance and that 64% is four times larger than 16%.

Error: Interpreting *r* in Terms of Arbitrary Descriptive Labels

Various schemes have been suggested to help students interpret correlation coefficients. A common but misleading scheme is the classification of certain *r* values as "very high" (for example, $r \geq .90$), "high" ($r = .70–.89$), "medium" ($r = .30–.69$), or "low" ($r = .30$). The problem with these classifications is that what constitutes a high or low correlation depends on what is being correlated with what and on the use to be made of *r* once it has been computed. This will be illustrated for the concepts of *reliability* and *validity*, two desirable characteristics of psychological tests. One type of reliability, called **test-retest reliability,** is determined by administering a test to a group of participants, waiting a suitable period of time, and then readministering the test to the same participants. The test's reliability, or consistency of measurement, is the correlation between the two sets of scores. Reliability coefficients of .90 or higher are common for tests of intellectual aptitude. A test-retest reliability coefficient below .80 would raise serious questions about the reliability of an intelligence test; however, the scheme for interpreting *r* described earlier would classify $r = .80$ as high. Equally misleading designations result when this classification scheme is used to interpret validity coefficients. The **validity** of a test is the degree to which it measures what it is supposed to measure. To assess the validity of, say, a college aptitude test, students' aptitude scores can be correlated with their grade-point averages. The best aptitude tests rarely have validity coefficients above .60. It is misleading to label a validity coefficient of .60 as medium when higher coefficients are seldom, if ever, obtained. An $r = .60$ is an extremely high validity coefficient but a very, very low reliability coefficient. As these examples illustrate, no single classification scheme for interpreting *r* is applicable to all situations.

Error: Inferring Causation from Correlation

Another common error in interpreting a correlation coefficient is to infer that because two variables are correlated, one causes the other.

> A nonzero correlation coefficient simply means that there is a **concomitant relationship** between X and Y—that is, variation in one variable is associated in some way with variation in the other.

It is true that if X causes Y, there must be a correlation between the variables. However, the converse of this statement is not true. A concomitant relationship is necessary but not sufficient for inferring causality. A concomitant relationship often exists because both variables are caused by a third variable. For example, it does not necessarily follow from the positive correlation between Sunday school attendance and honesty that attending Sunday school causes honesty. In all likelihood, both variables are caused by a third variable—parental reinforcement and modeling practices in the home.

It is easy to fall into the trap of inferring causality from correlation, especially when one variable occurs before the other. Consider the well-publicized positive correlation between years of formal education and income. Does such a correlation mean that going to college causes one to earn more money? Before giving an affirmative answer you would have to know how much college graduates would have earned if they had not gone to college. A causal relationship may in fact exist, but this cannot be ascertained from the correlation. Some or all of the correlation between education and income might be explained in terms of other causal variables. For example, colleges attract two kinds of students—the bright and the rich. We know that bright individuals tend to rise to better paying jobs whether or not they have gone to college and that few children of rich parents end up poor.

CHECK YOUR UNDERSTANDING OF SECTION 5.5

20. Which of the following are incorrect interpretations of a correlation coefficient and why?
    a. The strength of association between two forms (L and M) of a psychological test is .96.
    b. There is a medium correlation, $r = .67$, between the age at which babies can roll over and the age at which they can sit up alone.
    c. The correlation between women's scores on the Beck Depression Inventory and a self-report questionnaire measuring marital discord is .30; this correlation is twice as high as that for men, which is $r = .15$.
    d. We can conclude from the high correlation between risk for sexual assault and alcohol consumption by female victims that victimization is caused at least in part by consuming alcohol.
21. In an attempt to help children with low IQs improve their school performance, a special perceptual awareness program was instituted. Suppose that the program

was completely ineffective. The group's mean IQ before the program was 72. Would you expect it to change after the special program, and if so, in what direction? (*Hint:* If you don't see the issue, reread "A Bit of History" in Section 5.1.)

22. Terms to remember:
    a. Test-retest reliability   b. Validity
    c. Concomitant relationship

5.6 FACTORS THAT AFFECT THE SIZE OF A CORRELATION COEFFICIENT

Nature of the Relationship Between *X* and *Y*

There are many ways in which two variables can be related. It is sufficient for our purposes to classify them as a **linear** (straight line) relationship, or a **nonlinear** (curved line) relationship. Three examples showing the straight or curved lines of best fit for paired scores are presented in Figure 5.6-1. In general, the more closely data points cluster around the line of best fit, whether it is a straight or a curved line, the higher the correlation. You saw in Section 5.2 that when r is equal to $+1$ or -1, the data points fall on a straight line. If X and Y are normally distributed and have equal variances, as the absolute value of r decreases, the points form fatter and fatter ellipses until finally, when r is equal to 0, they tend to fall in a circle. The Pearson product-moment correlation always fits data points by a straight line. This works fine if the relationship is linear but not so well if the relationship is nonlinear, as in Figure 5.6-1(c). If a nonlinear relationship is fitted by a straight line, the data points will not cluster around the line as closely as they would an appropriate curved line; consequently, r underestimates the strength of association. In fact, an r equal to 0 can be obtained even though X and Y are highly correlated.

A different correlation measure called the **correlation ratio** or **eta squared**, η^2, has been developed for determining the strength of association between nonlinearly related variables.

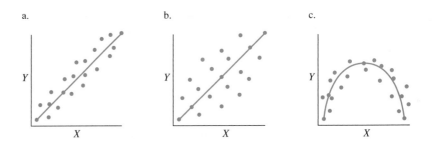

Figure 5.6-1. Parts a and b illustrate linear relationships; part c illustrates a nonlinear relationship. The higher the correlation, the closer the data points cluster around the line of best fit.

Eta squared fits data points by whatever line is appropriate. If the relationship is linear, a straight line is used, and $\eta^2 = r^2$. For nonlinear relationships in which the correlation is not equal to zero, η^2 fits the points by a curved line, and its value is always larger than that for r^2. A discussion of the correlation ratio can be found in more advanced texts.

How can you determine whether the relationship between X and Y is linear or nonlinear and hence whether to use r or η^2? You can use statistical tests;[3] however, the simplest method is to examine the scatterplot for evidence of nonlinearity—the so-called eyeball test. Usually, visual inspection is adequate to detect cases in which r would underestimate strength of association.

In summary, r is a measure of the linear relationship between two quantitative variables. If the relationship is not linear, r underestimates the strength of association.

Truncated Range

The size of the Pearson product-moment correlation coefficient is affected by the range of the X and Y variables. If the range of either variable is truncated—that is, restricted—the size of r will be reduced. Suppose that I have administered an aptitude test to assembly-line job applicants at a new factory. Because of the large number of jobs to be filled, all the applicants were hired regardless of their scores. Six months later I construct a scatterplot like the one in Figure 5.6-2, compute the correlation between aptitude scores and employee productivity, and find that r is equal to .55. This is a respectable validity coefficient. In the future if I had a surplus of applicants, I could improve productivity by hiring only those applicants with high aptitude scores. Suppose that instead of hiring all the applicants when the plant opened, I had

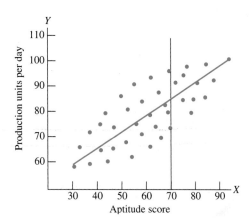

Figure 5.6-2. Scatterplot illustrating the effect on r of restricting the range of X to scores of 70 or above. The r for the unrestricted range is .55; that for the restricted range is .06.

[3] See, for example, Hays (1994, pp. 774–778).

artificially restricted the range of aptitude scores by hiring only applicants with scores of 70 or above. For this case, the correlation between aptitude and productivity would have been .06 instead of .55, and I would have incorrectly concluded that the test is of little value in selecting employees. The reason the restriction or truncation of the range of the X variable results in a misleadingly low correlation coefficient can be seen from Figure 5.6-2. The effect would have been the same had the range of the Y variable been truncated.

The truncated range problem is common in behavioral and education research because such research is often conducted with college students who have been carefully screened for intelligence and related variables and, consequently, constitute a relatively homogeneous population. It is not surprising that college aptitude scores do not correlate highly with grades because admission offices truncate the range by admitting only students with medium to high aptitude scores.

Spurious Effects Due to Subgroups with Different Means or Standard Deviations

A substantial correlation between X and Y can occur because the sample of participants contains two or more subgroups with means that differ for both variables. Suppose that I am interested in the correlation between school achievement (Y) and anxiety level (X) as measured by the Taylor Manifest Anxiety Scale, and I obtain random samples of students from lower- and middle-class families. The correlation coefficient computed for the combined samples will be much higher than that for either sample taken alone. This occurs because the means for the two subgroups differ with respect to both X and Y. The participants from middle-class families tend to perform better in school and to be somewhat more anxious than children from lower-class families. When the subgroups are combined, the correlation between achievement and anxiety is misleadingly high because of the differing means. The reason for this is evident from Figure 5.6-3(a), where the letters L and M denote data points for children from lower- and middle-class families, respectively. Figure 5.6-3(b) illustrates a situation in which the means of two subgroups, A and B, differ only on X. The correlation coefficient computed from the combined samples is lower than that for either sample taken alone.

A spurious correlation can occur when the standard deviations of the subgroups but not their means differ for one or both variables. This situation is depicted in Figure 5.6-3(c) and (d), where the letters A and B denote the subgroups. Figures 5.6–3(e) and (f) depict other ways in which subgroups can produce spurious correlations.

From the foregoing discussion it is apparent that the inclusion of subgroups with different means or standard deviations on X and Y can affect the size and the sign of r. Unfortunately, you are not always aware that the sample contains distinct subgroups. Your first clue may come when you construct a scatterplot and note in retrospect that the scores that cluster together tend to come from participants who have a common distinguishing attribute.

Sometimes a researcher intentionally conducts research with **extreme groups**— groups at opposite ends of a continuum. The use of introverts and extraverts, high

a. Combined *r* is spuriously high

b. Combined *r* is spuriously low

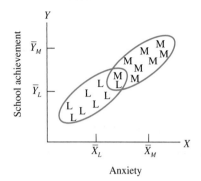
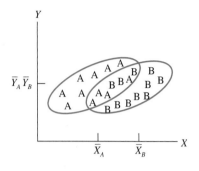
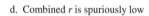

c. Combined *r* is spuriously
   high for B and low for A

d. Combined *r* is spuriously low

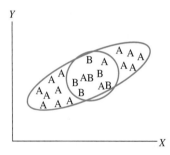
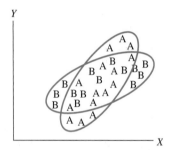

e.

f.

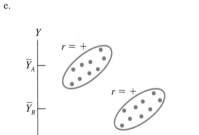
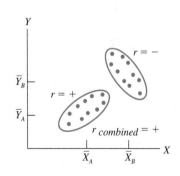

Figure 5.6-3. Scatterplots illustrating the effects on *r* of subsamples with means that differ on both variables (parts a, e, and f) or on only one variable (b). Parts (c) and (d) illustrate the effects of heterogeneous standard deviations. Parts (e) and (f) show that the sign of the coefficient for the combined samples may differ from that for one or both of the subsamples.

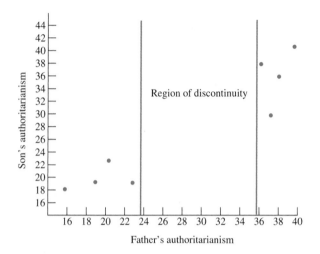

Figure 5.6-4. Scatterplot illustrating the effects on *r* of using extreme groups. The data are taken from Table 5.3-1, with the eight data points representing the four highest and the four lowest authoritarianism scores based on the father's data.

and low achievers, or normals and neurotics enhances the likelihood of detecting other variables on which the groups differ. This is a useful research strategy, but it may lead to spuriously high correlation coefficients. Frequently, the means of the groups differ on both *X* and *Y*, and the data points have the shape illustrated in Figure 5.6-4. The data were selected from Table 5.3-1 so as to contain two extreme groups: the four fathers with the highest authoritarianism scores and the four with the lowest scores. The correlation for all 20 father-son pairs in Table 5.3-1 is .85; the correlation based on the two extreme groups is .94.

Extreme groups constitute one type of **discontinuous distribution.** A discontinuous distribution also results when you restrict your sample to a relatively small number of points along a continuum or when your sample contains one or more outliers. As discussed in Section 4.5, outliers should be carefully examined. Their presence suggests errors in data recording, an equipment malfunction, or other sources of data contamination. It follows from this discussion that correlation coefficients involving discontinuous distributions should be carefully examined.

Non-normality and Heterogeneity of Array Variances

If the distributions of *X* and *Y* are markedly skewed, the value of *r* will be less than if the variables are approximately normally distributed. The reason for this is revealed in Figure 5.6-5, which shows various combinations of skewed *X* and *Y* distributions.

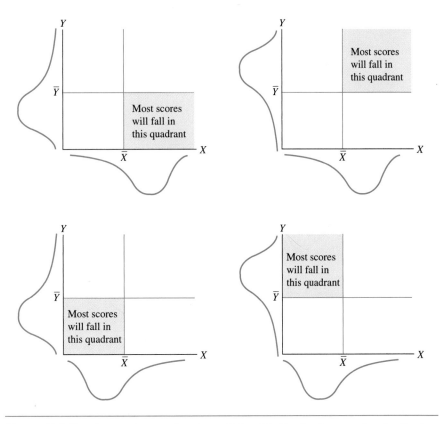

Figure 5.6-5. Effects of markedly skewed X and Y distributions on the distribution of data points in a scatterplot.

> The presence of skewed X and Y distributions is often accompanied by an unequal dispersion of the Y scores for different values of X and a similarly unequal dispersion of the X scores for different values of Y. This condition is called **heterogeneity of array** (row or column) **variances** or **heteroscedasticity.**

Heteroscedasticity is illustrated in Figures 5.6-6(a) and (b). Figures 5.6-6(c) and (d) illustrate the case in which the dispersions for X and for Y are uniform—a condition called **homogeneity of array variances** or **homoscedasticity.** Earlier, you learned that r reflects the average degree to which scores cluster around the line of best fit. If the dispersion around the line differs at different values along the X and Y measurement scales, the correlation coefficient will not have the same meaning as when the array variances are homogeneous. For example, in Figures 5.6-6(a) and (b), the correlation coefficient will underestimate the magnitude of association for low X scores and overestimate it for high X scores.

The use of r as a descriptive measure of association requires no assumptions regarding the shape of the X and Y distributions. As you have seen, however, if X and Y are markedly skewed, the value of r will be closer to zero than if the distributions

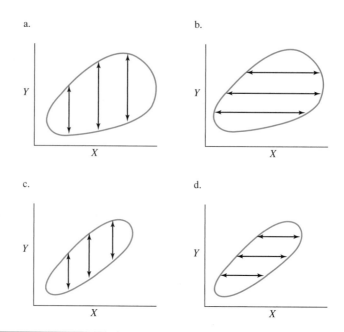

Figure 5.6-6. Parts a and b illustrate the heterogeneity of column and row dispersion, respectively; parts c and d illustrate the homogeneity of dispersion.

are approximately normal. Furthermore, under these conditions, the interpretation of r is altered because r no longer reflects the average degree to which the data points cluster around the line of best fit. Finally, the presence of skewed X and Y distributions is often accompanied by a nonlinear relationship between the variables. This condition calls for the computation of η^2 instead of r.

It is apparent from this discussion that the interpretation of r as a descriptive measure is simplified if X and Y are approximately normally distributed. I emphasize, however, that normality is not required for purely descriptive purposes because whatever the shapes of the X and Y distributions, r reflects the degree to which data points cluster around a straight line of best fit. You will learn in Chapter 12 that normality is required when the sample correlation is used in making inferences about the population correlation.

The factors that affect the size of r are summarized in Table 5.6-1.

TABLE 5.6-1   Factors That Affect the Size of r

r Underestimates Magnitude of Relationship When	r Overestimates Magnitude of Relationship When
1. The relationship between X and Y is nonlinear	1. The sample contains subgroups with means that differ for both variables
2. The range of either X or Y is truncated	2. The sample is composed of extreme groups
3. The distributions of X and Y are skewed	

CHECK YOUR UNDERSTANDING OF SECTION 5.6

23. What effects do the following factors have on r as a measure of strength of association? Draw figures like Figures 5.6-1 through 5.6-5 to represent the data.
    a. The relationship between X and Y looks like an inverted U. Assume that r is positive.
    b. The sample contains subgroups a and b with equal standard deviations and means $\overline{X}_a = 16$, $\overline{X}_b = 22$, $\overline{Y}_a = 31$, and $\overline{Y}_b = 37$. Assume that r is positive for both a and b.
    c. The sample contains subgroups a and b with equal means and standard deviations $S_{X_a} = 13$, $S_{X_b} = 22$, $S_{Y_a} = 22$, and $S_{Y_b} = 13$. Assume that r is positive for both a and b.
    d. The distribution of the X variable is negatively skewed; that for the Y variable is positively skewed. Assume that r is negative.
    e. The distributions of the X and Y variables are positively skewed. Assume that r is positive.
    f. The sample contains subgroups a and b with equal means and standard deviations $S_{X_a} = 9$, $S_{X_b} = 9$, $S_{Y_a} = 13$, and $S_{Y_b} = 21$. Assume that r is positive for both a and b.
    g. The sample contains subgroups a and b with equal standard deviations and means $\overline{X}_a = 12$, $\overline{X}_b = 18$, $\overline{Y}_a = 38$, and $\overline{Y}_b = 27$. Assume that r is positive for both a and b.
    h. The range of X is reduced by deleting participants with scores above $\overline{X}$. Assume that r is positive.
24. The correlation between IQ and ratings of the creativity of 50 highly creative individuals was .18. Can you conclude that IQ is a relatively unimportant factor in creativity? Discuss.
25. Terms to remember:
    a. Linear relationship
    c. Correlation ratio
    e. Truncated range
    g. Discontinuous distribution
    i. Heteroscedasticity
    k. Homoscedasticity
    b. Nonlinear relationship
    d. Eta squared
    f. Extreme groups
    h. Heterogeneity of array variance
    j. Homogeneity of array variance

5.7 SPEARMAN RANK CORRELATION

> The **Spearman rank correlation coefficient,** denoted by r_s, is used to describe the degree of agreement between paired data that are in the form of ranks.[4]

Such data may occur as a result of ranking scores, as when students' grade-point averages are converted to ranks in a graduating class, or because rank data are obtained in the original instance, as when freshman English themes are ranked from the most

---

[4] This coefficient was first used by Sir Francis Galton but was named for the British psychologist Charles Spearman, who made more extensive use of it.

to the least creative. Ranking is often used when it is difficult or impossible to apply more refined measuring procedures, as in assessing characteristics such as creativity, attractiveness, or tastiness.

The formula for r_s is

$$r_s = 1 - \frac{6\sum(R_{X_i} - R_{Y_i})^2}{n(n^2 - 1)}$$

where $R_{X_i} - R_{Y_i}$ is the difference between the ith person's ranks on X and Y and n is the number of pairs of ranks.

The computation of r_s is illustrated in Table 5.7-1, where 14 graduate school applicants have been ranked by tenured faculty (R_{X_i}) and nontenured faculty (R_{Y_i}).

The index r_s is a measure of the agreement between two sets of ranks and is interpreted in much the same way as the Pearson product-moment coefficient. The range of r_s is from -1 to $+1$. Values of r_s greater than 0 indicate that large R_X's tend to be paired with large R_Y's. Values less than 0 indicate that large R_X's are paired

TABLE 5.7-1   Computation of r_s for Ranks Assigned to Applicants by Tenured Faculty (R_{X_i}) and Nontenured Faculty (R_{Y_i})

(i) Data

Applicant	Rank, R_{X_i}	Rank, R_{Y_i}	$R_{X_i} - R_{Y_i}$	$(R_{X_i} - R_{Y_i})^2$
1	6	8	-2	4
2	3	2	1	1
3	4	5	-1	1
4	12	11	1	1
5	10	9	1	1
6	1	1	0	0
7	5	4	1	1
8	7	7	0	0
9	14	14	0	0
10	2	3	-1	1
11	8	10	-2	4
12	11	12	-1	1
13	9	6	3	9
14	13	13	0	0

$$\sum_{i=1}^{n}(R_{X_i} - R_{Y_i})^2 = 24$$

(ii) Computational procedure

$$r_s = 1 - \frac{6\sum_{i=1}^{n}(R_{X_i} - R_{Y_i})^2}{n(n^2 - 1)} = 1 - \frac{6(24)}{14[(14)^2 - 1]} = 1 - \frac{144}{2730} = .95$$

with small R_Y's, and so on. The coefficient is equal to 1 if and only if each person's X and Y ranks are equal. It can be shown that the formula for r_s is equivalent to that for r when two sets of consecutive untied ranks $1, \ldots, n$ are substituted for X_i and Y_i in the Pearson formula.[5] However, the use of ranks in place of scores alters the meaning of the correlation coefficient. This point is examined next.

Earlier you learned that r is a measure of the linear relationship between two quantitative variables; r_s is a measure of the **monotonic relationship** between two sets of ranks.

A function $Y = f(X)$ is said to be **strictly monotonic increasing** if an increase in the value of X is always accompanied by an increase in Y.[6] A **strictly monotonic decreasing function** is one in which an increase in X is accompanied by a decrease in Y.

Monotonic functions include linear functions ($Y = a + bX$) as well as a number of other functions that are nonlinear ($Y = X^3$; $Y = \log X$). Thus, Spearman's rank correlation coefficient does not necessarily reflect the linear relationship between two sets of ranks. It does reflect the strength of the monotonic relationship, a more general relationship. If r_s is equal to zero, either the variables represented by ranks are not related or the form of the relationship is nonmonotonic.

The Problem of Tied Ranks

Occasionally, two or more objects or individuals are assigned the same rank, which results in **tied ranks.** The usual practice is to give them the mean of the ranks they would have received collectively if they had been distinguishable. For example, if Jane, Elaine, and Bill are considered equally gregarious, each is given the mean of the ranks they would have occupied, say, $(1 + 2 + 3)/3 = 2$. Thus, Jane, Elaine, and Bill each are assigned the same mean rank of 2. Unfortunately, the presence of tied ranks violates the assumptions underlying the derivation of the computational formula for r_s. A correction for ties can be incorporated in the formula, but the computation is tedious. The most desirable solution is to force those making ratings to discern differences among the objects or individuals, thereby eliminating tied ranks. If this is done, the uncorrected formula can be used. If raters persist in assigning tied ranks, the next best solution is to treat the sets of ranks as though they were scores and to compute a Pearson product-moment correlation coefficient. The result can be regarded as a Spearman rank correlation coefficient that has been corrected for ties.

CHECK YOUR UNDERSTANDING OF SECTION 5.7

26. A random sample of freshman psychology majors ranked various fields of psychology according to vocational attractiveness. The students again ranked the fields when they were seniors. Compute the correlation between their freshman and senior rankings.

---

[5] The derivation is given by Kirk (1978, pp. 122–124).

[6] A strictly monotonic transformation preserves the order inherent in the original scores; it does not preserve information concerning the magnitude of differences among the original scores.

Field	Freshman Rank	Senior Rank
Social	5	2
Experimental	7	6
Human factors	6	7
Clinical	1	1
Statistics and measurement	8	8
Industrial	3	3
Educational	4	4
Counseling	2	5

27. The debate format can be a useful adjunct to traditional teaching methodologies for presenting complex issues. Graduate student nurses were exposed to a debate on the issue of third-party reimbursement. Researchers used a questionnaire to evaluate pre- and postdebate knowledge of 13 affirmative and negative arguments concerning the issue. The results are listed in the following table; a rank of 1 was assigned to the argument known by the most student nurses. Compute the correlation between the two sets of ranks. (Suggested by Archold, Patricia G., and Hoeffer, Beverly. [1981]. Reframing the issue: A debate on third-party reimbursement. *Nursing Outlook*, 423–427.)

Argument	Pretest Rank	Posttest Rank
Legitimize role and service of nurses	1	7
Increase health care cost	2	7
Increase access of consumer to nursing services	3	4.5
Nursing services are undefined and dependent on physicians	4	12.5
Decrease health care cost	6	4.5
Provide equal opportunity in a free-market system	6	11
Support health-care delivery system not based on need	6	7
Cumbersome process for individual nurses	8	12.5
Increase accountability of nurses for their services	9	9.5
Increase power and autonomy of nursing to influence health care delivery system	11.5	2
Support inequitable/discriminatory health-care delivery system	11.5	1
Elitist/divisive to nursing	11.5	3
No increase in accessibility	11.5	9.5

28. Which of the following are strictly monotonic functions?
    a. $Y = 1 + 2X$ b. $Y = X^2$
    c. $Y = 2 + X^3$ d. $Y = 1/(X + 4)$
29. Terms to remember:
    a. Spearman rank correlation coefficient
    b. Strictly monotonic increasing and decreasing functions
    c. Tied ranks

5.8 OTHER KINDS OF CORRELATION COEFFICIENTS

Three correlation coefficients have been mentioned thus far: r, η^2, and r_s. An extension of r to the case in which there are three or more variables is discussed in Section 6.7. This coefficient is called a multiple correlation coefficient. A fifth coefficient, Cramér's V, that is appropriate for unordered qualitative variables is discussed in Section 17.4. Other coefficients also are available, but they are beyond the scope of this book.

5.9 LOOKING BACK: WHAT HAVE YOU LEARNED?

The term *correlation* refers to the association or concomitance between two or more quantitative or ordered qualitative variables. A correlation coefficient is a measure of the degree of association. The presence of an association does not imply causality; it does, however, imply that as one variable changes, the other variable changes.

The two most widely used correlation coefficients in the behavioral sciences and education are the Pearson product-moment correlation coefficient, r, and the Spearman rank correlation coefficient, r_s. Pearson's r reflects the strength and the direction of the linear relationship between two quantitative variables. It is a number that varies between -1 and 1, with 0 indicating the absence of a linear relationship. Negative values indicate an inverse relationship between the variables; positive values indicate a positive or direct relationship. Spearman's r_s measures the strength and the direction of the monotonic relationship between two ordered qualitative variables—that is, ranked data. It, like r, varies between -1 and 1, with 0 indicating the absence of a monotonic relationship.

Two statistics, both functions of r, are useful in interpreting a particular r value: the coefficient of determination, r^2, and the coefficient of nondetermination, $k^2 = 1 - r^2$. For a given linear relationship between X and Y, r^2 reflects the proportion of the X-score variance that can be explained by the Y-score variance and vice versa; k^2 reflects the proportion that cannot be explained. If, for example, r is equal to .50, you know that, based on the linear relationship between the variables, 25% of the variance of one variable can be explained by the variance of the other variable, and 75% remains to be explained.

The Pearson product-moment correlation coefficient is appropriate for linearly related quantitative variables. For descriptive purposes, no other assumptions regarding the variables are required. However, in interpreting r, keep in mind that the size of r can be affected by such factors as the shape of the X and Y distributions, the presence of a truncated X or Y range, the presence of subgroups with standard deviations or means that differ for both variables, and the presence of a discontinuous distribution for X or Y or both.

REVIEW EXERCISES FOR CHAPTER 5

1. A job-satisfaction questionnaire was administered to a random sample of 36 men between the ages of 29 and 34. The researcher was interested in the relationship between number of years of formal education and job satisfaction. (a) Construct

a scatterplot for the data in the following table. (b) Does the relationship appear to be linear or nonlinear?

Participant	Years of Education	Job Satisfaction	Participant	Years of Education	Job Satisfaction
1	14	36	19	12	43
2	11	38	20	11	46
3	10	36	21	18	53
4	15	51	22	8	30
5	7	30	23	9	35
6	8	37	24	12	40
7	12	40	25	13	40
8	13	43	26	13	41
9	16	47	27	10	32
10	12	44	28	14	50
11	12	37	29	12	33
12	11	40	30	14	47
13	9	32	31	10	38
14	12	42	32	11	37
15	13	45	33	12	40
16	11	38	34	14	50
17	12	42	35	13	42
18	11	37	36	13	45

2. Distinguish between r and ρ.
3. Match the r values 1, -1, 0, .3, and $-.8$ with the scatterplots shown here.

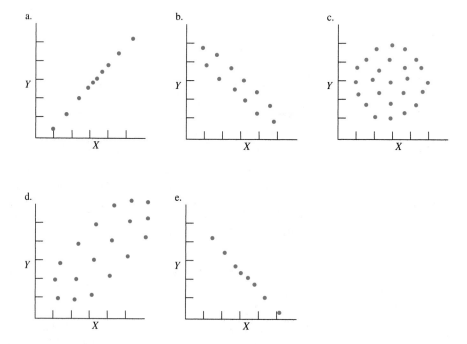

4. Would you expect the correlation between the following to be positive, negative, or essentially zero?
   a. Mechanical aptitude and birth order
   b. Verbal intelligence and number of trials to learn a list of nonsense syllables
   c. Grades in college and annual income 10 years after graduation
   d. Number of letters in last name and musical aptitude

5. The Alcohol Dependence Scale was developed to assist the World Health Organization in the classification of alcoholism. Fifteen alcoholics seeking counseling for alcohol-related disabilities took this scale and the Michigan Alcoholism Screening Test, which yields an index of problems related to drinking. The investigators obtained the following data. (Suggested by Skinner, Harvey A., and Allen, Barbara A. [1982]. Alcohol dependence syndrome: Measurement and validation. *Journal of Abnormal Psychology, 91*, 199–209.)

Counselee	Alcohol Dependence Scale	Michigan Alcoholism Screening Test
1	89	78
2	48	57
3	74	65
4	97	86
5	59	58
6	65	75
7	46	57
8	84	95
9	78	69
10	77	86
11	67	78
12	36	47
13	83	74
14	68	77
15	96	87

   a. Construct a scatterplot for these data and decide whether the data appear to be linearly related.
   b. Use the deviation formula or a calculator to compute r for these data.

6. Researchers have reported that lonely people often describe themselves as shy. To investigate the strength of the relationship between the two variables, investigators gave a modified version of the Stanford Shyness Survey and the UCLA Loneliness Scale to 20 male and 20 female college students. The order of administration of the instruments was randomized independently for each student. The researchers obtained the following data for the male students. (Experiment suggested by Maroldo, Georgetter K. [1981]. Shyness and loneliness among college men and women. *Psychological Reports, 48*, 885–886.)

Student	Stanford Shyness Survey	UCLA Loneliness Scale	Student	Stanford Shyness Survey	UCLA Loneliness Scale
1	36	51	11	30	29
2	39	52	12	30	40
3	30	33	13	33	45
4	23	35	14	32	30
5	28	55	15	28	42
6	41	52	16	34	45
7	29	32	17	21	35
8	27	38	18	41	35
9	28	40	19	23	30
10	28	33	20	39	51

    a. Construct a scatterplot for these data and decide whether the data appear to be linearly related.

    b. Use the deviation formula or a calculator to compute r for these data.

7. Use the deviation formula or a calculator to compute r for the education and job data in Exercise 1.

8. Calculate $\sum_{i=1}^{n}(X_i - \overline{X})(Y_i - \overline{Y})$ for the following data. In which quadrants of Figure 5.3-1 would the majority of the data points fall? Are the variables linearly related, and if so, is the relationship positive or negative?

a.

X	Y
14	18
6	11
10	15
10	16

b.

X	Y
10	17
10	15
12	15
8	13

c.

X	Y
9	17
11	14
13	10
7	19

d.

X	Y
9	17
11	17
13	13
7	13

9. For the data in Exercise 8, make figures like Figure 5.3-1.

10. For the data in Exercise 8, calculate the Pearson product-moment correlation coefficient using the deviation formula or a calculator.

11. What does covariance, S_{XY}, tell you about the relationship between X and Y? In computing r, why is S_{XY} divided by $S_X S_Y$?

12. For a set of data with $S_X = 4$ and $S_Y = 5$, what is the largest possible value that S_{XY} can be? (*Hint:* The maximum value of $r = +1$ and $r = S_{XY}/S_X S_Y$.)

13. The correlation coefficient for the following data is undefined. Why is this statement true?

X	Y
13	16
16	16
11	16
17	16
12	16

14. What do r^2 and k^2 tell you about the relationship between X and Y?
15. For the following experiments, compute r^2 and k^2 and interpret them verbally and by means of diagrams like those in Figure 5.34-1.
    a. The correlation between grades in introductory psychology and introductory statistics was .32.
    b. The correlation between the number of hours that rats had been deprived of food and the time to traverse a maze with sunflower seeds in the goal box was .80.
    c. The correlation between the last two digits of students' Social Security numbers and the number of trials to learn nonsense syllables was .02.
16. Which of the following are incorrect interpretations of a correlation coefficient, and why?
    a. The strength of association between scores on the Attitudes Toward Disabled Persons Scale and amount of exposure to persons with disabilities is .56.
    b. The correlation between height and weight at age 6 is .40; this correlation is twice as high as that at age 16, when $r = .20$.
    c. The correlation between reaction time and number of automobile accidents is .20; 96% of the variance in frequency of accidents is unaccounted for.
    d. You can conclude from the high correlation between level of motivation and number of elective offices sought that office-seeking behavior is caused at least in part by motivation.
17. What is wrong with interpreting r
    a. in direct proportion to its size?
    b. in terms of arbitrary descriptive labels?
    c. as indicating causality?
18. Employees with the highest accident rates were required to complete a safety course. Following the course, the employees had fewer accidents. Can you conclude that the course was effective? What controls could be used in the experiment to make the outcome easier to interpret?
19. What effects do the following factors have on r as a measure of strength of association? Draw figures like Figures 5.6-1 through 5.6-5 to represent the data.
    a. The relationship between X and Y looks like a U. Assume that r is positive.
    b. The range of X is reduced by deleting participants with scores below $\overline{X}$.
    c. The sample contains subgroups a and b with equal standard deviations and means $\overline{X}_a = 16$, $\overline{X}_b = 22$, $\overline{Y}_a = 42$, and $\overline{Y}_b = 31$. Assume that r is positive for both a and b.
    d. The sample contains subgroups a and b with equal standard deviations and means $\overline{X}_a = 20$, $\overline{X}_b = 26$, $\overline{Y}_a = 35$, and $\overline{Y}_b = 41$. Assume that r is positive for both a and b.
    e. The sample contains subgroups a and b with equal means and standard deviations $S_{X_a} = 15$, $S_{X_b} = 24$, $S_{Y_a} = 24$, and $S_{Y_b} = 15$. Assume that r is positive for both a and b.
    f. The sample contains subgroups a and b with equal means and standard deviations $S_{X_a} = 18$, $S_{X_b} = 18$, $S_{Y_a} = 26$, and $S_{Y_b} = 34$. Assume that r is positive for both a and b.

g. The distribution of the X variable is positively skewed; that for the Y variable is negatively skewed. Assume that r is positive.

h. The distributions of the X and Y variables are negatively skewed.

20. How can you detect cases in which η^2 should be used instead of r?

21. What are the potential advantages and disadvantages of using extreme groups in research?

22. The correlation between IQ and grade-point average (GPA) for high school seniors was .63. For seniors who went on to college, the correlation between IQ and college GPA was .51. Explain why this correlation is lower.

23. List the similarities and differences between r and r_s.

24. A psychiatric social worker and an occupational therapist ranked 11 Veterans Administration patients with respect to extent of recovery following 3 months of therapy. Compute the Spearman rank correlation between the two sets of rankings.

Patient	Social Worker	Occupational Therapist
1	7	7
2	2	1
3	1	2
4	3	5
5	8	9
6	10	10
7	4	3
8	9	8
9	11	11
10	6	6
11	5	4

25. Participants rated the attractiveness of one set of geometric shapes before smoking marijuana and a similar set after smoking marijuana. One shape in the two sets was the same. The following data are the ratings for that shape. A rating of 1 means very attractive; a rating of 20 means very unattractive. Transform the ratings to ranks, and compute the Spearman rank correlation between the two sets of ranks.

Participant	Smoking	After Smoking
1	6	3
2	8	7
3	14	16
4	7	2
5	10	12
6	9	15
7	5	1
8	15	20
9	12	17

26. Suppose that for the data in Exercise 25, participant 6 had assigned a rating of 12 instead of 15 to the geometric shape after smoking marijuana. This rating results in tied ranks. How would this affect the computational procedure for the correlation coefficient?

27. Which of the following are strictly monotonic functions?

 a. $Y = 3 + 3X$ b. $Y = 1 + X^2$

 c. $Y = X^3$ d. $Y = 1/X$

28. Use a statistical software package to compute the Pearson product-moment correlation between for the variables of number of years of formal education and job satisfaction in Exercise 1.

29. Use a statistical software package to compute the Pearson product-moment correlation between the Alcohol Dependence Scale data and the Michigan Alcoholism Screening Test data in Exercise 5.

30. Use a statistical software package to compute the Pearson product-moment correlation between the modified version of the Stanford Shyness Survey data and the UCLA Loneliness Scale data in Exercise 6.

6

Regression

6.1 Introduction to Regression
Looking Ahead: What Is This Chapter About?
An Overview of the Prediction Process

6.2 Criterion for the Line of Best Fit
Predicting Y from X
Predicting X from Y
Relationship between r and the Slopes of the Regression Lines
Check Your Understanding of Sections 6.1 and 6.2

6.3 Another Measure of Ability to Predict: The Standard Error of Estimate
An Alternative Formula for $S_{Y \cdot X}$
Descriptive Application of $S_{Y \cdot X}$

6.4 Assumptions Associated with Regression and the Standard Error of Estimate
Check Your Understanding of Sections 6.3 and 6.4

6.5 Multiple Regression and Multiple Correlation
Multiple Regression
Multiple Correlation
Check Your Understanding of Section 6.5

6.6 Looking Back: What Have You Learned?
Review Exercises for Chapter 6

6.1 INTRODUCTION TO REGRESSION

Looking Ahead: What Is This Chapter About?

This chapter is about making predictions. Consider Jean who wants to do well in law school. Her score on the Law School Aptitude Test (LSAT) is 69. She wonders what grade-point average she can expect to make in law school? Bertha is on a 750-calorie diet. How many pounds should she be able to lose in a month? Because the variables in each case are correlated, Jean can predict her GPA from her 69 LSAT score and Bertha can predict her weight loss from her 750-calorie diet with better than chance accuracy. As you will learn, the higher the correlation between the independent and dependent variables, the more accurate the prediction.

For r equal to $+1$ or -1, the dependent variable, denoted by Y, can be predicted from the independent variable, X, with perfect accuracy. If, however, r is equal to zero, a knowledge of X is useless in predicting Y. Although a correlation coefficient is indicative of our ability to predict, the actual prediction is made using regression analysis, the subject of this chapter.

> Strictly speaking, **regression analysis** applies to paired data (X_i, Y_i), where X is the independent variable with values X_i that are selected in advance, and Y is the dependent variable with values Y_i that are free to vary. However, regression procedures also are applicable when both X and Y are free to vary, as they are in correlation.

Often one's prediction can be improved by using more than one predictor. For example, Bertha could more accurately predict her weight loss by taking into account the amount of exercise she gets each day in addition to her calorie intake. The simultaneous use of two or more predictors in predicting a dependent variable is called **multiple regression.**

After reading the chapter, you should know the following:

- How to predict one variable from another
- How to determine the line of best fit
- The relationship between r and the slopes of the best-fitting regression lines
- What the standard error of estimate is and how to interpret it
- How to interpret multiple regression and multiple correlation

An Overview of the Prediction Process

George, who is taking statistics, copies down the grades from last semester's class and constructs the scatterplot shown in Figure 6.1-1. He finds that the correlation between the midterm and the final exam was .80. His midterm grade was 82, and he wonders how he'll do on the final. According to the scatterplot, two students in last semester's class made 82; the mean of their grades—and hence George's predicted grade, assuming that the two classes are comparable—is $(74 + 84)/2 = 79$.

Although this prediction method works, it has a serious disadvantage. The prediction is based on only the two Y scores corresponding to $X_i = 82$; the other 10 paired scores are ignored. Predictions based on such small samples tend to be unstable—that

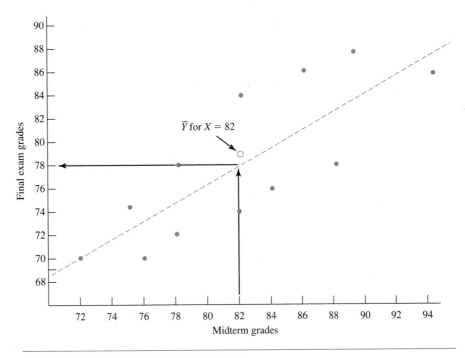

Figure 6.1-1. Scatterplot for paired midterm and final exam grades.

is, they tend to vary markedly from sample to sample. Prediction can be improved by utilizing all the data rather than a small subset. George notes that the relationship between the midterm and final grades appears to be linear, so he determines the best-fitting linear regression line. It is shown as a dashed line in Figure 6.1-1. To predict his final grade George draws a vertical line from $X_i = 82$ up to the regression line and then a horizontal line over to the Y axis. His predicted grade is 78.

Predictions based on the regression line take into account all the sample data and hence are more stable than those based on only the mean of the Y scores corresponding to a given X score. Both procedures presuppose that the population represented by the current sample (George's statistics class) does not differ from that represented by the earlier sample (last semester's class). Obviously, if this assumption isn't tenable, George can have little faith in the prediction. The regression approach also presupposes that the data points have been fitted by the correct regression equation—in this example, the equation for a straight line. Fortunately, one can easily check the tenability of this assumption by looking at the scatterplot.

6.2 CRITERION FOR THE LINE OF BEST FIT

Predicting *Y* from *X*

Earlier I referred to the best-fitting linear regression line without defining it. What is the best-fitting line for a set of data points? Best fit can be defined in a number of

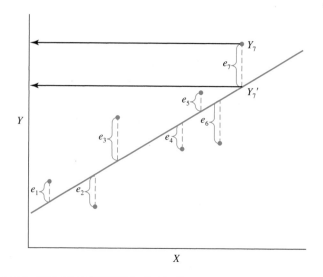

Figure 6.2-1. A prediction error, e_i, is the discrepancy between Y_i, the actual observed score for person i, and Y'_i, the predicted score based on the regression line—for example, $e_7 = Y_7 - Y'_7$

ways. It seems reasonable that the best-fitting line should minimize some function of the error in predicting Y_i from X_i.

A **prediction error** or **residual,** e_i, is defined as the difference between the ith person's actual score, Y_i, and the score predicted for that person, Y'_i—that is, $e_i = Y_i - Y'_i$.

Prediction errors are illustrated in Figure 6.2-1 and are represented as vertical distances along the Y axis. One definition of best fit widely used by mathematicians is based on the **principle of least squares** and is as follows:

The **line of best fit** is the one that minimizes the sum of the squared prediction errors—that is, the line for which $\sum e_i^2 = \sum (Y_i - Y'_i)^2$ is as small as it can be.

I will limit my discussion to linearly related data. For this case, the predicted values fall on a straight line called the **regression line**. The equation for a straight line is

$$Y'_i = a_{Y \cdot X} + b_{Y \cdot X} X_i$$

where

Y'_i is the predicted value,

$a_{Y \cdot X}$ is the point at which the line crosses the Y axis,

$b_{Y \cdot X}$ is the slope of the line, and

X_i is a value of the independent variable.

The subscript $Y \cdot X$ is read "Y given X" and indicates that I am predicting Y from X. According to the least squares criterion, I want values of the constants $a_{Y \cdot X}$ and $b_{Y \cdot X}$ such that

$$\Sigma e_i^2 = \Sigma (Y_i - Y_i')^2 = \Sigma [Y_i - (a_{Y \cdot X} + b_{Y \cdot X} X_i)]^2$$

is as small as it can be.

The values for $a_{Y \cdot X}$ and $b_{Y \cdot X}$ that make Σe_i^2 as small as it can be are given by

$$a_{Y \cdot X} = \overline{Y} - b_{Y \cdot X} \overline{X}$$

and

$$b_{Y \cdot X} = \frac{S_{XY}}{S_X^2} = \frac{\dfrac{\Sigma (X_i - \overline{X})(Y_i - \overline{Y})}{n}}{\dfrac{\Sigma (X_i - \overline{X})^2}{n}} = \frac{\Sigma (X_i - \overline{X})(Y_i - \overline{Y})}{\Sigma (X_i - \overline{X})^2}$$

In the formula for $b_{Y \cdot X}$, S_{XY} is the covariance of X and Y that was discussed in Section 5.3, and S_X^2 is the variance of X that was discussed in Section 5.4. An example showing the computation of $a_{Y \cdot X}$ and $b_{Y \cdot X}$ is given in Table 6.2-1 for the data in Figure 6.1-1. The values of the constants from part ii of the table are $a_{Y \cdot X} = 12.1868$ and $b_{Y \cdot X} = 0.8026$. Hence, the linear equation that minimizes the sum of the squared prediction errors is

$$Y_i' = a_{Y \cdot X} + b_{Y \cdot X} X_i$$
$$= 12.1868 + 0.8026 \, X_i$$

According to the equation, the line crosses the Y axis at 12.1868 (see Figure 6.2-2). In other words, when $X_i = 0$, the predicted value is $Y_i' = 12.1868$. The slope of the line is 0.8026, which means that as X increases 1 unit, Y increases 0.8026 unit (see Figure 6.2-2). Furthermore, the regression line goes through the point corresponding to the mean of X and the mean of Y, which is (82, 78); see the circle in Figure 6.2-3. If the regression line does not go through this point, the line is incorrect.

To determine the predicted Y value for, say, $X_i = 82$, I enter the X_i value in the regression equation and solve for Y_i' as follows:

$$Y_i' = a_{Y \cdot X} + b_{Y \cdot X} X_i$$
$$Y_i' = 12.1868 + 0.8026(82) = 78$$

The predicted value is 78. Alternatively, I can determine predicted values by graphic means, as George did in Figure 6.1-1. The first step is to draw the line of best fit. Because a straight line is defined by two points, I begin by solving for Y_i' when X_i is equal to 72 and when it is equal to 94 (the smallest and largest X scores, respectively). The corresponding Y_i' values are, respectively, 69.97 and 87.63. Once I draw a line connecting the (X_i, Y_i) points (72, 69.97 and 94, 87.63), I can use it to obtain

TABLE 6.2-1 Computation of Least Squares Values of Constants in a Linear Equation (Data from Figure 6.1-1)

(i) Data

X_i	Y_i	$(X_i - \overline{X})$	$(Y_i - \overline{Y})$	$(X_i - \overline{X})(Y_i - \overline{Y})$	$(X_i - \overline{X})^2$	$(Y_i - \overline{Y})^2$
72	70	−10	−8	80	100	64
75	74	−7	−4	28	49	16
76	70	−6	−8	48	36	64
78	72	−4	−6	24	16	36
78	78	−4	0	0	16	0
82	74	0	−4	0	0	16
82	84	0	6	0	0	36
84	76	2	−2	−4	4	4
86	86	4	8	32	16	64
88	78	6	0	0	36	0
89	88	7	10	70	49	100
94	86	12	8	96	144	64

$\Sigma X_i = 984$ $\Sigma Y_i = 936$ $\qquad \Sigma(X_i - \overline{X})(Y_i - \overline{Y}) = 374$ $\Sigma(X_i - \overline{X})^2 = 466$ $\Sigma(Y_i - \overline{Y})^2 = 464$

$\overline{X} = 984/12 = 82$ $\qquad \overline{Y} = 936/12 = 78$

(ii) Computation of $a_{Y \cdot X}$ and $b_{Y \cdot X}$

$$b_{Y \cdot X} = \frac{\Sigma(X_i - \overline{X})(Y_i - \overline{Y})}{\Sigma(X_i - \overline{X})^2} = \frac{374}{466} = 0.8026$$

$$a_{Y \cdot X} = \overline{Y} - b_{Y \cdot X}\overline{X} = 78 - 0.8026(82) = 12.1868$$

(iii) Computation of $a_{X \cdot Y}$ and $b_{X \cdot Y}$

$$b_{X \cdot Y} = \frac{\Sigma(X_i - \overline{X})(Y_i - \overline{Y})}{\Sigma(Y_i - \overline{Y})^2} = \frac{374}{464} = 0.8060$$

$$a_{X \cdot Y} = \overline{X} - b_{X \cdot Y}\overline{Y} = 82 - 0.8060(78) = 19.1320$$

Y_i' for other values of X_i. The two sets of points (72, 69.97 and 94, 87.63) are represented by squares in Figure 6.2-3.

A word of caution is in order here. I should restrict my prediction of Y to the range of X values for which I have paired data points. In this example, the smallest and largest X scores are, respectively, 72 and 94. Within this range of X scores, I know that the relationship between X and Y is linear. However, I have no

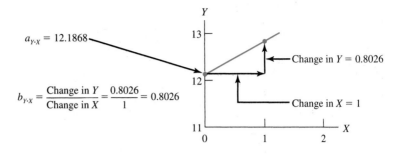

Figure 6.2-2. Illustration of $a_{Y \cdot X}$, the point at which the regression line crosses the Y axis, and $b_{Y \cdot X}$, the slope of the regression line. The slope of the regression line is the ratio of the change in Y divided by the change in X.

way of knowing from the data in Figure 6.2-3 whether or not the linear regression equation is appropriate for X scores outside the interval from 72 to 94. In the absence of such information, it is prudent to restrict the predictions to X scores between 72 and 94.

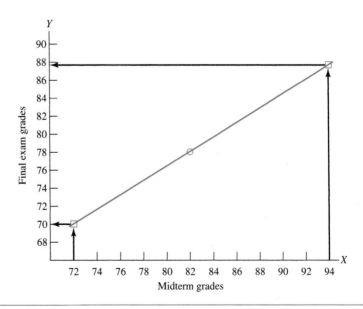

Figure 6.2-3. To obtain the line of best fit for predicting Y from X, the smallest and largest X values (72 and 94) were inserted in the equation $Y'_i = 12.1868 + 0.8026X_i$ to obtain the predicted values 70.0 and 87.6 (see the squares). A line drawn through these two points also passes through the mean of X and Y, which is represented by the circle.

Predicting X from Y

Prediction can go both ways. I have just shown how to predict the value of Y_i from X_i. Alternatively, I can predict the value of X_i from Y_i using the following equation:

$$X'_i = a_{X \cdot Y} + b_{X \cdot Y} Y_i$$

The subscript $X \cdot Y$ indicates that X is predicted from Y. As you will see, $a_{X \cdot Y}$ is different from $a_{Y \cdot X}$, and $b_{X \cdot Y}$ is different from $b_{Y \cdot X}$, because they apply to different regression lines. The constants of the linear equation for predicting X from Y are given by

$$a_{X \cdot Y} = \overline{X} - b_{X \cdot Y} \overline{Y}$$

and

$$b_{X \cdot Y} = \frac{S_{XY}}{S_Y^2} = \frac{\dfrac{\Sigma(X_i - \overline{X})(Y_i - \overline{Y})}{n}}{\dfrac{\Sigma(Y_i - \overline{Y})^2}{n}} = \frac{\Sigma(X_i - \overline{X})(Y_i - \overline{Y})}{\Sigma(Y_i - \overline{Y})^2}$$

The formulas for $a_{X \cdot Y}$ and $b_{X \cdot Y}$ were derived so as to minimize the sum of the squared prediction errors defined by $\Sigma e_i^2 = \Sigma(X_i - X'_i)^2$. These prediction errors are illustrated in Figure 6.2-4 and are represented as *horizontal distances* along the X axis. The computation of $a_{X \cdot Y}$ and $b_{X \cdot Y}$ is illustrated in Table 6.2-1. The regression equation is

$$X'_i = a_{X \cdot Y} + b_{X \cdot Y} Y_i$$

$$= 19.1320 + 0.8060 \, Y_i$$

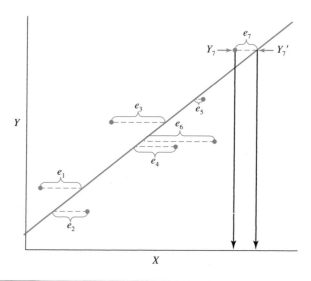

Figure 6.2-4. The error in predicting X_i from Y_i is the discrepancy between X_i, the actual observed value for person i, and X'_1, the predicted value based on the regression line—for example, $e_7 = X_7 - X'_7$.

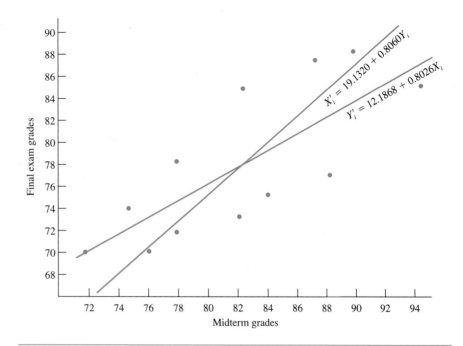

Figure 6.2-5. Regression line for predicting Y_i from X_i and X_i from Y_i (data from Table 6.2-1). Each regression line goes through the point defined by the X and Y means. In this example, that point is $\overline{X} = 82$ and $\overline{Y} = 78$. The equation for predicting Y_i' crosses the Y axis at $Y_i = 12.1868$. The equation for predicting X_i' crosses the X axis at $X_i = 19.1320$. These points are not shown in the figure because the X and Y axes have been shortened to save space.

According to the equation, the line crosses the X axis at 19.1320. In other words, when $Y_i = 0$, the predicted value is $X' = 19.1320$. The slope of the line is 0.8060, which means that as Y increases 1 unit, X increases 0.8060 unit.

To summarize, for any set of paired data points, I can compute two regression lines—the regression of Y on X, given by $Y_i' = a_{Y \cdot X} + b_{Y \cdot X} X_i$, and the regression of X on Y, given by $X_i' = a_{X \cdot Y} + b_{X \cdot Y} Y_i$. The two lines are shown in Figure 6.2-5 for the data in Table 6.2-1. There are two lines because in predicting Y from X I want to minimize one set of errors, $\sum (Y_i - Y_i')^2$, but in predicting X from Y I minimize a different set of errors, $\sum (X_i - X_i')^2$.

Relationship between *r* and the Slopes of the Regression Lines

There are a number of interesting relationships between *r* and the two regression coefficients $b_{X \cdot Y}$ and $b_{X \cdot Y}$. For example, it is a simple matter to show that

$$r \, (S_Y/S_X) = b_{Y \cdot X}$$

$$r \, (S_X/S_Y) = b_{X \cdot Y}$$

$$\pm \sqrt{b_{Y \cdot X} \, b_{X \cdot Y}} = r$$

For the latter relationship, r is positive when $b_{Y \cdot X}$ and $b_{X \cdot Y}$ are positive and negative when both coefficients are negative; $b_{Y \cdot X}$ and $b_{X \cdot Y}$ always have the same sign.

Because $b_{Y \cdot X} = r(S_Y/S_X)$, the linear equation for predicting Y_i from X_i can be rewritten using $r(S_Y/S_X)$ in place of $b_{Y \cdot X}$ as follows:

$$Y_i' = \overbrace{\overline{Y} - r\frac{S_Y}{S_X}\overline{X}}^{a_{Y \cdot X}} + \overbrace{r\frac{S_Y}{S_X}X_i}^{b_{Y \cdot X}X_i}$$

$$= \overline{Y} + r\frac{S_Y}{S_X}(X_i - \overline{X})$$

In this form you can see what happens when $r = 0$; you obtain

$$Y_i' = \overline{Y} + 0\frac{S_Y}{S_X}(X_i - \overline{X})$$

$$= \overline{Y}$$

This means that when r is equal to zero, the predicted value of Y is the mean of the Y scores regardless of the X value used to predict Y. In other words, knowing X_i does not help in predicting Y_i if r is equal to zero, because in every case the predicted Y value is $\overline{Y}$.

CHECK YOUR UNDERSTANDING OF SECTIONS 6.1 AND 6.2

1. In one sentence, state the primary purpose of a regression analysis.
2. If Y increases 2 units for every 4-unit increase in X, what is the slope of the regression line of Y on X?
3. In an experiment on gender-typed behavior, a random sample of boys ages 5 to 8 was given choices among such toys as a football, a doll carriage, a dump truck, and dishes. The number of gender-appropriate choices for boys at each age is listed in the table.

Age, X	Number of Appropriate Choices, Y	Age, X	Number of Appropriate Choices, Y
7.5	18	7.5	15
7.0	13	5.0	7
5.5	11	5.5	8
8.0	20	6.0	12
6.5	13	8.0	17
6.0	14	7.0	14
5.0	9	6.5	12
8.0	18	5.5	10
6.5	14	5.0	8
6.0	10	7.0	16
7.5	19		

    a. Construct a scatterplot and decide whether the data appear to be linearly related.

    b. Compute the values of $a_{Y \cdot X}$ and $b_{Y \cdot X}$ for the line of best fit, write the equation for predicting Y from X, and draw the line in the scatterplot. Compute r using the relationship $r = b_{Y \cdot X} (S_X/S_Y)$.

    c. Compute the values of $a_{X \cdot Y}$ and $b_{X \cdot Y}$ for the line of best fit, write the equation for predicting X from Y, and draw the line of best fit in the scatterplot. Which slope, $b_{Y \cdot X}$ or $b_{X \cdot Y}$, is the steepest? Compute r using the relationship $r = b_{X \cdot Y} (S_Y/S_X)$.

    d. Compute r using the relationship $r = \pm \sqrt{b_{Y \cdot X} b_{X \cdot Y}}$. Does your answer agree with the values you computed in parts b and c?

    e. For a six-year-old boy, estimate Y using both the regression equation and the line of best fit in the scatterplot.

4. In what sense is the regression line for predicting Y from X in Exercise 3 a best-fitting line?

5. For any set of data, there are two regression lines. Under what condition are the two lines identical?

6. If r is equal to zero, what value of Y should you predict for each value of X?

7. If $Y'_i = Y_i$ for all i, what do you know about r?

8. Terms to remember:

    a. Regression analysis   b. Prediction error (residual)

    c. Principle of least squares   d. Line of best fit

    e. Regression line   f. Slope of line

6.3 ANOTHER MEASURE OF ABILITY TO PREDICT: THE STANDARD ERROR OF ESTIMATE

Your ability to predict Y from X is a function of the degree of correlation between the two variables. The higher the correlation, the more closely the data points cluster around the regression line and the smaller the prediction error. A measure of the size of the prediction error is given by the **standard error of estimate,** which is denoted by $S_{Y \cdot X}$. Do not confuse $S_{Y \cdot X}$ with covariance, which is denoted by S_{XY}. The standard error of estimate is a kind of standard deviation. For comparison purposes, the formulas for the standard error of estimate and standard deviation are given here:

$$S_{Y \cdot X} = \sqrt{\frac{\Sigma (Y_i - Y'_i)^2}{n}} \quad \text{and} \quad S_Y = \sqrt{\frac{\Sigma (Y_i - \overline{Y})^2}{n}}$$

In computing $S_{Y \cdot X}$, the deviation $(Y_i - Y'_i)$ is from the predicted value or regression line, whereas for S_Y the deviation $(Y_i - \overline{Y})$ is from the mean of Y. The two deviations are illustrated in Figure 6.3-1.

    Let's look at $S_{Y \cdot X}$ more closely. The regression line denoted by Y' can be thought of as a kind of mean—a "running mean," which gives the predicted value of Y for a particular value of X. Whereas $\overline{Y}$ is the mean of all the Y's, Y' is the mean of Y for a particular value of X. Viewed in this light, $S_{Y \cdot X}$, like S_Y, is computed from the sum

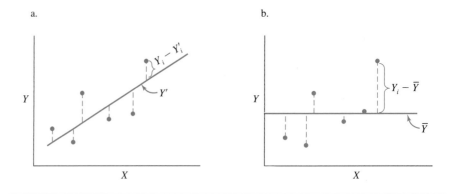

Figure 6.3-1. Comparison of the deviation $Y_i - Y'_i$ used to compute the standard error of estimate (part a) and the deviation $Y_i - \overline{Y}$ used to compute the standard deviation (part b).

of squared deviations from means and hence is a standard deviation. However, $S_{Y \cdot X}$ is the standard deviation of scores around the regression line, whereas S_Y is the standard deviation of scores around the mean. As you will see, $S_{Y \cdot X}$ can be interpreted in much the same way as a regular standard deviation.

An Alternative Formula for $S_{Y \cdot X}$

The formula for the standard error of estimate described above is not a convenient one to use. An equivalent formula[1] for the sample standard error of estimate that is much easier to use is

$$S_{Y \cdot X} = S_Y \sqrt{1 - r^2}$$

This formula has the added advantage of enabling you to easily determine the maximum and minimum possible values of $S_{Y \cdot X}$. The maximum value of $S_{Y \cdot X}$ occurs when r is equal to 0, in which case $S_{Y \cdot X}$ is equal to S_Y. I can show this as follows:

$$S_{Y \cdot X} = S_Y \sqrt{1 - (0)^2} = S_Y \sqrt{1} = S_Y$$

Thus, if r is equal to 0, the dispersion of Y scores around the regression line is as large as the standard deviation of Y. In this case, knowing the X score does not reduce your error in predicting Y. The minimum value of $S_{Y \cdot X}$ occurs when r is equal to 1, in which case $S_{Y \cdot X}$ is equal to 0. I can show this as follows:

$$S_{Y \cdot X} = S_Y \sqrt{1 - (1)^2} = S_Y \sqrt{0} = 0$$

Thus, if r is equal to 1, there is no dispersion around the regression line and no error in predicting Y from X.

[1] When the population standard error of estimate is estimated from sample data, a better estimator is

$$\hat{\sigma}_{Y \cdot X} = \sqrt{\frac{\Sigma (Y_i - Y'_i)^2}{n - 2}} = S_Y \sqrt{\frac{n}{n - 2}(1 - r^2)}$$

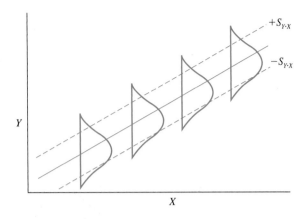

Figure 6.3-2. Illustration of the standard error of estimate. Approximately 68.3% of the Y scores fall within the interval given by $Y'_i \pm S_{X \cdot Y}$ if the distribution of Y scores at every X score is approximately normally distributed and all the Y-score distributions have the same dispersion.

To summarize, the maximum value of $S_{Y \cdot X}$ is S_Y and occurs when r is equal to 0; the minimum value of $S_{Y \cdot X}$ is 0 and occurs when r is equal to 1. Thus, the standard error of estimate can assume a value between 0 and S_Y.

Descriptive Application of $S_{Y \cdot X}$

As you have seen, the larger $S_{Y \cdot X}$, the greater the dispersion of Y scores around the regression line and hence the larger the average prediction error. If the distribution of Y scores at every X score is approximately normal and if all the Y-score distributions have the same dispersion, 68.3% of the Y scores will fall within the interval given by $Y' \pm S_{Y \cdot X}$. This information is illustrated in Figure 6.3-2. Similarly, 95.4% of the Y scores will fall within the interval given by $Y' \pm 2\ S_{Y \cdot X}$, and 99.7% will fall within the interval given by $Y' \pm 3\ S_{Y \cdot X}$. These percentages are based on the normal distribution; see Figure 4.4-1 in Chapter 4.

Although the standard error of estimate is most often used in inferential statistics, I will briefly mention a descriptive application. Suppose an experiment was conducted to determine the relationship between Y, the length of time (measured in hundredths of a second) necessary to reach a decision, and X, the number of alternative choices presented. The following data were obtained: $S_X = 1.5$, $S_y = 12.5$, $\overline{X} = 4.5$, $\overline{Y} = 46$, $r = .78$, and $n = 100$. Assume that the distribution of Y scores for every X score is approximately normal and that all the Y-score distributions have the same dispersion. The predicted reaction time for a person presented with a choice from among, say, three alternatives is given by the regression equation

$$Y' = \overline{Y} + r \frac{S_Y}{S_X}(X_i - \overline{X})$$

$$Y' = 46 + .78\frac{12.5}{1.5}(3 - 4.5)$$

$$= 46 + 6.5(- 1.5)$$

$$= 36.25$$

The use here of the regression equation $Y' = \overline{Y} + r(S_Y/S_X)(X_i - \overline{X})$ is convenient because of the statistics that are available. I would have arrived at the same predicted reaction time if I had used the equivalent equation $Y' = a + bX_i$. The standard error of estimate is

$$S_{Y \cdot X} = S_Y\sqrt{1 - r^2}$$

$$= 12.5\sqrt{1 - (.78)^2}$$

$$= 12.5(.6258)$$

$$= 7.82$$

I can conclude that approximately 68.3% of the participants in the three-choice condition had reaction times between 44.07 and 28.43, as I see from

$$Y' \pm S_{Y \cdot X} = 36.25 \pm 7.82 = 44.07 \text{ and } 28.43$$

Similarly, approximately 95.4% had reaction times between

$$Y' \pm 2S_{Y \cdot X} = 36.25 \pm 2(7.82) = 51.89 \text{ and } 20.61$$

The percentages 68.3 and 95.4 are based on the proportion of the normal distribution that lies in the interval from $\overline{X} - S$ to $\overline{X} + S$ and from $\overline{X} - 2S$ to $\overline{X} + 2S$, respectively, as shown in Figure 4.4-1.

6.4 ASSUMPTIONS ASSOCIATED WITH REGRESSION AND THE STANDARD ERROR OF ESTIMATE

When you make predictions using the regression equation $Y'_i = a + bX_i$, you assume only that the relationship between X and Y is linear. If the assumption is tenable, the principle of least squares ensures that $Y'_i = a + bX_i$ provides the best possible prediction line for the data. For prediction purposes, you do not have to make any assumptions regarding the shape of the X and Y distributions.

The use of the standard error of estimate involves more stringent assumptions. In addition to the linearity assumption, you must also assume that (1) for any value of X, the associated Y scores are approximately normally distributed and (2) the dispersions of the Y scores for different values of X are equal. The latter assumption is referred to as the *homoscedasticity* assumption. The converse situation, heteroscedasticity, in which the dispersions of the Y scores for different values of X are unequal, was discussed in Section 5.6.

In predicting X from Y the same assumptions are required, but they must be rephrased to reflect the reversed roles of X and Y.

CHECK YOUR UNDERSTANDING OF SECTIONS 6.3 AND 6.4

9. Chimpanzees were exposed to white noise eight hours a day for three months to determine whether the noise affected their hearing. Ten animals were randomly assigned to the following noise levels: 75 dBA, 85 dBA, 95 dBA, 105 dBA, and 115 dBA.

Animal	Noise Level (dBA), X	Hearing Loss (dBA at 1000 Hz), Y	Animal	Noise Level (dBA), X	Hearing Loss (dBA at 1000 Hz), Y
1	105	11	6	85	9
2	85	6	7	105	13
3	95	10	8	115	11
4	115	15	9	75	5
5	75	7	10	95	8

a. Compute $S_{Y \cdot X}$ using the formula $S_{Y \cdot X} = S_Y \sqrt{1 - r^2}$.

b. Assuming a large sample in which the distribution of Y scores for every X score is approximately normal and all the distributions have the same dispersion, compute the interval that will contain 68.3% of the scores for a noise level of 115 dBA.

c. Compute the value of $S_{Y \cdot X}$ for $r = 0$ and $r = 1$. Is the $S_{Y \cdot X}$ for these data relatively large, relatively small, or somewhere in between?

10. How is $S_{Y \cdot X}$ related to the magnitude of the prediction error? For the gender-typed data in Exercise 3 in "Check Your Understanding of Sections 6.1 and 6.2," what are the minimum and maximum values of $S_{Y \cdot X}$?

11. Term to remember:
a. Standard error of estimate

6.5 MULTIPLE REGRESSION AND MULTIPLE CORRELATION

Multiple Regression

At the beginning of the chapter I talked about Jean, who wanted to predict her grade-point average in law school based on her LSAT score. There are other variables that Jean might use to predict her GPA, such as her undergraduate GPA and her level of motivation for having a law career. It turns out that Jean could improve her prediction by using not just one, but several predictor variables.

> The simultaneous use of two or more independent variables in predicting a dependent variable is called **multiple regression.**

In Section 6.2 you learned that when there is one independent variable or predictor, the regression equation for predicting Y from X is

$$Y_i' = a + bX_i$$

When there are two independent variables,

$$Y_i' = a + b_1 X_{i1} + b_2 X_{i2}$$

where

Y_i' is the predicted value,

a is the Y intercept,

b_1 is the expected change in Y when X_1 changes one unit and X_2 remains constant,

X_1 is the value of the first independent variable,

b_2 is the expected change in Y when X_2 changes one unit and X_1 remains constant, and

X_2 is the value of the second independent variable.

The equation for two independent variables can be extended to any number of independent variables, say, k, as follows:

$$Y_i' = a + b_1 X_{i1} + b_2 X_{i2} + b_3 X_{i3} + \cdots + b_k X_{ik}$$

The simplest possible regression equation has one independent variable. For this equation, the line of best fit for predicting Y is a straight line such that the sum of the squared prediction errors, $\Sigma e_i^2 = \Sigma (Y_i - Y')^2$, is as small as it possibly can be. For the one-independent variable case, the relationship between X and Y can be represented by a two-dimensional scatterplot, where Y is plotted on the vertical axis and X on the horizontal axis. When there are two independent variables, the scatterplot requires three dimensions: one for Y, one for X_1, and one for X_2. For this case, the predicted values of Y fall on a **regression plane** or surface rather than a regression line. Furthermore, the orientation or slope of the plane is determined so that the sum of the squared prediction errors from the plane is as small as it possibly can be.

Perhaps an example will help to clarify the slope of a plane and prediction errors around this plane. Consider the data in Table 6.5-1(i), where there are two independent variables. As the data in the table shows, an observed score, Y_i, is equal to its predicted score, Y_i', plus its prediction error or residual, e_i,—that is,

$$Y_i = Y_i' + e_i$$

For example, the observed score for participant 1 is

$$Y_1 = Y_1' + e_1$$

$$3 = 3.90 + (-90)$$

The multiple regression equation is shown in part (ii) of the table. Formulas for computing a, b_1, and b_2 are complex and will not be given here because the values are usually computed with a computer.[2] The data in columns 2, 3, and 4 are plotted in the three-dimensional scatterplot in Figure 6.5-1(a). The predicted values of Y are

---

[2] The values in Table 6.5-1 were computed using the SPSS software package.

TABLE 6.5-1   Data for Multiple Regression with Two Independent Variables

(i) Data

Participant	(1) Observed score, Y	(2) Predictor No. One, X_1	(3) Predictor No. Two, X_2	(4) Predicted Score, Y'_i	(5) Prediction error, e_i
1	3	4	3	3.90	−0.90
2	1	2	6	1.02	−0.02
3	2	1	4	1.70	0.30
4	4	6	5	3.75	0.25
5	6	5	1	5.63	0.37

(ii) Multiple regression equation

$$Y'_i = a + b_1 X_{i1} + b_2 X_{i2}$$
$$Y'_i = 3.58 + 0.53 X_{i1} + (-0.60) X_{i2}$$
where $a = 3.58$
$$b_1 = 0.53$$
$$b_2 = -0.60$$

shown as five solid circles on a sloped plane. In part (b) of the figure, prediction errors (see column 5 of Table 6.5-1) are shown as deviations above or below the sloped plane. The prediction errors appear to deviate little from the plane; consequently, Y can be predicted from X_1 and X_2 with considerable accuracy. A measure

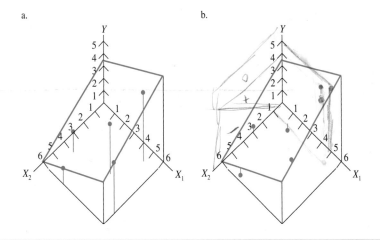

Figure 6.5-1. (a) The five predicted Y scores in the figure on the left fall on the surface of a plane. The coefficient for X_1 is positive ($b_1 = 0.53$), hence the surface of the plane slopes up relative to the X_1 axis; the coefficient for X_2 is negative ($b_2 = -0.60$), hence the plane slopes down relative to the X_2 axis. (b) Prediction errors in the figure on the right are plotted as deviations from the plane. Recall that prediction errors are deviations of the observed scores from the predicted scores.

of just how well Y can be predicted from a knowledge of X_1 and X_2 is given by the coefficient of multiple determination, which is discussed in the next section.

Multiple Correlation

The correlation between Y and the combined predictors $X_1, X_2, \ldots, X_k$ is called the **coefficient of multiple correlation** and is denoted by $R_{Y \cdot X_1 X_2}, \ldots, X_k$, or simply R.

The dot after Y in the notation separates the dependent variable, Y, from the independent variables, $X_1, X_2, \ldots, X_k$. For the two predictor case, $R_{Y \cdot X_1 X_2}$ is given by

$$R_{Y \cdot X_1 X_2} = \sqrt{\frac{r_{YX_1}^2 + r_{YX_2}^2 - 2r_{YX_1} r_{YX_2} r_{X_1 X_2}}{1 - r_{X_1 X_2}^2}}$$

where r_{YX_1}, r_{YX_2}, and $r_{X_1 X_2}$ are correlation coefficients for the respective variables. The multiple regression coefficient can assume values from 0 to 1, where 0 indicates the absence of a linear multiple correlation between Y and the independent variables and 1 indicates a perfect linear multiple correlation in which all of the observed Y's fall on the regression plane.

The proportion of variance in Y accounted for by the combined predictors X_1, $X_2, \ldots, X_k$ is obtained by squaring the multiple correlation coefficient and is called the **coefficient of multiple determination, R^2.** This coefficient is an extension of the coefficient of determination for one predictor, r^2, which was discussed in Section 5.4.

A comparison of the value of R^2 with that for r^2 indicates the improvement in predicting Y that can be achieved by using a multiple regression equation instead of a one-predictor regression equation. For the data in Table 6.5-1, the correlation between Y and X_1, Y and X_2, and X_1 and X_2 is given in Table 6.5-2. This form of presenting correlation coefficients is called a *correlation matrix*. According to Table 6.5-2, predictor variable X_2 has the highest correlation with Y ($r_{YX_2} = -.797$). This variable accounts for $r_{YX_2}^2 = (-.797)^2 = .64$ of the variance in Y. The multiple correlation coefficient that reflects the contributions of both X_1 and X_2 is

$$R_{Y \cdot X_1 X_2} = \sqrt{\frac{(.777)^2 + (-.797)^2 - 2[(.777)(-.797)(-.338)]}{1 - (-.338)^2}} = .962$$

TABLE 6.5-2   Intercorrelations among the Variables

		Variable	
Variable	Y	X_1	X_2
Y	1.000	.777	-.797
X_1		1.000	-.338
X_2			1.000

The coefficient of multiple determination is $R^2_{Y \cdot X_1 X_2} = (.962)^2 = .93$. Thus, the inclusion of a second predictor, X_1, in the regression equation enables me to account for an additional $R^2_{Y \cdot X_1 X_2} - r^2_{YX_2} = .93 - .64 = .29$ of the variance in Y over and above the variance accounted for by the best predictor, X_2. The proportion of variance in Y that is unaccounted for by X_1 and X_2 is given by $1 - R^2_{Y \cdot X_1 X_2} = 1 - .93 = .07$.

The coefficient of multiple determination will be relatively large when the correlation of each of the predictors with Y is large and the correlations among the predictors are 0 or very small. In fact, if the independent variables are uncorrelated, $R^2_{Y \cdot X_1 X_2, \ldots, X_k} = r^2_{YX_1} + r^2_{YX_2} + \cdots + r^2_{YX_k}$. If correlations exist among some or all of the independent variables, it is usually the case that $R^2_{Y \cdot X_1 X_2, \ldots, X_k} < r^2_{YX_1} + r^2_{YX_2} + \cdots + r^2_{YX_k}$. The presence of nonzero correlations among the independent variables is referred to as **multicollinearity.** Extreme multicollinearity occurs when one independent variable is a linear function of other independent variables; for example, X_2 might equal $3X_1$, or X_3 might equal $X_1 + X_2$. In the latter case, the inclusion of X_3 in the regression equation would not account for any variance in Y not already accounted for by X_1 and X_2. Ideally, you would like to have predictors that have high correlations with the dependent variable and zero correlations with each other. Unfortunately in the behavioral sciences, health sciences, and education, it is difficult to find predictors that meet these criteria. Once you have found three or four good predictors, it is often difficult to find additional predictors that are not highly correlated with at least one of the original predictors.

CHECK YOUR UNDERSTANDING OF SECTION 6.5

12. a. For each of the following correlation matrices, compute the coefficient of multiple determination.

(i)	Y	X_1	X_2
Y	1.00	.20	.30
X_1		1.00	.60
X_2			1.00

(ii)	Y	X_1	X_2
	1.00	.60	.50
		1.00	.30
			1.00

(iii)	Y	X_1	X_2
	1.00	.60	-.50
		1.00	-.10
			1.00

  b. For these correlation matrices, determine the improvement in prediction that can be achieved by using a multiple regression equation instead of a one-predictor regression equation.

13. Data were obtained for 46 college students who were enrolled in an intensive French language course. The course enables students to fulfill their foreign language degree requirement (14 semester hours) in one eight-week summer session. The purpose of the research was to develop a regression equation that would assist the professor in selecting and admitting only those students most likely to succeed in the rigorous course. The dependent variable was the student's grade for the intensive course. The following grading scale was used: A = 4.0, B+ = 3.5, B = 3.0, C+ = 2.5, C = 2.0, D = 1.0, and F = 0. The three most useful independent variables were found to be grade-point average, X_1; professor's rating, based on an interview with the student, of his or her

probable success in the course, X_2; and whether the student had previously taken a French course, X_3. The correlation matrix for these variables is as follows:

	Y	X_1	X_2	X_3
Y	1.00	.773	.681	.289
X_1		1.00	.544	.065
X_2			1.00	.083
X_3				1.00

The coefficient of multiple determination for these data is $R^2_{Y \cdot X_1 X_2 X_3} = (.862)^2 = .743$. The regression equation for predicting a student's course grade is

$$Y'_i = 1.069 + 0.742X_{i1} + 0.496X_{i2} + 0.323X_{i3}.$$

(Suggested by Currall, S. C., and Kirk, R. E. [1986]. Predicting success in intensive foreign language courses. *Modern Language Journal, 70,* 107–113.)

a. Three two-predictor coefficients of multiple correlation can be computed for these data: $R_{Y \cdot X_1 X_2}$, $R_{Y \cdot X_1 X_3}$, and $R_{Y \cdot X_2 X_3}$. How much does the addition of a third predictor improve the prediction of Y relative to the use of the best two-predictor multiple regression equation?

b. Data for participants 3, 16, 21, and 34 are as shown in the following table. Determine the predicted letter grade for these participants. Use the following scale; $\geq 3.75 =$ A, 3.25–3.74 = B+, 2.75–3.24 = B, 2.25–2.74 = C+, 1.75–2.24 = C, 0.75–1.74 = D, and $< 0.75 =$ F).

Participants	X_1	X_2	X_3
3	3.6	0	0
16	2.8	1	1
21	3.1	1	0
34	2.3	1	0

14. Terms to remember:
   a. Multiple regression
   b. Coefficient of multiple correlation
   c. Coefficient of multiple determination
   d. Regression plane
   e. Correlation matrix
   f. Multicollinearity

6.6 LOOKING BACK: WHAT HAVE YOU LEARNED?

This chapter is about making predictions using one or more predictors. You learned in Chapter 5 that Sir Francis Galton laid the foundation for regression and correlation in his classic studies on regression. He used the term *regression* to refer to the tendency for short parents to have offspring who are slightly taller than they and for tall parents to have offspring who are slightly shorter than they. Today the term has a broader meaning. It refers to any analysis of paired data $(X_1, Y_1), (X_2, Y_2), \ldots, (X_n, Y_n)$, where X is the independent variable and Y is the dependent variable.

In simple linear regression analysis, the line of best fit, called the regression line, is used to predict Y from a knowledge of X. The line of best fit according to the least squares principle is the one for which the sum of the squared prediction errors, the discrepancy between the observed value of Y_i and the predicted value, is as small as it can be.

If r is equal to 1 or -1, the value of Y_i can be predicted perfectly from the equation $Y'_i = a + bX_i$. If the value of r is between -1 and 1, there is likely to be some discrepancy between the observed value of Y_i and the predicted value of Y'_i. The discrepancy $Y_i - Y'_i$ is called a prediction error or residual. A measure of the magnitude of the prediction error is given by the standard error of estimate, $S_{Y \cdot X}$, which is a kind of standard deviation of errors around the regression line. The maximum value of $S_{Y \cdot X}$ is equal to the standard deviation of Y, S_Y, and it occurs when r is equal to 0. The minimum value of $S_{Y \cdot X}$ is 0, and it occurs when r is equal to 1.

In predicting Y from X, you assume only that the relationship between the variables is linear. Interpretations involving $S_{Y \cdot X}$ also assume that the distribution of the Y scores at every X score is approximately normal and that all the Y-score distributions have the same dispersion. When prediction involves different samples, as when the performance of one group of students is predicted from that of another, you also must assume that the populations represented by the two samples are identical with respect to the relevant characteristics. Of course, you should restrict your prediction of Y to the range of X values for which you have paired data points unless you are certain that the regression equation is appropriate for the additional X values.

The concepts in simple linear regression can be extended to data where there are two or more independent variables. The simultaneous use of two or more independent variables in predicting a dependent variable is called multiple regression. There is an important advantage in using multiple predictors instead of a single predictor—more accurate prediction. Prediction is most accurate when the predictors have high correlations with the dependent variable and zero correlations with each other. Unfortunately, good predictors are often highly correlated, a condition called multicollinearity. Because of multicollinearity, there is a point of diminishing returns after which adding new predictors to a multiple regression equation contributes little to the accuracy of prediction.

REVIEW EXERCISES FOR CHAPTER 6

1. If Y decreases five units for every two-unit increase in X, what is the slope of the regression line of Y on X?

2. In an experiment on gender-typed behavior, a random sample of girls ages 5 to 8 was given choices among such toys as a football, a doll carriage, a dump truck, and dishes. The number of gender-appropriate choices for girls at each age is listed in the table.

Age, X	Number of Appropriate Choices, Y	Age, X	Number of Appropriate Choices, Y
7.5	10	8.0	14
6.0	11	7.0	11
5.5	10	7.5	13
8.0	15	6.5	9
7.5	14	6.5	11
5.0	6	6.0	10
6.0	8	5.5	8

(table continued on the following page)

Age, X	Number of Appropriate Choices, Y	Age, X	Number of Appropriate Choices, Y
7.0	12	7.0	10
8.0	12	6.5	13
5.0	7	5.0	9
5.5	9		

  a. Construct a scatterplot and decide whether the data appear to be linearly related.

  b. Compute the values of $a_{Y \cdot X}$ and $b_{Y \cdot X}$ for the line of best fit, write the equation for predicting Y from X, and draw the line in the scatterplot. Compute r using the relationship $r = b_{Y \cdot X}(S_X/S_Y)$.

  c. Compute the values of $a_{X \cdot Y}$ and $b_{X \cdot Y}$ for the line of best fit, write the equation for predicting X from Y, and draw the line of best fit in the scatter plot. Which slope, $b_{Y \cdot X}$ or $b_{X \cdot Y}$, is the steepest? Compute r using the relationship $r = b_{X \cdot Y}(S_Y/S_X)$.

  d. Compute r using the relationship $r = \pm\sqrt{b_{Y \cdot X}b_{X \cdot Y}}$. Does your answer agree with the values you computed in parts b and c?

  e. Estimate Y for a six-year-old girl and X for a girl who made 11 "appropriate" choices using the lines of best fit in the scatter diagram.

3. In what sense are the regression lines in Exercise 2 best-fitting lines?

4. For any set of data, there are two regression lines. Explain.

5. What characteristics of the line of best fit do $a_{Y \cdot X}$ and $b_{Y \cdot X}$ describe?

6. Distinguish between $b_{Y \cdot X}$ and $b_{X \cdot Y}$.

7. In one sentence, describe a residual or prediction error. Under what conditions are all residuals equal to zero?

8. If r is equal to zero, the predicted Y score for all participants is the mean of Y. Draw a scatter diagram that illustrates this point.

9. a. If $Y' = a + bX_i$ for all i and $a = \overline{Y} - b\overline{X}$, prove that $\sum Y'_i = \sum Y_i$. Hint: Replace a with $\overline{Y} - b\overline{X}$ and take the sum of both sides of the equation—that is, $\sum Y'_i = \sum(\overline{Y} - b\overline{X} + bX_i)$.

  b. In words, what does it mean that $\sum Y'_i = \sum Y_i$?

10. Researchers investigated the relationship between birth order and participation in dangerous sports such as hang gliding, auto racing, and boxing. They screened college records to find four men who were first-born, four who were second-born, and so on. They then obtained the data in the following table.

Participant	Birth Order, X	Number of Dangerous Sports, Y	Participant	Birth Order, X	Number of Dangerous Sports, Y
1	4	1	11	1	0
2	3	1	12	2	0
3	2	0	13	3	2
4	4	2	14	5	1
5	1	0	15	3	1
6	5	2	16	2	1
7	1	0	17	5	2
8	4	1	18	1	1
9	2	1	19	3	1
10	5	3	20	4	2

   a. Compute $S_{Y \cdot X}$ using the formula $S_Y \sqrt{1 - r^2}$.

   b. Assuming a large sample in which the distribution of Y scores for every X score is approximately normal and all the distributions have the same dispersion, compute the limits that will contain 68.3% of the scores for fourth-born men.

   c. Compute the value of $S_{Y \cdot X}$ for $r = 0$ and $r = 1$. Is $S_{Y \cdot X}$ relatively large, relatively small, or somewhere in between?

11. In what sense is Y_i' a mean?

12. How is $S_{Y \cdot X}$ related to the magnitude of prediction error? For the gender-typed data in Exercise 2, what are the minimum and maximum values of $S_{Y \cdot X}$?

13. Describe the effect of changes in r on the value of $S_{Y \cdot X}$.

14. Compare the assumptions associated with predictions using r, Y', and $S_{Y \cdot X}$.

15. a. For each of the following correlation matrices, compute the coefficient of multiple determination.

(i)	Y	X_1	X_2	(ii)	Y	X_1	X_2	(iii)	Y	X_1	X_2
Y	1.00	.55	.35		1.00	.80	.70		1.00	.60	−.50
X_1		1.00	.15			1.00	.90			1.00	−.20
X_2			1.00				1.00				1.00

   b. For these correlation matrices, determine the improvement in prediction that can be achieved by using a multiple regression equation instead of a one-predictor regression equation.

16. Researchers hypothesized that there is a relationship among men's marital satisfaction and measures of gender role conflict and family environment. They obtained data for 70 married men who completed self-report instruments measuring marital satisfaction, the dependent variable, and restrictive emotionality (X_1), conflict between work or school and family relations (X_2), and family cohesion (X_3). The following correlation matrix reflects these variables.

	Y	X_1	X_2	X_3
Y	1.00	−.35	−.37	.56
X_1		1.00	.19	−.28
X_2			1.00	−.20
X_3				1.00

The coefficient of multiple determination for these data is $R^2_{Y \cdot X_1 X_2 X_3} = (.684)^2 = .468$. (Exercise suggested by Campbell, J. L., and Snow, B. M. [1992]. Gender role conflict and family environment as predictors of men's marital satisfaction. *Journal of Family Psychology, 6*, 84–87.)

   a. Compute the three two-predictor coefficients of multiple correlation that can be computed for these data: $R_{Y \cdot X_1 X_2}$, $R_{Y \cdot X_1 X_3}$, and $R_{Y \cdot X_2 X_3}$.

   b. How much does the addition of a third predictor improve the prediction of Y relative to the use of the best two-predictor multiple regression equation?

17. Use a statistical software package to obtain a scatterplot, regression equation, and coefficient of determination for the gender-typed data in Exercise 2.

18. Use a statistical software package to obtain a scatterplot, regression equation, and coefficient of determination for the birth-order and dangerous-sports data in Exercise 10.

7

Probability

7.1 Introduction to Probability
Looking Ahead: What Is This Chapter About?
The Subjective-Personalistic View of Probability
The Classical, or Logical, View of Probability
The Empirical Relative-Frequency View of Probability
Check Your Understanding of Section 7.1

7.2 Basic Concepts
Simple and Compound Events
Graphing Simple and Compound Events
Formal Properties of Probability
Check Your Understanding of Section 7.2

7.3 Probability of Combined Events
Addition Rule of Probability
Addition Rule for Mutually Exclusive Events
Multiplication Rule of Probability
Multiplication Rule for Statistically Independent Events
Common Errors in Applying the Rules of Probability
Check Your Understanding of Section 7.3

7.4 Counting Simple Events
Fundamental Counting Rule
Permutation of n Objects Taken n at a Time, $_nP_n$
Permutation of n Objects Taken r at a Time, $_nP_r$
Combination of n Objects Taken r at a Time, $_nC_r$
Check Your Understanding of Section 7.4

7.5 Looking Back: What Have You Learned?
Review Exercises for Chapter 7

7.1 INTRODUCTION TO PROBABILITY

Looking Ahead: What Is This Chapter About?

Everyone has some intuitive notion of what probability is. However, its definition is a topic for continuing debate among mathematicians. This chapter describes three views of probability: (1) the subjective-personalistic view, (2) the classical, or logical, view, and (3) the empirical relative-frequency view. Fortunately, the three views supplement one another.

You will learn how to compute the probability of combined events using the addition and multiplication rules and be introduced to the concept of statistical independence. The chapter ends with a description of several rules for counting the number of outcomes of simple experiments.

This focus on probability is motivated by practical considerations. You will discover that probability theory provides a set of tools for dealing with situations involving uncertainty, and that includes most research in the behavioral sciences, health sciences, and education. Probability theory also provides the foundation for statistical inference, the subject of the second half of this book. This chapter on probability and the two that follow on random variables and sampling distributions introduce ideas that you will use throughout your study of statistical inference.

After reading the chapter, you should know the following:

- How to compute the probability for the outcomes of simple experiments
- When to use the addition and multiplication rules of probability
- The meaning of statistical independence
- When and how to use different counting rules to determine the number of outcomes of simple experiments

The Subjective-Personalistic View of Probability

According to the **subjective-personalistic view,** probability is a measure of the strength of one's expectation that an event will occur.

For example, you might assert, "Chances are I'll pass statistics" or "I think I'll go home this weekend." Such assertions express a degree of belief concerning an event whose outcome is at the moment uncertain. Subjective probabilities affect our lives because they enter into our decision-making process. For most of us, the subjective probability of being struck by a car while crossing the street is low, so we proceed as if the event won't happen. But if our subjective probability of, say, being invited to a New Year's party is high enough, we will make all suitable preparations for the event's occurrence.

Although our behavior is influenced by subjective probability, there are difficulties in incorporating it into a formal decision-making process. Equally knowledgeable individuals often disagree on the probability that should be assigned to an event. We find that some people's subjective probabilities follow closely the rules of probability described later, but other people's do not. Hence, a subjective probability cannot be considered apart from the person holding it. The measurement of subjective probability poses another problem, although behavioral scientists are beginning to find solutions to this problem. Despite the problems, a formal approach to decision making that utilizes subjective probability has been developed. It is popular in economics and business management and is beginning to find acceptance in behavioral research. This approach, called **Bayesian inference,**[1] enables a researcher to make decisions about some true state of affairs using not only sample data but also any prior information that is available, either from previous samples or simply in the form of informed opinions or beliefs. You may encounter this approach again when you take advanced statistics courses.

The Classical, or Logical, View of Probability

Suppose that you want to know the probability of rolling a 2 with a fair die. You reason that because a fair die is symmetrical and dynamically balanced, all six faces are equally likely to appear. Of the six possible events, only one is a 2, and therefore the probability of rolling a 2, denoted by $p(2)$, is $1/6$.

According to the **classical,** or **logical, view,** the probability of an event, say, A, is given by the number of events favoring A, denoted by n_A, divided by the total number of equally likely events, n_S.[2] Thus, $p(A) = n_A/n_S$.

The value of $p(A)$ is always a number between 0 and 1 inclusive, because the number of events favoring A can never exceed the total number of events—that is, $n_A \leq n_S$.

The classical view of probability is based on logical analysis. You reason, for example, that when a fair coin is tossed, there are two possible outcomes—a head or a tail—and that the outcomes are equally likely. It follows that the probability of a head is $p(H) = n_H/n_S = 1/2$. The probabilities $1/2$ for a head and $1/6$ for a 2 in the die example were arrived at by logical analyses of these very simple experiments. In effect, you developed a mathematical model of the experiments based on a postulate and logic. You postulated that certain events are equally likely and deduced the consequences. If your logic is correct, the deductions $p(H) = 1/2$ and $p(2) = 1/6$ are formally correct. However, your deductions may not correspond to the empirical results of actually tossing a coin or rolling a die because for any particular coin or die the postulate that the outcomes are equally likely may be incorrect. For example, the coin may not be fair, or the die may be loaded. However, for fairly simple experiments such as coin tossing and die rolling, where the equally likely postulate is tenable, experience has demonstrated that the classical view generates probability estimates that closely approximate empirical probabilities. Consequently, the classical view of probability is useful for practical problems.

---

[1] Bayesian inference is named for the early 18th-century English clergyman Reverend Thomas Bayes (1702–1761), whose theorem laid the groundwork for the approach.

[2] The letter S, which denotes a sample space, is defined in Section 7.2.

The Empirical Relative-Frequency View of Probability

A third view of probability can be adopted for experiments that can be repeated without changing their characteristics, such as coin tossing and die rolling. Probability according to this view is estimated from experience—by performing an experiment and determining the ratio of the number of events of interest to the total number of events. This leads to my final definition of probability.

According to the **empirical relative-frequency view,** the probability of event A, $p(A)$, is a number approached by the ratio n_A/n as the total number of observations, n, approaches infinity.

For example, in a simple experiment such as tossing a coin, the probability of a head can be estimated by making many tosses of the coin and recording the outcomes. If a head is obtained 12 times in 20 tosses, your best estimate of the probability of heads is $n_A/n = {}^{12}/_{20} = .6$. If a head is obtained 120 times in 200 tosses, your confidence in the estimate ${}^{120}/_{200} = .6$ is even greater. As n gets larger and larger, you assume that the sample estimate n_A/n moves closer and closer to some "true probability" and thus you have greater confidence in larger samples.

Although on any particular coin toss, the outcome is uncertain until you have examined the result, a pattern of outcomes emerges in many repetitions of the toss. Many phenomena like coin tosses are random. However, the probabilities of their outcomes seem to approach fixed values in the long run over many tosses. Probabilities that are based on experience, empirical probabilities, are always approximations because they are based on a finite as opposed to an infinite number of trials.

The empirical view of probability is useful and intuitively simple, but it, too, has certain difficulties. It is meaningful to speak of the probability of rain tomorrow or the probability of getting an A on Tuesday's quiz; however, there is only one tomorrow and only one such quiz. The interpretation of probability as the number approached by n_A/n as the number of tomorrows approaches infinity is unconvincing.

In conclusion, none of the views of probability is completely adequate. Because they are all useful and they are not incompatible, they coexist amicably in the mathematician's bag of conceptual tools. The discussion that follows relies most on the classical and empirical views.

CHECK YOUR UNDERSTANDING OF SECTION 7.1

1. (a) According to the classical view, what is the probability of observing an odd number on the toss of a die? (b) What assumptions were required to arrive at the answer?
2. (a) What is the probability of drawing the queen of spades from a well-shuffled deck of 52 cards? (b) What assumptions were required to arrive at the answer?
3. (a) According to the relative-frequency view, what is the probability that a head will occur on the next toss of a fair coin if a head appeared on 52 of the last 100 tosses? (b) According to the classical view, what is the probability that a head will occur?

4. The English statistician Karl Pearson is reported to have tossed a coin 24,000 times and obtained 12,012 heads. (a) According to the relative-frequency view, what is the probability of a head? (b) What is the probability of a tail?

7.2 BASIC CONCEPTS

For behavioral scientists, health scientists, and educators, probability theory is a means to an end. It is a tool for making inferences about the characteristics of populations by observing samples drawn from the populations. Sample data are obtained by observing events in nature or performing experiments under controlled conditions. I will denote either procedure by the term **experiment.** In particular, I will focus on experiments whose outcomes cannot be predicted with certainty. For example, will desensitization therapy result in more symptom relief than symbolic modeling therapy? Will one cell phone advertisement produce more customers than another?

Simple and Compound Events

One of the simplest experiments you can perform is tossing a die and observing the number that appears on the upper face. Some of the possible outcomes are the following:

Event E_1—observe a 1

Event E_2—observe a 2

Event E_3—observe a 3

Event E_4—observe a 4

Event E_5—observe a 5

Event E_6—observe a 6

Event A—observe an odd number

Event B—observe an even number

Event C—observe a number less than 4

An **event** is an observable happening. Events A, B, and C are called **compound events** because they can be decomposed into simpler events. For example, event A (an odd number) is the occurrence of one of the simple events E_1, E_3, or E_5. Events $E_1, \ldots, E_6$ are called **simple events** because they cannot be decomposed. A list of simple events provides a breakdown of all possible outcomes of the experiment.

Graphing Simple and Compound Events

It is convenient to represent the simple events in an experiment by a graph called an Euler diagram.[3] An Euler diagram representing the simple events for the die-tossing

---

[3] The diagram was developed by Leonhard Euler (1707–1783), a Swiss mathematician.

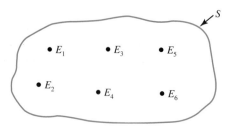

Figure 7.2-1. Euler diagram for the die-tossing experiment. The set of all sample points $E_1, \ldots, E_6$ defines the sample space S of the experiment.

experiment is shown in Figure 7.2-1. In the figure, each simple event is assigned a point called a **sample point.** The symbol E_i identifies the ith simple event.

The set of all sample points is called the **sample space** and is denoted by the letter S.

A compound event is represented in the diagram by encircling the sample points for that event. For example, earlier I defined event A as observing an odd number on the toss of a die and event C as a number less than 4. The two events are represented in Figure 7.2-2 by two subsets of the sample points. The probability of event A according to the classical view is $p(A) = n_A/n_S = 3/6$; the probability of event C is $p(C) = n_C/n_S = 3/6$.

By examining the sample space, you also can determine the probability for combined events. What is the probability that when a die is tossed the outcome will be an odd number, event A, *and* a number less than 4, event C? This probability is denoted by $p(A \text{ and } C)$. You could observe an odd number and a number less than 4 if either E_1 or E_3 occurred—two of the six simple events in Figure 7.2-2. Hence, the probability that the outcome will represent both events A and C is $2/6 = 1/3$.

You could observe an odd number *or* a number less than 4, event A or C or both A and C, in four ways: if E_1, E_2, E_3, or E_5 occurred—four of the simple events in Figure 7.2-2. Hence, the probability of A or C or both A and C is $4/6 = 2/3$. This

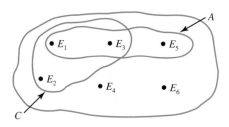

Figure 7.2-2. Euler diagram for event A, observing an odd number, and event C, observing a number less than 4.

probability is denoted by p(A or C). You have arrived at probabilities for the combined events p(A and C) and p(A or C) by a process of deduction. Section 7.3 describes several rules for computing the probabilities of combined events, but first I examine three properties of probabilities.

Formal Properties of Probability

Probability theory can be thought of as a system of definitions and operations pertaining to a sample space. According to the classical view described in Section 7.1, the probability of event A is the ratio of the number of sample points that are examples of A to the total number of sample points, provided all sample points are equally likely. For the die-tossing experiment represented in Figure 7.2-1, $p(E_1) = p(E_2) = \cdots = p(E_6) = \frac{1}{6}$. This follows from the assumption that all six faces are equally likely and the fact that there are six sample points in the sample space—that is, $n_S = 6$. To each event defined on the sample space, I can assign a number called the probability of E_i such that

1. $0 \leq p(E_i) \leq 1$ for all i,
2. $\sum_{i=1}^{n} p(E_i) = 1,$ and
3. $p(S) = 1$.

In words, these three properties of probability state that (1) the probability assigned to an event is a number greater than or equal to 0 and less than or equal to 1, (2) the sum of the probabilities over the sample space equals 1, and (3) the probability of the sure event, one of the events in S, is always 1.

CHECK YOUR UNDERSTANDING OF SECTION 7.2

5. An experiment consists of tossing three fair coins. (a) Represent the sample space by an Euler diagram, and encircle the sample points corresponding to observing two heads, event A, and observing at least one head, event B. (b) What is the probability of event A? (c) What is the probability of event B?
6. A class contains six psychology (P) majors, one sociology (S) major, and three history (H) majors. Assume that no students have double majors. (a) Represent the sample space by an Euler diagram. (b) If a student is selected at random, what is the probability that the student will be a psychology major? (c) What is the probability that the student will be a psychology or a sociology major?
7. Determine (a) the probability that a man chosen randomly from a group of 10 men is a psychologist if the group contains three psychologists and (b) the probability that you will win a car if you buy 6 raffle tickets and 10,000 tickets are sold.
8. Your package of M&Ms contains the following distribution of colored chocolate candies: four green (G), five red (R), six brown (Br), one orange (O), two blue (B), and seven yellow (Y). (a) Represent the sample space of the 25 events by an Euler diagram and encircle events G and B. (b) What is the probability of reaching into the M&M bag and drawing a green or blue candy?
9. Terms to remember:
   a. Subjective-personalistic view of probability
   b. Classical or logical view of probability

     c. Empirical-relative frequency view of probability
     d. Experiment
     e. Simple and compound events
     f. Euler diagram
     g. Sample point
     h. Sample space

7.3 PROBABILITY OF COMBINED EVENTS

This section describes rules for determining the probabilities of combined events. For example, you might want to know the probability that the outcome of an experiment will be event A or event B or both A and B. As noted earlier, I denote this probability by $p(A\ or\ B)$.[4] Alternatively, you might want to know the probability that the outcome will be both A and B. I denote this probability by $p(A\ and\ B)$.[5]

> The **union** of two events A and B is the set of elements that belong to A or to B or to both A and B. As you will see, the probability of the union of two events, $p(A\ or\ B)$, is computed by using the addition rule of probability. The **intersection** of two events A and B is the set of elements that belong to both A and B. You will see that the probability of the intersection of two events, $p(A\ and\ B)$, is computed by using the multiplication rule.

Addition Rule of Probability

> The **addition rule** states that the probability of the union of two events A and B, $p(A\ or\ B)$, is equal to
>
> $$p(A\ or\ B) = p(A) + p(B) - p(A\ and\ B)$$

For example, let event A be an even number when a die is tossed and event B, a number less than 5. The events are represented in Figure 7.3-1. Their probabilities are determined by counting sample points: $p(A) = n_A/n_S = {}^3/_6$; $p(B) = n_B/n_S = {}^4/_6$. The probability of event A and B is the ratio of the number of sample points that are examples of both A and B to the total number of sample points. In symbols, $p(A\ and\ B) = n_{A\ and\ B}/n_S = {}^2/_6$ because there are two simple events in both A and B and six in the sample space. Given this information,

$$p(A\ or\ B) = p(A) + p(B) - p(A\ and\ B)$$

$$= \frac{3}{6} + \frac{4}{6} - \frac{2}{6} = \frac{5}{6}$$

---

[4] Some books use the Boolean algebraic symbol $\cup$ in place of *or*.

[5] Some books use the Boolean algebraic symbol $\cap$ in place of *and*.

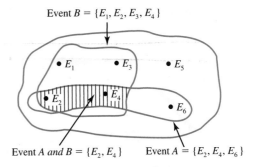

Event $B = \{E_1, E_2, E_3, E_4\}$

$\bullet\, E_1$ $\bullet\, E_3$ $\bullet\, E_5$

E_2 E_4 $\bullet\, E_6$

Event A and $B = \{E_2, E_4\}$ Event $A = \{E_2, E_4, E_6\}$

Figure 7.3-1. Euler diagram for event A, observing an even number, and event B, observing a number less than 5. The intersection of A and B is the shaded area.

Thus, the probability of observing an even number or a number less than 5 is $5/6$. In computing $p(A\ or\ B)$, the value $p(A\ and\ B) = 2/6$ is subtracted from $p(A) + p(B)$ to avoid counting the simple events E_2 and E_4 twice, because they are contained in event A and in event B.

The information contained in Figure 7.3-1 is presented in Table 7.3-1. This mode of presentation is easier to interpret, especially when the number of events exceeds two.

The addition rule leads to another important rule: the complement rule.

> For any event A, the event that A does not occur is called the **complement** of A and is written *Not A*. The probability that A does not occur, denoted by $p(Not\ A)$, is given by
>
> $$p(Not\ A) = 1 - p(A)$$

For the sample space in Figure 7.3-1, the probability of not observing an even number, event A, or a number less than five, event B, is

$$p[Not\ (A\ or\ B)] = 1 - p(A\ or\ B) = 1 - 5/6 = 1/6$$

TABLE 7.3-1   Tabular Presentation of Information in Figure 7.3-1

		Event		
		A	Not A	
Event	B	A and $B = \{E_2, E_4\}$	Not A and $B = \{E_1, E_3\}$	$B = \{E_1, E_2, E_3, E_4\}$
	Not B	A and Not $B = \{E_6\}$	Not A and Not $B = \{E_5\}$	Not $B = \{E_5, E_6\}$
		$A = \{E_2, E_4, E_6\}$	Not $A = \{E_1, E_3, E_5\}$	

Addition Rule for Mutually Exclusive Events

Two events may contain no sample points in common, in which case the events are said to be **mutually exclusive** or **disjoint.** For example, consider the following events: observe an even number on the toss of a die, event A, and observe an odd number, event B. An Euler diagram depicting the two events is shown in Figure 7.3-2. Because the intersection A *and* B contains no sample points, A and B are mutually exclusive.

> For mutually exclusive events, the addition rule can be simplified because for this case, $p(A \text{ and } B) = 0$. The addition rule $p(A \text{ or } B) = p(A) + p(B) - p(A \text{ and } B)$ becomes
>
> $$p(A \text{ or } B) = p(A) + p(B)$$

The probability of observing an even number or an odd number in tossing a die is $p(A \text{ or } B) = \frac{3}{6} + \frac{3}{6} = 1$. Because the probability is 1, we know that when a die is tossed, one of the events must occur.

> Events for which the probability of their union equals 1 are called **collectively exhaustive** or simply **exhaustive.**

Multiplication Rule of Probability

The multiplication rule is used to compute the probability of the joint occurrence, or intersection, of two or more events. For example, suppose that 100 psychology majors have been classified according to gender and class level. The number of students in each category is given in Table 7.3-2. If a student is selected by lottery, what is the probability that the student will be both a woman and a lowerclassman? As you will see, the multiplication rule lets you determine the probability that the student selected will be in the intersection *woman and lowerclassman*—that is, both a woman and a lowerclassman. This information differs from that given by the addition rule, which tells you the probability that the student selected will be a *woman* or a *lowerclassman* or a *woman lowerclassman*.

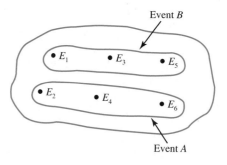

Figure 7.3-2. Euler diagram for event A, observing an even number, and event B, observing an odd number. Because the intersection A *and* B contains no sample points, the events are mutually exclusive.

TABLE 7.3-2   Number of Psychology Majors by Gender and Class Level

	Lowerclassman, L	Upperclassman, U	Marginal total
Women, W	10 $p(W \text{ and } L) = n_{W \text{ and } L}/n_S$ $= 10/100$ $= .10$	20	$n_W = 30$ $p(W) = n_W/n_S$ $= 30/100$ $= .30$
Men, M	40	30	$n_M = 70$ $p(M) = n_M/n_S$ $= 70/100$ $= .70$
Marginal total	$n_L = 50$ $p(L) = n_L/n_S$ $= 50/100$ $= .50$	$n_U = 50$ $p(U) = n_U/n_S$ $= 50/100$ $= .50$	$n_S = 100$

Before presenting the multiplication rule, I need to discuss the concept of conditional probability. Two events often are related so that the probability of one event depends on whether the other has or has not occurred. Consider these events: Your roommate reports that she feels bad, event A, and her temperature is 103, event B. The two events are obviously related because the probability of an elevated temperature, $p(B)$, is much higher if a person feels bad than if the person feels good. This type of relationship is a *conditional probability*.

The **conditional probability** of B given that A has occurred is denoted by $p(B \mid A)$ and is equal to

$$p(B \mid A) = p(A \text{ and } B)/p(A) = \left(\frac{n_{A \text{ and } B}}{n_S}\right)\Big/\left(\frac{n_A}{n_S}\right) = \frac{n_{A \text{ and } B}}{n_A}$$

The vertical line "$\mid$" in $(A \mid B)$ is read "given," or "given that." Similarly, the conditional probability of A given that B has occurred is

$$p(A \mid B) = p(A \text{ and } B)/p(B) = \left(\frac{n_{A \text{ and } B}}{n_S}\right)\Big/\left(\frac{n_B}{n_S}\right) = \frac{n_{A \text{ and } B}}{n_B}$$

The calculation of conditional probability will be illustrated using information in Table 7.3-2. The probability that a student selected by a lottery is a woman, given that you know the student is a lowerclassman, is

$$p(W \mid L) = \frac{n_{W \text{ and } L}}{n_L} = \frac{10}{50} = .20$$

You may find it helpful to realize that conditional probability always reduces the sample space of interest to a subspace of the original sample space. For example, the condition of being a lowerclassman reduces the sample space of interest to the left column of Table 7.3-2, which is a smaller sample space of size $n_L = 50$. The probability of selecting a woman is a subset of this smaller sample space, namely, 10 events out of 50. Thus, the probability of selecting a woman if you know that the student is a lowerclassman is $10/50 = .20$. However, the probability of selecting a woman in the absence of information about class level is $p(W) = 30/100 = .30$ (see Table 7.3-2). The events W and L are related because a knowledge of one event, class level, affects the probability of the other event, selecting a woman. In this example, $p(W \mid L) = .20$, but $p(W) = .30$.

The **multiplication rule** can be stated now. Given two events A and B, the probability of obtaining both A and B jointly is the product of the probability of obtaining one event, say A, times the conditional probability of the other event, B, given that A has occurred. In other words, the probability of the intersection of the events A and B, $p(A \text{ and } B)$, is given by

$$p(A \text{ and } B) = p(A)p(B \mid A)$$
$$= p(B)p(A \mid B)$$

For the events defined in Table 7.3-2, the probability of selecting a student who is both a woman and a lowerclassman is

$$p(W \text{ and } L) = p(W)p(L \mid W) = \left(\frac{n_W}{n_S}\right)\left(\frac{n_{W \text{ and } L}}{n_W}\right)$$

$$= \left(\frac{30}{100}\right)\left(\frac{10}{30}\right) = .10$$

$$= p(L)p(W \mid L) = \left(\frac{n_L}{n_S}\right)\left(\frac{n_{W \text{ and } L}}{n_L}\right)$$

$$= \left(\frac{50}{100}\right)\left(\frac{10}{50}\right) = .10$$

The multiplication rule may seem unnecessarily complicated because if $n_{W \text{ and } L}$ and n_S are known, $p(W \text{ and } L) = n_{W \text{ and } L} / n_S$. Sometimes only a **marginal probability,** $p(A)$ or $p(B)$, and a conditional probability, $p(A \mid B)$ or $p(B \mid A)$, are known. For example, suppose that you want to know the probability of drawing two aces from a 52-card deck that has been well shuffled. On the first draw, the probability of drawing an ace is $p(ace \text{ } on \text{ } first \text{ } draw) = 4/52$. If an ace is drawn on the first draw and is not replaced in the deck, the conditional probability of drawing an ace on the second draw is $p(ace \text{ } on \text{ } second \text{ } draw \mid ace \text{ } on \text{ } first \text{ } draw) = 3/51$. The probability of drawing two aces on two draws without replacement is

$$p(two \text{ } aces) = p(ace \text{ } on \text{ } first \text{ } draw) \times p(ace \text{ } on \text{ } second \text{ } draw \mid ace \text{ } on \text{ } first \text{ } draw)$$

$$= \left(\frac{4}{52}\right)\left(\frac{3}{51}\right) \cong 0.0045$$

Multiplication Rule for Statistically Independent Events

Two events A and B are **statistically independent** if the probability of one event's occurring is unaffected by the occurrence of the other. In other words, A and B are statistically independent if and only if $p(A \mid B) = p(A)$. Furthermore, if $p(A \mid B) = p(A)$, it also must be true that $p(B \mid A) = p(B)$.

The events $p(W)$ and $p(L)$ in Table 7.3-2 are not statistically independent because $p(W \mid L)$ is not equal to $p(W)$ as the following computations show.

$$p(W|L) = p(W \text{ and } L)/p(L) = \frac{n_{W \text{ and } L}}{n_L} = \frac{10}{50} = .20$$

is not equal to

$$p(W) = \frac{n_W}{n_S} = \frac{30}{100} = 30$$

I can easily construct an example in which the events are independent. Consider an experiment in which a fair coin is tossed and a fair die is rolled. Because the coin can land in one of two ways, H or T, and the die, in one of six ways, $1, \ldots, 6$, the possible outcomes are $H1, T1, H2, T2, \ldots, H6, T6$. The sample space for the experiment is shown in Figure 7.3-3. Let event A be a head and B a 5. The probabilities required to demonstrate independence of A and B are

$$p(A) = \frac{n_A}{n_S} = \frac{6}{12} = \frac{1}{2}$$

and

$$p(A|B) = \frac{n_{A \text{ and } B}}{n_B} = \frac{1}{2}$$

Because $p(A) = p(A \mid B) = 1/2$, the events are statistically independent; this agrees with our intuition that what happens on the roll of a die can in no way affect the outcome of tossing a coin.

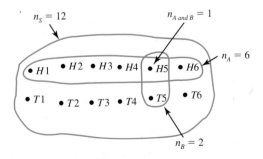

Figure 7.3-3. Euler diagram for event A, observing a head, and event B, observing a 5, when a coin and die are tossed.

For statistically independent events, the multiplication rule can be simplified because

$$p(A \mid B) = p(A) \quad \text{and} \quad p(B \mid A) = p(B)$$

The multiplication rule

$$p(A \text{ and } B) = p(A)p(B \mid A)$$
$$= p(B)p(A \mid B)$$

becomes

$$p(A \text{ and } B) = p(A)p(B)$$

As you just saw, the probability of observing a head and a 5 are independent; hence, the probability of their joint occurrence is

$$p(A \text{ and } B) = \left(\frac{n_A}{n_S}\right)\left(\frac{n_B}{n_S}\right) = \left(\frac{6}{12}\right)\left(\frac{2}{12}\right) = \frac{1}{12}$$

Common Errors in Applying the Rules of Probability

The probability rules described in this section often are used incorrectly. Some of the more common errors are the following:

1. Using the addition rule for mutually exclusive events, $p(A \text{ or } B) = p(A) + p(B)$, when the events are not mutually exclusive. For example, let event A be the classification "psychology major" and event B, "biology major." If $p(A) = .20$ and $p(B) = .15$, you might conclude that the probability that a student is either a psychology major or a biology major is $p(A \text{ or } B) = .20 + .15 = .35$. This is incorrect because some students have a double major, and these students have been counted twice—once in computing $p(A)$ and again in computing $p(B)$. Assume that $p(A \text{ and } B) = .03$; the correct probability is given by $p(A \text{ or } B) = p(A) + p(B) - p(A \text{ and } B) = .20 + .15 - .03 = .32$.
2. Using the addition rule when the multiplication rule should be used and vice versa. For example, on the toss of a die the probability of observing a 3, event A, or a 5, event B, is given by $p(A \text{ or } B) = p(A) + p(B) = 1/6 + 1/6 = 2/6$ and not by $p(A \text{ and } B) = p(A)p(B) = (1/6)(1/6) = 1/36$.
3. Using the multiplication rule for statistically independent events, $p(A \text{ and } B) = p(A)p(B)$, when the events are not statistically independent. Suppose the probability of seeing an advertisement for a product, event A, is .40 and the probability of buying the product, event B, is .30. If the dependency between A and B is ignored, the incorrect probability of both seeing an advertisement and buying the product is $p(A \text{ and } B) = (.40)(.30) = .12$. The correct probability takes in to account the conditional probability of buying the product given that the ad has been seen, $p(B \mid A) = .50$, so that $p(A \text{ and } B) = p(A)p(B \mid A) = (.40)(.50) = .20$.

CHECK YOUR UNDERSTANDING OF SECTION 7.3

10. A standard deck of cards contains 52 cards: 10 number cards of each suit (counting the ace as a 1) and three face cards of each suit. If someone draws a card from the deck at random, what is the probability that it will be (a) an ace, (b) a heart, (c) an ace or a heart or both, (d) a heart or a spade, (e) a face card, (f) a card less than 5, or (g) not an ace?

11. Events A and B are independent; $p(A) = .6$ and $p(B) = .8$. What is the probability that (a) both will occur? (b) Neither will occur? (c) One or the other or both will occur?

12. Highway accident statistics show that 10% of all automobile accidents and half of all fatal automobile accidents are caused by drunken drivers. Four in 1,000 reported accidents are fatal. (a) Fill in the table with the appropriate probabilities. (b) What is the joint probability that a fatal accident is caused by a drunken driver?

	Fatal, *F*	Nonfatal, *Not F*	
Drunken Driver, *D*	$p(D \text{ and } F) =$	$p(D \text{ and Not } F) =$	$p(D) =$
Other Cause, *O*	$p(O \text{ and } F) =$	$p(O \text{ and Not } F) =$	$p(O) =$
	$p(F) =$	$p(Not F) =$	

13. You ask your roommate to mail a letter. The probability that she will mail it is .98. The probability that the post office will fail to deliver it, given that it was mailed, is .15. What is the probability that the letter will be mailed and the post office will fail to deliver it?

14. Exercise 8 in "Check Your Understanding of Section 7.2" described the color of the candies in a package of M&Ms. If you draw a candy at random from the package, what is the probability that it will be (a) green, (b) red or yellow, (c) not green, and (d) colorless? After eating the first candy, you draw another from the package. What is the probability that you have (e) eaten a blue candy and drawn an orange candy, (f) eaten a blue candy and drawn an orange or brown candy?

15. Terms to remember:
    a. Union
    b. Intersection
    c. Addition rule
    d. Addition rule for mutually exclusive events
    e. Complement rule
    f. Mutually exclusive events
    g. Disjoint events
    h. Exhaustive events
    i. Conditional probability
    j. Multiplication rule
    k. Marginal probability
    l. Statistical independence
    m. Multiplication rule for mutually exclusive events
    n. Sampling with (without) replacement

7.4 COUNTING SIMPLE EVENTS

Listing all the simple events in an experiment can be tedious. Even a small experiment, such as recording the outcome of tossing three dice, has a large sample space, in this case $6 \times 6 \times 6 = 216$ sample points. Fortunately, it is not necessary to list all of the simple events to compute probabilities. The required information can be determined using the counting rules discussed in this section.

Fundamental Counting Rule[6]

> Suppose that an event can occur in n_1 ways and a second event can occur in n_2 ways and that each of the first event's n_1 ways can be followed by any of the second's n_2 ways. Then, according to the **fundamental counting rule,** event 1 followed by event 2 can occur in $n_1 n_2$ ways.

To illustrate, suppose that you toss a coin and then a die. The number of possible outcomes of the experiment is

$$n_1 n_2 = (2)(6) = 12$$

because a coin can land heads or tails ($n_1 = 2$) and a die has six faces ($n_2 = 6$). The simple events are shown in the tree diagram of Figure 7.4-1.

The fundamental counting rule can be extended to $k > 2$ events. If there are k events (event 1 having n_1 outcomes, followed by event 2 having n_2 outcomes, and so

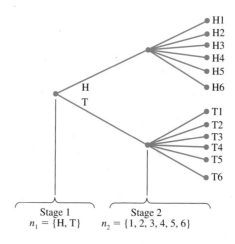

Figure 7.4-1. Tree diagram of possible outcomes of tossing a coin and then a die.

---

[6] Also called the **multiplication principle.**

forth), the outcome can occur in $n_1 n_2 \ldots n_k$ ways. For example, the number of possible outcomes of tossing three dice and a coin is $6 \times 6 \times 6 \times 2 = 432$.

Permutation of *n* Objects Taken *n* at a Time, $_nP_n$

Suppose that you have three distinct objects, and you want to find the number of different ordered sequences in which the objects can be arranged. For example, in how many ordered sequences can the letters *A*, *B*, and *C* be arranged? The answer is six: *ABC*, *ACB*, *BAC*, *BCA*, *CAB*, and *CBA*. Arranging *n* objects in an ordered sequence is equivalent to putting them into a long box with *n* ordered compartments. The first

1	2	3	$\cdots$	*n*
n ways	*n* − 1 ways	*n* − 2 ways		1 way

compartment can be filled in any of *n* ways, which uses up one of the objects; the second compartment can be filled in any of *n* − 1 ways, . . . , and the last compartment, in only one way. Applying the fundamental counting rule, the number of ordered arrangements of *n* objects is the product $n(n - 1)(n - 2) \cdots 1$. The quantity $n(n - 1)(n - 2) \cdots 1$ is denoted by the symbol *n*!, which is read "*n* factorial."

An ordered sequence of *n* distinct objects taken all together is called a **permutation** of the objects. The total number of such permutations, denoted by $_nP_n$, is given by

$$_nP_n = n! = n(n - 1)(n - 2) \cdots 1$$

The symbol $_nP_n$ is read "the permutation of *n* objects taken *n* at a time."

Suppose that I am doing a taste preference experiment in which a panel of 10 experts rates five nondairy coffee creamers. I want to control for sequence effects—the effects of presenting the five coffee creamers in a particular order. One way to control for sequence effects is to present the five coffee creamers in all possible sequences to each judge. In how many ordered sequences can coffee prepared with the five creamers be presented? The answer is 5! = 5 (4)(3)(2)(1) = 120. Finding 10 experts willing to sit through the 120 tasting sequences is probably impossible. I need to consider alternative designs for my experiment. Another and more practical way to control for sequence effects is to present the coffee creamers in 12 of the 120 sequences to one expert, in 12 different sequences to another expert, and so on. Following this procedure, all 120 of the sequences would be used, but each of the 10 expert judges would receive only 12 sequences.

Permutation of *n* Objects Taken *r* at a Time, $_nP_r$

I illustrated the computation of $_nP_n$ with an example in which I put *n* objects in a box with *n* ordered compartments. Suppose that the box only has *r* ordered compartments, where $r \leq n$.

The number of permutations of n distinct objects taken r at a time, where $r \leq n$, is denoted by $_nP_r$[7] and is equal to $n(n-1)(n-2) \cdots (n-r+1)$.

For example, the number of ordered sequences of five letters, A, B, C, D, and E, taken three at a time, is $_5P_3 = 5(5-1)(5-3+1) = (5)(4)(3) = 60$. The rationale behind the formula is as follows. Consider the box

1	2	3
n ways	$n-1$ ways	$n-(r-1)$ ways

with $r = 3$ ordered compartments. The first compartment can be filled in any of $n = 5$ ways and the second, in $n - 1 = 4$ ways. When you come to the $r = $ 3rd compartment, you have used $r - 1 = 2$ of the n letters so that $n - (r-1) = n - r + 1 = 3$ letters are left to fill the last compartment. According to the fundamental counting rule, the number of ordered sequences is the product $n(n-1) \cdots (n-r+1)$. Therefore, the number of ordered sequences of the five letters taken three at a time is $(5)(4)(3) = 60$.

An equivalent formula for computing $_nP_r$, is [8]

$$_nP_r = \frac{n!}{(n-r)!}$$

To illustrate, the permutations of five distinct objects taken three at a time is

$$_5P_3 = \frac{5!}{(5-3)!} = \frac{(5)(4)(2)(1)}{(2)(1)} = \frac{120}{2} = 60$$

This answer agrees with that obtained using $_nP_r = n(n-1)(n-2) \cdots (n-r+1)$.

The taste-preference experiment described earlier could be performed using the method of paired comparisons. In this method, an expert sips first one and then a second cup of coffee prepared with two of the creamers and indicates a preference. The procedure is repeated until each creamer has been compared twice with every other creamer, once in the first cup sipped and once in the second cup. In how many ordered sequences can five creamers be presented two at a time? The answer is given by

$$_5P_2 = 5(5-2+1) = 5(4) = 20$$

or

$$_5P_2 = \frac{5!}{(5-2)!} = \frac{(5)(4)(3)(2)(1)}{(3)(2)(1)} = \frac{120}{6} = 20$$

The method of paired comparisons would require each expert to make a total of 20 judgments—10 judgments in which a particular creamer in a pair is in the first cup sipped and 10 in which the creamer is in the second cup sipped.

---

[7] Also denoted by P_r^n, $P(n, r)$, and $(n)_r$.

[8] In computations involving $n!$, remember that $1! = 1$ and that by definition $0! = 1$.

Combination of *n* Objects Taken *r* at a Time, $_nC_r$

Sometimes you are not interested in the number of ordered sequences or permutations of *n* objects taken *r* at a time, but instead in the number of different combinations of *r* objects that can be selected from *n* distinct objects when order is ignored. This is referred to as the **combination** of *n* objects taken *r* at a time and is denoted by $_nC_r$.[9] The formula for $_nC_r$ is

$$_nC_r = \frac{n!}{r!(n-r)!}$$

The rationale for the formula is as follows. Consider four letters *A*, *B*, *C*, and *D* taken two at a time. The number of ordered sequences is $_4P_2 = 4!/(4-2)! = 12$. But suppose that you do not want to distinguish *AB* from *BA*, *BC* from *CB*, and so on. You note that any sequence of $r = 2$ objects can be permuted in $r! = 2(1) = 2$ ways. If you want to ignore the order of the *r* objects in $_nP_r$, you can divide $_nP_r$ by $r!$, which gives

$$_nC_r = \frac{_nP_r}{r!} = \left(\frac{\frac{n!}{(n-r)!}}{r!} \right) = \frac{n!}{r!(n-r)!}$$

The number of different sets of $r = 2$ letters that can be selected from $n = 4$ letters, *A*, *B*, *C*, *D*, is

$$_4C_2 = \frac{4!}{2!(4-2)!} = \frac{4(3)(2)(1)}{2(1)[2(1)]} = 6$$

The six sets are as follows: *AB*, *AC*, *AD*, *BC*, *BD*, and *CD*. Because the order of letters in a pair is of no interest, the six could just as well have been written *BA*, *CA*, *AD*, *CB*, *BD*, and *CD*.

The combination of *n* objects taken *r* at a time will be used in Chapter 8 to develop the binomial distribution, which describes the possible outcomes of a particular kind of experiment.

CHECK YOUR UNDERSTANDING OF SECTION 7.4

16. Determine the number of possible outcomes for the following: (a) Three coins are tossed. (b) Four dice are rolled. (c) A coin and a die are tossed.
17. If there are three candidates for governor and five for mayor, in how many ways can the two offices be filled?
18. The four Russian novels *War and Peace*, *Anna Karenina*, *Crime and Punishment*, and *The Brothers Karamazov* are to be placed on a shelf. In how many ordered sequences can the books be arranged?

---

[9] Also denoted by C_r^n, $C(n, r)$, and $\binom{r}{n}$.

19. How many different ways can 10 people be seated four at a time on a bench with only four seats?
20. Given nine areas from which to choose, in how many ways can a student select (a) a major-minor area? (b) a major and first and second minors? (c) a major and two minors if it is not necessary to designate the order of the minors?
21. Terms to remember:
    a. Fundamental counting rule
    b. Permutation
    c. n factorial
    d. Combination

7.5 LOOKING BACK: WHAT HAVE YOU LEARNED?

Probability is an abstract mathematical concept that can be defined in a number of ways. The three most useful views of probability are the subjective-personalistic view; the classical, or logical view; and the empirical relative-frequency view.

My interest in probability is pragmatic: I want to make statements about the likelihood of observing various outcomes in experiments. An experiment is any well-defined act or process that leads to an outcome. An outcome is either a compound event that can be decomposed into simple events, such as observing an even number on the toss of a die, or a simple event that cannot be decomposed. If I assign to each simple event a point called a sample point, the possible outcomes of an experiment can be represented by an Euler diagram. The set of all sample points is called the sample space, S.

Whatever one's view, probability is based on a system of definitions and operations pertaining to a sample space. If S is the sample space for an experiment and n_S is the number of sample points in S, I can associate with each event E_i a real number called the probability of E_i, $p(E_i)$, satisfying the following properties:

1. $0 \le p(E_i) \le 1$, for all i
2. $\sum_{i=1}^{n_S} p(E_i) = 1$
3. $p(S) = 1$

These properties describe probabilities, but they do not tell you how to compute them. If you adopt the classical view, the probability of an event A is computed from the formula $p(A) = n_A/n_S$, where n_A is the number of events favoring A and n_S is the total number of equally likely events in the sample space S. This view of probability is based on logical analysis. You reason that an experiment has n_S possible outcomes, the outcomes are equally likely, and n_A of the outcomes favor A. If your reasoning is correct, the value you compute for $p(A)$ will agree closely with that based on the relative-frequency view.

According to the relative-frequency view, the probability of event A is the number approached by n_A/n as the total number of observations, n, approaches infinity. The estimate n_A/n is based on experience because it is computed for a sample from the population of possible experiments. On average, the larger the sample, the closer the estimate is to the true probability.

Probabilities for combined events can be computed by the addition rule and the multiplication rule. The addition rule states that the probability that an event will be A or B or both is

$$p(A \text{ or } B) = p(A) + p(B) - p(A \text{ and } B)$$

For mutually exclusive events, $p(A\ and\ B) = 0$, and the rule simplifies to

$$p(A\ or\ B) = p(A) + p(B)$$

The multiplication rule states that the probability that an event will be both A and B is

$$p(A\ and\ B) = p(A)p(A|B)$$

For statistically independent events, $p(B|A) = p(B)$ and $p(A|B) = p(A)$, and the rule simplifies to

$$p(A\ and\ B) = p(A)p(B)$$

The number of simple events in an experiment can be determined either by enumeration, which is the hard way, or by using counting rules, which is the easy way. The key rules are as follows:

1. Fundamental counting rule. If there are k events, event 1 followed by event 2, . . . , followed by the kth event, the outcome can occur in $n_1 n_2 \cdots n_k$ ways.
2. Permutation of n objects taken n at a time. The number of ordered sequences of n distinct objects taken all together is $_n P_n = n! = n(n-1)(n-2) \cdots 1$.
3. Permutation of n objects taken r at a time. The number of ordered sequences of n distinct objects taken r at a time is $_n P_r = n!/(n-r)!$.
4. Combination of n objects taken r at a time. The number of different combinations of r objects that can be selected from n distinct objects when order is ignored is $_n C_r = n!/[r!\ (n-r)!]$.

REVIEW EXERCISES FOR CHAPTER 7

1. Why is subjective probability difficult to incorporate into a formal decision-making process?
2. To use the classical approach to probability, what information do you need to know?
3. (a) According to the classical view, what is the probability of observing a number less than 5 on the toss of a die? (b) What assumptions are required to arrive at the answer?
4. (a) According to the classical view, what is the probability of drawing the king of hearts from a well-shuffled deck of 52 cards? (b) What assumptions are required to arrive at the answer?
5. (a) According to the relative-frequency view, what is the probability that a head will occur on the next toss of a fair coin if a head appeared on 54 of the last 100 tosses? (b) According to the classical view, what is the probability that a head will occur?
6. An experiment consists of tossing two dice, one green and one red, and recording the outcome. (a) Represent the sample space by an Euler diagram, and encircle the sample points corresponding to observing a 7 as the sum of the dice. (b) What is the probability that the sum of two dice is 7? (c) What is the probability that the sum of two dice is less than 5?

7. A fair die is rolled once. You win $5 if the outcome is even, event A, or if it is divisible by 3, event B. (a) Represent the sample space by an Euler diagram and encircle events A and B. (b) What is the probability of winning the $5?

8. The following are properties of probabilities. In your own words, state what each property means. (a) $0 \leq p(E_i) \leq 1$, for all i. (b) $\sum_{i=1}^{n} p(E_i) = 1$. (c) $p(S) = 1$.

9. Events A, B, C, and D are mutually exclusive and exhaustive, each having a probability of $\frac{1}{4}$. Determine the following.
   a. $p(A \text{ or } C)$ c. $p[Not(A \text{ or } C)]$
   b. $p(A \text{ or } B \text{ or } C \text{ or } D)$ d. $p[Not(A \text{ or } B \text{ or } C)]$

10. For the data in the table, determine whether the events "attend college" and "man" are statistically independent.

	Attend college		
	Yes	No	
Man	.30	.20	.50
Woman	.10	.40	.50
	.40	.60	1.00

11. Data were obtained on the incidence of rheumatic disease and the presence of grimacing in schizophrenic patients. In a sample of 1942 patients, 6% had a known history of rheumatic disease, 21.8% grimaced, and 1.8% had a history of both rheumatic disease and grimacing. (a) Fill in the table with the appropriate probabilities. (b) What is the probability of grimacing, given a history of rheumatic disease? (c) Are grimacing and rheumatic disease statistically independent?

	Grimacing, G	No grimacing, $No\ G$
History of rheumatic disease, D		
No history of rheumatic disease, $No\ D$		

12. A smoker has 10 pipes, three of which are meerschaums. Of his six curved-stem pipes, two are meerschaums. He asks his son to bring him a curved-stem meerschaum. Because the boy does not know a meerschaum from other curved-stem pipes, he picks up a curved-stem pipe at random. (a) Fill in the table with the appropriate probabilities. (b) What is the probability that the son picked the right pipe?

	Meerschaum, M	Other Kind of Pipe, O	
Curved Stem, C	$p(C \text{ and } M) =$	$p(C \text{ and } O) =$	$p(C) =$
Straight Stem, S	$p(S \text{ and } M) =$	$p(S \text{ and } O) =$	$p(S) =$
	$p(M) =$	$p(O) =$	

13. One hundred students are enrolled in a university course. Fifty are men (M) and 50 are women (W). Of the 100 students, 60 are undergraduates (U) and 40 are graduate students (G). Of these 100 students, 20 are both men and undergraduates. For a student selected at random from the class, compute the following probabilities. (*Hint:* $p(U) = p(M \text{ and } U) + p(W \text{ and } U)$. It is helpful to construct a 2×2 table and fill in the information that is known.)
    a. $p(W \text{ and } U)$ d. $p(M \mid U)$
    b. $p(W \text{ and } G)$ e. $p(W \mid G)$
    c. $p(M \text{ and } G)$

14. A statistician who worked in operations research for the British Bomber Command during World War II determined that the probability that a member of a bomber crew sent on night raids over Germany would complete a standard tour of duty (30 missions) was equal to .30. (Suggested by Dyson, F. [1981]. *Disturbing the universe.* New York: Harper & Row.)
    a. What is the probability of a crewman not surviving ($p(Not \ S)$) a standard tour of duty?
    b. If successive tours of duty are treated as independent events, what is the probability of surviving two tours of duty?
    c. If successive tours of duty are treated as independent events, what is the probability of surviving the first tour of duty but not the second?
    d. If successive tours of duty are treated as independent events, what is the probability of not surviving three tours of duty?

15. In a survey of 100 couples who had recently had marital counseling, 80 of the couples reported that their relationship had improved (I). Sixty of the couples in the improved group had children (C). Assume that a couple is selected at random from the sample. Compute the following probabilities for that couple.
    a. $p(C \mid I)$
    b. $p(Not \ C \mid I)$
    c. Find two probabilities whose product gives $p(C \text{ and } I)$.

16. The Greasy Spoon menu offers a choice of five appetizers, four salads, eight entrees, seven vegetables, and nine desserts. If a meal consists of one from each category, in how many ways can you select a dinner?

17. Two different psychology books, four different statistics books, and three different sociology books are to be arranged on a shelf. (a) In how many ordered sequences can the books be arranged? (b) If the books in each subject must be kept together, how many ordered sequences are possible?

18. In how many different ways can eight people be seated four at a time on a bench with only four seats?

19. On a statistics examination consisting of 12 questions, a student may omit five. In how many ways can the student select the problems to answer?

20. (a) In how many ways can six people be seated in a row at the head banquet table? (b) Suppose the people are to be seated in pairs at separate tables; in how many ways can they be seated if we consider the arrangement AB to be different from BA? (c) In how many ways if you consider AB to be equivalent to BA?

21. How many different committees of three men and four women can be formed from eight men and six women?

8

Random Variables and Probability Distributions

8.1 Introduction
Looking Ahead:
What Is This
Chapter About?

8.2 Random Sampling
Defining the Population
Sampling with or without
Replacement
Random Sampling
Procedures
Using a Table of Random
Numbers
Check Your Understanding
of Section 8.2

**8.3 Random Variables and
Their Distributions**
Random Variables
Distribution of a Discrete
Random Variable
Expected Value of a
Discrete Random
Variable
Expected Value of a
Continuous Random
Variable
Standard Deviation of a
Discrete Random
Variable
Check Your Understanding
of Section 8.3

8.4 Binomial Distribution
Bernoulli Trial
Binomial Distribution
Expected Value and
Standard Deviation of
Binomial Distribution
Check Your Understanding
of Section 8.4

**8.5 Looking Back: What
Have You Learned?**
Review Exercises for
Chapter 8

8.1 INTRODUCTION

Looking Ahead: What Is This Chapter About?

You learned in Chapter 1 that a random sample is often used in research when it is not possible to observe all of the elements in the population. This chapter discusses how to draw a random sample. You also will learn about several important concepts that are used in inferential statistics: random variable, probability distribution, and sampling distribution. In the simplest terms, a *random variable* is the numerical outcome of an experiment. For example, the random variable could be the number of heads when I toss a coin once. The value of the random variable, number of heads, is either 0 or 1. A table showing the probability associated with the possible outcomes, 0 and 1, is called a *probability distribution*. If I toss a coin two or more times, I can count the number of heads on the $n \geq 2$ trials. Now the random variable is a statistic (count) based on the outcome of the n trials. A table showing the probability associated with each of the possible outcomes is called a *sampling distribution*. In this chapter you will learn how to describe the central tendency and dispersion of sampling distributions.

After reading this chapter, you should know the following:

- How to draw a random sample using a table of random numbers
- How to compute the expected value and standard deviation of discrete random variables
- The characteristics of a Bernoulli trial
- How a binomial random variable is obtained from n Bernoulli trials

8.2 RANDOM SAMPLING

Inferential statistics are used in reasoning from a sample to the population—that is, determining the characteristics of a population by observing a sample from the population. Some samples provide a sound basis for this process; others do not. The difference lies in the method by which the samples are selected.

> The method of drawing samples from a population so that every possible sample of a particular size has the same probability of being selected is called **random sampling,** and the resulting sample is called a **random sample.**

As the definition indicates, randomness is a property of the procedure rather than of the particular sample obtained. The term *random sample* simply refers to a sample produced by a random sampling procedure. Other sampling methods based on haphazard or purposeless choices such as enlisting volunteers, students enrolled in a psychology course, or every 10th name in an alphabetical list is called **nonrandom sampling.** The resulting samples, unlike random samples, do not provide a sound basis for determining the properties of populations.

As you will see, the inferential procedures described in subsequent chapters assume either random sampling from a population or random assignment of participants to the various conditions of an experiment.[1] If random sampling is used, there is no guarantee that a particular random sample will resemble the population, but in the long run, random samples are more likely to do so than nonrandom samples. Random assignment of participants to experimental conditions helps to ensure that systematic bias is not introduced, as it would be, for example, if the best participants were unwittingly assigned to the experimental conditions that are expected to be superior.

Defining the Population

The first step in drawing a random sample is to identify the population. A **population** was defined in Chapter 1 as the collection of all people, objects, events, or observations having one or more specified characteristics. The population is identified when you specify the common characteristics, for example, this year's freshmen at Oregon State University or the outcomes of tossing a die for eternity. A single person, object, event, or observation is called an **element** of the population. The elements of the population can be **finite**[2] (limited) in number, as in this year's freshmen at Oregon State, or **infinite** in number, as in the outcomes of tossing a die for eternity.

In practice, it is difficult to obtain a random sample from large populations like residents of a city or students at a university. There are two obstacles: obtaining an accurate list of the population elements and securing their participation once they have been selected. Some cities have lists of their residents, but unfortunately the information is not updated frequently. Telephone directories are more current but exclude certain segments of society more often than others. The use of either list introduces systematic bias into an experiment. A researcher faced with the choice between the two lists might prefer to redefine the population to fit the more current list. Instead of all city residents, the population is defined as all households in the telephone directory.

Sampling with or without Replacement

> After identifying the population, one must decide whether to sample with replacement or without replacement. In sampling **with replacement,** a sampled element is returned to the population so that it is available to be drawn again; in sampling **without replacement,** the element is not replaced and hence can be drawn only once.[3]

---

[1] Random assignment is discussed in Section 13.2.

[2] The probability of drawing a particular sample from a finite population is given by $1/(_nC_r)$ (see Section 7.4), where r denotes the sample size and n denotes the population size. For example, the probability for $r = 2$ and $n = 100$ is $1/\{100!/[2!(100 - 2)!]\} = 1/4{,}950 \cong .0002$.

[3] The number of different samples of size r that can be drawn without replacement from a population of size n is given by $_nC_r$. The number of different samples with replacement is given by $n_1n_2 \ldots n_r$.

Sampling with replacement is rarely appropriate for the kinds of problems investigated in the behavioral and medical sciences and education because the sampled elements may be significantly and permanently altered by participating in the experiment. For example, once a child has learned an arithmetic unit, that child is no longer a naïve learner with respect to the unit; once tissue has been surgically removed, it cannot be removed again should the organism happen to be sampled a second time.

Random Sampling Procedures

A variety of procedures can be used to draw a random sample. If the population is finite, each element can be identified on a slip of paper and the slips placed in a container, thoroughly mixed, and then drawn blindly from the container. If sampling with replacement is used, the identity of a selected element is noted and the slip is returned to the container; it is then available to be drawn again. The blind drawing-of-slips procedure seems simple enough, but in practice it is not always random—witness the December 1969 draft lottery for the Vietnam War. More slips containing birth dates in the later months of the year were drawn, much to the dismay of men with birthdays in September, October, November, and December who were sent off to fight an unpopular war. The problem with the sampling procedure was attributed to placing the slips in the bowl in chronological order and failing to shake the bowl thoroughly. Slips for the later months were the last ones in the bowl and the first ones drawn.

Another technique for drawing a random sample is to flip a coin or spin a roulette wheel, with the outcome of the random device determining whether an element is or is not included in the sample. This procedure is practical for selecting a small sample but becomes tedious for larger ones.

Most researchers prefer to use a table of random numbers to draw their samples. Random number tables like the one in Appendix Table D.1 were prepared so that integers from 0 to 9 occur with about equal frequency and appear in the table in a random order. The digits in Appendix Table D.1 are in groups of two to make them easier to read, but the grouping has no other significance.

Using a Table of Random Numbers

Suppose that I want a random sample of 30 speech-therapy majors. A printout listing 273 majors constituting the population is obtained from the computer center, and the students are numbered serially from 001 to 273. I turn to Appendix Table D.1 and note that it has two pages with 50 rows and 25 columns each. To decide where to begin in the table I close my eyes and drop my pencil on the table. Suppose the pencil lands on the second page with the point closest to the first number in row 21 and column 13. The numbers reading from left to right are 22 00 20 35 55 . . . . I let the first number, 2, identify the table page on which I will begin (I had numbered the pages 1 and 2, so I was looking for a one-digit number between 1 and 2); the next two digits, 20, identify the row in which I will begin (in this case I was looking for a two-digit number between 1 and 50); and the next two digits, 02, the column (here I was looking for a two-digit number between 1 and 25). Because I previously decided to read the numbers from left to right, although any sequence can be used, I proceed to draw my sample. I begin on page 2, row 20, and column 2 and read numbers in groups of three until I obtain 30 unique numbers between 001 and 273, inclusive. The first eight numbers from the table are 644, 359, 989, 877, 876, 807, 915, and 167. I ignore the first seven numbers because they are not between 001 and 273 and take as my first sample element the student identified as 167. To sample without replacement, I ignore numbers after their first appearance. The students corresponding to the 30 numbers between 001 and 273, inclusive, compose the sample.

In sampling from a list with many pages, such as a telephone directory or a student directory, it is not necessary to number each population element if the number of names on each page is about the same. Instead of numbering each name, you number each page and each position on the page. To select a sample element, pairs of numbers are drawn from a random number table; the first number identifies the directory page, and the second number identifies the position of the element on the page. Another procedure, called **systematic sampling,** is sometimes used to sample from a list. It involves sampling every nth element, say every 20th person, in the list. Despite the simplicity of this procedure, it cannot be recommended because it does not satisfy the definition of random sampling.

CHECK YOUR UNDERSTANDING OF SECTION 8.2

1. List the steps involved in drawing a random sample.
2. Drawing a random sample from a large population is difficult. What are the problems?
3. (a) How many different samples of size 5 can be drawn without replacement from a population of size 50? (b) How many different samples of size 5 can be drawn with replacement from a population of size 50?
4. A sample of four supermarkets is to be selected from a total of eight in a small town. (a) How many different random samples without replacement can be drawn? (b) What is the probability that a given sample will be selected? (c) How many different random samples with replacement can be drawn?
5. (a) Use the table of random numbers in Appendix D to draw two random samples of 10 students from the following population. For one sample use sampling with replacement; for the other use sampling without replacement. (b) Describe in detail how you used the table.

Helen	Gary	Keith	Brad	Joe	Jim
Mike	Betty	Judy	Kris	JoAnn	Jack
Chuck	Matthew	Tom	Jaime	Wade	Rita

6. Terms to remember:
   a. Random and nonrandom sampling
   b. Population
   c. Element
   d. Sampling with or without replacement
   e. Random number table
   f. Systematic sampling

8.3 RANDOM VARIABLES AND THEIR DISTRIBUTIONS

Random Variables

In rolling a pair of dice you can observe the total number of dots; in tossing a coin two times you can observe the total number of heads; in observing a naïve rat in a three-choice T maze you can view the total number of incorrect turns. The variable, number of dots or number of heads or number of incorrect turns, is called a **random variable** because it is quantitative and its value for a particular experiment is determined by chance. In the dice example, the random variable, number of dots, can assume values of 2, . . . , 12; in the coin example, the random variable can assume values of 0, 1, or 2 heads; in the T-maze example, the random variable can assume values of 0, 1, 2, or 3 errors. Random variables usually are denoted by a capital letter toward the end of the alphabet, for example X, Y, or Z. It helps to think of a random variable as the name for the number associated with the outcome of a random experiment before the experiment is performed. Performing the experiment converts the random variable into a specific number.

You may be wondering, why the fancy name? How does a random variable differ from just a plain old variable? I can contrast the two kinds of variables as follows:

1. The variable X is the name for any one of a set of permissible values.
2. The random variable X is the name for any one of a set of permissible numerical values of a random experiment.

Let's pursue the meaning of a random variable a bit further. In Section 7.2 you saw that all the possible outcomes of a random experiment can be represented by points in a sample space. A random variable associates one and only one numerical value with each point; hence, in the language of the mathematician, a random variable is a **function.** To understand this idea, recall from your algebra course that a function consists of two sets of elements and a rule that assigns to each element in the first set one and only one element in the second set. The definition of a function is quite general; $\{(a, 1), (b, 5), (c, 6)\}$ is a function, as are $\{$(Mike, tall), (Chuck, medium), (Jim, short)$\}$ and $\{$(no errors, 0), (one error, 1), (two errors, 2), (three errors, 3)$\}$. More simply stated, a function is a set of ordered pairs of elements, no two of which have the same first element. If the second element of a pair is a number, the function is said to be numerically valued. A random variable associates one and only one number with each point in a sample space. This discussion leads to the following formal definition of a random variable:

A random variable is a numerically valued function defined over a sample space.

Most readers will find the following definition easier to remember: A random variable is a numerical quantity whose value is determined by the outcome of a random experiment.

Random variables are classified according to the nature of the numbers they can assume.

A random variable is **discrete** if its range can assume only a finite number of values or an infinite number of values that is countable—for example, family size, number of dates per week, or scores on a test. A random variable is **continuous** if its range is uncountably infinite—for example, temperature in Chicago, duration of a kiss, or height.

It is important to distinguish between the values the random variable can assume and those yielded by your measuring instruments. A thermometer is usually calibrated in 1° steps, a stop watch in 0.1 second, and a ruler in 1/16 inch. Consequently, your measurement of continuous random variables is always approximate.

Distribution of a Discrete Random Variable

You learned in Chapter 2 that a frequency distribution associates a frequency with each value or class interval of a variable.

A similar representation that associates a probability with each value of a random variable is called a **probability distribution.**

A probability distribution for an experiment of tossing a die is shown in Table 8.3-1, and a graph of the distribution is shown in Figure 8.3-1. In the table, $p(X = r)$ denotes the probability that the random variable X is equal to the value r. The distribution in

TABLE 8.3-1   Probability Distribution for Outcome of Tossing a Die

Possible Values, r, of the Random Variable X	$p(X = r)$
1	1/6
2	1/6
3	1/6
4	1/6
5	1/6
6	1/6

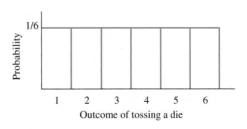

Figure 8.3-1. Histogram for probability distribution in Table 8.3-1.

Figure 8.3-1 is said to be uniform because each value of the random variable has the same probability. Notice that the probabilities sum to 1 because the events $X = 1, \ldots,$ 6 are mutually exclusive and collectively exhaustive.

Consider next the three-choice T-maze experiment mentioned earlier. Suppose that the correct series of turns is *right, left, right* (R, L, R). You know from the fundamental counting rule in Section 7.4 that a rat can traverse the maze in $2 \times 2 \times 2 = 8$ ways because three right-left choices must be made. The eight ways and the number of errors associated with each are listed in the table.

	Number of Errors, X
R, L, R	0
R, R, R	1
R, L, L	1
L, L, R	1
R, R, L	2
L, R, R	2
L, L, L	2
L, R, L	3

The probability of making 0, 1, 2, or 3 errors—the random variable—can be computed by $p(X = r) = n_r/n_s$, where n_r is the number of maze routes favoring r errors and n_s is the number of possible maze routes. For example, the probability of one error is ⅜ = .375 because there are three ways that a rat can make one error and there are eight possible maze routes. The probability distribution is given in Table 8.3-2 and a graph of the distribution, in Figure 8.3-2. The table and figure can be used to answer questions about the probability associated with the random variable—for instance, the probability that X is odd: $p(X = 1$ or $3) = .375 + .125 = .5$, or the probability that X is less than 3: $p(X < 3) = .125 + .375 + .375 = .875$.

A probability distribution is similar to a frequency distribution. The probability distribution associates a probability with each value of a random variable; the frequency distribution associates a frequency with each value of a variable. A probability distribution describes data that might be observed under certain well-specified conditions; hence, it is hypothetical or theoretical. A frequency distribution describes data that actually have been observed; it is empirical. You saw in Chapter 3 that the arithmetic mean often is used to describe the central tendency of a frequency distribution. A sim-

TABLE 8.3-2 Probability Distribution for Number of Errors in a Three-Choice T Maze

Possible Values, r, of the Random Variable X	p(X = r)
0	.125
1	.375
2	.375
3	.125

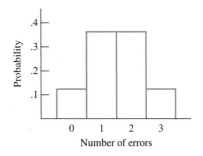

Figure 8.3-2. Histogram for probability distribution in Table 8.3-2.

ilar index of the central tendency of a probability distribution is called the **expected value.**[4] Let's now turn to the subject of how to compute expected values.

Expected Value of a Discrete Random Variable

If an extremely large number of naïve rats were to run the three-choice T maze, how many errors on the average would you expect them to make? Stated more formally, what is the *expected value* of the random variable?

If X is a discrete random variable that assumes values $X_1, X_2, \ldots, X_n$ with probabilities $p(X_1), p(X_2), \ldots, p(X_n)$, then the expected value of X denoted by $E(X)$ is defined as[5]

$$E(X) = p(X_1)X_1 + p(X_2)X_2 + \cdots + p(X_n)X_n$$

$$= \sum_{i=1}^{n} p(X_i)X_i$$

where $p(X_1) + p(X_2) + \cdots + p(X_n) = 1$.

For the T-maze example, $E(X)$ for the values in Table 8.3-2 is

$$E(X) = .125(0) + .375(1) + .375(2) + .125(3) = 1.5$$

where $p(X_1) = .125$, $p(X_2) = .375$, $p(X_3) = .375$, and $p(X_4) = .125$. Based on this computation, you would expect a rat to make on the average 1.5 errors in the maze. Note the similarity between the formula for $E(X)$ and that for the mean of an ungrouped frequency distribution:

$$\overline{X} = \frac{f_1}{n}X_1 + \frac{f_2}{n}X_2 + \cdots + \frac{f_k}{n}X_k$$

---

[4] The terms *expected value* and *expectation* are synonymous.

[5] This definition of $E(X)$ does not commit one to a particular view of probability because the $p(X_i)$'s can be subjective, classical, or empirical.

TABLE 8.3-3   Expected Value of a Bet

Possible Winnings, X_i	$p(X_i)$	$p(X_i)X_i$
+ \$35	$\dfrac{1}{38}$	$\dfrac{1}{38}(\$35) = \$\dfrac{35}{38}$
− \$1	$\dfrac{37}{38}$	$\dfrac{37}{38}(-\$1) = -\$\dfrac{37}{38}$

$$E(X) = \sum_{i=1}^{n} p(X_i)X_i = -\$\dfrac{2}{38} = -.053$$

Here, X is a discrete variable that assumes values $X_1, X_2, \ldots, X_k$ with frequencies $f_1, f_2, \ldots, f_k$, where $f_1 + f_2 + \cdots + f_k = n$. The statistic $\overline{X}$ and the parameter $E(X)$ differ in that $\overline{X}$ is the mean of a sample defined by its frequency distribution; $E(X)$ is the mean of a theoretical population defined by its probability distribution. The latter mean also is denoted by μ (Greek mu, pronounced "mew").

Originally, the expected value concept was used in games of chance to tell a player what the long-run average loss or gain per play would be. Consider the popular casino game of roulette. A player places a bet, the roulette wheel is spun, and the ball is set in motion. The ball can drop into one of 38 slots. Thirty-six slots are numbered from 1 to 36, with half red and half black. Two green slots are numbered 0 and 00. Suppose a player places \$1 on number 7. If the ball drops into the 7 slot, the player receives a \$35 payoff; otherwise the player loses the \$1 bet. I can calculate the player's expected winnings as shown in Table 8.3-3. According to the table, a player who makes \$1 bets indefinitely will lose an average of 5.3¢ per bet. On any given gamble, the player stands to either win \$35 or lose \$1. What the player may choose to ignore is that on the average \$35 is won in only 1 out of 38 gambles, whereas \$1 is lost in 37 out of 38.

The term *expected value* is misleading in one sense because $E(X)$ is often not one of the possible outcomes of an experiment. In the T-maze example, $E(X) = 1.5$, but the possible values of the random variable are 0, 1, 2, or 3 errors. Similarly, the gambler can win \$35 or lose \$1 on any given play, although $E(X) = -5.3$¢. In both examples, $E(X)$ is an average result, and in this respect it is like a sample mean, $\overline{X}$.

Expected Value of a Continuous Random Variable

Computing the expected value of a discrete random variable is fairly simple because you need only multiply random variable values, X_i, by probabilities, $p(X_i)$, and sum the products—that is, $E(X) = \sum_{i=1}^{n} p(X_i)X_i$. The continuous random variable case is more complicated because the variable can assume an infinite number of values. The probability that a continuous random variable X has a particular value is zero.[6]

---

[6] This is not obvious. For the rare student who wants an explanation, see Hays (1994, pp. 107–110).

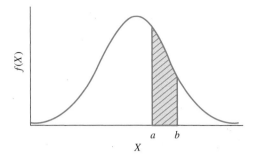

Figure 8.3-3. The probability that X will assume a value between a and b is equal to the area under the curve between those two points. For many random variables, tables are available that simplify the method for determining the area between two points (see Section 9.2).

Consequently, instead of referring to the probability that X has a particular value, I refer to the probability that X lies in an interval between two values of the random variable. This notion is illustrated in Figure 8.3-3. The expected value of a continuous random variable X is the sum of the products formed by multiplying each value that X can assume by the height of the probability distribution curve above that value of X. Because X can assume an infinite number of values, its expected value is not computed by actually physically multiplying each X by the height of the curve at X but instead by means of the integral calculus.[7] As you will discover, tables for most random variables of interest have been prepared; these tables simplify the calculation of the probability that X lies in an interval.

Standard Deviation of a Discrete Random Variable

In Chapter 4 you learned that the standard deviation is a useful measure of dispersion. One formula for computing a sample standard deviation is

$$S = \sqrt{\Sigma f_j (X_j - \overline{X})^2 / n}$$

A similar formula for computing the standard deviation of a discrete probability distribution is

$$\sigma = \sqrt{E\{[X - E(X)]^2\}} = \sqrt{\Sigma p(X_i)[X_i - E(X_i)]^2}$$

Note from the formula on the left that σ is the square root of the expected value of a squared deviation, $[X - E(X)]^2$. I compute this expected value in the same way we did for $E(X)$, where I multiplied each value of X_i by its probability. To compute $E\{[X - E(X)]^2\}$, I multiply each $[X - E(X)]^2$ by its probability $p(X_i)$ and sum the

---

[7] For those familiar with the calculus, the expected value is $E(X) = \int_{X\min}^{X\max} xf(x)dx$, where X_{min} is the smallest value of X and X_{max} is the largest value.

products. The computation of σ is illustrated for the T-maze data in Table 8.3-2; for these data, $E(X) = 1.5$. The standard deviation is

$$\sigma = \sqrt{.125(0-1.5)^2 + .375(1-1.5)^2 + .375(2-1.5)^2 + .125(3-1.5)^2}$$

$$= 0.866$$

The symbol σ is used instead of S because this standard deviation is a population parameter. The value $\sigma = 0.866$ together with $E(X) = 1.5$ provides a useful summary of the theoretical population of errors in the three-choice T maze.

CHECK YOUR UNDERSTANDING OF SECTION 8.3

7. (a) Construct a probability distribution for a four-choice T maze. Assume that the correct series of turns is *right, right, left, right.* (b) Graph the probability distribution.

8. Let the random variable X be the number of cars per household. Suppose that in Waco, Texas, X has the probability distribution listed in the table.

X	0	1	2	3	4	5
$f(X)$	.16	.54	.23	.05	.01	.01

For a household selected at random, compute the following.
a. $p(X \le 2)$ b. $p(X \ge 3)$ c. $p(1 \le X \le 2)$
d. $E(X)$ e. σ

9. What is the maximum you should be willing to pay to enter a game in which you can win $30 with probability .6 and $10 with probability .4? (*Hint:* Compute $E(X)$.)

10. The random variable X has the probability distribution listed in the table.

X	0	1	2	3	4
$f(X)$	0	$\frac{2}{5}$	$\frac{1}{5}$	$\frac{1}{5}$	$\frac{1}{5}$

a. Compute $E(X)$.   b. Compute σ.

11. Suppose that a fraternal organization plans to sell 1,000 lottery tickets for $1 each. The prize is a $750 DVD recorder. (a) If you purchase a ticket, what is the probability that you will win? (b) What is your expected gain? Remember to subtract the cost of the ticket from the value of the prize. (c) Does it make economic sense to purchase a ticket? (d) What is the maximum that you should be willing to pay for a ticket? (*Hint:* The maximum you should be willing to pay for a ticket is that amount for which $E(X) = 0$,—that is, the amount for which

there is no gain or loss over the long run. This amount, denoted by T, can be determined from

$$p(\text{win})(\text{gain value}) + p(\text{lose})(\text{loss value}) = 0$$

where the gain value is equal to $[750 + (-T)]$ and the loss value is equal to $-T$.)

12. Terms to remember:
    a. Discrete random variable
    b. Continuous random variable
    c. Probability distribution
    d. Expected value

8.4 BINOMIAL DISTRIBUTION

Bernoulli Trial

Many experiments have only two possible outcomes: a new drug is effective or it is not, an animal takes the correct turn or the wrong turn in a maze, a job is given to an applicant or it is not. These experiments have much in common with tossing a coin. In each case, the random variable is discrete and can assume only two values, often denoted "success" and "failure." Flipping a coin once and noting whether it landed heads or tails or randomly sampling one person from a population of former students and noting whether he or she graduated is called a **Bernoulli trial** or **Bernoulli experiment.**[8] The probability of observing a success on any given trial is denoted by p and the probability of a failure, by q. Because the two outcomes, success and failure, are mutually exclusive and exhaustive, $p + q = 1$. The characteristics of a Bernoulli trial can be summarized as follows:

1. A trial can result in one of two outcomes.
2. The probability of a success remains constant from trial to trial.
3. The outcomes of successive trials are independent.

Few real-life situations perfectly satisfy the requirements. Strictly speaking, the last two are satisfied only when sampling is done with replacement or from an infinite population. In most research, sampling is done without replacement from a finite population. This practical departure from the ideal is of little consequence as long as the population is large relative to the sample size.

I am usually interested in the outcome of several Bernoulli trials. I toss a coin n times and note the number of heads, or I randomly sample n persons and note the number of graduates. When there are n Bernoulli trials, the random variable of interest is the number of successes; its value can range from 0 to n.

The following section describes a binomial distribution in which the random variable is a sum—the number of successes observed on n greater than or equal to two Bernoulli trials. A binomial distribution is a relatively simple example of an important class of theoretical distributions or models that are referred to as sampling distributions.

---

[8] Both terms were named after James Bernoulli (1654–1705), who discussed such trials in his *Ars Conjectandi* (1713).

> The term **sampling distribution** is the special name given to a probability distribution where the random variable is a statistic based on the results of more than one trial.

For convenience, I will examine a simple binomial distribution here and defer discussion of the special properties of sampling distributions to Chapter 9.

The binomial distribution will be encountered repeatedly in subsequent chapters. It is the theoretical model for a variety of statistics, as you will see in Sections 12.3, 14.4, 14.5, 17.3, 17.4, and 17.5.

Binomial Distribution

> The number of successes observed on $n \geq 2$ identical Bernoulli trials is called a **binomial random variable,** and its probability distribution is called a **binomial distribution.**[9] Suppose you toss a fair coin five times. The probability of observing exactly r heads (successes) in n tosses is given by the function rule
>
> $$p(X = r) = {}_nC_r \, p^r q^{n-r}$$
>
> where $p(X = r)$ is the probability that the random variable X equals r heads, ${}_nC_r$ is the combination of n objects taken r at a time,[10] p is the probability of success (a head), and $q = 1 - p$.

For example, the probability that the random variable X equals four heads is

$$p(X = 4) = {}_5C_4 \left(\frac{1}{2}\right)^4 \left(\frac{1}{2}\right)^{5-4} = \frac{5!}{4!(5-4)!}\left(\frac{1}{2}\right)^4\left(\frac{1}{2}\right)^1 = \frac{5}{32}$$

The complete probability distribution is given in Table 8.4-1 and a graph of the distribution, in Figure 8.4-1. The probability that X equals or exceeds some value or that it lies in a given interval can be obtained by combining probabilities from the table or figure. For example, the probability of obtaining four or more heads in five tosses of a fair coin is

$$p(X \geq 4) = p(X = 4) + p(X = 5) = \frac{5}{32} + \frac{1}{32} = \frac{6}{32}$$

---

[9] The term was so named because the probabilities associated with the distribution can be obtained by raising a binomial (an algebraic expression containing two terms) to the nth power. For example,

$$(p + q)^n = p^n + np^{n-1}q + \frac{n(n-1)}{2(1)}p^{n-2}q^2 + \cdots + q^n$$

where p is the probability of success, $q = 1 - p$, and n is the number of Bernoulli trials. The first term, p^n, gives the probability of n successes; the second term, $np^{n-1}q$, the probability of $n - 1$ successes, and so on.

[10] The combination of n objects taken r at a time is discussed in Section 7.4.

TABLE 8.4-1 Binomial Distribution for $n = 5$ and $p = \frac{1}{2}$

Number of Heads, r	0	1	2	3	4	5
$(X = r)$	$\dfrac{1}{32}$	$\dfrac{5}{32}$	$\dfrac{10}{32}$	$\dfrac{10}{32}$	$\dfrac{5}{32}$	$\dfrac{1}{32}$

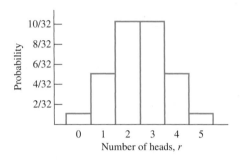

Figure 8.4-1. Histogram for the binomial distribution in Table 8.4-1.

The sampling (probability) distribution of a binomial random variable is completely specified by n, the number of trials, and the parameter p, the probability of success. When p is less than .5, a graph of the probability distribution is positively skewed; for p equal to .5, it is symmetrical, and for p greater than .5, it is negatively skewed. As n increases, the shape of the distribution approaches more and more closely that of the normal bell-shaped distribution. The binomial distribution is actually a family of distributions, one for each set of p and n values. The thread that binds the distributions into a family is their common function rule, $p(X = r) = {}_nC_r\, p^r\, q^{n-r}$.[11] The following example illustrates another member of the binomial family.

Suppose that I am interested in the probability that more than half of a random sample of six patients will show improvement following treatment. Let the probability of improvement, p, for any patient equal .7. The probability of observing exactly $r = 6$ successes in $n = 6$ patients is given by

$$p(X = r) = {}_nC_r p^r q^{n-r} = {}_6C_6(.7)^6(.3)^0 = \frac{6!}{6!(6-6)!}(.7)^6(.3)^0 = .118$$

---

[11] Other examples of families of discrete probability distributions are the uniform distribution, multinomial distribution, hypergeometric distribution, Poisson distribution, and negative binomial distribution. The first three distributions are briefly discussed in this text.

TABLE 8.4-2 **Distribution Showing Probability of Improvement Following Treatment**

Number Improved, r	0	1	2	3	4	5	6
$p(X = r)$	.001	.008	.059	.185	.324	.302	.118

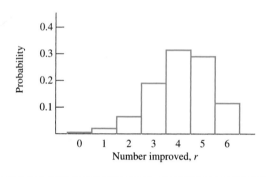

Figure 8.4-2. Histogram for the probability that patients will show improvement following treatment.

The complete probability distribution is given in Table 8.4-2 and graphed in Figure 8.4-2.

The probability that in a random sample of six patients more than half will show improvement is given by

$$p(X \geq 4) = p(X = 4) + p(X = 5) + p(X = 6) = .324 + .302 + .118 = .744$$

Expected Value and Standard Deviation of Binomial Distribution

The expected value of a discrete random variable always can be computed from $E(X) = \sum_{i=1}^{n} p(X_i) X_i$. For a binomial random variable, there is a simpler formula for computing the expected value of X (number of successes):

$$E(X) = np$$

where n is the number of trials and p is the probability of a success on any trial. For the probability distribution in Table 8.4-2, the expected number of patients showing improvement is $E(X) = 6(.7) = 4.2$. The same result is obtained using the longer formula $E(X) = \sum_{i=0}^{6} p(X_i)X_i = .001(0) + .008(1) + \cdots + .118(6) = 4.2$.

The standard deviation of a binomial distribution is given by $\sigma = \sqrt{npq}$. For the probability distribution in Table 8.4-2, the standard deviation is

$$\sigma = \sqrt{6(.7)(.3)} = 1.12$$

As you have seen, the binomial distribution is the appropriate model for a random variable when (1) there are n trials involving a population whose elements belong to one of two classes, (2) the probability of obtaining an element in a class remains constant from trial to trial, as when sampling with replacement or from an infinite population, and (3) the outcomes of successive trials are independent. When one or more of these conditions are not satisfied, two other models may be appropriate. These models, which are used in advanced statistical procedures, are the multinomial and the hypergeometric distributions. The **multinomial distribution**[12] represents an extension of the binomial distribution for the case in which a trial can result in an outcome from one of $k \geq 2$ classes and the probabilities associated with the classes remain constant as in sampling with replacement or sampling from an infinite population. The **hypergeometric distribution** applies to the case in which a trial also results in an outcome from one of $k \geq 2$ classes but the probabilities associated with the classes do not remain constant as in sampling without replacement from a finite population. Much research in the behavioral and medical sciences and education fits the latter set of conditions. Another model that describes the distribution of many random variables of interest to psychologists is the normal distribution. This important distribution is described in the next chapter.

CHECK YOUR UNDERSTANDING OF SECTION 8.4

13. Interpret the statement $p(X = 3) = .2$.
14. What are the three characteristics of a Bernoulli trial?
15. Let the random variable X be the number of men in a random sample of size 2 taken from a population that contains 60% men and 40% women. (a) Determine the probability of the sample's containing 0, 1, or 2 men. (b) Graph the probability distribution. (c) Compute $E(X)$ and σ.
16. Thirty percent of elementary students in a school system have a reading ability below the national standard for their grade level. (a) If 10 children are selected at random, what is the probability that no more than 1 will be functioning below grade level? (b) Compute $E(X)$ and σ.

---

[12] So named because the probabilities associated with the distribution can be obtained by raising a multinomial (an algebraic expression containing three or more terms) to the nth power.

17. Of 800 families with five children each, how many would you expect to have (a) three girls? (b) Five boys? (c) Either two or three girls? Assume equal probabilities for girls and boys.

18. Terms to remember:
    a. Bernoulli trial
    b. Binomial random variable
    c. Multinomial experiment
    d. Hypergeometric experiment

8.5 LOOKING BACK: WHAT HAVE YOU LEARNED?

Some kind of random procedure should be a part of all research in which samples are used to learn about populations. Most often the procedure takes the form of random sampling from a population or random assignment of participants to experimental conditions. Randomness is a property of a procedure rather than of a sample. Any procedure for drawing samples from a population so that every possible sample of a particular size has the same probability of being selected is called random sampling, and the resulting sample is called a random sample.

A random variable is a numerical quantity whose values are determined by the outcomes of a random experiment. A table showing the possible values of a random variable and the associated probabilities is called a probability distribution. Probability distributions and the frequency distributions discussed in Chapter 2 are similar—each associates a number with the possible values of a variable. However, for a frequency distribution, the number is a frequency; for a probability distribution, it is a probability. This reflects a fundamental difference between them. A frequency distribution describes a set of data that has been observed; it is empirical. A probability distribution describes data that might be observed under certain well-specified conditions; hence, it is hypothetical or theoretical. Probability distributions are used in inferential statistics as models of how random variables are expected to be distributed. If empirical data deviate appreciably from the predictions of a model, doubt is cast on the correctness of the model or its assumptions. For example, if you toss five coins and if the coins are fair, according to the binomial model you should observe five heads on the average once in every 32 trials. If instead of observing five heads once, you observe five heads in 10 of 32 tosses, you would probably question the assumption that the coin is fair.

The central tendency of a theoretical population defined by its probability distribution can be described in the same way as the central tendency of a sample—by a mean. The mean of a theoretical population is called an expected value and is given by $E(X) = \sum_{i=1}^{n} p(X_i) X_i$.

An experiment is called a Bernoulli trial if (1) its random variable has only two possible outcomes, denoted "success" and "failure," (2) the probability of a success remains constant from trial to trial, and (3) the outcomes of successive trials are independent. The probability distribution of a Bernoulli random variable could hardly be simpler because it represents the possible outcomes of a single trial. The number of successes in a series of n identical Bernoulli trials is a discrete random variable that can assume integer values from zero to n. The distribution of the number of successes in n identical Bernoulli trials is called a binomial distribution. The binomial distribution is one of the more useful models of how a discrete random variable should behave. Two other useful models, the multinomial distribution and the hypergeometric distribution, can be thought of as special extensions of the binomial distribution. The multinomial distribution applies to experiments in which a trial results in an outcome from one of $k \geq 2$ classes and sampling is done with replacement or from an infinite population. The hypergeometric distribution applies to experiments in which a trial also results in an outcome from one of $k \geq 2$ classes but sampling is done without replacement from a finite population. The latter conditions more closely approximate research in the behavioral and medical sciences and education.

REVIEW EXERCISES FOR CHAPTER 8

1. What advantages do random samples have over nonrandom samples?
2. (a) How many different samples of size 4 can be drawn without replacement from a population of size 30? (b) How many different samples of size 4 can be drawn with replacement from a population of size 30?
3. The probability of drawing a particular sample from a finite population is given by $1/(_nC_r)$. What is the probability of drawing a particular sample of size $r = 3$ from a population of size $n = 50$?
4. A sample of 5 students is to be selected from a class of 10. (a) How many different random samples without replacement can be drawn? (b) What is the probability that a given sample will be selected? (c) How many different random samples with replacement can be drawn?
5. (a) Use the table of random numbers in Appendix D to draw two random samples of 10 students from the following population. For one sample, use sampling with replacement; for the other, use sampling without replacement. (b) Describe in detail how you used the table.

Don	Sonja	Jimmy	Dick	Bob	Gary
Herb	Wallace	Martha	Clyde	Sylvia	Ruben
Henry	Bill	Mike	Chuck	Richard	Milton

6. Use the table of random numbers in Appendix D to draw a random sample without replacement of 30 students from the Student Database in Appendix E. (a) List the ID No., Stat Grade, and GPA for each person in your sample. Compute the mean of the variables labeled Stat Grade and GPA. (b) Compute the correlation between Stat Grade and GPA. (c) Develop a regression equation to predict Stat Grade from a knowledge of GPA. (d) If you have access to a computer and suitable software, develop a multiple regression equation for predicting Stat Grade from GPA and Math Test. How much does the addition of Math Test improve the prediction of Stat Grade?
7. Distinguish between a variable and a random variable.

8. Let the random variable X be the number of children in a family. Suppose that X has the probability distribution listed in the table.

X	0	1	2	3	4	5	6	7
$f(X)$	.40	.18	.15	.11	.09	.05	.01	.01

For a family selected at random, compute the following.
a. $p(X = 0)$ b. $p(X \geq 4)$ c. $p(X < 3)$
d. $p(2 \leq X \leq 5)$ e. $E(X)$ f. σ

9. How does an expected value differ from the mean of a frequency distribution?
10. What is the maximum you should be willing to pay to enter a game in which you can win $20 with probability .7 and $10 with probability .5? (*Hint:* Compute $E(X)$.)
11. If it rains, a fortuneteller loses $12 per day; if it is fair, she earns $110 per day. Assume that the probability of rain is .3. What are her expected earnings per day?
12. The random variable X has the probability distribution listed in the table.

X	0	1	2	3	4
$f(X)$	$\dfrac{1}{6}$	$\dfrac{2}{6}$	$\dfrac{1}{6}$	$\dfrac{1}{6}$	$\dfrac{1}{6}$

a. Compute $E(X)$.   b. Compute σ.

13. Suppose that the Lions Club plans to sell 2,000 lottery tickets for $5 each. The prize is a $4,000 trip for two to Cancun. (a) If you purchase a ticket, what is the probability that you will win? (b) What is your expected gain? Remember to subtract the cost of the ticket from the value of the prize. (c) Does it make economic sense to purchase a ticket? (d) What is the maximum that you should be willing to pay for a ticket? (*Hint:* The maximum you should be willing to pay for a ticket is that amount for which $E(X) = 0$—that is, the amount for which there is no gain or loss over the long run. This amount, denoted by T, can be determined from

$$p(\text{win})(\text{gain value}) + p(\text{lose})(\text{loss value}) = 0,$$

where the gain value is equal to $[4,000 + (-T)]$ and the loss value is equal to $-T$.)
14. Interpret the statement $p(X = 5) = .4$.
15. Compare a Bernoulli random variable with a binomial random variable.
16. Suppose that 20% of eligible voters in a given city voted in the last election. A random sample of 10 eligible voters is obtained to investigate reasons for the poor turnout. (a) If X is the number of people who did not vote, determine the probability distribution for X. (b) Compute $E(X)$ and σ.

17. Ten percent of patients fail to improve after being placed on medication. (a) If five patients are selected at random, what is the probability that two or more will not show improvement? (b) Compute $E(X)$ and σ.

18. What is the probability of guessing correctly at least 6 of 10 answers on a true-false examination?

9

Normal Distribution and Sampling Distributions

9.1 Introduction
Looking Ahead: What Is
This Chapter About?

9.2 The Normal Distribution
Characteristics of the
Normal Distribution
Converting Scores to
Standard Scores
Finding Areas under the
Normal Distribution
Finding Scores When the
Area Is Known
Normal Approximation
to the Binomial
Distribution
Check Your Understanding
of Section 9.2

**9.3 Interpreting Scores in
Terms of z Scores and
Percentile Ranks**
Standard Score
Percentile Rank
Relative Advantages of z
Scores and Percentile
Ranks
Other Kinds of Standard
Scores
Comparing Performance
on Different Tests
Check Your Understanding
of Section 9.3

9.4 Sampling Distributions
Looking Ahead to
Inferential Statistics
Sampling Distributions
Sampling Distribution of
the Mean
Central Limit Theorem
Standard Error of a
Statistic
Two Properties of Good
Estimators
Test Statistics
Check Your Understanding
of Section 9.4

**9.5 Looking Back: What
Have You Learned?**
Review Exercises for
Chapter 9

9.6 Supplementary Notes*
Explanation of Why the
Mean of a Distribution
of z Scores Is Zero and
the Standard Deviation
Is One
Demonstration Showing
That $\hat{\sigma}^2$ and $\hat{\sigma}^2_{est}$ Are
Unbiased Estimators
but S^2 Is a Biased
Estimator

9.1 INTRODUCTION

Looking Ahead: What Is This Chapter About?

In previous chapters, you learned about a number of different kinds of distributions. Some distributions, such as the sample distribution, describe data that have been observed. Other distributions, such as probability and sampling distributions, describe data that might be observed if an experiment is performed. They are hypothetical or theoretical in the sense that they do not represent the outcome of an actual experiment. These distributions are used in inferential statistics as models of the results that a researcher should expect if certain assumptions are tenable. For example, in the previous chapter the binomial distribution was used to describe the possible outcomes of tossing a coin five times under the assumption that the coin is fair. In this chapter, you will see how another important model, the normal distribution, is used to describe the possible outcomes of an experiment. In addition, several important new statistics are described: standard score, standard error, and test statistic.

After reading this chapter, you should know the following:

- How to convert scores to standard scores (z scores)
- How to use standard scores to find the size of areas under the normal distribution
- Three characteristics of the sampling distribution of the mean
- Two properties of good estimators
- The difference between sample statistics and test statistics

9.2 THE NORMAL DISTRIBUTION

Thus far you have seen numerous references to the normal distribution—and with good reason. The normal distribution is the most important probability distribution in statistics. One reason for the importance of the normal distribution is that many variables in science and nature have probability distributions that closely resemble it. Hence, it can serve as a model for such distributions. For example, people's heights and weights are approximately normally distributed, as are intelligence, mechanical aptitude, introversion, and most other psychological attributes. The normal distribution also is important because it is a convenient model for estimating probabilities for other theoretical distributions. You will see that it provides an excellent approximation to the binomial distribution when the number of trials is large.

Granted, the normal distribution is a useful model, but this hardly accounts for its preeminent position in statistical theory. To understand why it occupies this position, we must consider the distribution of a sample statistic such as the mean. Suppose that from a population you drew 100 random samples of size n (where n is fairly large), computed the mean of each sample, and constructed a histogram of the sample means. You would find that the resulting graph closely resembles the normal distribution. This might not surprise you if the sampled population was normally distributed, but the striking aspect is that if n is sufficiently large, the resemblance

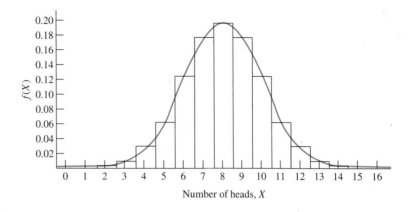

Figure 9.2-1. Comparison of the histogram for the probability distribution for tossing 16 fair coins and the normal curve.

holds regardless of the population's shape. The tendency for the distribution of a sample statistic to approximate a normal distribution as n (the number of observations in each random sample) increases plays a key role in inferential statistics. You will learn more about this tendency when I describe the central limit theorem in Section 9.4.

Serendipity—accidentally making discoveries—has produced many breakthroughs in science, and one of them is the normal distribution. Abraham de Moivre (1667–1754), a mathematics tutor, was searching for a shortcut method for computing probabilities for binomial random variables. In the process he derived the function rule for the ubiquitous normal distribution. If I toss 10 coins, it doesn't take too much effort to compute the probability of observing zero heads, one head, and so on. But suppose I toss 100 coins. The amount of work necessary to calculate the probabilities associated with 0 through 100 heads is significant. You will see, as de Moivre discovered over 270 years ago, that the task is greatly simplified by using the normal distribution.

Consider the graph of the probability distribution for tossing 16 fair coins in Figure 9.2-1. If I superimpose the graph of a normal distribution on the histogram, it provides a fairly good fit. The fit would be even better if I had graphed the distribution for tossing 50 coins. If the number of coins were increased indefinitely, the number of bars in the histogram would increase, and their outline would eventually coincide with that of the normal distribution. De Moivre derived the function rule for determining the height of the normal distribution, denoted by $f(X)$, for any value of the random variable X.

Characteristics of the Normal Distribution

A random variable X is said to be normally distributed if its probability distribution is given by the function rule for the normal distribution.

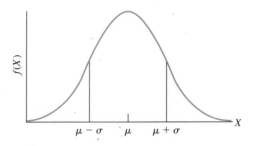

Figure 9.2-2. Graph of the normal distribution. The inflection points where the curve changes from being concave to convex and vice versa occur at $\mu - \sigma$ and $\mu + \sigma$.

The function rule for the **normal distribution** is

$$f(X) = \frac{1}{\sigma\sqrt{2\pi}} e^{-(X-\mu)^2/(2\sigma^2)}$$

where $f(X)$ is the height of the distribution at X, π is approximately 3.142, e (the base of the system of natural logarithms) is approximately 2.718, and μ and σ identify the mean and standard deviation of a particular normal distribution in the family of normal distributions.

Fortunately, you don't have to use the rule to determine the size of areas under the distribution between various values of X. As you will see, the size of areas can be determined from Appendix Table D.2.

The normal distribution is shaped like a bell. Because it is unimodal and symmetrical, its mean, median, and mode have the same value, and that value corresponds to the highest point on the curve. The mean plus or minus the standard deviation, as shown in Figure 9.2-2, defines the *inflection points* of the curve—that is, the points at which the curve changes from being concave to convex or vice versa. Although not shown in the figure, the tails of the curve extend indefinitely in both directions, never quite touching the horizontal axis. The total area under the curve is equal to 1.

Converting Scores to Standard Scores

There are as many normal distributions as there are possible values of μ and σ, the parameters that identify a particular distribution. To avoid having to develop an infinite number of tables, statisticians have made one particular normal distribution the standard. It has a mean equal to 0 and a standard deviation equal to 1 ($\mu = 0$ and $\sigma = 1$) and is called the **standard normal distribution.** This is the distribution whose areas are tabulated in Appendix Table D.2. Random variable values for this distribution are called **standard scores** and are denoted by z.

If as is usually the case the random variable you are interested in doesn't have a mean of 0 and standard deviation of 1, the random variable must be transformed into a standard score to use the standard normal distribution table in Appendix D.2. The transformation is accomplished by the formula

$$z = \frac{X - \overline{X}}{S}$$

where X is a random variable value, $\overline{X}$ is the sample mean, and S is the sample standard deviation.

If you apply this z-score transformation to each X in a distribution, will the resulting distribution of standard scores have a mean of 0, $\overline{z} = 0$, and a standard deviation of 1, $S_z = 1$? The answer is yes. The reason is given in Supplementary Note 9.6.

The transformation of X scores into z scores is simple. Suppose that the mean of a random variable you are interested in is 100 and its standard deviation is 15. The z score corresponding to an X score of 130 is $z = (X - \overline{X})/S = (130 - 100)/15 = 2$. A z score transformation alters the mean and standard deviation of the transformed random variable but not the relative location of scores in the distribution. For example, the X score of 130 is two standard deviations above the mean of 100 because $\overline{X} + 2(S) = 100 + 2(15) = 130$. Similarly, the corresponding z score of 2 is also two standard deviations above its mean of zero because $\overline{z} + 2(S_z) = 0 + 2(1) = 2$, where $\overline{z}$ denotes the mean of the z scores and S_z denotes the standard deviation of the z scores. If you were to graph the distribution of the X scores and the distribution of the z scores, you would find that they are identical in shape although they differ in central tendency and dispersion. Transforming scores to standard scores does not change the shape of the distribution or the relative position of scores, only the mean and the standard deviation. As Section 9.3 will show, standard scores are particularly useful for comparing the performance of individuals on psychological tests having different means or standard deviations.

For distributions that are approximately normal, most z scores are between -3 and $+3$. This follows from a fact you learned in Chapter 4, namely that 99.73% of the area under the normal distribution lies within ± 3 standard deviations of the mean.

Finding Areas under the Normal Distribution

If a random variable is approximately normally distributed, the standard normal distribution in Appendix Table D.2 can be used to find the proportion of the total area falling between any two scores. The areas tabulated in Appendix Table D.2 are shown in Figures 9.2-3(a) and (b).

1. *Area between μ and a score above it [area A in Figure 9.2-3(a)].* Suppose that the distribution of college students' IQs is approximately normal with $\mu = 115$ and $\sigma = 15$ and you want to know the proportion of students with IQs between $\mu = 115$ and $X = 130$. The first step is to convert $X = 130$ into a standard score: $z = (X - \mu)/\sigma = (130 - 115)/15 = 1$. According to Appendix Table D.2, the proportion of the area from μ to $z = 1$ is .3413; thus, approximately 34%

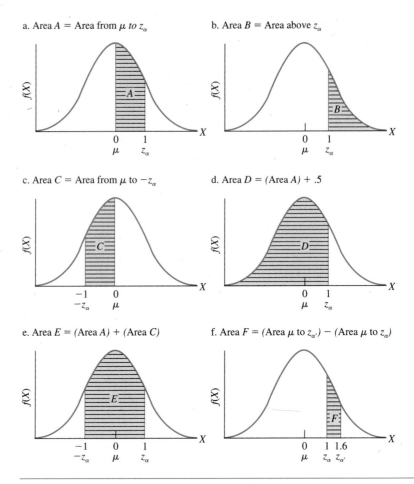

a. Area A = Area from μ to z_α

b. Area B = Area above z_α

c. Area C = Area from μ to $-z_\alpha$

d. Area D = (Area A) + .5

e. Area E = (Area A) + (Area C)

f. Area F = (Area μ to $z_{\alpha'}$) − (Area μ to z_α)

Figure 9.2-3. Illustration of the areas of the standard normal distribution. Areas A and B are given in Appendix Table D.2. A standard score is denoted by z_α, where α indicates the proportion of the standard normal distribution that falls above the score. In considering area D, recall that the mean divides the total area in half, so that .5 falls above the mean and .5 falls below the mean.

of students have IQs between μ = 115 and X = 130. This area is shown as area A in Figure 9.2-3(a).

2. *Smaller area in the tail [area B in Figure 9.2-3(b)].* The proportion of students with IQs above 130, which corresponds to a standard score of 1, is shown as area B in Figure 9.2-3 (b). This area is equal to .1587.

Standard scores are sometimes denoted by z and a subscript α that indicates the proportion of the normal distribution that lies to the right of (above) the z score. The symbol z_α denotes the standard score above which α proportion of the normal distribution falls. For example, the standard score of 1 is denoted by $z_{.1587}$ because .1587 of the area falls to the right of $z = 1$.

3. *Area between μ and a score below it [area C in Figure 9.2-3(c)].* To determine the proportion of the total area from μ to a score below the mean, say, a score of 100 using $\mu = 115$ and $\sigma = 15$ from example 1, you first convert the score to a z score: $z = (100 - 115)/15 = -1$. Appendix table D.2 gives areas only for positive z scores, but because the distribution is symmetrical, the size of the area from μ to $z = -1$ is the same as that from μ to $z = +1$. Thus, area C is obtained by ignoring the negative sign and looking up the z score in area A. The area from μ to $z = -1$ is .3413, and is it shown as area C in Figure 9.2-3(c).

4. *Larger area including the left half of the distribution [area D in Figure 9.2-3(d)].* To find area D for a score of, say, 130 (z score equals 1), you find area A and add .5 (the area below μ) to it. For example, area $D = .3413 + .5 = .8413$. A student with an IQ of 130 has a score above approximately 84% of college students.

5. *Area between scores on opposite sides of the mean [area E in Figure 9.2-3(e)].* To find the proportion of the total area between two scores on opposite sides of the mean, add areas A and C. For example, if the scores are 130 and 100, the z scores are 1 and -1. The sum of areas A and C is $.3413 + .3413 = .6826$.

6. *Area between scores on the same side of the mean [area F in Figure 9.2-3(f)].* Suppose that you want to determine the proportion of the total area between scores of 130 and 139. You first transform the scores to z scores: $(130 - 115)/15 = 1$ and $(139 - 115)/15 = 1.6$. Area A for $z = 1$ is .3413 and area A for $z = 1.6$ is .4452. Area F is the difference between these two areas and is given by (area μ to $z = 1.6$) $-$ (area μ to $z = 1$) $= .4452 - .3413 = .1039$.

Finding Scores When the Area Is Known

A different kind of problem arises when you have a percentile rank in mind or know the relative size of the area above or below a point in a distribution and you want to determine the untransformed score corresponding to that rank or point. If you know the size of the area, you can determine from Appendix Table D.2 the z score that marks the boundary of the area. In the previous examples, you knew X, μ, and σ and solved for z using the formula $z = (X - \mu)/\sigma$. If you know z, μ, and σ, it is a simple matter to solve for X. A little algebra is all that is needed to express the formula in the desired form:

$$z = \frac{X - \mu}{\sigma}$$

$$\sigma z = X - \mu$$

$$X = \mu + \sigma z$$

Suppose that you want to know the IQ score corresponding to the 80th percentile rank. You know that .80 of the area under the normal curve falls below the z score and that .20 of the area falls above the z score. To find the z score, you look in column 3 of Appendix Table D.2 until you locate .20. The corresponding z score is approximately 0.84. Knowing that $z_{.20} = 0.84$, $\mu = 115$ and $\sigma = 15$, you have all the information necessary to solve for X in the formula $X = \mu + \sigma z$. Substituting in the formula, you obtain $X = 115 + 15(0.84) = 127.6$. Thus, a score of 127.6 corresponds to the 80th percentile rank.

To take one more example, suppose that you want to know the IQ score corresponding to the 40th percentile rank. You know that the score is below the mean and that .40 of the area lies to the left of (below) the score and .60 lies above. To find the z score corresponding to the area below .40, you look in column 3 of Appendix Table D.2 until you locate .40 and find that $-z_{.60} \cong -0.25$. Remember that the sign of z scores below the mean is negative and that the subscript, .60, denotes the area above the z. Substituting in the formula $X = \mu + \sigma z$ gives $X = 115 + 15(-0.25) = 111.25$, the IQ score corresponding to the 40th percentile rank.

Normal Approximation to the Binomial Distribution

The normal distribution function rule was originally derived by de Moivre to estimate binomial distribution probabilities when the number of trials, n, is large. As you will see, the approximation is excellent even when n is small.

Consider an experiment in which a fair coin is tossed five times. The random variable of interest is the number of heads. A graph of the distribution for $n = 5$ and $p = .5$ is given in Figure 9.2-4. A normal distribution has been superimposed on the graph. The probability of observing four or more heads can be computed from the binomial distribution in Chapter 8, Table 8.4-1: $p(X \geq 4) = \frac{5}{32} + \frac{1}{32} = \frac{6}{32} = .1875$.

The probability of observing four or more heads can be estimated using the normal distribution table by finding the area including and to the right of four heads. Because you are using the continuous normal distribution to estimate a discrete random variable, you must think of four heads as occupying the interval from 3.5 to 4.5; the lower limit of the interval is 3.5 (see Figure 9.2-4). To find the area above the lower limit of four heads, you first convert the lower limit of four heads, 3.5, to a z score. Recall from Section 8.3 that the mean and standard deviation of a binomial distribution are given by, respectively, $E(X) = np$ and $\sigma = \sqrt{npq}$. For the example,

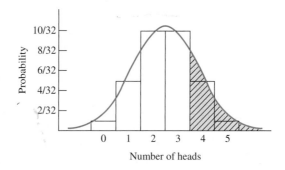

Figure 9.2-4. Histogram for binomial distribution with $n = 5$ and $p = .5$. A normal distribution is superimposed over the histogram. The normal distribution area corresponding to the probability of observing four or more heads is represented by the shaded area.

$E(X) = 5(.5) = 2.5$ and $\sigma = \sqrt{5(.5)(.5)} = 1.118$. The z score corresponding to observing four or more heads is

$$z = \frac{X - E(X)}{\sigma} = \frac{3.5 - 2.5}{1.118} = 0.894$$

According to Appendix Table D.2, the area above $z = 0.894$ is .1857, which is close to the exact value of .1875 computed from the binomial distribution. So you see that although the normal distribution approximation was not intended to be used for such a small n, it yielded a value quite close to the exact probability.

CHECK YOUR UNDERSTANDING OF SECTION 9.2

1. How does a standard normal distribution differ from other normal distributions?
2. Which of the following variables do you think approximate the normal distribution? For those that you do not think are normal, sketch the form of the distribution you would expect. (a) Amount of coffee per cup dispensed by a vending machine. (b) Extraversion scores of college students. (c) Incomes of families in the United States. (d) Time spent looking at a painting in a museum. (e) Ages of residents in Normal, Ohio. (f) The time at which students arrive for an 11 o'clock class.
3. A set of scores has a mean of 20 and a standard deviation of 5. Transform the following to z scores.
   a. 30   b. 12   c. 15   d. 27   e. 20
4. If z is a normally distributed random variable with $\mu = 0$ and $\sigma = 1$, determine the percentage of the area under the standard normal curve for the following.
   a. Above $z = 1.5$ b. Below $z = -2$
   c. From μ to $z = 3$ d. Between $z = 1$ and $z = 2$
   e. Between $z = 1$ and $z = -3$ f. Between $z = -1$ and $z = -3$
5. Determine the percentage of the area of the standard normal distribution that falls between $\mu - k\sigma$ and $\mu + k\sigma$, where k is equal to the following.
   a. 1.0   b. 1.645   c. 1.96   d. 2.58   e. 3.30
6. Compute the untransformed score corresponding to each of the following z scores. Assume that the original distribution had a mean of 150 and a standard deviation of 20.
   a. 2.0   b. -1.5 c. 3.1   d. 0   e. 0.5
7. Find the z score such that at least the following proportion of the area under the standard normal distribution falls above it.
   a. .50   b. .05   c. .40   d. .70   e. .95
8. Junior college grade-point averages (GPAs) have $\mu = 2.8$ and $\sigma = 0.24$. A university is considering raising its minimum entrance score from 2.2 to 2.5. If GPA is normally distributed, how will the proposed change affect the percentage of students eligible to enter the university from junior colleges?
9. Use the normal approximation to the binomial distribution to determine the probability of guessing correctly (a) at least 12 of 20 answers on a true-false examination and (b) at least 24 of 40 answers.

10. Suppose that 10% of physicians' diagnoses at a clinic are incorrect. Use the normal approximation to the binomial distribution to determine the probability that of 400 diagnoses (a) at most 30 will be incorrect, (b) between 30 and 50 will be incorrect, (c) more than 50 will be incorrect.
11. Terms to remember:
    a. Standard normal curve   b. Standard score (z)

9.3 INTERPRETING SCORES IN TERMS OF *Z* SCORES AND PERCENTILE RANKS

Your roommate announces that she got a 62 on the midterm. Not knowing whether to rejoice with her or to sympathize, you ask, "What was the class average?" "Forty-one," she replies. You press further: "What was the range?" The lowest score was 22 and the highest was 62. A celebration is in order.

This example illustrates a problem in interpreting scores. A score by itself is uninterpretable; you need a frame of reference to know whether a score is good or bad. The frame of reference in the example was provided by the central tendency of the distribution and its range. The score became interpretable when it was related to the performance of other students.

Standard Score

It would be convenient to have one number that provides all the information necessary to interpret a score instead of having to relate it to the mean and a dispersion measure such as the range or the standard deviation. I have already discussed two such numbers that can be used to interpret a score: standard score and percentile.

A **standard score** is a number that expresses the value of a score relative to the mean and the standard deviation of its distribution.

Suppose that a distribution has a $\overline{X} = 50$ and $S = 10$. A score of 70 corresponds to a z score of

$$z = \frac{X - \overline{X}}{S} = \frac{70 - 50}{10} = \frac{20}{10} = 2$$

which is two standard deviations above the mean. A standard score tells us the location of a score in standard deviation units relative to the mean. Furthermore, if the distribution of X is normally distributed, Appendix Table D.2 tells us that $0.4772 + 0.5000 = 0.9772$ of the scores fall below $X = 70$.

Percentile Rank

The second kind of number that can be used to interpret a score is percentile rank, which is discussed in Chapter 4.

The **percentile rank** of a score indicates the percentage of the scores of the distribution that falls below that score. For example, if a score has a percentile rank of 80, you know that 80% of scores fall below it and 20% fall above.

The range of the transformed scale is from the 0th percentile rank to the 100th percentile rank. The median is the 50th percentile rank. Transforming a score to a percentile rank locates the score on a scale from 0 to 100 and indicates the percentage of scores below. Thus, as in the case of a standard score, a single number, the percentile rank, is sufficient for interpreting a score.

Because percentile ranks are familiar to most people, they are used widely in presenting psychological test scores. Standard scores, on the other hand, are less familiar but, as you will see, possess a number of advantages over percentiles.

Relative Advantages of *z* Scores and Percentile Ranks

Consider the distribution of IQ scores in Figure 9.3-1 (a); it is slightly negatively skewed. A graph of the percentile ranks corresponding to scores in Figure 9.3-1 (a) is shown in part (b) of the figure. The percentile rank graph has a rectangular shape.

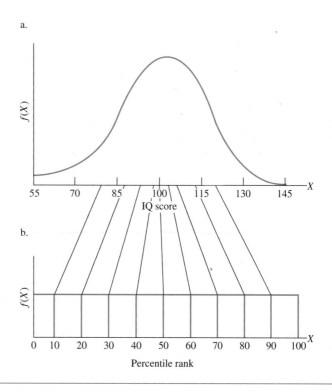

Figure 9.3-1. (a) Graph of distribution of IQ scores. (b) Graph of distribution of percentile ranks. The transformation of scores to percentile ranks alters the shape of the distribution.

You can see from the figure that the transformation of scores to percentile ranks has altered four characteristics of the distribution: (1) central tendency (for example, the transformed mean is 50), (2) dispersion, (3) skewness (the percentile graph is symmetrical), and (4) kurtosis. The only characteristic that is not changed by the transformation is the rank order of scores within the distribution. In addition, you see that the 10-point difference between, for example, the 50th and 60th percentiles corresponds to a relatively small difference between IQ scores, but a 10-point difference between the 80th and 90th percentiles corresponds to a larger difference between IQs. To put it another way, there is a greater difference in intellectual functioning between two individuals at the 80th and 90th percentiles than between individuals at the 50th and 60th percentiles. Thus, the interpretation of a 10-point difference between percentile ranks depends on where the difference is on the 0 to 100 scale. This problem does not occur with standard scores.

As you have seen, transforming scores to percentile ranks alters four characteristics of the distribution; a standard score transformation alters only two characteristics—central tendency and dispersion. Standard scores have the added advantage that they can be manipulated arithmetically. For these reasons, psychologists and educators who use or develop psychological tests prefer standard scores over percentile ranks even though they are less familiar to the average person.

Other Kinds of Standard Scores

The standard scores I have described range approximately from -3 to $+3$ and have a mean of 0 and a standard deviation of 1. It is a minor inconvenience to have to deal with negative scores, and fortunately this inconvenience can be avoided. If a sufficiently large constant is added to each z score, all the z scores will be positive, with a new mean equal to the constant. Similarly, if each z score is multiplied by a constant, the standard deviation is changed from one to the value of the constant. The formula

$$z' = \frac{X - \overline{X}}{S} S' + \overline{X}'$$

is used to change the mean and standard deviation of z scores to any desired values, where z' is the transformed standard score, S' is the value of the desired standard deviation, and $\overline{X}'$ is the value of the desired mean.

A surprising number of psychological test scores are actually transformed z scores. Many IQ tests, for example, yield scores that are actually z scores that have been multiplied by 15 and then had 100 added to the product. The resulting transformed z' scores have a mean equal to 100 and a standard deviation equal to 15. Other examples of transformed standard scores are shown in Figure 9.3-2.

Comparing Performance on Different Tests

Randy got a raw score of 68 in arithmetic and a 42 in English. He seems to be doing better in arithmetic than in English, but is he really? His teacher converts the class's arithmetic and English scores to standard scores with a mean of 50 and a standard deviation of 10. A different picture of Randy's performance emerges; his arithmetic

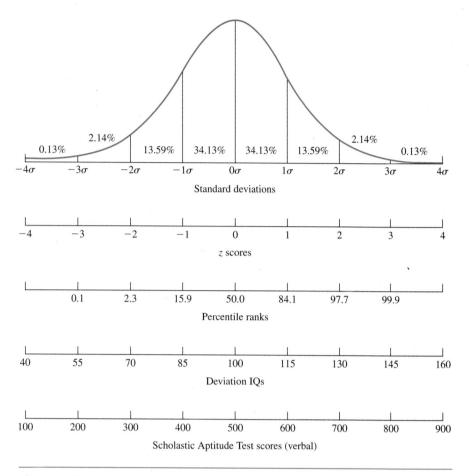

Figure 9.3-2. Comparison of percentiles and widely used systems of standard scores.

z score is 40, one standard deviation below the class mean, but his English score is 65, one and a half standard deviations above the mean. So Randy is doing much better in English than in arithmetic, relative to others in his class. As this example illustrates, *z* scores are useful for determining an individual's strengths and weaknesses—that is, for making intraindividual comparisons. *z* scores permit you to compare performance on different tasks that are measured on different scales, as were Randy's arithmetic and English tests. However, for the comparisons to be meaningful, the *z* scores for both variables should be based on the same or equivalent reference groups. Reference groups are equivalent with respect to a variable if their distributions have essentially the same mean, standard deviation, and shape. It would not have been possible to compare Randy's arithmetic and English *z* scores if he had been in an accelerated arithmetic class and a remedial English class. In this case, the references groups, accelerated arithmetic class and remedial English class, clearly would not be equivalent.

12. Suppose that three tests were given in your statistics course. The class means, standard deviations, and your scores are listed in the table.

Test	μ	σ	Your Scores
1	60	11	72
2	44	17	61
3	53	8	63

On which test did you do your best, and on which did you do your worst?

13. Your statistics professor returned the midterm exam and said that the mean was 82 and the standard deviation was 14. The top 15% of the test scores received an A. Assume that the distribution is normally distributed and that your score was 99. Did you get an A?

14. Suppose that the mean of a test was 22 and the standard deviation was 5. Transform a score of 18 to standard scores with the following means and standard deviations:

   a. $\overline{X} = 100$, $S = 15$ b. $\overline{X} = 50$, $S = 10$ c. $\overline{X} = 10$, $S = 2$

9.4 SAMPLING DISTRIBUTIONS

Looking Ahead to Inferential Statistics

So far you have covered descriptive statistics, probability, and probability distributions. These topics provide the necessary background for moving on to inferential statistics, the subject of the second half of this book. Inferential statistics are procedures for using sample data to make inferences about one or more population parameters. Two kinds of procedures are categorized under inferential statistics: estimation and hypothesis testing.

The term **estimation** is used in statistics in much the same way as it is used in everyday language. A student might estimate that the mean grade-point average of members of his sailing club is 2.9 or that it is between 2.7 and 3.1. The first type of estimate is called a **point estimate** because the one number representing the estimate can be associated with a point on the real number line (a straight line in which points are identified with real numbers). The second type, involving two numbers, is called an **interval estimate** because the two numbers and associated points define an interval on the real number line.

An **estimator** is a rule, usually in the form of a formula such as $\sum X_i / n$, that tells you how to calculate an estimate of a population parameter using sample information. The estimate is the numerical value that results from applying the rule to a sample.

The value of a point estimate varies from one random sample to the next; hence, the value for a particular sample is likely to differ from the population parameter. As you will see in Chapters 11 through 14, interval estimation is used in conjunction with point estimation to specify an interval on the real number line that has a high likelihood of containing the parameter of interest. In subsequent chapters, I will call this interval a **confidence interval.**

The other approach to statistical inference, **hypothesis testing,** is similar in many respects to the scientific method. A scientist observes nature, formulates a hypothesis, and then proceeds to test the hypothesis by comparing its predictions with data. Similarly, hypothesis testing begins with a question about nature that leads to a hypothesis regarding the value of one or more population parameters. The researcher obtains a sample from the population and compares the sample value with the hypothesized value of the population parameter. If the sample value is inconsistent with the hypothesized value, the hypothesis is rejected; otherwise, it is not rejected. These procedures are discussed in Chapters 10 and 12 through 14.

In summary, estimation is concerned with getting a reasonable idea of the value of a parameter. Hypothesis testing is concerned with deciding whether a hypothesis about a parameter is or is not tenable. In estimation, the result is a number or an interval bounded by two numbers. In hypothesis testing, the result is a decision about a hypothesis.

Before turning to hypothesis testing and confidence intervals, which are introduced in Chapters 10 and 11, respectively, I will lay a little more groundwork for statistical inference.

Sampling Distributions

As you have learned, inferential statistics are used to reason from a sample to the population—from the particular to the general. Such reasoning is based on a knowledge of the sample-to-sample variability of a statistic—that is, on its sampling behavior. Before data have been collected, you can speak of a sample statistic such as $\overline{X}$ in terms of probability. Its value is yet to be determined and will depend on which score values happen to be randomly selected from the population. Thus, at this stage of research, a sample statistic is a random variable because it will be computed from two or more score values obtained by random sampling.

> Like any random variable, a sample statistic has a probability distribution that gives the probability associated with each value of the statistic over all possible samples of the same size that could be drawn from the population. The probability distribution of a statistic is called a **sampling distribution** to distinguish it from a probability distribution for, say, a score value.

Sampling distributions play a key role in statistical inference because they describe the sample-to-sample variability of statistics computed from random samples. In subsequent chapters, you will use sampling distributions to (1) determine the tenability of the hypothesis that a population parameter is equal to a particular value and (2) specify a range of values that has a high likelihood of including the parameter.

Sampling Distribution of the Mean

Some of the important characteristics of a sampling distribution will be introduced by an example that, though obviously unrealistic, has the virtue of allowing a concrete approach to the topic. This discussion focuses on the sampling distribution of the mean, but the ideas developed apply to any sampling distribution. Suppose that I have a discrete, uniform (rectangular) population consisting of $N = 4$ scores: 1, 2, 3, and 4. A graph of the population is shown in Figure 9.4-1. The mean of the population is

$$\mu = \frac{\sum\limits_{i=1}^{N} X_i}{N} = \frac{1 + 2 + 3 + 4}{4} = 2.5$$

and its standard deviation is

$$\sigma = \sqrt{\frac{\sum\limits_{i=1}^{N} (X_i - \mu)^2}{N}}$$

$$= \sqrt{\frac{(1 - 2.5)^2 + (2 - 2.5)^2 + (3 - 2.5)^2 + (4 - 2.5)^2}{4}}$$

$$= 1.118$$

If I draw all possible samples of size $n = 2$ with replacement, $k = 16$ different samples can be drawn (see Table 9.4-1). This follows from the fundamental counting rule (see Section 7.4) because the first element can be drawn in any one of four ways and the second, in any one of four ways, making a total of $4 \times 4 = 16$ samples. The probability of drawing a particular sample is, according to the multiplication rule for independent events, $(\frac{1}{4})(\frac{1}{4}) = \frac{1}{16}$. The 16 equally likely samples and their means are given in Table 9.4-1. As shown in the table, the population mean of the 16 means, denoted by $\mu_{\bar{X}}$, is equal to 2.5; the population standard deviation of the means, denoted by $\sigma_{\bar{X}}$, is equal to 0.791. A chart depicting the sampling procedure along with

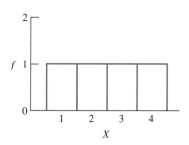

Figure 9.4-1. Histogram of a discrete uniform population.

TABLE 9.4-1 Listing of All Possible Samples of Size Two from the Population in Figure 9.4-1

(i) Data (the sample mean for each of the j = 1, . . . , k samples is given by $\overline{X}_j = \sum_{i=1}^{n} X_i/n$, where k = 16 and n = 2)

Sample Number	Sample Values	$\overline{X}_j$	Sample Number	Sample Values	$\overline{X}_j$
1	1, 1	1.0	9	2, 3	2.5
2	1, 2	1.5	10	3, 2	2.5
3	2, 1	1.5	11	2, 4	3.0
4	1, 3	2.0	12	4, 2	3.0
5	3, 1	2.0	13	3, 3	3.0
6	1, 4	2.5	14	3, 4	3.5
7	4, 1	2.5	15	4, 3	3.5
8	2, 2	2.0	16	4, 4	4.0

(ii) Mean and standard deviation of the means

$$\mu_{\overline{X}} = \frac{\sum_{j=1}^{k} \overline{X}_j}{k} = \frac{1.0 + 1.5 + \cdots + 4.0}{16} = \frac{40}{16} = 2.5$$

$$\sigma_{\overline{X}} = \sqrt{\frac{\sum_{j=1}^{k} (\overline{X}_j - \mu_{\overline{X}})^2}{k}} = \sqrt{\frac{(1.0 - 2.5)^2 + (1.5 - 2.5)^2 + \cdots + (4.0 - 2.5)^2}{16}} = 0.791$$

a graph of the sampling distribution of the mean is presented in Figure 9.4-2. The figure also gives concrete examples of three kinds of distributions that are often confused: population distribution, sample distribution, and sampling distribution. A population distribution is shown at the top of Figure 9.4-2—it contains all the score values in the population. Examples of sample distributions are shown in the middle of the figure—each sample distribution contains n = 2 score values from the population. A sampling distribution is shown at the bottom of Figure 9.4-2—it contains the 16 sample means that can be computed from random samples of size n = 2 from the population. A sampling distribution is the distribution of a statistic such as the mean. Population and sample distributions are distributions of score values.

Three characteristics of the sampling distribution are especially important:

1. The distribution of the sample means does not resemble the original population, which in this example was rectangular, but instead resembles the normal distribution. I could show that if the sample size was increased from n = 2 to n = 3, the number of possible $\overline{X}_j$ values would increase and the distribution of the $\overline{X}_j$'s would resemble more closely the normal distribution.
2. The population mean of the 16 sample means, $\mu_{\overline{X}} = 2.5$, equals the mean of the four score values in the population, $\mu = 2.5$.

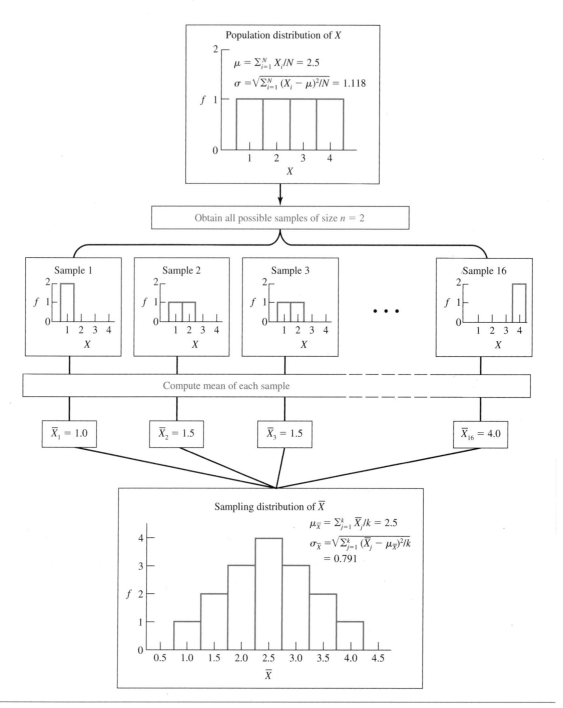

Figure 9.4-2. Graph of the sampling procedure used to construct a sampling distribution for samples of size $n = 2$ from a discrete, uniform population. Note that $\mu_{\overline{X}} = \mu = 2.5$ and that $\sigma_{\overline{X}} = \sqrt{\sum_{j=1}^{k}(\overline{X}_j - \mu_{\overline{X}})^2/k} = 0.791$, which is equal to $\sigma/\sqrt{n} = 1.118/\sqrt{2} = 0.791$.

3. The population standard deviation of the 16 sample means, $\sigma_{\overline{X}} = 0.791$, equals the standard deviation of the four scores in the population divided by the square root of the sample size—that is, $\sigma_{\overline{X}} = \sigma/\sqrt{n} = 1.118/\sqrt{2} = 0.791$.

Several implications of the third point are easily overlooked. It says in effect that you can compute the standard deviation of sample means in two ways—from $\sigma_{\overline{X}} = \sqrt{\sum_{j=1}^{k}(\overline{X}_j - \mu_{\overline{X}})^2/k}$ or from $\sigma_{\overline{X}} = \sigma/\sqrt{n}$. Because in practical situations the distribution of sample means is not available, you will rely on a knowledge of, or an estimate of, the population standard deviation, σ, and the formula $\sigma/\sqrt{n}$ in computing $\sigma_{\overline{X}}$. The formula $\sigma_{\overline{X}} = \sigma/\sqrt{n}$ also gives you a reason for having greater confidence in large samples. You know that the standard deviation of the population, σ, is a constant. Therefore, it follows from $\sigma_{\overline{X}} = \sigma/\sqrt{n}$ that as n (the sample size) increases, $\sigma_{\overline{X}}$ (the dispersion of sample means) decreases, and hence the closer a randomly selected sample mean is likely to be to μ. In other words, the larger the sample size, the more probable it is that the sample mean comes arbitrarily close to the population mean. This fact, referred to as the **law of large numbers,** is one justification for using random samples to learn about populations. If the sample is large enough, the sample information is likely to be very accurate.

Central Limit Theorem

The three characteristics of the sampling distribution of the mean just described are succinctly stated in the *central limit theorem*, one of the most important theorems in statistics.

> In one form, the **central limit theorem** states that if random samples are selected from a population with mean μ and finite standard deviation σ, as the sample size n increases, the distribution of $\overline{X}$ approaches a normal distribution with mean μ and standard deviation $\sigma/\sqrt{n}$.

Probably the most significant point is that regardless of the shape of the sampled population, the means of sufficiently large samples will be nearly normally distributed. Just how large is sufficiently large? This depends on the shape of the sampled population; the more a population departs from the normal form, the larger n must be. For most populations encountered in the behavioral sciences and education, a sample size of 100 is sufficient to produce a nearly normal sampling distribution of $\overline{X}$. The tendency for the sampling distributions of statistics to approach the normal distribution as n increases helps to explain why the normal distribution is so important in statistics.

Standard Error of a Statistic

The term *standard deviation* has been used here to refer to a measure of dispersion, both for scores in a frequency distribution and statistics in a sampling distribution. To avoid confusion, in the future, I will use the term **standard error** to denote the latter measure. The symbol for a standard error always includes a subscript indicating the statistic to which it applies—for example, $\sigma_{\overline{X}}$ (standard error of a mean),

σ_{Mdn} (standard error of a median), and σ_r (standard error of a correlation coefficient). There are as many standard errors as there are sample statistics, but they are all interpreted analogously to a standard deviation.

In the future, whenever you encounter a standard error, think of it simply as a measure of the sample-to-sample variability of the values of a statistic computed from a large number of random samples. The standard error reflects the dispersion of the values of a statistic computed from many samples; a standard deviation reflects the dispersion of scores computed from a sample.

Two Properties of Good Estimators

As I have discussed, the value of sample statistics varies from one random sample to the next. Consequently, it is unlikely that a given statistic will equal the population parameter it is used to estimate. This is a little frustrating, but it is something you have to live with. However, you can require that the mean of the distribution of estimates yielded by an estimator equals the parameter it estimates and that the estimates vary from one random sample to the next as little as possible. Statistics that satisfy these two intuitively reasonable requirements are said to be unbiased estimators and minimum variance estimators, respectively.

More formally, an estimator $\hat{\theta}$ is an **unbiased estimator** of the parameter θ if $E(\hat{\theta}) = \theta$. An estimator $\hat{\theta}$ is a **minimum variance estimator** of the parameter θ if the variance of $\hat{\theta}$, denoted by $\text{Var}(\hat{\theta})$, is smaller than that for any other unbiased estimator of θ.

The sample mean is a good estimator of μ because it satisfies both these requirements: $E(\overline{X}) = \mu$ and $\text{Var}(\overline{X})$ is a minimum—that is, the expected value of the sample mean equals the population mean and the variance of sample means is as small as it can be.

It can be shown that the sample median of normally distributed populations also is an unbiased estimator of μ, but it is not a minimum variance estimator. This can be seen by comparing the variance error (the square of the standard error) of the median with that for the mean. The variance of the median, $\text{Var}(Mdn)$, is equal to $1.57\sigma^2/n$. This variance is larger than the variance of the mean, $\text{Var}(\overline{X})$, which is equal to σ^2/n. This confirms what you learned in Section 3.5, namely that the sample mean is more stable than the sample median—the mean varies less from sample to sample than the median.

Some statistics are biased estimators. One example is the sample variance S^2. Its expected value, $E(S^2)$, does not equal σ^2. When you want to estimate σ^2 you should use $\hat{\sigma}^2 = \Sigma(X_i - \overline{X})^2/(n-1)$ because $E(\hat{\sigma}^2) = \sigma^2$. A demonstration showing that $\hat{\sigma}^2$ is an unbiased estimator but S^2 is a biased estimator is given in Supplementary Note 9.6.

Test Statistics

The statistics presented thus far—$\overline{X}$, Mdn, and so on—are useful for describing samples. If they are computed from a random sample, they also can be used to estimate population parameters, although, as you have seen, some are better for this purpose than others. Subsequent chapters describe in detail a different kind of statistic that is used to test hypotheses about the values of population parameters. These statistics are called **test statistics.** Consider a z test statistic that is used to test the hypothesis that the population mean, μ, is equal to some value denoted by μ_0. The formula for z is

$$z = \frac{\overline{X} - \mu_0}{\sigma_{\overline{X}}} = \frac{\overline{X} - \mu_0}{\sigma/\sqrt{n}}$$

where $\overline{X}$ is the mean of a random sample that is used to estimate the unknown population mean, μ_0 is the hypothesized value of the population mean, $\sigma_{\overline{X}}$ is the standard error of the mean, σ is the population standard deviation, and n is the size of the random sample. If the sampled population is normal or the sample size is sufficiently large and if you know the population standard deviation, it is possible to specify the sampling distribution of the z test statistic—it is the standard normal distribution whose μ is 0 and σ is 1. There is a marked similarity in appearance between this z test statistic ($z = (\overline{X} - \mu_0)/\sigma_{\overline{X}}$) and a z score ($z = (X - \overline{X})/S$). In both cases, z has the form

$$z = \frac{\text{Statistic} - \text{Mean of the statistic}}{\text{Standard deviation of the statistic}}$$

In words, the z's are obtained by subtracting the sample mean from a statistic, $X - \overline{X}$, or the hypothesized mean from a statistic, $\overline{X} - \mu_0$, and dividing the difference by a standard deviation—S in the case of X and $\sigma_{\overline{X}}$ in the case of $\overline{X}$.

Other test statistics that will be introduced in later chapters include $t = (\overline{X} - \mu_0)/(\hat{\sigma}/\sqrt{n})$ (also used to test a hypothesis about a population mean) and $F = \hat{\sigma}_1^2 / \hat{\sigma}_2^2$ (used to test the hypothesis that two population variances are equal).

CHECK YOUR UNDERSTANDING OF SECTION 9.4

15. A population consists of $N = 4$ scores: 0, 1, 2, and 3. (a) List the $(4)(4) = 16$ samples of size $n = 2$ that can be drawn with replacement from the population. (b) Compute the mean and standard error of the mean using the formulas $\mu = \sum_{i=1}^{N} X_i/N$ and $\sigma_{\overline{X}} = \sigma/\sqrt{n}$, where $\sigma = \sqrt{\sum_{i=1}^{N}(X_i - \mu)^2/N}$. (c) Compute the mean and standard error of the mean using the formulas $\mu_{\overline{X}} = \sum_{j=1}^{k} \overline{X}_j/k$ and $\sigma_{\overline{X}} = \sqrt{\sum_{j=1}^{k}(\overline{X}_j - \mu_{\overline{X}})^2/k}$. (d) Compare the results obtained in parts (b) and (c).

16. For the population in Exercise 15, (a) list the $_4C_2 = 6$ distinct samples of size two that can be drawn without replacement. (b) Compute the mean and standard error of the mean using the formulas $\mu = \sum_{i=1}^{N} X_i/N$ and $\sigma_{\overline{X}} = \sigma/\sqrt{n}$, where $\sigma = \sqrt{\sum_{i=1}^{N}(X_i - \mu)^2/N}$. (c) Compute the mean and standard error of the mean using the formulas $\mu_{\overline{X}} = \sum_{j=1}^{k} \overline{X}_j/k$ and $\sigma_{\overline{X}} = \sqrt{\sum_{j=1}^{k}(\overline{X}_j - \mu_{\overline{X}})^2/k}$. The means computed from the two formulas should be equal, but the standard error computed from $\sigma_{\overline{X}} = \sigma/\sqrt{n}$ overestimates the true value because it assumes an

infinite population or sampling with replacement. A correction for a finite population or when you are sampling without replacement can be made:

$$\sigma_{\overline{X}} = (\sigma/\sqrt{n})\sqrt{(N-n)/(N-1)}$$

where N is the number of scores in the population and n is the number in the sample. (d) Apply the correction to $\sigma/\sqrt{n}$ and compare the value with that obtained using $\sigma_{\overline{X}} = \sqrt{\sum_{j=1}^{k}(\overline{X}_j - \mu_{\overline{X}})^2/k}$. (e) One rule of thumb states that the finite population correction can be ignored when $n/N \le .05$. Use an example to show why this rule is reasonable.

17. How is the dispersion of the sampling distribution of $\overline{X}$ related to σ and n?

18. A sample of size n is to be drawn from a population with a mean of 100 and a standard deviation of 10. Complete the table.

n	$\sigma_{\overline{X}}$		n	$\sigma_{\overline{X}}$
a. 2			b. 4	
c. 8			d. 16	

19. The registrar claims that the mean IQ of students at a university (μ_0) is 120, with a standard deviation (σ) of 10. You obtain a random sample of 25 students and find that their mean ($\overline{X}$) is 115. What is the probability of obtaining a mean of 115 or lower if the true mean is 120? (*Hint*: Transform $\overline{X}$ to a z statistic, and use the standard normal distribution to find the area below 115.)

20. Terms to remember:
    a. Point estimate
    b. Interval estimate
    c. Estimator
    d. Confidence interval
    e. Sampling distribution
    f. Law of large numbers
    g. Central limit theorem
    h. Standard error
    i. Unbiased estimator
    j. Minimum variance estimator
    k. Test statistic

9.5 LOOKING BACK: WHAT HAVE YOU LEARNED?

This chapter described two theoretical distributions that provide a bridge between descriptive and inferential statistics: a probability distribution and its close relative, a sampling distribution. A probability distribution associates a probability with each value of a random variable where the random variable is a single population element. A sampling distribution associates a probability with each value of a random variable where the random variable is some function of two or more population elements, say, a mean, a sum, or a standard deviation.

The normal distribution is the most widely applicable theoretical model in statistics. It provides an excellent approximation to the binomial distribution and to other theoretical distributions whose probabilities are laborious to calculate when n is large. In addition, it serves as a model for the many variables in science and nature that are approximately normally distributed. But its most important use is as a model for the sampling distribution of statistics based on large n's. According to the central limit theorem, as the sample size n increases, the distribution of $\overline{X}$'s from random samples approaches a normal distribution, with mean μ and standard deviation $\sigma/\sqrt{n}$, whatever the shape of the original population.

The normal distribution is actually a family of distributions, one for each possible combination of μ and σ. The distribution with $\mu = 0$ and $\sigma = 1$ is called the standard normal distribution; it is the distribution whose areas are given in Appendix Table D.2. To use the standard normal distribution table, a score is transformed into a standard score (z score) by the formula $z = (X - \overline{X})/S$. The transformation does not affect the shape of the original distribution but does change its mean and standard deviation to 0 and 1, respectively. Standard scores are widely used for reporting psychological test scores because one number contains all the information necessary to interpret a score.

An important new measure of dispersion was introduced in this chapter—the standard error, which is the standard deviation of a statistic. It is the dispersion of a random variable that has been computed from two or more population elements. The standard error describes the dispersion of a statistic over all possible samples of the same size. It is denoted by σ, with a subscript identifying the statistic; for example, $\sigma_{\overline{X}}$ denotes the standard error of the mean. The following chapters describe how the elements—standard error, sampling distribution, and test statistic—are used in inferential statistics.

REVIEW EXERCISES FOR CHAPTER 9

1. Why is the normal distribution so important in statistics?
2. A set of scores has a mean of 50 and a standard deviation of 15. Transform the following to z scores.

   a. 65   b. 35   c. 50   d. 80   e. 45   f. 5

3. If z is a normally distributed random variable with $\mu = 0$ and $\sigma = 1$, determine the percentage of the area under the standard normal curve for the following.

   a. Above $z = 2$ b. Below $z = -3$
   c. From μ to $z = 2.5$ d. Between $z = 0.5$ and $z = 1$
   e. Between $z = 1$ and $z = -2$ f. Between $z = -2$ and $z = -3$
   g. From μ to $z = -1$ h. Between $z = -1$ and $z = 1.5$

4. Determine the percentage of the area of the standard normal distribution that falls between $\mu - k\sigma$ and $\mu + k\sigma$, where k is equal to the following.

   a. 0.5   b. 2.0   c. .67   d. 3.0   e. 2.33

5 Compute the score corresponding to each of the following z scores. Assume that the original distribution had a mean of 150 and a standard deviation of 20.

   a. 3.3   b. 2.5   c. -1.0 d. 1.8   e.   1.645

6. Find the z score such that at least the following proportion of the area under the standard normal distribution falls above it.

   a. .01   b. .16   c. .025   d. .84   e. .99

7. In the general population, Stanford-Binet IQs are nearly normally distributed, with a mean of 100 and a standard deviation of 16. (a) What is the probability that a randomly selected person will have an IQ between 100 and 124? (b) What proportion of the population will have IQs above 132?

8. Grading on the curve means assigning grades according to the normal distribution. The mean of a test is 50, with a standard deviation of 10. If 10% of the class receives A's, what is the lowest score that receives an A?

9. The time from conception to birth in humans is approximately normally distributed, with a mean of 280.5 days and a standard deviation of 8.4 days. In a paternity case it was proved that the time from the alleged conception to the birth of a 6.5-pound baby was at least 306 days. (a) Compute the proportion of women having this or a longer gestation time. (b) Discuss the significance of the evidence.

10. Suppose that 64% of stocks recommended by a broker increase in value within six months. Use the normal approximation to the binomial distribution to determine the probability that of 372 recommendations, (a) at least 225 will increase in value and (b) more than 250 will increase in value.

11. The statement "Jane got a 29 on the quiz" is uninterpretable. Discuss.

12. Compare the relative merits of standard scores and percentile ranks for interpreting scores.

13. On a mechanical aptitude test, Bill scored 110 and Elaine scored 85. The population mean for men is 104, with a standard deviation of 20. The comparable norms for women are 70 and 30. Which of the two did better, considering the norms for their genders?

14. Suppose that the mean of a test was 30 and the standard deviation was 8. Transform a score of 18 to standard scores with the following means and standard deviations.

  a. $\overline{X} = 100$, $S = 10$ b. $\overline{X} = 500$, $S = 100$ c. $\overline{X} = 80$, $S = 10$

15. Distinguish a sampling distribution from a sample (frequency) distribution.

16. A population consists of $N = 5$ scores: 0, 1, 2, 3, and 4. (a) List the $(5)(5) = 25$ samples of size two that can be drawn with replacement from the population. (b) Compute the mean and standard error of the mean using the formulas $\mu = \sum_{i=1}^{N} X_i / N$ and $\sigma_{\overline{X}} = \sigma/\sqrt{n}$, where $\sigma = \sqrt{\sum_{i=1}^{N}(X_i - \mu)^2 / N}$. (c) Compute the mean and standard error of the mean using the formulas $\mu_{\overline{X}} = \sum_{j=1}^{k} \overline{X}_j / k$ and $\sigma_{\overline{X}} = \sqrt{\sum_{j=1}^{k}(\overline{X}_j - \mu_{\overline{X}})^2 / k}$. (d) Compare the results obtained in parts (b) and (c).

17. For the population in Exercise 16, (a) list the $_5C_2 = 10$ distinct samples of size two that can be drawn without replacement. (b) Compute the mean and standard error of the mean using the formulas $\mu = \sum_{i=1}^{N} X_i / N$ and $\sigma_{\overline{X}} = \sigma/\sqrt{n}$, where $\sqrt{\sum_{i=1}^{N}(X_i - \mu)^2 / N}$. (c) Compute the mean and standard error of the mean using the formulas $\mu_{\overline{X}} = \sum_{j=1}^{k} \overline{X}_j / k$ and $\sigma_{\overline{X}} = \sqrt{\sum_{j=1}^{k}(\overline{X}_j - \mu_{\overline{X}})^2 / k}$. The means computed from the two formulas should be equal, but the standard error computed from $\sigma_{\overline{X}} = \sigma/\sqrt{n}$ overestimates the true value because it assumes an infinite population or sampling with replacement. A correction for a finite population or when you are sampling without replacement can be made:

$$\sigma_{\overline{X}} = (\sigma/\sqrt{n})\sqrt{(N-n)/(N-1)}$$

where N is the number of scores in the population and n is the number in the sample. (d) Apply the correction to $\sigma_{\overline{X}} = \sigma/\sqrt{n}$ and compare the value with that obtained using $\sigma_{\overline{X}} = \sqrt{\sum_{j=1}^{k}(\overline{X}_j - \mu_{\overline{X}})^2 / k}$. (e) One rule of thumb states that the finite population correction can be ignored when $n/N < .05$. Use an example to show why this rule is reasonable.

18. Distinguish a standard error from a standard deviation.

19. A sample of size n is to be drawn from a population with a mean of 63 and a standard deviation of 15. Complete the table.

n	$\sigma_{\overline{X}}$		n	$\sigma_{\overline{X}}$
a. 3			b. 9	
c. 27			d. 81	

20. An elevator has a maximum safe load of 1638 pounds. If men's weights are approximately normally distributed with a mean of 165 pounds and a standard deviation of 15 pounds, what is the probability that nine men (whose weights can be assumed to be independent) will overload the elevator?

9.6 SUPPLEMENTARY NOTES[†]

Explanation of Why the Mean of a Distribution of z Scores Is Zero and the Standard Deviation Is One

Information from Chapters 3 and 4 can be used to show that if a distribution of X scores is transformed into z scores, $z = (X_i - \overline{X})/S$, the distribution of z scores has a mean of 0 and standard deviation of 1. To show this, use two facts that were mentioned in Chapters 3 and 4. Review Exercise 21 in Chapter 3 showed that if a constant c is subtracted from each score in a distribution, $X_i - c$, the mean of the transformed distribution is equal to the original mean minus the constant—that is, $\overline{X}_{transformed} = \overline{X}_{original} - c$. Hence, if $c = \overline{X}_{original}$ is subtracted from each score, the mean of the transformed scores will equal 0 because $\overline{X}_{transformed} = \overline{X}_{original} - \overline{X}_{original} = 0$. Also, Review Exercise 11b in Chapter 4 showed that if each $(X_i - \overline{X})$ is divided by a positive constant c, the standard deviation of the transformed $(X_i - \overline{X})$'s is equal to the original standard deviation divided by the constant, that is, $S_{transformed} = S_{original}/c$. Hence, if each $(X_i - \overline{X})$ is divided by $c = S_{original}$, the transformed standard deviation of the $(X_i - \overline{X})$'s will equal 1 because $S_{transformed} = S_{original}/S_{original} = 1$. Thus, applying the transformation $(z = X_i - \overline{X}/S)$ to each X score results in a new variable called a standard score, whose mean is 0 and whose standard deviation is 1.

Demonstration Showing That $\hat{\sigma}^2$ and $\hat{\sigma}^2_{est}$ Are Unbiased Estimators but S^2 Is a Biased Estimator

Section 9.4 drew all possible samples of size two with replacement from a finite population to show that the standard error of the mean, $\sigma_{\overline{X}}$, is equal to the standard deviation

[†] These supplementary notes can be omitted without a loss of continuity.

of the population divided by the square root of the sample size—that is $\sigma_{\overline{X}} = \sigma/\sqrt{n}$. This supplementary note uses the same sampling procedure and data to show that $E(\hat{\sigma}^2) = \sigma^2$ and $E(S^2) \neq \sigma^2$, which means that $\hat{\sigma}^2$ is an unbiased estimator of the parameter σ^2 but S^2 is a biased estimator. The values of $\hat{\sigma}_j^2$ and S_j^2 are shown in Table 9.6-1 and are based on the population in Figure 9.4-1 and the random samples in Table 9.4-1. For the moment, ignore $\hat{\sigma}_{est\,j}^2$ in column 6 of Table 9.6-1. Because $\hat{\sigma}^2$ is a discrete random variable that assumes values $\hat{\sigma}^2, \hat{\sigma}_2^2, \ldots, \hat{\sigma}_k^2$ with probabilities $p(\hat{\sigma}_1^2)$, $p(\hat{\sigma}_2^2), \ldots, p(\hat{\sigma}_k^2)$, the expected value of $\hat{\sigma}^2$ is given by $E(\hat{\sigma}^2) = \sum_{j=1}^{k} p(\hat{\sigma}_j^2) \hat{\sigma}_j^2$. Similarly, the expected value of S^2 is given by $E(S^2) = \sum_{j=1}^{k} p(S_j^2) S_j^2$. You can see from the computations in Table 9.6-1 (part ii) that $\hat{\sigma}^2$ is an unbiased estimator of σ^2 because $E(\hat{\sigma}^2) = 1.25 = \sigma^2$. However, $E(S^2) = 0.625 \neq \sigma^2$, which means that S^2 is a biased estimator of σ^2. Thus, dividing $\sum_{i=1}^{n}(X_i - \overline{X})^2$ by $n - 1$ instead of by n provides an unbiased estimator of the population variance.

A second unbiased estimator of the population variance is $\hat{\sigma}_{est}^2$, where $\sum_{i=1}^{n}(X_i - \mu)^2$ is divided by n. According to Table 9.6-1 (part ii), $E(\hat{\sigma}_{est}^2) = 1.25 =$

TABLE 9.6-1   Computation of $\hat{\sigma}^2$, S^2, and $\hat{\sigma}_{est}^2$ for All Possible Samples of Size Two from the Population in Figure 9.4-1 (for This Population, $\mu = 2.5$ and $\sigma^2 = 1.25$)

(i) *Data (the three variance estimators, $\hat{\sigma}_j^2$, S_j^2, and $\hat{\sigma}_{est\,j}^2$ are each computed from $i = 1, \ldots,$ n scores, where $n = 2$. There are $j = 1, \ldots, k$ variance estimates, where $k = 16$).*

(1) Sample Number	(2) Sample Values	(3) $\overline{X}_j$	(4) $\hat{\sigma}_j^2 = \dfrac{\sum_{i=1}^{n}(X_i - \overline{X})^2}{n-1}$	(5) $S_j^2 = \dfrac{\sum_{i=1}^{n}(X_i - \overline{X})^2}{n}$	(6) $\hat{\sigma}_{est\,j}^2 = \dfrac{\sum_{i=1}^{n}(X_i - \mu)^2}{n}$
1	1,1	1.0	0.0	0.00	2.25
2	1,2	1.5	0.5	0.25	1.25
3	2,1	1.5	0.5	0.25	1.25
4	1,3	2.0	2.0	1.00	1.25
5	3,1	2.0	2.0	1.00	1.25
6	1,4	2.5	4.5	2.25	2.25
7	4,1	2.5	4.5	2.25	2.25
8	2,2	2.0	0.0	0.00	0.25
9	2,3	2.5	0.5	0.25	0.25
10	3,2	2.5	0.5	0.25	0.25
11	2,4	3.0	2.0	1.00	1.25
12	4,2	3.0	2.0	1.00	1.25
13	3,3	3.0	0.0	0.00	0.25
14	3,4	3.5	0.5	0.25	1.25
15	4,3	3.5	0.5	0.25	1.25
16	4,4	4.0	0.0	0.00	2.25

TABLE 9.6-1 *(continued)*

(ii) Computation of expected value

$$p(\hat{\sigma}_j^2) = p(S_j^2) = p(\hat{\sigma}_{est}^2) = \frac{1}{16} = .0625$$

$$E(\hat{\sigma}^2) = p(\hat{\sigma}_1^2)\hat{\sigma}_1^2 + p(\hat{\sigma}_2^2)\hat{\sigma}_2^2 + \cdots + p(\hat{\sigma}_k^2)\hat{\sigma}_k^2$$

$$= .0625(0) + .0625(0.5) + \cdots + .0625(0) = 1.25$$

$$E(S^2) = p(S_1^2)S_1^2 + p(S_2^2)S_2^2 + \cdots + p(S_k^2)S_k^2$$

$$= .0625(0) + .0625(0.25) + \cdots + .0625(0) = 0.625$$

$$p(\hat{\sigma}_{est}^2) = p(\hat{\sigma}_{est\,1}^2)\hat{\sigma}_{est\,1}^2 + p(\hat{\sigma}_{est\,2}^2)\hat{\sigma}_{est\,2}^2 + \cdots + p(\hat{\sigma}_{est\,k}^2)\hat{\sigma}_{est\,k}^2$$

$$= .0625(2.25) + .0625(1.25) + \cdots + .0625(2.25) = 1.25$$

(iii) Computation of variance

$$\text{Var}(\hat{\sigma}^2) = \sum_{j=1}^{k} p(\hat{\sigma}_j^2)[\hat{\sigma}_j^2 - E(\hat{\sigma}^2)]^2$$

$$= .0625(0 - 1.25)^2 + .0625(0.5 - 1.25)^2 + \cdots + .0625(0 - 1.25)^2$$

$$= 2.0625$$

$$\text{Var}(\hat{\sigma}_{est}^2) = \sum_{j=1}^{k} p(\hat{\sigma}_{est\,j}^2)[\hat{\sigma}_{est\,j}^2 - E(\hat{\sigma}_{est}^2)]^2$$

$$= .0625(2.25 - 1.25)^2 + .0625(1.25 - 1.25)^2 + \cdots + .0625(2.25 - 1.25)^2$$

$$= 0.5000$$

σ^2, which means that σ_{est}^2, like $\hat{\sigma}^2$, is an unbiased estimator. It is also a better estimator of σ^2 than is $\hat{\sigma}^2$ because $\hat{\sigma}_{est}^2$ varies less from sample to sample. This is shown in part iii of the table: $\text{Var}(\hat{\sigma}_{est}^2) = 0.5000 < \text{Var}(\hat{\sigma}^2) = 2.0625$. It turns out that $\hat{\sigma}_{est}^2$ is a minimum variance estimator.

To compute $\hat{\sigma}_{est}^2$, I need to know μ, one of the parameters of the population. Because μ is rarely known in real-life situations, I rely instead on $\hat{\sigma}^2$. In computing $\hat{\sigma}^2$, I used $\overline{X}$ to estimate the unknown population parameter μ. As a consequence, $\sum_{i=1}^{n}(X_i - \overline{X})^2$ must be divided by $n - 1$ (1 is the number of parameters estimated in the computation) instead of by n to obtain an unbiased estimator of σ^2.

In summary, I have just demonstrated that $\hat{\sigma}^2$ and $\hat{\sigma}_{est}^2$ are unbiased estimators of the population variance and that S^2 is a biased estimator. Furthermore, $\hat{\sigma}_{est}^2$ is a minimum variance estimator. Unfortunately, $\hat{\sigma}_{est}^2$ cannot be used in practice because it requires a knowledge of the population mean, μ. Consequently, I use $\hat{\sigma}^2$ to estimate σ^2. As you have just seen, $\hat{\sigma}^2$ has the desirable property of being unbiased, although it is not a minimum variance estimator.

10

Statistical Inference: One-Sample Hypothesis Test

10.1 Introduction to Hypothesis Testing
Looking Ahead: What Is This Chapter About?
Scientific Hypotheses
Why Statistical Inference?
Statistical Hypotheses
Hypothesis Testing and the Method of Indirect Proof
Rejection or Nonrejection of H_0: What Does It Mean?
The Role of Logic in Evaluating a Scientific Hypothesis
Check Your Understanding of Section 10.1

10.2 Hypothesis Testing
Step 1: Stating the Statistical Hypotheses
Step 2: Specifying the Test Statistic
Step 3: Specifying n and the Sampling Distribution
Step 4: Specifying the Significance Level, α
Step 5: Making a Decision
Check Your Understanding of Section 10.2

10.3 One-Sample t Test for a Mean
Some Experimental Design Considerations
Check Your Understanding of Section 10.3

10.4 More about Hypothesis Testing
One- and Two-Tailed Tests
Type I and Type II Errors
More about Type I and Type II Errors
Determining the n Required to Achieve an Acceptable α, $1 - \beta$, and $\mu - \mu_0$
Reporting p Values
Check Your Understanding of Section 10.4

10.5 Looking Back: What Have Your Learned?
Review Exercises for Chapter 10

10.1 INTRODUCTION TO HYPOTHESIS TESTING

Looking Ahead: What Is This Chapter About?

Evaluating the effectiveness of a new teaching technology or assessing attitudes toward violence on TV involves making a decision on the basis of incomplete information. The researcher's information is usually incomplete because it is impossible or impractical to observe all the people in the population of interest—for example, all schoolchildren or all TV viewers. Fortunately, there are procedures for making rational decisions about populations that use a sample containing only a small portion of the elements in the population. These procedures, called **statistical inference,** are the subject of this and subsequent chapters.

   Several approaches to making decisions about a population use information from a sample, but I will limit my discussion to classical statistical inference, which evolved from the work of Ronald A. Fisher and, more directly, Jerzy Neyman and Egon Pearson. Two complementary topics fall under classical statistical inference: null hypothesis significance testing, the subject of this chapter, and confidence interval estimation, which is described in the next chapter. I will examine hypothesis testing first because the procedure is so widely used in the behavioral sciences, health sciences, and education.

   In this chapter you will learn about a new sampling distribution called the *t* distribution. You also will learn how to use a *t* statistic to test a hypothesis about the mean of a population. You will use the concepts that you learn in this chapter throughout the remainder of the book.

   After reading this chapter, you should know the following:

- The difference between scientific hypotheses and statistical hypotheses
- The five steps used to test a statistical hypothesis
- How to use a *t* statistic to test a statistical hypothesis about a population mean
- The relative advantages of one- and two-tailed tests
- The two kinds of errors that can occur in testing a statistical hypothesis
- How to specify an appropriate sample size, *n*

Scientific Hypotheses

People are by nature inquisitive. We ask questions, develop hunches, and sometimes put our hunches to the test. Over the years, a formalized procedure for testing hunches has evolved—the scientific method. It involves (1) observing nature, (2) asking questions, (3) formulating hypotheses, (4) conducting experiments, and (5) developing theories and laws. Let's examine in detail the third characteristic, formulating hypotheses.

A **scientific hypothesis** is a testable supposition that is tentatively adopted to account for certain facts and to guide in the investigation of others. It is a statement about nature that requires verification.

Consider the following examples of scientific hypotheses: The child-rearing practices of parents affect the personalities of their offspring. Cognitive-behavioral therapy is an effective treatment for girls who are anorexic. Cigarette smoking is associated with high blood pressure. Children who feel insecure engage in overt aggression more frequently than do children who feel secure. These hypotheses have three characteristics in common with all scientific hypotheses: (1) they are intelligent, informed guesses about phenomena of interest; (2) they can be stated in the *if-then* form of an implication—for example, "*if* John smokes, *then* he will show signs of high blood pressure"; (3) their truth or falsity can be determined by observation and experimentation.

Many interesting hypotheses do not qualify as scientific hypotheses because they are not testable by recourse to experience. Questions such as "Can three or more angels dance on the head of a pin?" and "Does life exist in more than one galaxy in the universe?" cannot be investigated because no procedures presently exist for observing angels or life on other galaxies. This does not mean that the question concerning the existence of life in other galaxies can never be investigated. Indeed, with continuing advances in space science, it is likely that this question eventually will be answered.

Why Statistical Inference?

I have said that statistical inference is a form of reasoning whereby rational decisions about states of nature can be made on the basis of incomplete information. Rational decisions often can be made without resorting to statistical inference, as when a scientific hypothesis concerns some limited phenomenon that is directly observable—for example, "This rat will run under condition X." The truth or falsity of the hypothesis can be determined by observing the rat under condition X.

Many scientific hypotheses, on the other hand, refer to phenomena that cannot be directly observed. The population elements are so numerous that viewing all of them is impossible or impractical, for example, "All rats run under condition X." It is impossible to observe the entire population of rats under condition X. Likewise, it is impossible to observe all parents rearing their children, all anorexic girls, all smokers, or all insecure children. If a scientific hypothesis cannot be evaluated directly by observing all members of a population, it may be possible to evaluate the hypothesis indirectly by statistical inference. Statistical inference, which involves observing a sample from the population of interest, enables a researcher to make a rational decision concerning the probable truth or falsity of the scientific hypothesis.

Statistical Hypotheses

Scientific hypotheses are statements about phenomena of nature and humankind and are usually stated in fairly general terms—at least in the initial stages of an inquiry. Consider the scientific hypothesis that a new class registration procedure at Idle-on-in College will reduce the time required for students to register. Over the past several years, the dean of students has found that the mean time required to register using the current procedure is 3.10 hours. The dean's scientific hypothesis that the new procedure is better than the old procedure can be expressed in the form of a *statistical hypothesis.*

A **statistical hypothesis** is a statement about one or more parameters of a population distribution that requires verification.

---

we want to be able to reject the null

The statistical hypothesis corresponding to the dean's scientific hypothesis is $\mu < 3.10$, where μ is the unknown mean for the new registration procedure and 3.10 is the mean registration time for the current procedure. This statistical hypothesis states that the population mean, denoted by μ, is less than 3.10. It is possible that the new procedure is no better than the current procedure or that it is worse than the current procedure. Thus, another statistical hypothesis can be formulated that states that the mean for the new procedure is greater than or equal to 3.10—that is, $\mu \geq 3.10$. These two hypotheses, $\mu \geq 3.10$ and $\mu < 3.10$, are mutually exclusive and exhaustive; if one is true, the other must be false. They are examples, respectively, of the **null hypothesis,** denoted by H_0, and the **alternative hypothesis,** denoted by H_1. The null hypothesis, $H_0: \mu \geq 3.10$, is the one whose tenability is actually tested. If on the basis of this test the null hypothesis is rejected, only the alternative hypothesis, $H_1: \mu < 3.10$, remains tenable. According to convention, the alternative hypothesis is always formulated so that it corresponds to the researcher's scientific hypothesis. The process of choosing between the null and alternative hypotheses is called **hypothesis testing.**

The mean time required to register using the current procedure is 3.10; this mean is denoted by μ_0. The dean doesn't know the population mean, μ, or the population standard deviation, σ, for the new procedure. However, these population parameters can be estimated by conducting an experiment. The dean can have a random sample of n undergraduate students register using the new procedure. The sample statistics $\overline{X}$ and $\hat{\sigma}$ from the experiment are used to estimate the unknown μ and σ.

To summarize, the null hypothesis, $H_0: \mu \geq 3.10$, is contrary to what the dean believes to be true. The dean has followed the convention of equating the alternative hypothesis, $H_1: \mu < 3.10$, with the situation she believes to be true—that the new procedure is better than the old procedure. The scientific hypothesis and its negation are expressed as two mutually exclusive and exhaustive statistical hypotheses concerning the value of μ, the unknown population mean for the new procedure. The two statistical hypotheses cannot both be true. If the sample mean that is obtained in the experiment would be highly unlikely if the null hypothesis is true, the null hypothesis that $\mu \geq 3.10$ is a poor prediction of the population mean and should be rejected. In this case, only the alternative hypothesis remains credible.

Hypothesis Testing and the Method of Indirect Proof

You may marvel at the roundabout procedure whereby a researcher tests a null hypothesis that is believed to be untrue in the hope of rejecting it and thereby accepting the alternative hypothesis that is believed to be true. On reflection, you may recall a similar procedure taught in plane geometry and algebra—the method of indirect proof. This method consists of listing all possible answers or solutions to a problem and showing that all but one are contrary to known fact or lead to an absurdity. By a process of elimination, the one that is not contrary to known fact or absurd must be true. The success of the method of indirect proof depends on listing all possibilities and finding a contradiction for all but one. The comparable procedure in testing a null hypothesis consists of formulating the null and alternative hypotheses so that they exhaust all the possibilities concerning a population parameter. A sample is obtained from the population, and appropriate statistics, such as the sample mean and standard deviation, are computed. If it is highly improbable that the obtained value of the sample mean would have occurred if the null hypothesis were true, then the null hypothesis must be considered a poor prediction of the population mean and should be rejected in favor of the alternative hypothesis.

There is one important difference between the method of indirect proof and null hypothesis testing. In indirect proof, a possibility is rejected only if it is found to lead to a contradiction to known fact or is absurd. In hypothesis testing, the null hypothesis is rejected if the obtained value of a sample mean is very unlikely if the null hypothesis is indeed true. It follows that null hypothesis testing, unlike the method of indirect proof, does not provide incontrovertible proof because the null hypothesis is rejected because of the occurrence of an event that is improbable but not impossible.

Rejection or Nonrejection of H_0: What Does It Mean?

If the null hypothesis is not rejected, what conclusion can the researcher draw? Is the null hypothesis true? Not necessarily; there are always alternative reasons for why the null hypothesis is not rejected.

1. The null hypothesis is true and should not be rejected.
2. The null hypothesis is false and should be rejected, but the particular sample that was used to estimate μ and σ is not representative of the population.
3. The null hypothesis is false and should be rejected, but the experimental methodology is not sufficiently sensitive to detect the true situation.

An experimental methodology can lack sensitivity for a variety of reasons: the size of the sample is too small, the procedure used to measure the dependent variable is subject to large random or systematic errors, and so on.

Sometimes a random sampling procedure will produce a random sample that is not representative of the population and one that is consistent with the false null hypothesis. You know, for example, that a fair coin will, on occasion, produce 10 or even 20 or more consecutive heads. If the null hypothesis is not rejected, the researcher has two options: state that he or she failed to reject the null hypothesis, in which case it remains credible, or suspend judgment about the null and scientific hypotheses pending completion of a new, improved experiment.

On the other hand, if the null hypothesis is rejected, what does it mean? The researcher can conclude that the alternative hypothesis is probably true. Here, too, the possibility always exists that one's sample is not representative, but, as you will see later, the probability of erroneously rejecting a true null hypothesis is determined by the researcher and can be made as small as desired.

The Role of Logic in Evaluating a Scientific Hypothesis

I have just described the evaluation of statistical hypotheses. Let's now turn to the researcher's ultimate objective—evaluating a scientific hypothesis. This evaluation involves a chain of deductive and inductive logic that begins and ends with the scientific hypothesis. The chain is diagrammed in Figure 10.1-1. First, by means of deductive logic, the scientific hypothesis and its negation are expressed as two mutually exclusive and exhaustive statistical hypotheses that make predictions concerning a population parameter. These predictions, denoted by H_0 and H_1, are made about the population mean, median, variance, correlation, and so on. If, as is usually the case, all the elements in the population cannot be observed, a random sample is obtained from the population. The sample provides an estimate of the unknown population parameters.

> The process of deciding whether to reject the null hypothesis is called a **statistical test.** The decision is based on (1) a test statistic computed for a random sample from the population, (2) hypothesis testing conventions, and (3) a decision rule.

These three items are described in subsequent sections. The outcome of the statistical test is the basis for the final link in the chain shown in Figure 10.1-1: an inductive inference concerning the probable truth or falsity of the scientific hypothesis. Logic therefore plays a key role in hypothesis testing. It is the basis for arriving at both the statistical hypothesis that is tested and the final decision regarding the scientific hypothesis. If errors occur in the deductive or inductive links in the chain of logic, the statistical hypothesis that is tested may have little or no bearing on the original scientific hypothesis, or the inference concerning the scientific hypothesis

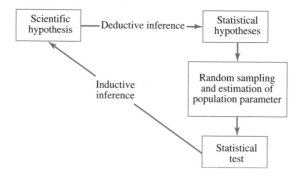

Figure 10.1-1. The evaluation of a scientific hypothesis using deductive and inductive logic.

may be incorrect, or both. Both creativity and deductive skill are required to formulate relevant statistical hypotheses.

CHECK YOUR UNDERSTANDING OF SECTION 10.1

1. Which of the following are scientific hypotheses?
   a. Right-handed people tend to be taller than left-handed people.
   b. Behavior therapy is more effective than hypnosis in helping smokers kick the habit.
   c. Most clairvoyant people are able to communicate with beings from outer space.
   d. Rats are likely to fixate an incorrect response if it is followed by an intense noxious stimulus.

2. Which of the following are examples of statistical hypotheses?
   a. $H_0: \mu = 100$ b. $H_0: S^2 \leq 50$
   c. $H_1: \rho \neq 0$ d. $H_0: \overline{X} \geq 100$
   e. $H_1: \sigma^2 > 0$ f. $H_1: \overline{X} \leq 15$
   g. $H_0: r = 0$ h. $H_0: \mu \geq 60$
   i. $H_0: \sigma^2 = 225$ j. $H_0: \rho = 0$

3. a. According to convention, which statistical hypothesis corresponds to the researcher's scientific hunch? alt
   b. Which is the hypothesis that actually is tested? null

4. Assume that a researcher has a hunch that insecure children engage in overt aggression more frequently than do children who feel secure. Let μ and μ_0 denote the mean daily number of aggressive acts, respectively, of insecure and secure children, where it is known that $\mu_0 = 8$. State H_0 and H_1 for the research. $H_0: \mu \leq 8$ $H_1: \mu > 8$

5. It was hypothesized that a sample of 139 women seeking treatment for marital discord at the University Marital Therapy Clinic would have a score above 14 on the Beck Depression Inventory (BDI). A score of 14 indicates depressive symptomatology or dysphoria. Let μ denote the BDI mean for women seeking treatment and let μ_0 represent the criterion for depressive symptomatology. State H_0 and H_1 for the research. $H_0: \mu \leq 14$ $H_1: \mu > 14$

6. Terms to remember:
   a. Statistical inference   b. Scientific hypothesis
   c. Statistical hypothesis   d. Null hypothesis
   e. Alternative hypothesis   f. Hypothesis testing
   g. Statistical test

10.2 HYPOTHESIS TESTING

I will now describe the procedures for testing statistical hypotheses. For the sake of clarity, I have organized these procedures around five steps and a decision rule. This should not suggest that hypothesis testing is a formal or a rigid procedure—it isn't.

However, as a researcher makes plans for doing research, each of the items in the following five steps must be considered. After I list the five steps and decision rule, I will discuss each in detail.

Step 1.   State the null and alternative hypotheses.

Step 2.   Specify the test statistic based on the hypothesis to be tested, information that is known about the population, and assumptions about the population that appear to be tenable.

Step 3.   Specify the size of the sample, n, to be obtained and make assumptions that permit specification of the sampling distribution of the test statistic, given that H_0 is true.

Step 4.   Specify an acceptable risk of rejecting the null hypothesis when it is true—that is, making a decision error.

Step 5.   Obtain a random sample of size n from the population, compute the test statistic, and make a decision about the null and alternative hypotheses and an inductive inference about the scientific hypothesis.

Decision rule:

Reject the null hypothesis if the test statistic falls in the specified region of the sampling distribution of the test statistic; otherwise, do not reject the null hypothesis. Rejecting the null hypothesis leads you to infer that the scientific hypothesis is true.

You may find it helpful to read the following discussion of the five steps and decision rule a number of times.

Step 1: Stating the Statistical Hypotheses

Let's return to the registration example mentioned earlier. Recall that the dean is interested in testing the scientific hypothesis that a new registration procedure will enable students to register in less time than with the old procedure. The corresponding statistical hypothesis is $H_1: \mu < \mu_0$, where μ denotes the unknown population mean for the new procedure and μ_0 denotes the population mean of the current procedure. The latter mean is known to equal 3.10—that is, $\mu_0 = 3.10$. The null and alternative hypotheses are

$$H_0: \mu \geq 3.10$$

$$H_1: \mu < 3.10$$

where μ_0 has been replaced by 3.10, the known mean for the current procedure. As written, the null hypothesis is inexact because it states a range of possible values for the population mean—all values greater than or equal to 3.10. However, one exact value is specified, $\mu = 3.10$, and that is the value actually tested. If the null hypothesis $\mu = 3.10$ can be rejected, then the hypothesis $\mu > 3.10$ is rejected automatically. Obviously, if $\mu = 3.10$ is considered improbable because the mean of the new registration procedure is less than 3.10, any population mean whose value is greater than 3.10 would be considered even less probable.

Step 2: Specifying the Test Statistic

Two test statistics can be used to evaluate hypotheses about a population mean. They are denoted by t and z. A test statistic is called a t *statistic* if its sampling distribution is the t distribution; a test statistic is called a z *statistic* if its sampling distribution is the standard normal distribution. As you will see, the choice of a test statistic is de-termined by (1) the hypothesis to be tested, (2) the information that is known about the population, and (3) the assumptions about the population that appear to be ten-able. Which of the two test statistics should be used to test the hypothesis $H_0: \mu \geq 3.10$? Because the hypothesis concerns the mean of a single population, the popula-tion standard deviation is unknown, and the population is assumed to be normally distributed; the appropriate test statistic is

$$t = \frac{\overline{X} - \mu_0}{\hat{\sigma}_{\overline{X}}} = \frac{\overline{X} - \mu_0}{\hat{\sigma}/\sqrt{n}}$$

where $\overline{X} = \Sigma X_i/n$ is used to estimate the unknown population mean for the new reg-istration procedure, $\hat{\sigma} = \sqrt{\Sigma(X_i - \overline{X})^2/(n-1)}$ is used to estimate the unknown population standard deviation, n is the size of the random sample used to estimate μ and σ, and $\hat{\sigma}_{\overline{X}} = \hat{\sigma}/\sqrt{n}$ is a sample estimate the standard error of the mean.

The use of the t statistic to test the hypothesis about the new registration proce-dure is appropriate if the population of registration times is normally distributed. I should say *approximately normal*, because random variables in experiments do not range from $-\infty$ to ∞ and, hence, they are never normally distributed. For simplicity, I often omit the qualifier "approximately." The tenability of the normality assump-tion can be checked by visually inspecting the distribution of one's random sample. Fortunately, the t test gives satisfactory results even when the distribution of X de-parts somewhat from a normal distribution. This is another way of saying that the t statistic is robust with respect to violation the normality assumption. If the sample distribution appears fairly symmetrical, it is probably safe to use the t statistic.[1]

Earlier, I mentioned that another test statistic, the z statistic, also can be used to test a hypothesis about the mean of a single population. To use this statistic, the pop-ulation standard deviation, σ, must be known and the population must be assumed to be approximately normal or the sample size must be quite large. The z test statistic is

$$z = \frac{\overline{X} - \mu_0}{\sigma_{\overline{X}}} = \frac{\overline{X} - \mu_0}{\sigma/\sqrt{n}}$$

---

[1] You should always examine a plot of your sample distribution for signs that the population might be markedly non-normal. Research by Micceri (1989) suggests that extreme non-normality in behavioral science data is more common than was once thought. Wilcox (1996) provides an excellent discussion of procedures for dealing with normality.

At first glance, the t and z test statistics look alike, but a difference can be seen on close inspection:

$$t = \frac{\overline{X} - \mu_0}{\hat{\sigma}/\sqrt{n}} = \frac{\text{Random variable} - \text{Constant}}{\text{Random variable}}$$

$$z = \frac{\overline{X} - \mu_0}{\sigma/\sqrt{n}} = \frac{\text{Random variable} - \text{Constant}}{\text{Constant}}$$

The z statistic is the ratio of a random variable to a constant; t is the ratio of two random variables. This follows because when n is less than ∞, both $\overline{X}$ and $\hat{\sigma}$ in the t statistic vary from sample to sample and hence are random variables. The difference in the nature of the z and t denominators has an important ramification that I will examine in the following step. I will have little more to say about this particular z statistic. It is rarely ever used because researchers generally do not know the population standard deviation.

Step 3: Specifying *n* and the Sampling Distribution

A number of factors enter into the specification of a sample size, n. I have developed a table that simplifies the task of choosing n; it is Appendix Table D.8. Before I can describe how to use the table, I need to introduce several new concepts. For the moment, I will simply specify that the sample size in the registration example should be $n = 27$. I will return to the topic of specifying a sample size in Section 10.4.

The sampling distribution of the t statistic was derived by William Sealey Gossett, an employee of the Guiness Brewing Company in Dublin, Ireland. Gossett published under the pseudonym *Student*; hence, the distribution is often referred to as **Student's *t* distribution.** The t sampling distribution—or, more simply, the t distribution—is symmetrical and centered over a mean of zero. In these respects, it is like the standard normal distribution described in the previous chapter. However, the dispersion of the t distribution—that is, the variance of t—depends on sample size or, more specifically, degrees of freedom. Before going any further, I need to discuss the concept of *degrees of freedom*, abbreviated *df*, and also denoted by ν (Greek nu, pronounced "new"). The term comes from the physical sciences, where it refers to the number of planes or directions in which an object is free to move.

In statistics, the term **degrees of freedom** refers to the number of scores whose values are free to vary.

To clarify, consider a sample of size $n = 3$, with mean $= 5$—that is, $\overline{X} = (X_1 + X_2 + X_3)/3 = 5$. If I arbitrarily specify that $X_1 = 4$ and $X_2 = 5$, then X_3 must equal 6, because $(4 + 5 + 6)/3 = 15/3 = 5$. Given the statement that $\overline{X} = 5$, I am free to assign any values to $n - 1 = 2$ of the scores, but having done so, the value of the remaining score is determined. Thus, the number of degrees of freedom associated with $\overline{X}$ is $n - 1$. Let us consider another example, one that is particularly relevant to the t statistic. The number of degrees of freedom associated with

$\hat{\sigma} = \sqrt{\sum(X_i - \overline{X})^2/(n-1)}$ is $n - 1$. This follows because once $n - 1$ of the n deviations $(X_i - \overline{X})$ have been arbitrarily specified, the remaining deviation is not free to vary because $\sum(X_i - \overline{X})$ must equal 0 as shown in Section 3.8 under "Proof That the Mean Is a Balance Point." The number of degrees of freedom for the t statistic in our registration example is $n - 1$, which is the number of degrees of freedom of $\hat{\sigma}$ in the denominator of t.

Now that I have introduced the concept of degrees of freedom, I can describe the dispersion of the t sampling distribution and compare its dispersion with that of the z sampling distribution. It can be shown that when n is greater than 3, the variance of the t distribution is

$$\text{Var}(t) = \frac{\nu}{\nu - 2}$$

where ν, the degrees of freedom, is equal to $n - 1$. According to the formula, if random samples of size $n = 5$ are obtained from a population, the variance of the resulting t distribution is

$$\text{Var}(t) = \frac{\nu}{\nu - 2} = \frac{4}{2} = 2$$

When n is equal to 5, the variance of the t distribution is 2, which is twice as large as the variance of the standard normal z distribution. Recall from Section 9.2 that the variance of the z distribution is equal to 1. As the number of degrees of freedom increases, the variance of the t distribution approaches more and more closely that of z. For example, when n is equal to 30,

$$\text{Var}(t) = \frac{29}{29 - 2} = 1.07$$

which differs only slightly from the variance of z. When ν is equal to ∞, the two sampling distributions are identical. Because the two sampling distributions are so similar for samples equal to or larger than 30, an n of 30 is often taken as the dividing point between large and small samples.

The t distribution is actually a family of distributions whose shapes depend on the associated number of degrees of freedom. Figure 10.2-1 compares three members of the t family and the z distribution. As this figure illustrates, the t and z sampling distributions are alike in that both have a mean of 0, are symmetrical, and are unimodal. The distributions differ when ν is less than ∞—the t distribution is more leptokurtic and has a larger variance.

An advantage of the t statistic relative to the z statistic is that the t statistic can be computed when the researcher does not know the population standard deviation. However, for the t statistic to be distributed as the t sampling distribution when the null hypothesis is true, it is necessary to assume that the population distribution of X is normal. The normality assumption serves two purposes. First, it permits a researcher to specify the sampling distribution of the numerator of the t statistic without regard to sample size: it is the normal distribution. This follows from the discussion of the central limit theorem and the sampling distribution of $\overline{X}$ in Section 9.4. Second, the normality assumption is a necessary condition for the numerator and

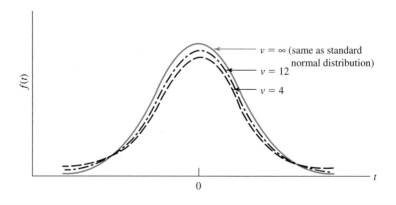

Figure 10.2-1. Graph of the distribution of t for 4, 12, and ∞ degrees of freedom. When $\nu = \infty$, the t distribution is identical to the z distribution.

denominator (both random variables) of the t statistic to be statistically independent, which means that the information contained in $\overline{X}$ does not affect the value of $\hat{\sigma}$ and vice versa. Independence was a simplifying assumption that Gossett made when he derived the sampling distribution of t. If the numerator and denominator of the t statistic are not independent, specifying the exact sampling distribution of t is extremely difficult. This problem does not occur with the z test statistic because its denominator is a constant rather than a random variable. According to the central limit theorem, the sampling distribution of the z test statistic is the standard normal distribution regardless of the shape of the population distribution of X if n is sufficiently large. Hence, the normality assumption plays a more important role in the derivation and use of t than in z.

Step 4: Specifying the Significance Level, α

In the registration example, the dean might decide that $\mu < 3.10$ when in fact $\mu \geq 3.10$. In this case, she would have made a decision error. The fourth step is to specify an acceptable risk of making this kind of error—that is, rejecting the null hypothesis when it is true. I will touch on this subject here and return to it later. Considering the sample-to-sample variability of random variables, I would not expect the mean, $\overline{X}$, of a single random sample to exactly equal the predicted value, μ_0, even though $\mu = \mu_0$. I would be willing to attribute a small discrepancy between $\overline{X}$ and μ_0 to chance. However, if the discrepancy is large enough, I would be inclined to believe that μ_0 is incorrect and that the null hypothesis should be rejected. According to hypothesis-testing conventions, a discrepancy between $\overline{X}$ and μ_0 that would be expected to occur five or fewer times in 100 replications of the experiment is considered to be large enough to warrant rejecting the hypothesis $\mu = \mu_0$. Stated another way, the null hypothesis $\mu = \mu_0$ should be rejected if the probability is equal to or less than .05 of observing a discrepancy between $\overline{X}$ and μ_0 as large as or larger than that observed.

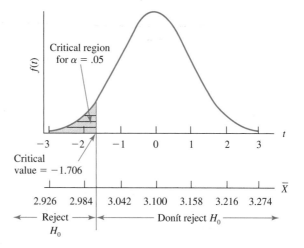

Figure 10.2-2. Sampling distribution of t given that H_0 is true. The lower scale gives the corresponding values of the sample means. The critical region, which corresponds in this example to the lower .05 portion of the sampling distribution, defines values of t and $\overline{X}$ that are improbable if the null hypothesis H_0: $\mu \geq 3.1$ is true. Hence, if the t test statistic falls in the critical region, the null hypothesis should be rejected. The value of t that cuts off the lower .05 portion of the sampling distribution is called the critical value. This value can be found in the table of Student's t distribution in Appendix Table D.3 and is $-t_{.05,\,26} = -1.706$. It can be shown that the sample mean corresponding to $-t_{.05,\,26} = -1.706$ is

$$\overline{X}_{.05} = \mu_0 - t_{.05,26}\hat{\sigma}/\sqrt{n} = 3.100 - 1.706(0.3013)/\sqrt{27} = 3.001$$

By convention a probability of .05 is the largest risk a researcher should be willing to take of rejecting a true null hypothesis—declaring, for example, that $\mu < 3.10$ when in fact $\mu \geq 3.10$. Such a probability, called a **significance level,** is denoted by the lowercase Greek letter alpha, α. For $\alpha = .05$ and H_1: $\mu < 3.10$, the region for rejecting H_0, called the **critical region,** is shown in Figure 10.2-2. The location and size of the critical region are determined, respectively, by H_1 and α.

A decision to adopt the .05 level of significance in experiments is based on hypothesis-testing conventions that have evolved since the 1920s. These conventions are so well entrenched that editors of scientific journals rarely publish articles that fail to meet the .05 significance criterion. In Section 10.4, I will return to the problem of selecting a significance level.

Step 5: Making a Decision

The fifth step in testing a statistical hypothesis is to obtain a random sample from the population of interest, compute the test statistic, and make a decision.

The **decision rule** is as follows: Reject the null hypothesis if the test statistic falls in the critical region; otherwise, do not reject the null hypothesis.

The value of t that cuts off the critical region of the sampling distribution of t is called the **critical value** (see Figure 10.2-2). The critical value of t that cuts off the upper α region (upper tail) of the t distribution for v degrees of freedom is given in Appendix Table D.3 and is denoted by $t_{\alpha, v}$. Because the t distribution is symmetrical, critical values in the lower tail of the t distribution are obtained by putting a negative sign in front of the upper tail values. For the registration example, the critical value of t is obtained from the row in Appendix Table D.3 labeled "Level of Significance for a One-Tailed Test" with $\alpha = .05$ and $v = 27 - 1 = 26$ and is $-t_{.05, 26} = -1.706$. According to the decision rule, the null hypothesis is rejected if the observed t test statistic is less than or equal to the critical value, $-t_{.05, 26} = -1.706$. Otherwise, the null hypothesis is not rejected.

If the null hypothesis is rejected, a researcher can conclude that the scientific hypothesis is probably true. But what if the null hypothesis is not rejected? A nonrejection can occur for a variety of reasons. For example, the null hypothesis may be true and should not be rejected. Alternatively, the null hypothesis may be false but the researcher's sample was not representative of the population or the experiment may have lacked adequate sensitivity to reject the null hypothesis because the sample was too small. Hence, a nonrejection should not be taken as evidence that the null hypothesis is true. Faced with a nonrejection, the researcher can either conclude that the evidence does not support the original scientific hypothesis or suspend judgment pending the completion of a new, improved experiment.

CHECK YOUR UNDERSTANDING OF SECTION 10.2

7. For the past several years, the mean arithmetic-achievement score for a population of ninth-grade students has been $\mu_0 = 45$. After participating in an experimental teaching program, a random sample of 121 students had a mean score of $\overline{X} = 50$ with a standard deviation of $\hat{\sigma} = 15$. (a) List the five steps you would follow to test the hypothesis that the new program leads to better arithmetic achievement than the old program, and supply the required information. Let $\alpha = .05$. (b) State the decision rule.

8. For the data in Exercise 7, draw the sampling distribution associated with the null hypothesis and indicate the regions that lead to rejection and nonrejection of the null hypothesis.

9. a. Which of the following statistical hypotheses actually is tested?

$$H_0: \mu \leq 15$$
$$H_1: \mu > 15$$

b. Which hypothesis corresponds to the researcher's scientific hypothesis?

10. List similarities and differences between the t and z sampling distributions.

11. What determines the size of the critical region and its location?

12. Use Appendix Table D.3 to determine the critical value for the following. Assume in each case that the null hypothesis is $H_0: \mu \leq \mu_0$, which means that the significance level is in the row labeled "one-tailed test."
   a. $n = 12, \alpha = .05$ b. $n = 12, \alpha = .01$
   c. $n = 25, \alpha = .05$ d. $n = 17, \alpha = .05$

13. Use Appendix Table D.3 to determine the critical value for the following. Assume in each case that the null hypothesis is $H_0\!: \mu \geq \mu_0$, which means that the significance level is in the row labeled "one-tailed test."
    - a. $n = 12$, $\alpha = .05$
    - b. $n = 12$, $\alpha = .01$
    - c. $n = 31$, $\alpha = .05$
    - d. $n = 61$, $\alpha = .05$
14. Terms to remember:
    - a. Student's *t* distribution
    - b. Degrees of freedom
    - c. Significance level
    - d. Critical region
    - e. Decision rule
    - f. Critical value

10.3 ONE-SAMPLE *t* TEST FOR A MEAN

I will now illustrate the use of the *t* statistic,

$$t = \frac{\overline{X} - \mu_0}{\hat{\sigma}/\sqrt{n}}$$

in testing a hypothesis about a population mean. Recall that $\overline{X}$ is the mean of a random sample from the population of interest, μ_0 is the mean specified in the null hypothesis, $\hat{\sigma}$ is the standard deviation of a random sample from the population, and n is the size of the sample used to compute $\overline{X}$ and $\hat{\sigma}$.

Again, consider the registration example at Idle-on-in College. Over the past several years, the mean time required to register has been 3.10 hours. The dean plans to do a trial run to test the new procedure using a random sample of $n = 27$ undergraduates. The steps she will follow in testing the null hypothesis and the decision rule are as follows.

Step 1.	State the statistical hypotheses:	$H_0\!: \mu \geq 3.10$ $H_1\!: \mu < 3.10$
Step 2.	Specify the test statistic:	$t = (\overline{X} - \mu_0)/(\hat{\sigma}/\sqrt{n})$ because she wants to test $\mu \geq 3.10$, σ is unknown, the sample is random, and she assumes the population distribution of X is approximately normal.
Step 3.	Specify the sample size: and the sampling distribution:	$n = 27$ t distribution with $\nu = n - 1 = 26$, because σ is unknown and must be estimated, and she assumes the population distribution of X is approximately normal.
Step 4.	Specify the significance level:	$\alpha = .05$
Step 5.	Obtain a random sample of size n, compute t, and make a decision.	

Decision rule:

Reject the null hypothesis if t falls in the lower 5% of the sampling distribution of t; otherwise, do not reject the null hypothesis. If the null hypothesis is rejected, conclude that the new class registration procedure reduces the time required to register; if the null hypothesis is not rejected, do not draw this conclusion.

The data for the trial run with a random sample of 27 undergraduate students are shown in Table 10.3-1. The mean registration time for the new procedure is $\overline{X} = 2.90$.

TABLE 10.3-1   Registration-Time Data

(i) Data

Student	Registration Time, X_i (Hours)	$(X_i - \overline{X})^2$	Student	Registration Time, X_i (Hours)	$(X_i - \overline{X})^2$
1	2.9	0	15	3.0	.01
2	2.7	.04	16	2.8	.01
3	2.4	.25	17	2.3	.36
4	3.0	.01	18	2.5	.16
5	2.6	.09	19	2.5	.16
6	2.9	0	20	3.2	.09
7	3.1	.04	21	3.2	.09
8	2.9	0	22	2.8	.01
9	3.0	.01	23	3.3	.16
10	2.7	.04	24	3.0	.01
11	2.9	0	25	3.2	.09
12	3.3	.16	26	3.5	.36
13	3.1	.04	27	2.5	.16
14	3.0	.01		$\Sigma X_i = 78.3$	$\Sigma(X_i - \overline{X})^2 = 2.36$

(ii) Computation

$$\overline{X} = \frac{\Sigma X_i}{n} = \frac{78.3}{27} = 2.90$$

$$\hat{\sigma} = \sqrt{\frac{\Sigma(X_i - \overline{X})^2}{n-1}} = \sqrt{\frac{2.36}{27-1}} = 0.3013$$

$$t = \frac{\overline{X} - \mu_0}{\hat{\sigma}/\sqrt{n}} = \frac{2.90 - 3.10}{0.3013/\sqrt{27}} = \frac{-0.20}{0.0580} = -3.449$$

$$\nu = n - 1 = 27 - 1 = 26$$

$$-t_{.05,26} = -1.706$$

This sample mean is consistent with the dean's scientific hypothesis. The value of the t statistic is $t(26) = -3.449$. In reporting the value of the t statistic, I have followed the convention of giving the degrees of freedom, 26, in parentheses immediately after t. Does the t statistic fall in the critical region? According to Appendix Table D.3, a t of -1.706 with $n - 1 = 26$ degrees of freedom cuts off the lower .05 region of the sampling distribution—that is, $-t_{.05, 26}$ is equal to -1.706. Because the computed $t(26) = -3.449$ in Table 10.3-1 is less than the critical value, $-t_{.05, 26} = -1.706$, the null hypothesis is rejected. The dean and other school administrators conclude that the new procedure is better than the old procedure.

Some Experimental Design Considerations

I will digress for a moment and explore some experimental design issues concerning the registration experiment at Idle-on-in College. The dean and other school administrators would like to believe that the new registration procedure is efficient and, if adopted for all students, would shorten the registration time. But consider some alternative explanations for the apparent greater efficiency of the new procedure. Because the 27 students were selected for the trial run, they may have felt that they should make a special effort to complete registration quickly—an effort they would not make once the new procedure was adopted and they were no longer under scrutiny. It also is possible that the personnel assisting in registration were more alert and tried to expedite the registration because they, too, were under scrutiny and because the procedure was a break from the usual routine. It is common for people to put forth special effort when they know that they are under scrutiny. The phenomenon even has a name—it is called the **John Henry effect** in honor of the steel driver who, when he learned that his performance was being compared with that of a steam drill, worked so hard that he outperformed the drill and died of overexertion.

Other explanations for the apparent greater efficiency of the new procedure could be advanced, and unless these explanations can be ruled out, the administrators may be disappointed if they adopt the new procedure. Once the novelty wears off, the new procedure may be no better, or may be even poorer, than the old one.

Designing an experiment whose outcome can be unambiguously interpreted requires careful planning.

It is customary in behavioral science research to use one or more **control groups.** These groups contain participants who do not receive the treatment. The purpose of control groups is to provide data on the effects of extraneous variables that affect the interpretation of the experiment.

For example, the design of the registration experiment could be improved by drawing a sample of 50 students, with half the students randomly assigned to use the new procedure and the other half assigned to the old procedure. This change in the design of the experiment would provide data on the effects of being specially selected to participate in the trial run. If this design modification were adopted, the appropriate test statistic is the two-sample t statistic for independent samples discussed in Section 13.2.

15. Assume that the Pd (Psychopathic deviate) scale of the Minnesota Multiphasic Personality Inventory has been given to a random sample of 30 men classified as habitual criminals. The researcher wants to test the hypothesis that habitual criminals have higher Pd scores than noncriminals. The latter population is known to be normally distributed, with mean and standard deviation equal to 50 and 10, respectively. (a) List the five steps you would follow in testing the scientific hypothesis. Let $\alpha = .05$. (b) State the decision rule.

16. Assume that the data in the following table have been obtained for the habitual criminals in Exercise 15. (a) Compute a t statistic for these data. (b) What conclusion can be drawn about the scientific hypothesis in Exercise 15?

Participant	Pd Score	Participant	Pd Score
1	50	16	55
2	51	17	56
3	54	18	48
4	55	19	45
5	25	20	41
6	61	21	82
7	64	22	65
8	55	23	67
9	55	24	75
10	52	25	40
11	71	26	61
12	57	27	35
13	59	28	56
14	54	29	56
15	55	30	55

17. If $\alpha = .005$ in Exercise 16, what conclusion would have been drawn about the scientific hypothesis?

18. One of the prison guards confessed that for a lark he filled out the Pd scale and used a prisoner's name, participant number 22. (a) Recompute the t statistic for the data in Exercise 16, eliminating participant 22's score. (b) What conclusion can be drawn about the scientific hypothesis?

19. Term to remember:
    a. John Henry effect

10.4 MORE ABOUT HYPOTHESIS TESTING

I described the steps used in testing a hypothesis in Section 10. 2, and these steps were illustrated in Section 10.3 by means of the one-sample t test. I now turn to several additional concepts that round out my discussion of null hypothesis significance testing.

One- and Two-Tailed Tests

A statistical test for which the critical region is in either the upper tail or the lower tail of the sampling distribution is called a **one-tailed test.** If the critical region is in both the upper and lower tails of the sampling distribution, the statistical test is called a **two-tailed test.**

A one-tailed test is used whenever the researcher makes a **directional** prediction concerning the phenomenon of interest—for example, that the new registration procedure takes less time than the current procedure. You know from Section 10.3 that the statistical hypotheses corresponding to this scientific hypothesis are

$$H_0: \mu \geq \mu_0$$
$$H_1: \mu < \mu_0$$

These hypotheses are called **directional** or **one-sided hypotheses.** The region for rejecting the null hypothesis is shown in Figure 10.2-2. If the scientific hypothesis stated that the mean registration time for the new procedure is longer than the current procedure, the following statistical hypotheses would be appropriate:

$$H_0: \mu \leq \mu_0$$
$$H_1: \mu > \mu_0$$

The region for rejecting this null hypothesis is shown in Figure 10.4-1(a). To be statistically significant, an observed t statistic would have to be greater than or equal to the critical value $t_{.05, 26} = 1.706$.

Often, researchers do not have sufficient information to make a directional prediction about a population parameter; they simply believe that the parameter is not equal to the value specified by the null hypothesis. For example, the dean may simply believe that the mean registration time for the new procedure is different from that for the current procedure. This situation calls for a two-tailed test. The statistical hypotheses for a two-tailed test have the following form:

$$H_0: \mu = \mu_0$$
$$H_1: \mu \neq \mu_0$$

These hypotheses are called **nondirectional** or **two-sided hypotheses.** For a two-tailed test, the region for rejecting the null hypothesis lies in both the upper and lower tails of the sampling distribution. Half of the significance level, $\alpha/2 = .025$, is assigned to the upper tail and half to the lower tail. The two critical regions are shown in Figure 10.4-1(b). To reject the null hypothesis at the .05 level of significance for a two-tailed test, the value of the t statistic in Table 10.3-1, $t(26) = -3.449$, must be greater than or equal to the two-tailed critical value $t_{.05/2, 26} = 2.056$ or less than or equal to $-t_{.05/2, 26} = -2.056$. The notation ".05/2" in $t_{.05/2, 26}$ indicates that half of the .05 critical region has been assigned to the upper tail of the sampling distribution of t and half to the lower tail. Note that the two-tailed null and alternative

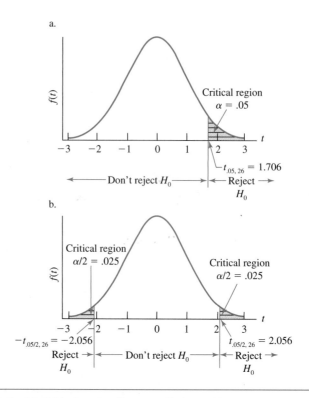

Figure 10.4-1. (a) Critical region for one-tailed test; $H_0: \mu \geq \mu_0$; $H_1: \mu < \mu_0$; $\alpha = .05$. (b) Critical regions for two-tailed test; $H_0: \mu = \mu_0$; $H_1: \mu \neq \mu_0$; $\alpha = .025 + .025 = .05$.

hypotheses also are mutually exclusive and exhaustive—if one is true, the other must be false.

In summary, a one-sided, or directional, hypothesis is called for when the researcher's original hunch is expressed in such terms as "more than," "less than," "increased," or "decreased." Such a hunch indicates that the researcher has quite a bit of knowledge about the research area. The knowledge could come from previous research, a pilot study, or perhaps theory. If the researcher is interested in determining only whether there is a difference, without specifying the direction of the difference, a two-tailed test should be used. Generally, significance tests in the behavioral sciences are two tailed, because most researchers lack the information necessary to formulate directional hypotheses.

How does the choice of a one- or two-tailed test affect the probability of rejecting a false null hypothesis? A researcher is more likely to reject a false null hypothesis with a one-tailed test than with a two-tailed test if the critical region has been placed in the correct tail. A one-tailed test places all of the α area, say .05, in one tail of the sampling distribution. A two-tailed test divides the $\alpha = .05$ area between the two tails with .025 in one tail and .025 in the other tail. In the registration example, the critical value of t that cuts off the lower .05 region for a one-tailed test is

$-t_{.05,26} = -1.706$. The critical values of t that cut off the lower and upper $.05/2 = .025$ regions for a two-tailed test are $-t_{.05/2,26} = -2.056$ and $t_{.05/2,26} = 2.056$, respectively. The critical regions and critical values for the two cases are shown in Figure 10.4-1(a and b). An inspection of this figure shows that the size of the difference $\overline{X} - \mu_0$ necessary to reach the critical region for a two-tailed test is larger than that required for a one-tailed test. Consequently, a researcher is less likely to reject a false null hypothesis with a two-tailed test than with a one-tailed test.

The term *power* refers to the probability of rejecting a false null hypothesis. A one-tailed test is more powerful than a two-tailed test if the researcher's hunch about the true difference $\mu - \mu_0$ is correct—that is, if the alternative hypothesis places the critical region in the correct tail of the sampling distribution. If the directional hunch is incorrect, the rejection region will be in the wrong tail, and the researcher will most certainly fail to reject the null hypothesis, even though it is false. A researcher is rewarded for making a correct directional prediction and is penalized for making an incorrect directional prediction. In the absence of sufficient information for using a one-tailed test, the researcher should play it safe and use a two-tailed test.

Type I and Type II Errors

When the null hypothesis is tested, a researcher's decision will be either correct or incorrect.

A researcher can arrive of an incorrect decision in two ways. The researcher can reject the null hypothesis when it is true; this is called a **Type I error.** Or the researcher can fail to reject the null hypothesis when it is false; this is called a **Type II error.** Likewise, a correct decision can be made in two ways. If the null hypothesis is true and the researcher does not reject it, a **correct acceptance** has been made. If the null hypothesis is false and the researcher rejects it, a **correct rejection** has been made.

The two kinds of correct decisions and the two kinds of errors are summarized in Table 10.4-1.

TABLE 10.4-1   Decision Outcomes Categorized

		True Situation	
		H_0 *true*	H_0 *false*
Researcher's Decision	*Fail to reject H_0*	Correct acceptance Probability $= 1 - \alpha$	Type II error Probability $= \beta$
	Reject H_0	Type I error Probability $= \alpha$	Correct rejection Probability $= 1 - \beta$

The probability of making a Type I error is determined by the researcher when the significance level, α, is specified. If α is specified as .05, the probability of making a Type I error is .05. The significance level also determines the probability of a correct acceptance of a true null hypothesis because this probability is equal to $1 - \alpha$.

The probability of making a Type II error, denoted by β, and the probability of making a correct rejection, denoted by $1 - \beta$, are determined by a number of variables: (1) the significance level adopted, (2) the size of the sample, (3) the size of the population standard deviation, (4) the magnitude of the difference between μ and μ_0, and (5) whether a one- or two-tailed test is used.

The probability of making a correct rejection, $1 - \beta$, is called the **power** of the statistical test.

To compute the probability of making a Type II error (β) and power ($1 - \beta$), it is necessary to know (1) μ, the true population mean, or to specify a value of μ that is sufficiently different from μ_0 to be worth detecting and (2) the population standard deviation. Researchers rarely know the population standard deviation, but, as you have seen, the parameter can be estimated from sample data. Also, researchers do not know the population mean, but they often are able to specify a population mean that is sufficiently different from μ_0 to be of interest to detect. I will denote such a mean by μ'. If the new registration procedure reduced the mean registration time by only three minutes (.05 hour), the dean probably would conclude that the time savings is not worth changing to the new procedure. However, if the new procedure reduced the mean time from $\mu_0 = 3.10$ to $\mu' = 2.95$ hours, the dean might be inclined to adopt the procedure. The difference $3.10 - 2.95 = 0.15$ corresponds to nine minutes. Nine minutes is the smallest difference that the dean would be interested in detecting if the new procedure is actually better than the current procedure. I will illustrate the computation of power for this difference. Figure 10.4-2 shows two sampling distributions, one associated with the null hypothesis where $\mu_0 = 3.10$ and the other associated with the alternative hypothesis where $\mu' = 2.95$. Recall from the registration example that $\alpha = .05$, $t_{.05, 26} = 1.706$, $\hat{\sigma} = 0.3013$, and $n = 27$. To compute an estimate of power, I need one more bit of information—the value of $\overline{X}$ that cuts off the lower .05 region of the null hypothesis sampling distribution. I'll denote this mean by $\overline{X}_{.05}$. I can estimate $\overline{X}_{.05}$ by rearranging the terms in the formula $t_{.05,26} = (\overline{X}_{.05} - \mu_0)/(\hat{\sigma}/\sqrt{n})$ as follows:

$$\overline{X}_{.05} = \mu_0 + t_{.05,26}(\hat{\sigma}/\sqrt{n})$$

$$= 3.10 + (-1.706)(0.3013)/\sqrt{27}$$

$$= 3.001$$

Thus, a mean of 3.001 cuts off the lower .05 region of the null hypothesis sampling distribution. In Figure 10.4-2, $\overline{X}_{.05} = 3.001$ falls on the boundary between the reject and nonreject regions. An estimate of the size of the region corresponding to a Type II error (labeled $\hat{\beta}$ in Figure 10.4-2) can be determined by computing a t statistic for the difference $\overline{X}_{.05} - \mu' = 3.001 - 2.95$. The t statistic for determining the size of the $\hat{\beta}$ area is

$$t = \frac{\overline{X}_{.05} - \mu'}{\hat{\sigma}/\sqrt{n}} = \frac{3.001 - 2.95}{0.3013/\sqrt{27}} = \frac{0.051}{0.058} = 0.880$$

According to Appendix Table D.3, the area above $t = 0.880$, which is the size of the $\hat{\beta}$ region, is .19. Thus, if the mean time to register using the new procedure is $\mu' = 2.95$, the dean's estimate of the probability of making a Type II error ($\hat{\beta}$) is .19, and her estimate of the probability of making a correct rejection (power) is $1 - \hat{\beta} = 1 - .19 = .81$. Figure 10.4-2 shows the regions corresponding to these two probabilities. The procedure for estimating power may seem complicated. Take heart; the Web contains numerous easy-to-use programs for computing power. The purpose of this example is to show that $\hat{\beta}$ and $1 - \hat{\beta}$ represent areas under the

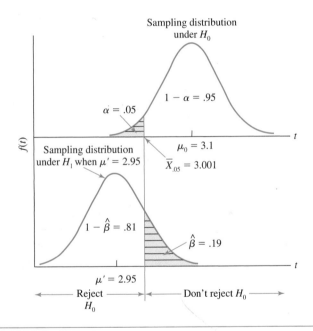

Figure 10.4-2. Regions corresponding to probabilities of making a Type I error (α) and a Type II error ($\hat{\beta}$). The mean that cuts off the lower .05 region of the sampling distribution under H_0 is denoted by $\overline{X}_{.05}$ and is equal to 3.001. The statistic

$$t = (\overline{X}_{.05} - \mu')/(\hat{\sigma}/\sqrt{n}) = (3.001 - 2.95)/(0.3013/\sqrt{27}) = 0.880$$

along with the t table (Appendix Table D.3) is used to determine the size of the region corresponding to a Type II error. The area that lies above $t = 0.880$ is .19.

The size and location of the region corresponding to a Type I error are determined by α and H_1, respectively. If the size of the α region is made smaller, say .01, the size of the $\hat{\beta}$ region increases. In other words, as the probability of a Type I error decreases, the probability of a Type II error increases.

TABLE 10.4-2   Probabilities Associated with the Decision Process

	True Situation	
	$\mu = 3.10$	$\mu' = 2.95$
$\mu \leq 3.10$	Correct acceptance $1 - \alpha = .95$	Type II error $\hat{\beta} = .19$
$\mu > 3.10$	Type I error $\alpha = .05$	Correct rejection $1 - \hat{\beta} = .81$

Researcher's Decision (row label)

sampling distribution of μ' just as α and $1 - \alpha$ represent areas under the sampling distribution of μ_0. The t statistic enables us to estimate the size of these areas.

A power of .81 in the registration example just exceeds the minimum power that by convention is considered acceptable, which is .80. When the power is .80, the probability of a Type II error is .20. The selection of .80 as the minimum acceptable power is a convenient rule of thumb and reflects the view that Type I errors are more serious than Type II errors. For example, when $\beta = .20$ and $\alpha = .05$, the probability of making a Type II error is $.20/.05 = 4$ times larger than the probability of making a Type I error.

Table 10.4-2 summarizes the probabilities associated with the possible decision outcomes when $\mu_0 = 3.10$ and $\mu' = 2,95$. In this example, the probability of making a correct decision is larger when the null hypothesis is true (Probability $= 1 - \alpha = .95$) than when the null hypothesis is false (Probability $= 1 - \hat{\beta} = .81$). It also is apparent that the probability of making a Type I error ($\alpha = .05$) is much smaller than the probability of making a Type II error ($\hat{\beta} = .19$). In most research situations, the researcher follows the convention of setting α equal to either .05 or .01. As the probability of a Type I error is made smaller and smaller, the probability of a Type II error increases and vice versa. We can see this result by examining Figure 10.4-2. If the vertical line cutting off the lower α region is moved to the left or to the right in the figure, the region designated $\hat{\beta}$ is made, respectively, larger or smaller.

More about Type I and Type II Errors

In many research situations, the cost of committing a Type I error can be large relative to that of a Type II error. For example, falsely deciding that a new medication is more effective than conventional therapies in halting the production of cancer cells and therefore can be used in place of conventional medical procedures—a Type I error—is a serious matter. On the other hand, falsely deciding that the new medication is not more effective—a Type II error—would result in withholding the medication from the public and further research. Eventually, after enough research, the effectiveness of the new medication would be demonstrated. In this example, a Type I error is more costly than a Type II error and is the error to be avoided. The probability of making a Type I error can be reduced by using the .01, .005, or even the .001

level of significance. However, in research situations that do not involve life and death, a Type I error may be less costly than a Type II error. For example, a researcher who makes a Type II error may discontinue a promising line of research, whereas a Type I error would lead to further exploration into a blind alley. Faced with these two alternatives, many researchers would adopt the .05 or even .10 level of significance, preferring to make a Type I error rather than a Type II error.

It is apparent that the costs and benefits associated with Type I and Type II errors must be known before one can make a rational choice of α. Unfortunately, researchers in the behavioral sciences, health sciences, and education generally are unable to specify the costs and benefits associated with the two kinds of errors, and therein lies the problem. The problem is resolved by using the conventional but arbitrary .05 or .01 level of significance.

I hope that this discussion has dispelled the magical aura that surrounds the .05 and .01 levels of significance—their use in hypothesis testing is simply a convention. A statistical test at the .05 level of significance addresses the question "Is chance a likely explanation for the results that have been obtained?" A null hypothesis significance test does not address the question "Are the results important, useful, or practically significant?" The researcher is probably the person best equipped to decide whether a statistically significant result is of any practical significance. Throughout the remainder of the book I will describe various guidelines for assessing the practical significance of research results.

Determining the n Required to Achieve an Acceptable α, $1 - \beta$, and $\mu - \mu_0$

Until now I have not said much about specifying sample size, n, except that it should be large enough—but not too large. There is a rational way to specify sample size. The factors discussed in connection with power (α, $1 - \beta$, $\hat{\sigma}$, n, and $\mu - \mu_0$) are interrelated. Values for α, $1 - \beta$, $\hat{\sigma}$, and $\mu - \mu_0$ can be entered into a formula to estimate n, but the procedure is complicated (Kirk, 1995, pp. 62–65). Fortunately, it is not necessary to use the formula. I have developed a table, Appendix Table D.8, which simplifies the determination of an appropriate sample size. To use the table, we have to specify the value of a measure popularized by Jack Cohen called an *effect size* (1988, pp. 20–27).

Cohen's **effect size,** denoted by d, expresses the magnitude of the absolute difference $\mu - \mu_0$ one wants to detect in units of the population standard deviation. The formula is

$$d = |\mu - \mu_0|/\sigma$$

Cohen assigned labels to three values of d as follows:

$d = 0.2$ is a small effect

$d = 0.5$ is a medium effect

$d = 0.8$ is a large effect

According to Cohen (1992), a medium effect of 0.5 is visible to the naked eye of a careful observer. A small effect of 0.2 is noticeably smaller than medium but not so small as to be trivial. Only an expert would be able to detect a small effect. A large effect of 0.8 is the same distance above medium as small is below it. A large effect would be obvious to anyone. Several surveys have found that 0.5 approximates the average size of observed effects in a number of fields including psychology. By assigning the labels small, medium, and large to the numbers 0.2, 0.5, and 0.8, respectively, Cohen provided researchers with guidelines for interpreting the size of differences between means.

To estimate an appropriate sample size using Appendix Table D.8, a researcher needs to specify the following:

1. An effect size: $d = 0.2, 0.5,$ or 0.8
2. A significance level: $\alpha = .05$ or $.01$
3. An acceptable power: $1 - \beta = .80, .90,$ or $.95$
4. Type of statistical hypothesis: one-tailed or two-tailed
5. Type of test: one- or two-sample test

In the registration example, suppose that the dean was only interested in adopting the new registration procedure if the difference between it and the current procedure was at least a medium size effect ($d = 0.5$). Suppose, also, that she adopted $\alpha = .05$ and $1 - \beta = .80$, and that she advanced a one-sided null hypothesis and planned to use a one-sample t statistic. According to Appendix Table D.8, the sample size necessary to detect a medium size effect for these conditions is $n = 27$. Since 27 is the size of the sample the dean used in the trial run, she obviously had consulted Appendix Table D.8. If the dean had been interested in detecting a large effect, according to the table she would have needed only $n = 12$ undergraduates for the trial run. The smaller sample size required to detect a large effect is consistent with our intuition—it is much easier to detect large differences than small differences.

It is obvious that one's sample can be too small, resulting in insufficient power. But n also can be too large, resulting in wasted time and resources. A researcher can avoid these problems by using Appendix Table D.8 to make a rational choice of sample size. This procedure has two other less obvious benefits: it focuses attention on the interrelationships among n, α, $1 - \beta$, σ, and $\mu - \mu_0$; and it forces the researcher to think about the size of the effect or difference that would be worth detecting.

It is important to distinguish between **statistical significance** that is concerned with whether a result is due to chance or sampling variability and **practical significance** that is concerned with whether the result is useful in the real world.

By estimating the n required to detect a useful result, a researcher increases the chances of obtaining both statistical significance and practical significance.

Reporting p Values

Most research reports and computer printouts contain a statistic called a **probability value** or, simply, a p **value.**

A *p* **value** is the probability of obtaining a value of the test statistic equal to or more extreme than that observed, given that the null hypothesis is true.

Students often confuse *p* values with significance levels. A significance level is the probability a researcher has specified an acceptable level of falsely rejecting a null hypothesis. This probability is the probability of making a Type I error and is commonly set at $\alpha = .05$ or .01. The other kind of probability, a *p* value, refers to the probability of obtaining a test statistic as extreme as or more extreme than the one that has been obtained, assuming that the null hypothesis is true. *p* values are usually obtained with the aid of a statistical calculator or computer. Alternatively, the tables in Appendix D can be used to approximate some *p* values. However, the range of test-statistic values available in the tables is limited. Microsoft's Excel program, which is installed on most computers, also can be used to obtain *p* values for a variety of sampling distributions. For example, to obtain *p* values for the *t* sampling distribution, you use the Excel TDIST function. To access this function, select "Insert" in Excel's menu bar and then the menu command "Function." You then can select the TDIST function from the list of functions. After you access the TDIST function,

$$TDIST(x, \text{deg\_freedom}, \text{tails}),$$

replace "*x*" with the absolute value of the *t* statistic, "deg_freedom" with the degrees of freedom for the *t* statistic, and "tails" with 1 for a one-tailed test and 2 for a two-tailed test. To illustrate, the *p* value for the one-tailed *t* statistic in Table 10.3-1 where $t(26) = -3.449$ and $\nu = 26$ is given by

$$TDIST(3.449, 26, 1)$$

and is equal to .001.

In presenting the results of null hypothesis significance tests in the text portion of publications, it is good statistical practice to report, in order, the test statistic that was used, say *t*, followed by the degrees of freedom in parentheses, the value of the test statistic, and finally the *p* value. For example, in describing the results of the registration experiment, the dean could report that "the mean difference between the current procedure and the new procedure was –0.15 hours. The difference was statistically significant, $t(26) = -3.449, p < .001$." If the results of a statistical test are presented in a table, the *p* value is usually reported as a table footnote—for example, "$*p < .001$." It is common practice to round *p* values to the next larger value of .001, .005, .01, .05, .10, .15, .20, and so on. The Excel TDIST function actually gave the *p* value for $|t(26)| = |-3.449|$ as $p = .0009652$; the dean rounded the *p* value to .001. It also is good statistical practice to provide descriptive statistics for the data such as the sample size, mean, and standard deviation. This information is often reported in a table as follows:

Descriptive Statistics for the Registration-Time Data

Sample Size	Mean	Standard Deviation
27	2.90	0.30

In Section 10.1, I formulated a hypothesis-testing decision rule in terms of a test statistic and the critical region: Reject the null hypothesis if the test statistic falls in the critical region—that is, if $t \le t_{\alpha, \nu}$; otherwise, do not reject the null hypothesis. A decision rule also can be formulated in terms of the p value and significance level. The rule is as follows: Reject the null hypothesis if the p value is less than or equal to the preselected significance level—that is, if $p \le \alpha$; otherwise, do not reject the null hypothesis. The inclusion of a p value in a research report provides useful information because it enables a reader to discern those significance levels for which the null hypothesis could have been rejected.

The p values provided in some computer printouts are appropriate for two-sided null hypotheses. If your null hypothesis is directional, the two-tailed p value in the computer printout should be divided by 2. For example, a computer gave a p value of .0001930 for the data in Table 10.3-1. Because the null hypothesis is directional, the correct value is $.0019304/2 = .0009652$. Before leaving the subject of p values, remember that a p value is related to statistical significance; it says nothing about the practical significance of results.

CHECK YOUR UNDERSTANDING OF SECTION 10.4

20. For each of the following statistical hypotheses, sketch the t sampling distribution, designate the critical region(s), indicate their size, and determine the critical value.

a. $H_0: \mu = 60$
   $H_1: \mu \ne 60$
   $\alpha = .01$
   $n = 31$

b. $H_0: \mu \le 100$
   $H_1: \mu > 100$
   $\alpha = .05$
   $n = 17$

c. $H_0: \mu \ge 25$
   $H_1: \mu < 25$
   $\alpha = .005$
   $n = 22$

21. Which of the null hypotheses in Exercise 20 are directional?

22. Indicate the type of error or correct decision for each of the following.
   a. A true null hypothesis was rejected.
   b. The researcher failed to reject a false null hypothesis.
   c. The null hypothesis is false and the researcher rejected it.
   d. The researcher did not reject a true null hypothesis.
   e. A false null hypothesis was rejected.
   f. The researcher rejected the null hypothesis when he or she should have failed to reject it.

23. The calculation of power was illustrated using the registration example. The dean was considering adopting the new procedure if the population mean, μ', was equal to 2.95. Recall that $\overline{X}_{.05} = 3.001$, $\hat{\sigma} = 0.3013$, and $n = 27$. If the mean was 2.95, the estimate of the probability of correctly rejecting the null hypothesis was .81. If μ' was 2.93 instead of 2.95, what would the power have been?

24. Prepare a table that summarizes the probabilities associated with the four possible decision outcomes in Exercise 23 for $\mu' = 2.93$ and $\mu_0 = 3.10$.

25. For the following conditions, use Appendix Table D.8 to determine the appropriate sample size.
    a. $d = 0.20$, $\alpha = .05$, $1 - \beta = .80$ b. $d = 0.5$, $\alpha = .01$, $1 - \beta = .80$
    c. $d = 0.80$, $\alpha = .01$, $1 - \beta = .80$ d. $d = 0.5$, $\alpha = .05$, $1 - \beta = .80$
26. Distinguish between statistical significance and practical significance.
27. For each of the following, determine the p value using (i) Appendix Table D.3 and (ii) the Microsoft Excel TDIST function.
    a. $t(16) = 2.231$, two-tailed test   b. $t(29) = 2.498$, one-tailed test
    c. $t(40) = 1.782$, one-tailed test   d. $t(19) = 2.916$, two-tailed test
28. Terms to remember:
    a. One-tailed test   b. Two-tailed test
    c. One-sided (directional) hypothesis   d. Two-sided (nondirectional)
    e. Type I error (α)   hypothesis
    g. Correct acceptance ($1 - \alpha$)   f. Type II error (β)
    i. Power ($1 - \beta$)   h. Correct rejection
    k. Statistical significance   j. Effect size
    m. p value   l. Practical significance

10.5 LOOKING BACK: WHAT HAVE YOU LEARNED?

Hypothesis-testing procedures, one form of statistical inference, use sample data to make a decision about a scientific hypothesis when it is impossible or impractical to observe all the elements in the population. The main features of hypothesis testing are as follows. A researcher formulates from a scientific hypothesis two mutually exclusive and exhaustive statistical hypotheses—the null hypothesis, H_0, and the alternative hypothesis, H_1—that make predictions about one or more parameters of a population distribution. The alternative hypothesis is formulated so that it agrees with the researcher's scientific hypothesis. The null hypothesis is contrary to the researcher's scientific hypothesis. A test of the null hypothesis consists of determining whether the obtained value of a sample statistic would be improbable if the null hypothesis is true. If the value would be improbable, then the null hypothesis is a poor prediction and should be rejected in favor of the alternative hypothesis.

The null hypothesis is tested using a test statistic. It is a simple matter to transform a sample mean into a t test statistic using the formula $t = (\overline{X} - \mu_0)/(\hat{\sigma}/\sqrt{n})$. The criterion for what constitutes improbable values of the t statistic is expressed in terms of a probability called a significance level and denoted by α. By convention, a researcher usually sets this probability equal to or less than .05. The significance level along with the alternative hypothesis identifies a range of values of the test statistic that would be improbable if the null hypothesis is true. This range of improbable values is called the critical region. If a test statistic falls in the critical region, the test statistic is said to be statistically significant, in which case the researcher rejects the null hypothesis and concludes that the scientific hypothesis is probably true. If a test statistic does not fall in the critical region, the null hypothesis remains tenable.

How does one determine whether a t statistic falls in the critical region? This can be determined with the aid of Appendix Table D.3 that gives values of the t statistic that cut off various regions of the t sampling distribution. For example, the value of t that cuts off the upper critical region of size α for ν degrees of freedom is called a critical value and is denoted by $t_{\alpha, \nu}$. Now to answer the question posed a moment ago. You can determine whether the t test statistic falls in the critical region by determining whether your obtained t is greater than or equal to the critical value—that is whether $t \geq t_{\alpha, \nu}$. Alternatively, if a statistical software package is used to obtain the value of the t statistic, the p value provided by the package can be compared with the researcher's significance level. If the p value is less than or equal to the significance level, $p \leq \alpha$, the t statistic falls in the critical region.

It is helpful to think of hypothesis testing as a series of steps that culminate in a decision about the scientific hypothesis. The steps can be summarized as follows:

Step 1.   State the null and alternative hypotheses.

Step 2.   Specify the test statistic based on the hypothesis to be tested, information that is known about the population, and assumptions about the population that appear to be tenable.

Step 3.   Specify the size n of the sample to be obtained and make assumptions that permit specification of the sampling distribution of the test statistic, given that the null hypothesis is true.

Step 4.   Specify an acceptable risk, denoted by α, of rejecting the null hypothesis when it is true.

Step 5.   Obtain a random sample of size n from the population, compute the test statistic, and make a decision about the null and alternative hypotheses and an inductive inference about the scientific hypothesis.

Decision rule:

Reject the null hypothesis if the test statistic falls in the critical region of the sampling distribution of the test statistic; otherwise, do not reject the null hypothesis. Rejection of the null hypothesis leads to the inductive inference that the scientific hypothesis is true, in which case the statistic is said to be statistically significant.

There is a tendency among researchers to impart surplus meaning to the term *statistical significance*. All the term really means is that a result has been obtained that is improbable if the null hypothesis is true. Statistical significance does not connote importance or usefulness, and it should not be confused with practical significance. In the simplest terms, a statistically significant result is one for which chance is an unlikely explanation.

REVIEW EXERCISES FOR CHAPTER 10

1. Which of the following are scientific hypotheses?
   a. Wives in unhappy marriages have lower problem-solving ability than wives in happy marriages.
   b. Officer workers who listen to music with iPods while working exhibit lower job turnover.
   c. Dominant chimpanzees in a colony have a better self-image than chimpanzees who are less dominant.

   d. Mice prefer the music of Mozart to that of Schönberg because Mozart's music is less dissonant.

2. Why is it often necessary to use the techniques of statistical inference in evaluating a scientific hypothesis?

3. Which of the following are examples of null hypotheses?

   a. $\mu = 22$ b. $r = 0$

   c. $\rho > 0$ d. $\mu < 50$

   e. $\sigma^2 < 0$ f. $\overline{X} = 15$

   g. $\mu \geq 60$ h. $S^2 \leq 16$

   i. $\sigma^2 = 100$ j. $\rho = .30$

4. Why might a researcher fail to reject a null hypothesis?

5. If a null hypothesis is correctly rejected, what does this imply about the experimental methodology?

6. Under what conditions is the sampling distribution of $t = (\overline{X} - \mu_0)/(\hat{\sigma}/\sqrt{n})$ the same as Student's t distribution?

7. Use Appendix Table D.3 to determine the t critical value for the following.

   a. $\mu \leq 61, n = 10, \alpha = .05$ b. $\mu = 35, n = 18, \alpha = .01$

   c. $\mu < 12, n = 31, \alpha = .05$ d. $\mu \leq 121, n = 17, \alpha = .05$

   e. $\mu = 12, n = 17, \alpha = .05$ f. $\mu \geq 28, n = 27, \alpha = .005$

8. Researchers hypothesized that a random sample of 28 drug abusers who were clients of the Narcotics Service Council in St. Louis would rate the credibility of drug information provided by social workers below that of ex-addicts. Let $\overline{X}$ denote the mean rating of social workers. The known rating of ex-addicts is $\mu_0 = 72.8$. The population standard deviation is not known. (a) List the five steps you would follow to test the hypothesis that the credibility rating of social workers is lower than that of ex-addicts, and supply the required information. Let $\alpha = .05$. (b) State the decision rule.

9. For the data in Exercise 8, sketch the sampling distribution associated with the null hypothesis, and indicate the region(s) that lead to rejection and nonrejection of the null hypothesis.

10. For the data in Exercise 8, suppose that the mean credibility rating of social workers is $\overline{X} = 58.2$ and the sample standard deviation is $\hat{\sigma} = 18$. (a) Compute a t statistic for these data. (b) What conclusion can be drawn about the scientific hypothesis?

11. If $\alpha = .01$ in Exercise 8, what conclusion would have been drawn about the scientific hypothesis?

12. Can you think of some reasons why a researcher should always specify H_0, H_1, α, and n before collecting data?

13. For each of the following statistical hypotheses, sketch the t sampling distribution associated with the null hypothesis, designate the critical region(s), and indicate their size.

   a. $H_0: \mu \leq 50$ b. $H_0: \mu = 20$

       $H_1: \mu \geq 50$ $H_1: \mu \neq 20$

       $\alpha = .05$ $\alpha = .01$

   c. $H_0: \mu \geq 65$

       $H_1: \mu < 65$

       $\alpha = .005$

14. Which of the null hypotheses in Exercise 13 are directional?

15. Under what condition is a one-tailed test less powerful than a two-tailed test?

16. Suppose that several first-grade teachers have complained that their classes this year are unusually slow in learning to read. The school principal has asked you to determine if the children are below average in intelligence—that is, have a mean IQ below 100. Because there are 362 first-grade children, giving each of them an individual intelligence test is not feasible. Instead, you administer the Wechsler Intelligence Scale for Children–Revised (WISC–R) to a random sample of 16 children. Assume that the data in the following table have been obtained. Let $\alpha = .05$.

a. List the steps you would follow in testing the scientific hypothesis.

b. Compute a t statistic for these data and make a decision about the scientific hypothesis.

c. Use Appendix Table D.8 to estimate the sample size needed to detect a large effect for $\alpha = .05$ and $1 - \beta = .80$.

d. Determine the p value of the t statistic using (i) Appendix Table D.3 and (ii) the Microsoft Excel TDIST function.

e. Construct a box plot for the data. Do the data contain outliers? Does the sample distribution appear to be relatively symmetrical?

Child	IQ	Child	IQ
1	89	9	86
2	96	10	88
3	86	11	92
4	92	12	101
5	78	13	87
6	110	14	93
7	82	15	97
8	69	16	74

17. (a) Make a frequency distribution for the data in Exercise 16. Use 10 class intervals, with a class interval size of five. (b) From a visual inspection of the frequency distribution, is it reasonable to assume that the population distribution is normal in form?

18. Use the table of random numbers in Appendix Table D.1 to draw a random sample without replacement of 31 students from the Student Database in Appendix E.

a. List the steps you would follow in testing the scientific hypothesis that the population mean of the variable labeled GPA is different from that for the previous year where $\mu_0 = 2.7$. Let $\alpha = .05$.

b. List the Participant Number and GPA for each person in your sample. Compute the mean and standard deviation of the variable labeled GPA.

c. Test the null hypothesis that $\mu = 2.7$, where 2.7 is the mean population GPA of students who enrolled in the statistics course last year.

d. Use Appendix Table D.8 to estimate the sample size needed to detect a large effect for $\alpha = .05$ and $1 - \beta = .80$.

e. Determine the p value of the t statistic using (i) Appendix Table D.3 and (ii) the Microsoft Excel TDIST function.

f. Construct a box plot for the data. Do the data contain outliers? Does the sample distribution appear to be relatively symmetrical?

19. Indicate the type of error or correct decision for each of the following:
    a. A false null hypothesis was rejected.
    b. The researcher did not reject a true null hypothesis.
    c. The null hypothesis is false and the researcher failed to reject it.
    d. The researcher rejected a true null hypothesis.
    e. A false null hypothesis was not rejected.
    f. The researcher rejected the null hypothesis when he or she should have rejected it.

20. The calculation of power was illustrated in Section 10.4 for the registration example. The dean was considering adopting the new procedure if the population mean, μ', was equal to 2.95. Recall that $\overline{X}_{.05} = 3.001$, $\hat{\sigma} = 0.3013$, and $n = 27$. If the mean was 2.95, an estimate of the probability of correctly rejecting the null hypothesis was .81. If μ' was 2.90 instead of 2.95, what would the power have been?

21. Prepare a table that summarizes the probabilities associated with the four possible decision outcomes in Exercise 20 for $\mu' = 2.90$ and $\mu_0 = 3.10$.

22. For the credibility data in Review Exercises 8 and 10, suppose that the population mean credibility rating of social workers is really $\mu = 60.1$. (a) Compute the power of the t test. (b) How large a sample of drug abusers would be required to detect a large effect and have a power of .80?

23. Prepare a table that summarizes the probabilities associated with the four possible decision outcomes in Exercise 22.

24. A random sample of 65 freshman college students was selected to participate in a new look-say teaching program designed to increase reading speed in French. The final exam consisted of a French passage that the students translated. The time required for each student to complete the translation was recorded. The sample statistics were $\overline{X} = 302$ sec and $\hat{\sigma} = 56$ sec. According to departmental records, the mean for students in conventional classes was 320 sec. Let $\alpha = .05$.
    a. List the steps you would use in testing the scientific hypothesis that the look-say program resulted in a decrease in time required to translate the French passage.
    b. Compute a t statistic and make a decision about the scientific hypothesis.
    c. Determine the p value of the t statistic using (i) Appendix Table D.3 and (ii) the Microsoft Excel TDIST function.
    d. How could the design of the experiment be improved?
    e. Use Appendix Table D.8 to determine whether the sample size is adequate to detect a medium-size effect if a power of .95 is desired.

25. List the ways in which a researcher can increase the power of an experimental methodology. What are their relative merits?

26. Use the table of random numbers in Appendix D.1 to draw a random sample without replacement of 25 men from the student database in Appendix E. (a) List the Subject Number and Stat Grade for each man in your sample. (b) Compute the mean of the variable labeled Statistics Grade. (c) Test the null hypothesis that $\mu = 2.662$. Let $\alpha = .05$.

11

Statistical Inference: One-Sample Confidence Interval

11.1 Introduction
Looking Ahead: What Is This Chapter About?
Criticisms of Null Hypothesis Significance Testing

11.2 Confidence Interval for μ
Computation of a Two-Sided Confidence Interval for μ
Interpretation of a Confidence Interval
Computation of a One-Sided Confidence Interval for μ
Interval Estimation versus Hypothesis Testing

11.3 Practical Significance
Check Your Understanding of Sections 11.2 and 11.3

11.4 Looking Back: What Have You Learned?
Review Exercises for Chapter 11

11.1 INTRODUCTION

Looking Ahead: What Is This Chapter About?

A sample mean is often used to estimate a population mean when it is not possible to observe all of the elements in the population. Unfortunately, sample means vary from one random sample to the next. Hence, the mean of a particular sample is unlikely to equal the population mean. In this chapter you will learn how to find a range of values called a *confidence interval* that is likely to include the unknown population mean.

Confidence intervals are not used as much as null hypothesis significance tests in the behavioral sciences, health sciences, and education. This is true even though confidence intervals are more informative. The American Psychological Association (2001, p. 22) recommends that researchers make greater use of confidence interval procedures. Because of this recommendation, the use of confidence intervals in psychology will likely increase.

After reading this chapter, you should know the following:

- Four common criticisms of null hypothesis significance testing
- How to use the *t* sampling distribution to construct a confidence interval for a population mean
- When and how to use one- and two-sided confidence intervals
- How Hedges's *g* statistic can help you assess practical significance
- The advantages of confidence intervals over null hypothesis significance tests

Criticisms of Null Hypothesis Significance Testing

Since the 1920s, null hypothesis significance testing has been the dominant approach to statistical inference. There is a growing awareness among researchers that this approach has some shortcomings. As you have seen, a null hypothesis significance test addresses the question "Is chance a likely explanation for the results that have been obtained?" The test does not address the question "Are the results important or useful?" There are other criticisms. For example, null hypothesis significance testing and scientific inference address different questions. In scientific inference, what you want to know is the conditional probability that the null hypothesis (H_0) is true, given that you have obtained a set of data (D)—that is, $\text{Prob}(H_0|D)$. What null hypothesis significance testing tells you is the conditional probability of obtaining these data or more extreme data if the null hypothesis is true, $\text{Prob}(D|H_0)$. Unfortunately, obtaining data for which $\text{Prob}(D|H_0)$ is low does not imply that $\text{Prob}(H_0|D)$ also is low.

A third criticism of null hypothesis significance testing is that it is a trivial exercise. John Tukey (1991) observed that "It is foolish to ask 'Are the effects of *A* and *B* different?' They are always different—for some decimal place (p. 100)." Hence, because all null hypotheses are false, Type I errors cannot occur and statistically significant results are assured if large enough samples are used. Bruce Thompson (1998) captured the essence of this view when he wrote, "Statistical testing becomes a tautological search for enough participants to achieve statistical significance. If we fail to reject, it is only because we've been too lazy to drag in enough participants

(p. 799)." Because the null hypothesis is always false, a decision to reject it simply indicates that the research methodology had adequate power to detect a true state of affairs, which may or may not be a large effect or even a useful effect.

A fourth criticism of null hypothesis significance testing is that by adopting a fixed significance level such as $\alpha = .05$, a researcher turns a continuum of uncertainty into a dichotomous reject-do-not-reject decision. Researchers ordinarily react to a p value of .06 with disappointment and even dismay, but not p values of .05 or smaller. Rosnow and Rosenthal's (1989) comment is pertinent: "Surely, God loves the .06 nearly as much as the .05 (p. 1277)." Many psychologists believe that an emphasis on null hypothesis significance tests and p values distracts researchers from the main business of science—understanding and interpreting the outcomes of research. The next section describes an alternative approach to statistical inference.

11.2 CONFIDENCE INTERVAL FOR μ

Section 10.1 noted that two complementary topics are subsumed under classical statistical inference: null hypothesis significance testing and confidence interval estimation. In many investigations, a researcher's primary interest is to obtain an estimate of some population parameter such as the mean. Because sample means vary from sample to sample, it is unlikely that any given sample mean will equal the population mean.

> Although a researcher can never know the value of a population mean except by measuring all the elements in the population, the researcher can use a random sample to specify a segment or interval on the number line[1] such that the population mean has a high probability of lying on the segment. The segment is called a **confidence interval.**

The previous chapter introduced one- and two-tailed null hypotheses. A one-tailed hypothesis is adopted when the researcher has made a directional prediction about the population mean; otherwise the researcher adopts a two-tailed hypothesis.

> Confidence intervals can be either one or two sided. A one-sided confidence interval is constructed when the researcher has made a directional prediction about the population mean; otherwise the researcher constructs a two-sided interval.

Let's now construct a two-sided confidence interval for a population mean, μ, so that the interval has a probability equal to $1 - \alpha$ of containing μ. The probability $(1 - \alpha)$, which is usually equal to $(1 - .05) = .95$, is called a **confidence coefficient** and, like the significance level, α, is specified by the researcher. This section describes the logic underlying the construction of a confidence interval in some detail. By following the logic, you will gain a better understanding of this

[1] A number line is a straight line on which points on the line are identified with real numbers, for example: ——•——•—— .
                                                                                     1   2

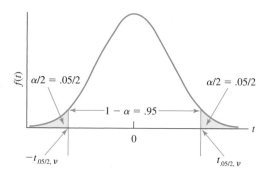

Figure 11.2-1. Sampling distribution of $t = (\overline{X} - \mu_0)/(\hat{\sigma}/\sqrt{n})$. If one t statistic is randomly sampled from this population of t's, the probability is .95 that the obtained t will come from the interval from $-t_{.05/2,\,\nu}$ to $t_{.05/2,\,\nu}$.

important approach to statistical inference. Consider the sampling distribution of $t = (\overline{X} - \mu)/(\hat{\sigma}/\sqrt{n})$ shown in Figure 11.2-1. Suppose I randomly sampled one t statistic from this population of t's. The probability is $1 - .05 = .95$ that the t statistic I obtained will come from the interval from $-t_{.05/2,\,\nu}$ to $t_{.05/2,\,\nu}$. This seems reasonable because .95 of the t's are in the interval from $-t_{.05/2,\,\nu}$ to $t_{.05/2,\,\nu}$. I can state this as follows:

$$\text{Prob}(-t_{.05/2,\,\nu} < t < t_{.05/2,\,\nu}) = 1 - .05 = .95$$

Next, I can replace the t in the probability statement with its formula, $t = (\overline{X} - \mu)/(\hat{\sigma}/\sqrt{n})$. This gives

$$\text{Prob}\left(-t_{.05/2,\,\nu} < \frac{\overline{X} - \mu}{\hat{\sigma}/\sqrt{n}} < t_{.05/2,\,\nu}\right) = .95$$

Multiply each term in the inequalities by $\hat{\sigma}/\sqrt{n}$ to obtain[2]

$$\text{Prob}\left(\frac{-t_{.05/2,\,\nu}\,\hat{\sigma}}{\sqrt{n}} < \overline{X} - \mu < \frac{t_{.05/2,\,\nu}\,\hat{\sigma}}{\sqrt{n}}\right) = .95$$

Subtracting $\overline{X}$ from each term in the inequalities, I obtain

$$\text{Prob}\left(-\overline{X} - \frac{t_{.05/2,\,\nu}\,\hat{\sigma}}{\sqrt{n}} < -\mu < -\overline{X} + \frac{t_{.05/2,\,\nu}\,\hat{\sigma}}{\sqrt{n}}\right) = .95$$

and multiplying by -1, which reverses the direction of the inequalities and the signs of the terms, gives

$$\text{Prob}\left(\overline{X} + \frac{t_{.05/2,\,\nu}\,\hat{\sigma}}{\sqrt{n}} > \mu > +\overline{X} - \frac{t_{.05/2,\,\nu}\,\hat{\sigma}}{\sqrt{n}}\right) = .95$$

---

[2] A review of inequalities is given in Appendix A, Section A.6.

For convenience, I can rearrange the terms in the inequality to form the confidence statement

$$\text{Prob}\left(\overline{X} - \frac{t_{.05/2,\,\nu}\,\hat{\sigma}}{\sqrt{n}} < \mu < \overline{X} + \frac{t_{.05/2,\,\nu}\,\hat{\sigma}}{\sqrt{n}}\right) = .95$$

In words, this statement says that the probability is .95 that the interval from

$$\overline{X} - t_{.05/2,\,\nu}\,\hat{\sigma}/\sqrt{n} \qquad \text{to} \qquad \overline{X} + t_{.05/2,\,\nu}\,\hat{\sigma}/\sqrt{n}$$

contains the parameter μ. The values $\overline{X} - t_{.05/2,\,\nu}\,\hat{\sigma}/\sqrt{n}$ and $\overline{X} + t_{.05/2,\,\nu}\,\hat{\sigma}/\sqrt{n}$ are the **lower** and **upper endpoints,** respectively, of the confidence interval. The endpoints also are called **confidence limits** and are denoted by L_1 and L_2, respectively. The value of the confidence coefficient, .95, reflects the degree of my confidence that μ does indeed lie in the specified interval.

The general form of a two-sided $100(1 - \alpha)\%$ confidence interval for μ is

$$\overline{X} - \frac{t_{\alpha/2,\,\nu}\hat{\sigma}}{\sqrt{n}} < \mu < \overline{X} + \frac{t_{\alpha/2,\,\nu}\hat{\sigma}}{\sqrt{n}}$$

where $t_{\alpha/2,\,\nu}$ is the value that cuts off the upper $\alpha/2$ region of the t sampling distribution for ν degrees for freedom.

In using the t statistic and t sampling distribution to construct a confidence interval, it is assumed that (1) a random sample of n observations is obtained from the population of interest, (2) the population is normally distributed, and (3) the population standard deviation is unknown. These are the same assumptions that are made in performing a null hypothesis significance test using the t statistic.

To summarize, it is impossible to know the value of a parameter such as μ without measuring all the elements in the population. However, it is possible to find two functions denoted by L_1 and L_2 of a random sample such that the probability that the interval between L_1 and L_2 will contain the parameter is equal to $1 - \alpha$. That is, I can be $100(1 - \alpha)\%$ confident that the interval contains the unknown parameter. The confidence interval tells me the margin of error associated with my sample estimate of μ.

Computation of a Two-Sided Confidence Interval for μ

Sections 10.3 and 10.4 of the previous chapter described an experiment used to determine whether a new registration procedure was better than the current procedure at Idle-on-in College. I will use the registration data to illustrate the computation of a $100(1 - .05)\% = 95\%$ two-sided confidence interval for μ. According to Table 10.3-1, the mean of a random sample of $n = 27$ student who used the new registration procedure in a trial run was $\overline{X} = 2.90$, and an estimate of the population standard deviation was $\hat{\sigma} = 0.3013$. A 95% two-sided confidence interval for μ is given by

$$\overline{X} - \frac{t_{.05/2,26}\,\hat{\sigma}}{\sqrt{n}} < \mu < \overline{X} + \frac{t_{.05/2,26}\,\hat{\sigma}}{\sqrt{n}}$$

$$2.90 - \frac{2.056(0.3013)}{\sqrt{27}} < \mu < 2.90 + \frac{2.056(0.3013)}{\sqrt{27}}$$

$$2.90 - 0.119 < \mu < 2.90 + 0.119$$

$$2.78 < \mu < 3.02$$

In words, this says that a 95% confidence interval for μ is from 2.78 to 3.02. You may find it helpful to visualize a confidence interval as a segment of the number line. In the following figure, the darkened segment corresponds to the 95% confidence interval for μ.

$$L_1 = 2.78 \qquad L_2 = 3.02$$

2.6	2.7	2.8	2.9	3.0	3.1	3.2

$$\mu$$

The confidence interval $2.78 < \mu < 3.02$ is called an **open interval** as opposed to a closed interval because neither endpoint, 2.78 nor 3.02, is included in the interval.[3] The dean can feel quite confident that the value of μ is greater than $L_1 = 2.78$ and less than $L_2 = 3.02$. The measure of the dean's confidence that the confidence interval does in fact contain μ is .95. If the dean wants to feel even more confident that she has specified L_1 and L_2 so that they contain μ, she can compute a $100(1 - .01)\%$ = 99% confidence interval. This is accomplished by substituting $t_{.01/2,26} = 2.779$ for $t_{.05/2,26} = 2.056$. The 99% confidence interval is given by

$$\overline{X} - \frac{t_{.01/2,26}\,\hat{\sigma}}{\sqrt{n}} < \mu < \overline{X} + \frac{t_{.01/2,26}\,\hat{\sigma}}{\sqrt{n}}$$

$$2.90 - \frac{2.779(0.3013)}{\sqrt{27}} < \mu < 2.90 + \frac{2.779(0.3013)}{\sqrt{27}}$$

$$2.90 - 0.161 < \mu < 2.90 + 0.161$$

$$2.74 < \mu < 3.06$$

Notice that as the dean's confidence that she has captured μ increases, so does the size of the interval from L_1 to L_2. This is illustrated in the following figures.

$$L_1 = 2.78 \qquad L_2 = 3.02$$

2.6	2.7	2.8	2.9	3.0	3.1	3.2

95% confidence interval for μ

$$L_1 = 2.74 \qquad L_2 = 3.06$$

2.6	2.7	2.8	2.9	3.0	3.1	3.2

99% confidence interval for μ

Interpretation of a Confidence Interval

When I developed the formula for the confidence interval for μ, I said that the probability is .95 that the interval from $\overline{X} - t_{.05/2, \nu}\,\hat{\sigma}/\sqrt{n}$ to $\overline{X} + t_{.05/2, \nu}\,\hat{\sigma}/\sqrt{n}$ contains μ.

---

[3] An interval in which the endpoints are included; for example, $2.78 \leq \mu \leq 3.02$, is called a **closed interval**.

When I computed the confidence interval for the registration data, I said that a 95% confidence interval for μ is from 2.78 to 3.02. I did not say that the probability is .95 that the interval from 2.78 to 3.02 contains μ. The latter statement would be incorrect, as I will now show. The probability statement

$$\text{Prob}(\overline{X} - t_{.05/2,\,\nu}\hat{\sigma}/\sqrt{n} < \mu < \overline{X} + t_{.05/2,\,\nu}\hat{\sigma}/\sqrt{n}) = .95$$

refers to the infinite set of confidence intervals that I could compute for μ. Ninety-five percent of these intervals will contain μ and 5% will not. The probability that a randomly selected interval from this infinite set will contain μ is .95. However, once I obtain a sample mean and construct a confidence interval for that mean, either the interval I compute does or does not contain μ. In other words, the probability is either 0 or 1, not .95. Hence, in describing a confidence interval you can say, for example, that a 95% confidence interval for μ is from 2.78 to 3.02, or that the degree of your confidence that μ lies in the open interval from 2.78 to 3.02 is .95, or, more simply, "You are 95% confident that μ is greater than 2.78 and less than 3.02."

Computation of a One-Sided Confidence Interval for μ

The confidence interval, $2.78 < \mu < 3.02$, is two-sided. Such an interval is used when the researcher is interested in the possibility, for example, that the new registration procedure is worse than or better than the current procedure. In a sense, this interval is analogous to the two-sided statistical hypotheses:

$$H_0\!: \mu = 3.10$$

$$H_1\!: \mu \neq 3.10$$

In the registration example, the dean was only interested in the possibility that the new procedure was better than the current procedure. The corresponding statistical hypotheses are

$$H_0\!: \mu \geq 3.10$$

$$H_1\!: \mu < 3.10$$

The analogous **one-sided confidence limit,** L_2, for these hypotheses with a confidence coefficient equal to $100(1 - .05)\% = 95\%$ is

$$\mu < \overline{X} + \frac{t_{.05,\,26}\hat{\sigma}}{\sqrt{n}}$$

$$\mu < 2.90 + \frac{1.706(0.3013)}{\sqrt{27}}$$

$$\mu < 2.90 + 0.099$$

$$\mu < 3.00$$

where $t_{.05,\,26} = 1.706$ is the value of t that cuts off the upper $\alpha = .05$ region instead of the .025 region of the t sampling distribution. The dean can be fairly confident that

μ is less than 3.00. This confidence interval corresponds to the darker segment of the real number line in the following figure:

If the dean were only interested in the possibility that the new procedure is worse than the current procedure, she could construct the following one-sided confidence limit, L_1, with confidence coefficient equal to $100(1 - .05)\% = .95\%$:

$$\overline{X} + \frac{t_{.05,\,26}\hat{\sigma}}{\sqrt{n}} < \mu$$

$$2.90 - \frac{1.706(0.3013)}{\sqrt{27}} < \mu$$

$$2.90 - 0.099 < \mu$$

$$2.80 < \mu$$

This confidence interval corresponds to the darker segment of the real number line in the following figure:

Interval Estimation versus Hypothesis Testing

In Section 10.3, the dean used a one-sample t statistic to test the null hypothesis H_0: $\mu \geq 3.10$. Recall that the hypothesis was rejected. The dean concluded that the alternative hypothesis was tenable—that is, $\mu < 3.10$. The dean's best guess regarding the value of μ for the new procedure is that it is equal to the sample mean $\overline{X} = 2.90$ obtained in the trial run. But sample means vary from sample to sample. Hence, it is unlikely that population mean is equal to $\overline{X} = 2.90$. Because the null hypothesis was rejected, the dean concluded that the population means was less than 3.10. The confidence interval for μ provides the dean with more precise information. Based on the one-sided 95% confidence interval, $\mu < 3.00$, the dean can be fairly confident that μ is less than 3.00. The confidence interval has enabled the dean to narrow the range of possible values for μ.

A two-sided confidence interval brackets the possible values for a population mean. Suppose that the dean had advanced the following two-sided statistical hypotheses:

$$H_0: \mu = 3.10$$
$$H_1: \mu \neq 3.10$$

Rejection of this null hypothesis would not be informative. The dean would know simply that the population mean for the new procedure is not equal to 3.10. A 95%

two-sided confidence interval for μ is $2.78 < \mu < 3.02$. This confidence interval would enable the dean to bracket the likely value of μ. She could be fairly confident that the population mean is greater than 2.78 and less than 3.02. It is apparent that the confidence interval provides more information than the null hypothesis significance test.

A confidence interval has another advantage. It can be used to test any null hypothesis for μ simply by looking at the interval. Consider the $100(1 - .05)\% = 95\%$ two-sided confidence interval $2.78 < \mu < 3.02$. Without doing a significance test, it is apparent from this interval that the null hypothesis $H_0: \mu = 3.10$ should be rejected at the .05 level of significance. This follows because 3.10 is not included in the interval from 2.78 to 3.02. However, the null hypothesis $H_0: \mu = 2.99$ would not be rejected because 2.99 is included in the 95% confidence interval.

The *Publication Manual of the American Psychological Association* strongly recommends the use of confidence intervals. The manual says, "Because confidence intervals combine information on location and precision and can be used to infer significance levels, they are, in general the best reporting strategy" (American Psychological Association, 2001, p. 22). Considering the advantages of confidence intervals and the APA recommendation, you may wonder why null hypothesis significance tests are given a prominent place in this and most other introductory statistics books. There are two reasons. Since the 1920s, null hypothesis significance testing has been the dominant approach to statistical inference. Hence, an understanding of this approach is necessary to read the literature in the behavioral sciences, health sciences, and education. Second, some statistical inference questions cannot be addressed using confidence intervals. In such cases, a researcher must resort to null hypothesis significance tests.

 To summarize, a sample mean and confidence interval provide an estimate of the population parameter and a range of values—the error variation—qualifying the estimate. A $100(1 - \alpha)\%$ confidence interval for μ contains all the values of μ_0 for which the null hypothesis would *not* be rejected at α level of significance. All values of μ_0 outside the confidence interval would be rejected.

11.3 PRACTICAL SIGNIFICANCE

As noted repeatedly, statistically significant results are not necessarily important, large, or even useful. What researchers need is a measure of the practical significance of results. Unfortunately, such a measure does not exist. However, effect magnitude statistics can assist a researcher in deciding whether results are practically significant (Kirk, 1996). Most **effect magnitude statistics** fall into one of two categories: measures of effect size and measures of strength of association.[4] A sample estimator of Cohen's (1988) effect size, *d,* is described here. A measure of strength of association for experiments with three or more samples is described in Chapter 15. According to the *Publication Manual of the American Psychological*

[4] In an article titled "Effect Size Measures, " I summarize more than 70 measures of effect magnitude that have been used in psychology and education journals (Kirk, 2005b).

Association (2001, pp. 25–26), researchers should always supplement reports of null hypothesis significance tests and confidence intervals with a measure of effect magnitude.

Cohen's effect size parameter, *d,* was introduced in Section 10.4. A estimator of the parameter has been described by Hedges and is denoted by g.[5] Hedges's estimator of *d* is

$$g = \frac{|\overline{X} - \mu_0|}{\hat{\sigma}}$$

g represents the size of the effect that a researcher has obtained in units of the sample standard deviation. The g statistic is interpreted the same as Cohen's *d*: $g = 0.2$ is a small effect, $g = 0.5$ is a medium effect, and $g = 0.8$ is a large effect.

For the registration data in Sections 10.3 and 10.4, the dean found that the new procedure reduced the registration time from $\mu_0 = 3.10$ hours to $\overline{X} = 2.90$ hours. The difference $2.90 - 3.10$ corresponds to a mean time savings of 12 minutes. Hedges's g for this difference is

$$g = \frac{|2.90 - 3.10|}{0.3013} = 0.66$$

This g just exceeds 0.5, which is Cohen's criterion for a medium effect size. Small and large effects correspond to registration times of 3.04 and 2.86 hours, respectively, as the following computations show:

$$g = \frac{|3.04 - 3.10|}{0.3013} = 0.2$$

$$g = \frac{|2.86 - 3.10|}{0.3013} = 0.8$$

Small and large effects correspond to a time savings, respectively, of 3.6 and 14.4 minutes. Most students would probably consider a savings of only 3.6 minutes to be a small effect, whereas a savings of 14.4 minutes would be viewed differently.

The practice of reporting a measure of effect size in research reports is far from universal. If a publication does not report an effect size, it is easy to compute the effect size if the t statistic and sample size are reported. The formula for computing g from a one-sample t statistic is

$$g = t/\sqrt{n}$$

As you just saw, the effect size for the registration experiment is $g = 0.66$. The same value can be obtained using the t statistic and sample size in Table 10.3-1 as follows:

$$g = \frac{t}{\sqrt{n}} = \frac{3.449}{\sqrt{27}} = 0.66$$

---

[5] Some authors use the letter *d* for both the parameter $|\mu - \mu_0|/\sigma$ and the statistic $|\overline{X} - \mu_0|/\hat{\sigma}$. To avoid confusion, here I use g to denote the statistic.

Researchers routinely report null hypothesis significance test results and p values in their publications. Researchers are also encouraged to report confidence intervals and measures of effect magnitude. I recommend reporting measures of effect magnitude even when the null hypothesis tests are not significant. The availability of effect magnitude statistics in publications is especially useful to those who do secondary analyses of research literature. The availability of effect magnitude statistics enables a researcher to aggregate the results of many studies in procedure called *meta-analysis*. In addition, publications should contain descriptive statistics such as means, standard deviations, and sample sizes, and, where appropriate, graphs such as box plots.

CHECK YOUR UNDERSTANDING OF SECTIONS 11.2 AND 11.3

1. What assumptions are associated with the following statement?

$$\text{Prob}\left(\overline{X} - \frac{t_{\alpha/2,\, v}\,\hat{\sigma}}{\sqrt{n}} < \mu < \overline{X} + \frac{t_{\alpha/2,\, v}\,\hat{\sigma}}{\sqrt{n}} \right) = 1 - \alpha$$

2. What are the advantages of confidence-interval procedures over null hypothesis-testing procedures?
3. a. A soft-drink machine is designed to dispense a measured amount of a popular drink. Construct a two-sided 99% confidence interval for μ if a random sample of 29 drinks has $\overline{X} = 7.2$ ounces. Assume that the distribution is approximately normal, with $\hat{\sigma} = 0.42$ ounces. Locate the confidence interval on the real number line.
   b. Machines of the same design are supposed to have a mean of 8 ounces. Does this machine need to be repaired?
   c. Compute Hedges's g and interpret.
4. If $23 < \mu < 36$ is a 95% confidence interval for μ, indicate which of the following statements are correct (C) and which are incorrect (I).
   a. The probability is .95 that the open interval from 23 to 36 contains the population mean.
   b. The probability that the open interval $\overline{X} \pm 1.99\hat{\sigma}\sqrt{n}$ contains μ is .95.
   c. $\text{Prob}(23 < \mu < 36)$ is .95.
   d. A researcher can be 95% confident that the open interval from 23 to 36 contains μ.
   e. A 95% confidence interval for μ is 23 to 36.
   f. $\text{Prob}(\overline{X} - 2.12\hat{\sigma}\sqrt{n} < \mu < \overline{X} + 2.12\hat{\sigma}\sqrt{n}) = .95$, where $\overline{X} = 29.5$ and $\hat{\sigma} = 6.1$.
5. How is the size of a confidence interval related to the following?
   a. Size of population standard deviation
   b. Sample size
   c. Confidence coefficient
6. Researchers investigated the effectiveness of a school and community-based violence prevention program for at-risk eighth-grade students in three public schools in Florida. The treatment group showed a significantly smaller number

of in-school suspensions relative to the population mean for the three schools, $t(57) = 2.86$, $p = .006$. Compute Hedges's g, and interpret the result.

7. Terms to remember:

   a. Confidence interval
   b. Confidence coefficient
   c. Lower and upper endpoints
   d. Confidence limits
   e. Open interval
   f. One-sided confidence limit
   g. Effect magnitude

11.4 LOOKING BACK: WHAT HAVE YOU LEARNED?

In many research situations, researchers want to know the value of a population mean. If, as is usually the case, it is not possible to observe all of the population elements, a researcher must resort to obtaining a random sample and computing the sample mean. The sample mean is the best guess that a researcher can make concerning the value of the population mean. Because of sampling variability, it is unlikely that the sample mean will equal the population mean. This is frustrating, but it is possible to find two functions, L_1 and L_2, of the sample data such that before the sample is drawn, the probability that the open interval from L_1 to L_2 will contain μ is equal to $1 - \alpha$. The open interval from L_1 to L_2 is called a confidence interval for μ with a confidence coefficient equal to $1 - \alpha$. The researcher can be $100(1 - \alpha)\%$ confident that μ is contained in the confidence limits from L_1 and L_2. Confidence intervals represent an alternative approach to statistical inference. They provide much more information about one's data than the more widely used null hypothesis significance tests.

The size of a confidence interval is determined by (1) the confidence coefficient that the researcher specifies, (2) the size of the sample, (3) the size of the sample estimate of the population standard deviation, and (4) whether the interval is one sided or two sided. The construction of a confidence interval involves the same assumptions as those of a null hypothesis significance test. However, a confidence interval has some important advantages over a significance test: (1) it provides a range of values that are likely to contain the population mean, and (2) any null hypothesis can be tested by looking at the confidence interval. By comparison, a null hypothesis significance test is less informative. Rejection of a null hypothesis, for example, indicates that μ is probably not equal to μ_0; nonrejection of the hypothesis indicates that μ_0 remains as a possible value of μ.

Regardless of which statistical inference approach one uses, it also is important to assess the practical significance of one's results. Although a measure of practical significance does not exist, several statistics can help a researcher make this kind of assessment. The statistics are called measures of effect magnitude. The one described in this chapter is Hedges's $g = |\overline{X} - \mu_0|/\hat{\sigma}$. Cohen's effect-size guidelines are helpful for interpreting g: 0.2 is a small effect, 0.5 is a medium effect, and 0.8 is a large effect. However, the determination of practical significance should not be ritualized. Ultimately, the researcher who collected and analyzed a set of data is in the best position to decide whether the results are small or large and whether the results are insignificant or important.

REVIEW EXERCISES FOR CHAPTER 11

1. List four criticisms of null hypothesis significance tests.
2. A random sample of 18 elementary schoolteachers in northeastern Ohio read a background profile of a seven-year-old boy who exhibited symptoms of inattention and hyperactivity. Each teacher assigned a rating on a 7-point scale of the likelihood of referring the child for an attention deficit hyperactivity disorder (ADHD) evaluation: 1 = definitely would not refer, 7 = definitely would refer. The following data were obtained. (Experiment suggested by Sciutto, M. J., Nolfi, C. J., and Bluhm, C. [2004]. Effects of child gender and symptom type on referrals for ADHD by elementary school teachers. *Journal of Emotional and Behavioral Disorders, 14,* 247–253.)

Teacher Ratings

1. 6	7. 5	13. 2
2. 4	8. 5	14. 7
3. 3	9. 3	15. 7
4. 6	10. 4	16. 2
5. 7	11. 5	17. 3
6. 6	12. 6	18. 4

   a. Construct a two-sided 95% confidence interval for μ.
   b. Locate the confidence interval on the real number line.
   c. Based on the confidence interval, list all the null hypotheses that could be rejected at the .05 level of significance.
   d. The population mean teacher rating for a seven-year-old girl whose background profile was identical to that of the seven-year-old boy was $\mu = 3.79$. Based on these data, do teachers treat boys differently from girls who exhibit the same background profile? Explain?
   e. Use Hedges's g to assess the effect size of the boy-girl rating difference and interpret the result.

3. Which of the following statements about a confidence interval are correct and which are incorrect? If a statement is incorrect, specify what is wrong with the statement.
   a. Prob($5.6 < \mu < 8.9$) = .95.
   b. I am 95% confident that μ lies in the open interval from 5.6 to 8.9.
   c. The degree of my confidence that μ is in the open interval from 5.6 to 8.9 is .95.
   d. The probability is .95 that μ lies in the open interval from 5.6 to 8.9.
4. Students desiring to enter graduate school at Kandykane Technical Institute (KTI) are required to submit Graduate Record Examination (GRE) scores with their applications. The verbal scores for the first 20 applications received this year are given in the table.

GRE Scores for Verbal Section of Test

402	390	429	391
381	407	410	403
430	413	406	398
376	424	382	410
395	360	410	404

a. If the first 20 applicants can be considered a random sample of applicants who will apply, what is the best estimate of the population mean for this year's applicants?

b. Construct a two-sided 95% confidence interval for μ. Locate the confidence interval on the real number line.

c. Based on the confidence interval, list all the null hypotheses that could be rejected.

d. Last year, the mean GRE verbal score of all KTI applicants was 428. Is the mean verbal aptitude for this year's applicants different from that for last year?

e. Use Hedges's g to assess the effect size of the difference between this year's and last year's scores and interpret the result.

f. Construct a box plot for the data. Do the data contain outliers?

5. A random sample of 65 junior college students was selected to participate in a new total immersion program designed to increase comprehension of spoken Spanish. The final exam consisted of a Spanish passage that the students transcribed. The number of words correctly transcribed by each student was recorded. The sample statistics were $\overline{X} = 302$ words transcribed with $\hat{\sigma} = 56$. According to departmental records, the mean for students in conventional classes was 320 words transcribed.

a. Construct a one-sided 95% confidence interval for μ for these data. Locate the confidence interval on the real number line.

b. Based on the confidence interval, list all null hypotheses that could be rejected.

c. Compute Hedges's g and interpret.

d. How could the design of the experiment be improved to remove the effects of potential confounding variables? (*Hint:* See Section 10.3, "Some Experimental Design Considerations.")

6. Use the table of random numbers in Appendix D.1 to draw a random sample without replacement of 25 women from the student database in Appendix E.

a. List the Subject Number and Stat Grade for each woman in your sample.

b. Compute the mean of the variable labeled Stat Grade.

c. Summarize the data by means of a box plot. Do the data contain outliers?

d. Construct a two-sided 95% confidence interval for μ. Is it reasonable to believe that the population mean is 2.805?

7. Use the table of random numbers in Appendix D.1 to draw a random sample without replacement of 25 men from the student database in Appendix E.

a. List the Subject Number and Stat Grade for each man in your sample.

b. Compute the mean of the variable labeled Stat Grade.

    c. Summarize the data by means of a box plot. Do the data contain outliers?

    d. Construct a two-sided 95% confidence interval for μ. Is it reasonable to believe that the population mean is 2.662?

8. Researchers investigated the relation between fraternity/sorority (Greek) membership and heavy alcohol use. They obtained self-report data regarding alcohol use for a random sample of 126 fraternity/sorority members at the University of Virginia. The sample data were compared with the population mean for non-Greeks. The survey found that throughout the college years, Greeks drank more heavily than non-Greeks, $t(125) = 3.028, p < .003$. Compute Hedges's g, and interpert the result.

12

Statistical Inference: Other One-Sample Test Statistics

12.1 Introduction to Other One-Sample Test Statistics
Looking Ahead: What Is This Chapter About?

12.2 One-Sample z Test and Confidence Interval for a Proportion
Computational Example for z Test for a Proportion
Confidence Interval for a Proportion
Computational Example for Confidence Interval for a Proportion
Choosing a Sample Size
Check Your Understanding of Section 12.2

12.3 One-Sample t Test and z Confidence Interval for a Correlation
Test of the Hypothesis That a Population Correlation Is Equal to Zero
Computational Example for Test of $\rho = 0$
Confidence Interval for a Correlation
Computational Example for Confidence Interval for a Correlation
Practical Significance of a Correlation
Check Your Understanding of Section 12.3

12.4 Looking Back: What Have You Learned?
Review Exercises for Chapter 12

12.1 INTRODUCTION TO OTHER ONE-SAMPLE TEST STATISTICS

Looking Ahead: What Is This Chapter About?

This chapter could be titled "Theme with Variations"—it applies the five-step null hypothesis-testing format and the confidence-interval procedures introduced in Chapters 10 and 11 to a sample proportion and correlation. Chapters 10 and 11 described procedures for using a sample mean to make decisions about a population mean. As you will discover, the same procedures, with slight modifications, are used to make decisions about a population proportion and a population correlation.

After reading this chapter, you should know the following:

- How to test a hypothesis and construct a confidence interval for a population proportion
- How to determine the sample n needed to estimate a population proportion and have an acceptable margin of error
- How to test a hypothesis and construct a confidence interval for a population correlation

12.2 ONE-SAMPLE z TEST AND CONFIDENCE INTERVAL FOR A PROPORTION

Researchers are often interested in testing a hypothesis about a population proportion. For example, an opinion pollster may want to know whether a majority of the voters favor a certain candidate, an automobile manufacturer may want to know whether at least .70 of new car buyers are willing to pay $150 for a safety device, or the United States Marine Corps may want to know whether at least .35 of its volunteers plan to reenlist.

Each of the examples has a large number of occasions, or independent trials, in which one of two outcomes can occur, and the probabilities associated with the two outcomes remain constant from trial to trial. For convenience, the outcomes are designated "success" and "failure," with probabilities p and $1 - p$, respectively.[1] What I have just described are the characteristics of a Bernoulli trial, which is discussed in Section 8.4. The number of successes on $n \geq 2$ Bernoulli trials is a binomial random variable.

In Section 9.2 you learned that the normal distribution can be used to approximate binomial probabilities. The approximation is excellent if n is large and p is equal to .5; as n becomes smaller or as p approaches either 0 or 1, the approximation becomes poorer. As a rule of thumb, the normal approximation is satisfactory if (1) the population is at least 10 times larger than the sample and (2) np_0 (the sample size multiplied by the value of the population proportion specified in the null hypothesis) and $n(1 - p_0)$ are both greater than 15.[2]

---

[1] This p denotes a population proportion and is not related to a p value. The meaning of p should be clear from the context in which it is used.

[2] In previous editions I used the number 5 instead of 15. Research by Brown, Cai, and DasGupta (2001) indicates that the number should be 15.

A z statistic for testing a null hypothesis about a population proportion is

$$z = \frac{\hat{p} - p_0}{\sqrt{p_0(p_0 - 1)/n}}$$

where $\hat{p}$ is the sample estimator of the population proportion and is given by

$$\hat{p} = \frac{\text{number of successes in the random sample}}{\text{number of observations in the random sample}}$$

p_0 is the value of the population proportion specified in the null hypothesis, and n is the size of the random sample used to compute $\hat{p}$.

The z statistic can be used to test null hypotheses of the form

$H_0: p = p_0$	$H_0: p \leq p_0$	$H_0: p \geq p_0$
$H_1: p \neq p_0$	$H_1: p > p_0$	$H_1: p < p_0$

Here, p denotes the unknown population proportion. The assumptions associated with using the z statistic to test these hypotheses are (1) random sampling from the population of interest, (2) binomial population, (3) np_0 and $n(1 - p_0)$ are both greater than 15, and (4) the population is at least 10 times larger than the sample. A null hypothesis is rejected if the z statistic falls in the critical region of the sampling distribution of the standard normal distribution given in Appendix Table D.2. The values of z that cut off the upper and lower critical regions for a two-sided null hypothesis are denoted by $z_{\alpha/2}$ and $-z_{\alpha/2}$, respectively. For a one-sided null hypothesis, the critical regions are denoted by z_α and $-z_\alpha$.

Computational Example for z Test for a Proportion

Suppose that the Committee for Better Student Housing has conducted a survey to determine whether the proportion of substandard apartments near the university campus has changed since the last survey five years ago. At that time, .30 of the apartments were classified as substandard. A random sample of 900 apartments was surveyed, and .34 were found to be substandard. Has the proportion changed since the last survey? The steps to be followed in testing the null hypothesis that the population proportion is equal to .30 are as follows:

Step 1. State the statistical hypotheses: $H_0: p = .30$
$H_1: p \neq .30$

Step 2. Specify the test statistic: $z = \dfrac{\hat{p} - p_0}{\sqrt{p_0(p_0 - 1)/n}}$ because the committee wants to test $p = .30$, the sample is random, and both $np_0 = (900)(.30) = 270$ and $n(1 - p_0) = (900)(1 - .30) = 630$ are greater than 15.

Step 3. Specify the sample size: $\quad n = 900$
and the sampling distribution: standard normal distribution.

Step 4. Specify the significance level: $\quad \alpha = .05$

Step 5. Obtain a random sample of size n,
compute z, and make a decision.

Decision rule:

Reject the null hypothesis if z falls in either the lower 2.5% or the upper 2.5% of the sampling distribution of z; otherwise, do not reject the null hypothesis. If the null hypothesis is rejected, conclude that the proportion of substandard apartments has changed since the last survey; if the null hypothesis is not rejected, do not draw this conclusion.

For $\hat{p} = .34$, the sample proportion of substandard apartments in the recent survey, the z statistic is

$$z = \frac{\hat{p} - p_0}{\sqrt{p_0(1 - p_0)/n}} = \frac{.34 - .30}{\sqrt{(.30)(1 - .30)/900}} = \frac{.04}{0.0153} = 2.62$$

According to Appendix Table D.2, $z_{.05/2} = 1.96$ and $-z_{.05/2} = -1.96$, respectively, cut off the upper and lower .025 regions of the sampling distribution. Because the computed $z = 2.62$ is greater than $z_{.05/2} = 1.96$, the null hypothesis is rejected. The students can conclude that the proportion of substandard apartments near the university campus has changed. In fact, data for the recent survey, $\hat{p} = .34$, suggest that the housing situation has deteriorated.

In reporting the results of the null hypothesis significance test in the text portion of a publication, the students might say, "It appears from a survey of 900 randomly sampled apartments near the university campus that the population proportion of substandard apartments is greater than it was five years ago. The sample proportion in the recent survey was .34; the proportion five years ago was .30. The z test was statistically significant, $z = 2.62$, $p < .01$." The p value, $(2)(.0044) = .0088$, was obtained from Appendix Table D.2. The students multiplied the value in the table by 2 because the null hypothesis was nondirectional. The value was rounded up to .01.

Confidence Interval for a Proportion

A two-sided $100(1 - \alpha)\%$ confidence interval for p is given by

$$\hat{p} - z_{\alpha/2}\sqrt{\frac{\hat{p}(1 - \hat{p})}{n}} < p < \hat{p} + z_{\alpha/2}\sqrt{\frac{\hat{p}(1 - \hat{p})}{n}}$$

where $\hat{p}$ is an estimator of the population proportion, n is the number of elements in a random sample used to compute $\hat{p}$, and $z_{\alpha/2}$ is the value of the standard normal distribution that cuts off the upper $\alpha/2$ region.

Lower and upper one-sided $100(1 - \alpha)\%$ confidence intervals for p are given by, respectively,

$$\hat{p} - z_\alpha \sqrt{\frac{\hat{p}(1 - \hat{p})}{n}} < p \quad \text{and} \quad p < \hat{p} + z_\alpha \sqrt{\frac{\hat{p}(1 - \hat{p})}{n}}$$

where z_α is the value of the standard normal distribution that cuts off the upper α region.

The assumptions associated with these interval are (1) random sampling from the population of interest, (2) binomial population, (3) $n\hat{p}$ and $n(1 - \hat{p})$ are both greater than 15, and (4) the population is at least ten times larger than the sample.

Notice that the formulas for estimating the **standard error of a proportion,**

$$\sigma_p = \sqrt{\frac{p(1 - p)}{n}}$$

where p is the unknown population proportion, are different for the z statistic and the confidence interval. The two formulas given earlier are

$$\hat{\sigma}_p = \sqrt{\frac{p_0(1 - p_0)}{n}} \qquad \hat{\sigma}_p = \sqrt{\frac{\hat{p}(1 - \hat{p})}{n}}$$

The z statistic uses the null hypothesis value, p_0, in estimating σ_p under the assumption that the null hypothesis is true—that is, $H_0: p = p_0$. The confidence interval assumes that the sample proportion, $\hat{p}$, provides the best estimate of p.

Computational Example for Confidence Interval for a Proportion

To illustrate the construction of a confidence interval for p, I will use the Committee for Better Student Housing data described earlier. Recall that the sample proportion of substandard apartments near the university campus was $\hat{p} = .34$ and $n = 900$. The statistical hypotheses were

$$H_0: p = .30$$

$$H_1: p \neq .30$$

An analogous two-sided $100(1 - .05)\% = 95\%$ confidence interval for these data is

$$\hat{p} - z_{.05/2} \sqrt{\frac{\hat{p}(1 - \hat{p})}{n}} < p < \hat{p} + z_{.05/2} \sqrt{\frac{\hat{p}(1 - \hat{p})}{n}}$$

$$.34 - 1.96 \sqrt{\frac{(.34)(1 - .34)}{900}} < p < .34 + 1.96 \sqrt{\frac{(.34)(1 - .34)}{900}}$$

$$.34 - .031 < p < .34 + .031$$

$$.31 < p < .37$$

This confidence interval corresponds to the darkened portion of the real number line as follows:

The students can be 95% confident that p is greater than .31 and less than 37. The margin of error in the students' estimate of p is $z_{.05/2}\sqrt{\hat{p}(1-\hat{p})/n} = .031$. The margin of error indicates how precisely a researcher can estimate the population proportion. Researchers often want the margin of error to be between .02 and .04.

Choosing a Sample Size

The Committee for Better Student Housing survey examined a random sample of $n = 900$ apartments. Could the students have used a smaller sample to estimate the population proportion of substandard dwelling units? To make a rational choice of sample size, you need to specify three things. First, you must decide on an acceptable margin of error, denoted by m^*, in estimating p. In other words, how close do you want your sample proportion to be to the population proportion? As mentioned earlier, investigators often use m^* values between .02 and .04. Second, you need to select a confidence level and associated z value from Appendix Table D.2. In practice, the 95% confidence level is commonly used. Finally, you need to make an educated guess about the likely value of p. I will denote this educated guess by the symbol p^*.

The formula for estimating the sample size is

$$n = \left(\frac{z_{\alpha/2}}{m^*}\right)^2 p^*(p^* - 1)$$

where $z_{\alpha/2}$ is the two-sided standard normal distribution value corresponding to a $100\%(1 - \alpha)$ confidence coefficient, m^* is the acceptable margin of error in estimating the population proportion, and p^* is the guessed value of the population proportion.

Suppose that in the housing survey, the students wanted to construct a 95% confidence interval for p with a margin of error equal to $m^* = .03$. The best guess that the students can make about the value of the population proportion is that $p^* = .30$. This guess is based on the earlier survey of apartments where $\hat{p}$ was found to be .30. For these conditions, the required sample size is

$$n = \left(\frac{1.96}{.30}\right)^2 (.30)(1 - .30) = 896.4$$

Rounding up, the required n is 897. This n is very close the sample size actually used, $n = 900$. In all likelihood, the students used the formula to estimate the required n.

To achieve a smaller margin of error, the students would have to use a much larger sample size. For example, if the students wanted the margin of error to only be $m^* = .02$, the required sample size would be $n = 2,017$, as the following computations show:

$$n = \left(\frac{1.96}{.02}\right)^2 (.30)(1 - .30) = 2,016.8$$

Sometimes, you may have no idea what value to guess for p. In such cases, you can obtain a conservative estimate of the sample size by assuming that the product $p^* \times (1 - p^*)$ is as large as it could possible be. It can be shown that this occurs when $p^* = .50$. Hence, a conservative n for a 95% confidence interval with a margin of error equal to $m^* = .03$ is

$$n = \left(\frac{1.96}{.03}\right)^2 (.50)(1 - .50) = 1,067.1$$

In the worst-case scenario where the population proportion is equal to .50, you need $n = 1,068$ units. If you have a basis for guessing that $p^* = .30$ and your guess is fairly close to the true population proportion, you need only $n = 897$ housing units.

CHECK YOUR UNDERSTANDING OF SECTION 12.2

1. If you want to use a z statistic to test a hypothesis about p, and p_0 is equal to .20, how large should n be to use the normal approximation to the binomial distribution?
2. The election is only days away and the latest Giddyup poll gives Mr. Jerry Mander 55% of the vote. Between periods of euphoria Mr. Mander ponders the question, should he or should he not cancel the expensive political advertisement planned for election eve? Is it possible that he does not have a majority, although the highly respected poll of $n = 1000$ randomly selected potential voters says he will win? Now, Mr. Mander is no statistician, but he knows that polls are subject to sampling error. With anxiety mounting, he decides to forego a vacation to Hawaii and use the campaign funds for their intended purpose.
   a. List the steps you would follow to test the scientific hypothesis that the population proportion is not equal to .50. Let $\alpha = .01$.
   b. Test the null hypothesis that $p = .50$.
   c. What does the use of the .01 instead of the .05 level of significance tell you about the relative importance that Mr. Mander assigned to Type I and II errors?
   d. What is the p value of the z statistic?
   e. Compute a $100(1 - .01)\% = 99\%$ confidence interval for p. Locate the confidence interval on the real number line. Was Mr. Mander's decision to forego the Hawaii vacation a good one?
   f. Specify all the null hypotheses that could be rejected.
   g. What was the margin of error for the confidence interval?
   h. How large should n be for the margin of error of a 99% confidence interval to equal .02 if $p^* = .50$?

3. Suppose that you are interested in testing babies' color preferences. On each of $n = 30$ trials, you offer a baby a choice between two balls—one red and one green. The baby chooses a red ball on 12 of the 20 trials.
    a. List the steps you would follow in testing the scientific hypothesis that the babies have a preference for one of the two colors. Let $\alpha = .05$.
    b. Can you conclude that the babies have a color preference?
    c. What is the p value of the test statistic?
    d. Compute a $100(1 - .05)\% = 95\%$ confidence interval for p. Locate the confidence interval on the real number line.
    e. Specify all the null hypotheses that could be rejected.
    f. What was the margin of error for the confidence interval?
    g. How large should n be for the margin of error of a 95% confidence interval to equal .04 if $p^* = .50$?

4. A national survey of 300 unmarried women between the ages of 15 and 19 found that 46% of the 19-year-olds had experienced sexual intercourse.
    a. List the steps you would follow in testing the scientific hypothesis that the population proportion has changed from an earlier survey in which $\hat{p} = .37$. Let $\alpha = .01$.
    b. Test the null hypothesis that $p = .37$.
    c. What is the p value of the z statistic?
    d. Compute a $100(1 - .01)\% = 99\%$ confidence interval for p. Locate the confidence interval on the real number line.
    e. Specify all the null hypotheses that could be rejected.
    f. What was the margin of error for the confidence interval?
    g. How large should n be for the margin of error of a 99% confidence interval to equal .03 if $p^* = .37$?
    h. In a paragraph, report the results of your analyses; follow good statistical practice.

5. Two hundred men who had suffered one heart attack participated in a supervised physical fitness program. Only sixteen of the men had a second attack during the 12 months after beginning the program. According to national statistics, the chances of a man having a second heart attack are 1 in 10 each year after the first seizure.
    a. List the steps you would follow in testing the scientific hypothesis that the supervised physical fitness program affected the chances of a man having a second heart attack. Let $\alpha = .05$.
    b. Test the null hypothesis. Was the physical fitness program effective? Why?
    c. What is the p value of the z statistic?
    d. Compute a $100(1 - .05)\% = 95\%$ confidence interval for p. Locate the confidence interval on the real number line.
    e. Specify all the null hypotheses that could be rejected.
    f. What was the margin of error for the confidence interval?
    g. How large should n be for the margin of error of a 95% confidence interval to equal .03 if $p^* = .10$?

6. Term to remember:
    a. Standard error of a proportion

12.3 ONE-SAMPLE *t* TEST AND *z* CONFIDENCE INTERVAL FOR A CORRELATION

Test of the Hypothesis That a Population Correlation Is Equal to Zero

Many research questions are concerned with whether two variables, say X and Y, are correlated. If the variables are not correlated, the population correlation coefficient is equal to 0. If the variables are correlated, the coefficient is not equal to zero. The hypotheses of interest to a researcher are

$$H_0: \rho = 0$$

$$H_1: \rho \neq 0$$

where ρ denotes the population correlation between the variables. A sample correlation coefficient, r, can differ from 0 due to chance sampling variability even though $\rho = 0$. Fortunately, the sample correlation coefficient can be used to determine whether the hypothesis $H_0: \rho = 0$ is or is not tenable.

Because the hypothesis $H_0: \rho = 0$ occurs so often in the behavioral sciences, health sciences, and education, a table has been developed that simplifies testing the hypothesis.[3] Appendix Table D.6 gives the values of Pearson's sample correlation coefficient, r, that are statistically significant for various significance levels and degrees of freedom. You enter the table with degrees freedom equal to $\nu = n - 2$, where n is the number of paired X and Y scores. The table tells you the minimum r that leads to rejecting $H_0: \rho = 0$ for either a one- or two-tailed test at various significance levels. If the absolute value of your sample r, $|r|$, is greater than or equal to the r value in the table, the hypothesis that ρ is equal to 0 is rejected.

The test of the null hypothesis, $H_0: \rho = 0$, assumes (1) random sampling, (2) the population distributions of X and Y are approximately normal, (3) the relationship between X and Y is linear, and (4) the distribution of Y for any value of X is normal with variance that does not depend on the X value selected (this is the homoscedasticity assumption discussed in Section 5.6) and vice versa. Under these conditions the sampling distribution of r is approximately normally distributed.

Computational Example for Test of $\rho = 0$

Suppose that a researcher wanted to determine whether a linear correlation exists between college grades and income 10 years after graduation. Assume that the researcher has obtained college grade-point averages and income for a random sample of 62 male graduates of Florida State University. The product-moment correlation between grade-point average and income for this sample is .28. Is it likely that a

---

[3] The table is based on the *t* sampling distribution and *t* statistic,

$$t = \frac{r\sqrt{n-2}}{\sqrt{1-r^2}}$$

with $\nu = n - 2$ degrees of freedom.

sample correlation coefficient of this size would have been obtained if the correlation between income and grades really is equal to 0? Assume that the researcher wants to perform a two-tailed test at $\alpha = .05$ level of significance. According to Appendix Table D.6, the minimum value of $|r|$ that is significant for $\nu = 62 - 2 = 60$ degrees of freedom is .25. Because $|r| = .28$ exceeds .25, the researcher concluded that the population correlation is not equal to zero.

In reporting the results of the null hypothesis significance test in the text portion of a publication, the researcher might say, "the linear correlation between college grade-point average and income for a random sample of 62 male graduates of Florida State University was .28. The correlation was statistically significant, $p < .05$."

Confidence Interval for a Correlation

When $\rho = 0$, the sampling distribution of r can be regarded as approximately normal. However, when ρ differs appreciably from zero, the sampling distribution of r becomes very skewed. The skewness occurs because the possible values of r are constrained—r cannot exceed $+1$ or -1.

As you saw earlier, Appendix Table D.6 can be used only when the sampling distribution of r is approximately normal. A procedure developed by Ronald A. Fisher does not have this limitation. Fisher's procedure can be used to construct confidence intervals for any value of ρ that is not too close to ± 1. The procedure uses a special function of r, rather than r. The function is called the **Fisher r-to-Z' transformation.** The Z' statistic does not have the same constraints as r; Z' can exceed $+1$ or -1. The transformation of r into Z' is easily accomplished by means of Appendix Table D.7. This table gives for each value of r the corresponding Z' statistic. For example, if r is equal to .50, the value of Z' from Table D.7 is 0.549. If $r = .85$, $Z' = 1.256$. Fisher showed that the sampling distribution of Z' is approximately normal if ρ is not too close to 1 or -1 and the sample n is greater than 10.

To construct a confidence interval for ρ, you begin by converting your sample r into Z' using Table D.7. You then construct a confidence interval for the population Z', denoted by Z'_{Pop}. Once you have obtained the interval for Z'_{Pop}, use Table D.7 to convert the lower and upper limits of the interval into a confidence interval for ρ.

A two-sided $100(1 - \alpha)\%$ confidence interval for Z'_{Pop} is given by

$$Z' - z_{\alpha/2}\sqrt{\frac{1}{n-3}} < Z'_{Pop} < Z' + z_{\alpha/2}\sqrt{\frac{1}{n-3}}$$

where Z' is the transformed sample r, $z_{\alpha/2}$ is the value of z from Appendix Table D.2 that cuts off the upper $\alpha/2$ region of the sampling distribution of z, and n is the size of the sample used to compute r.

Lower and upper one-sided $100(1 - \alpha)\%$ confidence intervals for Z'_{Pop} are given by, respectively,

$$Z' - z_{\alpha}\sqrt{\frac{1}{n-3}} < Z'_{Pop} \quad \text{and} \quad Z'_{Pop} < Z' + z_{\alpha}\sqrt{\frac{1}{n-3}}$$

where z_{α} is the value of z that cuts off the upper α region of the sampling distribution of z.

A confidence interval for ρ is obtained by converting the lower and upper limits for Z'_{Pop} into correlation coefficients using the Z'-to-r conversion in Appendix Table D.7. The confidence intervals assume (1) random sampling, (2) ρ is not too close to 1 or -1, (3) the population distributions of X and Y are approximately normal, (4) the relationship between X and Y is linear, (5) the distribution of Y for any value of X is normal with variance that does not depend on the X value that is selected and vice versa, and (6) the sample n is greater than 10.

Computational Example for Confidence Interval for a Correlation

Earlier, I used Appendix Table D.6 to test the null hypothesis that the correlation between college grades and income 10 years after graduation for a random sample of 62 graduates of Florida State University is equal to 0. The sample estimate of the population correlation coefficient was .28. I will use these data to construct a confidence interval for the population correlation coefficient. According to Appendix Table D. 7, the value of Z' that corresponds to $r = .28$ is $Z' = 0.288$. A two-sided $100(1 - .05)\% = 95\%$ confidence interval for Z'_{Pop} is given by

$$Z' - z_{.05/2}\sqrt{\frac{1}{n-3}} < Z'_{Pop} < Z' + z_{.05/2}\sqrt{\frac{1}{n-3}}$$

$$0.288 - 1.96\sqrt{\frac{1}{62-3}} < Z'_{Pop} < 0.288 + 1.96\sqrt{\frac{1}{62-3}}$$

$$0.288 - 0.255 < Z'_{Pop} < 0.288 + 0.255$$

$$0.033 < Z'_{Pop} < 0.543$$

Transforming the lower and upper limits of Z'_{Pop} into correlation coefficients yields the 95% confidence interval for ρ which is $.03 < \rho < .61$. Because the confidence interval does not include 0, a test of the null hypothesis that ρ is equal to 0 or any other null hypothesis in which ρ_0 is less than or equal to .03 or greater than or equal to 61 could be rejected. The confidence interval corresponds to the darkened portion of the real number line as follows:

The researcher's best guess concerning the value of ρ is that it is equal to .28—the value of the sample correlation coefficient. The researcher can be 95% confident that ρ is greater than .03 and less than 61.

Practical Significance of a Correlation

As discussed in Section 11.3, most measures of effect magnitude fall into one of two categories: measures of effect size such as d and measures of strength of association. Cohen (1988, pp. 77–83) has suggested using r, a measure of the linear strength of association between two variables, to assess effect magnitude. According to Cohen, $r = .10$ is a small strength of association, $r = .30$ is a medium strength of association, and $r = .50$ is a large strength of association. He has shown that the strengths of association represented by .10, .30, and .50 are roughly equivalent to the effect sizes represented by d values of .2, .5, and .8, respectively. Hence, the terms *small, medium,* and *large* mean about the same thing whether we are talking about strength of association or effect size.

Using Cohen's guidelines, the correlation ($r = .28$) between college grades and income 10 years after graduation represents a small strength of association.

CHECK YOUR UNDERSTANDING OF SECTION 12.3

7. Convert r into Z'.
   - a. $r = .46$
   - b. $r = -.23$
   - c. $r = -.96$
   - d. $r = .15$
8. Convert Z' into r.
   - a. $Z' = 0.549$
   - b. $Z' = -0.192$
   - c. $Z' = 0.245$
   - d. $Z' = -1.256$
9. Researchers hypothesized that the correlation between the scores of truck drivers on the realistic and artistic scales of the Career Assessment Inventory (CAI) is negligible. Assume that $r = .09$ has been computed for a random sample of 26 drivers.
   - a. Test the null hypothesis $H_0: \rho = 0$ using the critical value from Appendix Table D.6. Let $\alpha = .05$.
   - b. Compute a $100(1 - .05)\% = 95\%$ confidence interval for ρ. Locate the confidence interval on the real number line.
   - c. Specify all the null hypotheses that could be rejected.
   - d. Interpret the effect size.
10. The correlation between scores on the TAC (a college entrance test) and grade-point averages for a random sample of $n = 100$ freshmen was .54. Last year, the correlation for the freshman class was .61.
    - a. Compute a $100(1 - .05)\% = 95\%$ confidence interval for ρ. Locate the confidence interval on the real number line.
    - b. Specify all the null hypotheses that could be rejected.
    - c. Is the correlation between scores on the TAC and grade-point averages for this year's freshmen different from that for last year's freshmen?
    - d. Interpret the effect size.
11. Term to remember:
    - a. Fisher r-to-Z' transformation

12.4 LOOKING BACK: WHAT HAVE YOU LEARNED?

I have covered much ground in Chapters 10 through 12: the basic concepts of statistical inference and a variety of null hypothesis significance tests and confidence intervals for the one-sample case. Although the null hypothesis test statistics have different formulas and are used to test hypotheses about different parameters, they all use the same five-step format in arriving at a decision about a hypothesis. Similarly, the construction of confidence intervals follows the same pattern regardless of the parameter of interest. You will see that the logic underlying null hypothesis significance tests and confidence intervals described in Chapters 10 through 12 generalizes to the two-sample case and to more complex decision-making situations.

The test statistics and confidence intervals for the one-sample case are summarized in Tables 12.4-1 and 12.4-2, respectively. As the tables show, the assumptions of the test statistics and analogous confidence intervals are the same.

TABLE 12.4-1   Summary of One-Sample Test Statistics

Chapter Section	Statistical Hypotheses	Test Statistic	Assumptions
10.3	$H_0: \mu = \mu_0$ $H_1: \mu \neq \mu_0$	$t = \dfrac{\overline{X} - \mu_0}{\hat{\sigma}/\sqrt{n}}$ $\nu = n - 1$	1. Random sampling 2. Normality 3. Standard deviation is unknown
10.3	$H_0: \mu = \mu_0$ $H_1: \mu \neq \mu_0$	$z = \dfrac{\overline{X} - \mu_0}{\sigma/\sqrt{n}}$	1. Random sampling 2. Normality or large sample 3. Standard deviation is known
12.2	$H_0: p = p_0$	$z = \dfrac{\hat{p} - p_0}{\sqrt{p_0(1 - p_0)/n}}$	1. Random sampling 2. Binomial distribution 3. $np_0 > 15$, $n(1 - p_0) > 15$ 4. Population is at least 10 times larger than the sample
12.3	$H_0: p = p_0$ $H_0: p \neq p_0$	Table D.6 based on the t statistic $t = \dfrac{r\sqrt{n-2}}{\sqrt{1 - r^2}}$ $\nu = n - 2$	1. Random sampling 2. X and Y are normally distributed 3. Relationship between X and Y is linear 4. Homoscedasticity

TABLE 12.4-2   Summary of One-Sample Confidence Intervals

Chapter Section	Parameter	Confidence Interval	Assumptions
11.2	μ	$\overline{X} - \dfrac{t_{\alpha/2,\,\nu}\,\hat{\sigma}}{\sqrt{n}} < \mu < \overline{X} + \dfrac{t_{\alpha/2,\,\nu}\,\hat{\sigma}}{\sqrt{n}}$	1. Random sampling 2. Normality 3. Standard deviation is unknown

(continued)

TABLE 12.4-2   *(continued)*

Chapter Section	Parameter	Confidence Interval	Assumptions
12.2	p	$\hat{p} - z_{\alpha/2}\sqrt{\dfrac{\hat{p}(1-\hat{p})}{n}} < p < \hat{p} + z_{\alpha/2}\sqrt{\dfrac{\hat{p}(1-\hat{p})}{n}}$	1. Random sampling 2. Binomial distribution 3. $n\hat{p} > 15, n(1 - \hat{p}) > 15$ 4. Population is at least 10 times larger than the sample
12.3	ρ	$Z' - z_{\alpha/2}\sqrt{\dfrac{1}{n-3}} < Z'_{Pop} < Z' + z_{\alpha/2}\sqrt{\dfrac{1}{n-3}}$	1. Random sampling 2. ρ is not too close to $+1$ or -1 3. X and Y are normally distributed 4. Relationship between X and Y is linear 5. Homoscedasticity 6. Sample $n > 10$

REVIEW EXERCISES FOR CHAPTER 12

1. If you want to use a z statistic to test a hypothesis about p, and p_0 is equal to .40, how large should n be to use the normal approximation to the binomial distribution?

2. The probability of recovery for schizophrenic patients after receiving 6 months of conventional therapy at Happyfarm Hospital was .60. A token economy program was introduced for a random sample of 40 schizophrenic patients. At the end of the six-month trial period, 28 patients had improved.

    a. List the steps you would follow to test the scientific hypothesis that if the token economy program were used for all patients, the improvement probability would be higher than that for the conventional therapy. Let $\alpha = .05$.

    b. Can you conclude that the token economy program would result in a higher improvement probability than the conventional therapy?

    c. What is the p value of the test statistic?

    d. Compute a $100(1 - .05)\% = 95\%$ confidence interval for p. Locate the confidence interval on the real number line.

    e. Specify all the null hypotheses that could be rejected.

    f. What was the margin of error for the confidence interval?

    g. How large should n be for the margin of error of a 95% confidence interval to equal .04 if $p^* = .65$?

3. Sketch the sampling distribution for z in Review Exercise 2 and label the critical region.

4. In a random sample of 100 homes in Junction City, Oklahoma, researchers found that 84 have digital cameras.

    a. List the steps you would follow to test the scientific hypothesis that the proportion in Junction City differs from that in a nearby community where the proportion of homes with digital cameras is known to be .71. Let $\alpha = .05$.

    b. Test the null hypothesis. Does the proportion in Junction City differ from the other community?

    c. What is the p value of the z statistic?

    d. Compute a $100(1 - .05)\% = 95\%$ confidence interval for p. Locate the confidence interval on the real number line.

    e. Specify all the null hypotheses that could be rejected.

    f. What was the margin of error for the confidence interval?

    g. How large should n be for the margin of error of a 95% confidence interval to equal .04 if $p^* = .71$?

5. Convert r into Z'.

    a. $r = .39$ b. $r = -.19$

    c. $r = -.84$ d. $r = .11$

6. Convert Z' into r.

    a. $Z' = 0.576$ b. $Z' = -0.198$

    c. $Z' = 0.250$ d. $Z' = -1.499$

7. Researchers hypothesized that the correlation between the scores of accountants on the learning strategy and discriminability factors of the California Verbal Learning Test (CVLT) is negligible. Assume that $r = .12$ has been computed for a random sample of 29 accountants.

    a. Test the null hypothesis, H_0: $\rho = 0$, using the critical value from Appendix Table D.6. Let $\alpha = .05$.

    b. Compute a $100(1 - .05)\% = 95\%$ confidence interval for ρ. Locate the confidence interval on the real number line.

    c. Specify all the null hypotheses that could be rejected.

    d. Interpret the effect size.

8. Psychological Associates, a consulting firm, has revised a test that is used to select managers for a large chain of hamburger restaurants. The researcher believed that the revised test is better than the current test. The revised test was given to a random sample of 170 managers. The correlation between their test scores and a measure of their stores' net incomes was .31. The correlation for the old test was .19.

    a. Compute a one-sided $100(1 - .05)\% = 95\%$ confidence interval for ρ. Locate the confidence interval on the real number line.

    b. Specify all the null hypotheses that could be rejected.

    c. Should the revised test be used in selecting future managers for the chain? Why?

    d. Interpret the effect size.

9. The correlation between the recreational interests of a random sample of $n = 67$ pairs of husbands and wives who had contacted a large travel agency was .52.

    a. Compute a $100(1 - .01)\% = 99\%$ confidence interval for ρ. Locate the confidence interval on the real number line.

    b. Specify all the null hypotheses that could be rejected.

    c. Interpret the effect size.

10. The sampling distribution of r is not likely to be normal when ρ deviates appreciably from 0. From what you know about r, why is this true?

13

Statistical Inference: Two Samples

13.1 Introduction to Hypothesis Tests for Two Samples
Looking Ahead:
What Is This
Chapter About?

13.2 Two-Sample t Test and Confidence Interval for $\mu_1 - \mu_2$ Using Independent Samples
Computational Example
for t Test for $\mu_1 - \mu_2$
(Independent
Samples)
Two-Sample t' Test
for $\mu_1 - \mu_2$ with
Unequal Variances
(Independent
Samples)
Two-Sample z Test for
$\mu_1 - \mu_2$ (Independent
Samples)
Practical Significance
Determining the
Required Sample
Sizes (Independent
Samples)

t Confidence Interval
for $\mu_1 - \mu_2$
(Independent
Samples)
t' Confidence Interval
for $\mu_1 - \mu_2$ with
Unequal Variances
(Independent
Samples)
Check Your
Understanding
of Section 13.2

13.3 Two Randomization Strategies: Random Sampling and Random Assignment
The Strategy of Random
Sampling
The Strategy of Random
Assignment
Advantages and
Disadvantages of
the Two Research
Strategies
Check Your
Understanding of
Section 13.3

13.4 Two-Sample t Test and Confidence Interval for $\mu_1 - \mu_2$ Using Dependent Samples
Introduction to
Dependent Samples
t Test for $\mu_1 - \mu_2$
(Dependent Samples)
Computational Example
for t Test for $\mu_1 - \mu_2$
(Dependent Samples)
Practical Significance
Determining the
Required Sample Size
(Dependent Samples)
t Confidence Interval for
$\mu_1 - \mu_2$ (Dependent
Samples)
Group Matching:
A Research Strategy
to Be Avoided
Check Your
Understanding of
Section 13.4

13.5 Looking Back: What Have You Learned?
Review Exercises for
Chapter 13

13.1 INTRODUCTION TO HYPOTHESIS TESTS FOR TWO SAMPLES

Looking Ahead: What Is This Chapter About?

Are men able to withstand weightlessness better than women? Do disadvantaged children learn more quickly in a contingency management classroom than in a traditional classroom? Do people who jog have fewer heart attacks than those who don't? Is one antilitter slogan more effective than another? Each of these questions involves a comparison of two population distributions. Population distributions can differ in central tendency, dispersion, skewness, and kurtosis. Most questions in the behavioral sciences, health sciences, and education are concerned with central tendency and, more specifically, with whether the means of two populations differ.

You learned in Chapter 10 that scientific hypotheses often involve (1) predictions about populations whose elements are so numerous that viewing them all is impossible (all men and women in a weightless environment, all disadvantaged school children, all joggers and nonjoggers) or (2) predictions about phenomena that cannot be directly observed (the effectiveness of two antilitter slogans). In such cases you can use random samples from the populations to make inferences as to whether the means, variances, and so on of the populations differ. The inferences are based on null hypothesis testing and confidence-interval procedures that are straightforward extensions of those for the one-sample case described in Chapters 10 through 12.

After reading this chapter, you should know the following:

- How to use a t statistic to test a statistical hypothesis about two population means
- How to use the t sampling distribution to construct a confidence interval for the difference between two population means
- The relative advantages of random sampling and random assignment
- The power advantage of using dependent samples over independent samples
- How Hedges's g statistic can help you assess the practical significance of the difference between two means

13.2 TWO-SAMPLE t TEST AND CONFIDENCE INTERVAL FOR $\mu_1 - \mu_2$ USING INDEPENDENT SAMPLES

A t test statistic is used to test a hypothesis about the means, μ_1 and μ_2, of two populations. The statistic can be used to test any of the following null hypotheses:

$$H_0: \mu_1 - \mu_2 = \delta_0 \qquad H_0: \mu_1 - \mu_2 \leq \delta_0 \qquad H_0: \mu_1 - \mu_2 \geq \delta_0$$
$$H_1: \mu_1 - \mu_2 \neq \delta_0 \qquad H_1: \mu_1 - \mu_2 > \delta_0 \qquad H_1: \mu_1 - \mu_2 < \delta_0,$$

where, δ_0 (Greek lowercase delta) is the hypothesized difference between the population means. Usually, a researcher is interested in testing the hypothesis that the population means are equal, in which case δ_0 is equal to 0.

The *t* test statistic is given by

$$t = \frac{(\overline{X}_1 - \overline{X}_2) - \delta_0}{\hat{\sigma}_{\overline{X}_1 - \overline{X}_2}} = \frac{(\overline{X}_1 - \overline{X}_2) - \delta_0}{\sqrt{\dfrac{\hat{\sigma}^2_{Pooled}}{n_1} + \dfrac{\hat{\sigma}^2_{Pooled}}{n_2}}} = \frac{(\overline{X}_1 - \overline{X}_2) - \delta_0}{\sqrt{\hat{\sigma}^2_{Pooled}\left(\dfrac{1}{n_1} + \dfrac{1}{n_2}\right)}}$$

where δ_0 is the hypothesized difference between the population means and

$$\hat{\sigma}^2_{Pooled} = \frac{(n_1 - 1)\hat{\sigma}^2_1 + (n_2 - 1)\hat{\sigma}^2_2}{(n_1 - 1) + (n_2 - 1)}$$

If $\delta_0 = 0$, the *t* formula simplifies to

$$t = \frac{\overline{X}_1 - \overline{X}_2}{\hat{\sigma}_{\overline{X}_1 - \overline{X}_2}} = -\frac{\overline{X}_1 - \overline{X}_2}{\sqrt{\hat{\sigma}^2_{Pooled}\left(\dfrac{1}{n_1} + \dfrac{1}{n_2}\right)}}$$

The denominator, $\hat{\sigma}_{\overline{X}_1 - \overline{X}_2}$, of the *t* statistic is an estimator of the **standard error of the difference between two population means.**

The number of degrees of freedom, ν, for the *t* statistic is equal to $n_1 + n_2 - 2$. Sample 1 contributes $n_1 - 1$ degrees of freedom, the number of degrees of freedom associated with $\hat{\sigma}^2_1$, and, likewise, sample 2 contributes $n_2 - 1$ degrees of freedom, the number of degrees of freedom associated with $\hat{\sigma}^2_2$. The null hypothesis is rejected if the observed *t* statistic exceeds or equals the critical value of *t* given in Appendix Table D.3. Recall from Section 10.2 that one- and two-tailed critical values for *t* are denoted by, respectively, $t_{\alpha, \nu}$ and $t_{\alpha/2, \nu}$.

In using the *t* statistic, it is assumed that two random samples of size n_1 and n_2 have been obtained from the populations of interest or that participants have been randomly assigned to two groups often called experimental and control groups. These sampling procedures produce **independent samples** in which the selection of elements in one sample is not affected by the selection of elements in the other. The use of random sampling or random assignment helps to ensure that the samples are statistically independent. Random assignment also helps to distribute the unique, idiosyncratic characteristics of the participants equally to the two groups. Finally, it is assumed that the two populations are normally distributed and that the variances of the populations, σ^2_1 and σ^2_2, are unknown but are assumed to be equal.

The pooled variance, $\hat{\sigma}^2_{Pooled}$, in the *t* formula requires a word of explanation. Pooled sample variances are used whenever it is reasonable to assume that the unknown population variances, σ^2_1 and σ^2_2, are equal. If the equality assumption is tenable, the sample variances, $\hat{\sigma}^2_1$ and $\hat{\sigma}^2_2$, are both estimators of the same population variance, σ^2. Whenever two independent estimators of σ^2 are available, a pooled estimator is likely to provide a better estimate of the unknown population variance than either of the sample estimators taken alone. The pooled variance is simply a weighted mean of $\hat{\sigma}^2_1$ and $\hat{\sigma}^2_2$ where the weights are the respective degrees of freedom. This can be seen from the formula

$$\hat{\sigma}^2_{Pooled} = \frac{(n_1 - 1)\hat{\sigma}^2_1 + (n_2 - 1)\hat{\sigma}^2_2}{(n_1 - 1) + (n_2 - 1)}$$

The assumption that the variances of populations 1 and 2 are equal, called the **homogeneity of variance assumption,** is often reasonable. Researchers frequently begin an experiment with two groups of participants who are equivalent and then expose one group to an experimental treatment that is expected to raise or lower their scores by a constant amount. I showed in Section 4.2, Exercise 8, and Section 4.7, Exercise 11, that adding or subtracting a constant—the treatment effect—does not affect the standard deviation (or variance) of the scores.

But what if the variances of populations 1 and 2 are unequal? It has been shown that the two-sample t test for independent samples is robust with respect to violation of the assumption of equal population variances, provided that $n_1 = n_2$. This means that if the sample n's are equal, the t test gives fairly accurate p values even though the population variances are not equal. This is a good reason for always using equal sample sizes. However, if the population variances are unequal and the sample n's are unequal, the sample variances should not be pooled in computing a t statistic. A modified t statistic for this case is described later in the section called "Two-Sample t' Test for $\mu_1 - \mu_2$ with Unequal Variances (Independent Samples)."

The t statistic also is robust with respect to violation of the assumption that the two populations are normally distributed. If the two sample sizes are equal, the t test gives fairly accurate p values for a broad range of population distributions provided that the populations have similar shapes, are unimodal, and there are no outliers. This is true for sample sizes as small as $n_1 = n_2 = 5$. The tenability of the normality assumption can be checked by visually inspecting the two samples. Box plots are useful for detecting outliers. If the sample distributions appear to be fairly symmetrical and unimodal and there are no outliers, it is probably appropriate to use the t statistic. When n_1 and n_2 are both greater than 30, the normality assumption is no longer important because of the central limit theorem discussed in Section 9.4.

Computational Example for t Test for $\mu_1 - \mu_2$ (Independent Samples)

Let's suppose that a student in an experimental psychology course is investigating the hypothesis that distributed practice is superior to massed practice in developing skill on a mirror-tracing task. The task requires participants to trace a star pattern on a sheet of paper with their nonpreferred hand; they can see themselves tracing the pattern only by looking in a mirror. Forty students from an introductory psychology class are randomly assigned to the two practice conditions with the restriction that an equal number of students are assigned to each condition. Participants in the distributed condition have a three-minute rest period at the end of each practice trial. Participants in the massed condition have only a five-second pause at the end of each trial—just long enough to permit the researcher to place a new sheet of paper in the tracing apparatus. Both groups receive 15 practice trials. Because the groups may differ in amount of fatigue at the conclusion of practice, the dependent variable is measured the following day. The participants are given two warmup trials; the dependent variable is the time required to trace the star pattern on the next three trials.

The decision rule and the steps to be followed in testing the null hypothesis are as follows:

Step 1.   State the statistical hypotheses:

$H_0: \mu_1 - \mu_2 \geq 0$
$H_1: \mu_1 - \mu_2 < 0$,
where μ_1 and μ_2 denote the population means, respectively, for the distributed and massed conditions.

Step 2.   Specify the test statistic:

$t = (\overline{X}_1 - \overline{X}_2)/\hat{\sigma}_{\overline{X}_1 - \overline{X}_2}$ because the researcher wants to test $\mu_1 - \mu_2 \geq 0$, σ_1^2 and σ_2^2 are unknown, the samples are independent, random assignment is used, and the researcher assumes that the population distributions of X_1 and X_2 are approximately normal.

Step 3.   Specify the sample sizes:[1] and the sampling distribution:

$n_1 = 20$ and $n_2 = 20$; t distribution, because the population variances are estimated from sample data, the X_1 and X_2 populations are approximately normal, and there is no reason to believe that σ_1^2 does not equal σ_2^2.

Step 4.   Specify the significance level:

$\alpha = .05$.

Step 5.   Obtain random samples of size n_1 and n_2, compute t, and make a decision.

Decision rule:

Reject the null hypothesis if t falls in the lower .05 portion of the sampling distribution of t; otherwise, do not reject the null hypothesis. If the null hypothesis is rejected, conclude that distributed practice is superior to massed practice in developing skill on a mirror-tracing task; if the null hypothesis is not rejected, do not draw this conclusion.

The data for the experiment are shown in the top portion of Table 13.2-1. Before testing the null hypothesis, it is good statistical practice to examine the sample data for evidence of nonnormality, heterogeneity of variance, and outliers. It is apparent from part (ii) of Table 13.2-1 that the variances are very similar. Furthermore, the stacked box plots in Figure 13.2-1 indicate that the sample distributions are slightly positively skewed and that there are no outliers. The t test is robust to this small departure from symmetry, especially because the sample sizes are equal.

---

[1] The use of Appendix Table D.8 to estimate the required sample sizes is discussed later in this section.

TABLE 13.2-1   Mirror-Tracing Data

(i) Data

Student	Distributed Practice Time, X_{i1} (Seconds)	$(X_{i1} - \overline{X}_1)^2$	Student	Massed Practice Time, X_{i2} (Seconds)	$(X_{i2} - \overline{X}_2)^2$
1	16	1	21	18	1
2	17	0	22	19	0
3	20	9	23	17	4
4	16	1	24	19	0
5	22	25	25	25	36
6	15	4	26	18	1
7	15	4	27	17	4
8	24	49	28	26	49
9	23	36	29	23	16
10	21	16	30	24	25
11	18	1	31	16	9
12	13	16	32	12	49
13	11	36	33	13	36
14	19	4	34	22	9
15	18	1	35	20	1
16	17	0	36	22	9
17	17	0	37	19	0
18	12	25	38	14	25
19	9	64	39	16	9
20	17	0	40	20	1

$n_1 = 20$ $\Sigma X_{i1} = 340$ $\Sigma(X_{i1} - \overline{X}_1)^2 = 292$ $n_2 = 20$ $\Sigma X_{i2} = 380$ $\Sigma(X_{i2} - \overline{X}_2)^2 = 284$

$$\overline{X}_1 = \frac{\Sigma X_{i1}}{n_1} = \frac{340}{20} = 17 \qquad\qquad \overline{X}_2 = \frac{\Sigma X_{i2}}{n_2} = \frac{380}{20} = 19$$

(ii) Computation of variances

$$\hat{\sigma}_1^2 = \frac{\Sigma(X_{i1} - \overline{X}_1)^2}{n_1 - 1} \qquad\qquad \hat{\sigma}_2^2 = \frac{\Sigma(X_{i2} - \overline{X}_2)^2}{n_2 - 1}$$

$$= \frac{292}{20 - 1} \qquad\qquad = \frac{284}{20 - 1}$$

$$= 15.3684 \qquad\qquad = 14.9474$$

$$\hat{\sigma}_{Pooled}^2 = \frac{(n_1 - 1)\hat{\sigma}_1^2 + (n_2 - 1)\hat{\sigma}_2^2}{(n_1 - 1) + (n_2 - 1)} = \frac{(20 - 1)(15.3684) + (20 - 1)14.9474}{(20 - 1) + (20 - 1)}$$

$$= 15.1579$$

(continued)

(iii) Computation of t

$$t = \frac{\overline{X}_1 - \overline{X}_2}{\sqrt{\hat{\sigma}^2_{Pooled}(1/n_1 + 1/n_2)}} = \frac{17 - 19}{\sqrt{15.1579(1/20 + 1/20)}}$$

$$= \frac{-2}{1.2312} = -1.624$$

$$\nu = (n_1 - 1) + (n_2 - 1) = 19 + 19 = 38$$

$$-t_{.05,38} = -1.686$$

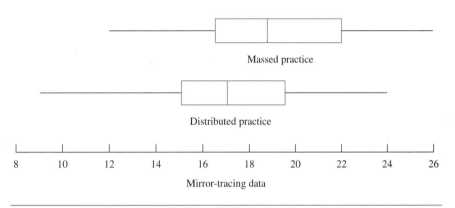

Figure 13.2-1. Stacked box plots for the mirror-tracing data in Table 13.2-1. The lower and upper ends of each box identify the first and third quartiles, respectively. The vertical centerline is the median.

The next step in analyzing the data is to compute a t statistic as shown in part (iii) of Table 13.2-1. The t statistic is $t(38) = -1.624$. According to Appendix Table D.3, the critical value that cuts off the lower .05 region of the t sampling distribution for 38 degrees of freedom is $-t_{.05,38} = -1.686$. Because the computed $t(38) = -1.624$ is not less than or equal to $t_{.05,38} = -1.686$, the student in the experimental psychology course did not reject the null hypothesis. The test does not warrant the inference that distributed practice leads to better performance on the tracing task than massed practice.

The student would have reached the same conclusion about the two practice conditions if she had compared the p value of the t statistic with her preselected level of significance ($\alpha = .05$). The p value of $t(38) = -1.624$ can be determined using Microsoft's Excel TDIST function. After accessing the Excel TDIST function

$$\text{TDIST}(x, \text{deg\_freedom}, \text{tails})$$

you replace x with the absolute value of $t = -1.624$, deg_freedom with 38 and replace tails with 1 as follows

$$\text{TDIST}(1.624, 38, 1)$$

The p value, rounded to two places, is .06. Because $p = .06$ is larger than $\alpha = .05$, the null hypothesis cannot be rejected.

Two-Sample t' Test for $\mu_1 - \mu_2$ with Unequal Variances (Independent Samples)

Sometimes you obtain data for which the sample variances differ enough to make you suspect that the population variances are not equal. If the sample sizes also are not equal, a modified t statistic should be used to test hypotheses about the population means. The modified statistic, denoted by t', is

$$t' = \frac{(\overline{X}_1 - \overline{X}_2) - \delta_0}{\sqrt{\hat{\sigma}_1^2/n_1 + \hat{\sigma}_2^2/n_2}}$$

with degrees of freedom given by

$$\nu' = \frac{\left(\dfrac{\hat{\sigma}_1^2}{n_1} + \dfrac{\hat{\sigma}_2^2}{n_2}\right)^2}{\dfrac{1}{n_1 - 1}\left(\dfrac{\hat{\sigma}_1^2}{n_1}\right)^2 + \dfrac{1}{n_2 - 1}\left(\dfrac{\hat{\sigma}_2^2}{n_2}\right)^2}$$

Notice that the denominator of the t' statistic does not use pooled sample variances. Pooling is only appropriate if it can be assumed that the two population variances are equal.

If both sample sizes are 5 or more, the t critical values in Appendix Table D.3 provide excellent approximations to the critical values of t'. The degrees of freedom for t' generally is not a whole number. Because Appendix Table D.3 does not provide fractional degrees of freedom, ν' can be truncated to the next smaller whole number.

The formula for ν' looks a little intimidating. The degrees of freedom for t' is bounded by the smaller of $n_1 - 1$ and $n_2 - 1$ at one extreme and by $n_1 + n_2 - 2$ at the other—that is,

$$\nu' \geq \text{Minimum of } n_1 - 1 \text{ and } n_2 - 1$$

and

$$\nu' \leq (n_1 + n_2 - 2)$$

This suggests a testing strategy that can eliminate the need to compute ν'. Appendix Table D.3 reveals that the critical value for t' decreases as ν' increases. The testing strategy is as follows. You begin by determining the critical value for t' as if ν' is at its minimum—the smaller of $n_1 - 1$ and $n_2 - 1$. If t' is significant for this degrees of freedom, it will certainly be significant for the larger correct value of ν'. If t' is not significant, you then determine the critical value as if ν' is at its maximum—$n_1 + n_2 - 2$. If t' is not significant at this point, you know that it would not be significant for the smaller correct value of ν'. Using this testing strategy, the only time that you need to compute ν' is when t' is not significant using the smaller of $n_1 - 1$ and $n_2 - 1$ degrees of freedom but is significant using the larger $n_1 + n_2 - 2$ degrees of freedom.

Many computer packages provide two t tests for $\mu_1 - \mu_2$. One test uses the t statistic illustrated in Table 13.2-1 in which the two sample variances are pooled. The other test uses the t' statistic in which it is assumed that the population variances are not equal and should not be pooled. The latter procedure is often referred to as the Welch or the Welch-Satterwaite procedure.

Two-Sample *z* Test for $\mu_1 - \mu_2$ (Independent Samples)

Some textbooks describe a *z* statistic,

$$z = \frac{(\overline{X}_1 - \overline{X}_2) - \delta_0}{\sigma_{\overline{X}_1 - \overline{X}_2}} = \frac{(\overline{X}_1 - \overline{X}_2) - \delta_0}{\sqrt{\sigma_1^2/n_1 + \sigma_2^2/n_2}}$$

for testing a hypothesis about two population means. The critical value for this *z* statistic for α level of significance is obtained from the standard normal distribution table in Appendix Table D.2. To use the *z* statistic, you need to know the values of the two population variances, σ_1^2 and σ_2^2. In practice, the values of the two variances are rarely ever know. Hence, the statistic cannot be computed. For this reason, I will say no more about this particular *z* statistic.

Practical Significance

Section 11.3 describes a one-sample estimator of Cohen's *d* effect size parameter. Hedges's has popularized a two-sample, *d*-like measure of effect size. The statistic can help a researcher decide whether research results are practically significant. The statistic is

$$g = \frac{|\overline{X}_1 - \overline{X}_2|}{\hat{\sigma}_{Pooled}}$$

where

$$\hat{\sigma}_{Pooled} = \sqrt{\frac{(n_1 - 1)\hat{\sigma}_1^2 + (n_2 - 1)\hat{\sigma}_2^2}{(n_1 - 1) + (n_2 - 1)}}$$

Hedges's *g* is interpreted like Cohen's *d*: $g = 0.2$ is a small effect, $g = 0.5$ is a medium effect, and $g = 0.8$ is a large effect.

I will illustrate the computation of *g* using the mirror-tracing data in Table 13.2-1. The effect size for the mirror-tracing data is

$$g = \frac{|\overline{X}_1 - \overline{X}_2|}{\hat{\sigma}_{Pooled}} = \frac{|17 - 19|}{3.8933} = 0.51$$

where

$$\hat{\sigma}_{Pooled} = \sqrt{\frac{(n_1 - 1)\hat{\sigma}_1^2 + (n_2 - 1)\hat{\sigma}_2^2}{(n_1 - 1) + (n_2 - 1)}}$$

$$= \sqrt{\frac{(20 - 1)(15.3684) + (20 - 1)(14.9474)}{(20 - 1) + (20 - 1)}} = 3.8933$$

According to Cohen's guidelines, the difference in tracing time between the distributed and massed practice conditions is a medium-size effect.

If the assumption that the population variances are equal is not tenable, the variances should not be pooled in computing *g*. For this situation, I recommend that the sample standard deviation of the control group, $\hat{\sigma}_c$, or the standard deviation of the group that is used as the baseline, $\hat{\sigma}_b$, be used in place of $\hat{\sigma}_{Pooled}$. The resulting measure is interpreted like Hedges's *g*.

If a research report does not provide a measure of effect size for the difference between two means, often you can compute Hedges's g from information in the report. The information you need is the value of the t statistic and the sizes of the two samples. The formulas for computing g from a two-sample t statistic where $n_1 = n_2$ or $n_1 \neq n_2$ are, respectively,

$$g = \frac{2|t|}{\sqrt{n}} \quad \text{and} \quad g = \frac{|t|\sqrt{n_1 + n_2}}{\sqrt{n_1 n_2}}$$

where $|t|$ denotes the absolute value of the t statistic and $n = n_1 + n_2$. The effect size for the mirror tracing experiment is $g = 0.51$. The same value can be obtained using the absolute value of the t statistic, $|t| = 1.624$, and sample sizes in Table 13.2-1 as follows:

$$g = \frac{2|t|}{\sqrt{n}} = \frac{2(1.624)}{\sqrt{40}} = 0.51$$

Determining the Required Sample Sizes (Independent Samples)

In Section 10.4, you learned how to use Appendix Table D.8 to make a rational choice of sample size for the one-sample t test. Appendix Table D.8 also can be used to select sample sizes for the two-sample t test. To estimate the required sample sizes, it is necessary to specify α, $1 - \beta$, and Cohen's d. Remember from Section 10.4 that $d = 0.2$ is a small effect, $d = 0.5$ is a medium effect, and $d = 0.8$ is a large effect. Consider the mirror-tracing experiment described earlier. Suppose that the researcher wanted to detect a medium-size effect ($d = 0.5$) and she wanted α to equal .05 and $1 - \beta$ to equal .80. According to Appendix Table D.8, the researcher should use 50 participants in each sample. The sample sizes actually used were only 20. Because the sample sizes were too small, it is likely that the t test lacked adequate power to reject the null hypothesis.

t Confidence Interval for $\mu_1 - \mu_2$ (Independent Samples)

The confidence-interval procedures for the one-sample case described in Chapter 11 generalize to the two-sample case.

A two-sided $100(1 - \alpha)\%$ confidence interval for $\mu_1 - \mu_2$ for independent samples is

$$(\overline{X}_1 - \overline{X}_2) - t_{\alpha/2, \nu}\sqrt{\hat{\sigma}^2_{Pooled}\left(\frac{1}{n_1} + \frac{1}{n_2}\right)} < \mu_1 - \mu_2$$

$$< (\overline{X}_1 - \overline{X}_2) + t_{\alpha/2, \nu}\sqrt{\hat{\sigma}^2_{Pooled}\left(\frac{1}{n_1} + \frac{1}{n_2}\right)}$$

where $t_{\alpha/2, \nu}$ is the value that cuts off the upper $\alpha/2$ region of the t sampling distribution for $\nu = (n_1 - 1) + (n_2 - 1)$ and

$$\hat{\sigma}^2_{Pooled} = \frac{(n_1 - 1)\hat{\sigma}^2_1 + (n_2 - 1)\hat{\sigma}^2_2}{(n_1 - 1) + (n_2 - 1)}$$

Lower and upper one-sided $100(1 - \alpha)\%$ confidence intervals for $\mu_1 - \mu_2$ for independent samples are given by, respectively,

$$(\overline{X}_1 - \overline{X}_2) - t_{\alpha, \nu}\sqrt{\hat{\sigma}^2_{Pooled}\left(\frac{1}{n_1} + \frac{1}{n_2}\right)} < \mu_1 - \mu_2$$

and

$$\mu_1 - \mu_2 < (\overline{X}_1 - \overline{X}_2) + t_{\alpha, \nu}\sqrt{\hat{\sigma}^2_{Pooled}\left(\frac{1}{n_1} + \frac{1}{n_2}\right)}$$

where $t_{\alpha, \nu}$ is the value that cuts off the upper α region of the t sampling distribution for $\nu = (n_1 - 1) + (n_2 - 1)$.

Earlier, I discussed the assumptions that underlie the use of the t statistic for $\mu_1 - \mu_2$. The same assumptions apply to confidence intervals.

Let's use the data in Table 13.2-1 ($\overline{X}_1 = 17$, $\overline{X}_2 = 19$, $\hat{\sigma}^2_{Pooled} = 15.1579$, and $n_1 = n_2 = 20$) to illustrate a one-sided confidence interval. The researcher's hypotheses for the mirror-tracing experiment were directional:

$$H_0: \mu_1 - \mu_2 \geq 0$$

$$H_1: \mu_1 - \mu_2 < 0$$

An analogous one-sided $100(1 - .05)\% = .95\%$ confidence interval for the difference $\mu_1 - \mu_2$ is

$$\mu_1 - \mu_2 < (\overline{X}_1 - \overline{X}_2) + t_{.5, 38}\sqrt{\hat{\sigma}^2_{Pooled}\left(\frac{1}{n_1} + \frac{1}{n_2}\right)}$$

$$\mu_1 - \mu_2 < (17 - 19) + 1.686\sqrt{15.1579\left(\frac{1}{20} + \frac{1}{20}\right)}$$

$$\mu_1 - \mu_2 < 0.08$$

This 95% confidence interval corresponds to the darkened portion of the real number line as follows:

The researcher hypothesized that the population mean for the distributed practice condition would be less than that for the massed condition—that is, $\mu_1 < \mu_2$. However, it is apparent from the confidence interval that the population mean for the distributed practice condition, μ_1, could be less than that for the massed practice condition, μ_2, or it could be equal to it or even larger.

t' Confidence Interval for $\mu_1 - \mu_2$ with Unequal Variances (Independent Samples)

Earlier you learned that the two-sample t test for independent samples is robust with respect to violation of the homogeneity of variance assumption provided that the sample sizes are equal. If your sample sizes are unequal and an examination of your sample variances leads you to suspect that the population variances are unequal, you should construct a confidence interval for $\mu_1 - \mu_2$ using $\sqrt{\hat{\sigma}_1^2/n_1 + \hat{\sigma}_2^2/n_2}$ from the t' statistic.

A two-sided $100(1 - \alpha)\%$ confidence interval for $\mu_1 - \mu_2$ for independent samples is

$$(\overline{X}_1 - \overline{X}_2) - t_{\alpha/2,\,\nu'}\sqrt{\left(\frac{\hat{\sigma}_1^2}{n_1} + \frac{\hat{\sigma}_2^2}{n_2}\right)} < \mu_1 - \mu_2$$

$$< (\overline{X}_1 - \overline{X}_2) + t_{\alpha/2,\,\nu'}\sqrt{\left(\frac{\hat{\sigma}_1^2}{n_1} + \frac{\hat{\sigma}_2^2}{n_2}\right)}$$

where $t_{\alpha/2,\,\nu'}$ is the value that cuts off the upper $\alpha/2$ region of the t sampling distribution with degrees of freedom given by

$$\nu' = \frac{\left(\dfrac{\hat{\sigma}_1^2}{n_1} + \dfrac{\hat{\sigma}_2^2}{n_2}\right)^2}{\dfrac{1}{n_1 - 1}\left(\dfrac{\hat{\sigma}_1^2}{n_1}\right)^2 + \dfrac{1}{n_2 - 1}\left(\dfrac{\hat{\sigma}_2^2}{n_2}\right)^2}$$

The variances for sample 1 and sample 2 are computed using

$$\hat{\sigma}_j^2 = \frac{\Sigma(X_{ij} - \overline{X}_j)^2}{n_j - 1}$$

where $j = 1$ or 2.

Lower and upper one-sided $100(1 - \alpha)\%$ confidence intervals for $\mu_1 - \mu_2$ for independent samples are given by, respectively,

$$(\overline{X}_1 - \overline{X}_2) - t_{\alpha,\,\nu'}\sqrt{\left(\frac{\hat{\sigma}_1^2}{n_1} + \frac{\hat{\sigma}_2^2}{n_2}\right)} < \mu_1 - \mu_2$$

and

$$\mu_1 - \mu_2 < (\overline{X}_1 - \overline{X}_2) + t_{\alpha,\,\nu'}\sqrt{\left(\frac{\hat{\sigma}_1^2}{n_1} + \frac{\hat{\sigma}_2^2}{n_2}\right)}$$

where $t_{\alpha,\,\nu}$ is the value that cuts off the upper α region of the t sampling distribution for ν' degrees of freedom.

CHECK YOUR UNDERSTANDING OF SECTION 13.2

1. The null hypothesis is sometimes written H_0: $\mu_1 = \mu_2$. What does this indicate about δ_0?
2. Under what condition is it appropriate to pool $\hat{\sigma}_1^2$ and $\hat{\sigma}_2^2$ in estimating $\sigma^2_{\overline{X}_1 - \overline{X}_2}$?
3. A researcher is interested in testing the hypothesis that members of fraternities have higher GPAs than nonmembers. Random samples of $n_1 = 50$ members and $n_2 = 52$ nonmembers are obtained from the respective populations. It is assumed that the populations are normally distributed. The sample standard deviations are $\hat{\sigma}_1 = 0.4$ and $\hat{\sigma}_2 = 0.5$. List the five steps you would follow to test the null hypothesis and state the decision rule. Let $\alpha = .05$.
4. a. Suppose that in Exercise 3, $\overline{X}_1 = 2.91$ and $\overline{X}_2 = 2.72$. Compute a t test statistic and make a decision.
   b. Determine the p value of the test statistic using Appendix Table D.3 and Excel's TDIST function.
   c. Compute Hedges's measure of effect size and interpret the measure.
   d. Use Appendix Table D.8 to determine if the sample size is adequate to detect a large-size effect if a power of .80 is desired. What is the minimum number of participants required?
   e. Compute a $100(1 - .05)\% = 95\%$ confidence interval for $\mu_1 - \mu_2$; assume that $t_{.05, 100} = 1.660$. Locate the confidence interval on the real number line.
   f. Specify all the null hypotheses that could be rejected.
5. It has been reported that employment interviewers spend more time talking to applicants who are hired than to applicants who are rejected. To determine whether this is true for college students seeking summer employment through a university placement center, a researcher posing as an applicant accompanied a random sample of referees to their job interviews and recorded the duration and outcome of $n = 49$ interviews.

Duration of Interview (Minutes)

Hired		Rejected	
30	23	19	17
21	24	18	18
24	26	22	19
25	27	13	22
29	24	15	15
24	22	18	19
23	25	17	17
24	26	20	20
28	23	18	18
25	24	19	17
24	27	23	
19	26	12	
25	25	18	

a. Construct box plots for the hired and rejected applicants and stack the plots one above the other. Do the data contain outliers? Do the sample distributions appear to be relatively symmetrical?

b. List the five steps you would follow to test the null hypothesis, and state the decision rule. Let $\alpha = .05$.

c. Compute a t' test statistic and make a decision about the researcher's hypothesis. Explain why the degrees of freedom is equal to $v' = n_2 - 1 = 22$.

d. Compute Hedges's measure of effect size using the hired students as the baseline group and interpret the measure.

e. Use Appendix Table D.8 to determine if the sample size is adequate to detect a large-size effect if a power of .80 is desired. What is the minimum number of participants required?

f. Compute a $100(1 - .05)\% = 95\%$ confidence interval for $\mu_1 - \mu_2$. Assume that for $v' = 44$, $t_{.05, 44} = 1.680$. Locate the confidence interval on the real number line.

g. Specify all the null hypotheses that could be rejected.

6. Researchers investigated the effect of early language experience on the discrimination of speech sounds. Twenty-eight 6- to 8-month-old infants raised in English- or Spanish-speaking homes were trained to turn their heads when they detected a change in a sound stimulus. Following the discrimination training, Spanish consonants involving a tapped and a trilled "r" were presented. The dependent measure was the number of head turns to stimuli involving a change minus the number of head turns on control trials divided by the number of experimental trials. The following data were obtained. (Suggested by Eilers, Rebecca E., Gavin, William J., and Oller, D. Kimbrough [1981]. Cross-linguistic perception in infancy: Early effects of linguistic experience. *Journal of Child Language*, 9, 289–302.)

English-Speaking Home	Spanish-Speaking Home
.0421	.1081
.0941	.0986
.1064	.1566
.0242	.1961
.1331	.1125
.0773	.1942
.0243	.1079
.0815	.1021
.1186	.1583
.0356	.1673
.0728	.1675
.0999	.1856
.0614	.1688
.0479	.1512

a. Construct box plots for English-speaking and Spanish-speaking homes and stack the plots one above the other. Assume that for the English-speaking homes $Mdn = 0.07285$, $Q_1 = 0.0421$, and $Q_3 = 0.0999$. Assume that for the Spanish-speaking homes $Mdn = 0.15665$, $Q_1 = 0.1081$, and $Q_3 = 0.1688$. Do the data contain outliers? Do the sample distributions appear to be relatively symmetrical?

b. List the five steps you would follow to test the null hypothesis that $\mu_1 - \mu_2 = 0$, where μ_1 and μ_2 denote, respectively, the population means for infants raised in English- and Spanish-speaking homes. State the decision rule. Let $\alpha = .001$.

   c. Use a t statistic to test the null hypothesis. What decision should the researcher make?

   d. Determine the p value of the test statistic using Appendix Table D.3 and Excel's TDIST function.

   e. Compute Hedges's measure of effect size and interpret the measure.

   f. Compute a $100(1 - .001)\% = 99.9\%$ confidence interval for $\mu_1 - \mu_2$; assume that $t_{.001/2, 26} = 3.707$. Locate the confidence interval on the real number line.

   g. Specify all the null hypotheses that could be rejected.

7. Use the table of random numbers in Appendix Table D.1 to draw random samples without replacement of 25 men and 25 women from the Student Database in Appendix E.

   a. List the participant number, gender, and stat grade for each person in your sample. For each gender, construct a box plot and stack the plots one above the other. Do the data contain outliers? Do the sample distributions appear to be relatively symmetrical?

   b. List the five steps you would follow to test the null hypothesis that the mean stat grades for the two populations are equal and state the decision rule. Let $\alpha = .05$.

   c. Test the null hypothesis that $\mu_1 - \mu_2 = 0$, where μ_1 and μ_2 denote, respectively, the population mean of men's and women's stat grade.

   d. Determine the p value of the test statistic using Appendix Table D.3 and Microsoft's Excel TDIST function.

   e. Compute a measure of effect size and interpret the measure.

   f. Use Appendix Table D.8 to determine if the sample size is adequate to detect a large-size effect if a power of .80 is desired.

   g. What is the minimum number of participants that is required?

   h. Compute a $100(1 - .05)\% = 95\%$ confidence interval for $\mu_1 - \mu_2$. Locate the confidence interval on the real number line.

   i. Specify all the null hypotheses that could be rejected.

   j. Write a paragraph summarizing your results and conclusions.

8. Terms to remember:

   a. Standard error of the difference between two means ($\hat{\sigma}_{\bar{X}_1 - \bar{X}_2}$)

   b. Independent samples

   c. Homogeneity of variance assumption

13.3 TWO RANDOMIZATION STRATEGIES: RANDOM SAMPLING AND RANDOM ASSIGNMENT

Two randomization strategies can be used in investigating scientific hypotheses. A researcher can obtain random samples from two existing populations of interest or randomly assign elements of a sample to experimental and control conditions. In rare cases, the two methods can be combined—that is, the researcher can obtain a random sample and randomly assign the sample elements to the experimental and control conditions.

The choice of a randomization strategy affects a researcher's conclusions, as you will now see.

The Strategy of Random Sampling

Consider the scientific hypothesis that men who jog have fewer heart attacks than those who do not. The statistical hypotheses are

$$H_0: \mu_1 - \mu_2 \geq 0$$
$$H_1: \mu_1 - \mu_2 < 0$$

where μ_1 and μ_2 denote the mean number of heart attacks of the populations of joggers and nonjoggers, respectively. The alternative hypothesis, which corresponds to the researcher's hunch, states that the mean number of heart attacks is smaller for joggers than for nonjoggers. To test the null hypothesis, a researcher could obtain a random sample of 70-year-old men who have jogged regularly since they were 40 and a second random sample of men the same age who have never jogged. Suppose that the mean number of heart attacks is 0.2 for the joggers and 1.1 for the nonjoggers and that the difference between the means, $0.2 - 1.1 = -0.9$, is significant at the .01 level. It can be concluded that the population of joggers has fewer heart attacks than the nonjoggers, and hence the scientific hypothesis is supported.

Can the researcher conclude that the difference between population means is due to jogging per se? Unfortunately, the answer is no because in all likelihood the two populations of men differ in other ways besides jogging. More than likely, men who jog are concerned about their health and about staying in good physical shape. Joggers are probably less obese, have better muscle tone, and have more healthful diets than nonjoggers. If our researcher had obtained random samples from populations of obese and nonobese men, or from men with good and poor muscle tone, or from men who are and are not diet conscious, the researcher probably also would have found a significant difference in the mean number of heart attacks.

The Strategy of Random Assignment

Suppose that a population of 40-year-old prisoners at Oops Penitentiary is available and that it is possible to exercise some control over their lives for a period of 30 years. The prisoners are randomly assigned to one of two groups, which we will call the experimental and control groups. Those assigned to the experimental group participate in a jogging program for 30 years; those in the control group do not participate in the jogging program. Suppose that at the end of 30 years the mean numbers of heart attacks for those in the experimental and control groups are, respectively, 0.3 and 1.4 and that the difference, $0.3 - 1.4 = -1.1$, is significant at the .01 level. As in the previous experiment, the scientific hypothesis is supported.

Can the researcher conclude that the difference between the experimental and control groups is due to jogging per se? Again the answer is no. What have we accomplished by using random assignment? Random assignment helps to make the experimental and control groups comparable on all extraneous variables at the beginning of the experiment, because before the experiment begins the two groups should differ no more than would be expected by chance. If at the conclusion of the experiment a significant difference exists between the groups in the incidence of heart attacks, the researcher can be confident that the difference is due to events that occurred after the experiment began rather than to unique characteristics of the participants that existed before the experiment. And if during the experiment all conditions except the independent variable of jogging are held constant, differences between the groups in number of heart attacks must be due to jogging per se. Unfortunately, in a 30-year experiment, it is unlikely that all conditions except the independent variable have been held constant.

Advantages and Disadvantages of the Two Research Strategies

> Many experiments in the behavioral sciences and education are designed to establish **casual relationships** rather than **concomitant relationships.** To establish that an independent variable X causes an effect Y, it is necessary to demonstrate that X is both necessary and sufficient for the occurrence of Y. To establish a concomitant relationship, it is only necessary to demonstrate that the occurrence or nonoccurrence of one event is accompanied by the occurrence or nonoccurrence of the other event.

Neither the random-sampling nor the random-assignment experiments just described have established that jogging per se results in fewer heart attacks—a causal relationship—but they have established that men who jog have, on the average, fewer heart attacks than nonjoggers—a concomitant relationship.

The strategy of drawing random samples from two existing populations that are known to differ in X cannot be used to establish causality, because the two populations also may differ on other variables. One or more of the other variables could be responsible for the observed difference. A researcher obtains random samples from two existing populations so that conclusions can be generalized to the populations. In many research situations, most notably opinion polling, the discovery of a concomitant relationship is sufficient for the researcher's purposes.

In the behavioral sciences, health sciences, and education, most researchers have neither the time nor the resources to obtain random samples. In the rare cases in which random samples are obtained, the populations are often so narrowly defined that they are of little interest. For example, human participants frequently are randomly sampled from a population of students enrolled in a college course, or from volunteers, and so forth. And researchers who work with animal subjects rarely attempt to obtain random samples.

The second strategy of randomly assigning participants to the experimental and control conditions can be used to establish the existence of a causal relationship if all conditions except the independent variable can be held constant. This is a big *if*, because the requirement is difficult to satisfy in nonlaboratory settings. An advantage of conducting experiments in a laboratory is that it is possible to exercise a high degree of control over extraneous variables. Hence, laboratory experiments are well suited to establishing causal relationships.

If a researcher wants to generalize findings to some population and also to obtain experimental and control groups that are comparable, the two research strategies can be combined. The researcher can obtain a random sample of participants from the population of interest and then randomly assign the participants to the two conditions. This combined strategy obviously cannot be used when a researcher samples from two populations that differ with respect to the independent variable, for example, populations of joggers and nonjoggers. Such populations are referred to as **intact populations.**

A final point: If a researcher wants to use statistical inference, the experimental design must include some form of randomization. Which randomization procedure is appropriate will depend on the objectives of the experiment.

CHECK YOUR UNDERSTANDING OF SECTION 13.3

9. Researchers investigated the effects of iPod use among office workers in a large retail organization on measures of employee performance and job satisfaction. Two hundred fifty-six employees were assigned to iPod and noniPod groups on the basis of their stated preference for using an iPod at work. The researchers found that the iPod group exhibited significant improvements in performance, organizational satisfaction, and mood states relative to the noniPod group. All of the t tests were significant beyond the .001 level. The researchers recommended that all employees be required to use iPods. (a) Comment on the appropriateness of the researchers' conclusion. (b) List some alternative explanations for the observed difference in performance and job satisfaction.

10. In Exercise 9, what does the fact that the test statistic was significant at the .001 level tell you about the magnitude of the difference between the population means?

11. What condition in the random assignment strategy must be satisfied to establish a causal relationship between the independent and dependent variables?

12. For each of the following research topics, indicate the research strategy—random sampling or random assignment—that seems most appropriate. Justify your choice.
    a. Relative resistance to extinction of a bar-pressing response acquired by rats under 100% reinforcement versus 50% reinforcement
    b. Difference between adult men and women in the incidence of alcohol use
    c. Relationship between grades in college and number of hours studied per week
    d. Difference in reaction time to the onset of a light versus the onset of a tone

13. Terms to remember:
    a. Concomitant relationship   b. Causal relationship
    c. Intact populations

13.4 TWO-SAMPLE *t* TEST AND CONFIDENCE INTERVAL FOR $\mu_1 - \mu_2$ USING DEPENDENT SAMPLES

Introduction to Dependent Samples

The significance tests and confidence intervals described earlier require the use of independent samples in which the selection of elements in one sample is not affected by the selection of elements in the other. Samples are independent if, for example, a researcher samples randomly from two populations or uses a random procedure to assign elements to two samples. In this section, you will learn that the use of dependent samples rather than independent samples almost always results in more powerful tests of false null hypotheses and to shorter confidence intervals.

Dependent samples can be obtained by any of the following research procedures:

1. Observing participants under both the experimental condition and the control condition—that is, obtaining **repeated measures** on each of the participants.
2. Forming pairs of participants who are similar with respect to a variable that is positively correlated with the dependent variable. This is called **participant matching.** One member of the pair is randomly assigned to the experimental condition and the other member to the control condition.
3. Obtaining sets of identical twins or litter mates and assigning one member of the pair randomly to the experimental condition and the other member to the control condition.
4. Obtaining pairs of participants who are matched by mutual selection, for example, husband-and-wife pairs or business partners. One member of the pair is randomly assigned to the experimental condition and the other member to the control condition.

Let us consider these procedures in more detail. The first procedure, observing a set of participants under both the experimental and control conditions, only can be used with independent variables that have relatively short-duration effects. The nature of the independent variable should be such that the effects of one condition dissipate before the participant is observed under the other condition. Otherwise, the second dependent measure will reflect the cumulative effects of two conditions rather than the effects of only the second condition. There is no such restriction, of course, when carryover effects such as learning or fatigue are the researcher's principal interest. The order of presentation of the two conditions should be randomized independently for each participant if possible. It is customary to randomize with the restriction that half the participants receive one condition first, whereas the other half receive the other condition first.

The remaining three procedures for obtaining dependent samples involve forming pairs of participants who are matched on some basis. In participant matching, a matching variable is used to pair up otherwise unrelated participants; the matching variable should be positively correlated with the dependent variable. For example, IQ and ability to learn verbal material are highly correlated; hence, participants can be assigned to pairs so that members of each pair have similar IQs and therefore similar verbal learning abilities. The higher the positive correlation between the matching variable and the dependent variable, the more effective the matching.

If identical twins or littermates are used, it can be assumed that participants within a pair are matched with respect to genetic characteristics. The aptitudes and abilities of identical twins, fraternal twins to some extent, and even siblings are more similar than those of unrelated participants.

When participants are matched by mutual selection, the researcher always must ascertain that the participants within pairs are in fact more similar with respect to the dependent variable than are unmatched participants. Knowing a husband's attitudes about abortion and legalization of marijuana, for example, may provide considerable information about his wife's attitudes on the issues and vice versa. However, knowing the husband's mechanical aptitude is not likely to provide information about his wife's mechanical aptitude.

t Test for $\mu_1 - \mu_2$ (Dependent Samples)

You probably wonder what difference it makes whether samples are dependent or independent. If the same participants are observed twice or if participants in one sample are paired with participants in another sample, the outcomes of X_1 and X_2 for each pair are not statistically independent. This does not affect the expectation of the difference between sample means; the expectation of $E(\overline{X}_1 - \overline{X}_2)$ is equal to $\mu_1 - \mu_2$. However, dependence within pairs affects the standard error of the difference between means. Section 13.2 defined the standard error of the difference between means for independent samples as

$$\hat{\sigma}_{\overline{X}_1 - \overline{X}_2} = \sqrt{\frac{\hat{\sigma}^2_{Pooled}}{n_1} + \frac{\hat{\sigma}^2_{Pooled}}{n_2}}$$

If the samples are dependent, the standard error the difference between means is

$$\hat{\sigma}_{\overline{X}_1 - \overline{X}_2} = \sqrt{\frac{\hat{\sigma}^2_{Pooled}}{n_1} + \frac{\hat{\sigma}^2_{Pooled}}{n_2} - 2r_{12}\left(\frac{\hat{\sigma}_{Pooled}}{\sqrt{n_1}}\right)\left(\frac{\hat{\sigma}_{Pooled}}{\sqrt{n_2}}\right)}$$

where r_{12} is the Pearson product-moment correlation between the two samples. An examination of the formula reveals that the larger the positive correlation, r_{12}, the smaller the dependent samples standard error, $\hat{\sigma}_{\overline{X}_1 - \overline{X}_2}$. Hence, if r_{12} is greater than 0, the *t* statistic for dependent samples will be larger than that for independent samples. You can see this by comparing the formulas for the independent and dependent samples *t* statistics:

Independent samples:

$$t = \frac{(\overline{X}_1 - \overline{X}_2) - \delta_0}{\hat{\sigma}_{\overline{X}_1 - \overline{X}_2}} = \frac{(\overline{X}_1 - \overline{X}_2) - \delta_0}{\sqrt{\frac{\hat{\sigma}^2_{Pooled}}{n_1} + \frac{\hat{\sigma}^2_{Pooled}}{n_2}}}$$

Dependent samples:

$$t = \frac{(\overline{X}_1 - \overline{X}_2) - \delta_0}{\hat{\sigma}_{\overline{X}_1 - \overline{X}_2}} = \frac{(\overline{X}_1 - \overline{X}_2) - \delta_0}{\sqrt{\dfrac{\hat{\sigma}^2_{Pooled}}{n_1} + \dfrac{\hat{\sigma}^2_{Pooled}}{n_2} - 2r_{12}\left(\dfrac{\hat{\sigma}_{Pooled}}{\sqrt{n_1}}\right)\left(\dfrac{\hat{\sigma}_{Pooled}}{\sqrt{n_2}}\right)}}$$

The important point is that the t formula for dependent samples provides a more powerful test of a false null hypothesis. This helps to explain why researchers like to use dependent samples.

The dependent samples t formula looks pretty complicated. Fortunately, a simpler alternative formula is available, one that does not require the computation of a correlation coefficient, r_{12}. The formula is simpler because it replaces each pair of scores X_1 and X_2 with one difference score D_i, where $D_i = X_{i1} - X_{i2}$, for each of the $i = 1, \ldots, n$ pairs of scores. In effect this converts the two-sample t formula for μ_1 and μ_2 into a one-sample t formula. Instead of testing one of the following null hypotheses,

$$H_0: \mu_1 - \mu_2 = \delta_0 \qquad H_0: \mu_1 - \mu_2 \leq \delta_0 \qquad H_0: \mu_1 - \mu_2 \geq \delta_0$$

you test an equivalent null hypothesis,

$$H_0: \mu_D = \delta_0 \qquad H_0: \mu_D \leq \delta_0 \qquad H_0: \mu_D \geq \delta_0$$

where μ_D is the population mean of difference scores.

The t test statistic for dependent samples using the difference-score approach is

$$t = \frac{\overline{X}_D}{\hat{\sigma}_{\overline{X}_D}} = \frac{\overline{X}_D}{\dfrac{\hat{\sigma}_D}{\sqrt{n}}} = \frac{\dfrac{\sum\limits_{i=1}^{n} D_i}{n}}{\dfrac{\sqrt{\dfrac{\sum\limits_{i=1}^{n}(D_i - \overline{X}_D)^2}{n-1}}}{\sqrt{n}}}$$

where $\overline{X}_D$ is the sample mean of the difference scores, D_i is equal to $X_{i1} - X_{i2}$ for the ith pair of scores, $\hat{\sigma}_D$ is the standard deviation of the difference scores, and n is the number of pairs of scores. The denominator of the t statistic, $\hat{\sigma}_{\overline{X}_D}$, is an estimator of the standard error of the mean of the population of difference scores.

The number of degrees of freedom, ν, for this test statistic is equal to $n - 1$, the degrees of freedom associated with $\hat{\sigma}_D$.

In using the t statistic, it is assumed that the population of differences, $D_i = X_{i1} - X_{i2}$, is normally distributed. These differences will be normally distributed if X_1 and X_2 are normally distributed. It also is assumed that the standard error of the mean of the difference scores, $\hat{\sigma}_{\overline{X}_D}$, is unknown and must be estimated from sample data.

If repeated measures are obtained, it is assumed that the participants are a random sample from the population of interest. The order in which the conditions are presented should be randomized for each participant if the nature of the independent variable permits it. If pairs of matched participants are used, the participants in each pair should be randomly assigned to the experimental and control conditions. The following example should help to clarify the meaning of the terms in the t statistic formula.

Computational Example for t Test for $\mu_1 - \mu_2$ (Dependent Samples)

The scientific hypothesis that the population mean for the distributed practice condition is smaller than that for the massed condition for the mirror-tracing task described in Section 13.2 could have been investigated using matched participants. Suppose that participants are tested on the mirror-tracing task using their preferred hand. The time required to trace the star pattern on the last three of five trials is used to form pairs of participants having comparable tracing times and hence similar motor skills. The participants in each pair are randomly assigned to the distributed and massed practice conditions. Then the experiment is carried out as described previously. Data for the experiment are shown in Table 13.4-1. According to Appendix Table D.3, a t of -1.729 with $\nu = 20 - 1 = 19$ cuts off the lower .05 region of the sampling distribution—that is, $-t_{.05, 19} = -1.729$. The computed $t(19) = -4.021$ in Table 13.5-1 is less than $-t_{.05, 19} = -1.729$. Hence, the researcher rejected the null hypothesis and concluded that distributed practice led to better performance on the task than massed practice. Of course, this inference applies only to the population represented by the participants in the experiment and to the particular practice conditions and task that were used.

In reporting the results of the research in the text portion of a publication, the researcher might say, "The mean mirror-tracing time for the distributed practice condition was shorter than that for the massed practice condition, $t(19) = -4.021$, $p < .0004$."

Has the researcher gained anything by using matched participants? To answer this question, I can compare the results in Table 13.4-1 with those obtained using independent samples in Table 13.2-1. The data in the two tables are identical; only the analysis procedures differ. The null hypothesis is rejected for the dependent-samples analysis, $t(19) = -4.021$, $p < .0004$, but not for the independent-samples analysis, $t(38) = -1.624$, $p < .06$. Clearly, the use of matched participants has resulted in a more powerful test of the false null hypothesis.

An examination of the data for the two practice conditions suggests that they are positively correlated; the Pearson product-moment correlation coefficient, r, is actually .84. This example illustrates an important principle: whenever the correlation between the samples is positive, the t statistic for dependent samples will be larger than the t for independent samples. As noted earlier, the use of dependent samples results in a more powerful test of a false null hypothesis. This statement must be qualified. The number of degrees of freedom for the independent t statistic, $(n_1 - 1) + (n_2 - 1) = 38$, is larger than that for the dependent t statistic, $n - 1 = 19$. The values of t that cut off the critical region for the independent and dependent samples are, respectively, $-t_{.05, 38} = -1.686$ and $-t_{.05, 19} = -1.729$. Now for

TABLE 13.4-1 Mirror-Tracing Data (Dependent Samples)

(i) Data

Student Pair	Distributed Practice Time, X_{i1} (Seconds)	Massed Practice Time, X_{i2} (Seconds)	Difference Score $D_i = X_{i1} - X_{i2}$	$(D_i - \overline{X}_D)^2$
1	16	18	−2	0
2	17	19	−2	0
3	20	17	3	25
4	16	19	−3	1
5	22	25	−3	1
6	15	18	−3	1
7	15	17	−2	0
8	24	26	−2	0
9	23	23	0	4
10	21	24	−3	1
11	18	16	2	16
12	13	12	1	9
13	11	13	−2	0
14	19	22	−3	1
15	18	20	−2	0
16	17	22	−5	9
17	17	19	−2	0
18	12	14	−2	0
19	9	16	−7	25
20	17	20	−3	1
$n = 20$	$\overline{X}_1 = 17$	$\overline{X}_2 = 19$	$\Sigma D_i = -40$	$\Sigma(D_i - \overline{X}_D)^2 = 94$

$$\overline{X}_D = \frac{\Sigma D_i}{n} = \frac{-40}{20} = -2$$

Computational check: $\overline{X}_1 - \overline{X}_2 = 17 - 19 = \overline{X}_D = -2$

(ii) Computation of $\hat{\sigma}_{\overline{X}_D}$ and t

$$\hat{\sigma}_{\overline{X}_D} = \frac{\sqrt{\dfrac{\Sigma(D_i - \overline{X}_D)^2}{n-1}}}{\sqrt{n}} = \frac{\sqrt{\dfrac{94}{20-1}}}{\sqrt{20}} = \frac{2.2243}{4.4721} = 0.4974$$

$$t = \frac{\overline{X}_D}{\hat{\sigma}_{\overline{X}_D}} = \frac{-2}{0.4974} = -4.021$$

$$\nu = n - 1 = 20 - 1 = 19$$

$$-t_{.05, \, 19} = -1.729$$

the qualification: For a t test with dependent samples to be more powerful than a t test with independent samples, the correlation between the dependent samples must be large enough to more than compensate for the smaller degrees of freedom and for the larger absolute value of t required for significance.

Practical Significance

In Section 13.2, I described Hedges's g statistic that is useful in assessing the practical significance of research results. The same formula and data are used to compute g for the dependent samples case:

$$g = \frac{|\overline{X}_1 - \overline{X}_2|}{\hat{\sigma}_{Pooled}} = \frac{|17 - 19|}{3.8933} = 0.51$$

where

$$\hat{\sigma}_{Pooled} = \sqrt{\frac{(n_1 - 1)\hat{\sigma}_1^2 + (n_2 - 1)\hat{\sigma}_2^2}{(n_1 - 1) + (n_2 - 1)}}$$

$$= \sqrt{\frac{(20 - 1)(15.3684) + (20 - 1)(14.9474)}{(20 - 1) + (20 - 1)}} = 3.8933$$

If a research report does not provide an effect size measure for the dependent samples case, you may be able to compute Hedges's g from information in the report. You need the following information: value of the dependent samples t statistic, sample estimators of the two population variances, and the sample estimator of the variance of the difference scores, $\hat{\sigma}_D^2$. The latter variance for the data in Table 13.4-1 is given by

$$\hat{\sigma}_D^2 = \frac{\sum_{i=1}^{n}(D_i - \overline{X}_D)^2}{n - 1}$$

$$= \frac{94}{20 - 1} = 4.9474$$

The dependent samples t statistic from Table 13.4-1 is $t = -4.021$; the sample estimators of the two population variances from Table 13.2-1 are $\hat{\sigma}_1^2 = 15.1579$ and $\hat{\sigma}_2^2 = 14.9474$. Hedges's effect size for the dependent samples case is

$$g = |t|\sqrt{\frac{2\hat{\sigma}_D^2}{n(\hat{\sigma}_1^2 + \hat{\sigma}_2^2)}} = 4.021\sqrt{\frac{(2)(4.9474)}{(20)(15.3684 + 14.9474)}} = 0.51$$

which is identical to that for the independent samples case in Section 13.2-1.

Determining the Required Sample Size (Dependent Samples)

I have repeatedly emphasized the importance of making a rational choice of sample size. Researchers do not want to use samples that are too small and possibly fail to reject a false null hypothesis because of low power. Alternatively, researchers do not want to use samples that are too large and waste the time of participants and other research resources. Appendix Table D.8 can be used to make a rational choice of sample sizes for the two-sample t test with dependent samples. To estimate the number of pairs of participants, n, it is necessary to specify α, $1 - \beta$, Cohen's d, and ρ, the correlation between the two populations. Because ρ is rarely known, its estimation must be based on previous research or informed judgment. Consider the mirror-tracing task with repeated measures on each participant described in this section. Suppose that the researcher wanted to detect a medium-size effect ($d = 0.5$) and she wanted α to equal .05 and $1 - \beta$ to equal .80. If she estimates that the population correlation between the distributed and massed practice times is at least .70, the required n according to Appendix Table D.8 is 16.

If researchers are not confident of their estimates of ρ, they can use a conservative estimate. For example, a researcher might believe that the population correlation is not less than .60. According to Appendix Table D.8, the required sample size for this correlation is 21 participants. The actual sample correlation between the distributed and massed practice times in Table 13.5-1 is .84. This sample correlation suggests the matching variable, mirror-tracing time for the last three of five trials, was an excellent choice.

t Confidence Interval for $\mu_1 - \mu_2$ (Dependent Samples)

A two-sided $100(1 - \alpha)\%$ confidence interval for $\mu_1 - \mu_2$ for dependent samples is

$$\overline{X}_D - t_{\alpha/2,\,\nu}\,\hat{\sigma}_{\overline{X}_D} < \mu_1 - \mu_2 < \overline{X}_D + t_{\alpha/2,\,\nu}\,\hat{\sigma}_{\overline{X}_D}$$

where $\overline{X}_D = \sum_{i=1}^{n} D_i/n$, $t_{\alpha/2,\,\nu}$ is the value that cuts off the upper $\alpha/2$ region of the sampling distribution of t for $\nu = n - 1$, and

$$\hat{\sigma}_{\overline{X}_D} = \frac{\sqrt{\dfrac{\sum\limits_{i=1}^{n}(D_i - \overline{X}_D)^2}{n - 1}}}{\sqrt{n}}$$

Lower and upper one-sided $100(1 - \alpha)\%$ confidence intervals for $\mu_1 - \mu_2$ are given by, respectively,

$$\overline{X}_D - t_{\alpha,\,\nu}\,\hat{\sigma}_{\overline{X}_D} < \mu_1 - \mu_2 \qquad \text{and} \qquad \mu_1 - \mu_2 < \overline{X}_D + t_{\alpha,\,\nu}\,\hat{\sigma}_{\overline{X}_D}$$

where $t_{\alpha,\,\nu}$ is the value that cuts off the upper α region of the sampling distribution of t for $\nu = n - 1$.

I will use the data in Table 13.4-1 ($\overline{X}_D = -2$, $\hat{\sigma}_{\overline{X}_D} = 0.4974$, and $n = 20$) to illustrate a one-sided confidence interval. The researcher's hypotheses for the mirror-tracing experiment were directional:

$$H_0\!: \mu_1 - \mu_2 \geq 0$$
$$H_1\!: \mu_1 - \mu_2 < 0$$

An analogous one-sided $100(1 - .05)\% = 95\%$ confidence interval for the difference $\mu_1 - \mu_2$ is

$$\mu_1 - \mu_2 < \overline{X}_D + t_{.05,19}\, \hat{\sigma}_{\overline{X}_D}$$

$$\mu_1 - \mu_2 < -2 + (1.729)(0.4974)$$

$$\mu_1 - \mu_2 < -1.14$$

This 95% confidence interval corresponds to the darkened portion of the real number line as follows:

The researcher can be 95% confident that the difference $\mu_1 - \mu_2$ is less than -1.14, which is consistent with the scientific hypothesis. Furthermore, it is reasonable to conclude that the medium-size effect, $g = |\overline{X}_1 - \overline{X}_2|/\hat{\sigma}_{Pooled} = |17 - 19|/3.8933 = .51$, is not attributable to chance (see "Practical Significance" in this section for the computation). The confidence interval for dependent samples is shorter than that for the case in which independent samples were used. For comparison purposes, the confidence interval for the independent samples case is shown as follows:

Group Matching: A Research Strategy to Be Avoided

A procedure called **group matching** is sometimes seen in the literature. It involves matching samples on one or more relevant characteristics so that the means and the standard deviations of the samples are approximately equal. No attempt is made to match individuals in one sample with those in another sample.

Group matching instead of individual matching is often used in ex post facto experiments. In an **ex post facto experiment,** the independent variable has occurred prior to the experiment. Thus, the independent variable is not under a researcher's control; rather, records or other information are used to construct two samples that differ with respect to the independent variable. For example, a researcher might be interested in determining whether the amount of community service (the dependent variable) of women who participated in Girl Scouts is greater than that for women who did not participate (participation-nonparticipation is the independent variable). Scout records can be used to identify those women who were Girl Scouts. In all likelihood the samples of former scouts and nonscouts differ on a variety of variables besides the independent variable. Group matching consists of adjusting the membership of each sample so that the samples' means and standard deviations are identical on a select set of extraneous variables. For example, high school records could be used to adjust the composition of the samples so as to equate the sample means and standard deviations on school achievement, number of extracurricular activities, and socioeconomic background.

You might expect that the use of group matching would result in a more powerful test than the use independent samples. This in not the case. Unfortunately, there are several problems inherent in using group matching. Although the procedure results in dependent samples, the *t* statistic for dependent samples cannot be used because individual participants are not matched. The data have to be analyzed using the *t* statistic for independent samples. This is not a good research strategy because (1) group matching restricts the ordinary variation between sample means that is expected on the basis of random sampling and (2) the denominator of the *t* statistic for independent samples overestimates the standard error of the mean of difference scores when the samples are dependent. Hence, the *t* statistic for independent samples gives a less powerful test than would have been obtained if group matching had not been used. An important experimental design principle emerges from this discussion—the sampling, randomization, and control procedures used in an experiment must be reflected in the statistical analysis and interpretation of data. If this is not possible, presumed refinements such as group matching should not be used.

CHECK YOUR UNDERSTANDING OF SECTION 13.4

14. If repeated measures are obtained, what restriction customarily is placed on the order of presentation of the conditions in the experiment?
15. (a) How is the size of the correlation between dependent samples related to the size of the standard error of the mean of difference scores? (b) How is the size of the correlation between dependent samples related to the probability of rejecting a false null hypothesis?
16. Before and after seeing a film about marijuana, 16 participants completed a questionnaire designed to assess their attitudes toward legalization of the drug. Researchers obtained the following data.

Favorableness of Attitude

Participant	Before	After	Participant	Before	After
1	13	16	9	19	20
2	16	18	10	16	18
3	10	12	11	15	18
4	14	18	12	14	15
5	15	18	13	12	12
6	12	15	14	13	17
7	11	12	15	14	16
8	18	20	16	15	17

a. Construct box plots for the before and after attitudes and stack the plots one above the other. Do the data contain outliers? Do the sample distributions appear to be relatively symmetrical?

b. List the five steps you would follow in testing the null hypothesis that $\mu_1 - \mu_2 \geq 0$, where μ_1 and μ_2 denote, respectively, the population means for the before and after attitudes. State the decision rule. Let $\alpha = .05$.

c. Use a t statistic to test the null hypothesis. What decision should the researcher make?

d. Determine the p value of the test statistic using Appendix Table D.3 and Microsoft's Excel TDIST function.

e. Compute Hedges's measure of effect size and interpret the measure.

f. Use Appendix Table D.8 to determine if the sample size is adequate to detect a large-size effect for $\alpha = .05$, $1 - \beta = .95$, and $\rho = .70$. What is the minimum number of participants required?

g. Compute a $100(1 - .05)\% = 95\%$ confidence interval for $\mu_1 - \mu_2$. Locate the confidence interval on the real number line.

h. Specify all the null hypotheses that could be rejected.

17. Expanding technology and the growth of knowledge in medicine require that nurses continually upgrade their skills. One way to accomplish this upgrading is through continuing-education workshops. The present study investigated the impact of a 60-hour workshop on a measure of the participants' cognitive knowledge. Twenty-two staff nurses took a paper-and-pencil pretest to evaluate their basic knowledge of cancer and cancer nursing prior to the 10-day workshop. The following data were obtained. (Suggested by Donovan, Marilee, Wolpert, Patricia, and Yasko, Joyce [1981]. Gaps and contracts. *Nursing Outlook*, 467–471.)

Knowledge Score

Participant	Pretest Score	Posttest Score
1	29	35
2	20	41
3	24	33
4	32	41
5	33	39
6	19	20
7	17	29
8	32	42
9	16	36
10	28	37
11	35	36
12	19	27
13	31	50
14	28	33
15	23	23
16	18	35
17	24	34
18	25	30
19	28	39
20	32	45
21	25	36
22	27	29

a. Construct box plots for the pretest and posttest scores and stack the plots one above the other. Do the data contain outliers? Do the sample distributions appear to be relatively symmetrical?

b. List the five steps you would follow in testing the null hypothesis that $\mu_1 - \mu_2 = 0$, where μ_1 and μ_2 denote, respectively, the population means for the pretest and posttest scores. State the decision rule. Let $\alpha = .01$.

c. Use a t statistic to test the null hypothesis. What decision should the researcher make?

d. Determine the p value of the test statistic using Appendix Table D.3 and Microsoft's Excel TDIST function.

e. Compute Hedges's measure of effect size and interpret the measure.

f. Use Appendix Table D.8 to determine if the sample size is adequate to detect a large-size effect for $\alpha = .01$, $1 - \beta = .80$, and $\rho = .50$. What is the minimum number of participants required?

g. Compute a $100(1 - .01)\% = 99\%$ confidence interval for $\mu_1 - \mu_2$. Locate the confidence interval on the real number line.

h. Specify all the null hypotheses that could be rejected.

i. For purposes of comparison, compute a t statistic for independent samples. Compare the result with the t statistic for dependent samples. Was the use of repeated measures an effective experimental design strategy?

j. In this experiment, the order of presentation of the pretest and the posttest obviously could not be randomized. Describe how a control group could be used in the experiment. How could the use of a control group help to clarify the interpretation of the results of the experiment?

18. Assume that a t statistic will be used to test the following null hypotheses. For (a), (b), and (c), estimate the total number of participants required; for (d), (e), and (f), estimate the number of pairs of dependent participants required.

a. $H_0: \mu_1 - \mu_2 \geq 0$
$\alpha = .05$
$1 - \beta = .80$
$d = 0.5$

b. $H_0: \mu_1 - \mu_2 = 0$
$\alpha = .01$
$1 - \beta = .90$
$d = 0.2$

c. $H_0: \mu_1 - \mu_2 = 0$
$\alpha = .05$
$1 - \beta = .95$
$d = 0.8$

d. $H_0: \mu_1 - \mu_2 \geq 0$
$\alpha = .05$
$1 - \beta = .80$
$d = 0.5$
$\rho = .6$

e. $H_0: \mu_1 - \mu_2 = 0$
$\alpha = .01$
$1 - \beta = .90$
$d = 0.2$
$\rho = .7$

f. $H_0: \mu_1 - \mu_2 = 0$
$\alpha = .05$
$1 - \beta = .95$
$d = 0.8$
$\rho = .5$

19. Terms to remember:

a. Dependent samples
b. Repeated measures
c. Participant matching
d. Group matching
e. Ex post facto experiment

13.5 LOOKING BACK: WHAT HAVE YOU LEARNED?

In this chapter, you have learned how to apply the hypothesis testing and confidence interval procedures for the one-sample case to the two-sample case for means. The tests are presented within the now familiar five-step hypothesis-testing format.

Two important topics related to the design of experiments also are discussed. The first concerns the relative merits of two randomization strategies: random sampling of participants from two populations versus random assignment of participants to experimental and control conditions. A researcher's research objectives determine whether one or the other procedure is sufficient or if both procedures are required. Remember that an experiment should contain some randomization procedure to justify using statistical inferential procedures.

The other topic related to the design of experiments concerns the use of independent samples versus dependent samples. It is advantageous to use dependent samples whenever the nature of the independent variable permits it. Matching participants on some variable that correlates positively with the dependent variable or observing the same participants under both the experimental and control conditions results in a more powerful test of a false null hypothesis than using independent samples. However, the use of group matching instead of individual matching is not recommended because the presumed refinement cannot be taken into account in the statistical analysis. This suggests an important general principle—the sampling, randomization, and control procedures used in an experiment must be reflected in the statistical analysis and interpretation.

The test statistics and confidence intervals that I have described in this chapter are summarized in Tables 13.5-1 and 13.5-2, respectively. As shown in the tables, the assumptions of the test statistics and analogous confidence intervals are the same.

TABLE 13.5-1   Summary of Two-Sample Test Statistics

Chapter Section	Statistical Hypotheses	Test Statistic	Assumptions
13.2	$H_0: \mu_1 - \mu_2 = \delta_0$ $H_1: \mu_1 - \mu_2 \neq \delta_0$	$t = \dfrac{(\overline{X}_1 - \overline{X}_2) - \delta_0}{\sqrt{\hat{\sigma}^2_{Pooled}(1/n_1 + 1/n_2)}}$ $\nu = (n_1 - 1) + (n_2 - 1)$	1. Random sampling or random assignment 2. Normality 3. Population variances are unknown but assumed equal 4. Independent samples
13.2	$H_0: \mu_1 - \mu_2 = \delta_0$ $H_1: \mu_1 - \mu_2 \neq \delta_0$	$t' = \dfrac{(\overline{X}_1 - \overline{X}_2) - \delta_0}{\sqrt{\hat{\sigma}^2_1/n_1 + \hat{\sigma}^2_2/n_2}}$ $\nu' = \dfrac{\left(\dfrac{\hat{\sigma}^2_1}{n_1} + \dfrac{\hat{\sigma}^2_2}{n_2}\right)^2}{\dfrac{1}{n_1-1}\left(\dfrac{\hat{\sigma}^2_1}{n_1}\right)^2 + \dfrac{1}{n_2-1}\left(\dfrac{\hat{\sigma}^2_2}{n_2}\right)^2}$	1. Random sampling or random assignment 2. Normality 3. Population variances are unknown but assumed unequal 4. Independent samples

(continued)

TABLE 13.5-1 *(continued)*

13.4	$H_0: \mu_1 - \mu_2 = \delta_0$	$t = \dfrac{\sum D_i / n}{\dfrac{\sqrt{\dfrac{\sum (D_i - \overline{X}_D)^2}{n-1}}}{\sqrt{n}}}$	1. Random sampling or random assignment 2. Normality 3. Population variances and correlation are unknown
	$H_1: \mu_1 - \mu_2 = \delta_0$	$v = n - 1$	4. Dependent samples

TABLE 13.5-2   Summary of Two-Sample Confidence Intervals

Chapter Section	Parameters	Confidence Interval	Assumptions
13.2	$\mu_1 - \mu_2$	$(\overline{X}_1 - \overline{X}_2) - t_{\alpha/2,\,v}\,\hat{\sigma}_{\overline{X}_1 - \overline{X}_2}$ $< \mu_1 - \mu_2 < (\overline{X}_1 - \overline{X}_2) + t_{\alpha/2,\,v}\,\hat{\sigma}_{\overline{X}_1 - \overline{X}_2}$ where $\hat{\sigma}_{\overline{X}_1 - \overline{X}_2} = \sqrt{\hat{\sigma}^2_{Pooled}(1/n_1 + 1/n_2)}$	1. Random sampling or random assignment 2. Normality 3. Population variances are unknown but assumed equal 4. Independent samples
13.4	$\mu_1 - \mu_2$	$\overline{X}_D - t_{\alpha/2,\,v}\,\hat{\sigma}_{\overline{X}_D}$ $< \mu_1 - \mu_2 < \overline{X}_D + t_{\alpha/2,\,v}\,\hat{\sigma}_{\overline{X}_D}$ where $\overline{X}_D = \sum D_i / n$ $\hat{\sigma}_{\overline{X}_D} = \dfrac{\sqrt{\dfrac{\sum (D_i - \overline{X}_D)^2}{n-1}}}{\sqrt{n}}$	1. Random sampling or random assignment 2. Normality 3. Population variances and correlation are unknown 4. Dependent samples

REVIEW EXERCISES FOR CHAPTER 13

1. A researcher is interested in testing the hypothesis that college freshmen who are on probation have lower academic aptitude scores than those not on probation. Random samples of $n_1 = 50$ probationers and $n_2 = 50$ nonprobationers are obtained from the respective populations. The populations are assumed to be normally distributed. Sample estimates of the standard deviations are $\hat{\sigma}_1 = 15.1$ and $\hat{\sigma}_2 = 15.3$. List the five steps you would follow to test the null hypothesis and state the decision rule. Let $\alpha = .05$.

2. (a) Suppose that in Exercise 1, $\overline{X}_1 = 112$, $\overline{X}_2 = 116$, and α has been set at .05. Compute the test statistic and make a decision; assume that $t_{.05,\,98} = 1.661$.
(b) Determine the p value of the test statistic using Appendix Table D.3 and Microsoft's Excel TDIST function.

3. Discuss the statement "The absolute magnitude of the t test statistic is indicative of the importance or practical significance of the difference between two sample means."

4. A researcher in Conception, Iowa, wished to determine whether there is a relationship between children's IQs and their mothers' ages when they were born. Using school records, a list was compiled of 10-year-olds whose mothers were over 35 at parturition, and a second list was compiled of 10-year-olds whose mothers were 20 or under at parturition. The researcher randomly sampled 50 children from each list and administered the Stanford-Binet intelligence test to them. The IQs were found to be considerably higher for the children of older mothers, and the difference was significant beyond the .001 level. The researcher concluded that a woman should postpone childbearing until later in life to ensure a high IQ for her offspring. (a) Comment on the appropriateness of the researcher's conclusion. (b) List some alternative explanations for the observed difference in IQs.

5. a. In Exercise 4, which sampling strategy did the researcher use?
   b. Would this strategy enable the researcher to establish a causal relationship between the IQs of children and the ages of their mothers at parturition?

6. In Exercise 4, what does the fact that the test statistic was significant at the .001 level tell you about the magnitude of the difference between the population means?

7. What are the advantages and disadvantages of random sampling and random assignment?

8. For each of the following research topics, indicate the research strategy that seems most appropriate. Justify your choice.
   a. Effects of two levels of feedback in acquiring a complex motor skill
   b. Classical music preferences of teenage boys and girls
   c. Relationship between the grades of college freshmen and the size of their high school graduation class
   d. Effects of 12 and 24 hours of food deprivation on the problem-solving skills of chimpanzees

9. A college dean believed that car ownership among students leads to lower grades. To test this hypothesis, she obtained a random sample of student car owners and nonowners and looked up their GPAs. She obtained the following data.

Grade Point Averages

Students Owning Cars			Students Not Owning Cars		
2.6	2.5	2.4	2.7	2.9	3.0
2.4	2.6	2.5	2.9	2.5	2.9
2.9	2.8	2.8	2.6	3.1	2.7
2.6	2.7	2.6	2.8	2.8	3.2
2.7	3.0	2.5	3.0	2.9	2.9
2.2	2.3	2.6	2.8	3.0	3.0

a. Construct box plots for car owners and nonowners and stack the plots one above the other. Do the data contain outliers? Do the sample distributions appear to be relatively symmetrical?
b. List the five steps you would follow in testing the null hypothesis and state the decision rule. Let $\alpha = .05$.

    c. Compute a t test statistic and make a decision about the researcher's hypothesis.

    d. Determine the p value of the test statistic using Appendix Table D.3 and Microsoft's Excel TDIST function.

    e. Compute Hedges's measure of effect size and interpret the measure.

    f. Use Appendix Table D.8 to determine if the sample size is adequate to detect a large-size effect if a power of .80 is desired. What is the minimum number of participants required?

    g. Construct a $100(1 - .05)\% = 95\%$ confidence interval for $\mu_1 - \mu_2$; assume that $t_{.05, 34} = 1.691$. Locate the confidence interval on the real number line.

    h. Specify all the null hypotheses that could be rejected.

10. In Exercise 9, the dean decided to prohibit freshmen from bringing cars to campus. (a) Do you think this action was justified by the data? (b) What other kinds of data about car owners and nonowners would be useful in helping the dean arrive at a rational car policy?

11. For children having problems in school, it was hypothesized that the mean IQ of those diagnosed as being depressed would be different from the IQ of those not diagnosed as being depressed. IQ data for 25 children who were referred to an educational diagnostic center because of problems in school are as follows. (Suggested by Brumback, R. A., Jackson, M. K., and Weinberg, W. A. [1980]. Relation of intelligence to childhood depression in children referred to an educational diagnostic center. *Perceptual and Motor Skills, 50,* 11–17.)

Full-Scale IQ

Depressed Children	Nondepressed Children	
117	110	106
102	112	85
104	100	105
89	97	106
84	106	105
128	92	
107	127	
102	121	
98	108	
92	108	

    a. Construct box plots for the depressed and nondepressed children and stack the plots one above the other. Do the data contain outliers? Do the sample distributions appear to be relatively symmetrical?

    b. List the five steps you would follow to test the null hypothesis and state the decision rule. Let $\alpha = .05$.

    c. Use a t' statistic to test the null hypothesis that $\mu_1 - \mu_2 = 0$, where μ_1 and μ_2 denote, respectively, the population means for depressed and nondepressed children. What decision should the researcher make?

    d. Compute Hedges's measure of effect size using the nondepressed children as the baseline group and interpret the measure.

12. Use the table of random numbers in Appendix D.1 to draw random samples without replacement of 25 men and 25 women from the student database in Appendix E.

   a. List the participant number, gender, and math test score for each person in your sample. For each gender, construct a box plot and stack the plots one above the other. Do the data contain outliers? Do the sample distributions appear to be relatively symmetrical?

   b. List the five steps you would follow in testing the null hypothesis that $\mu_1 - \mu_2 = 0$ and state the decision rule. Let $\alpha = .05$.

   c. Test the null hypothesis that $\mu_1 - \mu_2 = 0$, where μ_1 and μ_2 denote, respectively, the population mean of men's and women's math test scores.

   d. Determine the p value of the test statistic using Appendix Table D.3 and Microsoft's Excel TDIST function.

   e. Compute a measure of effect size and interpret the measure.

   f. Use Appendix Table D.8 to determine if the sample size is adequate to detect a large-size effect if a power of .80 is desired. What is the minimum number of participants required?

   g. Compute a $100(1 - .05)\% = 95\%$ confidence interval for $\mu_1 - \mu_2$. Locate the confidence interval on the real number line.

   h. Specify all the null hypotheses that could be rejected.

   i. Write a paragraph summarizing your results and conclusions.

13. (a) List three matching variables that you believe could be used to form pairs of participants in a learning experiment using nonsense syllables. (b) Which matching variable do you think would have the highest correlation with number of trials required to learn nonsense syllables?

14. It is well known that increasing room illumination up to some level increases reading speed. A random sample of 14 sixth-grade students read standardized passages under two levels of ambient room illumination: 5 foot-candles and 15 foot-candles. The order in which the conditions were presented was randomized independently for each participant, with the restriction that the conditions were presented first or second equally often. The reading sessions were separated by an interval of 2 hours.

Reading Speed (Words/Minute)

Participant	5 Foot-Candles	15 Foot-Candles	Participant	5 Foot-Candles	15 Foot-Candles
1	88	92	8	90	92
2	92	91	9	84	88
3	86	88	10	82	88
4	84	89	11	86	84
5	90	95	12	84	87
6	86	86	13	86	89
7	88	95	14	86	87

   a. Construct box plots for the 5- and 15-foot candle conditions and stack the plots one above the other. Do the data contain outliers? Do the sample distributions appear to be relatively symmetrical?

b. List the five steps you would follow to test the null hypothesis that $\mu_1 - \mu_2 \leq 0$, where μ_1 and μ_2 denote, respectively, the population means for the 5- and 15-foot-candle conditions. State the decision rule. Let $\alpha = .05$.

c. Use a t statistic to test the null hypothesis. What decision should the researcher make?

d. Determine the p value of the test statistic using Appendix Table D.3 and Microsoft's Excel TDIST function.

e. Compute Hedges's measure of effect size and interpret the measure.

f. Use Appendix Table D.8 to determine if the sample size is adequate to detect a large-size effect for $\alpha = .05$, $1 - \beta = .80$, and $\rho = .60$. What is the minimum number of participants required?

g. Compute a $100(1 - .05)\% = 95\%$ confidence interval for $\mu_1 - \mu_2$. Locate the confidence interval on the real number line.

h. Specify all the null hypotheses that could be rejected.

15. Researchers investigated the effect of a curriculum designed to develop children's critical viewing attitudes toward television programs. Eighteen second-grade children participated in the curriculum that dealt with such topics as the portrayal of violence on TV, commercials, stereotypes about gender and race, and the comprehension of magical effects on TV. The curriculum was presented in six 30- to 45-minute lessons and used brief videotape excerpts, class play activities, and homework assignments. A specially developed TV comprehension test was administered prior to the introduction of the curriculum and at its conclusion. The following data on the "impossible" characters subtest were obtained. (Suggested by Rapaczynski, Wanda, and Singer, Dorothy G. [1982]. Teaching television: A curriculum for young children. *Journal of Communication, 32* (2), 46–55.)

Score on "Impossible" Characters Subtest

Participant	Pretest Score	Posttest Score
1	1	1
2	3	3
3	0	3
4	2	4
5	1	2
6	2	4
7	3	3
8	3	2
9	2	4
10	2	3
11	1	4
12	3	3
13	1	2
14	2	2
15	3	4
16	3	4
17	1	2
18	2	4

a. Construct box plots for the pretest and posttest scores and stack the plots one above the other. Do the data contain outliers? Do the sample distributions appear to be relatively symmetrical?

b. List the five steps you would follow in testing the null hypothesis that $\mu_1 - \mu_2 \geq 0$, where μ_1 and μ_2 denote, respectively, the population means for the pretest and posttest scores. State the decision rule. Let $\alpha = .01$.

c. Use a t statistic to test the null hypothesis. What decision should the researcher make?

d. Determine the p value of the test statistic using Appendix Table D.3 and Microsoft's Excel TDIST function.

e. Compute Hedges's measure of effect size and interpret the measure.

f. Use Appendix Table D.8 to determine if the sample is adequate to detect a large effect for $\alpha = .01$, $1 - \beta = .80$, and $\rho = .40$. What is the minimum number of participants required?

g. Compute a $100(1 - .01)\% = 99\%$ confidence interval for $\mu_1 - \mu_2$. Locate the confidence interval on the real number line.

h. Specify all the null hypotheses that could be rejected.

i. For purposes of comparison, compute a t statistic for independent samples. Compare the result with the t statistic for dependent samples. Was the use of repeated measures an effective experimental design strategy?

16. Assume that a t statistic will be used to test the following null hypotheses. For (a), (b), and (c), estimate the total number of participants required; for (d), (e), and (f), estimate the number of pairs of dependent participants required.

a. $H_0: \mu_1 - \mu_2 \geq 0$	b. $H_0: \mu_1 - \mu_2 = 0$	c. $H_0: \mu_1 - \mu_2 = 0$
$\alpha = .05$	$\alpha = .01$	$\alpha = .05$
$1 - \beta = .90$	$1 - \beta = .80$	$1 - \beta = .80$
$d = 0.5$	$d = 0.2$	$d = 0.8$
d. $H_0: \mu_1 - \mu_2 \geq 0$	e. $H_0: \mu_1 - \mu_2 = 0$	f. $H_0: \mu_1 - \mu_2 = 0$
$\alpha = .05$	$\alpha = .01$	$\alpha = .05$
$1 - \beta = .90$	$1 - \beta = .80$	$1 - \beta = .80$
$d = 0.5$	$d = 0.2$	$d = 0.8$
$\rho = .6$	$\rho = .7$	$\rho = .5$

17. If the correlation between matched samples equals 0, the t test for dependent samples will be less powerful than the t test for independent samples. Explain why this assertion is true.

18. Use the table of random numbers in Appendix D.1 to draw random samples without replacement of 25 men and 25 women students from the student database in Appendix E. Use the variable of GPA to form 25 man-woman pairs of matched participants. The GPAs of men and women in a matched pair do not have to be equal, but the GPAs should be similar.

a. List the participant number, gender, and math test score for each matched pair in your sample. For each gender, construct a box plot and stack the plots one above the other. Do the data contain outliers? Do the sample distributions appear to be relatively symmetrical?

b. List the five steps you would follow in testing the null hypothesis that $\mu_1 - \mu_2 = 0$, where μ_1 and μ_2 denote, respectively, the population mean of men's and women's math test scores. State the decision rule. Let $\alpha = .05$.

c. Test the null hypothesis. What decision should the researcher make?

d. Determine the p value of the test statistic using Appendix Table D.3 and Microsoft's Excel TDIST function.

e. Compute Hedges's measure of effect size and interpret the measure.

f. Use Appendix Table D.8 to determine if the sample size is adequate to detect a large-size effect if $\rho = .70$ and a power of .80 is desired. What is the minimum number of participants required?

g. Compute a $100(1 - .05)\% = 95\%$ confidence interval for $\mu_1 - \mu_2$. Locate the confidence interval on the real number line. Specify all the null hypotheses that could be rejected.

h. Write a paragraph summarizing your results and conclusions.

i. If you did Exercise 12 in the Review Exercises for Chapter 13, compare the t statistic for independent samples with the t statistic for dependent samples. Was GPA an effective matching variable? Compute the correlation between the math test score and the GPA. Does the correlation shed any light on why the use of the dependent samples t statistic was or was not an effective research strategy?

19. Use the table of random numbers in Appendix D.1 to draw random samples without replacement of 30 men and 30 women students from the student database in Appendix E. Use the variable of GPA to form 30 man-woman pairs of matched participants. The GPAs of men and women in a matched pair do not have to be equal, but the GPAs should be similar.

a. List the participant number, gender, and number of math courses for each matched pair in your sample. For each gender, construct a box plot and stack th plots one above the other. Do the data contain outliers? Do the sample distributions appear to be relatively symmetrical?

b. List the five steps you would follow in testing the null hypothesis that $\mu_1 - \mu_2 = 0$, where μ_1 and μ_2 denote, respectively, the population mean of men's and women's No. of Math Courses variable. State the decision rule. Let $\alpha = .05$.

c. Test the null hypothesis that $\mu_1 - \mu_2 = 0$. What decision should the researcher make?

d. Determine the p value of the test statistic using Appendix Table D.3 and Microsoft's Excel TDIST function.

e. Compute Hedges's measure of effect size and interpret the measure.

f. Use Appendix Table D.8 to determine if the sample size is adequate to detect a large-size effect if $\rho = .40$ and a power of .80 is desired. What is the minimum number of participants required?

g. Compute a $100(1 - .05)\% = 95\%$ confidence interval for $\mu_1 - \mu_2$. Locate the confidence interval on the real number line. Specify all the null hypotheses that could be rejected.

h. Write a paragraph summarizing your results and conclusions.

i. Analyze the data using a t statistic for independent samples. Compare the results with the t statistic for dependent samples. Was GPA an effective matching variable? Compute the correlation between the No. of Math Courses variable and the GPA. Does the correlation shed any light on why the use of the dependent samples t statistic was or was not an effective research strategy?

20. Why should group matching be avoided?

Statistical Inference: Other Two-Sample Test Statistics

14.1 Introduction
Looking Ahead: What
Is This Chapter
About?

**14.2 Two-Sample *F* Test
and Confidence
Interval for Variances
Using Independent
Samples**
F Test for Two Variances
(Independent
Samples)
Computational Example
for *F* Test for
Two Variances
(Independent
Samples)
F Confidence Interval
for Two Variances
(Independent
Samples)
Computational Example
of Confidence Interval
for Two Variances
(Independent
Samples)
Check Your
Understanding
of Section 14.2

**14.3 Two-Sample *t* Test and
Confidence Interval
for Variances Using
Dependent Samples**
t Test for Two Variances
(Dependent Samples)
t Confidence Interval for
Two Variances
(Dependent Samples)
Check Your
Understanding
of Section 14.3

**14.4 Two-Sample *z* Test and
Confidence Interval for
Proportions Using
Independent Samples**
z Test for Two Proportions
(Independent Samples)
Computational Example
of *z* Test for Two
Proportions
(Independent Samples)
z Confidence Interval for
Two Proportions
(Independent Samples)
Computational Example
of Confidence Interval
for Two Proportions
(Independent Samples)

Check Your
Understanding
of Section 14.4

**14.5 Two-Sample *z* Test and
Confidence Interval
for Proportions Using
Dependent Samples**
z Test for Two Proportions
(Dependent Samples)
Computational Example
for *z* Test for Two
Proportions
(Dependent Samples)
z Confidence Interval
for Two Proportions
(Dependent Samples)
Computational Example
of Confidence Interval
for Two Proportions
(Dependent Samples)
Check Your
Understanding
of Section 14.5

**14.6 Looking Back: What
Have You Learned?**
Review Exercises for
Chapter 14

14.1 INTRODUCTION

Looking Ahead: What Is This Chapter About?

Two populations can differ in a variety of ways, such as central tendency, dispersion, skewness, and kurtosis. Often a researcher is primarily interested in whether the populations differ in central tendency. However, the researcher also may be interested in knowing whether the populations differ in dispersion. In this chapter you will learn about an F statistic and F sampling distribution that are used to test hypotheses about two variances. You also will learn how to use a z statistic to test hypotheses about two population proportions.

After reading this chapter, you should know the following:

- How to use an F statistic and independent samples to test a statistical hypothesis or construct a confidence interval for two population variances
- How to use a t statistic and dependent samples to test a statistical hypothesis or construct a confidence interval for two population variances
- How to use a z statistic and independent samples to test a statistical hypothesis or construct a confidence interval for two population proportions
- How to use a z statistic and dependent samples to test a statistical hypothesis or construct a confidence interval for two population proportions

14.2 TWO-SAMPLE F TEST AND CONFIDENCE INTERVAL FOR VARIANCES USING INDEPENDENT SAMPLES

F Test for Two Variances (Independent Samples)

Sometimes a researcher is interested in determining whether two populations differ in dispersion. For example, a researcher might want to know if placing disadvantaged children in a contingency management classroom results in less variability in the group's English-achievement scores than does placing them in a traditional classroom. Or the researcher might want to test one of the assumptions of the t test for independent samples—that two unknown population variances are equal.[1]

An F statistic for testing the following null hypotheses:

$$H_0: \sigma_1^2 = \sigma_2^2 \qquad H_0: \sigma_1^2 \geq \sigma_2^2 \qquad H_0: \sigma_1^2 \leq \sigma_2^2$$

$$H_1: \sigma_1^2 \neq \sigma_2^2 \qquad H_1: \sigma_1^2 < \sigma_2^2 \qquad H_1: \sigma_1^2 > \sigma_2^2$$

---

[1] Some books recommend always testing the assumption of equality of variances before performing a t test for $\mu_1 - \mu_2 = \delta_0$. Those who follow this advice should note that the t test is robust with respect to violation of the assumption of normalcy. However, the F test for $\sigma_1^2 = \sigma_2^2$ described in this section is almost as sensitive to non-normality as it is to nonequality of variances. Hence, a researcher may be dissuaded from using a t test when it is actually appropriate.

is

$$F = \frac{\hat{\sigma}^2_{larger}}{\hat{\sigma}^2_{smaller}}$$

where $\hat{\sigma}^2_{larger}$ and $\hat{\sigma}^2_{smaller}$ denote, respectively, the larger and smaller sample variance and each sample variance is computed using $\hat{\sigma}^2 = \Sigma(X_i - \overline{X})^2/(n-1)$. The degrees of freedom for the numerator and denominator are, respectively, $\nu_1 = n_{larger\,\hat{\sigma}^2} - 1$ and $\nu_2 = n_{smaller\,\hat{\sigma}^2} - 1$.

The sampling distribution of the F statistic was derived by R. A. Fisher in 1924 and given the name F in his honor by G. W. Snedecor. The F distribution, like the t distribution, is actually a family of distributions whose shape depends on its degrees of freedom. Unlike the z and t distributions that are symmetrical, the F distribution is positively skewed. The shape of the F distribution approaches the normal distribution for very large values of ν_1 and ν_2. Because F is a ratio of non-negative numbers, it can take values only from 0 to ∞. F values around 1 are expected if the null hypothesis that $\sigma_1^2 = \sigma_2^2$ is true. The assumptions associated with using the F statistic to test a null hypothesis are (1) the samples are independent, (2) the populations are normally distributed, and (3) the participants are random samples from the populations of interest or the participants have been randomly assigned to the conditions in the experiment.

The F test, unlike the t test, is not robust with respect to violation of the normality assumption. Hence, unless the normality assumption is fulfilled, the probability of making a Type I error will not equal the preselected value of α. Unfortunately, the lack of robustness of the F test does not improve in large samples. In summary, the F test should not be used unless you have good reason for believing that the population distributions of the two variables X_1 and X_2 are normal.

The critical value of F that cuts off the upper α region of the sampling distribution for ν_1 and ν_2 degrees of freedom is given in Appendix Table D.5 and is denoted by $F_{\alpha;\,\nu_1,\,\nu_2}$. The first ν in $F_{\alpha;\,\nu_1,\,\nu_2}$ denotes the numerator degrees of freedom of the F ratio; the second ν denotes the denominator degrees of freedom. To use Table D.5, you locate the column corresponding to the numerator degrees of freedom along the top of the table and the row corresponding to the denominator degrees of freedom along the side. The column-row intersection gives the critical values of F for $\alpha = .25, .10, .05,$ and $.01$. The critical value that cuts off the lower α region (lower tail of the distribution) is denoted by $F_{1-\alpha;\,\nu_1,\,\nu_2}$. Critical values for the lower tail are not given in the table.[2] By placing the larger sample variance in the numerator and the smaller sample variance in the denominator of the F statistic—that is, $F = \hat{\sigma}^2_{larger}/\hat{\sigma}^2_{smaller}$—you avoid the need to know the lower tail critical values. This follows because $F = \hat{\sigma}^2_{larger}/\hat{\sigma}^2_{smaller}$ is always in the upper tail. Of course, in testing directional hypotheses you must verify that the sizes of the sample variances are consistent with your alternative hypothesis.

---

[2] The critical value of F in the lower tail of the F distribution can be found by computing the reciprocal of the corresponding critical value in the upper tail with the degrees of freedom for numerator and denominator reversed—that is, $F_{1-\alpha;\,\nu_1,\,\nu_2} = 1/F_{\alpha;\,\nu_2,\,\nu_1}$. For example, the lower tail critical value for $\alpha = .05$, $\nu_1 = 24$, and $\nu_2 = 20$ is $F_{1-.05;\,24,\,20} = 1/F_{.05;\,20,\,24} = 1/2.03 = 0.49$.

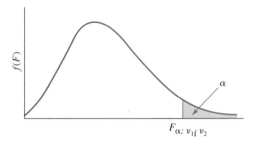

Figure 14.2-1. Sampling distribution of F. For $F = \hat{\sigma}^2_{larger}/\hat{\sigma}^2_{smaller}$, the critical region is in the upper tail of the sampling distribution.

The one-sided null hypotheses

$$H_0: \sigma_1^2 \le \sigma_2^2 \qquad\qquad H_0: \sigma_1^2 < \sigma_2^2$$
$$H_1: \sigma_1^2 > \sigma_2^2 \qquad\qquad H_1: \sigma_1^2 \ge \sigma_2^2$$

are rejected if $F = \hat{\sigma}^2_{larger}/\hat{\sigma}^2_{smaller}$ is greater than or equal to $F_{\alpha;\, \nu_1,\, \nu_2}$ and the sizes of the sample variances are consistent with the alternative hypothesis. The critical region for rejecting the null hypothesis is shown in Figure 14.2-1.

The two-sided null hypothesis

$$H_0: \sigma_1^2 = \sigma_2^2$$
$$H_1: \sigma_1^2 \ne \sigma_2^2$$

in which α is divided equally between the two tails of the F distribution is rejected if $F = \hat{\sigma}^2_{larger}/\hat{\sigma}^2_{smaller}$ is greater than or equal to $F_{\alpha/2;\, \nu_1,\, \nu_2}$. The F table in Appendix D.5 does not contain upper-tail values for $.05/2 = .025$. You can obtain the two-tailed critical value for, say, $F_{.05/2;\, 24,\, 20}$ by using Microsoft's Excel program that is installed on most computers. After accessing the Excel FINV function,

$$\text{FINV(probability,deg\_freedom1,deg\_freedom2)}$$

you replace the terms in parentheses as follows: FINV(.025,24,20). The two-tailed critical value is $F = 2.408$.

Computational Example for *F* Test for Two Variances (Independent Samples)

Suppose that 46 disadvantaged children were randomly assigned to contingency management and traditional classrooms: 25 children were placed in the contingency management classroom and 21 in the traditional classroom. At the end of the school year, an English-achievement test was administered to the two samples. The researcher believed that the children in the contingency management classroom would be more homogeneous in English achievement than the children in the traditional classroom. The steps in testing the null hypothesis are as follows:

Step 1. State the statistical hypotheses: $H_0: \sigma_1^2 \geq \sigma_2^2$

$H_0: \sigma_1^2 < \sigma_2^2$,

where σ_1^2 and σ_2^2 denote the population variances, respectively, for the contingency management and traditional classrooms.

Step 2. Specify the test statistic: $F = \hat{\sigma}_{\text{larger}}^2 / \hat{\sigma}_{\text{smaller}}^2$ because the researcher wants to test $H_0: \sigma_1^2 \geq \sigma_2^2$, the samples are random and independent, and the researcher assumes that the populations are approximately normal.

Step 3. Specify the sample sizes: and the sampling distribution: $n_1 = 25$ and $n_2 = 21$; F distribution.

Step 4. Specify the significance level: $\alpha = .05$.

Step 5. Obtain random samples of size n_1 and n_2, compute F, and make a decision.

Decision rule:

Reject the null hypothesis if F falls in the upper .05 portion of the sampling distribution of F; otherwise, do not reject the null hypothesis. If the null hypothesis is rejected and the sizes of the sample variances are consistent with the alternative hypothesis, conclude that the dispersion of English-achievement test scores is smaller for the population of children in the contingency management classroom than for children in the traditional classroom; if the null hypothesis is not rejected, do not draw this conclusion.

Assume that unbiased estimates of the population variances are $\hat{\sigma}_1^2 = 64$ and $\hat{\sigma}_2^2 = 196$ where $\hat{\sigma}_1^2$ and $\hat{\sigma}_2^2$ are computed from

$$\hat{\sigma}^2 = \frac{\sum_{i=1}^{n}(X_i - \overline{X})^2}{n-1}$$

The F test statistic is

$$F = \frac{\hat{\sigma}_{\text{larger}}^2}{\hat{\sigma}_{\text{smaller}}^2} = \frac{196}{64} = 3.062$$

The degrees of freedom are $\nu_{\text{larger } \hat{\sigma}^2} = n_2 - 1 = 20$ and $\nu_{\text{smaller } \hat{\sigma}^2} = n_1 - 1 = 24$. The null hypothesis is rejected because $F = 3.062$ exceeds the critical value $F_{.05; 20, 24} = 2.03$, and the sizes of the sample variances are consistent with the alternative hypothesis. The researcher concluded that placing disadvantaged children in a contingency management classroom resulted in smaller variance in English-achievement scores than placing them in a traditional classroom.

In reporting the results of the research in the text portion of a publication, the researcher might say, "The dispersion of English-achievement test scores was smaller for the population of children in the contingency management classroom than for children in the traditional classroom, $F(20, 24) = 3.062, p = .005$."

The F table in Appendix D.5 is not very useful for determining p values. I used Microsoft's Excel FDIST function to obtain the p value for the English-achievement experiment. After accessing the Excel FDIST function,

$$\text{FDIST}(x, \text{deg\_freedom1}, \text{deg\_freedom2})$$

I replaced "x" with the value of the F statistic (3.062), "deg_freedom1" with 20 and "deg_freedom2" with 24. To illustrate, the p value is given by

$$\text{FDIST}(3.062, 20, 24)$$

and is equal to .005.

F Confidence Interval for Two Variances (Independent Samples)

Let $\hat{\sigma}_1^2$ and $\hat{\sigma}_2^2$ be sample variances from independent, normal populations. Critical values for the F sampling distribution can be used to construct a confidence interval for the ratio σ_1^2 / σ_2^2.

A two-sided $100(1 - \alpha)\%$ confidence interval for σ_1^2/σ_2^2 for independent samples is

$$\frac{\hat{\sigma}_1^2}{\hat{\sigma}_2^2} \frac{1}{F_{\alpha/2; \nu_1, \nu_2}} < \frac{\sigma_1^2}{\sigma_2^2} < \frac{\hat{\sigma}_1^2}{\hat{\sigma}_2^2} F_{\alpha/2; \nu_2, \nu_1}$$

where $F_{\alpha/2; \nu_1, \nu_2}$ and $F_{\alpha/2; \nu_2, \nu_1}$ are the values of F that cut off the upper $\alpha/2$ region of the sampling distribution of F for $\nu_1 = n_1 - 1$ and $\nu_2 = n_2 - 1$. To find the critical value of $F_{\alpha/2; \nu_2, \nu_1}$ in Appendix Table D.5, the roles of ν_1 and ν_2 are reversed: ν_2 is the numerator degrees of freedom and ν_1 is the denominator degrees of freedom.

Lower and upper one-sided $100(1 - \alpha)\%$ confidence intervals for σ_1^2/σ_2^2 are given by, respectively,

$$\frac{\hat{\sigma}_1^2}{\hat{\sigma}_2^2} \frac{1}{F_{\alpha; \nu_1, \nu_2}} < \frac{\sigma_1^2}{\sigma_2^2} \qquad \text{and} \qquad \frac{\sigma_1^2}{\sigma_2^2} < \frac{\hat{\sigma}_1^2}{\hat{\sigma}_2^2} F_{\alpha; \nu_2, \nu_1}$$

where $F_{\alpha; \nu_1, \nu_2}$ and $F_{\alpha; \nu_2, \nu_1}$ are the values that cut off the upper α region of the sampling distribution of F.

The assumptions associated with constructing confidence intervals using the *F* distribution are the same as those described earlier for testing null hypotheses with the *F* statistic.

Computational Example of Confidence Interval for Two Variances (Independent Samples)

I will illustrate the computation of a one-sided confidence interval using the English-achievement test data of the 46 children who were randomly assigned to contingency management and traditional classrooms. Recall that $\hat{\sigma}_1^2 = 64$ was the sample variance of the 25 children in the contingency management classroom and $\hat{\sigma}_2^2 = 196$ was the sample variance of the 21 children in the traditional classroom. The statistical hypotheses were

$$H_0: \sigma_1^2 \geq \sigma_2^2$$
$$H_1: \sigma_1^2 < \sigma_2^2$$

An analogous one-sided $100(1 - .05)\% = .95$ confidence interval for the data where $\nu_1 = n_1 - 1 = 24$ and $\nu_2 = n_2 - 1 = 20$ is

$$\frac{\sigma_1^2}{\sigma_2^2} < \frac{\hat{\sigma}_1^2}{\hat{\sigma}_2^2} F_{.05;\, \nu_2,\, \nu_1}$$

$$\frac{\sigma_1^2}{\sigma_2^2} < \frac{64}{196} 2.03$$

$$\frac{\sigma_1^2}{\sigma_2^2} < 0.66$$

This confidence interval corresponds to the darkened portion of the real number line as follows:

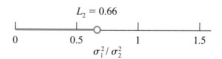

Because the interval does not include 1, the researcher can be confident that σ_1^2 is less than σ_2^2. The best guess the researcher can make regarding the ratio σ_1^2/σ_2^2 is that it is equal to $\hat{\sigma}_1^2/\hat{\sigma}_2^2 = 64/196 = 0.33$. The researcher can be 95% confident that the ratio is less than $L_2 = 0.66$.

CHECK YOUR UNDERSTANDING OF SECTION 14.2

1. Can $F = \hat{\sigma}_1^2/\hat{\sigma}_2^2$ be used to test hypotheses of the form $H_0: \sigma_1^2 - \sigma_2^2 = \delta_0$, where $\delta_0 \neq 0$? Explain.
2. In testing the tenability of the assumption $\sigma_1^2 = \sigma_2^2$ prior to using the *t* statistic to test $H_0: \mu_1 - \mu_2 = \delta_0$, it is common practice to set $\alpha = .15$ or .20. What

justification for this practice can you offer? (*Hint:* Consider how the size of α affects the power of the test.)

3. Exercise 5 in "Check Your Understanding of Section 13.2" described a study to determine whether interviewers spent more time talking to applicants who were hired than to applicants who were rejected. The data from the study are reproduced in the following table.

Duration of Interview (Minutes)

Hired		Rejected	
30	23	19	17
21	24	18	18
24	26	22	19
25	27	13	22
29	24	15	15
24	22	18	19
23	25	17	17
24	26	20	20
28	23	18	18
25	24	19	17
24	27	23	
19	26	12	
25	25	18	

a. Construct box plots for the hired and rejected applicants and stack the plots one above the other. Do the data contain outliers? Do the sample distributions appear to be relatively symmetrical?

b. Test the null hypothesis $H_0: \sigma_1^2 = \sigma_2^2$ using the statistic $F = \hat{\sigma}_{larger}^2 / \hat{\sigma}_{smaller}^2$. Let $\alpha = .05$. Assume that $F_{.05/2;\ 22,\ 25} = 2.269$. The F table in Appendix D.5 does not contain upper-tail values for $\alpha = .025$. I obtained the F two-tailed critical value, $F_{.05/2;\ 22,\ 25} = 2.269$, using Microsoft's Excel FINV function,

$$FINV(\text{probability,deg\_freedom1,deg\_freedom2})$$

I replaced the terms in parentheses as follows: FINV(.025,22,25).

c. Determine the p value of the F statistic using Microsoft's Excel FDIST function.

d. Compute a $100(1 - .05)\% = 95\%$ confidence interval for σ_2^2 / σ_1^2. Assume that $F_{.05/2;\ 22,\ 25} = 2.269$ and $F_{.05/2;\ 25,\ 22} = 2.320$. Locate the confidence interval on the real number line.

e. Is the confidence interval consistent with the null hypothesis significance test? Why?

4. Exercise 6 in "Check Your Understanding of Section 13.2" presented data on the discrimination of speech sounds for infants raised in English- or Spanish-speaking homes. The dependent measure was the number of head turns to stimuli involving a change minus the number of head turns on control trials divided

by the number of experimental trials. The data from the study are reproduced in the following table.

English-Speaking Home	Spanish-Speaking Home
.0421	.1081
.0941	.0986
.1064	.1566
.0242	.1961
.1331	.1125
.0773	.1942
.0243	.1079
.0815	.1021
.1186	.1583
.0356	.1673
.0728	.1675
.0999	.1856
.0614	.1688
.0479	.1512

a. Construct box plots for English-speaking (sample 1) and Spanish-speaking (sample 2) homes and stack the plots one above the other. Assume that for the English-speaking homes $Mdn = 0.07285$, $Q_1 = 0.0421$, and $Q_3 = 0.0999$. Assume that for the Spanish-speaking homes $Mdn = 0.15665$, $Q_1 = 0.1081$, and $Q_3 = 0.1688$. Do the data contain outliers? Do the sample distributions appear to be relatively symmetrical?

b. Test the null hypothesis $H_0: \sigma_1^2 \geq \sigma_2^2$ using the statistic $F = \hat{\sigma}_{\text{larger}}^2 / \hat{\sigma}_{\text{smaller}}^2$. Let $\alpha = .05$. Assume that $F_{.05; 13, 13} = 2.577$.

c. Determine the p value of the F statistic using Microsoft's Excel FDIST function.

d. Compute a $100(1 - .05)\% = 95\%$ confidence interval for σ_1^2 / σ_2^2. Locate the confidence interval on the real number line.

e. Is the interval consistent with the null hypothesis significance test? Why?

5. The nicotine content of random samples of two brands of cigarettes denoted by 1 and 2 was measured. The following data were obtained: $\overline{X}_1 = 18.6$ milligrams, $\overline{X}_2 = 16.1$ milligrams, $\hat{\sigma}_1 = 2.8$, $\hat{\sigma}_2 = 1.9$, $n_1 = 38$, and $n_2 = 35$.

a. Test the null hypothesis $H_0: \sigma_1^2 = \sigma_2^2$ using the statistic $F = \hat{\sigma}_{\text{larger}}^2 / \hat{\sigma}_{\text{smaller}}^2$. Let $\alpha = .05$. Assume that $F_{.05/2; 37, 34} = 1.962$.

b. Determine the p value of the F statistic using Microsoft's Excel FDIST function.

c. Compute a $100(1 - .05)\% = 95\%$ confidence interval for σ_1^2 / σ_2^2. Assume that $F_{.05/2; 37, 34} = 1.962$ and $F_{.05/2; 34, 37} = 1.943$. Locate the confidence interval on the real number line.

d. Is the confidence interval consistent with the null hypothesis significance test? Why?

e. Specify all the null hypotheses that could be rejected.

14.3 TWO-SAMPLE t TEST AND CONFIDENCE INTERVAL FOR VARIANCES USING DEPENDENT SAMPLES

t Test for Two Variances (Dependent Samples)

When the variances to be compared arise from dependent samples, for example, participants who are matched or observed on occasions 1 and 2, the appropriate statistic for testing a null hypothesis about σ_1^2 and σ_2^2 is t rather than F.

The t statistic is

$$t = \frac{\hat{\sigma}_1^2 - \hat{\sigma}_2^2}{\sqrt{[4\hat{\sigma}_1^2\hat{\sigma}_2^2/(n-2)](1 - r_{12}^2)}}$$

with degrees of freedom equal to $n - 2$, where n is the number of pairs of scores and r_{12} is the Pearson-product moment correlation coefficient for variables 1 and 2.

The assumptions associated with using the t statistic to test a null hypothesis are (1) the samples are dependent, (2) the populations are normally distributed, and (3) the dependent participants are a random sample from the population of interest or the dependent participants have been randomly assigned to the conditions in the experiment.

To illustrate the t test, suppose that 32 college freshmen who are enrolled in a psychology course titled Effective Personal Adjustment took the College Life Adjustment and Stress Survey. The survey is an interactive, computerized inventory designed to assess situation-specific stress, psychological distress, and satisfaction with support from family and friends. The test was administered on the first and last day of the class. Assume that the sample of students enrolled in the course is representative of the population of freshmen at the college. The college administrators want to know among other things if taking the course would affect the freshman population dispersion of scores on the support from family and friends scale. Suppose that the researchers obtained the following data for students enrolled in the course: pretest dispersion $\hat{\sigma}_1^2 = 256$, posttest dispersion $\hat{\sigma}_2^2 = 121$, $r_{12} = .60$, and $n = 32$. A test of the null hypothesis

$$H_0: \sigma_1^2 = \sigma_2^2$$

$$H_1: \sigma_1^2 \neq \sigma_2^2$$

is given by

$$t = \frac{\hat{\sigma}_1^2 - \hat{\sigma}_2^2}{\sqrt{[4\hat{\sigma}_1^2\,\hat{\sigma}_2^2/(n-2)](1 - r_{12}^2)}}$$

$$t = \frac{256 - 121}{\sqrt{[4(256)(121)/(32-2)][1 - (.60)^2]}} = \frac{135}{51.4129} = 2.626$$

with $\nu = 32 - 2 = 30$. According to Appendix Table D.3, a t of 2.042 cuts off the upper .025 region of the sampling distribution—that is, $t_{.05/2,\,30} = 2.042$. The computed $t(30) = 2.626$ is greater than $t_{.05/2,\,30} = 2.042$. Hence, the null hypothesis is rejected. The college administrators conclude that the dispersion of freshman scores on the support scale would be smaller if all freshmen at the college took the psychology course.

t Confidence Interval for Two Variances (Dependent Samples)

A two-sided $100(1 - \alpha)\%$ confidence interval for $\sigma_1^2 - \sigma_2^2$ for dependent samples is

$$(\hat{\sigma}_1^2 - \hat{\sigma}_2^2) - t_{\alpha/2,\,\nu}\sqrt{[4\hat{\sigma}_1^2\hat{\sigma}_2^2/(n-2)](1 - r_{12}^2)} < \sigma_1^2 - \sigma_2^2$$

$$< (\hat{\sigma}_1^2 - \hat{\sigma}_1^2) + t_{\alpha/2,\,\nu}\sqrt{[4\hat{\sigma}_1^2\hat{\sigma}_2^2/(n-2)](1 - r_{12}^2)}$$

where $t_{\alpha/2,\,\nu}$ is the value that cuts off the upper $\alpha/2$ region of the sampling distribution of t for $\nu = n - 2$.

Lower and upper one-sided $100(1 - \alpha)\%$ confidence intervals for $\sigma_1^2 - \sigma_2^2$ are given by, respectively,

$$(\hat{\sigma}_1^2 - \hat{\sigma}_2^2) - t_{\alpha,\,\nu}\sqrt{[4\hat{\sigma}_1^2\hat{\sigma}_2^2/(n-2)](1 - r_{12}^2)} < \sigma_1^2 - \sigma_2^2$$

and

$$\sigma_1^2 - \sigma_2^2 < (\hat{\sigma}_1^2 - \hat{\sigma}_2^2) + t_{\alpha,\,\nu}\sqrt{[4\hat{\sigma}_1^2\hat{\sigma}_2^2/(n-2)](1 - r_{12}^2)}$$

where $t_{\alpha,\,\nu}$ is the value that cuts off the upper α region of the sampling distribution of t for $\nu = n - 2$.

The assumptions associated with constructing confidence intervals using the t distribution are the same as those described earlier for testing null hypotheses with the t statistic.

I will use the data from the psychology class described earlier to illustrate the confidence interval. The college administrator's hypotheses for these data were nondirectional:

$$H_0: \sigma_1^2 = \sigma_2^2$$

$$H_0: \sigma_1^2 \neq \sigma_2^2$$

An analogous two-sided $100(1 - .05)\% = 95\%$ confidence interval for the difference $\sigma_1^2 - \sigma_2^2$ is

$$(\hat{\sigma}_1^2 - \hat{\sigma}_2^2) - t_{\alpha/2,\,\nu}\sqrt{\left(\frac{4\hat{\sigma}_1^2\hat{\sigma}_2^2}{n-2}\right)(1 - r_{12}^2)} < \sigma_1^2 - \sigma_2^2$$

$$< (\hat{\sigma}_1^2 - \hat{\sigma}_2^2) + t_{\alpha/2,\,\nu}\sqrt{\left(\frac{4\hat{\sigma}_1^2\hat{\sigma}_2^2}{n-2}\right)(1 - r_{12}^2)}$$

$$(256 - 121) - 2.042\sqrt{\left[\frac{4(256)(121)}{32 - 2}\right][1 - (.60)^2]} < \sigma_1^2 - \sigma_2^2$$

$$< (256 - 121) + 2.042\sqrt{\left[\frac{4(256)(121)}{32 - 2}\right][1 - (.60)^2]}$$

$$135 - 104.9851 < \sigma_1^2 - \sigma_2^2 < 135 + 104.9851$$

$$30.01 < \sigma_1^2 - \sigma_2^2 < 239.99$$

This 95% confidence interval corresponds to the darkened portion of the real number line as follows:

Because the interval does not include 0, the researcher can be confident that σ_1^2 is greater than σ_2^2. The best guess the college administrators can make regarding the difference $\sigma_1^2 - \sigma_2^2$ is that it is equal to $\hat{\sigma}_1^2 - \hat{\sigma}_2^2 = 135$. The administrators can be 95% confident that the difference is greater than $L_1 = 30.01$ and less than $L_2 = 239.99$. The margin of error, m, associated with the difference $\hat{\sigma}_1^2 - \hat{\sigma}_2^2 = 135$ is

$$m = t_{\alpha/2,\,\nu}\sqrt{\left(\frac{4\hat{\sigma}_1^2\hat{\sigma}_2^2}{n - 2}\right)(1 - r_{12}^2)} = 2.042\sqrt{\left[\frac{4(256)(121)}{32 - 2}\right][1 - (.60)^2]} = 104.99$$

CHECK YOUR UNDERSTANDING OF SECTION 14.3

6. Exercise 16 in "Check Your Understanding of Section 13.4" described a study to determine the effect of seeing a film about marijuana on attitudes toward legalization of the drug. The participants' attitudes were measured before and after seeing the film. The data from the study are reproduced in the following table.

Favorableness of Attitude

Participant	Before	After	Participant	Before	After
1	13	16	9	19	20
2	16	18	10	16	18
3	10	12	11	15	18
4	14	18	12	14	15
5	15	18	13	12	12
6	12	15	14	13	17
7	11	12	15	14	16
8	18	20	16	15	17

a. Construct box plots for the before and after attitudes and stack the plots one above the other. Do the data contain outliers? Do the sample distributions appear to be relatively symmetrical?

    b. Test the null hypothesis that the population variances are equal versus the alternative that they are not equal. Let $\alpha = .05$.

    c. Determine the *p* value of the *t* statistic using Appendix Table D.3 and Microsoft's Excel TDIST function.

    d. Compute a $100(1 - .05)\% = 95\%$ confidence interval for $\sigma_1^2 - \sigma_2^2$. Locate the confidence interval on the real number line.

    e. Is the confidence interval consistent with the null hypothesis significance test? Why?

7. Exercise 17 in "Check Your Understanding of Section 13.4" described a study to investigate the impact of a 60-hour workshop on nurses' knowledge of cancer and cancer nursing. The data from the study are reproduced in the following table.

	Knowledge Score	
Participant	Pretest Score	Posttest Score
1	29	35
2	20	41
3	24	33
4	32	41
5	33	39
6	19	20
7	17	29
8	32	42
9	16	36
10	28	37
11	35	36
12	19	27
13	31	50
14	28	33
15	23	23
16	18	35
17	24	34
18	25	30
19	28	39
20	32	45
21	25	36
22	27	29

    a. Construct box plots for the pretest and posttest scores and stack the plots one above the other. Do the data contain outliers? Do the sample distributions appear to be relatively symmetrical?

    b. Test the null hypothesis that $\sigma_1^2 \geq \sigma_2^2$, where σ_1^2 and σ_2^2 denote the pretest and posttest population variances, respectively. Let $\alpha = .05$.

    c. Determine the *p* value of the *t* statistic using Appendix Table D.3 and Microsoft's Excel TDIST function.

    d. Compute a $100(1 - .05)\% = 95\%$ confidence interval for $\sigma_1^2 - \sigma_2^2$. Locate the confidence interval on the real number line.

    e. Is the confidence interval consistent with the null hypothesis significance test? Why?

14.4 TWO-SAMPLE z TEST AND CONFIDENCE INTERVAL FOR PROPORTIONS USING INDEPENDENT SAMPLES

z Test for Two Proportions (Independent Samples)

Many variables in the behavioral sciences, health sciences, and education have two nonoverlapping and exhaustive classes and are qualitative in character, for example, men or women, cigarette smokers or nonsmokers, and pass or fail. In such cases p, the proportion in one class, and $1 - p$, the proportion in the other class, are useful descriptive measures. In Section 12.2, I described a z statistic for testing hypotheses about a single population proportion, p. The procedures described there can be modified to test any of the following null hypotheses about two independent population proportions, p_1 and p_2.

$$H_0: p_1 = p_2 \qquad H_0: p_1 \le p_2 \qquad H_0: p_1 \ge p_2$$
$$H_1: p_1 \ne p_2 \qquad H_1: p_1 > p_2 \qquad H_1: p_1 < p_2$$

The z statistic for testing a null hypothesis is

$$z = \frac{\hat{p}_1 - \hat{p}_2}{\sqrt{\hat{p}_{Pooled}(1 - \hat{p}_{Pooled})\left(\dfrac{1}{n_1} + \dfrac{1}{n_2}\right)}}.$$

$\hat{p}_1$ and $\hat{p}_2$ are the sample estimators of the population proportions p_1 and p_2, respectively; n_1 and n_2 are the sizes of the samples used to estimate the population proportions; and $\hat{p}_{Pooled}$ is a pooled estimator,

$$\hat{p}_{Pooled} = \frac{n_1\hat{p}_1 + n_2\hat{p}_2}{n_1 + n_2}$$

When both samples are large, the distribution of $\hat{p}_1 - \hat{p}_2$ is approximately normal, and the difference between the sample proportions is an unbiased estimator of the difference between the population proportions. The denominator of the z statistic is an estimator of

$$\sigma_{p_1 - p_2} = \sqrt{\frac{p_1(1 - p_1)}{n_1} + \frac{p_2(1 - p_2)}{n_2}}$$

which is the standard error of the difference between two population proportions.

The sampling distribution of the z statistic approaches a normal distribution if all the products $n_1\hat{p}_1$, $n_1(1 - \hat{p}_1)$, $n_2\hat{p}_2$, and $n_2(1 - \hat{p}_2)$ are greater than 5 and both populations are at least 10 times larger than their respective samples. The critical values of z for α and $\alpha/2$ levels of significance are obtained from Appendix Table D.2.

The use of a pooled estimator, $\hat{p}_{Pooled}$, in the z statistic requires a word of explanation. If the null hypothesis is true, the two population proportions are equal.

Hence, the two sample proportions, $\hat{p}_1$ and $\hat{p}_2$, are both estimators of the same population proportion. Whenever two independent estimators of a population proportion are available, a pooled estimator is likely to provide a better estimate than either sample proportion taken alone. The use of a pooled estimator is not new. Recall from Section 13.2 that a pooled estimator also was used to estimate a population variance in the formula for the independent samples t statistic.

Computational Example of z Test for Two Proportions (Independent Samples)

I will illustrate the z test with data from the landmark study of the effects of aspirin on the incidence of heart attacks in men. In the five-year study conducted at the Harvard Medical School, 22,071 men physicians took either an aspirin tablet or a placebo tablet every other day. The participants were randomly assigned to the two conditions: an aspirin group ($n_1 = 11,037$) and a placebo group ($n_2 = 11,034$). Neither the participants nor those who evaluated the results knew which tablet the participants took. This type of experiment is called a **double-blind study.** One hundred thirty-nine of the participants in the aspirin group suffered one or more heart attacks during the study, $\hat{p}_1 = 139/11,037 = .01259$. Two hundred thirty-nine in the placebo group suffered one or more heart attacks, $\hat{p}_2 = 239/11,034 = .0217$. The steps in testing the null hypothesis that the population proportions are equal are as follows:

Step 1. State the statistical hypotheses:

$H_0: p_1 = p_2$

$H_1: p_1 \neq p_2$

where p_1 and p_2 denote the population proportions, respectively, for the aspirin and placebo groups.

Step 2. Specify the test statistic:

z statistic because the researchers wanted to test $H_0: p_1 = p_2$; the samples were random and independent; $n_1\hat{p}_1$, $n_1(1 - \hat{p}_1)$, $n_2\hat{p}_2$, and $n_2(1 - \hat{p}_2)$ were greater than 5; and both populations were at least 10 times larger than their respective samples.

Step 3. Specify the sample sizes: and the sampling distribution:

$n_1 = 11,037$ and $n_2 = 11,034$; normal distribution.

Step 4. Specify the significance level:

$\alpha = .05$.

Step 5. Obtain random samples of size n_1 and n_2, compute z, and make a decision.

Decision rule:

Reject the null hypothesis if z falls in the lower or upper $.05/2 = .025$ portion of the standard normal distribution; otherwise, do not reject the null hypothesis. If the null hypothesis is rejected, conclude that the population proportion of participants in the aspirin group who suffered one or more heart attacks is not equal to that for the placebo group; if the null hypothesis is not rejected, do not draw this conclusion.

The z statistic for the Harvard Medical School data is

$$z = \frac{\hat{p}_1 - \hat{p}_2}{\sqrt{\hat{p}_{Pooled}(1 - \hat{p}_{Pooled})\left(\dfrac{1}{n_1} + \dfrac{1}{n_2}\right)}}$$

$$= \frac{.01259 - .02166}{\sqrt{.01712(1 - .01712)\left(\dfrac{1}{11{,}037} + \dfrac{1}{11{,}034}\right)}}$$

$$= \frac{-.00907}{.00175} = -5.19$$

where

$$\hat{p}_{Pooled} = \frac{n_1\hat{p}_1 + n_2\hat{p}_2}{n_1 + n_2} = \frac{(11{,}037)(.01259) + (11{,}034)(.02166)}{11{,}037 + 11{,}034} = .01712$$

and $z_{\alpha/2} = 1.96$. Because $|z| = 5.19 > z_{\alpha/2} = 1.96$, the null hypothesis that $p_1 = p_2$ is rejected. Participants who took the aspirin tablets had 0.91% fewer heart attacks than those who took the placebo. The researchers terminated the aspirin-placebo portion of the experiment prematurely. The reason given for the unusual termination was that "a statistically extreme beneficial effect" of the aspirin had been found. The difference, 0.91%, may appear to be a negligible, but the use of aspirin projected over a population of 100 million men in the United States could result in almost one million fewer heart attacks over a five-year period. The size of treatment effects always has to be interpreted in terms of the potential benefits.

z Confidence Interval for Two Proportions (Independent Samples)

A two-sided $100(1 - \alpha)\%$ confidence interval for $p_1 - p_2$ for independent samples is

$$(\hat{p}_1 - \hat{p}_2) - z_{\alpha/2}\sqrt{\frac{\hat{p}_1(1 - \hat{p}_1)}{n_1} + \frac{\hat{p}_2(1 - \hat{p}_2)}{n_2}} < p_1 - p_2$$

$$< (\hat{p}_1 - \hat{p}_2) + z_{\alpha/2}\sqrt{\frac{\hat{p}_1(1 - \hat{p}_1)}{n_1} + \frac{\hat{p}_2(1 - \hat{p}_2)}{n_2}}$$

where $z_{\alpha/2}$ is the value that cuts off the upper $\alpha/2$ region of the sampling distribution of z.

Lower and upper one-sided $100(1 - \alpha)\%$ confidence intervals for $p_1 - p_2$ are given by, respectively,

$$(\hat{p}_1 - \hat{p}_2) - z_\alpha \sqrt{\frac{\hat{p}_1(1 - \hat{p}_1)}{n_1} + \frac{\hat{p}_2(1 - \hat{p}_2)}{n_2}} < p_1 - p_2$$

and

$$p_1 - p_2 < (\hat{p}_1 - \hat{p}_2) + z_\alpha \sqrt{\frac{\hat{p}_1(1 - \hat{p}_1)}{n_1} + \frac{\hat{p}_2(1 - \hat{p}_2)}{n_2}}$$

where z_α is the value that cuts off the upper α region of the sampling distribution of z.

The confidence intervals are approximate because the standard error of the difference between two proportions depends on a knowledge of the parameters p_1 and p_2. Because p_1 and p_2 are unknown, sample estimates of the parameters are used in the confidence interval. The use of $\hat{p}_1$ and $\hat{p}_2$ in place of p_1 and p_2 is satisfactory if all the products $n_1\hat{p}_1$, $n_1(1 - \hat{p}_1)$, $n_2\hat{p}_2$, and $n_2(1 - \hat{p}_2)$ are greater than 10 and both populations are at least 10 times larger than their respective samples. The statistic

$$\hat{\sigma}_{p_1 - p_2} = \sqrt{\frac{\hat{p}_1(1 - \hat{p}_1)}{n_1} + \frac{\hat{p}_2(1 - \hat{p}_2)}{n_2}}$$

in the confidence interval is an estimator of the unknown standard error of the difference between two population proportions. Notice that the confidence interval does not use a pooled estimator as was done for the null hypothesis z test where

$$\hat{\sigma}_{p_1 - p_2} = \sqrt{\hat{p}_{Pooled}(1 - \hat{p}_{Pooled})\left(\frac{1}{n_1} + \frac{1}{n_2}\right)}$$

The null hypothesis z test assumes that the two population proportions are equal. This assumption is not made for the confidence interval. Hence, pooling is not appropriate.

Computational Example of Confidence Interval for Two Proportions (Independent Samples)

I will use the Harvard Medical School data described earlier to illustrate the computation of a confidence interval for $p_1 - p_2$. Recall that for the $n_1 = 11,037$ participants in the aspirin group, the proportion who had one or more heart attacks was $\hat{p}_1 = .01259$. For the $n_2 = 11,034$ participants in the placebo group, the proportion was $\hat{p}_2 = .01712$. A two-sided $100(1 - .05)\%$ confidence interval for $p_1 - p_2$ is

$$(.01259 - .02166) - 1.96\sqrt{\frac{(.01259)(1 - .01259)}{11,037} + \frac{(.02166)(1 - .02166)}{11,034}}$$

$$< p_1 - p_2$$

$$< (.01259 - .02166) + 1.96 \sqrt{\frac{(.01259)(1 - .01259)}{11,037} + \frac{(.02166)(1 - .02166)}{11,034}}$$

$$-.00907 - .00342 < p_1 - p_2 < -.00907 + .00342$$

$$-.012 < p_1 - p_2 < -.006$$

This confidence interval corresponds to the darkened portion of the real number line as follows:

$L_1 = -.012$ $L_2 = -.006$

$-.010$ $-.009$ $-.008$ $-.007$ $-.006$ $-.005$

$p_1 - p_2$

The researchers can be 95% confidant that the difference between the two population proportions is between $-.012$ and $-.006$. The margin of error, m, associated with the sample difference $\hat{p}_1 - \hat{p}_2 = .0091$ is .0034, as the following computations show:

$$m = z_{\alpha/2} \sqrt{\frac{\hat{p}_1(1 - \hat{p}_1)}{n_1} + \frac{\hat{p}_2(1 - \hat{p}_2)}{n_2}}$$

$$= 1.96 \sqrt{\frac{(.01259)(1 - .01259)}{11,037} + \frac{(.02166)(1 - .02166)}{11,034}} = .0034$$

CHECK YOUR UNDERSTANDING OF SECTION 14.4

8. In a 2006 Shuffle Poll of $n_2 = 500$ Americans over 18 years old, 29% said they had smoked pot. In 1996, the figure for a sample of $n_1 = 600$ was 22%.
   a. Test the hypothesis H_0: $p_1 = p_2$. Let $\alpha = .05$.
   b. Use Appendix Table D.2 to determine the p value of the z statistic.
   c. Compute a $100(1 - .05)\% = 95\%$ confidence interval for $p_1 = p_2$. Locate the confidence interval on the real number line.
   d. Is the confidence interval consistent with the null hypothesis significance test? Why?
   e. Specify all the null hypotheses that could be rejected.
9. In the 2006 survey cited in Exercise 8, 76% of the interviewees opposed legalization of marijuana. The figure in 1996 was 84%.
   a. Test the hypothesis H_0: $p_1 = p_2$. Let $\alpha = .05$.
   b. Use Appendix Table D.2 to determine the p value of the z statistic.
   c. Compute a $100(1 - .05)\% = 95\%$ confidence interval for $p_1 = p_2$. Locate the confidence interval on the real number line.
   d. Is the confidence interval consistent with the null hypothesis significance test? Why?
   e. Specify all the null hypotheses that could be rejected.

10. In a 2005 survey of 16-to 24-year-olds, 11% of the $n_1 = 300$ men and 8% of the $n_2 = 200$ women reported that they had tried marijuana.
    a. Test the null hypothesis that $H_0: p_1 = p_2$. Let $\alpha = .05$.
    b. Use Appendix Table D.2 to determine the *p* value of the *z* statistic.
    c. Compute a $100(1 - .05)\% = 95\%$ confidence interval for the difference between the proportion of pot smokers among men and women in 2004. Locate the confidence interval on the real number line.
    d. Is the confidence interval consistent with the null hypothesis significance test? Why?
11. Term to remember:
    a. Double-blind study

14.5 TWO-SAMPLE *z* TEST AND CONFIDENCE INTERVAL FOR PROPORTIONS USING DEPENDENT SAMPLES

z Test for Two Proportions (Dependent Samples)

If two samples are dependent, a statistic developed by McNemar (1947) can be used to test any of the following null hypotheses:

$$H_0: p_1 = p_2 \qquad H_0: p_1 \leq p_2 \qquad H_0: p_1 \geq p_2$$
$$H_1: p_1 \neq p_2 \qquad H_1: p_1 > p_2 \qquad H_1: p_1 < p_2$$

To test one of these hypotheses, the data are placed into a 2×2 table as follows:

		Sample 2		
		Category 0	Category 1	
Sample 1	Category 1	*a*	*b*	*a* + *b*
	Category 0	*c*	*d*	*c* + *d*
		a + *c*	*b* + *d*	*n*

The cell entry *a* denotes the number of elements classified in category 1 for sample 1 and in category 0 for sample 2; *b* denotes the number of elements that is classified in category 1 for both samples, and so on. The number of elements in each sample is *n*.

An estimator of the population proportion of individuals in category 1 for sample 1 is $\hat{p}_1 = (a + b)/n$. Similarly, the proportion in category 1 for sample 2 is $\hat{p}_2 = (b + d)/n$. The difference between the two populations can be expressed either as a proportion, $p_1 - p_2$, or as a frequency, $a - d$. It is easy to show that $n(\hat{p}_1 - \hat{p}_2) = a - d$:

$$\hat{p}_1 - \hat{p}_2 = \frac{a + b}{n} - \frac{b + d}{n} \qquad \text{by definition}$$

$$= \frac{1}{n}(a + b - b - d)$$

$$n(\hat{p}_1 - \hat{p}_2) = a - d$$

The use of frequencies instead of proportions results in a simpler z test statistic. If the null hypothesis is true, the z test statistic

$$z = \frac{a - d}{\sqrt{a + d}}$$

is approximately distributed as the standard normal distribution, provided that $(a + d) \geq 10$ for a two-tailed test and ≥ 30 for a one-tailed test.

Computational Example for z Test for Two Proportions (Dependent Samples)

Suppose that a researcher polls a random sample of 200 students at Thanatos University about whether they approve or disapprove of capital punishment. Following the survey, the students are shown a film depicting the effects of crime and acts of violence on the victims and their families. The researcher again polls the 200 students about capital punishment and hypothesizes that the proportion of students who approve of capital punishment will be higher after seeing the film than before. The statistical hypotheses are

$$H_0: p_1 \geq p_2$$

$$H_1: p_1 < p_2$$

where p_1 and p_2 denote, respectively, the before and after population proportions. The data, number of students who approve or disapprove of capital punishment before and after seeing the film, are shown in Table 14.5-1. It is apparent that the difference $a - d = -25$ is consistent with the alternative hypothesis. The two sample proportions are $\hat{p}_1 = .15$ and $\hat{p}_2 = .28$. According to Appendix Table D.2, $z_{.05} = 1.645$ cuts of the upper .05 region of the sampling distribution. Because $| z | = | -4.226 |$ is greater than $z_{.05} = 1.645$, the null hypothesis is rejected. The researcher concludes that for the population of students at Thanatos University a higher proportion would approve of capital punishment after seeing the film.

z Confidence Interval for Two Proportions (Dependent Samples)

A two-sided $100(1 - \alpha)$ confidence interval for $p_1 - p_2$ for dependent samples is

$$\frac{a - d}{n} - z_{\alpha/2} \sqrt{\frac{(a + d)(b + c) + 4ad}{n^3}} < p_1 - p_2$$

TABLE 14.5-1 Capital Punishment Data

(i) Data

		Sample 2		
		Disapprove	Approve	
Sample 1	Approve	$a = 5$	$b = 25$	$a + b = 30$
	Disapprove	$c = 140$	$d = 30$	$c + d = 170$
		$a + c = 145$	$b + d = 55$	$n = 200$

(ii) Computation

$$z = \frac{a - d}{\sqrt{a + d}} = \frac{5 - 30}{\sqrt{5 + 30}} = \frac{-25}{5.916} = -4.226$$

$$z_{.05} = 1.645$$

$$\hat{p}_1 = \frac{a + b}{n} = \frac{30}{200} = .15$$

$$\hat{p}_2 = \frac{b + d}{n} = \frac{55}{200} = .28$$

$$< \frac{a - d}{n} + z_{\alpha/2}\sqrt{\frac{(a + d)(b + c) + 4ad}{n^3}}$$

where a, b, c, and d denote cell frequencies as defined in Table 14.5-1, n is the number of elements in each sample, and $z_{\alpha/2}$ is the value that cuts off the upper $\alpha/2$ region of the sampling distribution of z.

Lower and upper one-sided $100(1 - \alpha)\%$ confidence intervals for $p_1 - p_2$ are given by, respectively,

$$\frac{a - d}{n} - z_\alpha\sqrt{\frac{(a + d)(b + c) + 4ad}{n^3}} < p_1 - p_2$$

and

$$p_1 - p_2 < \frac{a - d}{n} + z_\alpha\sqrt{\frac{(a + d)(b + c) + 4ad}{n^3}}$$

where z_α is the value that cuts off the upper α region of the sampling distribution of z.

These confidence intervals like those for the independent samples case are approximate. The approximation is satisfactory if $(a + d) \geq 30$.

Computational Example of Confidence Interval for Two Proportions (Dependent Samples)

I will use the experiment on attitudes toward capital punishment of Thanatos University students to illustrate the dependent-samples confidence interval for $p_1 - p_2$. The researcher's hypotheses were

$$H_0: p_1 \geq p_2$$

$$H_1: p_1 < p_2$$

An analogous one-sided $100(1 - .05)\% = 95\%$ confidence interval is

$$p_1 - p_2 < \frac{a - d}{n} + z_\alpha \sqrt{\frac{(a + d)(b + c) + 4ad}{n^3}}$$

$$p_1 - p_2 < \frac{5 - 30}{200} + 1.645 \sqrt{\frac{(5 + 30)(24 + 140) + 4(5)(30)}{(100)^3}}$$

$$p_1 - p_2 < -0.125 + 0.046$$

$$p_1 - p_2 < -0.079$$

The 95% confidence interval corresponds to the darkened portion of the real number line as follows:

The researcher can be 95% confident that $p_1 - p_2$ is less than $-.079$. Although the difference between p_1 and p_2 could be quite small, it is reasonable to believe that the population proportion of students who favor capital punishment would be larger after seeing the film. The best guess the researcher can make regarding the difference between $p_1 - p_2$ is that it is equal to $\hat{p}_1 - \hat{p}_2 = .15 - .28 = -.13$. The margin of error, m, associated with the sample difference $\hat{p}_1 - \hat{p}_2 = -.13$ is .046, as the following computations show:

$$m = z_\alpha \sqrt{\frac{(a + d)(b + c) + 4ad}{n^3}}$$

$$= 1.645 \sqrt{\frac{(5 + 30)(24 + 140) + 4(5)(30)}{(100)^3}} = .046$$

CHECK YOUR UNDERSTANDING OF SECTION 14.5

12. Attitudes of a sample of college students toward taking a required course in music appreciation were measured prior to taking the course and after completing the course. The following data were obtained:

Postcourse Attitude

		Unfavorable	Favorable	
	Favorable	13	24	37
Precourse Attitude				
	Unfavorable	19	27	46
		32	51	83

a. Compute p_1 and p_2, where the subscripts 1 and 2 denote, respectively, the pre- and postcourse attitudes.
b. Test the hypothesis H_0: $p_1 = p_2$. Let $\alpha = .05$.
c. Use Appendix Table D.2 to determine the p value of the z statistic.
d. Compute a $100(1 - .01)\% = 95\%$ confidence interval for $p_1 - p_2$. Locate the confidence interval on the real number line.
e. Is the confidence interval consistent with the null hypothesis significance test? Why?
f. Specify all the null hypotheses that could be rejected.

14.6 LOOKING BACK: WHAT HAVE YOU LEARNED?

In this chapter you learned how to test null hypotheses and construct confidence intervals for two variances and two proportions. You also were introduced to the important F statistic and its sampling distribution.

The z, t, and F statistics presented in Chapters 10 through 14 have a number of common characteristics that you might overlook because the formulas for the statistics are so different. Each statistic (1) assumes random sampling or random assignment of participants, (2) is used to test null hypotheses or construct confidence intervals for one or two parameters of the sampled populations, and (3) assumes, with the exception of the z statistic that is used with proportions, that the sampled population(s) is normally distributed. The z statistic assumes that the sampled population(s) is binomially distributed.

The test statistics and confidence intervals are summarized in Tables 14.6-1 and 14.6-2, respectively. As the tables show, the assumptions of the test statistics and analogous confidence intervals are similar.

TABLE 14.6-1 Summary of Two-Sample Test Statistics

Chapter Section	Statistical Hypotheses	Test Statistic	Assumptions
14.2	$H_0: \sigma_1^2 = \sigma_2^2$ $H_1: \sigma_1^2 \neq \sigma_2^2$	$F = \dfrac{\hat{\sigma}_{\text{larger}}^2}{\hat{\sigma}_{\text{smaller}}^2}$ $\nu_1 = n_{\text{larger }\hat{\sigma}^2} - 1$ $\nu_2 = n_{\text{smaller }\hat{\sigma}^2} - 1$	1. Random sampling or random assignment 2. Normality 3. Independent Samples
14.3	$H_0: \sigma_1^2 = \sigma_2^2$ $H_1: \sigma_1^2 \neq \sigma_2^2$	$t = \dfrac{\hat{\sigma}_1^2 - \hat{\sigma}_2^2}{\sqrt{[4\hat{\sigma}_1^2\hat{\sigma}_2^2/(n-2)](1 - r_{12}^2)}}$ $\nu = n - 2$	1. Random sampling or random assignment 2. Normality 3. Dependent samples
14.4	$H_0: p_1 = p_2$ $H_1: p_1 \neq p_2$ $z = \dfrac{\hat{p}_1 - \hat{p}_2}{\sqrt{\hat{p}_{\text{Pooled}}(1 - \hat{p}_{\text{Pooled}})\left(\dfrac{1}{n_1} + \dfrac{1}{n_2}\right)}}$		1. Random sampling or random assignment 2. Binomial distributions 3. Independent samples 4. $n_1\hat{p}_1$, $(1 - n_1\hat{p}_1)$, $n_2\hat{p}_2$, $(1 - n_2\hat{p}_2) > 5$ 5. Both populations are at least 10 times larger than their respective samples
14.5	$H_0: p_1 = p_2$ $H_1: p_1 \neq p_2$	$z = \dfrac{a - d}{\sqrt{a + d}}$	1. Random sampling or random assignment 2. Binomial distributions 3. Dependent samples 4. $a + d \geq 10$ for two-tailed test and ≥ 30 for one-tailed test

TABLE 14.6-2 Summary of Two-Sample Confidence Intervals

Chapter Section	Parameters	Confidence Interval	Assumptions
14.2	$\dfrac{\sigma_1^2}{\sigma_2^2}$	$\dfrac{\hat{\sigma}_1^2}{\hat{\sigma}_2^2}\dfrac{1}{F_{\alpha/2;\,\nu_1,\,\nu_2}} < \dfrac{\sigma_1^2}{\sigma_2^2} < \dfrac{\hat{\sigma}_1^2}{\hat{\sigma}_2^2}F_{\alpha/2;\,\nu_2,\,\nu_1}$ $\nu_1 = n_1 - 1, \nu_2 = n_2 - 1$	1. Random sampling or random assignment 2. Normality 3. Independent samples

(continued)

TABLE 14.6-2 (continued)

14.3	$\sigma_1^2 - \sigma_2^2$	$(\hat\sigma_1^2 - \hat\sigma_2^2) - t_{\alpha/2,\,\nu}\sqrt{\left(\dfrac{4\hat\sigma_1^2\hat\sigma_2^2}{n-2}\right)(1 - r_{12}^2)}$

$$< \sigma_1^2 - \sigma_2^2$$

$$< \left(\hat\sigma_1^2 - \hat\sigma_2^2\right) + t_{\alpha/2,\,\nu}\sqrt{\left(\dfrac{4\hat\sigma_1^2\hat\sigma_2^2}{n-2}\right)\left(1 - r_{12}^2\right)}$$

1. Random sampling random assignment
2. Normality
3. Dependent samples

14.4	$p_1 - p_2$	$(\hat p_1 - \hat p_2) - z_{\alpha/2}\sqrt{\dfrac{\hat p_1(1 - \hat p_1)}{n_1} + \dfrac{\hat p_2(1 - \hat p_2)}{n_2}}$

$$< p_1 - p_2$$

$$< (\hat p_1 - \hat p_2) + z_{\alpha/2}\sqrt{\dfrac{\hat p_1(1 - \hat p_1)}{n_1} + \dfrac{\hat p_2(1 - \hat p_2)}{n_2}}$$

1. Random sampling or random assignment
2. Binomial distributions
3. Independent samples
4. $n_1\hat p_1$, $(1 - n_1\hat p_1)$, $n_2\hat p_2$, $(1 - n_2\hat p_2) > 10$
5. Both populations are at least 10 times larger than their respective samples

---

14.5	$p_1 - p_2$	$\dfrac{a-d}{n} - z_{\alpha/2}\sqrt{\dfrac{(a+d)(b+c) + 4ad}{n^3}} < p_1 - p_2$

$$< \dfrac{a-d}{n} + z_{\alpha/2}\sqrt{\dfrac{(a+d)(b+c) + 4ad}{n^3}}$$

1. Random sampling or random assignment
2. Binomial distributions
3. Dependent samples
4. $a + d \geq 10$ for two-tailed test and ≥ 30 for one-tailed test

---

REVIEW EXERCISES FOR CHAPTER 14

1. What are the main factors a researcher should keep in mind when using an F test to determine the tenability of the assumption $\sigma_1^2 = \sigma_2^2$ prior to using a t statistic to test H_0: $\mu_1 - \mu_2 = \delta_0$?

2. A 95% confidence interval for σ_1^2/σ_2^2 is 0.6 to 2.7. Do you think that the population variances are unequal? Why?

3. An experiment was performed to compare disjunctive and simple reaction times. In the latter condition, a participant responded to a single light by pressing a button below the light; the disjunctive condition required a participant to press the right button if the right light was illuminated and the left button if the left light was illuminated. The two conditions were randomly assigned to 24 participants with the restriction that an equal number of participants participated under each condition. One participant in the simple reaction condition became ill during the experiment and had to withdraw. This reduced the sample size from 12 to 11.

Reaction Time (Hundredths of a Second)

Disjunctive			Simple		
27	34	35	24	24	24
31	32	31	27	26	22
28	30	32	23	24	25
37	30	31	25	23	

a. Construct box plots for the disjunctive and simple reaction time (RT) data and stack the plots one above the other. Do the data contain outliers? Do the sample distributions appear to be relatively symmetrical? Is it reasonable to believe that the populations are normally distributed?

b. Test the hypothesis H_0: $\sigma_1^2 = \sigma_2^2$ using the statistic $F = \hat{\sigma}_{larger}^2/\hat{\sigma}_{smaller}^2$. Let $\alpha = .05$. Assume that $F_{.05/2;\ 11,\ 10} = 3.665$. The F table in Appendix D.5 does not contain upper-tail values for $\alpha = .025$. I obtained the F two-tailed critical value, $F_{.05/2;11,\ 10} = 3.665$, using Microsoft's Excel FINV function,

$$\text{FINV(probability, deg\_freedom1, deg\_freedom2)}$$

I replaced the terms in parentheses as follows: FINV(.025,11,10).

c. Determine the p value of the F statistic using Microsoft's Excel FDIST function.

d. Compute a $100(1 - .05)\% = 95\%$ confidence interval for σ_1^2/σ_2^2. Locate the confidence interval on the real number line. Assume that $F_{.05/2;11,\ 10} = 3.665$ and $F_{.05/2;\ 10,\ 11} = 3.526$.

e. Is the confidence interval consistent with the null hypothesis significance test? Why?

f. Specify all the null hypotheses that could be rejected.

4. Use the table of random numbers in Appendix Table D.1 to draw random samples without replacement of 31 men (sample 1) and 41 women (sample 2) from the Student Database in Appendix E.

a. List the participant number, gender, and stat grade for each person in your sample. For each gender, construct a box plot and stack the plots one above the other. Do the data contain outliers? Do the sample distributions appear to be relatively symmetrical?

b. Test the hypothesis H_0: $\sigma_1^2 = \sigma_2^2$, where σ_1^2 and σ_2^2 denote, respectively, the population variances of men's and women's stat grade. Let $\alpha = .05$. Assume that $F_{.05/2;\ 30,\ 40} = 1.943$ and $F_{.05/2;\ 40,\ 30} = 2.009$.

c. Compute a $100(1 - .05)\% = 95\%$ confidence interval for σ_1^2/σ_2^2. Locate the confidence interval on the real number line.

d. Is the confidence interval consistent with the null hypothesis significance test? Why?

e. Write a paragraph summarizing your results and conclusions.

5. (a) For the data in Chapter 13, Table 13.2-1, test the tenability of the t test assumption that $\sigma_1^2 = \sigma_2^2$. Let $\alpha = .20$. (b) Explain why a researcher would use $\alpha = .20$ for this test instead of, say, $\alpha = .05$. (*Hint:* Consider how the size of α affects the power of the test.)

6. It is reasonable to expect 13-year-old boys to exceed 12-year-old boys in strength of grip. In all likelihood, the dispersion of strength of grip is greater for 13-year-olds than for 12-year-olds. To test this hypothesis, strength of grip was measured by means of a hand dynamometer for a random sample of 42 boys who had just turned 12. One year later, the same boys were remeasured. The variances for the first and second sets of measurements are 196 and 289, respectively. The correlation between the two sets of measurements is .83.
   a. Test the hypothesis H_0: $\sigma_1^2 \geq \sigma_2^2$. Let $\alpha = .05$.
   b. Determine the p value of the t statistic using Appendix Table D.3 and Microsoft's Excel TDIST function.
   c. Compute a $100(1 - .05)\% = 95\%$ confidence interval for $\sigma_1^2 - \sigma_2^2$. Locate the confidence interval on the real number line.
   d. Is the confidence interval consistent with the null hypothesis significance test? Why?
   e. Specify all the null hypotheses that could be rejected.
7. Use the table of random numbers in Appendix Table D.1 to draw random samples without replacement of 32 men and 32 women students from the student database in Appendix E. Use the variable of GPA to form 32 men-women pairs of matched participants. The GPAs of men and women in a matched pair do not have to be equal, but the GPAs should be similar.
   a. List the participant number, gender, and stat grade for each matched pair in your sample. For each gender, construct a box plot and stack the plots one above the other. Do the data contain outliers? Do the sample distributions appear to be relatively symmetrical?
   b. Test the hypothesis H_0: $\sigma_1^2 = \sigma_2^2$, where σ_1^2 and σ_2^2 denote, respectively, the population variances of men's and women's stat grade. Let $\alpha = .05$.
   c. Compute a $100(1 - .05)\% = 95\%$ confidence interval for $\sigma_1^2 - \sigma_2^2$. Locate the confidence interval on the real number line.
   d. Is the confidence interval consistent with the null hypothesis significance test? Why?
   e. Write a paragraph summarizing your results and conclusions.
   f. Compute the correlation between stat grade and GPA. Was GPA an effective matching variable? Does the correlation shed any light on why the use of the dependent samples t statistic was or was not an effective research strategy?
8. A national survey of 3,000 college and university students conducted by the American Council of Day-Care Centers found that 78% of West Coast freshmen return to college for their second year. The comparable figure for freshmen at southern schools is 85%. The percentages are based on $n_1 = 1,800$ and $n_2 = 1,200$ students, respectively.
   a. Test the hypothesis H_0: $p_1 = p_2$. Let $\alpha = .001$.
   b. Determine the p value of the z statistic using Appendix Table D.2.
   c. Compute a $100(1 - .001)\% = 99.9\%$ confidence interval for $p_1 - p_2$. Locate the confidence interval on the real number line.
   d. Is the confidence interval consistent with the null hypothesis significance test? Why?
   e. Specify all the null hypotheses that could be rejected.

9. A national survey of 1,000 unmarried women between the ages of 15 and 19 found that 46% of 19-year-olds and 26.6% of 17-year-olds had experienced sexual intercourse. The sample contained $n_1 = 200$ 19-year-olds and $n_1 = 150$ 17-year-olds.
   a. Test the hypothesis $H_0: p_1 = p_2$. Let $\alpha = .01$.
   b. Determine the p value of the z statistic using Appendix Table D.2.
   c. Compute a $100(1 - .01)\% = 99\%$ confidence interval for $p_1 - p_2$. Locate the confidence interval on the real number line.
   d. Is the confidence interval consistent with the null hypothesis significance test? Why?
   e. Specify all the null hypotheses that could be rejected.

10. A test comparing the detectability of two hues of stoplights under simulated fog conditions found that the relative frequencies of detection for red and yellow lights were $p_1 = .56$ and $p_2 = .62$, respectively. The participants were randomly assigned to view one or the other condition: 321 viewed the red light, and 315 viewed the yellow light.
    a. Test the hypothesis $H_0: p_1 = p_2$. Let $\alpha = .05$.
    b. Determine the p value of the z statistic using Appendix Table D.2.
    c. Compute a $100(1 - .01)\% = 95\%$ confidence interval for $p_1 - p_2$. Locate the confidence interval on the real number line.
    d. Is the confidence interval consistent with the null hypothesis significance test? Why?

11. Learning one task often enhances the learning of a similar task; this phenomenon is called *learning to learn*. To investigate this phenomenon, a researcher asked students to learn 20 lists of nonsense syllables. For the data in the table, test the hypothesis that p_1, the population proportion corresponding to students who learned lists 2 to 6 in less than 25 trials, and p_2, the population proportion corresponding to students who learned lists 16 to 20 in less than 25 trials, are equal. Let $\alpha = .05$. (b) What is the p value of the test statistic?

		Number of Students Who Learned Lists 16 to 20		
		In 25 Trials or More	In Fewer Than 25 Trials	
Number of Students Who Learned Lists 2 to 6	In Fewer Than 25 Trials	3	7	10
	In 25 Trials or More	13	13	26
		16	20	36

a. Compute p_1 and p_2, where the subscripts 1 and 2 denote, respectively, the students who learned lists 2 to 6 and lists 16 to 20.
b. Test the hypothesis H_0: $p_1 = p_2$. Let $\alpha = .05$.
c. Determine the p value of the z statistic using Appendix Table D.2.
d. Compute a $100(1 - .01)\% = 95\%$ confidence interval for $p_1 - p_2$. Locate the confidence interval on the real number line.
e. Is the confidence interval consistent with the null hypothesis significance test? Why?
f. Specify all the null hypotheses that could be rejected.

15

Introduction to the Analysis of Variance

15.1 Introduction
Looking Ahead: What Is This Chapter About?

15.2 Purpose of Analysis of Variance
The Omnibus Null Hypothesis
Analysis of Variance versus Doing Multiple *t* Tests
Check Your Understanding of Section 15.2

15.3 Basic Concepts in ANOVA
The Composite Nature of a Score
Model Equation for a Score
Partition of the Total Sum of Squares
Degrees of Freedom
Mean Squares and the *F* Statistic
The Nature of *MSBG* and *MSWG*
Check Your Understanding of Section 15.3

15.4 Completely Randomized Design
Computational Procedures for a CR-3 Design
Check Your Understanding of Section 15.4

15.5 Assumptions Associated with a CR-*p* Design
Assumption That the Model Equation $X_{ij} = \mu + (\mu_j - \mu) + (X_{ij} - \mu_j)$ Reflects All the Sources of Variation That Affect X_{ij}
Assumption of Random Sampling or Random Assignment
Assumption of Normally Distributed Populations
Assumption of Homogeneity of Variance
Check Your Understanding of Section 15.5

15.6 Multiple Comparison Procedures
Contrasts among Means
Fisher-Hayter Multiple Comparison Test
Scheffé's Multiple Comparison Test and Confidence Interval
Comparison of the Multiple Comparison Tests

15.7 Practical Significance
Check Your Understanding of Sections 15.6 and 15.7

15.8 Looking Back: What Have You Learned?
Review Exercises for Chapter 15

15.1 INTRODUCTION

Looking Ahead: What Is This Chapter About?

In this chapter, you will learn about one of the most frequently used statistical procedures in the behavioral sciences, health sciences, and education: the *analysis of variance*. The procedure was developed by R. A. Fisher in the early 1920s to test the null hypothesis that $p \geq 2$ population means are equal. All of the statistical procedures that you have learned up to now have involved either one or two population parameters. With analysis of variance, your statistical horizons are broadened—you can test hypotheses about any number of population means. The analysis of variance design described in this chapter, a completely randomized design, involves randomly assigning participants to two or more treatment conditions. The design has much in common with the two-sample t test for independent samples.

In this chapter you will learn about two multiple comparison statistics that are used to test hypotheses about differences among population means. You also will learn how to use a new measure of strength of association to assess the practical significance of the results of an analysis of variance.

After reading this chapter, you should know the following:

- How to use a completely randomized analysis of variance design to test the null hypothesis $H_0: \mu_1 = \mu_2 = \cdots = \mu_p$
- The distinction between pairwise and nonpairwise contrasts
- Which multiple comparison procedure to use in testing hypotheses about contrasts
- How to assess the practical significance of research results using a measure of strength of association

15.2 PURPOSE OF ANALYSIS OF VARIANCE

The Omnibus Null Hypothesis

Analysis of variance, often referred to as ANOVA (pronounced an-noh-va), is used to test null hypotheses of the form

$$H_0: \mu_1 = \mu_2 = \cdots = \mu_p$$

where $\mu_1, \mu_2, \ldots, \mu_p$ denote the means of $p \geq 2$ populations. If the null hypothesis is rejected, the alternative hypothesis is tenable. The alternative hypothesis is

$$H_1: \mu_j \neq \mu_{j'}$$

where the subscripts j and j' denote two different populations. If the null hypothesis is rejected, you know that at least two of the population means are not equal. Rejection of the null hypothesis does not mean that all of the population means are different—only two of the means may differ. If the null hypothesis is not rejected, it remains tenable. I like to think of the null hypothesis as an omnibus or overall hypothesis because it states that all of the $j = 1, \ldots, p$ population means are equal.

Analysis of Variance versus Doing Multiple *t* Tests

In Chapter 13 you learned how to use a *t* statistic to test a null hypothesis for two population means, $H_0: \mu_1 = \mu_2$. You may wonder why researchers don't test the ANOVA null hypothesis, say,

$$H_0: \mu_1 = \mu_2 = \mu_3$$

by performing three *t* tests of the following null hypotheses:

$$H_0: \mu_1 = \mu_2 \qquad H_0: \mu_1 = \mu_3 \qquad H_0: \mu_2 = \mu_3$$

If $\mu_1 = \mu_2$, $\mu_1 = \mu_3$, and $\mu_2 = \mu_3$, then it must be true that $\mu_1 = \mu_2 = \mu_3$. Although this research strategy seems reasonable, it has a serious flaw. If the researcher uses a *t* statistic to test each of the three null hypotheses at $\alpha = .05$ level of significance, the probability of making one or more Type I errors is close to .14. This probability is computed as follows:

$$\text{Prob. of one or more Type I errors} < [1 - (1 - \alpha)^C] = [1 - (1 - .05)^3] = .14$$

where $C = 3$ is the number of *t* tests. A probability of making one or more Type I errors that is close to .14 is unacceptable. In most research situations, you want the probability to not exceed $\alpha = .05$. Notice from the formula $1 - (1 - \alpha)^C$ that as the number of *t* tests, C, increases, the probability of making Type I errors also increases. Suppose your null hypothesis involves four means:

$$H_0: \mu_1 = \mu_2 = \mu_3 = \mu_4$$

You could use a *t* statistic to perform six *t* tests each at $\alpha = .05$ level of significance:

$$H_0: \mu_1 = \mu_2, \ H_0: \mu_1 = \mu_3, \ H_0: \mu_1 = \mu_4, \ H_0: \mu_2 = \mu_3, \ H_0: \mu_2 = \mu_4, \ H_0: \mu_3 = \mu_4$$

In this case, the probability of making one or more type one errors would be close to .26. The probability is given by

$$\text{Prob. of one or more Type I errors} < [1 - (1 - \alpha)^C] = [1 - (1 - .05)^6] = .26$$

Although you test each null hypothesis at $\alpha = .05$ level of significance, the probability of making a Type I error increases dramatically as the number, C, of hypotheses that are tested increases. The advantage of using analysis of variance to test the omnibus null hypothesis, $H_0: \mu_1 = \mu_2 = \cdots = \mu_p$, is that whatever the number of population means, the probability of making a Type I error is equal to α. For the special case in which an experiment contains only two experimental conditions and the null hypothesis is $H_0: \mu_1 = \mu_2$, the ANOVA and *t* approaches have the same probability of making a Type I error. The probability is the same because only one *t* test is performed.

CHECK YOUR UNDERSTANDING OF SECTION 15.2

1. Suppose that five methods of teaching foreign language vocabulary are compared in an experiment. The dependent variable is performance on a 25-item vocabulary test. (a) State the null hypothesis. (b) How many *t* tests would be required to test hypotheses of the form $H_0: \mu_j = \mu_{j'}$? (c) If $\alpha = .01$,

what is the probability of making one or more Type I errors using ANOVA? What is the probability when multiple t tests are performed? (d) If the omnibus null hypothesis is rejected by means of an ANOVA F test, what does this tell the researcher?

2. For experiments in which the number of experimental conditions is greater than two, what advantage does the ANOVA approach have over the multiple t approach?

15.3 BASIC CONCEPTS IN ANOVA

The material in this section provides a glimpse of some of the basic concepts associated with a completely randomized ANOVA, the simplest of all the ANOVA designs. The rationale underlying ANOVA is somewhat involved. The computations are straightforward but tedious. Fortunately, software packages are available that will do the computations for you. You may find it helpful to review this section after working through one of the ANOVA problems in Section 15.4.

The Composite Nature of a Score

The value of a score in an experiment is determined by a variety of variables. I will now examine this idea in some detail. A score can be thought of as a composite, reflecting, for example, the effects of the (1) independent variable, (2) individual characteristics of the participant or experimental unit, (3) chance fluctuations in the participant's performance, and (4) environmental and other uncontrolled variables. Similarly, the variability among the scores in an experiment also is a composite that reflects the effects of the same variables.

> **ANOVA** is a procedure for determining how much of the total variability among scores to attribute to various sources of variation and for testing hypotheses concerning some of the sources.

I will illustrate the composite nature of a score with an example. Consider an experiment to determine the effectiveness of three diets for obese teenage girls. Thirty girls who want to lose weight are randomly assigned to the three diets with the restriction that 10 girls are assigned to each diet. The independent variable is type of diet; the dependent variable is weight loss in pounds after being on a diet for one month.

> For notational convenience, the diets are called **treatment A.** The levels of treatment A, corresponding to the specific diets, are denoted by the lowercase letter a and numeric subscripts—a_1, a_2, and a_3. A particular but unspecified score is denoted by X_{ij}, where the first subscript designates one of the $i = 1, \ldots, n$ participants in a treatment level and the second subscript designates one of the $j = 1, \ldots, p$ levels of treatment A.

Let X_{72} denote Bella's weight-loss score in the diet experiment. The subscripts of X_{72} tell you that she is participant seven and that she used diet a_2. What factors have affected the value of her score? If she stuck to her diet, one major factor is the effectiveness of diet a_2. Other factors are her degree of obesity, day-to-day fluctuations in her eating and exercise habits, time of day that her weight loss was measured, and so on. In summary, Bella's weight loss score, X_{72}, reflects (1) the effect of treatment level a_2, (2) effects unique to her, (3) effects attributable to chance fluctuations in her behavior, and (4) effects attributable to environmental and other uncontrolled variables.

I can formulate a model equation that reflects the various factors that affect Bella's score. In the following section, I will present the results of the weight-loss experiment and illustrate the model equation that underlies Bella's score.

Model Equation for a Score

Suppose that the data in Table 15.3-1 have been obtained in the diet experiment. Notice that two subscripts are used to denote each score, X_{ij}, in the table. The first subscript denotes one of the $i = 1, \ldots, n$ participants in a treatment level. The second subscript denotes one of the $j = 1, \ldots, p$ levels of treatment A. The treatment means, $\overline{X}_{.1}, \overline{X}_{.2}, \overline{X}_{.3}$, and the grand mean, $\overline{X}_{..}$, in Table 15.3-1 also have two

Table 15.3-1 One-Month Weight Losses Measured to the Nearest Pound

(i) Data and notation (X_{ij} denotes a score for participant i in treatment level j; i = 1, . . . , n participants; j = 1, . . . , p levels of treatment A)

Treatment Levels (Diets)

	a_1	a_2	a_3
	7	10	12
	9	13	11
	8	9	15
	12	11	7
	8	5	14
	7	9	10
	4	8	12
	10	10	12
	9	8	13
	6	7	14

Sum of $i = 1, \ldots, n$ scores in each treatment level $\longrightarrow$ $\quad \sum_{i=1}^{n} X_{i1} = 80 \qquad \sum_{i=1}^{n} X_{i2} = 90 \qquad \sum_{i=1}^{n} X_{i3} = 120$

$$\text{Sum of all scores} \longmapsto \sum_{j=1}^{p} \sum_{i=1}^{n} X_{ij} = 290$$

Mean of each treatment level $\longrightarrow$ $\quad \overline{X}_{.1} = 8 \qquad \overline{X}_{.2} = 9 \qquad \overline{X}_{.3} = 12$

$$\text{Grand mean} \longmapsto \overline{X}_{..} = 9.67$$

subscripts. The dot in the subscript of $\overline{X}_{.1}$ indicates that the mean was obtained by averaging over the $i = 1, \ldots, n$ scores, X_{i1}. For example, the three treatment means are obtained as follows:

$$\overline{X}_{.1} = \frac{\sum\limits_{i=1}^{n} X_{i1}}{n} = \frac{X_{11} + X_{21} + X_{31} + \cdots + X_{10,1}}{n} = \frac{7 + 9 + \cdots + 6}{10} = \frac{80}{10} = 8$$

$$\overline{X}_{.2} = \frac{\sum\limits_{i=1}^{n} X_{i2}}{n} = \frac{X_{12} + X_{22} + X_{32} + \cdots + X_{10,2}}{n} = \frac{10 + 13 + \cdots + 7}{10} = \frac{90}{10} = 9$$

$$\overline{X}_{.3} = \frac{\sum\limits_{i=1}^{n} X_{i3}}{n} = \frac{X_{13} + X_{23} + X_{33} + \cdots + X_{10,3}}{n} = \frac{12 + 11 + \cdots + 14}{10} = \frac{120}{10} = 12$$

Notice that in computing each treatment mean, I averaged over the first subscript, i. That is the subscript that I replaced with a dot. The grand mean is obtained by averaging all the np scores:

$$\overline{X}_{..} = \frac{\sum\limits_{j=1}^{p}\sum\limits_{i=1}^{n} X_{ij}}{np} = \frac{X_{11} + X_{21} + X_{31} + \cdots + X_{10,3}}{np} = \frac{7 + 9 + \cdots + 14}{(10)(3)} = 9.67$$

The grand mean subscript has two dots because I averaged over both i and j.

Earlier I mentioned that each score is a composite. I will use the data in Table 15.3-1 to show that each score is composed of the following:

Grand mean = The mean of all of the np scores, $\overline{X}_{..}$

Treatment effect = The effect of the independent variable, $\overline{X}_{.j} - \overline{X}_{..}$—for example, the effect of diet a_2 on Bella's weight loss.

Error effect = The effects unique to participant i who received treatment level a_j and any other uncontrolled variables that affected the score, $X_{ij} - \overline{X}_{.j}$. For example, Bella's error effect includes her degree of obesity, day-to-day fluctuations in her eating and exercise habits, and the time of day that her weight loss was measured.

The **sample model equation** for a score can be written as

$$X_{ij} \quad = \quad \overline{X}_{..} \; + \; (\overline{X}_{.j} - \overline{X}_{..}) \; + \; (X_{ij} - \overline{X}_{.j})$$

| Score | Grand Mean | Treatment Effect | Error Effect |

The statistics in the sample model equation are unbiased estimators of three model parameters: population grand mean, μ; population treatment effect, $\mu_j - \mu$; and population error effect, $X_{ij} - \mu_j$:

$$X_{ij} = \overline{X}_{..} + (\overline{X}_{.j} - \overline{X}_{..}) + (X_{ij} - \overline{X}_{.j})$$

Model equation $\quad X_{ij} = \mu \quad + \quad (\mu_j - \mu) \quad + \quad (X_{ij} - \mu_j)$

Perhaps an example using Bella's score, X_{72}, will clarify the meaning of the terms in the sample model equation. According to Table 15.3-1, Bella lost 8 pounds ($X_{72} = 8$), which is 1.67 pounds less than the average weight loss for the 30 girls ($\overline{X}.. = 9.67$). Her weight loss can be expressed as follows:

$$X_{72} = \overline{X}.. + (\overline{X}_{.2} - \overline{X}..) + (X_{72} - \overline{X}_{.2})$$

$$8 = 9.67 + (9 - 9.67) + (8 - 9)$$

$$8 = 9.67 + (-0.67) + (-1)$$

| Bella's Score | Grand Mean | a_2 Treatment Effect | Bella's Error Effect |

This model equation gives us a bit more insight into why Bella's weight loss, $X_{72} = 8$ pounds, was 1.67 pounds less than the average weight loss. She used a less effective diet, $\overline{X}_{.2} - \overline{X}.. = 9 - 9.67 = -0.67$ pound, and, in addition, the diet was not as effective for her as it was for the average of the 10 girls who used it, $X_{72} - \overline{X}_{.2} = 8 - 9 = -1$ pound.

To summarize, the sample data allow you to compute three statistics that account for Bella's weight loss: (1) the average weight loss of all the girls, given by $\overline{X}.. = 9.67$ pounds, (2) the effect of diet a_2, given by $\overline{X}_{.2} - \overline{X}.. = -0.67$, and (3) the error effect that is unique to Bella and the testing conditions, given by $X_{72} - \overline{X}_{.2} = -1$.

The name *error effect* is an apt one because an error effect represents all of the effects not attributable to the grand mean and the treatment effect. In other words, Bella's error effect, $X_{72} - \overline{X}_{.2} = -1$, reflects characteristics that are peculiar to her, such as her degree of obesity and day-to-day fluctuations in her eating and exercise habits. Her error effect also reflects characteristics that are peculiar to the testing conditions, such as the time of day that Bella's weight loss was measured.

Partition of the Total Sum of Squares

Earlier, you saw that a score, X_{ij}, is a composite. The total variability among scores in the diet experiment,

$$SSTO = \sum_{j=1}^{p} \sum_{i=1}^{n} (X_{ij} - \overline{X}..)^2$$

called the **total sum of squares (SSTO),** also is a composite. It can be shown (see "Check Your Understanding of Section 15.3," Exercise 5) that the total sum of squares can be partitioned into two parts: variability between the treatment levels, called the **between-groups sum of squares (SSBG),**

$$SSBG = n \sum_{j=1}^{p} (\overline{X}_{.j} - \overline{X}..)^2$$

and variability within the treatment levels, called the **within-groups sum of squares (SSWG),**

$$SSWG = \sum_{j=1}^{p} \sum_{i=1}^{n} (X_{ij} - \overline{X}_{.j})^2$$

That is,

$$SSTO \qquad = \qquad SSBG \qquad + \qquad SSWG$$

$$\sum_{j=1}^{p}\sum_{i=1}^{n}(X_{ij}-\overline{X}..)^2 = n\sum_{j=1}^{p}(\overline{X}._j-\overline{X}..)^2 + \sum_{j=1}^{p}\sum_{i=1}^{n}(X_{ij}-\overline{X}._j)^2$$

Notice that $SSBG$ is computed from the treatment effects, $\overline{X}._j-\overline{X}..$, in an experiment. $SSWG$ is computed from the error effects, $X_{ij}-\overline{X}._j$, in an experiment.

Now I need to show what $SSBG$ and $SSWG$ have to do with testing the hypothesis that $H_0: \mu_1 = \mu_2 = \cdots = \mu_p$. But before I can do this, I must discuss the degrees of freedom associated with each of the sums of squares.

Degrees of Freedom

The term *degrees of freedom* refers to the number of observations whose values can be assigned arbitrarily, as you saw in Section 10.2. I now will determine the degrees of freedom associated with $SSBG$, $SSWG$, and $SSTO$. Consider $SSBG = n\sum_{j=1}^{p}(\overline{X}._j-\overline{X}..)^2$ and let n be the same for each of the sample means. If I have, say, $p = 3$ sample means, they are related to the grand mean by the equation

$$\frac{\overline{X}._1 + \overline{X}._2 + \overline{X}._3}{3} = \overline{X}..$$

If $\overline{X}.. = 6$ and I arbitrarily specify that $\overline{X}._1 = 6$ and $\overline{X}._2 = 8$, then $\overline{X}._3$ must equal 4, because $(6 + 8 + 4)/3 = 6$. Alternatively, if I specify that $\overline{X}._1 = 5$ and $\overline{X}._2 = 7$, then $\overline{X}._3$ must equal 6, because $(5 + 7 + 6)/3 = 6$. Given the value of the grand mean, I am free to assign any values to two of the three treatment means, but having done so, the third mean is determined.

Hence, the number of degrees of freedom associated with $SSBG$ is $p - 1$, one less than the number of treatment means.

The number of degrees of freedom associated with $SSWG$ is $p(n - 1)$.

To see why this is true, consider $SSWG = \sum_{j=1}^{p}\sum_{i=1}^{p}(X_{ij}-\overline{X}._j)^2$ and let $p = 3$ and $n = 8$. The eight scores in the jth treatment level, are related to the jth mean by

$$\frac{X_{1j} + X_{2j} + \cdots + X_{8j}}{8} = \overline{X}._j$$

Seven of the scores can take any value, but the eighth is determined because the sum of the scores divided by eight must equal $\overline{X}._j$. Hence, there are $n - 1 = 8 - 1 = 7$ degrees of freedom associated with the jth treatment level, and this is true for each of the $j = 3$ treatment levels. Thus, there are $p(n - 1) = 3(8 - 1) = 21$ degrees of freedom associated with $SSWG$. If the n_j's are not equal, the degrees of freedom for

$SSWG$ are $(n_1 - 1) + (n_2 - 1) + \cdots + (n_p - 1) = N - p$, where N is the total number of scores, $N = n_1 + n_2 + \cdots + n_p$.

The same line of reasoning can be used to show that when $n_1 = n_2 = \cdots = n_p$, the total sum of squares has $np - 1$ degrees of freedom. If the n_j's are not equal, the number of degrees of freedom is $(n_1 + n_2 + \cdots + n_p) - 1 = N - 1$.

This follows, because the $np = 8(3) = 24$ scores are related to the grand mean by

$$\frac{X_{11} + X_{21} + \cdots + X_{83}}{24} = \overline{X}_{..}$$

Hence, $np - 1 = 23$ of the scores can take any value, but the 24th score must be assigned so that the mean of the scores equals $\overline{X}_{...}$.

Mean Squares and the *F* Statistic

The term *mean square* (*MS*) is new, but the concept is not; mean square is simply another name for a sample variance, $\hat{\sigma}^2$.

A **mean square** (**MS**) is obtained by dividing a sum of squares (*SS*) by its degrees of freedom (*df*). Thus,

$$MSTO = SSTO/(np - 1) \text{ or } SSTO/(N - 1)$$

$$MSBG = SSBG/(p - 1)$$

$$MSWG = SSWG/[p(n - 1)] \text{ or } SSWG/(N - p)$$

I introduced the F statistic and F sampling distribution in Section 14.2. You learned that the F statistic, which is the ratio of two sample variances ($F = \hat{\sigma}^2_{\text{larger}}/\hat{\sigma}^2_{\text{smaller}}$), can be used to test the null hypothesis that two population variances are equal. As you have just seen, *MSBG* and *MSWG* also are sample variances. Hence, $F = MS_{BG}/MS_{WG}$ is an F statistic.

The null hypothesis $H_0: \mu_1 = \mu_2 = \cdots = \mu_p$ in analysis of variance is tested by means of an F statistic that is the ratio of the between-groups variance to the within-groups variance:

$$F = \frac{MSBG}{MSWG}$$

The degrees of freedom for the numerator and denominator of the F statistic are, respectively, $v_1 = p - 1$ and $v_2 = p(n - 1)$.

The F statistic is referred to the sampling distribution of F, which is tabled in Appendix Table D.5. If the F statistic is greater than or equal to the critical value, $F_{\alpha; v_1, v_2}$, the null hypothesis is rejected.

The Nature of *MSBG* and *MSWG*

It may seem paradoxical to test a hypothesis about population means by using the ratio of two sample variances, $F = MSBG/MSWG$. To show that this procedure is reasonable, I will describe the nature of the population variances estimated by *MSWG* and *MSBG* when the null hypothesis is true and when it is false.

You learned in Section 8.3 that $E(\overline{X}) = \mu$. In words this says that if you draw many, many random samples from a population and compute a mean for each sample, the long-run average of the sample means is equal to the population mean, μ. I call μ the expected value of $\overline{X}$, that is $E(\overline{X}) = \mu$. It can be shown for a completely randomized analysis of variance design that if the p population means are equal, the expected value of both *MSBG* and *MSWG* is σ_ε^2—that is,

$$E(MSBG) = E(MSWG) = \sigma_\varepsilon^2$$

where σ_ε^2 is the **population error variance.** When the p population means are equal, the F statistic is the ratio of two independent, sample error variances,

$$F = \frac{MSBG}{MSWG} = \frac{\hat{\sigma}_\varepsilon^2}{\hat{\sigma}_\varepsilon^2}$$

The F statistic should be close to 1 because both sample mean squares estimate the same population error variance. An F statistic close to 1 provides support for the null hypothesis that all of the population means are equal. When two or more of the population means are not equal, the expected values of *MSWG* and *MSBG* differ:

$$E(MSWG) = \sigma_\varepsilon^2$$

but

$$E(MSBG) = \sigma_\varepsilon^2 + n\sum(\mu_j - \mu)^2/(p-1)$$

Notice that the expected value of *MSBG* includes a function of population treatment effects, $\mu_j - \mu$. Hence, when two or more of population means are unequal, the F statistic,

$$F = \frac{MSBG}{MSWG} = \frac{\hat{\sigma}_\varepsilon^2 + \text{a function of the treatment effects}}{\hat{\sigma}_\varepsilon^2}$$

should be larger than 1 because *MSBG* estimates σ_ε^2 plus treatment effects but *MSWG* estimates only σ_ε^2. F statistics larger than 1 provide evidence against the null hypothesis and support for believing that the treatment effects are not all equal to zero.

How much larger than one should $F = MSBG/MSWG$ be for a researcher to feel confident in rejecting the null hypothesis $H_0\colon \mu_1 = \mu_2 = \cdots = \mu_p$? The usual practice is to reject the null hypothesis if F falls in the upper $\alpha = .05$ region of the sampling distribution of F.

Before concluding this section, let me reexamine the nature of *MSWG* and *MSBG* from a different perspective. It would be nice if you came away from this discussion with an intuitive feel for the sources of variation that are being measured by the two mean squares. An examination of the *MSWG* formula $\sum_{j=1}^{p}\sum_{i=1}^{n}(X_{ij} - \overline{X}_{\cdot j})^2/$

$[p(n-1)]$ and Figure 15.3-1 suggests that *MSWG* estimates the variation among participants who have been treated alike. This follows because the deviations of the scores in each treatment level are taken from their respective treatment means. All of the girls in, say, a_1 used the same diet. Hence, they were treated alike. On the other hand, *MSBG* estimates the variation among girls who were treated differently—that is, assigned to different treatment levels. This follows because the deviations of the treatment means in the formula $n\sum_{j=1}^{p}(\overline{X}_{\cdot j}-\overline{X}..)^2/(p-1)$ are taken from the grand mean. If, in Figure 15.3-1, the three treatment conditions really had no effect on the dependent variable, the variation among the treatment means reflects nothing more than chance variation and should be about the same size as the variation among the scores within each treatment condition. In this case, the *F* statistic should be close to 1. If,

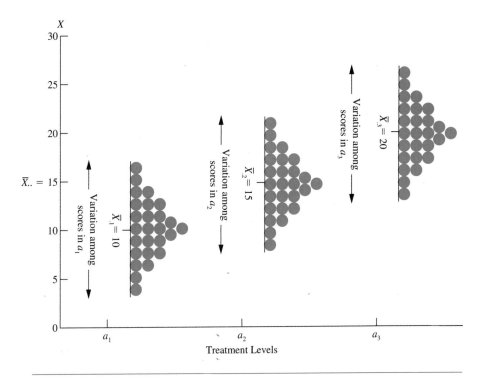

Figure 15.3-1. As shown in the figure, there is variation among the scores, denoted by ● and among the three sample means. The within-groups mean square, $MSWG = \sum\sum(X_{ij}-\overline{X}_{\cdot j})^2/[p(n-1)]$, reflects only the variation among the scores of participants who have been treated the same. For example, all participants in a_1 receive the same treatment condition. The between-groups mean square, $MSBG = n\sum(\overline{X}_{\cdot j}-\overline{X}..)^2/(p-1)$, reflects the variation among the means of participants who have been treated differently. If the three treatment conditions have no effect on the dependent variable, the amount of variation among the three means should be about the same as the variation of participants who have been treated the same. In this case, $F = MSBG/MSWG$ should be close to 1. If, however, one or more of the treatment conditions affects the dependent variable, $F = MSBG/MSWG$ should be greater than 1.

however, the treatment conditions do affect the dependent variable, the variation among the treatment means should be larger than the variation among the scores within each treatment condition. In this case, the F statistic should be larger than 1. The labels "within groups" and "between groups" are appropriate because they describe the deviations that are used to compute the two means squares.

CHECK YOUR UNDERSTANDING OF SECTION 15.3

3. Suppose that an experiment has been performed over a period of six months to evaluate the effectiveness of three exercise programs denoted by a_1, a_2, and a_3 for developing muscle mass. Sixty 21-year-old men have been randomly assigned to the three programs with 20 in each program. Let X_{42} denote the change in muscle mass of participant 4 who was assigned to exercise program a_2. What specific factors do you think affected the value of his score?

4. Identify the following.
   a. a_2
   b. X_{24}
   c. $X_{16,1}$
   d. $\overline{X}_{.4}$
   e. $\overline{X}_{..}$
   f. $X_{73} = \overline{X}_{..} + (\overline{X}_{.3} - \overline{X}_{..}) + (X_{73} - \overline{X}_{.3})$
   g. $\overline{X}_{.2} - \overline{X}_{..}$
   h. $X_{13} - \overline{X}_{..} - \overline{X}_{.3}$

5. The total sum of squares, $\sum_{j=1}^{p}\sum_{i=1}^{n}(X_{ij} - \overline{X}_{..})^2$, can be partitioned into sum of squares between groups, $n\sum_{j=1}^{p}(\overline{X}_{.j} - \overline{X}_{..})^2$, and sum of squares within groups, $\sum_{j=1}^{p}\sum_{i=1}^{n}(X_{ij} - \overline{X}_{.j})^2$. For equations that are preceded by (a) through (f), describe in words the operation that was performed. I begin the derivation with the sample model equation for the completely randomized design.

$$X_{ij} = \overline{X}_{..} + (\overline{X}_{.j} - \overline{X}_{..}) + (X_{ij} - \overline{X}_{.j})$$

a.
$$X_{ij} - \overline{X}_{..} = \overline{X}_{..} + (\overline{X}_{.j} - \overline{X}_{..}) + (X_{ij} - \overline{X}_{.j}) - \overline{X}_{..}$$
$$= (\overline{X}_{.j} - \overline{X}_{..}) + (X_{ij} - \overline{X}_{.j})$$

b.
$$(X_{ij} - \overline{X}_{..})^2 = [(\overline{X}_{.j} - \overline{X}_{..}) + (X_{ij} - \overline{X}_{.j})]^2$$

c.
$$\sum_{j=1}^{p}\sum_{i=1}^{n}(X_{ij} - \overline{X}_{..})^2 = \sum_{j=1}^{p}\sum_{i=1}^{n}[(\overline{X}_{.j} - \overline{X}_{..}) + (X_{ij} - \overline{X}_{.j})]^2$$

d.
$$= \sum_{j=1}^{p}\sum_{i=1}^{n}[(\overline{X}_{.j} - \overline{X}_{..})^2 + 2(\overline{X}_{.j} - \overline{X}_{..})$$
$$\times (X_{ij} - \overline{X}_{.j}) + (X_{ij} - \overline{X}_{.j})^2]$$

e.
$$= n\sum_{j=1}^{p}(\overline{X}_{.j} - \overline{X}_{..})^2 + 2\sum_{j=1}^{p}(\overline{X}_{.j} - \overline{X}_{..})\sum_{i=1}^{n}(X_{ij} - \overline{X}_{.j})$$
$$+ \sum_{j=1}^{p}\sum_{i=1}^{n}(X_{ij} - \overline{X}_{.j})^2$$

f.
$$\sum_{j=1}^{p}\sum_{i=1}^{n}(X_{ij} - \overline{X}_{..})^2 = n\sum_{j=1}^{p}(\overline{X}_{.j} - \overline{X}_{..})^2 + \sum_{j=1}^{p}\sum_{i=1}^{n}(X_{ij} - \overline{X}_{.j})^2$$

$$\text{SSTO} \quad = \quad \text{SSBG} \quad + \quad \text{SSWG}$$

6. For the following alternative hypotheses in ANOVA, indicate whether the hypothesis is correctly or incorrectly stated.
   a. $\mu_j - \mu_{j'} \neq 0$ for some j and j'
   b. $\mu_1 \neq \mu_2 \neq \mu_3$
7. Express the following scores in terms of the ANOVA model equation: (a) X_{83}, (b) X_{52}, (c) X_{24}.
8. Calculate the degrees of freedom for *MSTO*, *MSBG,* and *MSWG* for the following conditions.
   a. $p = 4, n = 21$
   b. $p = 5, n = 11$
   c. $p = 4, n = 8$
   d. $p = 3, n_1 = 6, n_2 = 5, n_3 = 6$
   e. $p = 4, n_1 = 10, n_2 = 10, n_3 = 9, n_4 = 8.$
9. a. Under what conditions do both *MSBG* and *MSWG* estimate only the population error variance, σ_ε^2?
   b. Under what condition would you expect *MSBG* to be bigger than *MSWG*?
10. Terms to remember:

a. ANOVA	b. Treatment *A*
c. Grand mean	d. Treatment effect
e. Error effect	f. Model equation
g. Total sum of squares	h. Between-groups sum of squares
i. Within-groups sum of squares	j. Mean square
k. Population error variance	

15.4 COMPLETELY RANDOMIZED DESIGN

This section presents the computational procedures associated with the simplest of all ANOVA designs—the completely randomized design. Here you will see how nicely some of the complex ideas presented previously fit together to produce a decision about the null hypothesis. In fact, after pondering over the three tables in this section, you will see that the computational procedures for ANOVA are tedious but not difficult to carry out. Fortunately, computer packages are available for doing the number crunching.

The completely randomized design is appropriate for experiments with one treatment (independent variable) with $p \geq 2$ treatment levels. The $N = n_1 + n_2 + \cdots + n_p$ participants in an experiment should be randomly assigned to the p treatment levels. As you will see, it is desirable but not necessary to assign the same number of participants to each treatment level.

The **completely randomized design** is so named because the assignment of participants to the treatment levels is completely random. Each participant is assigned to only one level. For convenience the design is referred to as a **CR-*p* design,** where p denotes the number of levels of treatment *A*.

A CR-*p* design with more than two treatment levels can be thought of as an extension of a *t* test for independent samples. For both designs, *N* participants are randomly assigned to the treatment conditions. A comparison of the layouts for a *t* test

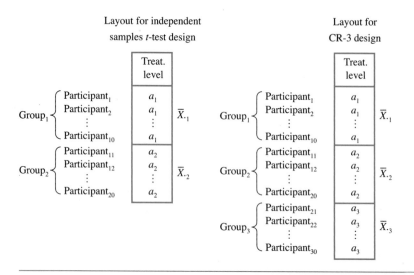

Figure 15.4-1. Comparison of layouts for a *t*-test design for independent samples shown on the left and a completely randomized ANOVA design on the right. For the *t*-test design, 20 participants were randomly assigned to the two levels of treatment *A;* for the CR-3 design, 30 participants were randomly assigned to the three levels of treatment *A*.

and a CR-3 design is shown in Figure 15.4-1. When a CR-*p* design has two treatment levels, the layouts are identical. For this case, it can be shown that the value of the *t* statistic is equal to $\sqrt{F}$ for the CR-*p* design.

Computational Procedures for a CR-3 Design

I will use the data from the diet experiment to illustrate the computational procedures associated with a completely randomized design. You will recall that 30 girls were randomly assigned to three diets, with the restriction that 10 girls were assigned each diet. The amount of weight loss for each girl was measured one month after going on a diet. The steps to follow in testing the null hypothesis and the decision rule are as follows.

Step 1.   State the statistical hypotheses: $H_0: \mu_1 = \mu_2 = \mu_3$
$H_1: \mu_j \neq \mu_{j'}$ for some j and j'.

Step 2.   Specify the test statistic: $F = MSBG/MSWG$ because the researcher wants to test $H_0: \mu_1 = \mu_2 = \mu_3$, random assignment was used, and the researcher assumes that the three populations are approximately normally distributed with equal variances.

Step 3.   Specify the sample size:[1] $np = 30$;
and the sampling distribution: F distribution with $v_1 = p - 1$ and $v_2 = p(n - 1)$.

Step 4.   Specify the significance level: $\alpha = .05$.

Step 5.   Obtain a random sample of np participants or randomly assign np participants to p treatment levels, compute F, and make a decision.

Decision rule:

Reject the null hypothesis if F falls in the upper 5% of the sampling distribution of F; otherwise, do not reject the null hypothesis. If the null hypothesis is rejected, conclude that the weight loss population means for the three diets are not equal; if the null hypothesis is not rejected, do not draw this conclusion.

Before testing the null hypothesis, it is good statistical practice to first compute descriptive statistics for one's data. The stacked box plots in Figure 15.4-2 indicate that the weight-loss data do not contain outliers and are relatively symmetrical. The symmetry of the sample distributions suggests that the populations also are probably symmetrical. This is useful information because, as you will see in Section 15.5, the ANOVA F test is robust to non-normality if the populations are relatively symmetrical. The sample means and standard deviations for the weight-loss data are shown in Table 15.4-1. These descriptive statistics should be included in reports of the results

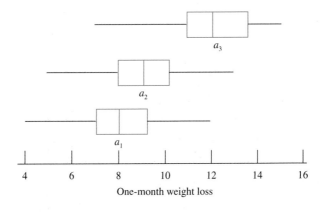

Figure 15.4-2. Stacked box plots for the weight-loss data in Table 15.2-1. The sample distributions are relatively symmetrical and have about the same amount of dispersion. There are no outliers.

---

[1] A discussion of procedures for making a rational specification of sample size for a completely randomized design is beyond the scope of this book. The interested reader should consult Cohen (1988, chap. 8) and Kirk (1995, pp. 182–188).

Table 15.4-1   Descriptive Statistics for Weight-Loss Data

	Diet		
	a_1	a_2	a_3
$\overline{X}_{\cdot j}$	8.00	9.00	12.00
$\hat{\sigma}_j$	2.21	2.21	2.31

of your experiment. It appears that there are sizable differences among several of the weight-loss sample means. For example, diet a_3 resulted in a much greater weight loss than the other two diets. If the differences are statistically significance—that is, cannot be attributed to chance—they would be practically significant. If the three sample means had been 8.00, 8.16, and 8.25, there would be little point in testing the null hypothesis because a weight-loss difference of only 0.25 pounds after one month of dieting is of no practical value. I also note from Table 15.4-1 that the three sample standard deviations are similar. The researcher can conclude that the population variances are probably homogeneous. Homogeneity of population variances is one of the assumptions of ANOVA discussed in Section 15.5. After examining Figure 15.4-1 and Table 15.4-1, a researcher would probably feel comfortable proceeding to test the ANOVA null hypothesis.

Table 15.4-2 presents the details of the computational procedures. In Section 15.3, I introduced formulas for computing *SSTO, SSBG,* and *SSWG.* These formulas are useful for understanding the nature of the three sums of squares, but they are not the most convenient for computational purposes. More convenient formulas are illustrated in Table 15.4-2.

The results of the analysis are summarized in the ANOVA table shown in Table 15.4-3. The sums of squares (*SS*) in Table 15.4-3 were obtained from Table 15.4-2. The mean squares (*MS*) were obtained by dividing the sums of squares by their respective degrees of freedom. The *F* statistic was obtained by dividing *MSBG* in row 1 by *MSWG* in row 2; this operation is indicated in the table by the symbol $[\frac{1}{2}]$.

Appendix Table D.5 does not contain *F* critical values for $\nu_1 = 2$ and $\nu_2 = 27$ degrees of freedom. I obtained $F_{.05;\,2,\,27} = 3.35$ using Microsoft's Excel FINV function,

$$\text{FINV(probability,deg\_freedom1,deg\_freedom2)}$$

I replaced the terms in parentheses as follows: FINV(.05,2,27). Because the computed $F(2,\,27) = 8.60$ is greater than $F_{.05;\,2,\,27} = 3.35$, the null hypothesis is rejected and the researcher concludes that at least two of the diets are not equally effective.

The results of the *F* test can be presented either by means of a table as in Table 15.4-3 or as a statement in the text portion of a publication. Using the latter method of presentation, the researcher might say, "I conclude from the analysis of variance that the weight-loss population means for the three diets are not all equal, $F(2,\,27) = 8.60$, $p < .002$."[2] When the results are presented in the text, it is

---

[2] I obtained the *p* value using Microsoft's Excel FDIST function,

$$\text{FDIST(x,deg\_freedom1,deg\_freedom2)}$$

I replaced the terms in parentheses with the value of the *F* statistic and degrees of freedom as follows: FDIST(8.60,2,27). The *p* value, .001299, was rounded up to .002.

Table 15.4-2 Computational Procedures for a CR-3 Design

(i) Data and notation [X_{ij} denotes a score for participant i in treatment level j; i = 1, . . . , n participants (s_i); j = 1, . . . , p treatment levels (a_j)]

AS Summary Table[a]

	a_1	a_2	a_3
	7	10	12
	9	13	11
	8	9	15
	12	11	7
	8	5	14
	7	9	10
	4	8	12
	10	10	12
	9	8	13
	6	7	14
$\sum_{i=1}^{n} X_{ij} = 80$		90	120
$\overline{X}_{.j} = 8$		9	12

(ii) Computational symbols[b]

$$\sum_{j=1}^{p} \sum_{i=1}^{n} X_{ij} = 7 + 9 + 8 + \cdots + 14 = 290.000$$

$$\sum_{j=1}^{p} \sum_{i=1}^{n} X_{ij}^2 = [AS] = (7)^2 + (9)^2 + (8)^2 + \cdots + (14)^2 = 3026.000$$

$$\frac{\left(\sum_{j=1}^{p} \sum_{i=1}^{n} X_{ij}\right)^2}{np} = [X] = \frac{(290)^2}{(3)(10)} = 2803.333$$

$$\sum_{j=1}^{p} \frac{\left(\sum_{i=1}^{n} X_{ij}\right)^2}{n} = [A] = \frac{(80)^2}{10} + \cdots + \frac{(120)^2}{10} = 2890.000$$

(iii) Computational formulas

$$SSTO = [AS] - [X] = 3026.000 - 2803.333 = 222.667$$

$$SSBG = [A] - [X] = 2890.000 - 2803.333 = 86.667$$

$$SSWG = [AS] - [A] = 3026.000 - 2890.000 = 136.000$$

[a] *A* denotes treatment *A*, and *S* denotes subjects; the table is so named because it reflects variation attributable to treatment levels (*A*) and subjects (*S*).
[b] The symbols [*AS*], [*X*], and [*A*] are used to simplify the computational formulas in part (iii).

Table 15.4-3   ANOVA Table for a CR-3 Design

Source	SS	df	MS	F
1. Between groups (*BG*) (three diets)	86.667	$p - 1 = 3 - 1 = 2$	43.334	$[\frac{1}{2}]\,8.60^*$
2. Within groups (*WG*)	136.000	$p\,(n - 1) = 3\,(10 - 1) = 27$	5.037	
3. Total	222.667	$n\,p - 1 = (3)(10) - 1 = 29$		

$[\frac{1}{2}]$ indicates that F was obtained by dividing the value of the *MS* in row 1 by the value of the *MS* in row 2.
$^*p < .002$

customary to provide (1) the value of the F statistic, (2) degrees of freedom (in parentheses) associated with the F statistic, and (3) p value. A decision to reject the null hypothesis should always be based on the researcher's preselected level of significance, $\alpha = .05$ in our example. The inclusion of the p value in the text or in a footnote to the ANOVA table permits a reader to, in effect, set his or her own level of significance.

In addition to providing information about the F test, the text portion of a publication of your results also should include a descriptive summary of the data like Table 15.4-1, the results of multiple comparison tests (see Section 15.6), and an assessment of the practical significance of your results (see Section 15.7).

If the omnibus null hypothesis $H_0: \mu_1 = \mu_2 = \cdots = \mu_p$ is rejected in ANOVA, the researcher knows that at least one difference among the population means is not equal to 0. The next question is "Which difference(s) isn't equal to 0?" Procedures for answering this question are described in Section 15.6. Before turning to that topic, I will examine the assumptions underlying the F test for a completely randomized design.

CHECK YOUR UNDERSTANDING OF SECTION 15.4

11. a. Fill in the blanks in the following ANOVA table.

Source	SS	df	MS	F
Between groups	168.000	( )	( )	( )
Within groups	( )	76	( )	
Total	1,384.000	79		

   b. Determine the p value of the F statistic using Microsoft's Excel FDIST function.

12. An experiment was performed to investigate the effects of meaningfulness, or association value, of nonsense syllables on learning. Thirty-two participants were randomly assigned to four treatment levels with the restriction that 8 were assigned to each level. The nonsense syllables were selected from the list compiled by C. E. Noble. The association values of the lists were 25% for a_1, 50% for a_2, 75% for a_3, and 100% for a_4. The dependent variable was time (in minutes)

needed to learn the list well enough to recite it correctly twice. The researcher obtained the following data.

a_1	a_2	a_3	a_4
22	22	18	18
21	20	20	17
20	18	17	16
21	21	16	18
22	20	18	19
24	19	19	15
22	21	18	16
23	19	17	17

a. Construct stacked box plots for the data. Are the sample distributions relatively symmetrical? Do the data contain outliers?

b. Compute descriptive statistics, $\overline{X}_{.j}$'s and $\hat{\sigma}_j$'s, for the data and construct a table similar to Table 15.4-1.

c. Are the sample data consistent with the researcher's alternative hypothesis $H_1 = \mu_j \neq \mu_{j'}$ for some j and j'?

d. Test the null hypothesis $H_0: \mu_1 = \mu_2 = \mu_3 = \mu_4$. Let $\alpha = .05$. Construct an ANOVA summary table. Determine the p value of the F statistic using Microsoft's Excel FDIST function.

e. Summarize the results of the ANOVA in a sentence or two.

13. List the steps used to test the null hypothesis in Exercise 12, and state the decision rule.

14. A researcher investigated the reaction time to red, green, and yellow instrument-panel warning lights. Thirty-one participants were randomly assigned to the three colors of warning lights. The participants pressed a microswitch as soon as they noticed the onset of the warning light. The dependent variable was reaction time in hundredths of a second. The researcher obtained the following data; decimal points have been omitted.

a_1 (Yellow)	a_2 (Red)	a_3 (Green)
20	23	21
20	20	21
21	21	20
22	21	23
21	23	22
20	22	20
19	22	21
21	21	22
19	22	22
20	22	20
		19

a. Construct stacked box plots for the data. Are the sample distributions relatively symmetrical? Do the data contain outliers?

b. Compute descriptive statistics, $\overline{X}_{.j}$'s and $\hat{\sigma}_j$'s, for the data and construct a table similar to Table 15.4-1.

    c. Are the sample data consistent with the researcher's alternative hypothesis $H_1: \mu_j \neq \mu_{j'}$ for some j and j'?

    d. Test the null hypothesis $H_0: \mu_1 = \mu_2 = \mu_3$. Let $\alpha = .05$. Construct an ANOVA summary table. Determine the p value of the F statistic using Microsoft's Excel FDIST function.

    e. Summarize the results of the ANOVA in a sentence or two.

15. List the steps used to test the null hypothesis in Exercise 14, and state the decision rule.

15.5 ASSUMPTIONS ASSOCIATED WITH A *CR-p* DESIGN

As with all statistical tests, the F test of the omnibus null hypothesis in analysis of variance involves assumptions. I will list the assumptions and then describe the effects of violating them.

1. The model equation $X_{ij} = \mu + (\mu_j - \mu) + (X_{ij} - \mu_j)$ reflects all the sources of variation that affect X_{ij}.
2. Participants are random samples from the respective populations or the participants have been randomly assigned to the treatment levels.
3. The $j = 1, \ldots, p$ populations are normally distributed.
4. The variances of the $j = 1, \ldots, p$ populations are equal.

At the outset, note that for real data some of the assumptions will always be violated. For example, the underlying populations from which samples are drawn are never exactly normally distributed. The important question then is not whether the assumptions are violated but rather whether minor violations seriously affect the significance level and power of the F test. Fortunately, the F test in ANOVA is robust with respect to violation of a number of assumptions—that is, the test is not very sensitive to departures from some of its assumptions. Unfortunately, the F test is not as robust to violation of certain assumptions as was once thought.

Assumption That the Model Equation $X_{ij} = \mu + (\mu_j - \mu) + (X_{ij} - \mu_j)$ Reflects All the Sources of Variation That Affect X_{ij}

Assumption 1 states that a score, X_{ij}, is the sum of three components: the grand mean, the effect of treatment j, and the error effect associated with participant i. The latter effect includes all effects not attributable to treatment level j, such as chance fluctuations in the participant's behavior, variations in the administration of the treatment condition, and any other conditions that are not held constant.

A completely randomized design is appropriate for experiments with one treatment in which the participants are randomly assigned to only one treatment level. If, for example, an experiment contains two or more treatments—say, treatment A with p levels and treatment B with q levels—or if a researcher wants to observe the participants under more than one treatment level, the researcher must choose a different ANOVA design. Designs appropriate for these situations are described in

Chapter 16. The choice of an incorrect design can seriously affect the probability of a Type I error and the power of the *F* test.

Assumption of Random Sampling or Random Assignment

Assumption 2 states that the participants in an experiment have been randomly sampled from populations of interest or have been randomly assigned to treatment levels. This is an important assumption. The use of random sampling or random assignment helps to distribute the unique characteristics of participants randomly over the treatment levels so that the characteristics do not selectively bias the outcome of an experiment.[3] In the absence of randomization, there is always the possibility that some variable other than the treatment produced the observed differences among the sample means. Hence, the interpretation of the results of experiments that do not use randomization involves some ambiguity.

Assumption of Normally Distributed Populations

Assumption 3 states that the populations are normally distributed. In the real world, this assumption is never satisfied because, for example, observations do not take values from $-\infty$ to $+\infty$. Fortunately, the *F* test in ANOVA, like the *t* test, is robust with respect to departures from normality. This is especially true when the populations are symmetrical and the samples sizes are equal and greater than 12 (Clinch and Keselman, 1982; Tan, 1982). Studies indicate that even if the treatment populations are asymmetrical or are flatter or more peaked than normal, the actual probability of making a Type I error will be fairly close to the nominal or specified probability if all of the populations have the same shape.

A rough check on the normality assumption can be made by constructing a frequency distribution for the scores in each treatment level and inspecting the distributions for evidence of skewness and kurtosis. Box plots also are useful for detecting marked departures from symmetry. Marked departures from normality in the samples raise questions concerning normality of the populations.

Assumption of Homogeneity of Variance

Assumption 4 states that the $j = 1, \ldots, p$ population variances are equal to σ_ε^2—that is, $\hat{\sigma}_1^2 = \hat{\sigma}_2^2 = \cdots = \hat{\sigma}_p^2 = \sigma_\varepsilon^2$. This assumption is referred to as the **homogeneity of variance assumption.**

Box (1954) reported that the ANOVA *F* test is robust with respect to violation of the homogeneity of variance assumption provided (1) there is an equal number of observations in each of the treatment levels, (2) the populations are normal, and (3)

---

[3] Sometimes factors beyond the researcher's control preclude the random assignment of participants to treatment levels and the control of important extraneous variables. Cook and Campbell (1979) referred to such experiments as "quasi-experimental designs."

the ratio of the largest variance to the smallest variance does not exceed 3. Considering these restrictions and the fact that it is not unusual for the ratio of the largest to smallest sample variance to exceed 3, it seems prudent to question the reputed robustness of ANOVA with respect to unequal (heterogeneous) variances. Indeed, numerous investigators have shown that even when sample sizes are equal, the ANOVA F test is not robust with respect to the variance heterogeneity often encountered in behavioral and educational research. In the face of this evidence, it is clear that researchers should not ignore violations of the homogeneity of variance assumption. Fortunately, there are robust alternatives to the ANOVA F test statistic that can be used when heterogeneous population variances are suspected. These procedures are described by Clinch and Keselman (1982) and Wilcox (1996).

CHECK YOUR UNDERSTANDING OF SECTION 15.5

16. Qualify the statement "The F test in ANOVA is robust with respect to departures from normality."
17. A rough but adequate check on the tenability of the normality assumption consists of making a frequency distribution of the scores in each treatment level and inspecting them for evidence of skewness and kurtosis. Decide on the tenability of this assumption for the data in (a) Exercises 12 and (b) Exercise 14 of "Check Your Understanding of Section 15.4."
18. In words, what is the assumption of homogeneity of variance?
19. Term to remember:
    a. Homogeneity of variance

15.6 MULTIPLE COMPARISON PROCEDURES

As you have seen, the ANOVA F test is used to determine the tenability of the omnibus null hypothesis $H_0: \mu_1 = \mu_2 = \cdots = \mu_p$. If this hypothesis is rejected, usually the next question is, which population means are not equal? A number of test statistics have been developed for answering this question—that is, for ferreting out significant differences among population means, or, as it is often called, **data snooping** Because the tests are performed after observing one's sample data, the tests also are referred to as **a posteriori** or **post hoc tests.** Statisticians have developed a variety of statistics called **multiple-comparison statistics** for performing such tests. In the following paragraphs, I will describe two especially useful multiple-comparison statistics. But first I will define a contrast among means.

Contrasts among Means

A **contrast** or **comparison** among means is a difference among the means, with appropriate algebraic signs. I use the symbols ψ_i and $\hat{\psi}$ to denote, respectively, the

ith contrast among population means and a sample estimate of the ith contrast. For example, the population contrast $\mu_1 - \mu_2$ is denoted by the symbol ψ_1; the sample contrast $\overline{X}_1 - \overline{X}_2$, by $\hat{\psi}$. If an experiment contains $p = 3$ means, contrasts involving two and three population means may be of interest, for example,

$$\psi_1 = \mu_1 - \mu_2 \qquad \psi_4 = \frac{\mu_1 + \mu_2}{2} - \mu_3$$

$$\psi_2 = \mu_1 - \mu_3 \qquad \psi_5 = \frac{\mu_1 + \mu_3}{2} - \mu_2$$

$$\psi_3 = \mu_2 - \mu_3 \qquad \psi_6 = \frac{\mu_2 + \mu_3}{2} - \mu_1$$

The contrasts on the left involve a difference between two means. Those on the right involve the average of two means versus a third mean. Contrast $\psi_4 = (\mu_1 + \mu_2)/2 - \mu_3$, for example, could represent the average of two experimental-group means, μ_1 and μ_2, versus a control-group mean, μ_3.

All contrasts have a set of underlying coefficients, denoted by $c_1, c_2, \ldots, c_p$, that define the contrast. Consider an experiment with three treatment levels. The coefficients for contrast $\psi_1 = \mu_1 - \mu_2$ are $c_1 = 1, c_2 = -1$, and $c_3 = 0$:

$$\psi_1 = (c_1)\mu_1 + \quad (c_2)\mu_2 + (c_3)\mu_3$$

$$\psi_1 = (1)\mu_1 + (-1)\mu_2 + (0)\mu_3 = \mu_1 - \mu_2$$

The coefficients for contrast $\psi_4 = (\mu_1 + \mu_2)/2 - \mu_3$ are $c_1 = 1/2, c_2 = 1/2$, and $c_3 = -1$:

$$\psi_4 = (c_1)\mu_1 + \quad (c_2)\mu_2 + (c_3)\mu_3$$

$$\psi_4 = (^1/_2)\mu_1 + (^1/_2)\mu_2 + (-1)\mu_3 = \frac{\mu_1 + \mu_2}{2} - \mu_3$$

Ordinarily, researchers do not bother to write the coefficients unless they are numbers other than 1, -1, and 0. Notice that I needed the coefficients $c_1 = c_2 = {}^1\!/_2$ to define contrast 4.

The difference $(\mu_1 + \mu_2)/2 - \mu_3$ is a contrast, but $(\mu_1 + \mu_2) - \mu_3$ is not. Why? For a difference among means to be a contrast, the coefficients must satisfy the following condition.

The **coefficients of a contrast,** $c_1, c_2, \ldots, c_p$, must be numbers such that the coefficients sum to 0—that is, $\sum_{i=1}^{p} c_j = c_1 + c_2 + \cdots + c_p = 0.$

The coefficients of the difference $(\mu_1 + \mu_2)/2 - \mu_3$ sum to zero: $1/2 + 1/2 + (-1) = 0$. Hence, this difference is a contrast. However, the difference

$(\mu_1 + \mu_2) - \mu_3$ is not a contrast because the coefficients do not sum to zero: $1 + 1 + (-1) = 1$.

For convenience, coefficients of contrasts usually are chosen so that the sum of their absolute values is equal to 2—that is,

$$\sum_{j=1}^{p} |c_j| = 2$$

where $|c_j|$ indicates that the sign of c_j is always taken to be positive. All six of the contrasts described earlier satisfy this property. For example, the sums of the absolute value of the coefficients for ψ_1 and ψ_4 are, respectively,

$$|c_1| + |c_2| + |c_3| = |1| + |-1| + |0| = 1 + 1 + 0 = 2$$

and

$$|c_1| + |c_2| + |c_3| = |\tfrac{1}{2}| + |\tfrac{1}{2}| + |-1| = \tfrac{1}{2} + \tfrac{1}{2} + 1 = 2$$

Contrasts for which $\sum_{i=1}^{p} |c_j| = 2$ are expressed on the same scale or metric and can be compared with one another.

When all of the coefficients of a contrast except two are equal to 0, the contrast is called a **pairwise contrast.** Otherwise, the contrast is a **nonpairwise contrast.** For example, contrast

$$\psi_1 = (1)\mu_1 + (-1)\mu_2 + (0)\mu_3 = \mu_1 - \mu_2$$

is a pairwise contrast. However, contrast

$$\psi_4 = (^1/_2)\mu_1 + (^1/_2)\mu_2 + (-1)\mu_3 = \frac{\mu_1 + \mu_2}{2} - \mu_3$$

is a nonpairwise contrast.

Fisher-Hayter Multiple Comparison Test

A variety of multiple comparison procedures have been developed to test null hypotheses about contrasts. I will describe two multiple comparison tests: the Fisher-Hayter test and Scheffé's (pronounced Shef-fay) test. The Fisher-Hayter test is appropriate for testing all pairwise contrasts among p means.[4] Scheffé's test can be used for making pairwise and nonpairwise tests. Both tests control the probability of making one or more Type I errors for the collection of tests at or less than α.

The Fisher-Hayter multiple comparison test is a two-step procedure. The first step consists of using the ANOVA F statistic to test the omnibus null hypothesis, $H_0: \mu_1 = \mu_2 = \cdots = \mu_p$, at α level of significance. If the ANOVA F test is not significant, the omnibus null hypothesis is not rejected and it is concluded that none of the pairwise contrasts differ from 0. If the omnibus null hypothesis is rejected, each of the pairwise contrasts is tested using the Fisher-Hayter test statistic.

[4] Tukey's HSD test is widely used for testing pairwise contrasts. I do not discuss Tukey's test here because the Fisher-Hayter test is more powerful and can be used when the various sample n' are not equal (Kirk, 1994).

The formula for the **Fisher-Hayter test statistic,** denoted by qFH, is

$$qFH = \frac{\overline{X}_{.j} - \overline{X}_{.j'}}{\sqrt{\dfrac{MSWG}{2}\left(\dfrac{1}{n_j} + \dfrac{1}{n_{j'}}\right)}}$$

where $\overline{X}_{.j}$ and $\overline{X}_{.j'}$ are two sample means, $MSWG$ is the denominator of the ANOVA F statistic, and n_j and $n_{j'}$ are the sizes of the samples used to compute the sample means.

A pairwise, nondirectional null hypothesis, H_0: $\mu_j = \mu_{j'}$, is rejected if the absolute value of the Fisher-Hayter qFH statistic exceeds or equals the critical value $q_{\alpha;\, p-1,\, \nu}$, where $q_{\alpha;\, p-1,\, \nu}$ is obtained from the distribution of the studentized range in Appendix Table D.9. Notice that Appendix Table D.9 is entered for $p - 1$ means instead of the actual number of means in the experiment. The meaning of the other subscripts in $q_{\alpha;\, p-1,\, \nu}$ is as follows: α is the two-tailed probability of making one or more Type I errors for the collection of all possible pairwise contrasts, and ν is the degrees of freedom associated with $MSWG$, which is equal to $p(n - 1)$ for the completely randomized ANOVA design. Ordinarily, I would use $\alpha/2$ instead of α to denote a two-tailed probability in $q_{\alpha;\, p-1,\, \nu}$. It is common to depart from this convention when a statistic is only appropriate for performing two-tailed tests. Neither the Fisher-Hayter test nor Scheffé's test is appropriate for one-tailed tests because the tests are performed after examining the data.

I will use the weight-loss data in Tables 15.4-2 and 15.4-3 to illustrate the computational procedures for the Fisher-Hayter test. The sample means in Table 15.4-2 are $\overline{X}_{.1} = 8.00$, $\overline{X}_{.2} = 9.00$, and $\overline{X}_{.3} = 12.00$; $MSWG = 5.037$ from Table 15.4-3, and $n = 10$. The .05 level of significance is adopted. Hence, the probability of making one or more Type I errors for the collection of all pairwise contrasts will not exceed .05.

The first step is to test the omnibus null hypothesis using an ANOVA F test. The F test is summarized in Table 15.4-3 and is significant. Because the F test is significant, the next step is to compute

$$qFH = \frac{\overline{X}_{.j} - \overline{X}_{.j'}}{\sqrt{\dfrac{MSWG}{2}\left(\dfrac{1}{n_j} + \dfrac{1}{n_{j'}}\right)}}$$

for each pairwise contrast.

$$qFH = \frac{8.00 - 9.00}{\sqrt{\dfrac{5.037}{2}\left(\dfrac{1}{10} + \dfrac{1}{10}\right)}} = -1.41 \qquad (\hat{\psi}_1 = \overline{X}_{.1} - \overline{X}_{.2})$$

$$qFH = \frac{8.00 - 12.00}{\sqrt{\dfrac{5.037}{2}\left(\dfrac{1}{10} + \dfrac{1}{10}\right)}} = -5.64 \qquad (\hat{\psi}_2 = \overline{X}_{.1} - \overline{X}_{.3})$$

$$qFH = \frac{9.00 - 12.00}{\sqrt{\dfrac{5.037}{2}\left(\dfrac{1}{10} + \dfrac{1}{10}\right)}} = -4.23 \qquad (\hat{\psi}_3 = \overline{X}_{.2} - \overline{X}_{.3})$$

To reject a null hypothesis, the absolute value $|qFH|$ must exceed or equal $q_{.05;\,3-1,\,27}$ $\cong 2.90$. Because $|qFH(27)| = 5.64$ for contrast 2 and 4.23 for contrast 3 are greater than $q_{.05;\,3-1,\,27} \cong 2.90$, the null hypotheses for $H_0\!: \mu_1 = \mu_3$ and $H_0\!: \mu_2 = \mu_3$ are rejected. The researcher can conclude from the sample means that for the population of girls represented in the experiment, diet a_3 would produce a greater weight loss than diets a_1 and a_2. Based on the data, the researcher's best guess is that a person following diet a_3 would lose 4 more pounds than would a person following diet a_1 and 3 more pounds than would a person following diet a_2.

The assumptions associated with the Fisher-Hayter statistic are as follows:

1. Random sampling or random assignment of participants to the treatment levels.
2. The $j = 1, \ldots, p$ populations are normally distributed.
3. The variances of the $j = 1, \ldots, p$ populations are equal.

Scheffé's Multiple Comparison Test and Confidence Interval

I turn now to Scheffé's test—one of the more versatile multiple comparison tests. The test should be used if any of the researcher's null hypotheses involves a non-pairwise contrasts—that is, a contrast of the form

$$\psi_i = c_1\mu_1 + c_2\mu_2 + \cdots + c_p\mu_p$$

where three or more of the c_j coefficients are not 0. If a researcher is only interested in hypotheses involving pairwise contrasts, the Fisher-Hayter test should be used because of its greater power.

After examining the weight-loss data in Table 15.3-1, a researcher might be interested in the following nondirectional null hypotheses: $H_0\!: \mu_1 - \mu_3 = 0$, $H_0\!: \mu_2 - \mu_3 = 0$, and $H_0\!: (\mu_1 + \mu_2)/2 - \mu_3 = 0$.

The formula for **Scheffé's test statistic,** denoted by FS, is

$$FS = \frac{(c_1\overline{X}_{.1} + c_2\overline{X}_{.2} + \cdots + c_p\overline{X}_{.p})^2}{MSWG\left(\dfrac{c_1^2}{n_1} + \dfrac{c_2^2}{n_2} + \cdots + \dfrac{c_p^2}{n_p}\right)}$$

where $c_1, c_2, \ldots, c_p$ are coefficients that define a contrast; $\overline{X}_{.1}, \overline{X}_{.2}, \ldots, \overline{X}_{.p}$ are sample means; $MSWG$ is the denominator of the ANOVA F statistic; and $n_1, n_2, \ldots, n_p$ are the sizes of the samples used to compute the sample means.

Scheffé's test, unlike the Fisher-Hayter test, does not have to be preceded by a test of the omnibus null hypothesis. However, if the omnibus null hypothesis is not rejected, Scheffé's test will not find any significant pairwise or nonpairwise contrasts. A nondirectional null hypothesis for $\psi_i = c_1\mu_1 + c_2\mu_2 + \cdots + c_p\mu_p$ is rejected if the absolute value of Scheffé's *FS* statistic exceeds or equals the critical value $(p-1)F_{\alpha;\,\nu_1,\,\nu_2}$, where p is the number of means in the experiment and $(p-1)F_{\alpha;\,\nu_1,\,\nu_2}$ is obtained from Appendix Table D.5. The meaning of the subscripts in $(p-1)F_{\alpha;\,\nu_1,\,\nu_2}$ is as follows: α is the value that cuts off the upper α region from Appendix Table D.5, ν_1 is equal to $p-1$, and $\nu_2 = p(n-1)$.

The Scheffé *FS* statistics for the weight-loss data in Tables 15.4-2 and 15.4-3 are as follows:

$$FS = \frac{[(1)8.00 + (0)9.00 + (-1)12.00]^2}{5.037\left(\frac{(1)^2}{10} + \frac{(0)^2}{10} + \frac{(-1)^2}{10}\right)} = 15.88 \qquad (\hat{\psi}_1 = \overline{X}_{.1} - \overline{X}_{.3})$$

$$FS = \frac{[(0)8.00 + (1)9.00 + (-1)12.00]^2}{5.037\left(\frac{(0)^2}{10} + \frac{(1)^2}{10} + \frac{(-1)^2}{10}\right)} = 8.93 \qquad (\hat{\psi}_2 = \overline{X}_{.2} - \overline{X}_{.3})$$

$$FS = \frac{[(^1/_2)8.00 + (^1/_2)9.00 + (-1)12.00]^2}{5.037\left(\frac{(^1/_2)^2}{10} + \frac{(^1/_2)^2}{10} + \frac{(-1)^2}{10}\right)} = 16.21 \qquad \left(\hat{\psi}_3 = \frac{\overline{X}_{.1} + \overline{X}_{.2}}{2} - \overline{X}_{.3}\right)$$

To reject a null hypothesis, the value of *FS* must exceed or equal $(3-1)F_{.05;\,2,\,27} = (2)(3.35) = 6.70$. Because $FS = 15.88, 8.93$, and 16.21 for contrasts 1 through 3 are greater than 6.70, the null hypotheses $H_0{:}\ \mu_1 = \mu_3$, $H_0{:}\ \mu_2 = \mu_3$, and $H_0{:}\ (\mu_1 + \mu_2)/2 = \mu_3$ can be rejected.

Scheffé's statistic also can be used to construct confidence intervals for all contrasts of interest.

A two-sided $100(1 - \alpha)\%$ confidence interval for $\psi_i = c_1\mu_1 + c_2\mu_2 + \cdots + c_p\mu_p$ is given by

$$\hat{\psi}_i - \sqrt{(p-1)F_{\alpha;\,\nu_1,\,\nu_2}}\sqrt{MSWG\sum_{j=1}^{p}\frac{c_j^2}{n_j}} < \psi_i$$

$$< \hat{\psi}_i + \sqrt{(p-1)F_{\alpha;\,\nu_1,\,\nu_2}}\sqrt{MSWG\sum_{j=1}^{p}\frac{c_j^2}{n_j}}$$

where $\hat{\psi}_i = c_1\overline{X}_{.1} + c_2\overline{X}_{.2} + \cdots + c_p\overline{X}_{.p}$; $c_1, c_2, \ldots, c_p$ are coefficients that define a contrast; $\overline{X}_{.1}, \overline{X}_{.2}, \ldots, \overline{X}_{.p}$ are sample means; p is the number of means in the experiment; $F_{\alpha;\,\nu_1,\,\nu_2}$ is the value that cuts off the upper α region from Appendix Table D.5; $\nu_1 = p - 1$; $\nu_2 = p(n - 1)$; $MSWG$ is the denominator of the ANOVA F statistic; and $n_1, n_2, \ldots, n_p$ are the sizes of the samples used to compute the sample means.

I will use the data from the diet experiment to illustrate a two-sided $100(1 - .05)\% = 95\%$ confidence interval for $\psi = (^1/_2)\mu_1 + (^1/_2)\mu_2 + (-1)\mu_3$. Recall that the weight-loss means were $\overline{X}_{\cdot 1} = 8.0$, $\overline{X}_{\cdot 2} = 9.0$, $\overline{X}_{\cdot 3} = 12.0$; $MSWG = 5.037$, $(3 - 1)F_{.05; 2, 27} = (2)(3.35) = 6.70$, and $n_1 = n_2 = n_3 = 10$:

$$[(^1/_2)8.0 + (^1/_2)9.0 + (-1)12.0]$$

$$-\sqrt{(2)(3.35)}\sqrt{(5.037)\left[\frac{(^1/_2)^2 + (^1/_2)^2 + (-1)^2}{10 + 10 + 10}\right]} < \psi$$

$$< [(^1/_2)8.0 + (^1/_2)9.0 + (-1)12.0]$$

$$+ \sqrt{(2)(3.35)}\sqrt{(5.037)\left[\frac{(^1/_2)^2 + (^1/_2)^2 + (-1)^2}{10 + 10 + 10}\right]}$$

$$-5.45 < \psi < -1.55$$

Because the 95% confidence interval does not include 0, a test of the null hypothesis that the contrast $\psi = (\mu_1 - \mu_2)/2 - \mu_3$ is equal to 0 would be rejected. For the population of girls represented in the experiment, the researcher can be 95% confident that the mean weight loss for girls who use diets a_1 and a_2 versus the mean for those who use a_3 is between -5.46 and -1.55 pounds. The 95% confidence interval corresponds to the darkened portion of the real number line as follows:

The assumptions associated with Scheffé's statistic and confidence interval are as follows:

1. Random sampling or random assignment of participants to the treatment levels.
2. The $j = 1, \ldots, p$ populations are normally distributed.
3. The variances of each of the $j = 1, \ldots, p$ populations are equal.

A robust alternative test that can be used when the population variances are unequal (assumption 3) is described by Kirk (1995, p. 155).

Comparison of the Multiple Comparison Tests

I have described two multiple comparison tests. Each of the tests controls the probability of making one or more Type I errors at or less than α for a collection of tests, but they differ in the nature of the collection.

1. The Fisher-Hayter test controls the Type I error for the collection of all pairwise contrasts.
2. Scheffé's test controls the Type I error for the collection of all pairwise and nonpairwise contrasts.

Table 15.6-1 Comparison of Multiple-Comparison Tests

	Fisher-Hayter	*Scheffé*
Type of contrast	Pairwise	Pairwise and nonpairwise
Confidence intervals available	No	Yes
Two-tailed test only	Yes	Yes
Requires equal n's	No	No
Assumes random sampling or random assignment, normal populations, and equal variances	Yes	Yes

Other similarities and differences between the tests are summarized in Table 15.6-1. As noted earlier, the tests differ in power. The Fisher-Hayter test is more powerful than Scheffé's test. However, Scheffé's test can be used to test nonpairwise contrasts.

15.7 PRACTICAL SIGNIFICANCE

In Section 11.3, I observed that most measures of effect magnitude fall into one of two categories: measures of effect size and measures of strength of association. A measure of strength of association that is used with the ANOVA F test is **omega squared,** denoted by $\hat{\omega}^2$. The formula for $\hat{\omega}^2$ is

$$\hat{\omega}^2 = \frac{(p-1)(F-1)}{(p-1)(F-1)+np}$$

Omega squared estimates the proportion of the population variance in the dependent variable that is accounted for by the p treatments levels. Omega squared is similar to the coefficient of determination, r^2, that is described in Section 5.4. The latter statistic describes the proportion of the sample variance in, say, variable Y, that is accounted for by variable, X.

Cohen (1988, pp. 284–288) has suggested the following guidelines for interpreting strength of association:

$\omega^2 = .010$ is a small association.

$\omega^2 = .059$ is a medium association.

$\omega^2 = .138$ or larger is a large association.

For the diet data in Table 15.4-3, an estimate of the proportion of the population weight-loss variance accounted for by the three diets is

$$\hat{\omega}^2 = \frac{(p-1)(F-1)}{(p-1)(F-1)+np} = \frac{(3-1)(8.60-1)}{(3-1)(8.60-1)+(10)(3)} = .34$$

According to Cohen's guidelines, the strength of association between the diets and weight loss is large—34% of the variance in weight loss is associated with the diets; $100\% - 34\% = 66\%$ is associated with factors other than the diets.

Some researchers do not follow the recommended practice of always reporting omega squared in their publications along with F and p values. If omega squared is not given in a publication, you can compute it if the value of F, p (number of treatment levels), and N or np (total number of participants) are reported.

Hedges's g statistic, described in Section 13.2, can be used to determine the effect size of contrasts among the diets. The g statistic is

$$g = \frac{|\overline{X}_{.j} - \overline{X}_{.j'}|}{\hat{\sigma}_{Pooled}}$$

where

$$\hat{\sigma}_{Pooled} = \sqrt{MSWG}$$

For the weight-loss data in Tables 15.4-2 and 15.4-3, the researcher used the Fisher-Hayter statistic to test three pairwise contrasts. The effect sizes for these contrasts are as follows:

$$g = \frac{|8 - 9|}{2.244} = 0.45 \qquad (\hat{\psi}_1 = \overline{X}_{.1} - \overline{X}_{.2})$$

$$g = \frac{|8 - 12|}{2.244} = 1.8 \qquad (\hat{\psi}_2 = \overline{X}_{.1} - \overline{X}_{.3})$$

$$g = \frac{|9 - 12|}{2.244} = 1.3 \qquad (\hat{\psi}_3 = \overline{X}_{.2} - \overline{X}_{.3})$$

where $\hat{\sigma}_{Pooled} = \sqrt{MSWG} = \sqrt{5.037} = 2.244$. According to Cohen's guidelines for interpreting d-like measures of effect size in Section 10.4, the two contrasts that were significant, $\hat{\psi}_2$ and $\hat{\psi}_3$, represent large effects. This suggests that the difference between diets a_1 and a_3 and between diets a_2 and a_3 is large enough to be of practical value. Indeed, what dieter wouldn't want to use diet a_3, which produced a one-month weight loss of 4 pounds more than diet a_1 and 3 pounds more than diet a_2?

CHECK YOUR UNDERSTANDING OF SECTIONS 15.6 AND 15.7

20. For an experiment with $p = 4$ treatment levels, list the coefficients, c_j, for the following population contrasts.
    a. μ_1 versus μ_2
    b. μ_2 versus μ_4
    c. μ_1 versus the mean of μ_2 and μ_3
    d. μ_1 versus the mean of μ_2, μ_3, and μ_4
    e. mean of μ_1 and μ_2 versus the mean of μ_3 and μ_4
    f. μ_1 versus the weighted mean of μ_2 and μ_3, where μ_2 is weighted twice as much as μ_3

21. Which of the following are contrasts?

    a. $\mu_1 - \mu_2$

    b. $2\mu_1 - \mu_2 - \mu_3$

    c. $(1)\mu_1 + (-\frac{1}{3})\mu_2 + (-\frac{1}{3})\mu_3$

    d. $(1\frac{1}{2})\mu_1 + (-\frac{1}{2})\mu_2 + (-1)\mu_3$

    e. $(3)\mu_1 + (-3)\mu_2 + (0)\mu_3$

    f. $(\frac{1}{2})\mu_1 + (\frac{1}{2})\mu_2 + (-\frac{1}{2})\mu_3 + (-\frac{1}{2})\mu_4$

22. Which of the sets of means in Exercise 21 satisfy $|c_1| + |c_2| + \cdots + |c_p| = 2$?

23. Determine the value of $q_{\alpha; p-1, \nu}$ for the Fisher-Hayter test for (a) $p = 4$, $n = 11$, $\alpha = .01$; (b) $p = 5$, $n = 13$, $\alpha = .05$; and (c) $p = 3$, $n = 6$, $\alpha = .05$.

24. Determine the value of $(p - 1)F_{\alpha; \nu_1, \nu_2}$ for Scheffé's test for (a) $p = 4$, $n = 11$, $\alpha = .01$; (b) $p = 5$, $n = 13$, $\alpha = .05$; and (c) $p = 3$, $n_1 = 6$, $n_2 = 7$, $n_3 = 8$, $\alpha = .05$.

25. Researchers investigated the effects of three dosages of ethylene glycol on the reaction time of chimpanzees. The animals were randomly assigned to the dosage levels so that five animals received 2 cc of the drug, treatment level a_1; five received 4 cc, a_2; and five received 6cc, a_3. The sample means were $\overline{X}_{.1} = 0.29$ sec, $\overline{X}_{.2} = 0.31$ sec, and $\overline{X}_{.3} = 0.39$ sec; $MSWG = .002$ and $\nu_2 = 3(5 - 1) = 12$. The hypothesis $H_0: \mu_1 = \mu_2 = \mu_3$ was rejected at the .05 level of significance using a CR-3 design.

    a. Perform all pairwise contrasts using the Fisher-Hayter test.

    b. Use Hedges's g statistic to determine the effect size of the contrasts. Interpret g for those tests that were significant.

26. A researcher investigated the effectiveness of three approaches to drug education in junior high school. The approaches were scare tactics, treatment level a_1; providing objective scientific information about physiological and psychological effects, a_2; and examining the psychology of drug use, a_3. Forty-one students who did not use drugs were randomly assigned to each treatment level. At the conclusion of an educational program, the students evaluated its effectiveness; a high score signified effectiveness. The sample means were $\overline{X}_{.1} = 23.1$, $\overline{X}_{.2} = 23.8$, and $\overline{X}_{.3} = 26.7$; $MSWG = 16.4$ and $\nu_2 = 3(41 - 1) = 120$.

    a. After examining the data, the researcher decided to use Scheffé's statistic to determine which of the following contrasts are not equal to 0: $\psi_1 = \mu_1 - \mu_2$, $\psi_2 = \mu_1 - \mu_3$, $\psi_3 = \mu_2 - \mu_3$, and $\psi_4 = (\mu_1 + \mu_2)/2 - \mu_3$. Test the null hypotheses for these contrasts; let $\alpha = .01$.

    b. Construct confidence intervals for each of the contrasts and locate the confidence intervals on the real number line.

    c. Use Hedges's g statistic to determine the effect size of the contrasts. Interpret g for those confidence intervals that do not include 0.

27. Exercise 12 in "Check Your Understanding of Section 15.4" described an experiment to investigate the effects of meaningfulness of nonsense syllables on learning.

    a. Estimate the proportion of the population variance in the dependent variable that is accounted for by the four treatments levels and interpret the result.

    b. Use the Fisher-Hayter test to determine which pairwise contrasts among means are not equal to zero. Let $\alpha = .05$.

    c. Use Hedges's g statistic to determine the effect size of the contrasts. Interpret g for those tests that were significant.

28. Terms to remember:
    a. Data snooping
    b. A posteriori (post hoc) tests
    c. Multiple-comparison statistic
    d. Contrast (comparison)
    e. Coefficients of a contrast
    f. Pairwise contrast
    g. Nonpairwise contrast
    h. Fisher-Hayter test statistic
    i. Scheffé's test statistic
    j. Omega squared

15.8 LOOKING BACK: WHAT HAVE YOU LEARNED?

Analysis of variance, ANOVA, is a statistical procedure for (1) determining how much of the total variability among scores to attribute to each source of variation in an experiment and for (2) testing hypotheses about some of these sources. The principal application of ANOVA is testing the omnibus null hypothesis that two or more population means are equal. This chapter describes a completely randomized design (CR-p), the simplest ANOVA design. It is appropriate for experiments that meet the following conditions:

1. One treatment or independent variable with two or more treatment levels.
2. Random assignment of participants to treatment levels, with each participant designated to receive only one level; alternatively, the treatments can be composed of participants obtained by random sampling.

Although ANOVA appears to be a complicated procedure, the basic notions are relatively simple. A score X_{ij} in a completely randomized design is a composite. Similarly, the total variation among the scores, designated by SSTO, is a composite and can be partitioned into two parts: the sum of squares between groups, SSBG, and the sum of squares within groups, SSWG. A variance, or mean square, is obtained by dividing a sum of squares by its degrees of freedom, for example, $SSBG/df_{BG} = MSBG$ and $SSWG/df_{WG} = MSWG$. The statistic for testing the omnibus null hypothesis, H_0: $\mu_1 = \mu_2 = \cdots = \mu_p$, is $F = MSBG/MSWG$. To use the ratio of two variances to test a hypothesis about means may seem a bit strange. It does make sense if you consider the expected values of MSBG and MSWG for the case in which the null hypothesis is true and the case in which it is false. If the null hypothesis is true, all the population treatment means are equal, in which case

$$\frac{E(MSBG)}{E(MSWG)} = \frac{\sigma_\varepsilon^2}{\sigma_\varepsilon^2}$$

If the null hypothesis is false, at least two of the population treatment means are not equal, in which case

$$\frac{E(MSBG)}{E(MSWG)} = \frac{\sigma_\varepsilon^2 + n\Sigma(\mu_j - \mu)^2/(p-1)}{\sigma_\varepsilon^2}$$

The larger the ratio $F = MSBG/MSWG$, the more likely it is that two or more population means are not equal. How large should the F statistic be to reject the null hypothesis? According to hypothesis-testing conventions, the null hypothesis is rejected if F falls in at least the upper 5% region of the F sampling distribution.

If the omnibus null hypothesis is rejected, the researcher must still decide which population means are not equal. Multiple comparison tests are used for this purpose. Two particularly useful multiple comparison tests are the Fisher-Hayter test and the Scheffé test. The Fisher-Hayter test is used for testing hypotheses about all pairwise contrasts. Scheffé's test is used for testing hypotheses about contrasts when at least one of the contrasts is a nonpairwise contrast.

Both multiple comparison tests control the probability of making one or more Type I errors at or less than α for a collection of tests. When these multiple comparison tests are used, the probability of erroneously rejecting one or more null hypotheses does not increase as a function of the number of hypotheses tested, which is a problem with Student's t test.

It is not enough to perform a null hypothesis significance test or construct a confidence interval. Researchers should routinely assess the practical significance of their data. Such a measure for the ANOVA omnibus null hypothesis is omega squared. Omega squared estimates the proportion of variance in the dependent variable that is accounted for by the independent variable. If multiple comparisons have been performed, Hedges's g can help a researcher decide whether statistically significant contrasts are practically significant.

REVIEW EXERCISES FOR CHAPTER 15

1. A researcher compared five colors of warning lights on an automobile instrument panel. The dependent measure was reaction time to the onset of a light. (a) State the null hypothesis. (b) How many t tests would be required to test hypotheses of the form $H_1: \mu_j = \mu_{j'}$? (c) If $\alpha = .01$, what is the probability of making one or more Type I errors using ANOVA? What is the probability of making one or more Type I errors when performing multiple t tests? (d) If the overall null hypothesis is rejected, what does this tell the researcher?

2. Under what conditions do the ANOVA and t approaches lead to the same probability of making a Type I error?

3. (a) Give two examples of independent variables for which the ANOVA and multiple t approaches would lead to identical conclusions. (b) What characteristic do the examples have in common?

4. Identify the following.
   a. a_3
   b. X_{44}
   c. $X_{12,2}$
   d. $\overline{X}_{\cdot 3}$
   e. $(X_{61} - \overline{X}_{\cdot 1})$
   f. $X_{42} = \mu + (\mu_2 - \mu) + (X_{42} - \mu_2)$
   g. $\overline{X}_{\cdot 4} - \overline{X}_{\cdot \cdot}$
   h. $\overline{X}_{\cdot j}$

5. For the following null hypotheses, indicate whether the hypothesis is correctly or incorrectly stated.
   a. $\mu_j - \mu_{j'} = 0$ for all j and j'
   b. $\mu_1 = \mu_2 = \mu_3$

6. Express the following scores in terms of an ANOVA model equation: (a) X_{31}, (b) X_{35}, (c) $X_{11,4}$.

7. Calculate the degrees of freedom for *MSTO*, *MSBG*, and *MSWG* for the following conditions.
   a. $p = 5, n = 15$
   b. $p = 4, n = 22$
   c. $p = 3, n = 24$
   d. $p = 4, n_1 = 8, n_2 = 8, n_3 = 6, n_4 = 6$
8. Under what conditions does $F = MSBG/MSWG$ tend to be larger than 1?
9. Under what conditions is a completely randomized design appropriate?
10. a. Fill in the blanks in the following ANOVA table.

Source	SS	df	MS	F
Between groups	36.000	3	( )	( )
Within groups	( )	( )	( )	
Total	164.000	35		

   b. Determine the *p* value of the *F* statistic using Microsoft's Excel FDIST function.
11. The learning of one task enhances the learning of different but similar tasks. To investigate this phenomenon (called *learning to learn*), 30 participants were randomly assigned to three conditions subject to the restriction that an equal number were assigned to each condition. Participants in condition a_1 learned 2 lists of nonsense syllables, those in a_2 learned 8 lists, and those in a_3 learned 14 lists. The next day all the participants learned another list. The dependent variable was the number of trials required to learn this list. The investigator obtained the following data.

a_1	a_2	a_3
7	6	3
9	5	2
5	7	3
7	3	6
8	4	3
7	5	4
6	6	5
8	5	5
7	4	4
6	5	4

   a. Construct stacked box plots for the data. Are the sample distributions relatively symmetrical? Do the data contain outliers?
   b. Compute descriptive statistics, $\overline{X}_{.j}$'s and $\hat{\sigma}_j$'s, for the data and construct a table similar to Table 15.4-1.
   c. Are the sample data consistent with the researcher's hypothesis that $H_1: \mu_j \neq \mu_{j'}$ for some j and j'?

d. Test the null hypothesis H_0: $\mu_1 = \mu_2 = \mu_3$. Let $\alpha = .05$. Construct an ANOVA summary table. Determine the p value of the F statistic using Microsoft's Excel FDIST function.

e. Summarize the results of the ANOVA in a sentence or two.

12. List the steps used in testing the null hypothesis in Exercise 11, and state the decision rule.

13. Presidents of companies employing between 5,000 and 8,000 employees were randomly sampled from five geographic areas: a_1 = southeast, a_2 = east, a_3 = midwest, a_4 = southwest, and a_5 = west. Use ANOVA to test the null hypothesis that mean income for the presidents is the same in different areas of the country. The investigator obtained the following data, representing thousands of dollars.

a_1	a_2	a_3	a_4	a_5
40	42	37	36	46
31	40	46	40	40
32	46	45	34	45
35	45	42	34	48
37	37	42	33	46
38	43	43	39	47
35	43	40	38	
33	44	39	37	
35	42		34	
37	39			

a. Construct stacked box plots for the data. Are the sample distributions relatively symmetrical? Do the data contain outliers?

b. Compute descriptive statistics, $\overline{X}_{.j}$'s and $\hat{\sigma}_j$'s, for the data and construct a table similar to Table 15.4-1.

c. Are the sample data consistent with the researcher's hypothesis that H_1: $\mu_j \neq \mu_{j'}$ for some j and j'?

d. Test the null hypothesis H_0: $\mu_1 = \mu_2 = \mu_3 = \mu_4 = \mu_5$. Let $\alpha = .05$. Construct an ANOVA summary table. Determine the p value of the F statistic using Microsoft's Excel FDIST function.

e. Summarize the results of the ANOVA in a sentence or two.

14. List the steps used in testing the null hypothesis in Exercise 13, and state the decision rule.

15. What does the use of random sampling or random assignment in an experiment accomplish?

16. A rough but adequate check on the tenability of the normality assumption consists of making a frequency distribution of the scores in each treatment level and inspecting them for evidence of skewness and kurtosis. Decide on the tenability of this assumption for the data in Exercise 11 of "Review Exercises for Chapter 15."

17. Comment on the statement "The F test in ANOVA is robust with respect to heterogeneity of variance."

18. For an experiment with $p = 5$ treatment levels, list the coefficients, c_j, for the following population contrasts:
   a. μ_1 versus μ_2
   b. μ_1 versus μ_3
   c. μ_2 versus μ_3
   d. μ_1 versus the mean of μ_2 and μ_4
   e. mean of μ_1 and μ_2 versus the mean of μ_3, μ_4, and μ_5
   f. the weighted mean of μ_1 and μ_2 versus the weighted mean of μ_3 and μ_4, where μ_1 and μ_3 are weighted twice as much as μ_2 and μ_4.

19. Which of the following are contrasts?
   a. $(2)\mu_1 + (-1)\mu_2 + (0)\mu_3$
   b. $(5)\mu_1 + (-2)\mu_2 + (-3)\mu_3$
   c. $(\frac{1}{2})\mu_1 + (-1)\mu_2 + (\frac{1}{2})\mu_3$
   d. $(\frac{1}{2})\mu_1 + (-\frac{1}{4})\mu_2 + (-\frac{1}{4})\mu_3$
   e. $(2)\mu_1 + (0)\mu_2 + (0)\mu_3$
   f. $(\frac{3}{5})\mu_1 + (\frac{2}{5})\mu_2 + (-\frac{1}{2})\mu_3 + (-\frac{1}{2})\mu_4$

20. Which of the sets of means in Exercise 19 satisfy $|c_1| + |c_2| + \cdots + |c_p| = 2$?

21. Determine the value of $q_{\alpha;\, p-1,\, v}$ for the Fisher-Hayter test for (a) $p = 3$, $n = 9$, $\alpha = .05$; (b) $p = 6$, $n = 11$, $\alpha = .05$; (c) $p = 4$, $n = 6$, $\alpha = .01$.

22. Determine the value of $(p - 1)F_{\alpha;\, v_1,\, v_2}$ for Scheffé's test for (a) $p = 3$, $n = 7$, $\alpha = .01$; (b) $p = 5$, $n = 25$, $\alpha = .05$; (c) $p = 4$, $n_1 = 5$, $n_2 = 5$, $n_3 = 6$, $n_4 = 8$, $\alpha = .05$.

23. Exercise 11 described an experiment to investigate the phenomenon called learning to learn.
   a. Estimate the proportion of the population variance in the dependent variable that is accounted for by the three treatments levels.
   b. Use the Fisher-Hayter test to determine which pairwise contrasts among means are not equal to zero. Let $\alpha = .05$.
   c. Use Hedges's g statistic to determine the effect size of the contrasts. Interpret g for those tests that were significant.

24. Exercise 13 described an experiment to investigate mean income of company presidents from five geographic areas.
   a. Estimate the proportion of the population variance in the dependent variable that is accounted for by the five treatments levels.
   b. Use the Scheffé statistic to test the following null hypotheses: $\psi_1 = \mu_1 - \mu_4 = 0$, $\psi_2 = \mu_3 - \mu_4 = 0$, and $\psi_3 = (\mu_2 + \mu_5) - (\mu_1 + \mu_4) = 0$. Let $\alpha = .05$.
   c. Use Hedges's g statistic to determine the effect size of the contrasts. Interpret g for those tests that were significant.
   d. Construct confidence intervals for each of the contrasts and locate the confidence intervals on the real number line.

25. A researcher sought to investigate the religious dogmatism of four church denominations in a large Midwestern city. A random sample of 31 members from each denomination took a paper-and-pencil test of dogmatism. The sample means were $\overline{X}_{.1} = 64$, $\overline{X}_{.2} = 73$, $\overline{X}_{.3} = 61$, and $\overline{X}_{.4} = 49$; $MSWG = 120$ and $v_2 = 4(31 - 1) = 120$.

    a. Use Scheffé's test to evaluate the following hypotheses at the .05 level of significance.

$$H_0: \mu_2 - \mu_3 = 0$$
$$H_0: (1)\mu_2 + (-\tfrac{1}{2})\mu_1 + (-\tfrac{1}{2})\mu_3 = 0$$
$$H_0: (\tfrac{1}{2})\mu_1 + (\tfrac{1}{2})\mu_3 + (-1)\mu_4 = 0$$

    b. Use Hedges's g statistic to determine the effect size of those contrasts for which the null hypothesis was rejected and interpret the results.

    c. Construct confidence intervals for each of the contrasts and locate the confidence intervals on the real number line.

26. List the requirements for using the Fisher-Hayter and Scheffé multiple comparison tests.

16

Other Analysis of Variance Designs

16.1 Introduction
Looking Ahead: What Is This Chapter About?

16.2 Basic Experimental Design Concepts
Definition of Experimental Design
Controlling Nuisance Variables
Procedures for Forming Blocks
Check Your Understanding of Section 16.2

16.3 Randomized Block Design
Model Equation for a Score
Computational Procedures for RB-3 Design
Multiple Comparison Procedures
Computational Example for the Fisher-Hayter Multiple Comparison Procedure
Practical Significance
Assumptions Associated with a Randomized Block Design
Check Your Understanding of Section 16.3

16.4 Completely Randomized Factorial Design
Introduction to Factorial Designs
Model Equation for a Score
Computational Procedures for CRF-23 Design
Interpreting Interactions
Multiple Comparison Procedures
Computational Example for the Fisher-Hayter Multiple Comparison Procedure
Practical Significance
Relative Merits of Factorial Designs
Assumptions Associated with a Completely Randomized Factorial Design
Check Your Understanding of Section 16.4

16.5 Looking Back: What Have You Learned?
Review Exercises for Chapter 16

429

16.1 INTRODUCTION

Looking Ahead: What Is This Chapter About?

In this chapter you will learn about three approaches to controlling or minimizing undesired sources of variation in experiments. You also will learn about two more analysis of variance designs: a randomized block design and a completely randomized factorial design. The randomized block design is appropriate for experiments with one treatment and one block variable. The design uses the blocking procedure introduced in connection with a t test for dependent samples to isolate an undesired source of variation in an experiment. The completely randomized factorial design enables you to test hypotheses about two or more treatments and the interaction between the treatments. The latter hypothesis about interactions is unique to factorial designs.

After reading this chapter, you should know the following:

- The relative merits of three approaches to controlling or minimizing undesired sources of variation in experiments
- How to lay out and analyze data using a randomized block design
- How to lay out and analyze data using a completely randomized factorial design
- How to interpret an interaction between two treatments
- How to compute and interpret partial omega squared

16.2 BASIC EXPERIMENTAL DESIGN CONCEPTS

Definition of Experimental Design

> The term **experimental design** refers to a randomization plan for assigning participants to experimental conditions and the statistical analysis associated with the plan.

The simplest experimental design is the randomization and analysis plan that is used with a t test for independent samples. I discussed this plan in Section 13.2. A t test for dependent samples uses a more complex randomization plan, but the added complexity is usually accompanied by greater power, as I noted in Section 13.4. The next level of design complexity is the randomization and analysis plan that is used with a completely randomized ANOVA design (CR-p design). As discussed in Chapter 15, this design is appropriate for an experiment that has one treatment with $p \geq 2$ levels. As you will see, the randomized block design and the completely randomized factorial design described in this chapter utilize features of the designs discussed earlier. Before describing the randomized block and completely randomized factorial designs, I will discuss several ways to control nuisance variables.

Controlling Nuisance Variables

In the behavioral sciences, health sciences, and education, differences among participants or experimental units can make a significant contribution to error variance,

$\hat{\sigma}_{\varepsilon}^{2}$. Recall from Section 15.3 that if the null hypothesis for a completely randomized design is false, the F statistic is the ratio of the following sample variances:

$$F = \frac{MSBG}{MSWG} = \frac{\hat{\sigma}_{\varepsilon}^{2} + \text{a function of treatment effects}}{\hat{\sigma}_{\varepsilon}^{2}}$$

A large error variance, $\hat{\sigma}_{\varepsilon}^{2}$, can mask or obscure the effects of a treatment. Hence, in designing an experiment, you want to minimize variables that contribute to error variance. Other variables that can contribute to error variance include administering the levels of a treatment under different environmental conditions—say, at different times of the day or locations—and having different researchers administer the treatment levels. Variation in the dependent variable that is attributable to such sources is called **nuisance variation.** Three approaches to controlling or minimizing these undesired sources of variation are as follows:

1. Hold the nuisance variables constant—for example, use only 19-year-old women participants—and have the same researcher administer the treatment levels at the same time of day and in the same research facility.
2. Assign the participants randomly to the treatment levels so that known and unsuspected sources of variation among the participants are distributed over the entire experiment and thus do not affect just one or a limited number of treatment levels. If the treatment levels must be administered at different times of the day or in different locations, randomize the assignment of treatment levels to times and locations. This research strategy, along with the strategy of holding some variables constant, is used in the completely randomized design.
3. Include the nuisance variable as one of the factors in the experiment. The randomized block design uses this research strategy in conjunction with the two just described.

To include a nuisance variable as one of the factors in an experiment, it is necessary to form **blocks** of participants so that the participants within a block are more homogeneous with respect to the nuisance variable than those in different blocks. Perhaps an example will help to clarify the procedure. In Chapter 15, I described an experiment to determine the effectiveness of three diets for obese teenage girls. In that example, 30 girls who wanted to lose weight were randomly assigned to three diets with the restriction that 10 girls were assigned to each diet. Because of random assignment, one would expect that nuisance variables such as the average initial weight of the girls assigned to each diet would be approximately the same. Initial weight is an important nuisance variable because it is positively correlated with the dependent variable of weight loss. The more overweight a girl is, the easier it is for her to lose weight.

When samples are small as in the diet experiment, random assignment of participants to treatment levels does not always distribute the nuisance variables evenly over the levels. For example, one treatment level may have a disproportionately large number of very obese girls. A researcher can minimize the likelihood of this occurring by assigning participants to blocks so that those assigned to the same block are similar with respect to the nuisance variable. A simple way to form the

a. Layout for randomized block design (RB − 3 design)

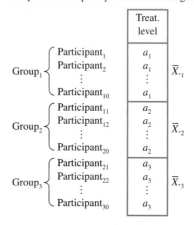

	Treat. level	Treat. level	Treat. level	
Block$_1$	a_1	a_2	a_3	$\bar{X}_{1.}$
Block$_2$	a_1	a_2	a_3	$\bar{X}_{2.}$
Block$_3$	a_1	a_2	a_3	$\bar{X}_{3.}$
⋮	⋮	⋮	⋮	
Block$_{10}$	a_1	a_2	a_3	$\bar{X}_{10.}$
	$\bar{X}_{.1}$	$\bar{X}_{.2}$	$\bar{X}_{.3}$	

b. Layout for completely randomized design (CR − 3 design)

		Treat. level	
Group$_1$	⎧ Participant$_1$	a_1	
	Participant$_2$	a_1	$\bar{X}_{.1}$
	⋮	⋮	
	⎩ Participant$_{10}$	a_1	
Group$_2$	⎧ Participant$_{11}$	a_2	
	Participant$_{12}$	a_2	$\bar{X}_{.2}$
	⋮	⋮	
	⎩ Participant$_{20}$	a_2	
Group$_3$	⎧ Participant$_{21}$	a_3	
	Participant$_{22}$	a_3	$\bar{X}_{.3}$
	⋮	⋮	
	⎩ Participant$_{30}$	a_3	

Figure 16.2-1. Comparison of layouts for RB-3 and CR-3 designs. In the RB-3 design, each of the 10 blocks contains three matched participants who are randomly assigned the treatment levels within a block. In the CR-3 design, 30 participants are randomly assigned to the three treatment levels.

blocks is to rank the girls from heaviest to lightest. The three heaviest girls become block 1, the next three heaviest girls become block 2, and so on. The matching procedure continues until all 30 girls have been assigned to one of 10 blocks. The three girls within a block are then randomly assigned to the diets. The layout for this randomized block design is shown in Figure 16.2-1(a). For comparison purposes, the layout for the completely randomized design described in Chapter 15 also is shown. An advantage of the randomized block design, as you will see, is that it removes the effects of the nuisance variable from the denominator of the F statistic. This results in a more powerful test of a false null hypothesis.

Another approach to minimizing the effect of nuisance variables that was mentioned earlier is to hold them constant. For example, measure each girl's weight loss using the same weight scale and at the same time of day. Some variables are not easy to hold constant, such as genetic predisposition to obesity and amount of daily exercise. These and other unsuspected nuisance variables are usually controlled by random assignment. The larger the sample, the more confident a researcher can be that the effects of nuisance variables have been evenly distributed across the treatment conditions. The randomized block design enables a researcher to use all three strategies for controlling nuisance variables.

Procedures for Forming Blocks

Any variable that is positively correlated with the dependent variable other than the independent variable is a candidate for becoming a blocking variable.

In forming blocks it is important to assign participants to blocks so that those in a given block are as similar as possible with respect to a variable that is positively correlated with the dependent variable. Participants in different blocks should be less similar. Any one of the four procedures described in Section 13.4 for obtaining dependent samples can be used to form blocks. These procedures are as follows:

1. Observing participants under all of the conditions in the experiment—that is, obtaining repeated measures on each participant.
2. Forming blocks of participants who are similar with respect to a nuisance variable that is positively correlated with the dependent variable. This is called participant matching.
3. Forming blocks that are composed of identical twins or littermates and assigning members of a pair or a litter randomly to the conditions in the experiment.
4. Forming blocks of participants who are matched by mutual selection such as husband and wife couples or business partners.

In the diet experiment, the use of participant matching appears to be the most appropriate blocking strategy for controlling the nuisance variable of initial weight. In general, however, participant matching is used less often than obtaining repeated measures on each participant. If each block consists of one participant who is observed p times, it is desirable if possible to randomize the order in which the p treatment levels are administered. The effects of some treatments such as a medication for an illness remain in a participant's system for some time. In such cases, it is necessary to provide a "washout period" between administrations of the medications to allow the effects of the previous medication to dissipate.

When researchers consider potential blocking variables, they often overlook characteristics of the environmental setting such as time of day. For example, if an experiment has three treatment levels and the researcher plans to test participants between the hours of 1 P.M. and 6 P.M., the blocks might represent the following afternoon time periods:

Block 1	1:00–1:10	1:15–1:25	1:30–1:40
Block 2	1:45–1:55	2:00–2:10	2:15–2:25
⋮	⋮	⋮	⋮
Block 8	5:15–5:25	5:30–5:40	5:45–5:55

The time periods within a block are randomly assigned to the three treatment levels. This blocking procedure ensures that the administration of treatment levels is evenly distributed over the testing period from 1 P.M. to 6 P.M. Time of day is a particularly effective blocking variable because it can isolate a number of additional sources of variability: fluctuation in daily body cycles, fatigue, changes in weather conditions, and drifts in the calibration of electronic equipment, to mention only a few. The use of time of day or other blocking variables such as day of the week, season, room location, and experimental apparatus can significantly decrease error variance (also called **variance of the error effects**).

CHECK YOUR UNDERSTANDING OF SECTION 16.2

1. Describe the nature of nuisance variables and three ways to control or minimize them.
2. In selecting a blocking variable, what should a researcher look for?
3. A researcher investigated the effects of three kinds of instruction on first-grade students' tendency to help another child. Forty-two boys were randomly assigned to one of three kinds of instructions, denoted by a_1, a_2, and a_3, with the restriction that 14 boys were assigned to each kind of instruction. Boys in the a_1 group (indirect responsibility group) were told that there was another boy alone in an adjoining room who had been told not to climb on a chair. Boys in the a_2 group were told the same story and in addition were told that they were being left in charge and to take care of anything that happened (direct responsibility group 1). All of the boys were given a simple task to perform. Shortly after the researcher left the room, there was a loud crash in the adjoining room followed by a minute of crying and sobbing. Boys in the a_3 group were given the same instructions as those in group a_2, but the sounds from the adjoining room included calls for help (direct responsibility group 2). The researcher observed the boys from behind a one-way mirror and rated their behavior in terms of the amount of help offered: 1 = no help to 5 = went to the adjoining room. (Experiment suggested by Staub, E. [1970]. A child in distress: The effect of focusing of responsibility on children on their attempts to help. *Developmental Psychology, 2,* 152–153.)
   a. Identify the independent and dependent variables.
   b. Identify nuisance variables that were held constant.
   c. Can you think of some nuisance variables that were controlled by randomization?
   d. Suppose that scores on the Conforming-Compulsive scale of the Millon Clinical Multiaxial Inventory are available for each of the 42 children and that the scale is known to be positively correlated with the dependent variable. Describe in detail how you could use this information.
4. Terms to remember:
   a. Experimental design   b. Nuisance variation
   c. Block   d. Variance of error effects (error variance)

16.3 RANDOMIZED BLOCK DESIGN

A **randomized block design** with p treatment levels, denoted by the letters RB-p, uses the blocking procedure to reduce the variance of the error effects and thereby obtain a more powerful test of a false null hypothesis. Recall from Section 15.3 that error effects include effects that are unique to a participant, effects attributable to chance fluctuations in the participant's performance, and effects attributable to environmental and other uncontrolled conditions. One of the goals of blocking in a randomized block design is to minimize the variance of error effects.

Every ANOVA design has a unique model equation. The model equation for a randomized block design is described next.

Model Equation for a Score

A score, X_{ij}, in a randomized block design is a composite that reflects all of the sources of variation that affect the score. You saw in Section 15.3 that a score for a completely randomized ANOVA design is the sum of three terms in the sample model equation: $X_{ij} = \overline{X}.. + (\overline{X}._j - \overline{X}..) + (X_{ij} + \overline{X}._j)$. In a randomized block design, a score is equal to the sum of four terms. The sample model equation is

$$X_{ij} = \overline{X}.. + (\overline{X}._j - \overline{X}..) + (\overline{X}_i. - \overline{X}..) + (X_{ij} - \overline{X}_i. - \overline{X}._j + \overline{X}..)$$

| Score | Grand Mean | Treatment Effect | Block Effect | Error Effect (Residual) |

Notice that the sample model equation contains one more effect than the model equation for a completely randomized design—the block effect. The statistics in the sample model equation are unbiased estimators of four model parameters: population grand mean, μ; population treatment effect, $\mu._j - \mu$; population block effect, $\mu_i. - \mu$; and population error effect, $X_{ij} - \mu_i. - \mu._j + \mu$. The correspondence between the statistics and the parameters that they estimate is as follows:

$$X_{ij} = \overline{X}.. + (\overline{X}._j - \overline{X}..) + (\overline{X}_i. - \overline{X}..) + (X_{ij} - \overline{X}_i. - \overline{X}._j + \overline{X}..)$$

Model equation $\quad X_{ij} = \mu \quad + (\mu._j - \mu) \quad + (\mu_i. - \mu) \quad + (X_{ij} - \mu_i. - \mu._j + \mu)$

A randomized block design has $j = 1, \ldots, p$ levels of treatment A and $i = 1, \ldots, n$ blocks. The total sum of squares and total degrees of freedom for the design can be partitioned into three parts as follows:

$$SS \text{ Total} = SS \text{ Treatment } A + SS \text{ Blocks} + SS \text{ Residual}$$

$$\sum_{j=1}^{p}\sum_{i=1}^{n}(X_{ij} - \overline{X}..)^2 = n\sum_{j=1}^{p}(\overline{X}._j - \overline{X}..)^2 + p\sum_{i=1}^{n}(\overline{X}_i. - \overline{X}..)^2 + \sum_{j=1}^{p}\sum_{i=1}^{n}(X_{ij} - \overline{X}_i. - \overline{X}._j + \overline{X}..)^2$$

| df_{TO} | $=$ | df_A | $+$ | df_{BL} | $+$ | df_{RES} |
| $np - 1$ | $=$ | $p - 1$ | $+$ | $n - 1$ | $+$ | $(n-1)(p-1)$ |

A test of the null hypothesis that the population means for treatment A are equal,

$$H_0: \mu_{.1} = \mu_{.2} = \cdots = \mu_{.p}$$

$$H_1: \mu_{.j} \neq \mu_{.j'}$$

is given by

$$F = \frac{SSA/(p-1)}{SSRES/[(n-1)(p-1)]} = \frac{MSA}{MSRES}$$

The degrees of freedom for the numerator and denominator of the F statistic are, respectively, $\nu_1 = p - 1$ and $\nu_2 = (n-1)(p-1)$.

The F statistic is referred to the sampling distribution of F, which is tabled in Appendix Table D.5. If F is greater than or equal to the critical value $F_{\alpha; \nu_1, \nu_2}$, the null hypothesis is rejected.

A test of the null hypothesis that the population means for blocks, BL, are equal is given by

$$F = \frac{SSBL/(n-1)}{SSRES/[(n-1)(p-1)]} = \frac{MSBL}{MSRES}$$

The degrees of freedom for the numerator and denominator of the F statistic are, respectively, $\nu_1 = n - 1$ and $\nu_2 = (n-1)(p-1)$.

The null hypothesis that the block population means are equal is rejected if $F \geq F_{\alpha; \nu_1, \nu_2}$. Ordinarily, a test of the null hypothesis for blocks is of little interest because the blocks represent a nuisance variable whose means are expected to differ. In the following section, you will see how to compute the required mean squares and F statistics.

Computational Procedures for RB-3 Design

For purposes of comparison, I will reanalyze the weight-loss data in Table 15.4-2 as if the randomization plan appropriate for a randomized block design had been used. I want to form 10 blocks of girls who are matched in terms of initial weight. Earlier, I described a simple way to accomplish this. The 30 girls are ranked from heaviest to lightest. The three heaviest girls become block 1, the next three heaviest girls become block 2, and so on. The matching procedure continues until all 30 girls have been assigned to one of 10 blocks. The three girls in each block are then randomly assigned to the three diets. Assume that the 30 girls in the diet experiment have been assigned to 10 blocks following this procedure. The data are shown in Table 16.3-1. The data in Table 16.3-1 for the RB-3 design and the data in Table 15.4-2 for the CR-3 design contain the same numbers. This will allow me to compare the results of the two designs.

TABLE 16.3-1   Computational Procedures for RB-3 Design

(i) Data and notation [X_{ij} denotes a score for the participant in block i and treatment level j; i = 1, . . . , n blocks (s_i); j = 1, . . . , p treatment levels (a_j)]

AS Summary Table[a]

	a_1	a_2	a_3	$\sum_{j=1}^{p} X_{ij}$
s_1	7	13	14	34
s_2	9	9	10	28
s_3	10	10	12	32
s_4	12	10	12	34
s_5	8	9	15	32
s_6	7	8	14	29
s_7	9	11	13	33
s_8	8	8	12	28
s_9	4	7	7	18
s_{10}	6	5	11	22
$\sum_{i=1}^{n} X_{ij} = 80$		90	120	

(ii) Computational symbols[b]

$$\sum_{j=1}^{p}\sum_{i=1}^{n} X_{ij} = 7 + 9 + 10 + \cdots + 11 = 290.000$$

$$\sum_{j=1}^{p}\sum_{i=1}^{n} X_{ij}^2 = [AS] = (7)^2 + (9)^2 + (10)^2 + \cdots + (11)^2 = 3026.000$$

$$\frac{\left(\sum_{j=1}^{p}\sum_{i=1}^{n} X_{ij}\right)^2}{np} = [X] = \frac{(290)^2}{(10)(3)} = 2803.333$$

$$\sum_{j=1}^{p}\frac{\left(\sum_{i=1}^{n} X_{ij}\right)^2}{n} = [A] = \frac{(80)^2}{10} + \cdots + \frac{(120)^2}{10} = 2890.000$$

$$\sum_{i=1}^{n}\frac{\left(\sum_{j=1}^{p} X_{ij}\right)^2}{p} = [S] = \frac{(34)^2}{3} + \cdots + \frac{(22)^2}{3} = 2888.667$$

(iii) Computational formulas

$$SSTO = [AS] - [X] = 3026.000 - 2803.333 = 222.667$$

$$SSA = [A] - [X] = 2890.000 - 2803.333 = 86.667$$

(continued)

TABLE 16.3-1 *(continued)*

$$SSBL = [S] - [X] = 2888.667 - 2803.333 = 85.333$$

$$SSRES = [AS] - [A] - [S] + [X] = 3026.000 - 2890.000 - 2888.667 + 2803.333$$

$$= 50.667$$

[a] *A* denotes treatment *A*, and *S* denotes subjects or blocks; the table is so named because it reflects variation attributable to treatment levels (*A*) and subjects (*S*).
[b] The symbols [*AS*], [*X*], [*A*], and [*S*] are used to simplify the computational formulas.

TABLE 16.3-2 ANOVA Table for RB-3 Design

Source	SS	df	MS	F
1. Treatment *A* (three diets)	86.667	$p - 1 = 2$	43.334	$\left[\frac{1}{3}\right]$ 15.39**
2. Blocks (initial weight)	85.333	$n - 1 = 9$	9.481	$\left[\frac{2}{3}\right]$ 3.37*
3. Residual	50.667	$(n - 1)(p - 1) = 18$	2.815	
4. Total	222.667	$npq - 1 = 29$		

*$p < .02$.
**$p < .0002$.

$\left[\frac{1}{3}\right]$ indicates that the *F* statistic was obtained by dividing *MSA* in row 1 by *MSRES* in row 3; Whereas $\left[\frac{2}{3}\right]$ indicates that the *F* statistic was obtained by dividing *MSBL* in row 2 by *MSRES* in row 3.

As discussed in Section 15.4, it is good statistical practice to compute descriptive statistics for one's data prior to testing an omnibus null hypothesis. A descriptive summary in the form of stacked box plots and a table of means and standard deviations for the weight-loss data are given in Figure 15.4-2 and Table 15.4-1 of the previous chapter. As discussed in Section 15.4, there was nothing in the descriptive summary that dissuaded the researcher from proceeding to test the omnibus null hypothesis.

The data and computational procedures for the randomized block design are shown in Table 16.3-1. The formulas in Table 16.3-1 are more convenient for computing the sums of squares than those given earlier. The .05 level of significance is adopted for the two *F* tests. According to Table 16.3-2, the null hypotheses for treatment *A* and blocks can be rejected.

You are probably wondering "What, if anything, has been gained by using a randomized block design instead of a completely randomized design?" The answer is greater power. A comparison of Tables 15.4-3 and 16.3-2 shows that the *F* statistics for testing the null hypothesis for the three diets are

$$\text{Completely randomized design } F = \frac{MSBG}{MSWG} = \frac{43.334}{5.037} = 8.60$$

$$\text{Randomized block design } F = \frac{MSA}{MSRES} = \frac{43.334}{2.815} = 15.39$$

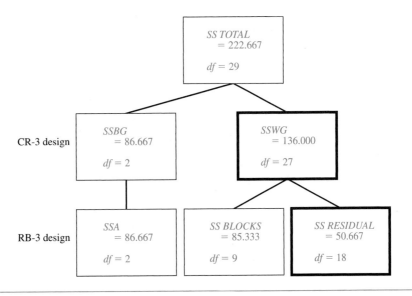

Figure 16.3-1. Partition of the total sum of squares and degrees of freedom for a CR-3 design and an RB-3 design. The sum of squares that appears in the denominator of the F statistic for each design is indicated by the rectangle with the thicker lines. Notice that for the RB-3 design, the nuisance variable of blocks has been isolated and removed from the F denominator. In other words,

$$
\begin{aligned}
SS\ RESIDUAL &= SSWG - SS\ BLOCKS \\
50.667 &= 136.000 - 85.333 \\
df_{Residual} &= df_{WG} - df_{Blocks} \\
18 &= 27 - 9
\end{aligned}
$$

The F statistic for the randomized block design is larger because its denominator ($MSRES = 2.815$) is about half as large as the denominator for the completely randomized design ($MSWG = 5.037$). The reduction in the F denominator has been accomplished by isolating the nuisance variable of the girls' initial weight (MS Blocks). Consequently, this nuisance variable does not contribute to $MSRES$ for the randomized block design. This point is graphically illustrated in Figure 16.3-1 where the partition of the total sum of squares for the two designs is shown. As this figure suggests, all sources of variation not specifically identified in the model equation contribute to the F denominator.

> The effectiveness of the blocking procedure is determined by how well participants in each block are matched. The better the matching, the higher the mean correlation between all pairs of treatment levels and the more powerful the randomized block design relative to a completely randomized design.

Let's use the weight-loss data in Table 16.3-1 to illustrate what I mean. For these data, the Pearson product-moment correlations among the three treatment levels are

$r_{12} = .477$ for a_1 and a_2, $r_{13} = .370$ for a_1 and a_3, and $r_{23} = .479$ for a_2 and a_3. The mean correlation, $\bar{r}$, is

$$\bar{r} = \frac{.477 + .370 + .479}{3} = .442$$

The F denominator for the randomized block design, $MSRES$, is equal to

$$MSRES = MSWG(1 - \bar{r})$$

where $MSWG$ is the F denominator for a completely randomized design. The value of $MSWG$ from Table 15.4-3 is 5.037. For the weight-loss data, $MSRES$ is, within rounding error, equal to

$$MSRES = MSWG(1 - \bar{r}) = 5.037(1 - .442) = 2.811$$

An examination of the equation $MSRES = MSWG(1 - \bar{r})$ reveals that the larger the mean correlation among the treatment levels, $\bar{r}$, the smaller is $MSRES$ relative to $MSWG$. What this means is that by carefully matching the participants in each of the block, a researcher can greatly increase the power of the randomized block design relative to that of a completely randomized design.

Multiple Comparison Procedures

After rejecting the omnibus null hypothesis for treatment A in a randomized block design, a researcher would probably want to determine which contrasts among the population means are significant. The Fisher-Hayter and Scheffé multiple comparison procedures described in Section 15.6 can be used for this purpose. The Scheffé procedure also can be used to construct confidence intervals.

The Fisher-Hayter and Scheffé formulas for a randomized block design are slightly different than those for a completely randomized design.

The formula for the Fisher-Hayter test statistic is

$$qFH = \frac{\overline{X}_{\cdot j} - \overline{X}_{\cdot j'}}{\sqrt{\dfrac{MSREG}{n}}}$$

where $\overline{X}_{\cdot j}$ and $\overline{X}_{\cdot j'}$ are sample means for treatment A, $MSREG$ is the denominator of the F statistic for the randomized block design, and n is the number of blocks.

The formula for the Scheffé test statistic is

$$FS = \frac{(c_1 \overline{X}_{\cdot 1} + c_2 \overline{X}_{\cdot 2} + \cdots + c_p \overline{X}_{\cdot p})^2}{MSREG\left(\dfrac{c_1^2}{n} + \dfrac{c_2^2}{n} + \cdots + \dfrac{c_p^2}{n}\right)}$$

where $c_1, c_2, \ldots, c_p$ are coefficients that define a contrast for treatment A, $\overline{X}_{\cdot 1}$, $\overline{X}_{\cdot 2}, \ldots, \overline{X}_{\cdot p}$ are sample means for treatment A, $MSREG$ is the denominator of the F statistic for the randomized block design, and n is the number of blocks.

The Fisher-Hayter test is a two-step procedure. The first step consists of using the ANOVA F statistic to test the omnibus null hypothesis for treatment A at α level of significance. If the ANOVA F test is not significant, the omnibus null hypothesis is not rejected and it is concluded that none of the pairwise contrasts for treatment A differ from 0. If the omnibus null hypothesis is rejected, each of the pairwise contrasts is tested using the Fisher-Hayter statistic. The null hypothesis, $H_0: \mu_{.j} = \mu_{.j'}$, is rejected if the absolute value of qFH exceeds or equals the critical value $q_{\alpha; p-1, \nu}$, where $q_{\alpha; p-1, \nu}$ is obtained from the distribution of the Studentized range in Appendix Table D.9. The table is entered for $p-1$ means, where p is the number of treatment A means in the experiment.

The Scheffé test for a treatment A contrast, $H_0: c_1\mu_{.1} + c_2\mu_{.2} + \cdots + c_p\mu_{.p} = 0$, is rejected if the absolute value of FS exceeds or equals the critical value $(p-1)F_{\alpha; \nu_1, \nu_2}$, where p is the number of treatment A means in the experiment and $F_{\alpha; \nu_1, \nu_2}$ is obtained from Appendix Table D.5.

Scheffé's statistic also can be used to construct confidence intervals for all contrasts of interest.

A two-sided $100(1-\alpha)\%$ confidence interval for the treatment A contrast, $\psi_i = c_1\mu_{.1} + c_2\mu_{.2} + \cdots + c_p\mu_{.p}$, is given by

$$\hat{\psi}_i - \sqrt{(p-1)F_{\alpha; \nu_1, \nu_2}}\sqrt{MSRES \sum_{j=1}^{p} \frac{c_j^2}{n}} < \psi_i$$

$$< \hat{\psi}_i + \sqrt{(p-1)F_{\alpha; \nu_1, \nu_2}}\sqrt{MSRES \sum_{j=1}^{p} \frac{c_j^2}{n}}$$

where $\hat{\psi}_i = c_1\overline{X}_{.1} + c_2\overline{X}_{.2} + \cdots + c_p\overline{X}_{.p}$; $c_1, c_2, \ldots, c_p$ are coefficients that define a contrast for treatment A; $\overline{X}_{.1}, \overline{X}_{.2}, \ldots, \overline{X}_{.p}$ are sample means; p is the number of treatment A means in the experiment; $F_{\alpha; \nu_1, \nu_2}$ is the value that cuts off the upper α region from Appendix Table D.5; $\nu_1 = p-1$, $\nu_2 = (n-1)(p-1)$; $MSRES$ is the denominator of the F statistic for a randomized block design; and n is the number of blocks.

Computational Example for the Fisher-Hayter Multiple Comparison Procedure

The omnibus null hypothesis for the weight-loss data in Tables 16.3-1 and 16.3-2 was rejected. After examining the sample means, the researcher decided to use the Fisher-Hayter multiple comparison statistic to test the following null hypotheses:

$$H_0: \mu_{.1} = \mu_{.2} \qquad H_0: \mu_{.1} = \mu_{.3} \qquad H_0: \mu_{.2} = \mu_{.3}$$

The weight-loss sample means are $\overline{X}_{.1} = 8.00$, $\overline{X}_{.2} = 9.00$, $\overline{X}_{.3} = 12.00$; $MSRES = 2.815$; and $n = 10$. Because the ANOVA F test was significant, the next step is to test the three pairwise contrasts using

$$qFH = \frac{\overline{X}_{.j} - \overline{X}_{.j'}}{\sqrt{\dfrac{MSREG}{n}}}$$

The test statistics are

$$qFH = \frac{8.00 - 9.00}{\sqrt{\dfrac{2.815}{10}}} = -1.88 \qquad (\hat{\psi}_1 = \overline{X}_{\cdot 1} - \overline{X}_{\cdot 2})$$

$$qFH = \frac{8.00 - 12.00}{\sqrt{\dfrac{2.815}{10}}} = -7.54 \qquad (\hat{\psi}_2 = \overline{X}_{\cdot 1} - \overline{X}_{\cdot 3})$$

$$qFH = \frac{9.00 - 12.00}{\sqrt{\dfrac{2.815}{10}}} = -5.65 \qquad (\hat{\psi}_3 = \overline{X}_{\cdot 2} - \overline{X}_{\cdot 3})$$

To reject a null hypothesis, the absolute value $|qFH|$ must exceed or equal $q_{\alpha; p-1, v} = q_{.05; 3-1, 18} = 2.97$, where $v = (n-1)(p-1)$. Because $|qFH(18)| = 7.54$ and 5.65 are greater than $q_{.05; 3-1, 18} = 2.97$, the null hypotheses for $H_0: \mu_1 = \mu_3$ and $H_0: \mu_2 = \mu_3$ are rejected. The researcher can conclude that for the population of girls represented in the experiment, diet a_3 would produce a greater weight loss than diets a_1 and a_2. Based on the sample data, the researcher's best guess is that the use of diet a_3 would result in losing 4 more pounds than diet a_1 and 3 more than diet a_2.

Practical Significance

In Section 15.7, I described omega squared, a measure of strength of association that is reported with the ANOVA F test. Omega squared estimates the proportion of variance in the dependent variable that is accounted for by the p treatments levels. For a randomized block design, a researcher wants to estimate the proportion of variance in the dependent variable that is accounted for by the p treatments levels while ignoring the nuisance variable of blocks. The appropriate measure of strength of association between the dependent variable X and treatment A is **partial omega squared,** denoted by $\hat{\omega}^2_{X|A\cdot BL}$. The subscript $X|A\cdot BL$ indicates that the association is between the dependent variable X and treatment A; the dot indicates that the effects of blocks are ignored. The formula for $\hat{\omega}^2_{X|A\cdot BL}$ is

$$\hat{\omega}^2_{X|A\cdot BL} = \frac{(p-1)(F_A - 1)}{(p-1)(F_A - 1) + np}$$

where F_A is the F statistic for treatment A ($F_A = MSA/MSRES$). For the weight-loss data in Table 16.3-2, an estimate of the proportion of the population weight-loss variance accounted for by the three diets is

$$\hat{\omega}^2_{X|A\cdot BL} = \frac{(3-1)(15.394 - 1)}{(3-1)(15.394 - 1) + (10)(3)} = .49$$

According to Cohen's guidelines for interpreting omega squared in Section 15.7, the strength of association between the diets and weight loss is large—49% of the variance in weight loss is associated with the diets; $100\% - 49\% = 51\%$ is associated with factors other than the diets.

Hedges's g statistic, described in Sections 13.2 and 15.7, can be used to assess the effect size of contrasts among the diet means. The g statistic is

$$g = \frac{|\overline{X}_{.j} - \overline{X}_{.j'}|}{\hat{\sigma}_{Pooled}}$$

where

$$\hat{\sigma}_{Pooled} = \sqrt{\frac{(n_1 - 1)\hat{\sigma}_1^2 + (n_2 - 1)\hat{\sigma}_2^2 + \cdots + (n_p - 1)\hat{\sigma}_p^2}{(n_1 - 1) + (n_2 - 1) + \cdots + (n_p - 1)}}$$

For a randomized block design, a simpler formula for computing $\hat{\sigma}_{Pooled}$ is

$$\hat{\sigma}_{Pooled} = \sqrt{\frac{SSBL + SSRES}{p(n-1)}}$$

where $SSBL$ and $SSRES$ are obtained from a randomized block ANOVA table. For the weight-loss data in Tables 16.3-1 and 16.3-2, the effect sizes for $\hat{\psi}_1$, $\hat{\psi}_2$, and $\hat{\psi}_3$ are, respectively,

$$g = \frac{|\overline{X}_{.j} - \overline{X}_{.j'}|}{\hat{\sigma}_{Pooled}}$$

$$g = \frac{|8 - 9|}{2.244} = 0.45 \qquad (\hat{\psi}_1 = \overline{X}_{.1} - \overline{X}_{.2})$$

$$g = \frac{|8 - 12|}{2.244} = 1.8 \qquad (\hat{\psi}_2 = \overline{X}_{.1} - \overline{X}_{.3})$$

$$g = \frac{|9 - 12|}{2.244} = 1.3 \qquad (\hat{\psi}_3 = \overline{X}_{.2} - \overline{X}_{.3})$$

where

$$\hat{\sigma}_{Pooled} = \sqrt{\frac{85.333 + 50.667}{3(10 - 1)}} = 2.244$$

The Fisher-Hayter multiple comparison procedure identified two significant pairwise contrast: $\hat{\psi}_2 = \mu_1 - \mu_3$ and $\hat{\psi}_3 = \mu_2 - \mu_3$. According to Cohen's guidelines for interpreting d-like measures of effect size in Section 10.4, $\hat{\psi}_2$ and $\hat{\psi}_3$ represent large effects. This suggests that the weight-loss difference between diets a_1 and a_3 and between diets a_2 and a_3 is large enough to be of practical value. This conclusion is consistent with our intuition—what girl wouldn't want to use a diet that results in losing 3 or 4 more pounds per month than less effective diets?

Assumptions Associated with a Randomized Block Design

The assumptions for the simplest ANOVA design, the completely randomized design, were described in detail in Section 15.5. The randomized block design shares several of the assumptions, as the following list shows:

1. The model equation $X_{ij} = \mu + (\mu_{.j} - \mu) + (\mu_{i.} - \mu) + (X_{ij} - \mu_{i.} - \mu_{.j} + \mu)$ reflects all the sources of variation that affect X_{ij}.
2. The blocks represent a random sample from a population of blocks. The population block effects within each block population are normally distributed, and the variances of the block populations are homogeneous. Furthermore, the block effects are independent of each other and other effects in the model equation.
3. The population variances of differences for all pairs of treatment levels, $\sigma_{a_j}^2 + \sigma_{a_{j'}}^2 - 2\sigma_{a_j a_{j'}}$, are homogeneous; $\sigma_{a_j a_{j'}}$ is the covariance (see Section 5.3) of treatment levels a_j and $a_{j'}$.
4. The population error effects are normally distributed and the variances of the error effects, σ_ε^2, are homogeneous. Furthermore, the error effects are independent of each other and other effects in the model equation.

Assumptions 1 and 4 are discussed in Section 15.5 in connection with a completely randomized design; assumptions 2 and 3 are new. Assumption 2 states, among other things, that the blocks in an experiment are a random sample from a population of blocks. In many experiments, a researcher does not actually obtain a random sample of block. In such cases, the conclusions from the experiment are restricted to the population represented by the blocks in the experiment. Recall that blocks represent a nuisance variable whose effects a researcher wants to control. In the weight-loss experiment, the blocks represented 10 levels of initial obesity and were not randomly sampled from a population of levels of initial obesity. Instead, 30 volunteers who wanted to lose weight were recruited. The levels of initial obesity were determined by the initial weights of the 30 girls. The researcher was not interested in the specific levels of obesity but instead focused on controlling for the effects of initial obesity. Although a random sample of blocks was not obtained, a population of girls must exist that would have produced the blocks in the experiment if a random sample had been obtained. The results of the experiment apply to this hypothetical population of blocks. To the extent that the blocks in an experiment are representative of a population of interest, the results may generalize to that population. However, in the absence of random sampling, generalizations to other block populations involve a leap of faith.

Assumption 3 states that the population variances of differences between all pairs of treatment levels are homogeneous. For the weight-loss data, this means that

$$\sigma_{a_1}^2 + \sigma_{a_2}^2 - 2\sigma_{a_1 a_2} = \sigma_{a_1}^2 + \sigma_{a_3}^2 - 2\sigma_{a_1 a_3} = \sigma_{a_2}^2 + \sigma_{a_3}^2 - 2\sigma_{a_2 a_3}$$

Violation of this assumption, which is called the *sphericity condition*, can seriously affect the probability of making a Type I error and the power of the F test. Procedures for testing the assumption and adjustments to compensate for observed violations are complicated and beyond the scope of this book. The interested reader is referred to Kirk (1995, pp. 274–282).

The model equation and associated assumptions that have been described are called a *mixed model* and underlie most randomized block designs. For a discussion of other models, the reader can consult Howell (2002, p. 442) and Kirk (1995, pp. 265–268).

CHECK YOUR UNDERSTANDING OF SECTION 16.3

5. Fill in the missing values in the following table. Use Microsoft's Excel FDIST function to determine the p value of the F statistics.

Source	SS	df	MS	F
1. Treatment A	51.765	3	( )	$[\frac{1}{3}]$( )*
2. Blocks	( )	20	( )	$[\frac{2}{3}]$( )**
3. Residual	271.500	( )	( )	
4. Total	484.765	( )		

*$p < $( ).
**$p < $( ).

6. Brain-damaged patients are expected to score lower on the Willner Unusual Meanings Vocabulary Test (*WUMV*), which measures knowledge of unusual meanings of familiar words, and the Willner-Sheerer Analogy Test (*WSA*) than on the vocabulary items of the Wechsler Adult Intelligence Scale (*WAIS*). A random sample of 12 brain-damaged patients took all three tests. The order of administration of the tests was randomized independently for each patient. The dependent variable was the participant's standard score on each test. According to the test manual, all three tests have a mean of 10 and a standard deviation of 3. The following data were obtained. (Experiment suggested by Willner, W. [1965]. Impairment of knowledge of unusual meanings of familiar words in brain damage and schizophrenia. *Journal of Abnormal Psychology, 70,* 405–411.)

	a_1 WAIS	a_2 WUMV	a_3 WSA
s_1	15	12	11
s_2	10	11	8
s_3	6	4	3
s_4	7	7	5
s_5	9	6	6
s_6	16	14	10
s_7	11	10	7
s_8	13	9	4
s_9	12	10	8
s_{10}	10	8	7
s_{11}	11	9	9
s_{12}	14	11	10

a. Construct stacked box plots for the data. Are the sample distributions relatively symmetrical? Do the data contain outliers?
b. Compute descriptive statistics, $\overline{X}_{\cdot j}$'s and $\hat{\sigma}_j$'s, for the data and construct a table similar to Table 15.4-1.
c. What do the descriptive statistics in (b) tell you?
d. Test the null hypothesis H_0: $\mu_{\cdot 1} = \mu_{\cdot 2} = \mu_{\cdot 3}$. Let $\alpha = .05$. Determine the p value of the F statistics for treatment A and Blocks using Microsoft's Excel FDIST function.
e. Estimate the proportion of the population variance in the dependent variable that is accounted for by treatment A and interpret the result.
f. Use the Fisher-Hayter statistic to determine which population means differ.
g. Use Hedges's g statistic to measure the effect size for the three pairwise contrasts and interpret the results.
h. Summarize the results of the ANOVA in a sentence or two.
i. Ignore the blocking variable and analyze the data as if the randomization plan for a CR-3 design had been used. Compare the results of the two analyses by constructing a figure similar to Figure 16.3-1. Was the blocking procedure effective? Explain.
7. Terms to remember:
a. Randomized block design
b. Partial omega squared

16.4 COMPLETELY RANDOMIZED FACTORIAL DESIGN

Introduction to Factorial Designs

The two ANOVA designs discussed thus far involve one treatment, but often a researcher wants to test hypotheses about two or more treatments. This can be accomplished by performing two or more separate experiments, but this is inefficient. An alternative approach is to use a factorial ANOVA design to simultaneously test hypotheses about two or more treatments in a single experiment.

> A **factorial design** is distinguished from other ANOVA designs in that it has two or more treatments and the levels of each treatment are investigated in combination with those of other treatments.

For example, a participant's performance on a learning task might be observed for the combined conditions of large monetary reward for good performance (one level of treatment A) and absence of distractions in the learning environment (one level of treatment B). A participant in a factorial design is always simultaneously exposed to one level each of two or more treatments. The combination of conditions to which a participant is simultaneously exposed is called a **treatment combination.** The number of observations in each treatment combination, n, must be the same for each combination. Special procedures can be used when the treatment combination n's are unequal, but the procedures are beyond the scope of this book.

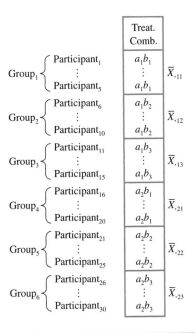

Figure 16.4-1. Layout for a CRF-23 design. Thirty participants were randomly assigned to the $2 \times 3 = 6$ combinations of treatments A and B.

The levels of the treatments in a factorial design are **completely crossed,** meaning that each level of one treatment occurs once with each level of the other treatments and vice versa. I will describe a **completely randomized factorial design** with two treatments: treatment A and treatment B. The design is designated by the letters CRF-pq, where p denotes the number of levels of treatment A, and q denotes the number of levels of treatment B.[1] Perhaps the following example will clarify the main features of a CRF-pq design.

Consider an experiment to investigate the effects of treatments A and B on reading speed. Suppose that treatment A consists of two levels of room illumination: a_1 is 15 foot-candles and a_2 is 30 foot-candles. Treatment B consists of three levels of type size: b_1 is 6-point type, b_2 is 12-point type, and b_3 is 18-point type. Each level of A is combined with all levels of B to form $2 \times 3 = 6$ treatment combinations: $a_1b_1, a_1b_2, a_1b_3, \ldots, a_2b_3$. The layout for this CRF-23 design with five participants in each treatment combination is shown in Figure 16.4-1.

The randomization plan for the design is as follows. Thirty participants are randomly assigned to $p \times q = 2 \times 3 = 6$ treatment combinations with the restriction

---

[1] Some writers refer to this design as a *two-way* or *two-factor ANOVA*. Unfortunately, these designations are imprecise because they could refer to any one of 10 different kinds of factorial designs. Kirk discusses this point (2005a, pp. 66–83).

that five participants are assigned to each combination. Before presenting the computational procedures for this design, I will describe the model equation for a CRF-pq design.

Model Equation for a Score

A participant's score in a CRF-pq design is represented by X_{ijk}, where i denotes one of the n participants, j denotes one of the p levels of treatment A, and k denotes one of the q levels of treatment B. As in all ANOVA designs, the score X_{ijk} is composite. It is equal to the sum of five terms. The sample model equation is

$$X_{ijk} = \overline{X}... + (\overline{X}_{\cdot j\cdot} - \overline{X}...) + (\overline{X}_{\cdot\cdot k} - \overline{X}...) + (\overline{X}_{\cdot jk} - \overline{X}_{\cdot j\cdot} - \overline{X}_{\cdot\cdot k} + \overline{X}...) + (X_{ijk} - \overline{X}_{\cdot jk})$$

| Score | Grand Mean | A Treatment Effect | B Treatment Effect | AB Interaction Effect | Within Cell Error Effect |

The statistics in the sample model equation are unbiased estimators of five model parameters: population grand mean, μ; population A treatment effect, $\mu_{j\cdot} - \mu$; population B treatment effect, $\mu_{\cdot k} - \mu$; population AB interaction effect, $\mu_{jk} - \mu_{j\cdot} - \mu_{\cdot k} + \mu$; and population error effect, $X_{ijk} - \mu_{jk}$. The correspondence between the statistics and the parameters that they estimate is as follows:

$$X_{ijk} = \overline{X}... + (\overline{X}_{\cdot j\cdot} - \overline{X}...) + (\overline{X}_{\cdot\cdot k} - \overline{X}...) + (\overline{X}_{\cdot jk} - \overline{X}_{\cdot j\cdot} - \overline{X}_{\cdot\cdot k} + \overline{X}...) + (X_{ijk} - \overline{X}_{\cdot jk})$$

$$X_{ijk} = \mu + (\mu_{j\cdot} - \mu) + (\mu_{\cdot k} - \mu) + (\mu_{jk} - \mu_{j\cdot} - \mu_{\cdot k} + \mu) + (X_{ijk} - \mu_{jk})$$

The sample model equation allows a researcher to partition the total sum of squares and total degrees of freedom ($npq - 1$) into four parts as follows:

$$SS\text{ Total} = SS\,A\text{ Treatment} + SS\,B\text{ Treatment} + SS\,AB\text{ Interaction} + SS\text{ Within Cell}$$

$$
\begin{array}{ccccccccc}
df_{TO} & = & df_A & + & df_B & + & df_{AB} & + & df_{WCELL} \\
npq - 1 = & & p - 1 & + & q - 1 & + & (p-1)(q-1) & + & pq(n-1)
\end{array}
$$

The following null hypotheses can be tested in this two-treatment factorial design:

$H_0: \mu_{1\cdot} = \mu_{2\cdot} = \cdots = \mu_{p\cdot}$.   (Treatment A population means are equal)

$H_0: \mu_{\cdot 1} = \mu_{\cdot 2} = \cdots = \mu_{\cdot q}$ (Treatment B population means are equal)

$H_0: \mu_{jk} - \mu_{j'k} - \mu_{jk'} + \mu_{j'k'} = 0$ for all j, j', k, k' (Treatments A and B do not interact)

The first two null hypotheses are familiar; the third null hypothesis is new. I will have more to say about the interaction hypothesis later.

Computational Procedures for CRF-23 Design

Descriptive summaries of the data for the reading-speed experiment are presented in Figure 16.4-2 and Table 16.4-1. Mean reading speed appears to be fastest for the 30 foot-candle condition and the larger type sizes. The standard deviations appear to

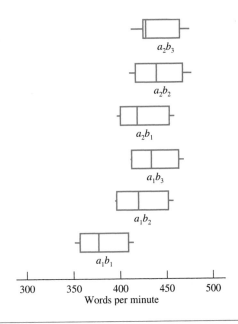

Figure 16.4-2. Treatment A is illumination level: $a_1 = 15$ ft-c, $a_2 = 30$ ft-c. Treatment B is type size: $b_1 = 6$ pt, $b_2 = 12$ pt, $b_3 = 18$ pt. With the exception of treatment combination a_2b_3, the distributions are relatively symmetrical. The data do not contain outliers.

TABLE 16.4-1 **Descriptive Summary of the Reading-Speed Data. Means and Standard Deviations Are Expressed in Words per Minute**

Illumination Level		*Type Size* $b_1 = 6\text{-}pt$	$b_2 = 12\text{-}pt$	$b_3 = 18\text{-}pt$	$\overline{X}_{\cdot j \cdot}$	$\hat{\sigma}_{j \cdot}$
$a_1 = 15$ ft-c	$\overline{X}_{\cdot jk} =$	382	423	436	413.7	35.1
	$\hat{\sigma}_{jk} =$	28.2	29.1	26.2		
$a_2 = 30$ ft-c	$\overline{X}_{\cdot jk} =$	423	442	441	435.3	27.8
	$\hat{\sigma}_{jk} =$	28.4	29.6	27.0		
	$\overline{X}_{\cdot \cdot k} =$	402.5	432.5	438.5		
	$\hat{\sigma}_{\cdot k} =$	34.3	29.4	25.2		

be fairly homogeneous. Researchers should always examine a descriptive summary of their data before proceeding to compute inferential statistics. The examination may uncover suspicious outliers, unexpected promising lines of investigation, or assumptions of the design that do not appear to be tenable.

TABLE 16.4-2   Computational Procedures for CRF-23 Design

(i) *Data and notation [X_{ijk} denotes a score for participant i in treatment combination jk; i = 1, ..., n participants (s_i); j = 1, ..., p levels of treatment A (a_j); k = 1, ..., q levels of treatment B (b_k)]*

ABS Summary Table[a]
Table entry is X_{ijk}

a_1 b_1	a_1 b_2	a_1 b_3	a_2 b_1	a_2 b_2	a_2 b_3
378	454	432	415	439	426
408	394	411	396	467	428
357	452	466	451	477	464
353	396	411	455	410	412
414	419	460	398	417	475
$\sum_{i=1}^{n} X_{ijk} = 1910$	2115	2180	2115	2210	2205

AB Summary Table
Table entry is $\sum_{i=1}^{n} X_{ijk}$

	b_1	b_2	b_3	$\sum_{i=1}^{n}\sum_{k=1}^{q} X_{ijk}$
a_1	1910	2115	2180	6205
a_2	2115	2210	2205	6530
$\sum_{i=1}^{n}\sum_{j=1}^{p} X_{ijk} = 4025$	4325	4385		

(ii) *Computational symbols*

$$\sum_{i=1}^{n}\sum_{j=1}^{p}\sum_{k=1}^{q} X_{ijk} = 378 + 408 + \cdots + 475 = 12{,}735.000$$

$$\sum_{i=1}^{n}\sum_{j=1}^{p}\sum_{k=1}^{q} X_{ijk}^2 = [ABS] = (378)^2 + (408)^2 + \cdots + (475)^2 = 5{,}437{,}581.000$$

$$\frac{\left(\sum_{i=1}^{n}\sum_{j=1}^{p}\sum_{k=1}^{q} X_{ijk}\right)^2}{npq} = [X] = \frac{(12{,}735)^2}{(5)(2)(3)} = 5{,}406{,}007.500$$

$$\sum_{j=1}^{p} \frac{\left(\sum_{i=1}^{n}\sum_{j=1}^{q} X_{ijk}\right)^2}{nq} = [A] = \frac{(6{,}205)^2}{(5)(3)} + \frac{(6{,}530)^2}{(5)(3)} = 5{,}409{,}528.333$$

(continued)

TABLE 16.4-2 *(continued)*

$$\sum_{k=1}^{q} \frac{\left(\sum_{i=1}^{n}\sum_{j=1}^{p} X_{ijk}\right)^2}{np} = [B] = \frac{(4{,}025)^2}{(5)(2)} + \cdots + \frac{(4{,}385)^2}{(5)(2)} = 5{,}413{,}447.500$$

$$\sum_{j=1}^{p}\sum_{k=1}^{q} \frac{\left(\sum_{i=1}^{n} X_{ijk}\right)^2}{n} = [AB] = \frac{(1{,}910)^2}{(5)} + \cdots + \frac{(2{,}205)^2}{(5)} = 5{,}418{,}615.000$$

(iii) Computational formulas

$$SSTO = [ABS] - [X] = 5{,}437{,}581.000 - 5{,}406{,}007.500 = 31{,}573.500$$
$$SSA = [A] - [X] = 5{,}409{,}528.333 - 5{,}406{,}007.500 = 3{,}520.833$$
$$SSB = [B] - [X] = 5{,}413{,}447.500 - 5{,}406{,}007.500 = 7{,}440.000$$
$$SSAB = [AB] - [A] - [B] + [X]$$
$$= 5{,}418{,}615.000 - 5{,}409{,}528.333 - 5{,}413{,}447.500 + 5{,}406{,}007.500$$
$$= 1{,}646.667$$
$$SSWCELL = [ABS] - [AB] = 5{,}437{,}581.000 - 5{,}418{,}615.000 = 18{,}966.000$$

[a] *A* denotes treatment *A*, *B* denotes treatment *B*, and *S* denotes subjects or participants; the table is so named because it reflects variation attributable to treatments *A* and *B* and subjects (*S*).

TABLE 16.4-3   ANOVA Table for CRF-23 Design

Source	SS	df	MS	F
1. Treatment *A* (illumination level)	3520.833	$p - 1 = 1$	3520.833	$\left[\frac{1}{4}\right]$ 4.46[*]
2. Treatment *B* (size of type)	7440.000	$q - 1 = 2$	3720.000	$\left[\frac{2}{4}\right]$ 4.71[*]
3. *AB* Interaction	1646.667	$(p - 1)(q - 1) = 2$	823.334	$\left[\frac{3}{4}\right]$ 1.04
4. Within Cell	18966.000	$pq(n - 1) = 24$	790.250	
5. Total	31573.500	$npq - 1 = 29$		

[*]$p < .05$; $\left[\frac{1}{4}\right]$ indicates that the *F* was obtained by dividing *MSA* in row 1 by *MSWCELL* in row 4, and so on.

The computational procedures for the two-treatment completely randomized factorial design are shown in Table 16.4-2. The .05 level of significance is adopted for each of the tests. The results of the analysis are summarized in Table 16.4-3. It is apparent from Table 16.4-3 that the null hypotheses for treatments *A* and *B* can be rejected. I know from the significant test of treatment *A* and the means in Table 16.4-1 that reading speed is faster under 30 foot-candles of illumination than under 15 foot-candles. A researcher probably would be interested in determining which type-size means are unequal. Before addressing this question using the Fisher-Hayter multiple comparison procedure, I will describe the nature and interpretation of an interaction.

Interpreting Interactions

The test of the AB interaction in Table 16.4-3 is not significant. This tells you that there is no reason for believing that the difference between the population means for treatment A is unequal across the three levels of treatment B. Similarly, there is no reason for believing that the differences among the population means for treatment B are not the same at each level of treatment A. To put it another way, if you graphed the population means for a_1 and a_2 at each level of treatment B, lines connecting the means would be parallel. Consider the graph of the sample means in Figure 16.4-3. The lines for the sample data are not parallel. The nonsignificant interaction, however, tells you that the departure from parallelism in Figure 16.4-3 is not greater than would be expected by chance.

An interaction test is unique to factorial designs. Two treatments are said to **interact** if differences in performance under the levels of one treatment are different at two or more levels of the other treatment.

A significant interaction is always a signal that the interpretation of tests of treatments A and B must be qualified. Consider the population means in Table 16.4-4. The means for the two levels of treatment A are equal, as are those for treatment B. An analysis of variance performed on sample data from these populations undoubtedly would support this conclusion and also detect the interaction between the two treatments. A graph of the interaction is shown in Figure 16.4-4(a). As expected,

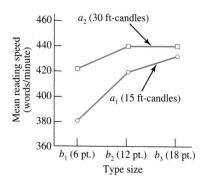

Figure 16.4-3. Graph of the interaction between treatment A (level of illumination) and treatment B (size of type) for the data in Table 16.4-1.

TABLE 16.4-4 **Population Means for Treatments *A* and *B***

		Treatment B		
		b_1	b_2	$\mu_{j\cdot}$
Treatment A	a_1	10	20	15
	a_2	20	10	15
	$\mu_{\cdot k} =$	15	15	

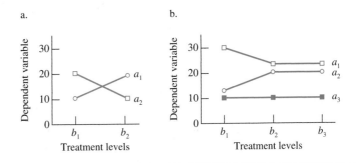

Figure 16.4-4. Part (a) illustrates the interaction between treatment *A* and treatment *B* for the data in Table 14.4-4. Part (b) illustrates interaction between treatment *A* and treatment *B* for a hypothetical set of data. Notice that a significant interaction does not mean that all lines throughout their length are nonparallel. A significant interaction does mean that there are at least two nonparallel lines between at least two levels of the other treatment.

the lines connecting the means are anything but parallel. Also, you can see how misleading are the nonsignificant tests for treatments *A* and *B*. Clearly, there is a difference between the *A* means at b_1 as well as at b_2, and between the *B* means at a_1 as well as at a_2.

If an *F* test indicates that two treatments interact, a graph like those in Figures 16.4-3 and 16.4-4 is helpful for interpreting the interaction. You know that the graph will reveal at least two nonparallel lines between at least two levels of a treatment. A significant interaction does not mean that all lines throughout their length are nonparallel. Such a case is shown in Figure 16.4-4(b). In this figure, the value of the contrast between a_1 and a_2 at b_1 ($30 - 12 = 18$) is different from its value at b_2 ($25 - 21 = 4$), but the value of the contrast is the same at b_2 ($25 - 21 = 4$) and b_3 ($25 - 21 = 4$). To put it another way, the lines are nonparallel over only a portion of their length. Before leaving the topic of interactions, two points should be emphasized: (1) the presence of an interaction is a signal that the interpretation of tests of the associated treatments is usually misleading and hence of little interest and

(2) one of the most useful procedures for understanding and interpreting an interaction is to graph it.[2]

The ability to test interactions is an important feature of a factorial design. But the design has other features that help to account for its wide use. Before describing these features, I will illustrate the use of the Fisher-Hayter multiple-comparison procedure to determine which population means for treatment B differ.

Multiple Comparison Procedures

Section 15.6 describes two multiple comparison tests: the Fisher-Hayter test and the Scheffé test. The Fisher-Hayter test can be used to test hypotheses involving pairwise contrasts; Scheffé's test can be used to test hypotheses involving both pairwise and nonpairwise contrasts.

The Fisher-Hayter statistics for testing contrasts for treatments A and B are, respectively,

$$qFH = \frac{\overline{X}_{.j.} - \overline{X}_{.j'.}}{\sqrt{\dfrac{MSWCELL}{nq}}} \quad \text{and} \quad qFH = \frac{\overline{X}_{..k} - \overline{X}_{..k'}}{\sqrt{\dfrac{MSWCELL}{np}}},$$

where $\overline{X}_{.j.}$, $\overline{X}_{.j'.}$, $\overline{X}_{..k}$, and $\overline{X}_{..k'}$ are sample means, $MSWCELL$ is the denominator of the F statistic for the completely randomized factorial design, and n is the number of participants in each treatment combination.

The Scheffé statistics for testing contrasts for treatments A and B are, respectively,

$$FS = \frac{(c_1\overline{X}_{.1.} + c_2\overline{X}_{.2.} + \cdots + c_p\overline{X}_{.p.})^2}{MSWCELL\left(\dfrac{c_1^2}{nq} + \dfrac{c_2^2}{nq} + \cdots + \dfrac{c_q^2}{nq}\right)}$$

and

$$= \frac{(c_1\overline{X}_{..1} + c_2\overline{X}_{..2} + \cdots + c_q\overline{X}_{..q})^2}{MSWCELL\left(\dfrac{c_1^2}{np} + \dfrac{c_2^2}{np} + \cdots + \dfrac{c_q^2}{np}\right)}$$

where $c_1, c_2, \ldots, c_p$ are coefficients that define a contrast for treatment A and $c_1, c_2, \ldots, c_q$ are coefficients that define a contrast for treatment B.

The Fisher-Hayter test is only performed if the omnibus ANOVA null hypothesis, $H_0: \mu_1 = \mu_2 = \cdots = \mu_p$, is rejected. The null hypothesis for a treatment A contrast is rejected if the absolute value of qFH exceeds or equals the critical value $q_{\alpha; p-1, \nu}$, where $q_{\alpha; p-1, \nu}$ is obtained from the distribution of the Studentized range

---

[2] Kirk (1995, pp. 377–389) discussed more advanced techniques for interpreting interactions.

in Appendix Table D.9, and $\nu = pq(n-1)$. The table is entered for $p-1$ means, where p is the number of treatment A means in the experiment. The null hypothesis for a treatment B contrast is rejected if the absolute value of qFH exceeds or equals the critical value $q_{\alpha;\, q-1,\, \nu}$. The table is entered for $q-1$ means, where q is the number of treatment B means in the experiment.

For the Scheffé test, the null hypothesis for a treatment A contrast is rejected if the absolute value of FS exceeds or equals $(p-1)F_{\alpha;\, \nu_1,\, \nu_2}$, where p is the number of treatment A means in the experiment, $\nu_1 = p-1$, $\nu_2 = pq(n-1)$, and $F_{\alpha;\, \nu_1,\, \nu_2}$ is obtained from Appendix Table D.5. The null hypothesis for a treatment B contrast is rejected if the absolute value of FS exceeds or equals $(q-1)F_{\alpha;\, \nu_1,\, \nu_2}$, where q is the number of treatment B means in the experiment, $\nu_1 = q-1$, and $\nu_2 = pq(n-1)$.

Scheffé's statistic can be used to construct confidence intervals for all treatment A and treatment B contrasts.

A two-sided $100(1-\alpha)\%$ confidence interval for a treatment A contrast, $\psi_i = c_1\mu_1. + c_2\mu_2. + \cdots + c_p\mu_p.$, is given by

$$\hat{\psi}_i - \sqrt{(p-1)F_{\alpha;\, \nu_1,\, \nu_2}}\sqrt{MSWCELL\sum_{j=1}^{p}\frac{c_j^2}{nq}} < \psi_i$$

$$< \hat{\psi}_i + \sqrt{(p-1)F_{\alpha;\, \nu_1,\, \nu_2}}\sqrt{MSWCELL\sum_{j=1}^{p}\frac{c_j^2}{nq}}$$

where $\hat{\psi}_i = c_1\overline{X}_{.1.} + c_2\overline{X}_{.2.} + \cdots + c_p\overline{X}_{.p.}$; $c_1, c_2, \ldots, c_p$ are coefficients that define a contrast; $\overline{X}_{.1.}, \overline{X}_{.2.}, \ldots, \overline{X}_{.p.}$ are treatment A sample means; p is the number of treatment A means in the experiment; $F_{\alpha;\, \nu_1,\, \nu_2}$ is the value that cuts off the upper α region from Appendix Table D.5; $\nu_1 = p-1$; $\nu_2 = pq(n-1)$; $MSWCELL$ is the denominator of the F statistic for a completely randomized factorial design; n is the number of participants in each treatment combination; and q is the number of levels of treatment B.

A two-sided $100(1-\alpha)\%$ confidence interval for a treatment B contrast, $\psi_i = c_1\mu_{.1} + c_2\mu_{.2} + \cdots + c_q\mu_{.q}$, is given by

$$\hat{\psi}_i - \sqrt{(q-1)F_{\alpha;\, \nu_1,\, \nu_2}}\sqrt{MSWCELL\sum_{k=1}^{q}\frac{c_k^2}{np}} < \psi_i$$

$$< \hat{\psi}_i + \sqrt{(q-1)F_{\alpha;\, \nu_1,\, \nu_2}}\sqrt{MSWCELL\sum_{k=1}^{q}\frac{c_k^2}{np}}$$

where $\hat{\psi}_i = c_1\overline{X}_{..1} + c_2\overline{X}_{..2} + \cdots + c_q\overline{X}_{..q}$; $c_1, c_2, \ldots, c_q$ are coefficients that define a contrast; $\overline{X}_{..1}, \overline{X}_{..2}, \ldots, \overline{X}_{..q}$ are treatment B sample means; q is the number of treatment B means in the experiment; $F_{\alpha;\, \nu_1,\, \nu_2}$ is the value that cuts off the upper α region from Appendix Table D.5; $\nu_1 = q-1$; and $\nu_2 = pq(n-1)$.

Computational Example for the Fisher-Hayter Multiple Comparison Procedure

The null hypotheses for the reading-speed data for treatments A and B were rejected. After examining the three sample means for treatment B, the researcher might want to test the following null hypotheses: H_0: $\mu_{\cdot 1} = \mu_{\cdot 2}$, H_0: $\mu_{\cdot 1} = \mu_{\cdot 3}$, and H_0: $\mu_{\cdot 2} = \mu_{\cdot 3}$. The reading-speed sample means are $\overline{X}_{\cdot \cdot 1} = 402.50$, $\overline{X}_{\cdot \cdot 2} = 432.50$, $\overline{X}_{\cdot \cdot 3} = 438.50$; $MSWCELL = 790.250$, $p = 2$, $q = 3$, and $n = 5$. Because the ANOVA F test for treatment B was significant, the next step in understanding the data is to test the three pairwise contrasts using

$$qFH = \frac{\overline{X}_{\cdot \cdot k} - \overline{X}_{\cdot \cdot k'}}{\sqrt{\dfrac{MSWCELL}{np}}}$$

The test statistics are

$$qFH = \frac{402.50 - 432.50}{\sqrt{\dfrac{790.250}{(5)(2)}}} = -3.37 \qquad (\hat{\psi}_1 = \overline{X}_{\cdot \cdot 1} - \overline{X}_{\cdot \cdot 2})$$

$$qFH = \frac{402.50 - 438.50}{\sqrt{\dfrac{790.250}{(5)(2)}}} = -4.05 \qquad (\hat{\psi}_2 = \overline{X}_{\cdot \cdot 1} - \overline{X}_{\cdot \cdot 3})$$

$$qFH = \frac{432.50 - 438.50}{\sqrt{\dfrac{790.250}{(5)(2)}}} = -0.67 \qquad (\hat{\psi}_3 = \overline{X}_{\cdot \cdot 2} - \overline{X}_{\cdot \cdot 3})$$

To reject a null hypothesis, the absolute value $|qFH|$ must exceed or equal $q_{\alpha; q - 1, \nu} = q_{.05; 3 - 1, 24} = 2.92$, where q denotes the number of levels of treatment B and $\nu = pq(n - 1)$. Because $|qFH| = 3.37$ and 4.05 are greater than $q_{.05; 3 - 1, 24} = 2.92$, the null hypotheses for H_0: $\mu_{\cdot 1} = \mu_{\cdot 2}$ and H_0: $\mu_{\cdot 1} = \mu_{\cdot 3}$ are rejected. The researcher can conclude that for the population of participants represented in the experiment and the levels of illumination employed, the use of 12- and 18-point type sizes (treatment levels b_2 and b_3) results in faster reading speeds than the 6-point type (treatment level b_1). Based on the sample data given in Table 16.4-1, the researcher's best guess is that the use of 12-point type would result in reading 30 more words per minute than the use of 6-point type. The use of 18-point type would result in reading 36 more words per minute than the use of 6-point type.

Practical Significance

You can use partial omega squared, as described in Section 16.3, to estimate the proportion of variance in the dependent variable for a CRF-pq design that is accounted for by each of the treatments and interaction. An estimate of the strength of association between the dependent variable X and treatment A while ignoring treatment B and the AB interaction is given by

$$\hat{\omega}^2_{X|A \cdot B, \, AB} = \frac{(p-1)(F_A - 1)}{(p-1)(F_A - 1) + npq}$$

$$= \frac{(2-1)(4.46-1)}{(2-1)(4.46-1) + (5)(2)(3)} = .10$$

where F_A denotes the value of the F statistic for treatment A. An estimate of the strength of association between the dependent variable X and treatment B while ignoring treatment A and the AB interaction is given by

$$\hat{\omega}^2_{X|B \cdot A, \, AB} = \frac{(q-1)(F_B - 1)}{(q-1)(F_B - 1) + npq}$$

$$= \frac{(3-1)(4.71-1)}{(3-1)(4.71-1) + (5)(2)(3)} = .20$$

where F_B denotes the value of the F statistic for treatment B. Treatment B accounts for more of the variance in reading speed than treatment A. According to Cohen's guidelines in Section 15.7 for interpreting omega squared, treatment A is a medium-size association; treatment B is a large association. The strength of the association between the dependent variable X and the AB interaction while ignoring treatments A and B is given by

$$\hat{\omega}^2_{X|AB \cdot A, \, B} = \frac{(p-1)(q-1)(F_{AB} - 1)}{(p-1)(q-1)(F_{AB} - 1) + npq}$$

$$= \frac{(2-1)(3-1)(1.04-1)}{(2-1)(3-1)(1.04-1) + (5)(2)(3)} = .003$$

where F_{AB} denotes the value of the F statistic for the AB interaction. The strength of association is clearly negligible.

Hedges's g statistic, described in Section 11.3, can be used to measure the effect size of contrasts among the means for treatments A and B. The g statistic for the treatment A contrast, $\hat{\psi}_1 = \overline{X}_{\cdot 1 \cdot} - \overline{X}_{\cdot 2 \cdot}$, is

$$g = \frac{|\overline{X}_{\cdot j \cdot} - \overline{X}_{\cdot j' \cdot}|}{\hat{\sigma}_{Pooled}} = \frac{|413.667 - 435.333|}{28.111} = \frac{21.666}{28.111} = 0.77$$

where $\hat{\sigma}_{Pooled} = \sqrt{MSWCELL} = \sqrt{790.250} = 28.111$.

The g statistic for the treatment B contrasts is

$$g = \frac{|\overline{X}_{\cdot \cdot k} - \overline{X}_{\cdot \cdot k'}|}{\hat{\sigma}_{Pooled}}$$

The effect sizes for the treatment B contrasts are

$$g = \frac{|\overline{X}_{..1} - \overline{X}_{..2}|}{\hat{\sigma}_{Pooled}} = \frac{|402.50 - 432.50|}{28.111} = \frac{30.00}{28.111} = 1.07 \quad (\hat{\psi}_{.1} = \overline{X}_{..1} - \overline{X}_{..2})$$

$$g = \frac{|\overline{X}_{..1} - \overline{X}_{..3}|}{\hat{\sigma}_{Pooled}} = \frac{|402.50 - 438.50|}{28.111} = \frac{36.00}{28.111} = 1.28 \quad (\hat{\psi}_{.2} = \overline{X}_{..1} - \overline{X}_{..3})$$

$$g = \frac{|\overline{X}_{..2} - \overline{X}_{..3}|}{\hat{\sigma}_{Pooled}} = \frac{|432.50 - 438.50|}{28.111} = \frac{6.00}{28.111} = 0.21 \quad (\hat{\psi}_{.3} = \overline{X}_{..2} - \overline{X}_{..3})$$

According to Cohen's guidelines for interpreting d-like measures of effect size in Section 10.4, the contrast for treatment A is a medium-size effect; those for the first two treatment B contrasts are both large effects. These results are consistent with our intuition that the mean reading-rate difference of 21.7 words per minute for the treatment A contrast is large enough to be of interest. Furthermore, the treatment B reading-rate contrasts of $\hat{\psi}_{.1} = 30$ and $\hat{\psi}_{.2} = 36$ words per minute are quite large. The third contrast for treatment B, $\hat{\psi}_{.3} = \overline{X}_{..2} - \overline{X}_{..3} = -6$ words per minute is too small to be of interest.

Relative Merits of Factorial Designs

A two-treatment, completely randomized factorial design is the simplest of the factorial designs.[3] It also is one of the more widely used designs. There are good reasons for its popularity. First, the design permits a researcher to test hypotheses about interactions, as you have just seen. Second, the design makes efficient use of participants. For example, the CRF-23 design described previously uses all 30 participants simultaneously in evaluating the effects of treatments A and B. If treatment A were evaluated by using of a CR-2 design and treatment B, by a separate CR-3 design, 60 participants—30 in each experiment—would be required to achieve the power of the CRF-23 design. In view of these two advantages, it is easy to understand the popularity of factorial designs. But the design has some disadvantages:

1. If numerous treatments are included in an experiment, the number of participants required may be prohibitive. For example, a four-treatment CRF-2433 design has $2 \times 4 \times 3 \times 3 = 72$ treatment combinations. If each combination were assigned to only two participants, the experiment would require $72 \times 2 = 144$ participants.
2. The interpretation of the analysis is not straightforward if the test of the interaction is significant. The presence of significant interaction effects always calls for some qualification of the test of the associated treatments.

---

[3] A completely randomized factorial design can be used for designs with more than two treatments. A discussion of the analysis procedures for designs with three or more treatments is beyond the scope of this book. The interested reader should consult books by Howell (2002), Hays (1994), Kirk (1995), and Maxwell and Delaney (2004).

3. The use of a factorial design commits a researcher to a relatively large experiment. Small one-treatment exploratory experiments may indicate much more promising lines of investigation than those originally envisioned. Relatively small experiments permit greater freedom in the pursuit of serendipity.

Assumptions Associated with a Completely Randomized Factorial Design

The assumptions for a two-treatment completely randomized factorial design represent extensions of the assumptions for a completely randomized design. These assumptions, which are discussed in Section 15.5, can be summarized as follows:

1. The model equation $X_{ijk} = \mu + (\mu_{j\cdot} - \mu) + (\mu_{\cdot k} - \mu) + (\mu_{jk} - \mu_{j\cdot} - \mu_{\cdot k} + \mu) + (X_{ijk} - \mu_{jk})$ reflects all the sources of variation that affect X_{ijk}.
2. Participants are random samples from the respective populations or the participants have been randomly assigned to the treatment combinations.
3. The population for each of the pq treatment combinations is normally distributed.
4. The variances of each of the pq treatment combinations are equal.

As discussed in Section 15.5, the F test is robust with respect to violation of assumption 3. However, violation of the other assumptions can undermine the interpretation of the results of an experiment and seriously affect the probability of making Type I and II errors. For more information about the effects of violating the assumptions, see Section 15.5.

CHECK YOUR UNDERSTANDING OF SECTION 16.4

8. List the treatment combinations for the following completely randomized factorial designs.
   a. CRF-22 design   b. CRF-32 design   c. CRF-33 design
9. How many participants are required for the following completely randomized factorial designs? Assume that n is equal to 4.
   a. CRF-24 design   b. CRF-43 design   c. CRF-33 design
10. Fill in the missing values in the following table. Use Microsoft's Excel FDIST function to determine the p value of the F statistics.

Source	SS	df	MS	F
1. Treatment A	273.000	4	( )	$[\frac{1}{4}]$ ( )**
2. Treatment B	263.550	2	( )	$[\frac{2}{4}]$ ( )***
3. AB Interaction	302.400	( )	( )	$[\frac{3}{4}]$ ( )*
4. Within Cell	( )	( )	( )	
5. Total	2413.950	74		

*$p < ($ $)$.
**$p < ($ $)$.
***$p < ($ $)$.

11. Researchers hypothesized that people who are required to evaluate someone they have just hurt tend to denigrate the victim as a means of justifying the harmful act. To investigate this hypothesis, white male college students were required to give a series of either painful or mild electric shocks (treatment A) as feedback for errors made by a confederate who was learning a task in another room. Shocks were not actually delivered to the confederate, but he acted as if he were being shocked. The participants were told that the confederate was either white or black (treatment B). Each participant had a brief telephone conversation with the confederate at the start of the experiment. Before and after administering the shocks, the participants rated the confederate in terms of likeability, intelligence, and personal adjustment. The dependent variable was the change in ratings from the pretest to the posttest. The four treatment combinations were randomly assigned to random subsamples of five participants each. The researchers obtained the following data. The constant 20 has been added to each score to avoid negative numbers. (Experiment suggested by Katz, I., Glass, D.C., and Cohn, S. [1973]. Ambivalence, guilt, and the scapegoating of minority group victims. *Journal of Experimental Social Psychology, 9*, 423–436.)

a_1 b_1	a_1 b_2	a_2 b_1	a_2 b_2
34	20	14	29
30	12	18	13
22	16	10	25
18	28	2	21
26	24	6	17

a_1 = Mild shock
a_2 = Strong shock
b_1 = Black confederate
b_2 = White confederate

a. Construct stacked box plots for the four treatment combinations. Are the sample distributions relatively symmetrical? Do the data contain outliers?

b. Prepare descriptive statistics, means, and standard deviations for the data and construct a table similar to Table 16.4-1.

c. What do the descriptive statistics in part (b) tell you?

d. Test the following null hypotheses: H_0: $\mu_{1\cdot} = \mu_{2\cdot}$, H_0: $\mu_{\cdot1} = \mu_{\cdot2}$, and H_0: $\mu_{jk} - \mu_{j'k} - \mu_{jk'} + \mu_{j'k'} = 0$ for all j, j', k, k'. Let $\alpha = .05$. Determine the p value of each of the significant F statistics using Microsoft's Excel FDIST function.

e. Graph the AB interaction. Is the graph consistent with the test of the AB interaction?

f. Estimate the proportion of variance in the dependent variable that is accounted for by the AB interaction and interpret the result.

g. Analyze the data for treatments A and B separately as if the randomization plan for a CR-2 design had been used. In analyzing treatment A, each level of A will have 10 participants instead of 5; the same is true for treatment B.

The analysis of treatment *A*, for example, ignores the levels of treatment *B*. Compare the results of the two CR-2 designs with the CRF-22 design. Which of the designs is preferable? Explain.

12. What are the main advantages and disadvantages of a completely randomized factorial design?

13. Terms to remember:
    a. Factorial design
    b. Treatment combination
    c. Completely crossed treatments
    d. Completely randomized factorial design
    e. Interaction

16.5 LOOKING BACK: WHAT HAVE YOU LEARNED?

The simplest experimental design involves a single treatment with two treatment levels. If participants are randomly assigned to the treatment levels, the data can be analyzed using a *t* statistic for independent samples. Alternatively, blocks of two matched participants can be formed. The participants in each block are then randomly assigned to the treatment levels. The data for this design can be analyzed using a dependent-samples *t* test. These two simple *t*-test designs have ANOVA analogs—they are the completely randomized design and the randomized block design, respectively.

A randomized block design uses the blocking procedure to analyze data for experiments having one treatment with two or more levels. The blocking procedure isolates the effects of a nuisance variable and typically results in a more powerful test of a false null hypothesis than a completely randomized design. The effectiveness of the blocking procedure is determined by the size of the mean correlation between the treatment levels. The higher the mean correlation, the greater the power.

A completely randomized factorial design enables a researcher to test hypotheses about two or more treatments and associated interactions in a single experiment. For example, instead of testing hypotheses about treatments *A* and *B* in two separate experiments—a CR-3 design and a CR-4 design—a researcher can use one CRF-34 design. An interaction test is unique to factorial designs. Two treatments are said to interact if differences in performance under the levels of one treatment are different at two or more levels of the other treatment. The presence of significant interaction effects is a clear indication that the interpretation of tests of the treatments must be qualified. Inevitably such tests are misleading. A good way to understand an interaction is to graph it.

Throughout my discussion of analysis of variance designs, I have emphasized two ideas: (1) each ANOVA design involves a unique randomization plan and statistical analysis and (2) each score is a composite that reflects all of the effects that affect the score. I formalized the latter idea by expressing a score as the sum of the statistics of a model equation. Associated with each model equation is a set of assumptions. As you saw, ANOVA is robust with respect to violation of some assumptions. However, research suggests that ANOVA is not as robust with respect to violations of other assumptions such as the homogeneity of variance assumption as was once thought. Violation of these assumptions can seriously affect the probability of making a Type I error and the power of the F test. Fortunately, there are robust alternatives that can be used when the tenability of the assumptions is suspect.[4]

REVIEW EXERCISES FOR CHAPTER 16

1. In a study to investigate the effects of three student-teacher ratios on reading performance of second-grade students, the researcher wanted to control the nuisance variable of IQ. Describe the simplest way to accomplish this. Assume that IQ scores are available for all of the children in the study.

2. Fill in the missing values in the following table. Determine the p value of the F statistics for treatment A and blocks using Microsofts's Excel FDIST function.

Source	SS	df	MS	F
1. Treatment A	( )	4	( )	$[\frac{1}{3}]$ 4.12**
2. Blocks	( )	7	41.053	$[\frac{2}{3}]$ ( )*
3. Residual	( )	( )	16.825	
4. Total	( )	( )		

**$p < ($).
*$p < ($).

3. Researchers investigated the effect of strenuous to exhaustive physical exercise on the performance of a discrimination task. Seven men performed a line-matching task while jogging at various speeds on a motor-driven treadmill. A new set of lines was presented immediately following the participant's response, making the task self-paced. The dependent variable was the number of responses made during a 3-minute period. The periods consisted of a pretest resting stage (level a_1), 2.5 mph exercise at 12% grade (level a_2), 3.4 mph exercise at 14% grade (level a_3), 4.2 mph exercise at 16% grade (level a_4), 5.0 mph exercise at 18% grade (level a_5), and a posttest resting stage (level a_6). The order of administration of the conditions, with the exception of the pretest and posttest conditions, was randomized independently for each participant. The following data were obtained. (Experiment suggested by McGlynn, G. H., Laughlin, N. T., and Bender, V. L. [1977]. Effect of strenuous to exhaustive exercise on a discrimination task. *Perceptual and Motor Skills, 44,* 1139–1147.)

	a_1 Pretest	a_2 2.5 mph	a_3 3.4 mph	a_4 4.2 mph	a_5 5.0 mph	a_6 Posttest
s_1	45	47	48	50	51	44
s_2	48	50	58	54	61	51
s_3	46	54	51	57	56	48
s_4	40	37	44	40	45	34
s_5	34	41	38	48	41	38
s_6	42	45	46	43	48	41
s_7	55	58	54	60	57	55

[4] Wilcox (1996) describes many of these procedures.

   a. Construct stacked box plots for the data. Are the sample distributions relatively symmetrical? Do the data contain outliers?

   b. Compute descriptive statistics, $\overline{X}_{.j}$'s and $\hat{\sigma}_j$'s, for the data and construct a table similar to Table 15.4-1.

   c. What do the descriptive statistics in (b) tell you?

   d. Test the null hypothesis H_0: $\mu_{.1} = \mu_{.2} = \cdots = \mu_{.6}$. Let $\alpha = .05$. Determine the p value of the F statistics using Microsoft's Excel FDIST function.

   e. Use the Fisher-Hayter statistic to determine which population means differ.

   f. Use Hedges's g statistic to determine the effect size of the contrasts. Interpret the effect sizes for the statistically significant contrasts.

   g. Summarize the results of the ANOVA in a sentence or two.

   h. Ignore the blocking variable and analyze the data as if the randomization plan for a CR-6 design had been used. Compare the results of the two analyses by constructing a figure similar to Figure 16.3-1. Was the blocking procedure effective? Explain.

4. List the treatment combinations for the following completely randomized factorial designs.

   a. CRF-23 design   b. CRF-42 design   c. CRF-24 design

5. How many participants are required for the following completely randomized factorial designs? Assume that n is equal to 5.

   a. CRF-34 design   b. CRF-35 design   c. CRF-44 design

6. Fill in the missing values in the following table.

Source	SS	df	MS	F
1. Treatment A	( )	( )	22.100	$\left[\frac{1}{4}\right]$ ( )**
2. Treatment B	( )	3	( )	$\left[\frac{2}{4}\right]$ 3.30*
3. AB Interaction	( )	6	( )	$\left[\frac{3}{4}\right]$ 3.20**
4. Within Cell	( )	( )	4.250	
5. Total	( )	71		

$^{*}p < (\ )$.
$^{**}p < (\ )$.

7. Researchers hypothesized that focusing on helping others versus focusing on accomplishing a task (treatment A) and instructions designed to vary the perceived need to hurry (treatment B) would affect the likelihood of a person behaving as a Good Samaritan. To test this hypothesis, 30 seminary students were asked to prepare and record a short message describing their work and the satisfactions of their profession. Half of the students, the task-relevant group, received no other instructions. The other half, the helping-relevant group, was given the same instructions and, in addition, had their attention directed to the parable of the Good Samaritan from the Revised Standard Version of the Bible (Luke 10:29–37). In the process of telling the students how to get to the recording studio that was in another building, one-third were told to hurry because they were running late, one-third were told to go right on over to the studio, and one-third were told that it would be a few minutes until the recording session but they might as well go on to the studio. The seminary students were

randomly assigned to the six treatment combinations with five students in each combination. On the way to the recording studio, the students passed the "victim" sitting in a doorway, head down, coughing and groaning. If a student offered help, the victim mumbled a prepared statement about pills, a condition, and resting. The dependent variable was the victim's rating of the helping behavior that was offered: 0 = failed to notice, . . . , 5 = stopped to render aid and refused to leave the victim or offered to take him to the infirmary. The researchers obtained the following data. (Experiment suggested by Darley, J. M., and Batson, C. D. [1973]. From Jerusalem to Jerico: A study of situational and dispositional variables in helping behavior. *Journal of Personality and Social Psychology*, 27, 100–108.)

a_1 b_1	a_1 b_2	a_1 b_3	a_2 b_1	a_2 b_2	a_2 b_3
4	1	0	0	1	0
4	5	0	4	0	0
5	1	4	1	2	0
1	0	0	1	5	2
5	2	2	4	1	0

a_1 = helping-relevant group
a_2 = task-relevant group
b_1 = no rush instruction
b_2 = go-on-over instruction
b_3 = hurry instruction

a. Visually inspect the treatment-combination distributions. Do they appear to be symmetrical?
b. Prepare descriptive statistics, means and standard deviations, for the data and construct a table similar to Table 16.4-1.
c. What do the descriptive statistics in (b) tell you?
d. Test the following null hypotheses: H_0: $\mu_{1.} = \mu_{2.}$, H_0: $\mu_{.1} = \mu_{.2} = \mu_{.3}$, and H_0: $\mu_{jk} - \mu_{j'k} - \mu_{jk'} + \mu_{j'k'} = 0$ for all j, j', k, k'. Let $\alpha = .05$. Determine the p value of the F statistics using Microsoft's Excel FDIST function.
e. Graph the AB interaction. Is the graph consistent with the test of the AB interaction?
f. Estimate the proportion of variance in the dependent variable that is accounted for by treatment B and interpret the result.
g. Use the Fisher-Hayter statistic to determine which population means for treatment B differ.
h. Use Hedges's g statistic to determine the effect size of the contrasts. Interpret the effect sizes for which the Fisher-Hayter statistic is significant.
i. Summarize the results of the ANOVA in a sentence or two.
j. Analyze the data for treatments A and B separately as if the randomization plan for a CR-2 design and a CR-3 design had been used. In analyzing

treatment A, each level of A will have 15 participants instead of 5; in analyzing treatment B, each level of B will have 10 participants. The analysis of treatment A, for example, ignores the levels of treatment B. Compare the results of the two CR-p designs with the CRF-23 design. Which of the designs is preferable? Explain.

17

Statistical Inference for Frequency Data

17.1 Introduction
Looking Ahead: What Is
This Chapter About?

**17.2 Three Applications of
Pearson's Chi-Square
Statistic**

17.3 Testing Goodness of Fit
Computational Example
Characteristics of
Pearson's Statistic
Degrees of Freedom
when E_j's Are Based
on a Theoretical
Distribution
Practical Significance
Assumptions of the
Goodness-of-Fit Test
Check Your
Understanding of
Sections 17.2 and 17.3

17.4 Testing Independence
Computational Example
Degrees of Freedom for
a Contingency Table
Statistical Hypotheses
Contingency Tables with
Three or More Rows
or Columns
Practical Significance
Assumptions of the
Independence Test
Check Your
Understanding of
Section 17.4

**17.5 Testing Equality of
$c \geq 2$ Proportions**
Computational Example
Comparison of Designs
for Testing
Independence and
Equality of
Proportions
Extension of the Test of
Equality to More Than
Two Response
Categories
Check Your
Understanding of
Section 17.5

**17.6 Looking Back: What
Have You Learned?**
Review Exercises for
Chapter 17

17.7 Supplementary Note
Special Computational
Procedure for a 2×2
Contingency Table

17.1 INTRODUCTION

Looking Ahead: What Is This Chapter About?

Some variables of interest to psychologist are difficult to measure. For example, it is difficult to measure an act of kindness, the unpleasantness of a purge episode, or the severity of a marital conflict. However, it is easy to count acts of kindness, purge episodes, and marital conflicts. The test statistics described in previous chapters are appropriate for measured characteristics such as IQ, reaction time, blood pressure, and time to learn a list of nonsense syllables. When the dependent variable is a frequency count, investigators use different test statistics. The test statistic described in this chapter was developed by the British statistician Karl Pearson in 1900. The statistic is called **Pearson's chi-square statistic** and is denoted by χ^2 (Greek lower-case chi). The statistic is approximately distributed as the chi-square sampling distribution. As you will learn, the statistic can be used to test three distinct null hypotheses.

After reading this chapter, you should know the following:

- How to use the chi-square statistic to test the hypothesis that a set of observed frequencies in $k \geq 2$ categories is equal to a set of expected frequencies
- How to use the chi-square statistic to test the hypothesis that two variables are statistically independent
- How to use the chi-square statistic to test the hypothesis that the proportions in each of $c \geq 2$ populations are equal
- How to compute and interpret Cramér's correlation coefficient
- How to compute and interpret Cohen's $\hat{w}$ effect size measure

17.2 THREE APPLICATIONS OF PEARSON'S CHI-SQUARE STATISTIC

Pearson's chi-square statistic is very versatile. I will describe three applications of the statistic: testing goodness of fit, testing independence, and testing the equality of c population proportions. The three applications are often confused because they all use the same Pearson test statistic and involve similar statistical analyses. However, once you know what to look for, it is easy to distinguish the experimental designs for the three applications—each application involves a distinct randomization plan. The major features of the three applications are as follows.

1. *Testing goodness of fit.* Pearson's chi-square statistic can be used to determine whether the population distribution estimated by a single random sample containing n independent observations is identical to some hypothesized or expected population distribution. Depending on the researcher's interests, expectations may be based on one of the theoretical distributions (such as the normal distribution) or on the results of an earlier empirical investigation. Pearson's chi-square statistic is used to test the null hypothesis that the observed frequencies $O_1, O_2, \ldots, O_k$ in k mutually exclusive categories of a population are equal to a set of expected frequencies $E_1, E_2, \ldots, E_k$. The randomization plan

consists of obtaining one random sample of n elements and classifying each element in terms of membership in one of the k mutually exclusive categories.

2. *Testing independence.* Another use of Pearson's chi-square statistic is in determining whether two variables are statistically independent. This is accomplished by classifying each of n independent observations for a single random sample in terms of two variables, denoted by A and B. Recall from Section 7.3 that A and B are statistically independent if the conditional probability of A given B, $p(A \mid B)$, is equal to the probability of A, $p(A)$. For example, variable A might represent a person's gender and variable B, his or her political affiliation (Democrat, Republican, independent, or other). The variables are independent if $p(\text{Man} \mid \text{Democrat}) = p(\text{Man})$, $p(\text{Man} \mid \text{Republican}) = p(\text{Man})$, and so on, which means that a knowledge of political affiliation tells you nothing about the individual's gender and vice versa. The randomization plan for testing independence consists of obtaining one random sample of n elements and classifying each element in terms of two variables, where each variable has two or more categories.

3. *Testing equality of $c \geq 2$ population proportions.* A final use of Pearson's chi-square statistic is to test the null hypothesis that c population proportions are equal—that is, $H_0: p_1 = p_2 = \cdots = p_c$.[1] The randomization plan consists of obtaining c random samples from c populations where $c \geq 2$ and for each sample classifying the elements in terms of membership in one of $r = 2$ mutually exclusive categories. When r, the number of categories, is greater than 2, the test is referred to as a *test of homogeneity of proportions.*

The distinguishing characteristics of the three applications of Pearson's chi-square statistic are summarized in Table 17.2-1.

TABLE 17.2-1   Comparison of Tests That Use Pearson's Chi-Square Statistic

Purpose	Null Hypothesis	Randomization Plan
1. Testing goodness of fit	$H_0: O_{Pop\ 1} = E_{Pop\ 1}, O_{Pop\ 2} = E_{Pop\ 2}, \ldots, O_{Pop\ k} = E_{Pop\ k}$	One random sample of n elements; each element is classified in terms of membership in one of k mutually exclusive categories.
2. Testing independence	$H_0: p(A \text{ and } B) = p(A)p(B)$	One random sample of n elements; each element is classified in terms of two variables, denoted by A and B, where each variable has two or more categories.

(continued)

---

[1] The letter p is used to denote a proportion as well as a probability. The meaning of the letter will be stated if it is not clear from the context.

TABLE 17.2-1   *(continued)*

Purpose	Null Hypothesis	Randomization Plan
3a. Testing equality of proportions	$H_0: p_1 = p_2 = \cdots = p_c$	c random samples, where $c \geq 2$; for each sample, the elements are classified in terms of membership in one of $r = 2$ mutually exclusive categories.
3b. Testing homogeneity of proportions	$$H_0 := \begin{bmatrix} p_{a_1\|b_1} = p_{a_1\|b_2} = \cdots = p_{a_1\|b_c} \\ p_{a_2\|b_1} = p_{a_2\|b_2} = \cdots = p_{a_2\|b_c} \\ \vdots \\ p_{a_r\|b_1} = p_{a_r\|b_2} = \cdots = p_{a_r\|b_c} \end{bmatrix}$$	c random samples, where $c \geq 2$; for each sample, the elements are classified in terms of membership in one of $r > 2$ mutually exclusive categories.

17.3 TESTING GOODNESS OF FIT

Tests of the three null hypotheses just described all use the chi-square sampling distribution. This sampling distribution was derived by F. R. Helmert in 1876. Karl Pearson first used the distribution to test hypotheses in 1900. The chi-square distribution, like the t and F distributions, is actually a family of distributions whose shape depends on its degrees of freedom, ν. The chi-square distribution like the F distribution is positively skewed, but as ν increases, the distribution approaches a normal distribution with mean and variance, respectively,

$$E(\chi_\nu^2) = \nu \qquad \text{and} \qquad \text{Var}(\chi_\nu^2) = 2\nu$$

Because χ^2 is a squared quantity, it can range over only non-negative numbers, zero to positive infinity, whereas t and z can range over all real numbers. The chi-square distributions for several different degrees of freedom are shown in Figure 17.3-1. The three applications of Pearson's chi-square statistic described here use the upper α region of the chi-square sampling distribution. The critical value of χ^2 for ν degrees of freedom is given in Appendix Table D.4 and is denoted by $\chi_{\alpha, \nu}^2$. A null hypothesis is rejected if χ^2 is greater than or equal to $\chi_{\alpha, \nu}^2$.

The goodness-of-fit test was developed to test the hypothesis that a population distribution estimated by a random sample is identical to a hypothesized or expected distribution. Let $O_1, O_2, \ldots, O_k$ represent observed sample frequencies and $E_1, E_2, \ldots, E_k$ represent expected frequencies. The null hypothesis is rejected if Pearson's statistic,

$$\chi^2 = \sum_{j=1}^{k} \frac{(O_j - E_j)^2}{E_j}$$

exceeds or equals the critical value of chi square, $\chi_{\alpha, \nu}^2$, at α level of significance for $\nu = k - 1$ degrees of freedom.

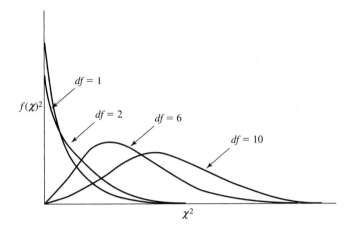

Figure 17.3-1. Chi-square distributions for different degrees of freedom. The critical region for rejecting a null hypothesis is in the upper tail of the distribution.

The three chi-square tests are approximate tests because they use the continuous chi-square distribution to estimate a probability for a discrete sampling distribution. If the expected frequencies are sufficiently large, the **approximate test** is quite accurate. An alternative **exact test** also can be used. When k is equal to 2, the exact test is based on the binomial distribution; when k is greater than 2, the exact test is based on the multinomial distribution. Exact tests usually require a prohibitive amount of computation and should be performed with a computer.

Computational Example

Suppose that the director of the clinical psychology program wants to know whether the distribution of the Graduate Record Examination (GRE) scores for this year's graduate school applicants differs from that for past years. The director classified this year's $n = 200$ applicants into one of $j = 1, \ldots, k$ categories, denoted by O_j, as shown in column 2 of Table 17.3-1. The table also shows the proportions for the previous years' applicants, denoted by p'_j. In column 4, these proportions are converted into expected frequencies by multiplying each of the previous years' proportions by $n = 200$. For example, the E_j for previous years' applicants in the 1400–1499 category is given by $E_j = np'_j = 200(.04) = 8$. The statistical hypotheses for Pearson's test are as follows:

$$H_0: O_{Pop\ 1} = E_{Pop\ 1}, O_{Pop\ 2} = E_{Pop\ 2}, \ldots, O_{Pop\ k} = E_{Pop\ k}$$

$$H_1: O_{Pop\ j} \neq E_{Pop\ j} \text{ for one or more of the } j = 1, \ldots, k \text{ categories}$$

The null hypothesis states that the observed population frequency in category $j = 1, \ldots, k$ equals the expected frequency in category j. The null hypothesis also can be stated in terms of proportions because frequencies are readily converted into proportions and vice versa. An observed population proportion in the jth

TABLE 17.3-1   Computation of Pearson's Chi-Square Statistic for $n = 200$ Graduate School Applicants

(1) GRE Score	(2) O_j	(3)[a] p'_j	(4) $np'_j = E_j$	(5) $O_j - E_j$	(6) $\dfrac{(O_j - E_j)^2}{E_j}$
1400–1499	13	.04	$200(.04)^a = 8$	5	3.125
1300–1399	35	.14	$200(.14) = 28$	7	1.750
1200–1299	49	.20	$200(.20) = 40$	9	2.025
1100–1199	57	.32	$200(.32) = 64$	−7	0.766
1000–1099	38	.22	$200(.22) = 44$	−6	0.818
900–999	8	.08	$200(.08) = 16$	−8	4.000
				0^b	$\chi^2(5, n = 200) = 12.484^*$
					$\chi^2_{.05,\,5} = 11.070$

[a] $p_{j'}$ denotes the proportions for previous year's applicants.
[b] Computational check: $\Sigma(O_j - E_j)$ should equal 0.
*$p < .03$.

category, denoted by p_j, can be computed from an observed population frequency by $p_j = O_{Pop\,j}/n$. Using proportions instead of frequencies, the statistical hypotheses are as follows:

$$H_0 {:}\ p_1 = p'_1,\ p_2 = p'_2,\ \dots,\ p_j = p'_j$$

$$H_1 {:}\ p_j \ne p_{j'} \text{ for one or more of the } j = 1, \dots, k \text{ categories}$$

where p_j and p'_j denote, respectively, the population observed and expected proportions in the jth category.

The director wants to know whether the proportions in the six categories for the population represented by the sample differ from the proportions for the population of previous applicants. The director is faced with a minor interpretation problem—this year's applicants were not obtained by random sampling. The director circumvents the problem by assuming that there is a population for which random sampling could have produced the sample she obtained. Conclusions about equality of the proportions apply to this population.

The computation of Pearson's statistic is illustrated in column 6 of Table 17.3-1. The degrees of freedom is equal to one less than the number of categories, $k - 1 = 6 - 1 = 5$. The director adopted the .05 level of significance; the critical value of $\chi^2_{.05,\,5}$ is 11.070. This critical value is found in Appendix Table D.4. Although the null hypothesis is nondirectional, the critical region always lies in the upper tail of the sampling distribution of χ^2. According to Table 17.3-2, the computed chi-square statistic with 5 degrees of freedom and $n = 200$ independent observations, $\chi^2 (5, n = 200) = 12.484$, exceeds the critical value, $\chi^2_{.05,\,5} = 11.070$. Hence, the null hypothesis is rejected.

The chi-square test is an omnibus or overall test. It tells you that one or more of the observed frequencies differs from the corresponding expected frequency. If the omnibus test is significant, it is useful to examine the data to determine where the discrepancies occurred. You can do this by comparing observed and expected frequencies—which categories have more or fewer observed frequencies than expected. You also can look to see which categories contributed most to the chi-square statistic. The program director would be pleased to note from Table 17.3-1 that there were more observed than expected applicants in the GRE categories of 1200–1299 and above. Furthermore, the category that contributed most to the chi-square statistic, 900–999 with $(O_1 - E_1)^2/E_1 = 4.00$, had fewer applicants than expected: 8 observed versus 16 expected. Such observations about the data must be regarded as tentative—they are not based on the outcome of significance tests.

In reporting the results to her department chairperson, the program director could say, "The population distribution of GRE scores for this year's applicants differs from the distribution of applicants from previous years, $\chi^2(5, n = 200) = 12.484$, $p < .03$. Furthermore, the data suggest that a higher proportion of this year's applicants have GRE scores above 1200 than previous applicants." The program director's description of the results follows the recommendations in the *Publication Manual of the American Psychological Association* (2001). The manual says to (1) provide the value of the test statistic, (2) enclose both the degrees of freedom and sample size in parentheses, and (3) provide the p value (APA, 2001, pp. 22, 139).

Appendix Table D.4 can be used to approximate some p values. However, the range of test-statistic values and degrees of freedom in the table is limited. Microsoft's Excel program, which is available on most computers, can be used to obtain p values for any combination of χ^2 test statistics and degrees of freedom. To obtain p values for the chi-square sampling distribution, you use the Excel CHIDIST function. To access this function, select "Insert" in Excel's menu bar and then the menu command "Function." You then can select the CHIDIST function from the list of functions. After you access the CHIDIST function,

$$CHIDIST(x,deg\_freedom)$$

you replace "x" with the value of the χ^2 statistic and "deg_freedom" with the degrees of freedom for the χ^2 statistic. The function gives the size of the area, p value, above the χ^2 statistic. For the data in Table 17.3-1, the χ^2 statistic is 12.484 with $\nu = 5$. The CHIDIST function gives

$$CHIDIST(12.484,5) = .029$$

In reporting the p value, the program director rounded .029 up to .03.

Characteristics of Pearson's Statistic

An examination of the formula $\sum_{j=1}^{k}(O_j - E_j)^2/E_j$ for Pearson's statistic reveals the following:

1. The statistic is never negative, because all $O_j - E_j$ discrepancies are squared. Because the statistic makes no distinction between positive and negative discrepancies, the hypothesis tested is nondirectional. This is true

even though the critical region of the sampling distribution of χ^2 is always in the upper tail.

2. The only way the statistic can equal 0 is for each observed frequency to equal the corresponding expected frequency.

3. The larger the $O_j - E_j$ discrepancies, the larger χ^2. Large values of χ^2 are evidence against the null hypothesis because they indicate that the observed frequencies are far from what you would expect if the null hypothesis were true. However, the contribution of a discrepancy to χ^2 is affected by the size of E_j, because $(O_j - E_j)^2$ is divided by E_j. This seems reasonable. If I tossed 10 coins and observed 9 heads where the expected number is 5, the discrepancy of 4 heads would lead me to question the fairness of the coins. If the discrepancy of 4 heads occurred when I tossed 100 coins, where the expected frequency is 50, I wouldn't be surprised. A discrepancy of 4 heads is viewed one way when E is equal to 5 and a different way when E is equal to 50. The formula takes this into account by expressing the size of the discrepancy relative to the magnitude of the expected frequency.

4. The larger the number of categories, the larger the degrees of freedom and the computed χ^2. As the number of degrees of freedom increases, the chi-square value required for significance also increases. Thus, the test procedure takes the number of categories into account.

Degrees of Freedom when E_j's Are Based on a Theoretical Distribution

A modification of the goodness-of-fit test is required if parameters of a theoretical distribution must be estimated in computing the expected frequencies. In the previous example, the expected frequencies, E_j's, were computed from actual data—previous years' GRE scores. Hence, no distribution parameters were estimated. For this case, $\nu = k - 1$, where k is the number of categories. Suppose, however, that the program director compared a set of observed frequencies with those predicted by, say, the normal distribution. The director would have to use sample data to estimate two parameters of the normal distribution, μ and σ, in order to compute the expected frequencies. For each parameter estimated from sample data, the degrees of freedom are reduced by one. The formula for degrees of freedom is $\nu = k - 1 - e$, where e is the number of distribution parameters estimated from sample data. Except for this modification, the test procedure is the same as that described previously.

Practical Significance

As with any null hypothesis significance test, it is important to know if the result is practically significant. Cohen (1988, p. 216) has described a statistic that can help a researcher or consumer of statistics make this judgment. The statistic, which is an effect size measure, is

$$\hat{w} = \sqrt{\sum_{j=1}^{k} \frac{(\hat{p}_j - p'_j)^2}{p'_j}}$$

where $\hat{p}_j$ is the observed proportion in the jth category and p'_j is the expected proportion for that category. When each of the observed proportions equals its expected proportion, the effect size is zero. It is apparent from the formula that the contribution of a discrepancy $(\hat{p}_j - p'_j)^2$ to $\hat{w}$ is expressed relative to its expected proportion. A simpler equivalent formula for $\hat{w}$ is

$$\hat{w} = \sqrt{\frac{\chi^2}{n}}$$

Cohen has suggested the following guidelines for interpreting w, the population effect size:

0.1 is a small effect.

0.3 is a medium effect.

0.5 is a large effect.

The computation of $\hat{w}$ for the graduate school data in Table 17.3-1 is

$$\hat{w} = \sqrt{\frac{\chi^2}{n}} = \sqrt{\frac{12.484}{200}} = 0.25$$

According to Cohen's guidelines, 0.25 is a small effect. Thus, although the difference between this year's applicants for graduate school and previous applicants is statistically significant, $p < .03$, the effect is small, $\hat{w} = 0.25$. A comparison of the observed and expected frequencies in Table 17.3-2 supports this conclusion.

Assumptions of the Goodness-of-Fit Test

The goodness-of-fit test can be used to compare observed frequencies with expected frequencies for any population distribution, provided the distribution is discrete or can be grouped into a manageable number of categories. The assumptions of the test are minimal: (1) every sample observation must fall in one and only one category, (2) the observations must be independent, and (3) the sample n must be large.

How large is large? This is difficult to specify because the adequacy of Pearson's chi-square statistic in approximating the exact multinomial probability (see Section 8.4) depends on (1) n, (2) the true proportion in the k categories, and (3) the number of degrees of freedom, among other things. Furthermore, Pearson's statistic is not exactly distributed as the chi-square distribution unless n is infinitely large. A conservative rule of thumb states that the approximation to the exact multinomial probability is satisfactory if, when the degrees of freedom equal 1, each expected frequency is at least 10. When the degrees of freedom are greater than 1, each expected frequency should be at least 5. One remedy if k is greater than 2 and expected frequencies are below the minimum is to combine categories where it is reasonable to do so until all expected frequencies are at least 5.[2]

---

[2] An alternative approach is to use the Kolmogorov-Smirnov goodness-of-fit test. This test, which has greater power than Pearson's test, is discussed by Hays (1994, pp. 854−855).

When the test has one degree of freedom, **Yates' correction for continuity**[3] can be applied to make the sampling distribution of the test statistic, which is discrete, more consistent with the chi-square distribution, which is continuous. Recall from Section 1.4 that a continuous variable can assume any value in an interval. Such is not the case for a discrete variable. For example, the number of children in a family can assume only one value in the interval 2.5–3.5, namely 3; values such as 2.5, 2.7, or 3.2 are not possible. The continuity problem arises whenever a researcher uses a continuous distribution to obtain probabilities for a discrete distribution. The continuity correction for the chi-square goodness of fit statistic consists of reducing the absolute value of each difference $O_j - E_j$ by 0.5. The correction can be included in the test statistic as follows:

$$\chi^2 = \sum_{j=1}^{k} \frac{(|O_j - E_j| - 0.5)^2}{E_j}$$

It is good practice to apply the correction when the degrees of freedom equal 1 and any expected frequency is not appreciably greater than 10.

CHECK YOUR UNDERSTANDING OF SECTIONS 17.2 AND 17.3

1. What are the distinguishing features of the tests for goodness of fit, independence, and equality of proportions?
2. If the critical value for a test for goodness of fit in which socioeconomic indices for this year are compared with those for last year is $\chi^2_{.05, 6} = 12.592$, how many mutually exclusive categories were used?
3. A random sample of students was asked if they favor a change from the semester system to the quarter system. Thirty-three said yes; 17 said no.
   a. List the steps you would follow to test the null hypothesis that opinion is equally divided on the issue. Let $\alpha = .05$.
   b. Do the data suggest that opinion is not equally divided on this issue?
   c. Determine the p value of the χ^2 statistic using Microsoft's Excel CHIDIST function.
   d. Compute the size of the effect. If χ^2 was significant, interpret the effect size.
4. According to the most recent public opinion poll in Johnson County, 71 eligible voters were Democrats, 52 were Republicans, and 33 belonged to other parties. Traditionally, the ratio of Democrats to Republicans to others has been 4: 3: 2.
   a. Does the poll suggest a change in party affiliation? Let $\alpha = .05$.
   b. Determine the p value of the χ^2 statistic using Microsoft's Excel CHIDIST function.
   c. Compute the size of the effect. If χ^2 was significant, interpret the effect size.
5. A student in a statistics class tossed a die 300 times and obtained the results shown in the table. The outcome denotes the number of dots, 1 through 6, shown on the upper face of the die.

[3] Proposed by Frank Yates, a British statistician.

Outcome	1	2	3	4	5	6
Frequency	53	41	60	47	38	61

a. Is the die fair? Let $\alpha = .05$.
b. Determine the p value of the χ^2 statistic using Microsoft's Excel CHIDIST function.
c. Compute the size of the effect and interpret the result.

6. Terms to remember:
  a. Approximate and exact tests
  b. Yates' correction for continuity

17.4 TESTING INDEPENDENCE

Pearson's statistic,

$$\chi^2 = \sum_{i=1}^{r} \sum_{j=1}^{c} \frac{(O_{ij} - E_{ij})^2}{E_{ij}}$$

can be used to obtain an approximate test of the null hypothesis that two variables, say; A and B, are statistically independent. Recall from Section 7.3 that A and B are statistically independent if the probability of, say, A occurring is unaffected by the occurrence of B. The first step in computing Pearson's chi-square statistic is to classify each of n independent observations for a single random sample in terms of variable A with $i = 1, \ldots, r$ rows and variable B with $j = 1, \ldots, c$ columns.

Computational Example

Suppose that a random sample of 200 engineering students has been obtained and that each student has been classified in terms of gender, variable A, and whether they reported frequently feeling or not feeling stressed, variable B. A table representing the classification of each of n elements in terms of two or more variables is called a **contingency table.** A contingency table for the 200 students has $i = 2$ rows for variable A and $j = 2$ columns for variable B. A partial summary of the gender and stress data is given in Table 17.4-1. If the two variables in the population are independent, what frequencies should be in the cells of the contingency table? You know from Section 7.3 that if two variables are independent, $p(A \mid B) = p(A)$, in which case $p(A \text{ and } B) = p(A)p(B)$. Typically, the population proportions are unknown, but you can use the sample marginal proportions, $p(a_1), p(a_2)$, and so on, in Table 17.4-1 to estimate the expected cell frequencies, denoted by $E_{a_i \text{ and } b_j}$. Using the relationship

$$E_{a_i \text{ and } b_j} = np(a_i \text{ and } b_j) = np(a_i)p(b_j)$$

TABLE 17.4-1 Partial Summary of Gender and Feeling-Stressed Data

	Stressed, b_1	Not Stressed, b_2	
Woman, a_1			$n_{a_1} = 40; \quad p(a_1) = \dfrac{40}{200} = .20$
Man, a_2			$n_{a_2} = 160; \quad p(a_2) = \dfrac{160}{200} = .80$

$$n_{b_1} = 72 \qquad\qquad n_{b_2} = 128 \qquad\qquad n = 200$$

$$p(b_1) = \frac{72}{200} \qquad\qquad p(b_2) = \frac{128}{200}$$

$$= .36 \qquad\qquad\qquad = .64$$

you can estimate each of the expected cell values, as follows:

$$E_{a_1 \text{ and } b_1} = np(a_1)p(b_1) = 200(.20)(.36) = 14.4$$

$$E_{a_1 \text{ and } b_2} = np(a_1)p(b_2) = 200(.20)(.64) = 25.6$$

$$E_{a_2 \text{ and } b_1} = np(a_2)p(b_1) = 200(.80)(.36) = 57.6 \text{ and}$$

$$E_{a_2 \text{ and } b_2} = np(a_2)p(b_2) = 200(.80)(.64) = 102.4$$

These are the cell frequencies you would expect if variables A and B were independent. The expected cell frequencies also can be computed directly from the marginal frequencies by the formula

$$E_{a_i \text{ and } b_j} = \frac{n_{a_i} n_{b_j}}{n}$$

because

$$E_{a_i \text{ and } b_j} = np(a_i)p(b_j) = n\left(\frac{n_{a_i}}{n}\right)\left(\frac{n_{b_j}}{n}\right) = \frac{n_{a_i} n_{b_j}}{n}$$

For example, $E_{a_1 \text{ and } b_1} = (40)(72)/200 = 14.4$. The expected cell frequencies, along with the observed cell frequencies, are given in Table 17.4-2. The computation of the chi-square statistic is illustrated in the table.[4]

The advisability of using Yates' correction for a 2×2 contingency table is the subject of continuing debate among statisticians (Conover, 1974a, 1974b; Grizzle, 1967; Mantel, 1974; Miettinen, 1974; Plackett, 1964; Starmer, Grizzle, & Sen, 1974)

---

[4] Supplementary Note 17.7-1 presents a simpler computational formula for a 2×2 contingency table.

TABLE 17.4-2 Gender and Feeling-Stressed Data

(i) *Data (O_{ij} and E_{ij} denote observed and expected frequencies for the $i = 1, \ldots, r$ rows of variable A and $j = 1, \ldots, c$ columns of variable B)*

	Stressed, b_1	Not Stressed, b_2	
Woman, a_1	$O_{11} = 8$ $E_{11} = 14.4$	$O_{12} = 32$ $E_{12} = 25.6$	$n_{a_1} = 40$
Man, a_2	$O_{21} = 64$ $E_{21} = 57.6$	$O_{22} = 96$ $E_{22} = 102.4$	$n_{a_2} = 160$
	$n_{b_1} = 72$	$n_{b_2} = 128$	$n = 200$

(ii) *Computation of chi-square statistic*

O_{ij}	E_{ij}	$O_{ij} - E_{ij}$	$\left(\dfrac{O_{ij} - E_{ij}}{E_{ij}}\right)^2$
8	14.4	-6.4	2.844
64	57.6	6.4	0.711
32	25.6	6.4	1.600
96	102.4	-6.4	0.400
		0^a	$\chi^2(1, n = 200) = 5.555^*$
			$\chi^2_{.05,\,1} = 3.841$

[a] Computational check: $\Sigma(O_{ij} - E_{ij})$ should equal 0.
[*] $p < .02$.

and therefore is not illustrated in Table 17.4-2. If the correction is desired, it can be incorporated in the chi-square formula as follows:

$$\chi^2 = \sum_{i=1}^{r} \sum_{j=1}^{c} \frac{(|O_{ij} - E_{ij}| - 0.5)^2}{E_{ij}}$$

Degrees of Freedom for a Contingency Table

How many degrees of freedom are associated with the chi-square statistic for testing independence? For the goodness-of-fit test, you saw that the degrees of freedom are $k - 1 - e$, where e is the number of distribution parameters that is estimated from sample data. A 2×2 table is a special case of an $r \times c$ contingency table where r and c equal 2. I will develop the degrees-of-freedom formula for the more general case in which r or c is greater than 2.

If I denote the number of rows by r and the number of columns by c, an $r \times c$ contingency table has $k = rc$ categories. Because there are r categories for variable A, I must estimate $r - 1$ of the expected row frequencies for this variable. Once

I have estimated $r - 1$ of the expected row frequencies, the remaining one can be obtained by subtracting the $r - 1$ expected frequencies from n, the total number of frequencies. This follows because the sum of the r expected row frequencies must equal n. By the same line of reasoning it follows that I must estimate $c - 1$ expected column frequencies for variable B. In all, I must make $e = (r - 1) + (c - 1)$ estimates. Thus, the number of degrees of freedom for an $r \times c$ contingency table is

$$
\begin{aligned}
df &= k - 1 - e \\
&= rc - 1 - [(r - 1) + (c - 1)] \\
&= rc - 1 - r + 1 - c + 1 \\
&= rc - r - c + 1 \\
&= (r - 1)(c - 1)
\end{aligned}
$$

Hence, for a 2×2 contingency table, the degrees of freedom are $(2 - 1)(2 - 1) = 1$.

Statistical Hypotheses

The statistical hypotheses for the data in Table 17.4-2 are

$$H_0: p(A \text{ and } B) = p(A)p(B)$$

$$H_1: p(A \text{ and } B) \neq p(A)p(B)$$

The hypothesis of statistical independence is rejected if the computed χ^2 exceeds or equals the critical value at α level of significance for $\nu = (r - 1)(c - 1)$ degrees of freedom. For the data in Table 17.4-2, the computed chi-square with 1 degree of freedom, $\chi^2(1, n = 200) = 5.555$, exceeds the critical value, $\chi^2_{.05, 1} = 3.841$. Hence, the null hypothesis is rejected, and the researcher concludes that gender and frequently feeling or not feeling stressed are not independent. An examination of the data suggests that the men reported frequently feeling stressed more than expected; the opposite is true for the women.

A chi-square test tells you how strong the evidence is that an association between variables A and B exists in the population. The test does not tell you the strength of the association or whether the association is practically significant. Earlier you learned how to compute Cohen's $\hat{w}$, a measure of effect size. Before describing an index of strength of association, I will show how to apply a test of independence to contingency tables with more than two rows or columns.

Contingency Tables with Three or More Rows or Columns

The test for independence can be extended to the case in which the row variable, A, has $r > 2$ mutually exclusive categories, $a_1, a_2, \ldots, a_i, \ldots, a_r$, and the column variable, B, has $c > 2$ mutually exclusive categories, $b_1, b_2, \ldots, b_j, \ldots, b_c$.

Suppose you want to know if a college graduate's starting salary is independent of the size of the university from which he or she graduated. Data for a random sample of 200 graduates are given in Table 17.4-3. The expected frequencies are computed from

$$E_{a_i \text{ and } b_j} = \frac{n_{a_i} n_{b_j}}{n}$$

TABLE 17.4-3 University Size and Starting Salaries of Graduates

(i) Data (O_{ij} and E_{ij} denote observed and expected frequencies for the $i = 1, \ldots, r$ rows of variable A and $j = 1, \ldots, c$ columns of variable B)

	Less Than $20,000, b_1	$20,000–30,000 b_2	Greater Than $30,000, b_3	
Small University, a_1	$O_{11} = 13$ $E_{11} = 10.08$	$O_{12} = 28$ $E_{12} = 34.44$	$O_{13} = 15$ $E_{13} = 11.48$	$n_{a_1} = 56$
Medium-size University, a_2	$O_{21} = 11$ $E_{21} = 13.14$	$O_{22} = 40$ $E_{22} = 44.90$	$O_{23} = 22$ $E_{23} = 14.96$	$n_{a_2} = 73$
Large University, a_3	$O_{31} = 12$ $E_{31} = 12.78$	$O_{32} = 55$ $E_{32} = 43.66$	$O_{33} = 4$ $E_{33} = 14.56$	$n_{a_3} = 71$
	$n_{b_1} = 36$	$n_{b_2} = 123$	$n_{b_3} = 41$	$n = 200$

(ii) Computation of chi-square statistic

O_{ij}	E_{ij}	$O_{ij} - E_{ij}$	$\dfrac{(O_{ij} - E_{ij})^2}{E_{ij}}$
13	10.08	2.92	0.846
11	13.14	−2.14	0.349
12	12.78	−0.78	0.048
28	34.44	−6.44	1.204
40	44.09	−4.90	0.535
55	43.66	11.34	2.945
15	11.48	3.52	1.079
22	14.96	7.04	3.313
4	14.56	−10.56	7.659
		0^a	$\chi^2(4, n = 200) = 17.978^*$
			$\chi^2_{.05, 4} = 9.488$

^{a} Computational check: $\Sigma(O_{ij} - E_{ij})$ should equal 0.
$^*p < .002$.

The degrees of freedom are $(r - 1)(c - 1) = (3 - 1)(3 - 1) = 4$. For a test at the .05 level of significance, the value of $\chi^2_{.05, 4}$ is 9.488. Because the $\chi^2(4, n = 200) = 17.978$ in Table 17.4-3 is greater than $\chi^2_{.05, 4} = 9.488$, the null hypothesis is rejected. You conclude that starting salary and university size are not independent.

Finding a significant χ^2 often is just the first step in understanding your data. It is helpful to look for large discrepancies between observed and expected frequencies in the contingency table and to examine the contribution of each cell to the chi-square statistic. An inspection of Table 17.4-3 suggests that graduates of large universities are less likely than expected to have starting salaries over $30,000, whereas the converse is true for those from medium and small universities. The largest contribution to the chi-square statistic come from cell a_3 and b_3, $(O_{33} - E_{33})^2/E_{33} = 7.659$. This also suggests that graduates of large universities are less likely than expected to have starting salaries over \$30,000. Inferences such as these must be regarded as tentative because they are not based on the outcome of significance tests. The significant chi-square test statistic applies to the data taken as a whole and provides no clue as to which cells are responsible for significance.

In the following section, I describe several statistics that can help a researcher assess the practical significance of an association between row and column variables.

Practical Significance

If the null hypothesis $p(A \ and \ B) = p(A)p(B)$ is rejected, you know that the variables are correlated. Several correlation coefficients were discussed in Chapter 5 (r, r_s, and η^2), but none of them is appropriate for unordered qualitative variables. One coefficient that is appropriate is **Cramér's measure of association**, denoted by V.

The formula for computing an estimate, $\hat{V}$, of Cramér's measure of association is

$$\hat{V} = \frac{\hat{\phi}_{observed}}{\hat{\phi}_{maximum}} = \frac{\sqrt{\chi^2/n}}{\sqrt{s-1}} = \sqrt{\frac{\chi^2}{n(s-1)}}$$

where s is the smaller of the number of rows and columns.[5]

Cramér's statistic is a relative measure, because it is the ratio of an observed statistic, $\hat{\phi}_{observed} = \sqrt{\chi^2/n}$, to its maximum possible value, $\hat{\phi}_{maximum} = \sqrt{s-1}$. The statistic can range from 0 (indicating complete independence) to 1 (indicating complete dependence, or perfect correlation).

Cramér's statistic is computed when the chi-square test is significant. A nonsignificant chi-square test suggests that any $\hat{V}$ greater than 0 could be due to chance. Put another way, a test of the null hypothesis H_0: $p(A \ and \ B) = p(A)p(B)$ is equivalent to a test of the null hypothesis H_0: $V = 0$. Unfortunately, Cramér's statistic does not have a simple, intuitively useful interpretation as, say, the proportion of explained variance between two variables. It should be thought of as reflecting magnitude of association on a scale of 0 to 1; the larger the number, the stronger the association. Cramér's statistic for the data in Tables 17.4-2 and 17.4-3 are, respectively,

$$\hat{V} = \sqrt{\frac{5.555}{200(2-1)}} = .17 \qquad and \qquad \hat{V} = \sqrt{\frac{17.978}{200(3-1)}} = .21$$

Both correlations fall in the lower range of Cramér's $\hat{V}$.

---

[5] For a 2×2 contingency table, $\hat{V} = \sqrt{\chi^2/n}$, because $\sqrt{s-1} = \sqrt{2-1} = 1$. In this special case, $\hat{V}$ is identical to another measure of strength of association called the *phi coefficient*, $\hat{\phi}$. Both $\hat{V}$ and $\hat{\phi}$ are related to the Pearson product-moment correlation coefficient. Suppose that the two categories of variables A and B are considered to be ordered and are assigned scores of 0 and 1, where 1 is assigned to the higher category. Under these conditions, the formula for r is algebraically equivalent to that for $\hat{V}$ and $\hat{\phi}$ (Hays, 1994, pp. 866–869).

You know from Tables 17.4-2 and 17.4-3 that the chi-square statistics for the feeling-stressed data and the salary data are both statistically significant, but are they practically significant? Cohen's $\hat{w}$, which was introduced in Section 17.3, can help a researcher make this assessment.

The $\hat{w}$ statistic can be computed using the formulas

$$\hat{w} = \sqrt{\sum_{i=1}^{r} \sum_{j=1}^{c} \frac{(\hat{p}_{ij} - p'_{ij})^2}{p'_{ij}}} = \sqrt{\frac{\chi^2}{n}}$$

where $\hat{p}_{ij}$ is the observed proportion in the ijth cell and p'_{ij} is the expected proportion. For data in a contingency table, $\hat{w}$ also can be computed from

$$\hat{w} = \hat{V}\sqrt{s-1}$$

where $\hat{V}$ is an estimate of Cramér's V and s is the smaller of the number of rows and columns in the contingency table.

Cohen's $\hat{w}$ for the data in Tables 17.4-2 and 17.4-3 is, respectively,

$$\hat{w} = \sqrt{5.555/200} = 0.17 \qquad \text{and} \qquad \hat{w} = \sqrt{17.978/200} = 0.30$$

Recall from Section 17.3 that $w = .1$ is a small effect, $w = .3$ is a medium effect, and $w = .5$ is a large effect. Thus, the effect size for the gender and feeling-stressed data is small. The effect size for the university size and starting salaries data is medium. These examples illustrate the maxim that statistical significance and practical significance address different questions. The chi-square test statistic for the variables of university size and starting salaries of graduates, for example, is large enough to be significant beyond the .002 level. However, the effect size is barely medium ($\hat{w} = .30$). The point cannot be made too often that statistical significance only means that chance is an unlikely explanation for an observed result. Other procedures must be used to assess the usefulness or practical significance of the result.

Assumptions of the Independence Test

The assumptions associated with the test for independence and the estimation of strength of association and effect size are as follows. (1) Every observation must fall in one and only one cell of the contingency table. (2) The observations must be independent. One situation in which the second assumption is likely to be violated occurs when an individual is represented more than once in a cell or in more than one cell. (3) The sample n should be large enough so that every expected frequency is at least 10 when there is one degree of freedom and at least 5 when there is more than one degree of freedom.[6]

---

[6] Fisher's exact test for a 2×2 contingency table can be used to test independence when n is small and expected cell frequencies are less than 10. The test is described by Hays (1994, pp. 863–865).

CHECK YOUR UNDERSTANDING OF SECTION 17.4

7. List the similarities and differences between Pearson's product-moment correlation coefficient and Cramér's measure of association.

8. Two hundred women between the ages of 19 and 25 were asked if they favored the use of the morning-after pills (plan B). The women were classified according to attitude and religious preference.

	Protestants	Roman Catholic	Non-Christians	Sum
Favor	58	30	28	116
Oppose	8	23	5	36
Undecided	10	15	23	48
Sum	76	68	56	200

   a. For the data in the table, list the steps you would use in testing the null hypothesis. Let $\alpha = .001$.
   b. What is your decision concerning the null hypothesis?
   c. Determine the p value of the χ^2 statistic using Microsoft's Excel CHIDIST function.
   d. If the null hypothesis is rejected, compute Cramér's statistic.
   e. Compute the size of the effect. If χ^2 was significant, interpret the effect size.

9. A random sample of 200 college students was classified according to class year and political conservatism as follows.

	Conservative	Neutral	Liberal	Sum
Freshman	38	22	6	66
Sophomore	22	24	5	51
Junior	11	12	19	42
Senior	7	13	21	41
Sum	78	71	51	200

   a. Are the variables independent? Let $\alpha = .05$.
   b. Determine the p value of the χ^2 statistic using Microsoft's Excel CHIDIST function.
   c. If the null hypothesis is rejected, compute Cramér's statistic.
   d. Compute the size of the effect. If χ^2 was significant, interpret the effect size.

10. Use the table of random numbers in Appendix D to draw a random sample without replacement of 40 students from the student database in Appendix E.
   a. List the participant number, gender, and course grade for each participant in your sample.
   b. For the variables of gender (A) and course grade (B), construct a contingency table.
   c. Test the hypothesis that the two variables are independent. Let $\alpha = .05$.
   d. Determine the p value of the χ^2 statistic using Microsoft's Excel CHIDIST function.

    e. If the null hypothesis is rejected, compute Cramér's $\hat{V}$.

    f. Compute the size of the effect. If χ^2 was significant, interpret the effect size.

    g. Write a paragraph summarizing the results of your analyses and your conclusions.

  11. Terms to remember:

    a. Contingency table

    b. Cramér's measure of association

17.5 TESTING EQUALITY OF $c \geq 2$ PROPORTIONS

The last application of Pearson's chi-square statistic that I will describe is testing the equality of $c \geq 2$ population proportions.

If a random sample is obtained from each of $j = 1, \ldots, c$ binomially distributed populations, the sample proportions $\hat{p}_1, \hat{p}_2, \ldots, \hat{p}_c$ can be used to test the null hypothesis

$$H_0: p_1 = p_2 = \cdots = p_c$$

versus

$$H_1: p_j \neq p_{j'} \text{ for some } j \text{ and } j', \text{ where } j \neq j'$$

The null hypothesis is rejected if $\chi^2 = \sum_{i=1}^{r} \sum_{j=1}^{c} (O_{ij} - E_{ij})^2 / E_{ij}$ exceeds or equals the critical value, $\chi^2_{\alpha, \nu}$, at α level of significance for $\nu = c - 1$ degrees of freedom.

Rejection of the null hypothesis means that some population proportions are not equal. It does not mean that they are all unequal; perhaps only one is discrepant. This test, like the two described earlier, is approximate, because the continuous chi-square distribution is used to estimate a probability for a discrete sampling distribution. The sample proportions $\hat{p}_1, \hat{p}_2, \ldots, \hat{p}_c$, which may be based on unequal sample sizes, are assumed to represent independent observations for c independent binomially distributed random variables. Like all binomial experiments, each trial must result in one of two outcomes. Later, you will see that the test can be extended to the multinomial case in which each trial can result in one of three or more outcomes.

Computational Example

Suppose a researcher surveyed older people living in public housing in Borborygme, Texas, to determine whether satisfaction with living conditions is related to age heterogeneity of people in their neighborhood. Neighborhoods were categorized as high, medium, or low in heterogeneity of residents' ages. Random samples of $n_j = 100$ elderly women from each category were interviewed (equal sample n_j's are not required) and asked, among other things, "Are you satisfied with your living conditions?" The answers were classified as "satisfied" or "not satisfied." It was

TABLE 17.5-1   Satisfaction and Age Heterogeneity

(i) Data (O_{ij} and E_{ij} denote observed and expected frequencies for the $i = 1, \ldots, r$ rows of variable A and $j = 1, \ldots, c$ columns of variable B)

	Age Heterogeneity			
	Low, b_1	Medium, b_2	High, b_3	
Satisfied, a_1	$O_{11} = 56$ $E_{11} = 50.67$	$O_{12} = 58$ $E_{12} = 50.67$	$O_{13} = 38$ $E_{13} = 50.67$	$n_{a_1} = 152$
Not Satisfied, a_2	$O_{21} = 44$ $E_{21} = 49.33$	$O_{22} = 42$ $E_{22} = 49.33$	$O_{23} = 62$ $E_{23} = 49.33$	$n_{a_2} = 148$
	$n_{b_1} = 100$	$n_{b_2} = 100$	$n_{b_3} = 100$	$n = 300$

(ii) Computation of chi-square statistic

O_{ij}	E_{ij}	$O_{ij} - E_{ij}$	$\dfrac{(O_{ij} - E_{ij})^2}{E_{ij}}$
56	50.67	5.33	0.561
44	49.33	−5.33	0.576
58	50.67	7.33	1.060
42	49.33	−7.33	1.089
38	50.67	−12.67	3.168
62	49.33	12.67	3.254
		0^a	$\chi^2(2, n = 200) = 9.708^*$
			$\chi^2_{.05, 2} = 5.991$

^{a} Computational check: $\Sigma(O_{ij} - E_{ij})$ should equal 0.
$^*p < .008$.

anticipated that satisfaction would be different for the three neighborhood categories. Responses to the question are given in Table 17.5-1, which includes the computation of Pearson's chi-square statistic. The procedure is identical to that for an $r \times c$ contingency table for testing independence (see Section 17.4). The degrees of freedom are equal to $c - 1 = 2$, the number of age-heterogeneity categories minus one. Alternatively, the degrees of freedom can be computed from $(r - 1)(c - 1) = (2 - 1)(3 - 1) = 2$. For a test at the .05 level of significance, the critical value of $\chi^2_{.05, 2}$ is 5.991. This value is obtained from Table D.4. The computed chi-square with two degrees of freedom, $\chi^2(2, n = 300) = 9.708$, exceeds the critical value, $\chi^2_{.05, 2} = 5.991$. Hence, the null hypothesis is rejected. The researcher can conclude that at least two of the population proportions are not equal.[7]

---

[7] Marascuilo and McSweeney (1977, pp. 141–147) described a procedure for determining which population proportions are unequal. The procedure is based on Scheffé's method, which is described in Section 15.6.

The effect size for the c sample proportions can be computed using Cohen's $\hat{w}$,

$$\hat{w} = \sqrt{\sum_{i=1}^{r} \sum_{j=1}^{c} \frac{(\hat{p}_{ij} - p'_{ij})^2}{p'_{ij}}} = \sqrt{\frac{\chi^2}{n}}$$

For the satisfaction and age data in Table 17.5-1, the effect size is

$$\hat{w} = \sqrt{\frac{9.708}{300}} = 0.18$$

According to Cohen's guidelines, this is a small effect.

Comparison of Designs for Testing Independence and Equality of Proportions

The experimental design for the test of equality of $c \geq 2$ proportions and the experimental design for the test of independence use the same Pearson test statistic and the same formula for computing degrees of freedom, and both are approximately distributed as the chi-square distribution. It is not surprising then that the two designs are often confused. There is no reason for confusion if you know what to look for.

The key differences between the two designs are the randomization plan and the way the sample elements are classified. In the design for testing independence, (1) a single random sample is obtained from a population and (2) the elements are classified in terms of two variables, where each variable has two or more categories. In the design for testing equality of proportions, (1) c random samples are obtained and (2) for each sample, the elements are classified in terms of membership in one of $r = 2$ mutually exclusive categories such as satisfied versus not satisfied. The important distinction is that each element's status with respect to the second variable—say, degree of neighborhood heterogeneity—has been predetermined by sampling from the appropriate population. In the design for testing independence, the status of the sample elements is not predetermined for either variable. Because of differences in the randomization plans and classification procedures, the hypotheses tested by the two designs are different—H_0: $p(A \text{ and } B) = p(A)p(B)$ for the test of independence and H_0: $p_1 = p_2 = \cdots = p_c$ for the test of equality of proportions.

Extension of the Test of Equality to More Than Two Response Categories

The test illustrated in Table 17.5-1 can be extended to the case in which variable A has r greater than two row categories: for example, very satisfied, somewhat satisfied, somewhat dissatisfied, very dissatisfied. When the number of rows is greater than 2, the test is referred to as a *test of homogeneity of proportions*. A proportion in row i and column j, denoted by $p_{a_i | b_j}$, is assumed to represent an observation for an independent multinomial random variable instead of a binomial random variable. The statistical hypotheses can be expressed as follows:

$$H_0: \begin{bmatrix} p_{a_1|b_1} = p_{a_1|b_2} = \cdots = p_{a_1|b_c} \\ p_{a_2|b_1} = p_{a_2|b_2} = \cdots = p_{a_2|b_c} \\ \vdots \\ p_{a_r|b_1} = p_{a_r|b_2} = \cdots = p_{a_r|b_c} \end{bmatrix}$$

H_1: $p_{a|b_j} \neq p_{a|b_{j'}}$ in at least one row for columns j and j'.

In words, the null hypothesis states that the proportions in the first row are equal across the c columns, the proportions in the second row are equal across the c columns, and so on. If the null hypothesis is rejected, you know that at least two proportions in at least one row are not equal. That is, there is some row for which the jth and j'th proportions are not equal. Ordinarily, numerical values are not specified in the null hypothesis; but if they were, a null hypothesis for $i = 1, \ldots, 4$ rows and $j = 1, \ldots, 3$ columns might look like

$$H_0: \begin{bmatrix} .20 = .20 = .20 \\ .40 = .40 = .40 \\ .30 = .30 = .30 \\ .10 = .10 = .10 \end{bmatrix}$$

At the risk of telling you more than you wanted to know about writing null hypotheses, let me contrast the preceding hypotheses for the multinomial case with that for a test of equality of proportions for the binomial case. If variable A has only two categories, the null hypothesis can be written as

$$H_0: p_{a_1|b_1} = p_{a_1|b_2} = \cdots = p_{a_1|b_c}$$

or simply

$$H_0: p_1 = p_2 = \cdots = p_c$$

For this binomial case, the null hypothesis does not need a second row of proportions because q, the proportion in the second category, is equal to $1 - p$. It follows that if $p_1 = p_2 = \cdots = p_c$, then $q_1 = q_2 = \cdots = q_c$.

The computation of Pearson's statistic for testing homogeneity of proportions is the same as that for testing equality of proportions. The number of degrees of freedom for the homogeneity test is equal to $(r - 1)(c - 1)$. The general assumptions discussed in connection with an $r \times c$ contingency table apply as well to the homogeneity test.

CHECK YOUR UNDERSTANDING OF SECTION 17.5

12. Company executives were classified as smokers or nonsmokers. Investigators gathered random samples from the two populations and tested for the presence of lung cancer. They obtained the following data.

	Smoker	Nonsmoker	Sun
Cancer present	16	5	21
Cancer absent	14	25	39
Sum	30	30	60

a. State the statistical hypotheses.
b. Test the null hypothesis. Let $\alpha = .01$.
c. Determine the p value of the χ^2 statistic using Microsoft's Excel CHIDIST function.
d. Compute the size of the effect. If χ^2 was significant, interpret the effect size.

13. State in words the meaning of the hypothesis

$$H_0: \begin{bmatrix} .30 = .30 = .30 \\ .60 = .60 = .60 \\ .10 = .10 = .10 \end{bmatrix}$$

14. New employees on an assembly line were randomly assigned to one of four groups and given different amounts of training. After two weeks on the job, their supervisor rated their performance as follows.

Amount of Training (Days)

Rating	1	2	5	10	Sum
Excellent	4	4	6	6	20
Good	5	3	10	11	29
Fair	9	9	5	8	31
Poor	7	9	4	0	20
Sum	25	25	25	25	100

a. State the statistical hypotheses.
b. Test the null hypothesis. Let $\alpha = .05$.
c. Determine the p value of the χ^2 statistic using Microsoft's Excel CHIDIST function.
d. Compute the size of the effect. If χ^2 was significant, interpret the effect size.

15. A program of home-care services designed to enable the elderly to postpone the need for long-term institutional care is available to all residents of Manitoba, Canada. Researchers used a structured interview to investigate differences in terms of perceived health between the elderly in Manitoba who use these services and those who do not. They obtained a random sample of 400 community residents aged 65 or older from each of the populations. A portion of the data is as follows. (Experiment suggested by Chappell, N. L. [1985]. Social support and the receipt of home-care services. *The Gerontologist, 25,* 47–54.)

Perceived Health	Home-Care User	Non-Home-Care User	Sum
High	26	112	138
Medium	129	187	316
Low	233	97	330
Sum	388*	396*	784

*Numbers do not equal 400 because of missing data.

   a. State the statistical hypotheses.
   b. Test the null hypothesis. Let $\alpha = .05$.
   c. Determine the p value of the χ^2 statistic using Microsoft's Excel CHIDIST function.
   d. Compute the size of the effect. If χ^2 was significant, interpret the effect size.

16. Use the table of random numbers in Appendix Table D.1 to draw a random sample without replacement of 20 men and 20 women students from the student database in Appendix E.
   a. List the participant number, gender, and stat grade (use only letter grades $A = 4$, $B+ = 3.5$, $B = 3, \ldots, F = 0$) for each participant in your sample.
   b. For the variables of gender (A) and stat grade (B), construct a contingency table.
   c. State the statistical hypotheses.
   d. Test the hypothesis that the proportion of A's, B's, and so on in the population are equal for men and women. Let $\alpha = .05$.
   e. Determine the p value of the χ^2 statistic using Microsoft's Excel CHIDIST function.
   f. Compute the size of the effect. If χ^2 was significant, interpret the effect size.
   g. Write a paragraph summarizing the results of your analysis and your conclusions.

17.6 LOOKING BACK: WHAT HAVE YOU LEARNED?

Pearson's chi-square test statistic is appropriate for frequency data. It provides an approximate test when an exact test based on the binomial or multinomial distributions would require a prohibitive amount of computation. The statistic is versatile. The three applications I have described are testing goodness of fit, independence, and equality of proportions. These applications are summarized in Table 17.6-1. In each application, a set of observed frequencies is compared with a set of expected frequencies. However, the apparent simplicity of the statistic $\Sigma(O - E)^2/E$ is deceptive. Its use involves important assumptions that novice researchers often overlook or misunderstand. The problem is compounded because all three applications use the same statistic for testing different hypotheses. The main points to consider in using Pearson's chi-square statistic are the following:

1. A single random sample is used to test goodness of fit and independence; more than one random sample is used to test equality of population proportions.

TABLE 17.6-1 Applications of Pearson's Chi-Square Statistic

Purpose	Null hypothesis	Degrees of freedom	Requirements
1. Testing goodness of fit	$H_0: p_1 = p_1', \ldots, p_k = p_k'$ or $O_{Pop\,1} = E_{Pop\,1}, O_{Pop\,2} = E_{Pop\,2}, \ldots, O_{Pop\,k} = E_{Pop\,k}$	$k - 1 - e$	1. One random sample. 2. If $\nu = 1$, every expected frequency should exceed 10. If $\nu > 1$, every expected frequency should exceed 5. 3. Random variable is binomially distributed for $k = 2$ and multinomially distributed for $k > 2$.
2. Testing independence	$H_0: p(A \text{ and } B) = p(A)p(B)$	$(r-1)(c-1)$	1. One random sample. 2. If $\nu = 1$, every expected frequency should exceed 10. If $\nu > 1$, every expected frequency should exceed 5. 3. Random variable is binomially distributed when A and B have two categories and is multinomially distributed otherwise.
3a. Testing equality of proportions	$H_0: p_1 = p_2 = \cdots = p_c$	$c - 1$	1. $c \geq 2$ random samples. 2. If $\nu = 1$, every expected proportions frequency should exceed 10. If $\nu > 1$, every expected frequency should exceed 5. 3. Random variable is binomially distributed.
3b. Testing homogeneity of proportions	$H_0: \begin{bmatrix} p_{a_1\mid b_1} = p_{a_1\mid b_2} = \cdots = p_{a_1\mid b_c} \\ p_{a_2\mid b_1} = p_{a_2\mid b_2} = \cdots = p_{a_2\mid b_c} \\ \vdots \\ p_{a_r\mid b_1} = p_{a_r\mid b_2} = \cdots = p_{a_r\mid b_c} \end{bmatrix}$	$(r-1)(c-1)$	1. c random samples, where $c \geq 2$; for each sample, the elements are classified in terms of one of $r > 2$ mutually exclusive categories. 2. Every expected frequency should exceed 5. 3. Random variable is multinomially distributed.

2. Each observation must be assigned to one and only one category or one cell of a contingency table.
3. Each participant or observational element should be represented only once. Multiple observations on the same participant almost always result in violation of the assumption of independence of observations.

4. The Pearson chi-square approximation to exact binomial or multinomial probabilities is generally unsatisfactory for very small samples. As a conservative rule of thumb, if the degrees of freedom are equal to 1, all expected frequencies should be at least 10; if the degrees of freedom are greater than 1, all expected frequencies should be at least 5.

5. A nonsignificant chi-square test of independence suggests that a $\hat{V}$ greater than 0 for the data could be due to chance.

6. The hypothesis tested by Pearson's statistic is nondirectional even though the region for rejection always lies in the upper tail of the sampling distribution.

REVIEW EXERCISES FOR CHAPTER 17

1. Why is the hypothesis tested by Pearson's statistic always nondirectional?

2. College students ($n = 197$) voted at a student-center booth for a beauty queen from among six photographs equivalent in physical attractiveness as determined by rankings of 35 students at a nearby university. The pictures were randomly assigned names that the 35 students had previously judged to be desirable (Kathy, Jennifer, Christine) or undesirable (Ethel, Harriet, Gertrude). The total number of votes for the photographs having the desirable names was 158; the number for the photographs having the undesirable names was 39. (Experiment suggested by Garwood, S. C., Cox, L., Kaplan, V., Wasserman, N., and Sulzer, Jefferson L. [1980]. Beauty is only "name" deep: The effect of first-name on ratings of physical attraction. *Journal of Applied Social Psychology, 10*, 431–435.)

   a. List the steps you would follow to test the null hypothesis that for the population represented by the sample of students who voted, the number of votes is evenly divided between the photographs assigned the attractive and unattractive names. Let $\alpha = .01$.

   b. Is it necessary to apply Yates' correction? Why?

   c. Perform the test and make a decision.

   d. Determine the p value of the χ^2 statistic using Microsoft's Excel CHIDIST function.

   e. Compute the size of the effect. If χ^2 was significant, interpret the effect size.

3. The dean believes that students in M–W–F classes are more likely to be absent on Monday and Friday than on Wednesday. A random sample of 200 students revealed that 68 were absent on Monday, 48 on Wednesday, and 84 on Friday.

   a. List the steps you would follow to test the hypothesis that the ratio of absences is M: W: F = 3: 2: 3. Let $\alpha = .05$.

   b. Perform the test and make a decision.

   c. Determine the p value of the χ^2 statistic using Microsoft's Excel CHIDIST function.

   e. Compute the size of the effect. If χ^2 was significant, interpret the effect size.

4. A random sample of 300 music majors took a test of creativity. Their scores and the expected number of scores based on the normal distribution are as follows.

Test Score	O_j	E_j
140 and above	0	5.0
130–139	32	20.2
120–129	48	54.2
110–119	76	83.8
100–109	90	78.4
90–99	36	42.4
80–89	18	13.4
Less than 80	0	2.7

    a. Test the hypothesis that the scores are normally distributed. Let $\alpha = .01$. The E_j column in the table presents expected frequencies, given that the null hypothesis is true; the O_j column presents the observed frequencies.
    b. How many degrees of freedom does the test have?
    c. Determine the p value of the χ^2 statistic using Microsoft's Excel CHIDIST function.
    d. Compute the size of the effect. If χ^2 was significant, interpret the effect size.
5. What is Yates' correction and why is it used?
6. State in your own words the meaning of the null hypothesis H_0: $p(A \text{ and } B) = p(A)p(B)$. If the null hypothesis is rejected, what do you know about the variables?
7. Why is Cramér's measure of association only computed when the null hypothesis $p(A \text{ and } B) = p(A)p(B)$ is rejected?
8. Three hundred divorced men were classified by age at time of first marriage and duration of first marriage as follows.

Duration of Marriage (Years)

Age at Mariage	<5	5–9	10–14	≥15	Sum
<19	41	31	15	15	102
19–24	30	27	22	21	100
25–34	11	7	16	16	50
≥35	13	14	9	12	48
Sum	95	79	62	64	300

    a. List the steps you would use to test the null hypothesis that the two variables are independent. Let $\alpha = .05$.
    b. Perform the test and make a decision.
    c. Determine the p value of the χ^2 statistic using Microsoft's Excel CHIDIST function.
    d. If the null hypothesis is rejected, compute Cramér's statistic.
    e. Compute the size of the effect. If χ^2 was significant, interpret the effect size.
9. Hip fractures in elderly patients are known to be associated with a high incidence of mortality. Researchers collected data for 225 elderly patients who had undergone hip surgery and measured the following variables: mortality,

number of previous hip injuries (antecedents), and patient's age. (Experiment suggested by Banna, S. E., Raynal, L., and Gerebzof, A. [1984]. Fractures of the hip and medico-social considerations. *Archives of Gerontology and Geriatrics, 3*, 311–319.)

Medical Antecedents	Died	Survived	Sum
No antecedent	8	27	35
1 antecedent	20	62	82
2 antecedents	21	25	46
3 antecedents	13	23	36
≥ 4 antecedents	20	5	25
Sum	82	142	224[a]

Age	Died	Survived	Sum
56–65	2	12	14
66–75	10	32	42
76–85	40	64	104
86–95	30	20	50
Sum	82	128	210[a]

[a]*n* does not equal 225 because of missing data.

a. For the data in the table, test the hypotheses that mortality is independent of the number of antecedents and age. Let $\alpha = .05$.
b. Determine the *p* value of the χ^2 statistics using Microsoft's Excel CHIDIST function.
c. If the null hypothesis is rejected, compute Cramér's statistic.
d. Compute the size of the effect for number of antecedents and age. If either χ^2 was significant, interpret the effect size.

10. Investigators performed an analysis on federal court cases in which a complainant charged that the Age Discrimination in Employment Act of 1967 and subsequent amendments had been violated. They examined data for 120 cases in terms of the outcome of the discrimination suit and the gender of the complainant. (Experiment suggested by Schuster, M., and Miller, C. S. [1984]. An empirical assessment of the age discrimination in employment act. *Industrial and Labor Relations Review, 38*, 64–74).

	Outcome of Suit		
Gender	Won	Lost	Sum
Man	19	15	34
Woman	21	65	86
Sum	40	80	120

a. Test the null hypothesis that the variables of gender and suit outcome are independent. Let $\alpha = .05$.

b. If the null hypothesis is rejected, compute Cramér's statistic.

c. Determine the p value of the χ^2 statistic using Microsoft's Excel CHIDIST function.

d. Compute the size of the effect. If χ^2 was significant, interpret the effect size.

11. The equality of proportions chi-square test and the independence chi-square test are applicable to an $r \times c$ contingency table, and both use the same test statistic. How do they differ?

12. Students were given a choice of writing or not writing a paper for extra credit. Half of the students, selected randomly, were made to feel coerced; the other half were not pressured. The number who chose to write or not to write a paper is as follows.

	Coerced	*Not Coerced*	*Sum*
Wrote paper	13	9	22
Did not write paper	17	21	38
Sum	30	30	60

a. List the steps you would use to test the null hypothesis. Let $\alpha = .05$.

b. Test the null hypothesis that the variables of paper writing and coercion are independent.

c. Determine the p value of the χ^2 statistic using Microsoft's Excel CHIDIST function.

d. Did the conditions affect paper writing?

e. Compute the size of the effect. If χ^2 was significant, interpret the effect size.

13. State in words the meaning of the hypothesis

$$H_0: \begin{bmatrix} .20 = .20 = .20 \\ .30 = .30 = .30 \\ .50 = .50 = .50 \end{bmatrix}$$

14. Random samples of seventh-, eighth-, and ninth-grade students were interviewed following one year of busing. They were asked, "Did black and white students mix more than, the same as, or less than last year?" The following data were obtained.

		Grade		
Response	7	8	9	*Sum*
More	26	12	4	42
Same	18	25	35	78
Less	6	13	11	30
Sum	50	50	50	150

a. State the statistical hypotheses.

b. Test the null hypothesis. Let $\alpha = .05$.

c. Determine the p value of the χ^2 statistic using Microsoft's Excel CHIDIST function.
d. Compute the size of the effect. If χ^2 was significant, interpret the effect size.

15. Use the table of random numbers in Appendix Table D.1 to draw a random sample without replacement of 20 men and 20 women students from the Student Database in Appendix E.

a. List the participant number, gender, and math test score for each participant in your sample.
b. For the variables of gender (A) and math test score (B), construct a contingency table. Assign the math test scores to one of the following class intervals: 0–9, 10–19, 20–29, 30–39, and 40–48.
c. Test the hypothesis that the population proportion in each of the five class intervals is equal for men and women. Let $\alpha = .05$.
d. Write the null and alternative hypotheses.
e. Compute the size of the effect. If χ^2 was significant, interpret the effect size.
f. Write a paragraph summarizing the results of your analysis and your conclusions.

†17.7 SUPPLEMENTARY NOTE

Special Computational Procedure for a 2 × 2 Contingency Table

A simpler procedure for computing Pearson's chi-square statistic can be used when a contingency table has 2 rows and 2 columns—a 2 × 2 contingency table. This procedure has the advantage of not requiring the computation of expected frequencies. Consider the following 2 × 2 table in which observed frequencies are denoted by

Variable 2

	a	b	$a + b$
Variable 1			
	c	d	$c + d$
	$a + c$	$b + d$	

the letters a, b, c, and d. The formula for Pearson's statistic using only observed cell frequencies is

$$\chi^2 = \frac{n(ad - bc)^2}{(a + b)(c + d)(a + c)(b + d)}$$

---

† This supplementary note can be omitted without loss of continuity.

For the data in Table 17.4-2, the formula yields

$$\chi^2 = \frac{200[(8)(96) - (32)(64)]^2}{(8+32)(64+96)(8+64)(32+96)} = 5.555$$

which is identical to the answer obtained using the conventional formula. If desired, Yates' correction for continuity can be included in the formula as follows:

$$\chi^2 = \frac{n(|ad - bc| - n/2)^2}{(a+b)(c+d)(a+c)(b+d)}$$

Statistical Inference for Ranked Data

18.1 Introduction
Looking Ahead: What Is
This Chapter About?

**18.2 Assumption-Freer
Tests**

**18.3 Mann-Whitney *U* Test
for Two Independent
Samples**
Computational
Procedure for Small
Samples
Computational
Procedures When One
or Both *n*'s Exceed 20
Measures of Relative
Efficiency
Relative Efficiency of the
Mann-Whitney *U* Test
Check Your
Understanding of
Sections 18.2 and 18.3

**18.4 Wilcoxon *T* Test for
Dependent Samples**
Computational
Procedure for Small
Samples
Computational
Procedures When *n*
Is Greater Than 50
Check Your
Understanding
of Section 18.4

**18.5 Comparison of
Parametric Tests and
Assumption-Freer
Tests for Ranked Data**
Check Your
Understanding of
Section 18.5

**18.6 Looking Back: What
Have You Learned?**
Review Exercises for
Chapter 18

18.1 INTRODUCTION

Looking Ahead: What Is This Chapter About?

This chapter describes two test statistics that are appropriate for testing hypotheses about the equality of populations where the data are in the form of ranks or can be converted to ranks. Some variables such as physical attractiveness, progress of group therapy participants, and tastiness of pizzas are difficult to measure, but they are easy to rank. The variables are difficult to measure because each is determined by numerous factors. For example, the tastiness of a pizza is determined by, among other things, the quality of the cheese, the crust, and the toppings. In spite of this, you and I have little difficulty ranking pizzas.

An advantage of tests in which the datum is a rank is that the tests make fewer assumptions about the underlying population distributions than do the test described in Chapters 10 through 16. For example, the two test statistics in this chapter do not assume that the populations are normally distributed and have equal variances.

After reading this chapter, you should know the following:

- How to use the Mann-Whitney U statistic and independent samples to test the hypothesis that two population distributions are identical
- How to use the Wilcoxon T statistic and dependent samples to test the hypothesis that two population distributions are identical
- The advantages and disadvantages of tests based on ranks

18.2 ASSUMPTION-FREER TESTS

So far I have presented procedures for testing hypotheses about a variety of population parameters. In most cases it was necessary to assume that the sampled population had a probability distribution of a particular shape—usually normal or binomial. For many variables, such an assumption seems warranted. For other variables, however, a researcher may not know the shape of the underlying population distribution and may be unwilling to make an assumption about it. The procedures I presented in Chapters 10–16 also require other assumptions. For example, the independent-samples t statistic for testing the null hypothesis $H_0: \mu_1 - \mu_2 = 0$ assumes that the population variances are equal. To avoid having to make such assumptions, nonparametric and distribution-free tests have been developed that are assumption freer—that is, they require less stringent assumptions. Before describing the tests, let me review the three kinds of distributions about which assumptions are made: (1) the sampled population (for example, the population of the observation statistic X), (2) the sampling distribution of the descriptive statistic used in the test (for example, $\overline{X}$), and (3) the sampling distribution of the test statistic (for example, t). Nonparametric and distribution-free tests are assumption freer with respect to the distribution of the sampled population.

> A statistical test is **nonparametric** if it does not test a hypothesis about one of the parameters of the sampled population. It is **distribution-free** if it makes no assumptions about the shape of the sampled population.

Most distribution-free tests, however, do assume that the sampled population is continuous. Although the distinction between nonparametric and distribution-free tests seems clear enough, in practice the distinction is frequently blurred. Consequently, many statisticians use the terms interchangeably. I will follow Ury's (1967) lead and denote both kinds of tests by the more descriptive label *assumption-freer tests*.

Several assumption-freer tests have already been described. The chi-square tests in Chapter 17, for example, are assumption-freer tests for frequency data. The two tests to be described in this chapter are assumption-freer tests for ranked data (ordered qualitative variables).

Assumption-freer tests differ from parametric tests in a number of important respects. I will mention one difference now and defer a complete discussion until Section 18.5. Parametric tests utilize the magnitude information contained in observations (scores), but assumption-freer tests ignore this information. Instead, assumption-freer tests use either the frequency with which observations occur, as in the case of the chi-square tests in Chapter 17, or their rank (ordinal position), as in the case of the tests in this chapter. One advantage of focusing on either the categorical or ordinal information contained in observations has already been mentioned: a researcher can avoid having to make assumptions regarding the shape of the sampled population. But as you will see, this freedom is bought at a price. Assumption-freer tests tend to be less efficient than parametric tests when the assumptions of the parametric tests are fulfilled.

Another advantage of assumption-freer tests is that they require less sophisticated measurement procedures. One of the simplest measurement procedures is ranking people or objects with respect to some characteristic. You observe, for example, that John is a better quarterback than Fred, who is better than Elmer; this piece of pie looks better than that one; or Jane is more resourceful than Dennis. It is convenient to use numbers to denote rank order. For example, John is 1; Fred is 2; and Elmer is 3. However, the numbers do not reflect the magnitude of differences in quarterbacking skill or whether the difference between John and Fred is the same as that between Fred and Elmer. Presumably, measuring instruments could be devised that would assign numbers that reflect the magnitude of differences in quarterbacking skill, pie attractiveness, and resourcefulness. This has been done in the area of intellectual assessment: the measuring instrument is an intelligence test. But such instruments are difficult to develop, which is why researchers frequently resort to counting or ranking.

Two test statistics that utilize only the ordinal information contained in observations are described in Sections 18.3 and 18.4. They are regarded as assumption-freer alternatives to the independent and dependent two-sample *t* tests for means. There are many other assumption-freer tests. The interested reader is referred to Siegel and Castellan (1988).

18.3 MANN-WHITNEY *U* TEST FOR TWO INDEPENDENT SAMPLES

requires n<20, use z test if n>20

The Mann-Whitney *U* test is used to test the hypothesis that two population distributions are identical.[1] The test assumes that the populations are continuous and that random samples have been drawn from the respective populations or the participants have been randomly assigned to two conditions. The test statistic is based on the ranks of observations rather than on their numerical values, and hence it is appropriate for most data in the behavioral sciences and education. Because of the *U* test's modest assumptions, it is widely used as an assumption-freer alternative to the two-sample *t* test for independent samples.

Computational Procedure for Small Samples

The computational procedures described here for the Mann-Whitney *U* statistic can be used when both sample sizes, n_1 and n_2, are 20 or less. When either of the samples contains more than 20 scores, a *z* statistic described later can be used.

Suppose an experiment was performed to determine whether the amount of aggressive behavior exhibited by children is affected by observing aggression on TV. A sample of $n = 21$ six-year-old girls was randomly assigned to one of two conditions: viewing a television program containing numerous aggressive acts, the experimental condition, and viewing a program without aggression, the control condition. Following the television viewing, each girl was observed at play, and her aggressive acts were counted.

The data for the experiment are given in Table 18.3-1 along with the computational procedures for the *U* statistic. The first step in the analysis is to rank-order the scores. In assigning ranks to the scores, the data for the experimental and control groups are treated as one sample. The scores, frequency of aggressive acts for each girl, are ordered from the smallest to the largest. The first *n* positive integers are then substituted for the scores, with the smallest score receiving a rank of 1 and the largest receiving a rank of *n*. For example, one of the girls exhibited 0 aggressive act, which is the fewest number. This 0 is assigned the rank of 1. Another girl exhibited 1 aggressive act, the next fewest number. This 1 is assigned the rank of 2, and so on. If two or more observations have the same value (tied scores), they are assigned the mean of the ranks they would have occupied. For example, two girls exhibited 13 aggressive acts. These two 13's would occupy ranks 12 and 13. So each 13 is assigned the mean of ranks 12 and 13, which is 12.5. The ranks associated with the experimental and control groups are added separately. The Mann-Whitney test statistic, *U*, is based on the sum of ranks as indicated in part (ii) of Table 18.3-1.

No assumptions regarding the shape of the populations are required because the test statistic is based not on scores but on ranks. The null hypothesis states that the

---

[1] The test was originally developed by Frank Wilcoxon in 1945 and called the Wilcoxon rank-sum test. Since then, various forms of the test have appeared: a form, by Festinger in 1946, the Mann-Whitney form in 1947, and a form by White in 1952. The Wilcoxon rank-sum test should not be confused with the Wilcoxon matched-pairs signed ranks test discussed in Section 18.4.

TABLE 18.3-1 Computational Procedure for Mann-Whitney U test

(i) Data (n = 21 girls were randomly assigned to two conditions. The two samples were treated as one combined sample, and the scores were ranked from 1 to n, with the smallest score receiving a rank of 1 and the largest, a rank of 21. Two or more scores with the same value [tied scores] were assigned the mean of the ranks they would have received. For example, the two scores of 13 would have received ranks of 12 and 13; instead, they both received the mean rank of 12.5.)

Number of Aggressive Acts for Experimental Group	Rank, R_1	Number of Aggressive Acts for Control Group	Rank, R_2
2	3	8	8
19	17	1	2
13	12.5	0	1
9	9	10	10
17	15	20	18
18	16	5	6
24	21	11	11
15	14	7	7
22	20	3	4
21	19	13	12.5
		4	5
$n_1 = 10$	$\Sigma R_1 = 146.5$	$n_2 = 11$	$\Sigma R_2 = 84.5$

(ii) Computational check

$$\Sigma R_1 + \Sigma R_2 = \frac{N(N+1)}{2} \text{ where } N = n_1 + n_2$$

$$146.5 + 84.5 = 231 \quad \frac{21(21+1)}{2} = 231$$

(iii) Computation of U

$$U(n_1, n_2) = \text{Smaller of} \left[\begin{array}{l} n_1 n_2 + \frac{n_1(n_1+1)}{2} - \Sigma R_1 \\ n_1 n_2 + \frac{n_2(n_2+1)}{2} - \Sigma R_2 \end{array} \right]$$

$$U(10, 11) = \text{Smaller of} \left[\begin{array}{l} (10)(11) + \frac{10(10+1)}{2} - 146.5 = 18.5 \\ (10)(11) + \frac{11(11+1)}{2} - 84.5 = 91.5 \end{array} \right] = 18.5$$

To be significant at α level of significance, the computed $U(10, 11)$ must be less than or equal to the critical value $U_{\alpha/2; n_1, n_2}$ in Table D.12. This value is $U_{.05/2; 10, 11} = 26$. Because $U(10, 11) = 18.5$ is less than $U_{.05/2; 10, 11} = 26$, the null hypothesis is rejected.

distribution of aggressive acts for girls in the experimental population is identical to that for girls in the control population. The statistical hypotheses are as follows:[2]

> H_0: Population distributions for the experimental and control groups are identical.
>
> H_1: Population distributions are not identical.

The .05 level of significance is adopted. To be significant at the .05 level, the computed value of the test statistic, $U(n_1, n_2)$, must be *less than* or *equal* to the critical value, $U_{.05/2; \, n_1, \, n_2}$, obtained from Appendix Table D.10. For the data in Table 18.3-1, the computed value of the Mann-Whitney statistic, $U(10, 11) = 18.5$, is less than the critical value, $U_{.05/2; \, 10, \, 11} = 26$. Hence, the researcher can conclude that the two populations are not identical. Inspection of the data indicates that the girls who watched a television program containing aggression engaged in more aggressive acts than those who did not.

The Mann-Whitney U test also can be used to test directional hypotheses if the population distributions are symmetrical. The U test statistic is computed as before. However U must be less than or equal to the one-tailed critical value from Table D.10. In addition, the relative position of the sample distributions must be consistent with the alternative hypothesis. For example, if the alternative hypothesis states that the population distribution for the experimental group is displaced (shifted) above that for the control group, the sample distributions must exhibit a similar displacement.

Computational Procedures When One or Both *n*'s Exceed 20

Table D.10 in Appendix D provides critical values of U for n_1 and n_2 from 3 to 20. When either of the samples contains more than 20 scores, a z statistic that is approximately normally distributed can be used. The approximate procedure is satisfactory if both n's are greater than 10. The z test statistic is

$$z = \frac{(U + c) - E(U)}{\sigma_U} = \frac{(U + c) - n_1 n_2 / 2}{\sqrt{(n_1 n_2)(n_1 + n_2 + 1) / 12}}$$

where U is defined in Table 18.3-1 and n_1 and n_2 are the two sample sizes. The c term in the formula is a correction for continuity and is equal to 0.5. The decision rule for the z test is as follows: Reject the null hypothesis if z falls in the critical region of the normal distribution; otherwise, do not reject the null hypothesis. Because of the way U is defined, the computed value of z will always be negative regardless of whether the test is one tailed or two tailed. To be significant, the absolute value of the z test statistic must be greater than or equal to $z_{\alpha/2}$ for a two-tailed test or greater than or equal to z_α for a one-tailed test.

As noted earlier, if two or more observations have the same value (tied scores), they are assigned the mean of the ranks they would have occupied. The denominator, σ_U, of the z statistic can be corrected for ties; the corrected formula is

$$\sigma_U = \sqrt{\frac{(n_1 n_2)(n_1 + n_2 + 1)}{12} \left[1 - \frac{\sum (t_i^3 - t_i)}{(n_1 + n_2)^3 - (n_1 + n_2)} \right]}$$

[2] If it can be assumed that the two population distributions are symmetrical, the Mann-Whitney U test is a test of the hypothesis that the population medians are equal.

where t_i is the number of tied observations in a particular set. The term ($- t_i$) is computed for each set and then is summed for the sets. In Table 18.3-1, there is one set of two tied scores. The two tied scores are 13 and 13. For this set, $t_i^3 - t_i = 2^3 - 2 = 6$. If $n_1 + n_2$ is large and the number of ties is small, the correction can be ignored.

The computation of the z statistic will be shown using the data in Table 18.3-1. The test statistic is

$$z = \frac{(U + c) - nh_1 n_2/2}{\sqrt{\frac{(n_1 n_2)(n_1 + n_2 + 1)}{12}\left[1 - \frac{\Sigma(t_i^3 - t_i)}{(n_1 + n_2)^3 - (n_1 + n_2)}\right]}}$$

$$= \frac{(18.5 + 0.5) - (10)(11)/2}{\sqrt{\frac{(10)(11)(10 + 11 + 1)}{12}\left[1 - \frac{2^3 - 2}{(10 + 11)^3 - (10 + 11)}\right]}}$$

$$= \frac{-36.00}{\sqrt{201.667(0.999)}} = -2.54$$

The critical value of z for a two-tailed test at the $\alpha = .05$ level of significance is $z_{.05/2} = 1.96$. Because the absolute value of the computed test statistic, $|z| = 2.54$, is greater than the critical value, $z_{.05/2} = 1.96$, the null hypothesis is rejected. The absolute value of the z test statistic is large enough to be significant at the .02 level. A similar conclusion would be reached using the small-sample exact test procedure. As expected, the correction for ties, which is $\sqrt{0.999}$, has virtually no effect on the test. The uncorrected z statistic is 2.5363 versus 2.5350 for the corrected statistic.

Earlier, I mentioned that assumption-freer tests tend to be less efficient than parametric tests when the assumptions of the parametric tests are fulfilled. Several statistics can be used to compare the relative efficiency of two tests. A simple relative index called *power efficiency* is described next.

Measures of Relative Efficiency

You saw in Section 10.4 that power is determined by four factors: (1) level of significance, (2) sample size, (3) population dispersion, and (4) magnitude of the difference between the true and hypothesized parameters. Furthermore, any desired power can be achieved for a given significance level and true alternative hypothesis by obtaining a sufficiently large sample. If one test statistic requires a smaller sample size to achieve a desired power than does another statistic, it is said to be more efficient.

One index for comparing the efficiency of two test statistics when both are used to test the same null hypothesis at α significance level against the same alternative hypothesis is called **power efficiency.** It is given by

$$Power\ efficiency = \frac{100(n_S)}{n_L}$$

where n_L is the sample size required by test L to equal the power of the more efficient test S, based on n_S observations.

Suppose, for example, that test S requires 40 participants to reject the null hypothesis in favor of the alternative hypothesis at α significance level with power equal to .90, and that test L requires 80 participants. The power efficiency, PE, of test L relative to S is

$$PE = \frac{100(40)}{80} = 50\%$$

The PE index has a drawback. Its value is determined by the particular values of α, power, H_0, H_1, and the sample size of the more efficient comparison test statistic. Statisticians prefer another index called **asymptotic relative efficiency,** or ARE, that does not depend on qualifying conditions that vary from one situation to the next. A description of the index is beyond the scope of this book. It turns out that when the two indexes, PE and ARE, are used to rank-order various test statistics in terms of efficiency, the results are almost identical.

Relative Efficiency of the Mann-Whitney U Test

In general, when the assumptions of parametric tests are met, they are more efficient than assumption-freer tests. This is true for the two-sample t test for independent samples when compared with the Mann-Whitney U test. The two provide tests of the same hypothesis if observations are randomly sampled from a normal population, because in that case the population mean is equal to the population median. Recall from footnote 2 that when the populations are symmetrical, the Mann-Whitney U test is a test of the hypothesis that the population medians are identical. The power efficiency of the U test relative to that for the t test is 95.5%. When the distribution assumptions of the t test are violated, the relative efficiency of the U test can exceed that for t. Thus, the U test is an excellent alternative to the t test. It has two important advantages: it is applicable to ranked data and it assumes only random assignment or random sampling from continuous populations.

CHECK YOUR UNDERSTANDING OF SECTIONS 18.2 AND 18.3

1. Compare the assumptions of the Mann-Whitney U test with those for the two-sample t test for independent samples. What are the relative merits of the tests?
2. Researchers investigated the effect of administering a noxious stimulus (an electric shock) at random intervals on the exploratory behavior of gerbils during infancy. They randomly assigned animals to the experimental condition (shock) or the control condition (nonshock) and measured the dependent variable (duration in minutes of exploratory behavior during one day) when the animals were six months old. For the data in the table, test the hypothesis that the experimental and control populations are identical. Let $\alpha = .05$.

Control Group				Experimental Group		
40	42	25	30	32	26	30
33	31	34		16	24	20

3. The effect on motor skill development of playing with educational toys for six months was investigated. The participants were four- and five-year-olds. Half of the participants were randomly assigned to the play group; the remaining half did not play with the toys. For the following data, test the hypothesis that the two populations are identical. Let $\alpha = .01$. Perform the test with and without a correction for ties.

Motor Skill Scores for Play Group				Motor Skill Scores for Control Group			
28	22	19	15	27	18	17	13
26	21	18	14	25	18	17	10
25	20	18	12	23	18	16	8
24	19	17	11	21	17	16	7
23	19	16	9	20	17	16	6

4. What are the qualifying conditions associated with the PE index?
5. Under what conditions can the z test be used instead of the U test to test the null hypothesis that two population distributions are identical?
6. Suppose that the two-sample t test required 82 participants to reject the nondirectional null hypothesis at the .01 level of significance with power equal to .80, and the Mann-Whitney U test required 86 participants. (a) What is the PE of the Mann-Whitney test? (b) What are the qualifying conditions associated with your estimate?
7. Terms to remember:
   a. Nonparametric tests
   b. Distribution-free tests
   c. Assumption-freer tests
   d. Power efficiency
   e. Asymptotic relative efficiency

18.4 WILCOXON *T* TEST FOR DEPENDENT SAMPLES

The Wilcoxon matched-pairs signed-ranks test is used to test the hypothesis that two population distributions are identical. It is appropriate for dependent samples. Such samples can result from (1) obtaining repeated measures on the same participants, (2) using participants matched on a variable that is known to be correlated with the dependent variable, (3) using identical twins or littermates, or (4) obtaining pairs of participants who are matched by mutual selection.[3] The Wilcoxon test assumes that the populations are continuous and that a random sample of paired elements has been obtained or that the paired elements have been randomly assigned to the conditions. The test's power efficiency relative to that of the two-sample t test for dependent samples is 95.5% when the latter test's assumptions are met. When the t test's assumptions are not met, Wilcoxon's relative efficiency can equal or exceed that for the t test. Thus, Wilcoxon's test is an excellent alternative to the t test for dependent samples.

---

[3] Procedures for obtaining dependent samples are discussed in Section 13.4.

The Wilcoxon test statistic, denoted by T, is based on the rank of the absolute difference between paired observations rather than on the numerical value of the difference. Consequently, the test is appropriate for observations that represent ordinal information.

Computational Procedure for Small Samples

The computational procedure described here for the Wilcoxon T statistic can be used when the sample contains 50 or fewer pairs of scores. When the sample contains more than 50 pairs of scores, a z statistic described later can be used.

Suppose that a test of assertiveness was administered to women college students and the scores were used to form 16 pairs of women matched on assertiveness. One woman in each pair was randomly assigned to participate in an assertiveness-training group; the other member of the pair participated in a psychology seminar, the control condition. It was hypothesized that women in the assertiveness-training group would become more assertive relative to those in the control group. The statistical hypotheses are as follows:

H_0: The population distributions of assertiveness scores are identical for the two groups.

H_1: The population distribution of scores for women in the training group is displaced (shifted) above that for the control group.

The alternative hypothesis calls for a one-tailed test in which the sample distribution for the training group is displaced above that for the control group. The .05 level of significance is adopted. The data are given in Table 18.4-1, along with the computational procedures.

The computations in Table 18.4-1 for Wilcoxon's T test are easy to perform. First, the magnitude of the difference between each pair of observations is determined (see column 4). These differences are rank-ordered in column 5 in terms of their absolute size—that is, their signs are ignored. The smallest difference receives a rank of 1; the largest, a rank of n. Finally, two columns, 6 and 7, containing the ranks, respectively, for the positive and negative differences are formed. The T test statistic is the smaller of the sum of the positive ranks and the absolute value of the sum of the negative ranks.

The presence of zero differences requires a computational adjustment. If the number of zero differences is even, each zero difference is assigned the average rank for the set, and then half are arbitrarily given a positive sign and half are given a negative sign. If an odd number of zero differences occurs, one randomly selected difference is discarded, and the procedure for an even number of zero differences is followed. When a score is discarded, the sample size, n, is reduced by one.

To be significant, the computed $T(n)$ for the data in Table 18.4-1 must be *less than* or *equal* to the one-tailed critical value $T_{\alpha, n}$ in Appendix Table D.11. The n in $T(n)$ is the number of pairs of observations. For this one-tailed test, the training

TABLE 18.4-1 Computational Procedure for Wilcoxon *T* Test

(i) Data (n = 16 pairs of women matched on assertiveness were formed. The women in each matched pair were randomly assigned to the training and control groups.)

(1) *Pair*	(2) *Training Group*	(3) *Control Group*	(4) *Difference*	(5) *Rank of Difference, Ignoring Sign*	(6) *Rank Associated with Positive Difference,* R_+	(7) *Rank Associated with Negative Difference,* R_-
1	34	32	2	6.5	6.5	
2	36	26	10	16.0	16.0	
3	31	28	3	8.5	8.5	
4	42	41	1	4.0	4.0	
5	47	47	0	1.5		-1.5^a
6	32	33	−1	4.0		−4.0
7	33	29	4	10.0	10.0	
8	39	41	−2	6.5		−6.5
9	31	26	5	11.0	11.0	
10	34	28	6	12.0	12.0	
11	32	29	3	8.5	8.5	
12	41	41	0	1.5	1.5	
13	35	28	7	13.0	13.0	
14	45	44	1	4.0	4.0	
15	31	23	8	14.0	14.0	
16	33	24	9	15.0	15.0	
	$\Sigma X_T = 576$	$\Sigma X_C = 520$			$\Sigma R_+ = 124.0$	$|\Sigma R_-| = 12.0$

(ii) Computational check

$$\Sigma R_+ + |\Sigma R_-| = \frac{n(n+1)}{2}$$

$$124 + 12 = 136 \qquad \frac{16(16+1)}{2} = 136$$

(iii) Test statistic

$$T(16) = (\text{Smaller of } \Sigma R_+ \text{ and } |\Sigma R_-|) = 12.0$$

To be significant at $\alpha = .05$ level of significance, the computed $T(16)$ must be less than or equal to the one-tailed critical value, $T_{.05,\,16}$, in Appendix Table D.13 and the training group must be displaced above the control group. Because $T(16) = 12.0 < T_{.05,\,16} = 36$ and the training group is displaced above the control group, the null hypothesis is rejected.

---

[a] See the text for an explanation of why this zero difference is assigned a negative sign.

group must be displaced above the control group. Inspection of the data indicates that the latter condition is satisfied. The computed value of the Wilcoxon statistic in Table 18.4-1, $T(16) = 12$, is less than the critical value, $T_{.05, 16} = 35$. Hence, the researcher can conclude that the two populations are not identical; the training group is displaced above the control group.

Computational Procedures When n Is Greater Than 50

Table D.11 in Appendix D provides critical values of Wilcoxon's T for n from 5 to 50. When the sample n is greater than 50, a z statistic that is approximately normally distributed can be used. The approximate procedure is satisfactory for n's as small as 10. The z statistic is

$$z = \frac{(T + c) - E(T)}{\sigma_T} = \frac{(T + c) - n(n + 1)/4}{\sqrt{n(n + 1)(2n + 1)/24}}$$

where T is defined in Table 18.4-1 and n is the number of pairs of scores. The c term in the formula is a correction for continuity and is equal to 0.5. The decision rule for the z test is as follows: Reject the null hypothesis if the absolute value of z is greater than or equal to z_α; otherwise, do not reject the hypothesis. Because of the way T is defined, the computed value of z will always be negative, whether the test is one tailed or two tailed.

If two or more ranks have the same value, they are assigned the mean of the ranks they would have occupied. The denominator, σ_T, of the z statistic can be corrected for ties; the formula with the correction is

$$\sigma_T = \sqrt{\frac{n(n + 1)(2n + 1)}{24} - \frac{\Sigma(t_i^3 - t)}{48}}$$

where t_i is the number of tied observations in a particular set. The term $(t_i^3 - t_i)$ is computed for each set and then summed for the sets. If n is large and the number of ties is small, the correction can be ignored.

The z test will be illustrated using the data in Table 18.4-1. The procedure provides a satisfactory approximation when n is greater than or equal to 10. The test statistic is

$$z = \frac{(T + c) - n(n + 1)/4}{\sqrt{\dfrac{n(n + 1)(2n + 1)}{24} - \dfrac{\Sigma(t_i^3 - t)}{48}}}$$

$$z = \frac{(12 + 0.5) - \dfrac{16(16 + 1)}{4}}{\sqrt{\dfrac{16(16 + 1)[(2)(16) + 1]}{24} - \dfrac{(2^3 - 2) + (2^3 - 2) + (2^3 - 2)}{48}}}$$

$$= \frac{-55.5}{\sqrt{374 - 0.375}} = -2.87$$

The critical value of z for a one-tailed test at $\alpha = .05$ level of significance is 1.645. Because $|z| = 2.87$ is greater than $z_{.05} = 1.645$ and the training group is displaced above the control group, the null hypothesis is rejected. The absolute value of the z test statistic is large enough to be significant at the .003 level. The table of critical values for T does not have significance levels beyond .005, but the computed T is small enough to be significant at the .003 level.

CHECK YOUR UNDERSTANDING OF SECTION 18.4

8. Researchers investigated the effect on one's sense of well-being of participating in a transactional analysis group. Participants completed a questionnaire before and after participating in the group. For the data in the table, test the hypothesis that the two populations are identical. Let $\alpha = .05$. The higher the score, the higher the individual's sense of well-being.

Participant	Score before Participation	Score after Participation	Participant	Score before Participation	Score after Participation
1	50	56	8	36	40
2	46	50	9	35	34
3	45	50	10	35	34
4	43	48	11	34	34
5	40	44	12	34	32
6	37	40	13	33	33
7	36	38	14	31	31

9. A researcher investigated the absolute threshold for a 1000-Hertz tone under the effects of a hallucinogen, hashish, and a placebo. The order of administration of the conditions was randomized independently for each participant. For the data in the table, test the hypothesis that the two populations are identical versus the alternative that the placebo population is displaced above the hallucinogen population. Let $\alpha = .05$. Scores are dB re. 0.0002 dyne/cm^2.

Participant	Hashish	Placebo	Participant	Hashish	Placebo
1	4	6	9	0	0
2	0	0	10	5	8
3	1	1	11	−1	−2
4	0	−1	12	6	7
5	0	1	13	2	2
6	1	2	14	1	1
7	3	3	15	4	5
8	−1	0	16	2	4

10. It has been claimed that the grades of college students improve following marriage. To test the hypothesis, the variables of college aptitude, gender, and size

of high school attended were used to form matched pairs of students: one student of a pair had been married for at least two semesters and the other was unmarried. For the data in the table, test the hypothesis that the populations are identical versus the alternative that the married population is displaced above the unmarried population. Use the z statistic to analyze the data. Let $\alpha = .05$. Do not use the correction for ties.

Pair	Married	Unmarried		Pair	Married	Unmarried
1	3.7	3.8		19	3.1	3.1
2	3.4	3.2		20	3.8	3.6
3	2.9	3.1		21	3.6	3.3
4	2.9	2.7		22	3.6	3.8
5	3.0	2.8		23	3.5	3.1
6	2.2	2.3		24	3.1	3.0
7	3.1	2.7		25	2.8	2.9
8	3.2	2.7		26	2.6	2.8
9	3.4	3.4		27	2.5	2.3
10	3.5	3.4		28	3.6	3.4
11	3.3	2.6		29	3.5	3.0
12	2.7	3.1		30	3.4	3.5
13	3.2	3.1		31	3.3	3.6
14	1.8	2.3		32	3.2	3.0
15	3.4	3.0		33	3.5	2.2
16	3.9	3.4		34	3.4	2.6
17	3.3	3.2		35	2.0	2.4
18	3.2	2.6				

11. Use the z statistic to analyze the data in Exercise 9. Use the correction for ties. Let $\alpha = .05$.

12. Suppose the two-sample t test required 122 participants to reject the nondirectional null hypothesis at the .01 level of significance with power equal to .95, and the Wilcoxon T test required 128 participants. (a) What is the power efficiency (PE) of the Wilcoxon test? (b) What qualifying conditions are associated with your estimate?

18.5 COMPARISON OF PARAMETRIC TESTS AND ASSUMPTION-FREER TESTS FOR RANKED DATA

When assumption-freer tests first appeared, they were regarded as no more than quick and dirty substitutes for parametric tests because their power efficiency was thought to be inferior. Now researchers have a clearer understanding of the differences between the two kinds of tests, which mainly involve (1) their assumptions, (2) the level of mathematics necessary to understand their rationale, (3) their computational simplicity, and (4) the nature of the hypothesis they test. I will now examine these differences.

Most parametric test statistics assume that (1) the population elements are randomly sampled or that the elements are randomly assigned to experimental conditions and (2) the population is normally distributed. Some test statistics require a third assumption if the null hypothesis concerns two or more populations—that the population variances are equal.

Assumption-freer test statistics make fewer assumptions and hence can be used in situations for which parametric methods are not appropriate. Most assumption-freer procedures assume that (1) the population elements are randomly sampled or that the elements are randomly assigned to experimental conditions and (2) the sampled population is continuous, which implies that no two population elements have the same value (that is, no tied values).[4] It is relatively easy to determine whether the assumptions of assumption-freer tests are satisfied. For example, a sampling procedure is under a researcher's control—the researcher knows whether it is random. And one can decide on logical grounds whether or not the population is continuous.

On the other hand, the parametric assumptions of normality and equal variances are more difficult to check because in any practical situation the population is not available for examination. Statistical tests can be applied to sample data to test these assumptions. However, for the small samples typically used in the behavioral sciences, health sciences, and education, the tests may lack the power necessary to detect departures from normality and equal variances.

If all the assumptions of parametric tests are met, these tests are more efficient than or as efficient as their assumption-freer counterparts. If, however, the assumptions of parametric tests are not met, they do not provide as precise control of the probability of making a Type I error as do assumption-freer tests. When their assumptions are not met, parametric tests are only approximate and the probability of making a Type I error can be considerably larger than α. Fortunately, some parametric tests are relatively insensitive to violation of some of their assumptions.[5] Nevertheless, one may prefer to use an assumption-freer test for which the probability of making a Type I error is known rather than relying on an inexact parametric test.

The second major way in which parametric and assumption-freer tests differ is in the level of mathematics necessary to understand their rationale. The derivation of parametric tests involves mathematics beyond the training of most researchers in the behavioral sciences and education. Many assumption-freer tests, however, can be derived using high-school algebra and elementary probability and counting rules. This is a real plus because most researchers want to understand the rationale for the procedures they use rather than having to accept their validity and appropriateness on faith.

Third, assumption-freer tests differ from parametric tests in being easier to apply. For example, the chi-square tests discussed in Chapter 17 use the simplest kind of

---

[4] This follows because the probability of randomly drawing the same value twice in a finite sample from a continuous population is 0. However, even if the population is continuous, the same sample value may occur more than once because the measuring instrument is calibrated in discrete units.

[5] This point is discussed in Sections 10.2, 13.2, 15.5, and 16.4.

measurement—counting the number of observations in categories—and a test statistic that is easy to compute. The tests in this chapter also use a simple measuring procedure—ranking—and statistics that are easy to compute.

The fourth difference is in the nature of the hypothesis tested. Two-sample parametric procedures, for example, test hypotheses about particular population parameters; most assumption-freer methods test hypotheses about equality of population distributions. As you have seen, populations can differ in a number of ways, such as central tendency, dispersion, skewness, and kurtosis. To test the null hypothesis H_0: $\mu_1 - \mu_2 = 0$ using a t statistic, you must assume that the populations have equal variances and are symmetrical and mesokurtic. Thus, to test a hypothesis about one population parameter, you must be willing to make assumptions about other parameters. Assumption-freer tests do not require such assumptions and, accordingly, are much less specific in what they tell you.

CHECK YOUR UNDERSTANDING OF SECTION 18.5

13. Summarize the differences between assumption-freer tests and parametric tests.
14. What assumptions do most assumption-freer tests make? How do these assumptions differ from those for parametric tests?

18.6 LOOKING BACK: WHAT HAVE YOU LEARNED?

Test statistics are often classified according to whether they are parametric, nonparametric, or distribution-free. The classification scheme is not entirely satisfactory because some tests fall into more than one category. A test is parametric if it tests a hypothesis concerning one of the parameters of the sampled population and if it requires stringent assumptions regarding the shape of the sampled population; if not, it is nonparametric. A test is distribution-free if it makes no assumptions about the shape of the sampled population. The Mann-Whitney U test and the Wilcoxon T test fit into both categories, because they do not require assumptions about the shape of the sampled population nor do they test hypotheses about parameters of the sampled population. Certainly, a classification scheme is less useful if its categories are not mutually exclusive. Even the parametric–distribution-free distinction becomes blurred under some conditions. For example, many parametric tests that assume that the sampled population is normally distributed are approximately distribution-free for very, very large samples. Little is gained by trying to distinguish between nonparametric and distribution-free tests; it is more useful to label the two categories collectively as assumption freer.

The Mann-Whitney U test is used to test the hypothesis that two population distributions are identical. It is an excellent alternative to the two-sample t test for independent samples, because its power efficiency is 95.5%. The Wilcoxon T test often is used in place of the two-sample t test for dependent samples when the assumptions of the latter are not tenable. Although it involves less stringent assumptions, Wilcoxon's T is nearly as efficient as the two-sample t—its power efficiency is

95.5%. Like the *U* test, it tests the hypothesis that two population distributions are identical.

The major differences between assumption-freer and parametric tests can be summarized as follows: The assumption-freer methods based on ranks (1) require less-stringent assumptions, (2) involve assumptions that are easier to verify, (3) are usually less powerful when the assumptions of corresponding parametric tests are satisfied, (4) are easier to compute, (5) require simpler mathematical procedures for their derivation and understanding, (6) usually test hypotheses about population distributions instead of parameters, and (7) utilize information regarding rank order instead of the numerical value of individual observations.

REVIEW EXERCISES FOR CHAPTER 18

1. Recognizing that in practice the distinction between nonparametric and distribution-free tests is often blurred, indicate the principle differences between them. How do these tests differ from parametric tests?

2. A paired-associates learning task is one in which participants are presented with stimulus-response paired items and must learn to give the second item in each pair when the first is presented. Researchers investigated the effect on learning of having as the stimulus item a dirty word versus a neutral word. Participants were randomly assigned to the conditions. For the recall scores listed in the table, test the hypothesis that the populations are identical. Let $\alpha = .05$.

Dirty Stimulus Item	Neutral Stimulus Item
12 14 16 13	11 10 7 5
10 18 19	8 13 9

3. Researchers investigated the effect on motor skill development of playing with educational toys for six months. The participants were eight- and nine-year-olds. Half of the participants were randomly assigned to the play group; the remaining half did not play with the educational toys. For the data in the table, test the hypothesis that the two populations are identical. Let $\alpha = .05$. Perform the test with and without a correction for ties.

Motor Skill Scores for Play Group				Motor Skill Scores for Control Group			
47	36	43	32	36	23	26	16
46	35	39	31	34	21	25	15
44	34	37	30	32	20	25	14
45	33	37	29	29	19	24	11
44	32	26	27	27	18	24	12
48							

4. To measure the effect of time of day on test performance, a multiple-choice general knowledge test was administered to a sample of 24 college students. Half of the students was tested at 7:30 A.M. on Saturday; the other half was tested at 4:00 P.M. on the same day. The participants were randomly assigned to the two testing times, with the restriction that the number of students assigned to each time was equal. Investigators obtained the following data representing number of correct answers on the test. (Suggested by Hughey, Arron Wilson. [1982]. Effects of scheduling test administration on the academic performance of college students. *Psychological Reports, 50*, 1346.)

7:30 A.M. Group					4:00 P.M. Group			
90	80	89	94		88	91	85	80
90	97	92	95		96	88	86	77
93	82	87	83		84	79	81	78

a. Compute the medians for the two samples.
b. Use the Mann-Whitney U statistic to test the hypothesis that the two population medians are equal. Let $\alpha = .05$.
c. What assumption must be tenable to use the Mann-Whitney U statistic to test the hypothesis of equal medians? Does the assumption appear to be tenable?

5. Suppose the two-sample t test required 101 participants to reject the nondirectional null hypothesis at the .05 level of significance with power equal to .90, and the Mann-Whitney U test required 106 participants. (a) What is the PE of the Mann-Whitney test? (b) What are the qualifying conditions associated with your estimate?

6. Compare the assumptions of the Wilcoxon T test with those for the two-sample t test for dependent samples. What are the relative merits of the tests?

7. An experiment was performed to determine the effects of sustained physical activity on hand steadiness. For the data in the table, test the hypothesis that the two populations are identical. Let $\alpha = .01$.

Participant	Steadiness before Activity	Steadiness after Activity	Participant	Steadiness before Activity	Steadiness after Activity
1	14	12	9	13	9
2	12	11	10	11	10
3	16	13	11	14	12
4	6	6	12	13	11
5	13	14	13	9	6
6	15	10	14	11	9
7	14	10	15	13	12
8	12	12			

8. Use the z statistic to analyze the data in Exercise 7. Use the correction for ties. Let $\alpha = .01$.

9. Suppose the two-sample t test required 57 participants to reject the nondirectional null hypothesis at the .05 level of significance with power equal to .80, and the Wilcoxon T test required 60 participants. (a) What is the PE of the Wilcoxon test? (b) What qualifying conditions are associated with your estimate?

10. Briefly describe the four major ways in which assumption-freer tests differ from parametric tests.

APPENDIX A

Review of Basic Mathematics

This appendix provides a brief review of selected arithmetic and algebraic concepts. You have, no doubt, been exposed to this material in the past, but chances are you have forgotten some of it. If so, this review should refresh your memory.

The following test is designed to appraise your knowledge of basic mathematics and help you pinpoint concepts that you should review. Answers are given at the end of the test, along with references to relevant review sections. A table of test norms in Section A.3 lets you compare your performance with that of students, mostly psychology majors, at Baylor University.

A.1 TEST OF MATHEMATICAL SKILLS

Round the following numbers to three digits.

1. 2.576___*2.58*___   2. 100.4___*100*___

3. 1.645___*1.65*___   4. 2.328___*2.33*___

5. 15.35___*15.4*___   6. 16.25___*16.3*___

Perform the following basic operations.

7. $|-3| + |3|$ = ___*6*___

8. $-5 + 2$ = ___*-3*___

9. $3 - 2 + 4 - 8$ = ___*-3*___

10. $-6 - 3$ = ___*-9*___

11. $5 - (-1)$ = ___*6*___

12. $-9 - (-4)$ = ___*-5*___

519

13. $(-2)(-6)$ $= \underline{\ 12\ }$

14. $10/(-2)$ $= \underline{\ -5\ }$

15. $0/6$ $= \underline{\ 0\ }$

16. $9/0$ $= \underline{\ \text{undefined}\ }$

17. $(a/b)(n/n)$ $= \underline{\ \frac{a}{b}\ }$

18. $(a/b)^2$ $= \underline{\ \frac{a^2}{b^2}\ }$

19. $(2/5)(3/6)$ $= \underline{\ 6/30 = 1/5\ }$

20. $(\tfrac{3}{4})/\,2$ $\tfrac{3}{4}\ \tfrac{1}{2}$ $= \underline{\ 3/8\ }$

21. $3/(\tfrac{1}{2})$ $3\tfrac{2}{4}$ $\tfrac{}{1}$ $= \underline{\ 6/4\ }$

22. 2^0 $= \underline{\ 1\ }$

23. $(X)(X^2)$ $= \underline{\ X^3\ }$

24. $(X^2)^3$ $= \underline{\ X^6\ }$

25. 2^{-1} $= \underline{\ (1)/(2)\ }$

26. 3^{-2} $= \underline{\ (1)/(3)^{(2)}\ }$

27. $3^2/3^4$ $= \underline{\ (3)^{(-2)}\ }$

28. $3\sqrt{15}$ $= \underline{\ \sqrt{(9)15}\ }$

29. Factor $X^2 - 2XY + Y^2$ $= \underline{\ (X-Y)^2\ }$

30. Factor $pn - p$ $= \underline{\ p(n-1)\ }$

31. $3!$ $\ 321$ $= \underline{\ 6\ }$

32. $0!$ $= \underline{\ 1\ }$

Remove the parentheses.

33. $X + (Y - Z)$ $\underline{\ X+Y-Z\ }$ 34. $X - (Y + C)$ $\underline{\ X-Y-C\ }$

35. $nS(1 - R^2)$ $\underline{\ nS - nSR^2\ }$ 36. $(X - Y)S + M$ $\underline{\ SX - SY + M\ }$

$$\frac{3x}{3} = \frac{18}{3} = x = 6$$

Solve the equations and inequalities.

37. $3X - 6 = 12$ $X = \underline{6}$ [handwritten: $+6 \ +6$]

38. $2a/3 = 6$ $a = \underline{9}$ [handwritten: $\frac{2a}{2} = \frac{18}{2}$, $\times 3 \ \times 3$]

39. $X = \dfrac{a+b}{n}$ $a = \underline{Xn - b}$ [handwritten: $Xn = a + b$, $Xn - b = a$]

40. $z = (X - Y)/S$ $X = \underline{Sz + Y}$ [handwritten: $Sz + Y = X$, $\times S$]

41. $Y = a + bX$ $X = \underline{\dfrac{Y - a}{b}}$ [handwritten: $Y - a = bX$, $\dfrac{Y - a}{b} = \dfrac{bX}{b}$]

42. $S = R/\sqrt{2n}$ $R = \underline{S\sqrt{2n}}$ [handwritten: $S\sqrt{2n} = R$]

43. $S = a\sqrt{1 - b^2}$ $b = \underline{\hphantom{xxxxx}}$ [handwritten: $\dfrac{S}{a}$, $\dfrac{a}{a}$; $\left(\dfrac{S}{a}\right) = \sqrt{1 - b^2}$; $\left(\dfrac{S}{a}\right)^2 = 1 - b^2$; $-\left(\dfrac{S}{a}\right)^2 + 1 = \sqrt{b^2}$; $-1\left(\left(\dfrac{S}{a}\right)^2 - 1\right)$]

44. $X = [(n - 1)S]/b$ $S = \underline{\dfrac{bX}{(n-1)}}$ [handwritten: $\times b$, $\dfrac{[(n-1)S]}{X} \leq b$, $bX = \dfrac{(n-1)S}{(n-1)}$]

45. $2X - 1 < 3$ $X < \underline{2}$ [handwritten: $+1 \ +1$, $\dfrac{2X}{2} < \dfrac{4}{2}$]

46. $-3 < \dfrac{16 - X}{7} < 5$ $\underline{-19 < X < 37}$ [handwritten: $-21 < 16 - X < 35$, $-37 < -X < 19$, $\dfrac{}{-1}$, $37 > X > -19$]

47. $-z < \dfrac{X - M}{S} < z$ $\underline{-ZS + X < M < ZS + X}$ [handwritten: $-ZS < X - M < ZS$, $-X \ -X$, $-ZS - X < -M < ZS - X$, $\dfrac{}{-1}$, $ZS + X > M > -ZS + X$]

48. $[(n - 1)S]/b \leq X$ $b \geq \underline{\dfrac{[(n-1)S]}{X}}$

[handwritten left margin: $\dfrac{[(n-1)S]}{X} \leq b$]

A.2 ANSWERS TO TEST OF MATHEMATICAL SKILLS

[handwritten: $bX = \dfrac{(n-1)S}{(n-1)}$]

The answers to the skills test follow. The numbers in parentheses refer to the review sections that discuss the principle involved.

Principles discussed in Section A.4 (Rounding Numbers)

1. 2.58   (1)   2. 100   (2)   3. 1.64   (3)
4. 2.33   (1)   5. 15.4   (3)   6. 16.2   (3)

Principles discussed in Section A.5 (Basic Operations)

7. 6   (5b, 6a)   8. -3 (6b)   9. -3 (6c)
10. -9 (7)   11. 6   (7)   12. -5 (7)
13. 12   (8)   14. -5 (8)   15. 0   (9c)
16. Undefined   (9d)   17. a/b (10c-iii)   18. a^2/b^2 (10c-iv)
19. $^6/_{30}$ (10c-i) 20. $^3/_8$ (10d-i)   21. $^6/_4$ (10d-ii)
22. 1   (11d)   23. X^3 (11b-i)   24. X^6 (11b-ii)
25. $^1/_2$ or 0.5   (11c-i)   26. $1/3^2$ (11c-i)   27. 3^{-2} (11c-iv)
28. $\sqrt{9}$(15)   (12c)   29. $(X - Y)^2$ (13)   30. $p(n - 1)$ (13)
31. 6   (14a)   32. 1   (14b)

Principles discussed in Section A.6 (Order of Performing Operations)

33. $X + Y - Z$ (17a)   34. $X - Y - C$ (17b)
35. $nS - nSR^2$ (17c)   36. $XS - YS + M$ (17c)

Principles discussed in Section A.7 (Equations)

37. 6 (19c, 20, 21, 22)   38. 9 (19c, 20, 22)
39. $nX - b$ (19c, 20, 21, 22)   40. $zS + Y$ (19c, 20, 21, 22)
41. $(Y - a)/b$ (19c, 20, 21, 22)   42. $S\sqrt{2n}$ (19c, 20, 22)
43. $\sqrt{1 - S^2/d^2}$ (19c, 20, 21, 22)   44. $Xb/(n - 1)$ (19c, 20, 22)

Principles discussed in Section A.8 (Inequalities)

45. 2 (25)   46. $-19 < X < 37$ (25, 26)
47. $X - zS < M < X + zS$ (25, 26)   48. $[(n - 1)S]/X$ (25, 27)

A.3 HOW DID YOU DO ON THE TEST?

Table A.3-1 provides norms for the Test of Mathematical Skills based on approximately 2000 students who have taken my introductory statistics course since the mid-1990s.

TABLE A.3-1   Norms for the Test of Mathematical Skills

Test Score	Percentile Rank	Test Score	Percentile Rank
48	100.0	30	24.2
47	97.1	29	21.8
46	94.1	28	18.7
45	89.4	27	16.7
44	84.6	26	14.9
43	80.3	25	13.4
42	75.3	24	12.2
41	70.2	23	10.7
40	65.0	22	9.1
39	59.2	21	7.8
38	53.4	20	6.6
37	48.9	19	5.4
36	45.0	18	4.3
35	40.7	17	3.4
34	36.7	16	2.7
33	33.3	15	2.2
32	30.5	14	1.5
31	27.3	13	1.1

A.4 ROUNDING NUMBERS

The number of significant digits in a number (all digits except 0 when it is used only to position the decimal point) should reflect the precision of a measurement.

Therefore, numbers should be rounded to give a correct impression of the measurement precision actually achieved. Rounding involves dropping digits if they are to the right of the decimal or replacing them with 0 if they are to the left of the decimal.

1. When the digit to be dropped is greater than 5 or is a 5 with nonzero digits to the right, the digit to the left of it is increased by 1.

   Examples   246.36 rounded to four significant digits becomes 246.4
   386 rounded to two significant digits becomes 390
   0.0068 rounded to one significant digit becomes 0.007
   6.51 rounded to one significant digit becomes 7

2. When the digit to be dropped is less than 5, no change is made in the digit to the left of it.

   Examples   246.31 rounded to four significant digits becomes 246.3
   384 rounded to two significant digits becomes 380
   0.0063 rounded to one significant digit becomes 0.006

3. When the digit to be dropped is 5 or is 5 with only zeros to the right, the digit to the left of 5 is increased by 1 if it is odd and is not changed if it is even. (Not all calculators follow this convention; some always increase the digit to the left of 5.)

   Examples   75 rounded to one significant digit becomes 80
   935.35 rounded to four significant digits becomes 935.4
   674.5 rounded to three significant digits becomes 674
   912.5 rounded to three significant digits becomes 912

4. If the final result of a computation is to be rounded to s digits to the right of the decimal, at least $s + 1$ digits to the right should be retained in intermediate computational steps.

   Example $(115 - 110)/(14/\sqrt{26}) = 5/(14/5.099) = 5/2.746 = 1.82$

A.5 BASIC OPERATIONS

5. Numbers
   a. A signed number—for example, 4, -2, 9, -11—indicates (1) direction and (2) size. The sign, $+$ or $-$, indicates the direction of movement away from a starting point, 0. Zero has no direction. The number part of the signed number indicates the extent or size of movement away from 0.

   Example   The size and direction of movement for -2 and 4 are shown here.

b. The absolute value of a number, denoted by | |, indicates size but not direction. The absolute value is always positive for nonzero numbers. The general rule is

$$|a| = \begin{cases} a \text{ if } a \geq 0 \\ -a \text{ if } a < 0 \end{cases}$$

The second part of the rule appears contradictory but isn't. If a is less than 0, it is a negative number, and a minus sign in front of a negative number makes it positive.

Examples $|3| = 3$; $|-3| = 3$; $|0| = 0$; $|-1.96| = 1.96$;
$|X| = X$ if X is a positive number, and $|X| = -X$ if X is a negative number.

6. Addition
   a. Two numbers of like sign: add the absolute values of the numbers and attach the common sign to the sum.

   Examples $3 + 2 = 5$; $-3 + (-2) = -5$

   b. Two numbers of unlike sign: determine the difference between their absolute values and attach the sign of the larger number.

   Examples $3 + (-2) = 1$; $-3 + 2 = -1$

   c. More than two numbers with unlike signs: add the absolute values of the positive numbers, as in Rule 6a, and do the same for the negative numbers; then determine the difference between their absolute values and attach the sign of the larger of the two, as in Rule 6b.

   Example $3 + 2 + (-5) + (-3) + (-1) = 5 + (-9) = -4$

7. Subtraction
   To subtract one number from another, change the sign of the number to be subtracted and proceed as in addition.

   Examples
   $$3 - (2) = 3 + (-2) = 1$$
   $$3 - (-2) = 3 + 2 = 5$$
   $$-3 - (2) = -3 + (-2) = -5$$
   $$-3 - (-2) = -3 + 2 = -1$$

8. Multiplication and division
   Multiplying two numbers results in another number called a *product*; dividing one number by another results in another number called a *quotient*. When two numbers have like signs, their product and quotient are positive; when they have unlike signs, their product and quotient are negative.

   Examples
   $$(6)(3) = 18 \qquad 6/3 = 2$$
   $$(6)(-3) = -18 \qquad 6/-3 = -2$$
   $$(-6)(3) = -18 \qquad -6/3 = -2$$
   $$(-6)(-3) = 18 \qquad -6/-3 = 2$$

9. Operations with zero
   a. If 0 is added to or subtracted from any number, the result is the number itself.

      Examples $3 + 0 = 3$; $9 - 0 = 9$

   b. The product of 0 and any other number is equal to 0.

      Examples $(3)(0) = 0$; $(2)(3)(0) = 0$

   c. $0/a = 0$ for all nonzero values of a.

      Examples $\dfrac{0}{3} = 0$; $\dfrac{0}{7} = 0$

   d. The use of 0 as a divisor results in a fraction that cannot be evaluated.

      Example $\dfrac{5}{0}$ is undefined.

10. Fractions
    a. A fraction, for example, 6/2 or a/b, is the result of dividing one number or expression by another. The upper part of the fraction is called the *numerator*; the lower part (the divisor) is called the *denominator*.
    b. Addition and subtraction
       i. To add or subtract fractions with the same denominator, perform the indicated operation on the numerator and leave the denominator unchanged.

          Examples $\dfrac{a}{c} + \dfrac{b}{c} = \dfrac{a+b}{c}$; $\dfrac{a}{c} - \dfrac{b}{c} = \dfrac{a-b}{c}$; $\dfrac{2}{3} + \dfrac{4}{3} = \dfrac{6}{3}$; $\dfrac{2}{3} - \dfrac{4}{3} = \dfrac{-2}{3}$

       ii. To add or subtract fractions with different denominators, find a common denominator, change all fractions accordingly, and proceed as in part i. Some multiple of all the original denominators is selected as the common denominator; each new numerator is formed by multiplying the original numerator by the number of times the original denominator divides into the common denominator.

          Examples $\dfrac{a}{b} + \dfrac{c}{d} = \dfrac{ad}{bd} + \dfrac{bc}{bd} = \dfrac{ad+bc}{bd}$; $\dfrac{1}{2} + \dfrac{3}{4} = \dfrac{4}{8} + \dfrac{6}{8} = \dfrac{10}{8}$

       iii. In general, if the same quantity is added to or subtracted from both the numerator and the denominator, the value of the fraction is changed.

          Examples $\dfrac{a}{b} \neq \dfrac{a+n}{b+n}$ unless $a = b$ or $n = 0$;

          $\dfrac{3}{4} \neq \dfrac{3+2}{4+2} = \dfrac{5}{6}$

    c. Multiplication
       i. To multiply two or more fractions, multiply their numerators together and their denominators together to obtain, respectively, the numerator and the denominator of the product.

Examples $\left(\dfrac{a}{b}\right)\left(\dfrac{c}{d}\right) = \dfrac{ac}{bd}$; $\left(\dfrac{2}{3}\right)\left(\dfrac{3}{4}\right) = \dfrac{(2)(3)}{(3)(4)} = \dfrac{6}{12}$

ii. Multiplying anything by 1 leaves its value unchanged.

Examples $\dfrac{a}{b}(1) = \dfrac{a}{b}$; $\dfrac{3}{2}(1) = \dfrac{3}{2}$

iii. Multiplying both the numerator and the denominator of a fraction by the same quantity other than 0 does not change its value.

Examples $\left(\dfrac{a}{b}\right)\left(\dfrac{n}{n}\right) = \dfrac{an}{bn} = \dfrac{a}{b}$; $\left(\dfrac{3}{4}\right)\left(\dfrac{2}{2}\right) = \dfrac{(3)(2)}{(4)(2)} = \dfrac{3}{4}$

iv. In general, squaring a fraction or taking its square root changes its value.

Examples $\dfrac{a}{b} \neq \left(\dfrac{a}{b}\right)^2$ and $\dfrac{a}{b} \neq \dfrac{\sqrt{a}}{\sqrt{b}}$ unless $a = b$;

$$\dfrac{4}{9} \neq \left(\dfrac{4}{9}\right)^2 = \dfrac{16}{81}\quad \text{and}\quad \dfrac{4}{9} \neq \dfrac{\sqrt{4}}{\sqrt{9}} = \dfrac{2}{3}$$

d. Division

  i. To divide a fraction by a quantity, multiply the denominator of the fraction by that quantity.

Examples $\dfrac{a/b}{c} = \dfrac{a}{bc}$; $\dfrac{2/3}{4} = \dfrac{2}{(3)(4)} = \dfrac{2}{12}$

  ii. To divide a quantity by a fraction, invert the fraction and multiply.

Examples $\dfrac{a}{b/c} = a\dfrac{c}{b} = \dfrac{ac}{b}$; $\dfrac{2}{3/4} = 2\left(\dfrac{4}{3}\right) = \dfrac{8}{3}$

  iii. To divide a fraction by another fraction, invert the second fraction and multiply.

Examples $\dfrac{a/b}{c/d} = \left(\dfrac{a}{b}\right)\left(\dfrac{d}{c}\right) = \dfrac{ad}{bc}$; $\dfrac{2/3}{4/5} = \left(\dfrac{2}{3}\right)\left(\dfrac{5}{4}\right) = \dfrac{10}{12}$

  iv. Any quantity (other than 0) divided by itself equals 1.

Examples $a/a = 1$ if $a \neq 0$; $3/3 = 1$

  v. Dividing any quantity by 1 leaves its value unchanged.

Examples $\dfrac{a/b}{1} = \dfrac{a}{b}$; $\dfrac{3/2}{1} = \dfrac{3}{2}$

11. Exponents

  a. The number of times a number, the *base*, is multiplied by itself is denoted by a superscript, the *exponent*.

Examples $a^1 = a$; $a^2 = (a)(a)$; $a^3 = (a)(a)(a)$

b. Laws of positive exponents

   i. $a^n a^m = a^{n+m}$ *Example* $(2)^2(2)^3 = 2^{2+3} = 2^5$

   ii. $(a^n)^m = a^{nm}$ *Example* $(2^2)^3 = 2^{(2)(3)} = 2^6$

   iii. $a^n b^n = (ab)^n$ *Example* $(2)^2(4)^2 = [(2)(4)]^2 = 8^2$

c. Laws of negative exponents and mixed exponents

   i. $a^{-1} = \dfrac{1}{a}$ *Example* $2^{-1} = \dfrac{1}{2}$

     $a^{-2} = \dfrac{1}{a^2}$ *Example* $2^{-2} = \dfrac{1}{2^2}$

     $a^{-n} = \dfrac{1}{a^n}$

   ii. $(a^n)^{-1} = (a^{-1})^n = a^{(-1)(n)} = a^{-n}$

     Examples $(2^3)^{-1} = 2^{(3)(-1)} = 2^{-3}$

   iii. $\left(\dfrac{a}{b}\right)^n = a^n\left(\dfrac{1}{b}\right)^n = a^n(b^{-1})^n = a^n b^{-n} = \dfrac{a^n}{b^n}$

     Example $\left(\dfrac{2}{4}\right)^2 = \dfrac{(2)^2}{(4)^2}$

   iv. $\dfrac{a^n}{b^m} = a^n a^{-m} = a^{n-m}$

     Example $\dfrac{(2)^2}{(2)^3} = 2^{2-3} = 2^{-1}$

d. A number not equal to 0 with a 0 exponent, a^0, is equal to 1. This follows, because according to 11c-iv, $a^n/a^n = a^{n-n} = a^0$, and according to 10d-iv, $a^n/a^n = 1$; therefore $a^0 = 1$.

  Examples $a^0 = 1$ for $a \neq 0$; $2^0 = 1$, $5^0 = 1$

e. Do not confuse exponents and coefficients. When multiplying terms with coefficients and exponents, add exponents and multiply coefficients.

  Examples $(3X^2)(2X^3) = 6X^5$; $(3X)(5X^2) = 15X^3$

12. Radicals

a. A radical is used to indicate a specific root of a quantity, as, for example, in the expression $b = \sqrt[n]{a}$; b is said to be the nth root of a, $\sqrt{}$ is a radical sign, n is the index of the radical, and a is the radicand. If n is not specified, it is understood to equal 2, in which case $b = \sqrt{a}$ is called the square root of a.

b. To multiply two radicals with the same index where both radicands are positive, multiply their radicands under one radical. Similarly, to divide one radical by another, divide (under one radical) the radicand of the first by the radicand of the second.

  Examples $\sqrt{a}\sqrt{b} = \sqrt{ab}$; $\sqrt{2}\sqrt{3} = \sqrt{(2)(3)}$

             $\sqrt{a}/\sqrt{b} = \sqrt{a/b}$; $\sqrt{2}/\sqrt{3} = \sqrt{2/3}$

c. To multiply or divide a radical of the *n*th order by a number *a* not equal to 0, place the number raised to the *n*th power under the radical and multiply or divide the radicand by it.

Examples $a\sqrt{b} = \sqrt{a^2 b}$; $2\sqrt{3} = \sqrt{2^2(3)}$; $2\sqrt[3]{3} = \sqrt[3]{2^3(3)}$

$$\sqrt{a/c} = \sqrt{a/c^2}; \quad \sqrt{3/2} = \sqrt{3/2^2}$$

d. Note that the *n*th root of a sum is not equal to the sum of the respective *n*th roots.

Examples $\sqrt{a^2 + b^2} \neq \sqrt{a^2} + \sqrt{b^2}$; $\sqrt{3^2 + 4^2} = 5 \neq \sqrt{3^2} + \sqrt{4^2} = 7$

13. Factoring
Factoring an expression consists of dividing it into smaller terms or expressions that, when multiplied, will yield the original expression.

Examples $ab - a = a(b - 1)$;
$a^2 - b^2 = (a + b)(a - b)$;
$a^2 - 5a - 6 = (a + 1)(a - 6)$;
$a^2 - 5a + 6 = (a - 2)(a - 3)$

14. Factorials
a. The product of the first *n* natural numbers (positive integers) is called *n factorial* and is denoted by *n*!, which equals $n(n - 1)(n - 2) \cdots (3)(2)(1)$.

Example $4! = 4(4 - 1)(4 - 2)(4 - 3) = (4)(3)(2)(1) = 24$

b. For $n = 0$, 0! is defined as 1.

A.6 ORDER OF PERFORMING OPERATIONS

15. The order in which numbers are added does not affect the result.

Examples $a + b = b + a$; $2 + 3 = 3 + 2 = 5$;
$(a + b) + c = a + (b + c)$; $(2 + 3) + 5 = 2 + (3 + 5) = 10$
$a + b = b + a$ illustrates the *commutative law of addition.*
$(a + b) + c = a + (b + c)$ illustrates the *associative law of addition.*

16. The order in which numbers are multiplied does not affect the result.

Example $ab = ba$; $(2)(3) = (3)(2) = 6$; $(ab)c = a(bc)$;
$[(2)(3)]5 = 2[(3)(5)] = 30$
$ab = ba$ illustrates the *commutative law of multiplication.*
$(a\,b)c = a(bc)$ illustrates the *associative law of multiplication.*

17. Parentheses ( ), braces{ }, brackets [ ], and the radical sign $\sqrt{\ }$ indicate that the enclosed expression is to be treated as a single number. The bar of a fraction has a similar effect: the numerator and the denominator are treated as single numbers.

Examples $10(16 - 14) = 10(2) = 20$; $(3 - 1)4.21 = (2)4.21 = 8.42$

$$\frac{2 + 4}{3 - 1} = \frac{6}{2} = 3$$

a. When a plus sign ($+$) precedes parentheses, the parentheses may be removed without changing the signs of terms within the parentheses.

Examples $a + (b + c) = a + b + c;\ 2 + (3 + 5) = 2 + 3 + 5 = 10$

b. If a minus sign ($-$) precedes parentheses and the parentheses are removed, the sign of every term within the parentheses must be changed.

Examples $(a + b) - (c + d) = a + b - c - d;\ 2 - (3 + 5) =$
$2 - 3 - 5 = -6$

c. When a quantity within parenthesis is to be multiplied by a number, each term within the parentheses must be so multiplied.

Examples $a(b + c) = ab + ac;$

$$10(16 - 14) = 10(16) - 10(14) = 160 - 140 = 20;$$

$$10\left(\frac{1}{20} + \frac{6}{24}\right) = \frac{10}{20} + \frac{60}{24} = \frac{1}{2} + \frac{5}{2} = 3$$

$a(b + c) = ab + ac$ illustrates the *distributive law.*

18. Unless specifically altered (for example, by parentheses) the order for performing operations is as follows: first, exponentiation (raising a number to a power); next, multiplication and division; and last, addition and subtraction.

Examples $Mdn = 44.5 + 10\left(\dfrac{30/2 - 14}{3}\right) = 44.5 + 10\left(\dfrac{15 - 14}{3}\right)$

$$= 44.5 + 10\left(\frac{1}{3}\right) = 44.5 + 3.33 = 47.8;$$

$$S = \sqrt{\frac{10(32) - (16)^2}{(10)^2}} = \sqrt{\frac{320 - 256}{100}} = \sqrt{\frac{64}{100}} = 0.8;$$

$$F = \frac{320/(3 - 1)}{1350/[3(10) - 3]} = \frac{320/2}{1350/27} = \frac{160}{50} = 3.2$$

A.7 EQUATIONS

19. An equation is a statement asserting that what is on the left side of the equal sign is equal to what is on the right.

Examples $2 + 4 = 6$ is an example of an *arithmetic equation*, because it contains only numbers.

$2X - 5 = 7$ is an example of an *algebraic equation*, because it contains a symbol.

a. An equation in which both sides have the same numerical value or one that is true for all values of the variables employed is called an *identity*.

Examples $2 + 4 = 6;\ 3a + 4a = 7a$

One that is true only when certain values are substituted for variables is called a *conditional equation.*

> *Examples* $2X = 6$; $3X - 4 = X + 6$

b. To solve for an unknown in an algebraic equation, find the set of values (called *roots*) that, when substituted for the unknown, makes the two sides of the equation numerically equal. For $2X - 5 = 7$, the root is 6, because $2(6) - 5 = 7$, that is, $7 = 7$.

c. To find the roots of an equation, perform a series of manipulations that place the unknown alone on the left side (see Rules 20–23).

> *Example* $2X - 5 = 7$

$$2X - 5 + 5 = 7 + 5 \quad \text{Add 5 to both sides (see Rule 21)}$$

$$\frac{2X}{2} = \frac{7+5}{2} \quad \text{Divide both sides by 2 (see Rule 22)}$$

$$X = \frac{12}{2}$$

$$X = 6$$

20. An operation performed on one side of an equation must also be performed on the other. The condition of equality is not affected by the following:
    a. Adding the same quantity to both sides
    b. Subtracting the same quantity from both sides
    c. Multiplying both sides by the same quantity
    d. Dividing both sides by the same nonzero quantity
    e. Raising both sides to the same power if both sides have the same sign
    f. Taking the same root of both sides if both sides have the same sign

21. Any term on one side of an equation may be transposed to the other side by changing its sign. In essence, the term to be transposed is either added to or subtracted from both sides of the equation.

> *Example*   Solving for *a*:

$$a + b = c$$
$$a + b - b = c - b$$
$$a = c - b$$

22. A quantity that multiplies one side of an equation may be transposed to divide the other side or vice versa. In essence, both sides of the equation are subjected to the same operation—either multiplication or division.

> *Examples*   Solving for *a*:   Solving for *X*:

$$ab = c \qquad\qquad \left(\frac{X-a}{S}\right)b + c = z$$

$$\frac{ab}{b} = \frac{c}{b} \qquad\qquad \left(\frac{X-a}{S}\right)b = z - c$$

$$a = \frac{c}{b}$$

$$\frac{X - a}{S} = \frac{z - c}{b}$$

$$X - a = \left(\frac{z - c}{b}\right)S$$

$$X = \left(\frac{z - c}{b}\right)S + a$$

23. When each side of an equation consists of a fraction, the fractions can be removed by cross-multiplying.

Example $\dfrac{a}{b} = \dfrac{c}{d}$

$ad = bc$

A.8 INEQUALITIES

24. Two or more expressions connected by one of the ordering symbols $<, >, \leq$, or $\geq$ is an *inequality*.

Examples $a \leq b;\ -1.96 < t < 1.96;\ z > 2.576$

25. The solutions to an inequality are not affected by the following operations:
    a. Adding the same quantity to both sides
    b. Subtracting the same quantity from both sides
    c. Multiplying both sides by a positive quantity
    d. Dividing both sides by a positive quantity

Example $4X + 2 \geq 10$

$$4X \geq 10 - 2$$

$$X \geq 2$$

26. If both sides of an inequality are multiplied or divided by the same negative number, a new inequality is formed, with direction opposite to that of the original.

Examples $-a < b$ $-3 < 2$

$-1\,(-a < b)$ $-1\,(-3 < 2)$

$a > -b$ $3 > -2$

Find μ if $-3 \leq \dfrac{2 - \mu}{5} \leq 8$.

$-3(5) \leq 2 - \mu \leq 8(5)$ Multiply each member by 5

$-15 - 2 \leq -\mu \leq 40 - 2$ Subtract 2 from each member

$-1(-17 \leq -\mu \leq 38)$ Multiply by -1

$$17 \geq \mu \geq -38$$

$$-38 \leq \mu \leq 17 \qquad\qquad \text{Rearrange terms}$$

27. Taking the reciprocal of, or inverting, all expressions in an inequality results in a new inequality with direction opposite to that of the original.

Examples $a > b$ implies that $\dfrac{1}{a} < \dfrac{1}{b}$ if $ab > 0$;

$$a < \frac{(n-1)b}{c} < d \quad \text{implies that} \quad \frac{1}{a} > \frac{c}{(n-1)b} > \frac{1}{d}$$

if a times $\dfrac{(n-1)b}{c} > 0$ and $\dfrac{(n-1)b}{c}$ times $d > 0$

Glossary of Symbols

MATHEMATICAL SYMBOLS

Symbol	Example	Meaning[1]
$+$	$X + Y$	X and Y are added (A.5)
$-$	$X - Y$	Y is subtracted from X (A.5)
$()()$, $\times$	$(X)(Y)$, $X \times Y$, or XY	X and Y are multiplied (A.5)
$/$, $\div$	X/Y or $X \div Y$	X is divided by Y (A.5)
$=$	$X = Y$	X is equal to Y (A.7)
$\neq$	$X \neq Y$	X is not equal to Y
$\cong$	$X \cong Y$	X is approximately equal to Y (2.2)
$>$	$X > Y$	X is greater than Y (A.8)
$\geq$	$X \geq Y$	X is greater than or equal to Y (A.8)
$<$	$X < Y$	X is less than Y (A.8)
$\leq$	$X \leq Y$	X is less than or equal to Y (A.8)
$< \ <$	$W < X < Y$	X is greater than W and less than Y (A.8)
$\leq \ \leq$	$W \leq X \leq Y$	X is greater than or equal to W and less than or equal to Y (A.8)
$\sum_{i=1}^{n}$	$\sum_{i=1}^{n} X_i$	Sum of X_i, letting i equal 1, . . . , n (3.3, 3.8)
. . .	1, 2, 3, . . . , 6	Continue the pattern—that is, 1, 2, 3, 4, 5, 6 in this case
$\lvert\ \rvert$	$\lvert X \rvert$	Absolute value of X; for $X = 0$, $\lvert X \rvert = 0$, and for $X \neq 0$, $\lvert X \rvert$ is equal to the positive member of the couple X, $-X$ (A.5)
$\sqrt{}$	$\sqrt{X}$	Square root of X (A.5)
$!$	$n!$	n factorial, $n(n - 1)(n - 2) \cdots (3)(2)(1)$ (A.5)

[1] The letter or number in parentheses refers to the section in which the symbol is discussed. The letter A denotes Appendix A.

GREEK LETTERS

Symbol	Meaning
α (alpha)	Probability of a Type I error (10.4); significance level (10.2)
β (beta)	Probability of a Type II error (10.4)
δ_0 (delta)	Value of the difference between two population parameters specified by the null hypothesis (13.2)
η^2 (eta squared)	Correlation ratio (5.6)
θ (theta)	Population parameter (9.4); a caret over the symbol, $\hat{\theta}$, denotes an estimator of θ (9.4)
μ (mu)	Population mean (3.3)
$\mu_j, \mu_{j'}$	Means for populations j and j', $j \neq j'$ (15.2)
μ_0	Value of the population mean specified by the null hypothesis (9.4)
$\mu_{\bar{X}}$	Mean of means (9.4)
μ'	Population mean of interest (10.4)
ν (nu)	Degrees of freedom (10.2)
ν'	Degrees of freedom for t' (13.2)
π (pi)	Ratio of the circumference of a circle to the diameter, approximately 3.1416 (9.2)
ρ (rho)	Pearson product-moment population correlation parameter (5.2)
Σ (sigma)	Summation (3.3)
Σf_a	Number of scores above the upper limit of the class interval that contains the median (3.4)
Σf_b	Number of scores below the lower limit of the class interval that contains the median (3.4)
ΣR_1 and ΣR_2	Sum of ranks, respectively, for variables 1 and 2 (18.3)
ΣR_+ and ΣR_-	Sum, respectively, of positive and negative ranks (18.4)
σ (sigma)	Population standard deviation (4.2); a caret over the symbol, $\hat{\sigma}$, denotes an estimator of σ (4.2)
σ_r	Standard error of a correlation coefficient (9.4)
σ_T	Standard error of T (18.4)
σ_U	Standard error of U (18.3)
$\sigma_{\bar{X}}$	Standard error of a mean (9.4); a caret over the symbol, $\sigma_{\bar{X}}$, denotes an estimator of $\sigma_{\bar{X}}$ (10.2)
$\hat{\sigma}_{\bar{X}_D}$	Estimator of the standard error of the mean of difference scores (13.4)
$\sigma_{\bar{X}_1 - \bar{X}_2}$	Standard error of the difference between means (13.2); a caret over the symbol, $\hat{\sigma}_{\bar{X}_1 - \bar{X}_2}$, denotes an estimator of $\sigma_{\bar{X}_1 - \bar{X}_2}$ (13.2)
$\hat{\sigma}_{Y \cdot X}$	Estimator of the population standard error of estimate (6.3)
σ^2	Population variance (4.2); a caret over the symbol, $\hat{\sigma}^2$, denotes an estimator of σ^2 (4.2)

σ_ε^2	Population error variance (15.3)
$\hat{\sigma}_{est}^2$	Estimator of the population variance (9.6)
$\hat{\sigma}_{larger}^2$	Larger sample variance (14.2)
$\hat{\sigma}_{Pooled}^2$	Weighted estimator of the population variance (13.2)
$\hat{\sigma}_{smaller}^2$	Smaller sample variance (14.2)
ϕ' (phi)	Cramér's measure of association; also denoted by V (17.4); a caret over the symbol, $\hat{\phi}'$, denotes an estimator of ϕ' (17.4)
χ^2 (chi)	Pearson's chi-square statistic (17.3)
$\chi_{\alpha,\nu}^2$	Value that cuts off the upper α region of the sampling distribution of χ^2 for ν degrees of freedom (17.3)
ψ (psi)	Contrast among population means (15.6); a caret over the symbol, $\hat{\psi}$, denotes an estimator of ψ (15.6)
$\hat{\omega}^2$ (omega squared)	Strength of association for the ANOVA F test (15.7)
$\hat{\omega}_{X\mid A\cdot BL}^2$	Partial omega squared (16.3)

ENGLISH LETTERS

Letter	Meaning
ANOVA	Analysis of variance (15.2)
ARE	Asymptotic relative efficiency (18.3)
a_j	Level j of treatment A (15.4)
$a_{Y\cdot X}$	Y intercept of a line (6.2)
b_k	Level k of treatment B (16.4)
$b_{Y\cdot X}$	Sample slope coefficient of linear regression of Y on X (6.2)
b_1	Expected change in Y when X_1 changes one unit and X_2 remains constant (6.5); level 1 of treatment B
b_2	Expected change in Y when X_2 changes one unit and X_1 remains constant (6.5); level 2 of treatment B
C	Number of t tests performed among $p > 2$ means (15.2)
CR-p	Completely randomized ANOVA design (15.4)
CRF-pq	Completely randomized factorial ANOVA design (16.4)
Cum f	Cumulative frequency (2.2)
Cum prop. f	Cumulative proportionate frequency (2.2)
Cum % f	Cumulative percentage frequency (2.2)
$_nC_r$	Combination of n objects taken r at a time (7.4)
c	A constant (3.8); number of qualitative categories (4.2, 17.5); correction for continuity (18.3)
c_j	Coefficient of a linear contrast (15.6)
D	Index of dispersion (4.2)
DP	Number of distinguishable pairs (4.2)
DP_{max}	Number of distinguishable pairs when observations are equally divided among categories (4.2)

D_i	Difference between scores for the ith pair of elements (13.4)
d	Cohen's effect size (10.4)
df	Degrees of freedom; also denoted by ν (10.2)
$E(MSBG)$ and $E(MSWG)$	Expected value of $MSBG$ and $MSWG$ (15.3)
$E(S^2)$	Expected value of S^2 (9.6)
$E(T)$	Expected value of T in the Wilcoxon T statistic (18.4)
$E(U)$	Expected value of U in the Mann-Whitney U statistic (18.3)
$E(X)$	Expected value of X (8.3)
E_i	ith event (7.2); sample point for the ith event (7.2)
E_j	Expected frequency in the jth category (17.3)
$E(\hat{\theta})$	Expected value of an estimator (9.4)
$E(\hat{\sigma}^2)$	Expected value of $\hat{\sigma}^2$ (9.6)
$E(\chi_\nu^2)$	Expected value of a chi-square statistic (17.3)
e	Base of the system of natural logarithms, approximately 2.7183 (9.2); number of distribution parameters estimated (17.3)
e_i	Prediction error for the ith element; difference between the observed and predicted scores (6.2)
F	F statistic (14.2)
FS	Scheffé's multiple comparison test statistic (15.6)
$F_{\alpha;\,\nu_1,\,\nu_2}$ and $F_{1-\alpha;\,\nu_1,\,\nu_2}$	Values that cut off, respectively, the upper and lower α regions of the sampling distribution of F (14.2)
f_a and f_b	Number of scores, respectively, above the real upper limit of a class interval and below the real lower limit of a class interval (3.4)
f, f_j	Frequency of a measurement or event class (2.2); frequency of scores in the jth class interval (3.3); number of scores in the class interval containing the median (3.4)
f_i	Number of scores in the class interval containing a particular statistic such as the median (3.4)
g	Hedges's effect size (11.3)
H_0	Null hypothesis (10.1)
H_1	Alternative hypothesis (10.1)
i	Class interval size (2.2); index of summation (3.3); an unspecified level of blocks (16.3)
j	An unspecified level of treatment A (15.3)
Kur	Kurtosis index (4.6)
k	Number of class intervals in a frequency distribution (3.3); an unspecified level of treatment B (16.4)
k^2	Coefficient of nondetermination (5.4)
L_1 and L_2	Lower and upper endpoints, respectively, of a confidence interval (11.2)
MSA, MSB	Treatment A (16.3) or treatment B (16.4) mean squares

MSBG	Between-groups mean squares (15.3)
MSBL	Blocks mean squares (16.3)
MSRES	Residual mean squares (16.3)
MSWCELL	Within-cell mean squares (16.4)
MSWG	Within-groups mean squares (15.3)
Mdn	Sample median (3.4)
Mo	Sample mode (3.2)
m^*	Acceptable margin of error (12.2)
N	Total number of scores (15.3)
n	Number of observations in a sample (2.2); number of trials in a binomial experiment (8.4); terminal value of summation (3.3)
n!	*n* factorial (7.4)
n_A	Number of equally likely events favoring *A* (7.1)
n_L and n_S	Sample size of tests *L* and *S* (18.3)
n_S	Total number of equally likely events (7.1)
O_j	Number of observations in the *j*th category (17.3)
%f	Percentage frequency (2.2)
PE	Power efficiency (18.3)
Prop *f*	Proportionate frequency (2.2)
P_R	Percentile rank (4.2)
$P_\%$	Percentile point (4.2)
$_nP_n$	Permutation of *n* objects taken *n* at a time (7.4)
$_nP_r$	Permutation of *n* objects taken *r* at a time (7.4)
p	Probability of a success (8.4); population proportion (12.2); a caret over the symbol, $\hat{p}$, denotes an estimator of *p* (12.2); number of levels of treatment *A* (15.3)
p^*	Guessed value of the population proportion (12.2)
p_j	Population proportion of observations in the *j*th category (17.3); a caret over the symbol, $\hat{p}_j$, denotes an estimator of p_j (17.3)
p_j'	Value of the population proportion specified by the null hypothesis (17.3)
p_0	Value of the population proportion specified by the null hypothesis (12.2)
$\hat{p}_{Pooled}$	Weighted mean of two population proportion estimators (14.4)
p(*A*)	Probability of event *A* (7.1)
p(*A*|*B*)	Conditional probability of *A* given *B* (7.3)
p(*A* and *B*)	Probability of the intersection of events *A* and *B* (7.3)
p(*A* or *B*)	Probability of the union of events *A* and *B* (7.3)
$p(E_i)$	Probability of event E_i (7.2)
p(Not *A*)	Probability of the complement of *A* (7.3)
p(*X* = *r*)	Probability that *X* is equal to *r* (8.4)
Q	Semi-interquartile range (4.2)
Q_1, Q_2, Q_3	First, second, and third quartile points, respectively (4.2)

q	Probability of a failure (8.4); number of levels of treatment B (16.4)
qFH	Fisher-Hayter multiple comparison test statistic (15.6)
$q_{\alpha;\, p-1,\, \nu}$	Value that cuts off the $\alpha/2$ region of the sampling distribution of q for p treatment levels and ν degrees of freedom (15.6)
R	Sample range (4.2)
RB-p	Randomized block ANOVA design (16.3)
$R_{Y \cdot X_1 X_2, \ldots, X_k}$	Coefficient of multiple correlation (6.5)
R_X and R_Y	Ranks, respectively, for variables X and Y (5.7)
$R^2_{Y \cdot X_1 X_2, \ldots, X_k}$	Coefficient of multiple determination (6.5)
r	Sample Pearson product-moment correlation coefficient (5.2); number of successes in a binomial experiment (8.4)
r_s	Spearman rank correlation coefficient for a sample (5.7)
r^2	Sample coefficient of determination (5.4)
S	Sample standard deviation (4.2)
S^2	Sample variance (4.2)
S'	Desired sample standard deviation (9.3)
SSA, SSB	Treatment A (16.3) or treatment B (16.4) sum of squares
$SSBG$	Between-groups sum of squares (15.3)
$SSBL$	Blocks sum of squares (16.3)
$SSRES$	Residual sum of squares (16.3)
$SSTO$	Total sum of squares (15.3)
$SSWCELL$	Within-cell sum of squares (16.4)
$SSWG$	Within-groups sum of squares (15.3)
S_{cX}	Standard deviation that has been altered by multiplying each score by a constant (4.2)
S_X and S_Y	Sample standard deviations, respectively, of X and Y (5.3)
S_X^2 and S_Y^2	Sample variances, respectively, of X and Y (5.4)
S_{X+c}	Standard deviation that has been altered by adding a constant to each score (4.2)
S_{XY}	Sample covariance (5.3)
$S_{Y \cdot X}$	Standard error of estimate for predicting Y from X (6.3)
Sk	Skewness index (4.6)
s_i	ith block (16.3)
T	Wilcoxon's T statistic (18.4)
$T_{\alpha,\, n}$ and $T_{\alpha/2,\, n}$	Values that cut off, respectively, the α and $\alpha/2$ regions of the sampling distribution of Wilcoxon's T for n pairs of observations (18.4)
t	Student's t statistic (10.2)
t_i	Number of tied observations in a set (18.3)
$t_{\alpha,\, \nu}$ and $t_{\alpha/2,\, \nu}$	Values that cut off, respectively, the α and $\alpha/2$ regions of the sampling distribution of t for ν degrees of freedom (10.2)

t'	Modified t statistic (13.2)
U	Mann-Whitney U statistic (18.3)
$U_{\alpha;\,n_1,\,n_2}$ and $U_{\alpha/2;\,n_1,\,n_2}$	Values that cut off, respectively, the α and $\alpha/2$ regions of the sampling distribution of U for n_1 and n_2 observations in samples 1 and 2 (18.3)
V	A variable (3.8); Cramér's measure of association, also denoted by ϕ' (17.4); a caret over the symbol, $\hat{V}$, denotes an estimator of V (17.4)
$\mathrm{Var}(Mdn)$	Variance of sample medians (9.4)
$\mathrm{Var}(\overline{X})$	Variance of sample means (9.4)
$\mathrm{Var}(t)$	Variance of Student's t statistic (10.2)
$\mathrm{Var}(\chi_v^2)$	Variance of a chi-square statistic (17.3)
$\mathrm{Var}(\hat{\sigma}^2)$	Variance of $\hat{\sigma}^2$ (9.6)
$\mathrm{Var}(\hat{\sigma}_{est}^2)$	Variance of $\hat{\sigma}_{est}^2$ (9.6)
W	A variable (3.8)
$\hat{w}$	Cohen's effect size (17.3)
X	A score (1.4); the independent variable in an experiment (5.1)
X_i	A score for the ith measurement or event class (3.3); value of independent variable (6.2)
X_n	A score for the nth measurement or event class (3.3)
X_{ij}	A score for the ith subject in the jth treatment condition (15.3)
X_{ijk}	A score for the ith subject in the jkth treatment combination (16.4)
X_j	Value of the jth class interval (3.3)
X_{ll}	Real lower limit of a score (4.2) or class interval (3.4)
X_{ul}	Real upper limit of a score (4.2) or class interval (3.4)
X'_j	A predicted X score (6.2)
$\overline{X}$	Sample arithmetic mean (3.3)
$\overline{X}_D$	Mean of difference scores (13.4)
$\overline{X}'$	Desired sample mean (9.3)
$\overline{X}_{i\cdot}$	Arithmetic mean of the ith level of blocks (16.3)
$\overline{X}_{\cdot\cdot}$ and $\overline{X}_{\cdots}$	Arithmetic mean of all scores, grand mean (15.3, 16.4)
$\overline{X}_{\cdot j}$ and $\overline{X}_{\cdot j\cdot}$	Arithmetic mean of the jth level of treatment A (15.3, 16.4)
$\overline{X}_{\cdot\cdot k}$	Arithmetic mean of the kth level of treatment B (16.4)
$\overline{X}_{\cdot jk}$	Arithmetic mean of the jkth treatment combination (16.4)
$\overline{X}_W$	Weighted mean of two or more sample means (3.7)
Y	A score (1.4); the dependent variable in an experiment (5.1)
Y'_i	Value of predicted Y score (6.2)
$\overline{Y}$	Sample arithmetic mean (3.3)
Z'	Fisher's transformation of r (12.3)

Z'_0 — Value of population Z' specified by the null hypothesis (12.3)

z — Standard score (9.2); z statistic (10.2)

z_α and $z_{\alpha/2}$ — Values that cut off, respectively, the upper α and $\alpha/2$ regions of the sampling distribution of z (12.2)

7. a.

X	f	X	f
210–212	1	192–194	3
207–209	0	189–191	5
204–206	1	186–188	6
201–203	2	183–185	4
198–200	2	180–182	1
195–197	2		
			$n = 27$

X	f	X	f
210–211	1	194–195	1
208–209	0	192–193	3
206–207	0	190–191	3
204–205	1	188–189	4
202–203	2	186–187	4
200–201	0	184–185	4
198–199	2	182–183	0
196–197	1	180–181	1
			$n = 27$

b. The distribution with $i = 3$ is better than the one with $i = 2$. The larger class interval size provides a clearer picture of the distribution of scores because the number of scores is relatively small.

8.

X	Prop f	X	Prop f
95–99	.03	60–64	.06
90–94	.03	55–59	.11
85–89	.11	50–54	.14
80–84	.14	45–49	.09
75–79	.11	40–44	.06
70–74	.06	35–39	.03
65–69	.03		

9.

X	f	Cum f	X	f	Cum f
16	1	32	10	7	17
15	0	31	9	4	10
14	1	31	8	3	6
13	2	30	7	2	3
12	5	28	6	1	1
11	6	23			
					$n = 32$

10.

X	f	Cum f	Cum Prop f	X	f	Cum f	Cum Prop f
13	1	23	1.00	6	2	19	.83
12	0	22	.96	5	4	17	.74
11	0	22	.96	4	6	13	.57
10	1	22	.96	3	3	7	.30
9	1	21	.91	2	2	4	.17
8	0	20	.87	1	1	2	.09
7	1	20	.87	0	1	1	.04
							$n = 23$

11.

X	f
Graduate	1
Senior	8
Junior	10
Sophomore	6
Freshman	4
	$n = 29$

12. When the order of the class intervals is arbitrarily determined, it is meaningless to construct a cumulative frequency distribution.

13. See Section 2.2 for the meaning of the terms.

14.

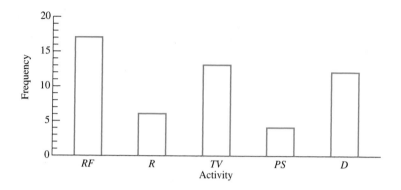

15.

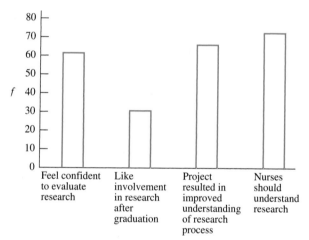

16.

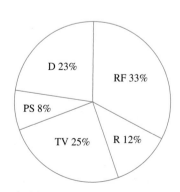

Favorite leisure time activity of college students

17.

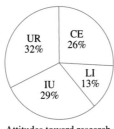

CE = Feel confident to
     evaluate research

LI = Like involvement in
     research after graduation

IU = Project resulted in improved
     understanding of research process

UR = Nurses should understand
     research

Attitudes toward research

18. See Section 2.4 for the meaning of the terms.

19.

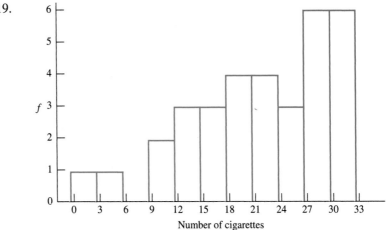

Histogram for number of cigarettes smoked per day by mothers whose first babies were stillborn.

20.

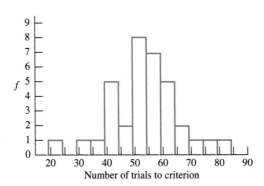

Histogram for number of trials required by rats to reach the criterion of eight consecutive correct responses.

21. a. 22   b. 9.5   c. 132.5   d. 22

22.

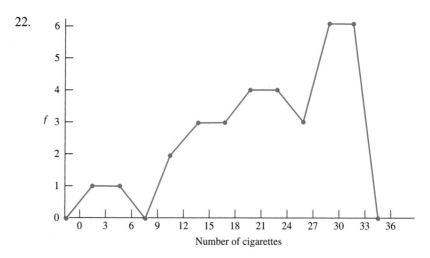

Frequency polygon for number of cigarettes smoked by mothers whose first babies were stillborn.

23.

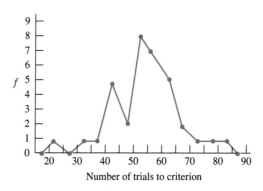

Frequency polygon for number of trials required by rats to reach the criterion of eight consecutive correct responses.

24.

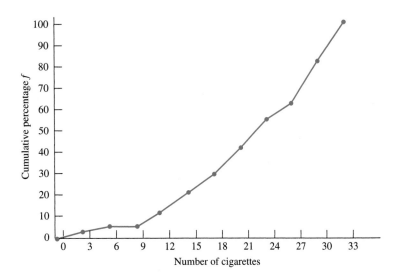

Cumulative percentage frequency polygon for number of cigarettes smoked per day by mothers whose first babies were stillborn.

25. A cumulative polygon will have an S shape if there are more scores in the middle of the corresponding frequency distribution than at the extremes.

26.

Stems (Class Intervals)	Leaves (Scores)
0–2	0
3–5	3
6–8	
9–11	9 0
12–14	2 3 4
15–17	5 6 6
18–20	8 9 9 0
21–23	1 1 2 3
24–26	5 5 6
27–29	7 7 7 8 8 9
30–32	0 0 0 1 1 2

27. See Section 2.5 for the meaning of the terms.
28. a. true   b. true   c. false   d. true   e. false

29. a.

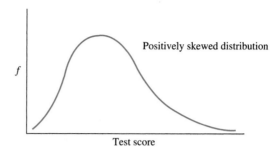

Positively skewed distribution

f

Test score

b.

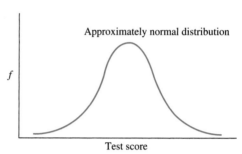

Approximately normal distribution

f

Test score

c.

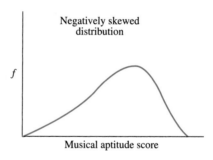

Negatively skewed distribution

f

Musical aptitude score

d.

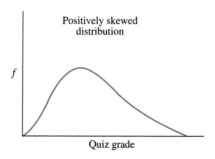

Positively skewed distribution

f

Quiz grade

30. See Section 2.6 for the meaning of the terms.

31.

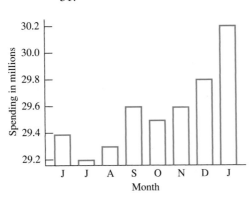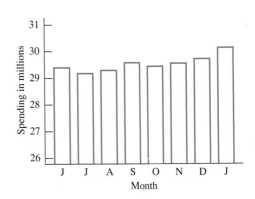

32. See Section 2.7 for the meaning of the term.

CHAPTER 3

1. a. $Mo = S$ b. ordered qualitative variable
2. a. the distribution is bimodal; the maximum values occur at 1 and 3
   b. unordered qualitative variable
3. The value of the mode computed from a grouped frequency distribution depends on the scheme used to group the data.
4. a. X score for element one   b. X score for element i
   c. mean of population one   d. X score for element j
5. a. $X_1 + X_2 + \cdots + X_n$ b. $(f_1 X_1 + f_2 X_2 + \cdots + f_k X_k)/n$
   c. $(Z_1 + Z_2 + Z_4)/3$
6. $\overline{X} = 78/17 = 4.59$
7. $\overline{X} = 340/36 = 9.44$
8.

X_j	f_j	$f_j X_j$
9	1	9
8	0	0
7	2	14
6	2	12
5	4	20
4	3	12
3	2	6
2	2	4
1	1	1

$$n = 17 \qquad \sum_{j=1}^{k} f_j X_j = 78$$

$$\overline{X} = 78/17 = 4.59$$

9.

X_j	f_j	$f_j X_j$
22	1	22
21	0	0
20	0	0
19	0	0
18	0	0
17	0	0
16	1	16
15	0	0
14	2	28
13	1	13
12	3	36
11	4	44
10	6	60
9	5	45
8	5	40
7	3	21
6	0	0
5	2	10
4	0	0
3	1	3
2	1	2
1	0	0
0	1	0

$$n = 36 \qquad \sum_{j=1}^{k} f_j X_j = 340$$

$$\overline{X} = 340/36 = 9.44$$

10. See Section 3.3 for the meaning of the terms.
11. a. 9   b. 18   c. 3.25   d. 3.75

12.

X_j	f_j	$Cum\ f$
22	1	36
21	0	35
20	0	35
19	0	35
18	0	35

(Continued)

X_j	f_j	*Cum f*
17	0	35
16	1	35
15	0	34
14	2	34
13	1	32
12	3	31
11	4	28
10	6	24
9	5	18
8	5	13
7	3	8
6	0	5
5	2	5
4	0	3
3	1	3
2	1	2
1	0	1
0	1	1

$$n = 36$$
$$Mdn = 8.5 + 1[(18 - 13)/5] = 9.5$$

13. X_{ul} = real upper limit of class interval containing the median, i = class interval size, n = number of scores, Σf_a = number of scores above X_{ul}, f_i = number of scores in the class interval containing the median.

14. $Mdn = 8.5 - 1[(4 - 2)/3] = 7.83$

15. a. Compute the mean because the data are quantitative and the distribution is relatively symmetrical.
    b. Compute the mean because the data are quantitative and the distribution is relatively symmetrical.
    c. Compute the median because the data contain an extreme score, $X = 23$.

16. a. $\overline{X} = 1$, $Mdn = 2$, $Mo = 3$ b. Only the *Mo* is appropriate.

17. See Section 3.5 for the meaning of the terms.

18. a. positively skewed   b. positively skewed   c. bimodal
    d. symmetrical   e. negatively skewed   f. multimodal

19. a. 43.33   b. 26.25

20. See Section 3.7 for the meaning of the term.

21. a. $X_1 + X_2 + X_3$
    b. $Y_1 + Y_2 + Y_3 + Y_4$
    c. $f_1 X_1 + f_2 X_2 + f_3 X_3$
    d. $f_1 X_1 + f_2 X_2 + \cdots + f_k X_k$
    e. $a X_1 + a X_2 + a X_3 = a(X_1 + X_2 + X_3)$
    f. $(X_1 + a) + (X_2 + a) + \cdots + (X_n + a) = (X_1 + X_2 + \cdots + X_n) + na$

22. a. $3(2) = 6$ b. $4(3) = 12$ c. 9
    d. 16   e. 5   f. $2(2 + 3 + 4) = 18$
    g. $(2 + 3 + 4) + 3(2) = 15$ h. $(1 + 2 + 4 + 9) + 4(2) - 4(3) = 12$
    i. $(2 + 3) + 2(2) = 9$

23. a. $\sum_{i=1}^{n}(X_i + c) = \sum_{i=1}^{n}X_i + \sum_{i=1}^{n}c$ Rules 3.8-4 and 3.8-2

         $= \sum_{i=1}^{n}X_i + nc$ Rule 3.8-1

    b. $\sum_{i=1}^{n}(cX_i) = c\sum_{i=1}^{n}X_i$ Rule 3.8-3

CHAPTER 4

1. a. 16   b. 16   c. 10   d. 14
2. The range is determined only by the two most extreme scores.
3. a. $Mdn = 27.33, Q = 1.33$ b. $P_{10} = 24.70, P_{90} = 30.30$

c.

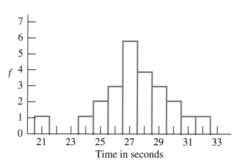

Time in seconds required to notice the onset of a warning light during the performance of a simulated driving test.

4. $P_R = 87.50$
5. a. $\overline{X} = 2.4667, S = 1.26$
   b. The calculator should give the same value for S.
6. a. $\overline{X} = 50.8667, S = 8.84$
   b. The calculator should give the same value for S.
7. a. $Mo =$ moderately desire career, $D = .97$

b.

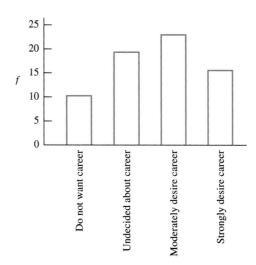

8. a. $\displaystyle\sum_{i=1}^{n}(X_i + c)/n = \sum_{i=1}^{n}X_i/n + \sum_{i=1}^{n}c/n$ Rule 3.8-4

   $\displaystyle\sum_{i=1}^{n}c/n = nc/n$ Rule 3.8-1

   b. $\displaystyle\sum_{i=1}^{n}cX_i/n = c\sum_{i=1}^{n}X_i/n$ Rule 3.8-3

   $\displaystyle\sum_{i=1}^{n}c^2(X_i - \overline{X})^2 = c^2\sum_{i=1}^{n}(X_i - \overline{X})^2$ Rule 3.8-3

9. a. Approximately 68% of the scores fall between 85 and 115.
   b. Approximately 50% of the scores fall between 58 and 82.
   c. A range of four includes all of the scores; the most frequent score is 16.
   d. The number of distinguishable pairs of categories is 25% of the maximum number; the most frequent category is Pizza Inn pizza.

10. See Section 4.2 for the meaning of the terms.

11. a. Compute the mean and the standard deviation because the variable is quantitative and the distribution is relatively symmetrical.
   b. Compute the median and the semi-interquartile range because the distribution is skewed.
   c. Compute the mode and the index of dispersion because the variable is qualitative.
   d. Compute the mode and index of dispersion because the variable is qualitative.

12. a. 84.13%   b. 99.73%   c. 97.72   d. 15.87
13. See Section 4.4 for the meaning of the term.
14. a. $Mdn \pm 2(Q_3 - Q_1) = 5.0 \pm 2(6.5 - 3.5) = 5.0 \pm 6.0 = 0$ and 11. Note that a socioeconomic score cannot be negative and is set equal to zero. There is no reason to believe that the data contain outliers.
    b. $Mdn = 5.0$
       $Q_1 - 1.5(Q_3 - Q_1) = 3.5 - 1.5(6.5 - 3.5) = 0$. Note that the value cannot be negative and is set equal to zero.
       $Q_3 + 1.5(Q_3 - Q_1) = 6.5 + 1.5(6.5 - 3.5) = 11.0$

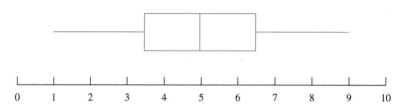

The two criteria lead to the same conclusion that the data do not contain outliers.

15. a. $Mdn \pm 2(Q_3 - Q_1) = 27.33 \pm 2(28.83 - 26.17) = 32.6$ and 22.0. There is reason to believe that $X = 21$ is an outlier.
    b. $\overline{X} \pm 2.5S = 27.375 \pm 2.5(2.306) = 33.1$ and 21.6. This criterion leads to the same decision as the criterion in (a).
    c. $Mdn = 27.33$
       $Q_1 - 1.5(Q_3 - Q_1) = 26.17 - 1.5(28.83 - 26.17) = 22.18$
       $Q_3 + 1.5(Q_3 - Q_1) = 28.83 + 1.5(28.83 - 26.17) = 32.82$

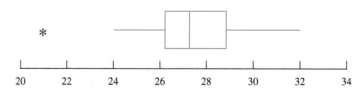

All of the criteria lead to the same conclusion: $X = 21$ is an outlier.

16. See Section 4.5 for the meaning of the terms.
17. a. $Sk = -1.02$; distribution is negatively skewed.

b.

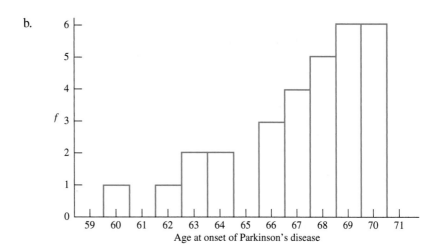

Age at onset of Parkinson's disease

c. yes

18. a. Because $Kur = -0.04$, the data do not support the prediction.

b. The data are slightly negatively skewed; $Sk = -0.09$.

19. $Kur = 0.23$; distribution is leptokurtic.

20. See Section 4.6 for the meaning of the terms.

CHAPTER 5

1. a.

Test A	Test B									
	30	31	32	33	34	35	36	37	38	39
33										1
32										1
31								1		
30									1	
29							1	1		
28						1	1			
27					1	1	1			
26			1		2	1	1			
25				1	2		1			
24			1		1					
23			1							
22				1						
21			1							
20	1									

b. linear

2. The term means that extreme scores for one variable—that is, scores that differ considerably from their mean—are likely to be paired with less extreme scores for the other variable.

3. See Section 5.1 for the meaning of the terms.
4. a. 1   b. 0   c. −1   d. .4   e. −.9
5. a. positive   b. positive   c. zero   d. positive
6. See Section 5.2 for the meaning of the terms.
7. $r = .86$
8. a. Data appear to be linearly related.   b. $r = -.53$
   c. The faster the music tempo, the slower the rate of sipping.
9. $r = .90$
10. a. $\sum_{i=1}^{n}(X_i - \overline{X})(Y_i - \overline{Y}) = 18$, quadrants 1 and 3, variables are positively related.
    b. $\sum_{i=1}^{n}(X_i - \overline{X})(Y_i - \overline{Y}) = 0$, quadrants 1, 2, 3, and 4, variables are not related.
    c. $\sum_{i=1}^{n}(X_i - \overline{X})(Y_i - \overline{Y}) = -15$, quadrants 2 and 4, variables are inversely related.
    d. $\sum_{i=1}^{n}(X_i - \overline{X})(Y_i - \overline{Y}) = 13$, quadrants 1 and 3, variables are positively related.
11.

a.
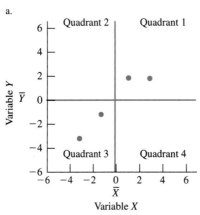

b.
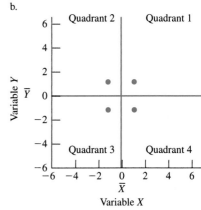

c.
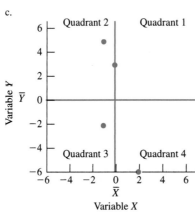

d.
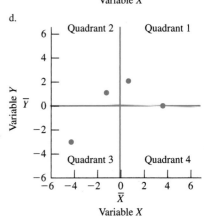

12. a. $r = .95$ b. $r = .0$ c. $r = -.71$ d. $r = .60$
13. a. The cross product reflects both the nature and the degree of relationship between X and Y.

   b. By dividing the cross product by n, you obtain a measure that is independent of the number of pairs of scores.

14. The largest possible value of S_{XY} is 30.

15. a. The possible values of r are 1 and -1. If both scores are equal to the mean of either X or Y, the correlation coefficient is undefined because $S_X S_Y = 0$.

   b.

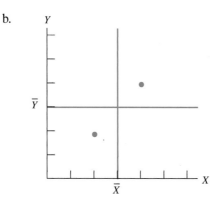 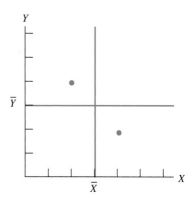

16. The value of S_X is equal to zero, hence the denominator of $r = S_{XY}/S_X S_Y$ is equal to zero and the ratio is undefined.

17. See Section 5.3 for the meaning of the terms.

18. a. The proportion of variance in English grades explained by variation in physical education grades is .048; the proportion that is not explained is .952.

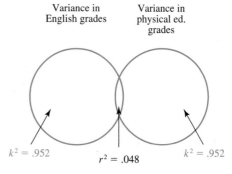

   b. The proportion of variance in family cohesion explained by men's marital satisfaction is .314; the proportion that is not explained is .686.

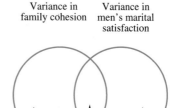

c. The proportion of variance in Social Security numbers explained by total fiber consumed is .001; the proportion that is not explained is .999.

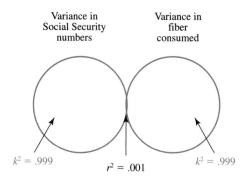

19. See Section 5.4 for the meaning of the terms.
20. a. This is the correct interpretation.
    b. This interpretation is incorrect because it uses an arbitrary descriptive label, medium, to denote r's between .30 and .69.
    c. This interpretation is incorrect because a .15 unit increase from 0 to .15 does not represent the same increase in correlation as that from .15 to .30.
    d. This interpretation is incorrect because a nonzero correlation indicates a concomitant relationship but not a causal relationship.
21. The mean IQ should increase because of regression toward the mean.
22. See Section 5.5 for the meaning of the terms.
23. a. r underestimates the magnitude of the relationship.

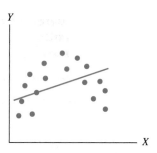

b. The combined r overestimates the magnitude of the relationship for either group.

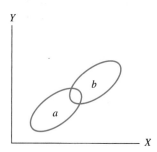

c. The combined r underestimates the magnitude of the relationship for either group.

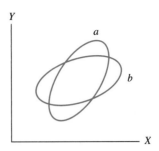

d. r underestimates the magnitude of the relationship for small values of X and large values of Y; the converse is true for large values of X and small values of Y.

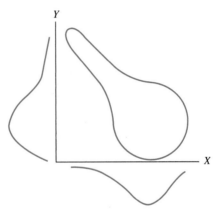

e. r underestimates the magnitude of the relationship for large values of X and Y; the converse is true for small values of X and Y.

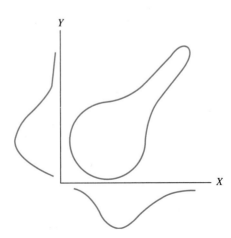

f. The combined r overestimates the magnitude of the relationship for a and underestimates the magnitude of the relationship for b.

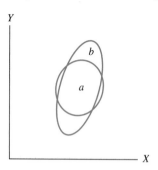

g. The combined r is negative although the r for both a and b is positive.

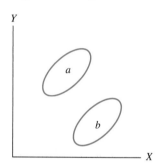

h. r underestimates the value of the relationship.

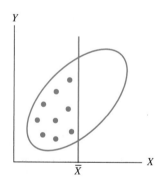

24. The correlation between IQ and creativity for the sample of highly creative individuals may be misleadingly low because the range of creativity is truncated.
25. See Section 5.6 for the meaning of the terms.
26. $r_s = .76$
27. An estimate of r_s using the Pearson product-moment correlation formula is $-.30$.
28. a. strictly monotonic   b. nonmonotonic
    c. strictly monotonic   d. strictly monotonic
29. See Section 5.7 for the meaning of the terms.

CHAPTER 6

1. The primary purpose of a regression analysis is to predict the value of a dependent variable from the value of an independent variable.
2. a. $b_{Y \cdot X} = 2/4 = 0.5$

3. a.

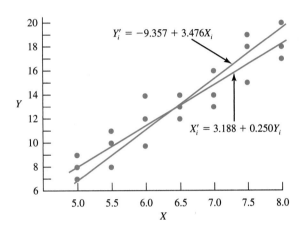

The data appear to be linearly related.
   b. $a_{Y \cdot X} = -9.357$ $b_{Y \cdot X} = 3.476$ $Y'_i = -9.357 + 3.476X_i$
      $r = 3.476(1.000/3.728) = .93$
   c. $a_{X \cdot Y} = 3.188$ $b_{X \cdot Y} = 0.250$ $X'_i = 3.188 + 0.250Y_i$
      The slope $b_{Y \cdot X} = 3.476$ is steepest. $r = 0.250(3.728/1.000) = .93$
   d. $r = \sqrt{(3.476)(0.250)} = .93$; yes
   e. Estimate based on the regression equation is 11.5; estimate based on the line of best fit is 11.5.
4. It is a best fitting line in the sense that it minimizes the sum of the squared prediction errors.
5. The regression lines are identical when $|r|$ is equal to one.
6. Predict that $Y_i = \bar{Y}$ for all i.
7. You know that r is equal to 1 or -1.
8. See Sections 6.1 and 6.2 for the meaning of the terms.
9. a. $S_{Y \cdot X} = 1.42$
   b. $13.2 \pm 1.42 = 11.78$ and 14.62
   c. For $r = 0$, the maximum value of $S_{Y \cdot X} = 2.97$; for $r = 1$, the minimum value of $S_{Y \cdot X} = 0$. The observed value of $S_{Y \cdot X} = 1.42$ is somewhere in between.
10. The larger $S_{Y \cdot X}$, the larger the average prediction error. The minimum value of $S_{Y \cdot X}$ is 0; the maximum value of S_Y is 3.728.
11. See Sections 6.3 and 6.4 for the meaning of the term.

12. a.   (i) $R^2_{Y \cdot X_1 X_2} = \dfrac{(.20)^2 + (.30)^2 - 2(.20)(.30)(.60)}{1 - (.60)^2} = .091$

      (ii) $R^2_{Y \cdot X_1 X_2} = \dfrac{(.60)^2 + (.50)^2 - 2(.60)(.50)(.30)}{1 - (.30)^2} = .473$

      (iii) $R^2_{Y \cdot X_1 X_2} = \dfrac{(.60)^2 + (-.50)^2 - 2(.60)(-.50)(-.10)}{1 - (-.10)^2} = .556$

   b.   (i) $R^2_{Y \cdot X_1 X_2} - r^2_{YX_2} = .091 - .090 = .001$

      (ii) $R^2_{Y \cdot X_1 X_2} - r^2_{YX_1} = .473 - .360 = .113$

      (iii) $R^2_{Y \cdot X_1 X_2} - r^2_{YX_1} = .556 - .360 = .196$

13. a. $R^2_{Y \cdot X_1 X_2} = \dfrac{(.773)^2 + (.681)^2 - 2(.773)(.681)(.544)}{1 - (.544)^2} = .694$

      $R^2_{Y \cdot X_1 X_3} = \dfrac{(.773)^2 + (.289)^2 - 2(.773)(.289)(.065)}{1 - (.065)^2} = .655$

      $R^2_{Y \cdot X_2 X_3} = \dfrac{(.681)^2 + (.289)^2 - 2(.681)(.289)(.083)}{1 - (.083)^2} = .518$

      $R^2_{Y \cdot X_1 X_2 X_3} - R^2_{Y \cdot X_1 X_2} = .743 - .694 = .049$

   b. $Y'_3 = 1.069 + 0.742(3.6) + 0.496(0) + 0.323(0) = 3.74$; the predicted letter grade is B+.
$Y'_{16} = 1.069 + 0.742(2.8) + 0.496(1) + 0.323(1) = 3.97$; the predicted letter grade is A.
$Y'_{21} = 1.069 + 0.742(3.1) + 0.496(1) + 0.323(0) = 3.87$, the predicted letter grade is A.
$Y'_{34} = 1.069 + 0.742(2.3) + 0.496(1) + 0.323(0) = 3.27$, the predicted letter grade is B.

14. See Section 6.5 for the meaning of the terms.

CHAPTER 7

1. a. $p(\textit{odd number}) = {}^3/_6 = {}^1/_2$
   b.   It is assumed that there are six possible outcomes, they are equally likely, and the number of outcomes favoring an odd number is three.
2. a. $p(\textit{queen of spades}) = {}^1/_{52}$
   b.   It is assumed that there are 52 possible outcomes, they are equally likely, and only one of them is a queen of spades.
3. a. $p(\textit{head}) = 52/100 = .52$ b. $p(\textit{head}) = .5$
4. a. $p(H) = .5005$ b. $p(T) = 1 - p(H) = 1 - .5005 = .4995$

5. a.

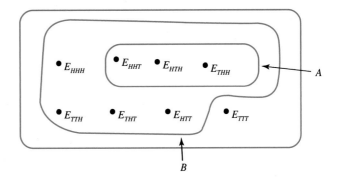

    b. $p(A) = 3/8$ c. $p(B) = 7/8$
6. a.

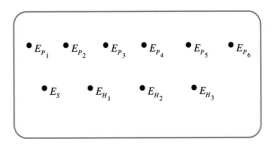

    b. $p(psychology\ major) = 6/10$
    c. $p(psychology\ or\ sociology\ major) = 7/10$
7. a. $p(psychologist) = 3/10$ b. $p(win\ a\ car) = 6/10,000$
8. a.

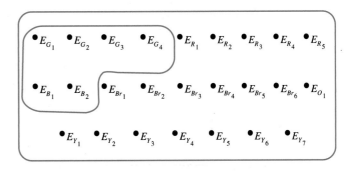

    b. 6/25
9. See Section 7.2 for the meaning of the terms.
10. a. $p(ace) = 4/52 = 1/13$ b. $p(heart) = 13/52$
    c. $p(ace\ or\ heart) = 16/52 = 4/13$ d. $p(heart\ or\ spade) = 26/52 = 1/2$
    e. $p(face\ card) = 12/52 = 3/13$ f. $p(card < 5) = 16/52 = 4/13$
    g. $p(not\ ace) = 1 - 4/52 = 48/52 = 12/13$

11. a. $p(A \text{ and } B) = p(A)\, p(B) = (.6)(.8) = .48$
    b. $p(\text{Not } A \text{ and Not } B) = [1 - p(A)][1 - p(B)] = (1 - .6)(1 - .8) = (.4)(.2) = .08$
    c. $p(A \text{ or } B) = p(A) + p(B) - p(A \text{ and } B) = .6 + .8 - .48 = .92$

12. a.

	Fatal, F	Nonfatal, $Not\ F$	
Drunken driver, D	$p(D \text{ and } F) = .002$	$p(D \text{ and Not } F) = .098$	$p(D) = .100$
Other cause, O	$p(O \text{ and } F) = .002$	$p(O \text{ and Not } F) = .898$	$p(O) = .900$
	$p(F) = .004$	$p(Not\ F) = .996$	

   b. $p(D \text{ and } F) = .002$

13. $p(M) = .98,\ p(\text{Not } D \mid M) = .15;\ p(M \text{ and Not } D) = (.98)(.15) = .147$

14. a. $p(G) = 4/25$ b. $p(R \text{ or } Y) = 12/25$ c. $p(\text{Not } G) = 1 - 4/25 = 21/25$
    d. $p(\text{Not}(G \text{ or } R \text{ or } Br \text{ or } O \text{ or } B \text{ or } Y)) = 1 - 25/25 = 0$
    e. $p(B \text{ and } O) = (2/25)(1/24) = 2/600 = 1/300$
    f. $p[B \text{ and } (O \text{ or } Br)] = (2/25)(7/24) = 14/600 = 7/300$

15. See Section 7.3 for the meaning of the terms.

16. a. $n_1 n_2 n_3 = (2)(2)(2) = 8$ b. $n_1 n_2 n_3 n_4 = (6)(6)(6)(6) = 1296$
    c. $n_1 n_2 = (2)(6) = 12$

17. $n_1 n_2 = (3)(5) = 15$

18. $n! = 4! = (4)(3)(2)(1) = 24$

19. $_{10}P_4 = 10!/(10 - 4)! = 5040$

20. a. $n_1 n_2 = (9)(8) = 72$ b. $n \times_8 P_2 = 9[8!/(8 - 2)!] = 504$
    c. $n \times_8 C_2 = 9\{8!/[2!(8 - 2)!]\} = 252$

21. See Section 7.4 for the meaning of the terms.

CHAPTER 8

1. Identify the population, decide whether to sample with or without replacement, and select elements using a random sampling procedure.
2. The two problems are obtaining an accurate list of the population elements and securing their participation once they have been selected.
3. a. $_{50}C_5 = 50!/[5!(50 - 5)!] = 2,118,760$ b. $n^r = (50)^5 = 312,500,000$
4. a. $_8C_4 = 8!/[4!(8 - 4)!] = 70$ b. $1/_8C_4 = 1/\{8!/[4! (8 - 4)!]\} = .0143$
   c. $n^r = (8)^4 = 4096$
5. See the section titled "Using a Table of Random Numbers" for a description of how to use the table.
6. See Section 8.2 for the meaning of the terms.
7. a. _____

r	$p(X = r)$
0	.0625
1	.2500
2	.3750
3	.2500
4	.0625

b.

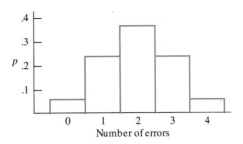

Number of errors

8. a. $p(X \le 2) = .93$ b. $p(X \ge 3) = .07$ c. $p(1 \le X \le 2) = .77$
   d. $E(X) = .16(0) + .54(1) + \cdots + .01(5) = 1.24$
   e. $\sigma = \sqrt{.16(0 - 1.24)^2 + .54(1 - 1.24)^2 + \cdots + .01(5 - 1.24)^2} = 0.88$
9. $E(X) = .6(30) + .4(10) = 22$. The maximum you should be willing to pay is $22.
10. a. $E(X) = 0(0) + 2/5(1) + \cdots + 1/5(4) = 2.20$
    b. $\sigma = \sqrt{0(0 - 2.2)^2 + 2/5(1 - 2.2)^2 + \cdots + 1/5(4 - 2.2)^2} = 1.17$
11. a. $p(W) = 1/1000$
    b. $E(X) = (1/1000)[750 + (-1.00)] + (999/1000)(-1.00) = -.25$
    c. no
    d. The maximum you should be willing to pay for a ticket is an amount such that the expected value is equal to zero—that is,

    $$E(X) = (1/1000)[750 + (-T)] + (999/1000)(-T) = 0$$

    Solving for T gives

    $$.75 - \frac{T}{1000} - \frac{999\,T}{1000} = 0$$

    $$T = .75$$

12. See Section 8.3 for the meaning of the terms.
13. The probability is .2 that the value of X is equal to 3.
14. A trial can result in one of three outcomes. The probability of success remains constant from trial to trial. The outcomes of successive trials are independent.
15. a. $p(X = 0) = .16, p(X = 1) = .48, p(X = 2) = .36$
    b.

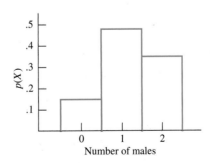

Number of males

    c. $E(X) = np = 2(.6) = 1.2, \sigma = \sqrt{npq} = \sqrt{2(.6)(.4)} = 0.693$

16. a. $p(X \leq 1) = {}_{10}C_0(.3)^0(.7)^{10} + {}_{10}C_1(.3)^1(.7)^9 = .028 + .121 = .149$

    b. $E(X) = np = 10(.3) = 3, \sigma = \sqrt{npq} = \sqrt{10(.3)(.7)} = 1.45$

17. a. $p(3 \ girls) = {}_5C_3(.5)^3(.5)^2 = .3125$. The number of families with three girls is .3125(800) = 250.

    b. $p(5 \ boys) = {}_5C_0(.5)^0(.5)^5 = .0312$. The number of families with five boys is .0312 (800) = 25.

    c. $p(2 \ girls) = {}_5C_2(.5)^2(.5)^3 = .3125$; $p(2 \ or \ 3 \ girls) = .3125 + .3125 = .625$. The number of families with two or three girls is .625(800) = 500.

18. See Section 8.4 for the meaning of the terms.

CHAPTER 9

1. The standard normal distribution has a $\mu = 0$ and $\sigma = 1$; this is not necessarily true for other normal distributions.

2. a. normal   b. normal   c.   d. normal

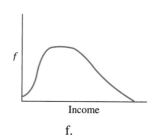

Income

e.   f.

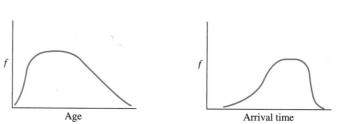

Age   Arrival time

3. a. 2   b. −1.6   c. −1   d. 1.4   e. 0
4. a. .0668   b. .0228   c. .4987   d. .1359   e. .8400
   f. .1574
5. a. .6826   b. .9000   c. .9500   d. .9902   e. .9990
6. a. 190   b. 120   c. 212   d. 150   e. 160
7. a. 0   b. 1.645   c. 0.25   d. −0.53   e. −1.645
8. $z = (2.2 - 2.8)/0.24 = -2.50$, $z = (2.5 - 2.8)/0.24 = -1.25$. The area between z's of −2.50 and −1.25 is .0994. If the university raises its minimum entrance GPA to 2.5, the percentage of eligible junior college students will decrease by 9.94%.
9. a. $E(X) = np = 20(.5) = 10, \sigma = \sqrt{npq} = \sqrt{20(.5)(.5)} = 2.24.$ $z = (11.5 - 10)/2.24 = .67$; the area beyond $z = .67$ is approximately .25.

    b. $E(X) = np = 40(.5) = 20, \sigma = \sqrt{npq} = \sqrt{40(.5)(.5)} = 3.16.$ $z = (23.5 - 20)/3.16 = 1.11$; the area beyond $z = 1.11$ is approximately .13.

10. a. $E(X) = np = 400(.1) = 40$, $\sigma = \sqrt{npq} = \sqrt{400(.1)(.9)} = 6.0$, $z = (30.5 - 40)/6.0 = -1.58$; the area beyond $z = -1.58$ is approximately .06.
    b. $z = (29.5 - 40)/6.0 = -1.75$, $z = (50.5 - 40)/6.0 = 1.75$; the area between the two z's is approximately .92.
    c. $z = (49.5 - 40)/6.0 = 1.58$; the area beyond $z = 1.58$ is approximately .06.

11. See Section 9.2 for the meaning of the terms.

12. $z_1 = (72 - 60)/11 = 1.09$, $z_2 = (61 - 44)/17 = 1.0$, $z_3 = (63 - 53)/8 = 1.25$. Performance on test 3 was best, and performance on test 2 was poorest.

13. $z = (99 - 82)/14 = 1.21$; the area beyond $z = 1.21$ is .11. A score of 99 is in the top 11.3% of test scores, hence you get an A.

14. a. $z = [(18 - 22)/5]15 + 100 = 88$ b. $z = [(18 - 22)/5]10 + 50 = 42$
    c. $z = [(18 - 22)/5]2 + 10 = 8.4$

15. a.

Sample No.	Sample Values	$\overline{X}_j$	Sample No.	Sample Values	$\overline{X}_j$
1	0, 0	0.0	9	2, 0	1.0
2	0, 1	0.5	10	2, 1	1.5
3	0, 2	1.0	11	2, 2	2.0
4	0, 3	1.5	12	2, 3	2.5
5	1, 0	0.5	13	3, 0	1.5
6	1, 1	1.0	14	3, 1	2.0
7	1, 2	1.5	15	3, 2	2.5
8	1, 3	2.0	16	3, 3	3.0

    b. $\mu = \sum_{i=1}^{N} X_i/N = 6/4 = 1.5$, $\sigma_{\overline{X}} = \sigma/\sqrt{n} = 1.11803/\sqrt{2} = 0.7906$
    c. $\mu_{\overline{X}} = \sum_{j=1}^{k} \overline{X}_j/k = 24/16 = 1.5$, $\sigma_{\overline{X}} = \sqrt{\sum_{j=1}^{k}(\overline{X}_j - \mu_{\overline{X}})^2/k} = 0.7906$
    d. The results are the same.

16. a.

Sample No.	Sample Values	$\overline{X}_j$
1	0, 1	0.5
2	0, 2	1.0
3	0, 3	1.5
4	1, 2	1.5
5	1, 3	2.0
6	2, 3	2.5

    b. $\mu = \sum_{i=1}^{N} X_i/N = 6/4 = 1.5$, $\sigma_{\overline{X}} = \sigma/\sqrt{n} = 1.11803/\sqrt{2} = 0.7906$
    c. $\mu_{\overline{X}} = \sum_{j=1}^{k} \overline{X}_j/k = 9/6 = 1.5$, $\sigma_{\overline{X}} = \sqrt{\sum_{j=1}^{k}(\overline{X}_j - \mu_{\overline{X}})^2/k} = 0.6455$
    d. $\sigma_{\overline{X}} = \sigma/\sqrt{n}\sqrt{(N - n)/(N - 1)} = .7906\sqrt{(4 - 2)/(4 - 1)} = 0.6455$. The results are the same.
    e. Consider a population with $N = 340$. A sample of $n = 17$ yields $17/340 = .05$. The correction for a finite population is $\sqrt{(340 - 17)/(340 - 1)} = .9761$. Applying this correction would have little effect on $\sigma_{\overline{X}}$.

17. The larger the value of σ and the smaller the value of n, the greater is the dispersion of a sampling distribution.

18. a. $\sigma_{\overline{X}} = 10/\sqrt{2} = 7.07$ b. $\sigma_{\overline{X}} = 10/\sqrt{4} = 5.00$
    c. $\sigma_{\overline{X}} = 10/\sqrt{8} = 3.54$ d. $\sigma_{\overline{X}} = 10/\sqrt{16} = 2.50$

19. $(115 - 120)/(10/\sqrt{25}) = -2.5$; the probability of obtaining a mean of 115 or lower if the mean is really 120 is .0062.

20. See Section 9.4 for the meaning of the terms.

CHAPTER 10

1. a. scientific hypothesis   b. scientific hypothesis   c. not a scientific hypothesis
   d. scientific hypothesis

2. a. yes   b. no   c. yes   d. no   e. yes   f. no
   g. no   h. yes   i. yes   j. yes

3. a. alternative hypothesis   b. null hypothesis

4. $H_0: \mu \leq 8, H_1: \mu > 8$

5. $H_0: \mu \leq 14, H_1: \mu > 14$

6. See Section 10.1 for the meaning of the terms.

7. a. State the null and alternative hypotheses: $H_0: \mu \leq 45, H_1: \mu > 45$.
   Specify the test statistic: $t = (\overline{X} - \mu_0)/(\hat{\sigma}/\sqrt{n})$
   because the researcher wants to test $\mu \leq 45$, σ is unknown, and the researcher assumes the population distribution of X is approximately normal.

   Specify the sample size: $n = 121$,
   and the sampling distribution: t distribution with $\nu = 120$ degrees of freedom because σ is unknown and must be estimated and the researcher assumes the population distribution of X is approximately normal.

   Specify the level of significance: $\alpha = .05$.
   Obtain a random sample of size n,
   compute t, and make a decision.

   b. Reject the null hypothesis if t falls in the upper 5% of the sampling distribution of t; otherwise do not reject the null hypothesis. If the null hypothesis is rejected, conclude that the new program is superior to the old program; if the null hypothesis is not rejected, do not draw this conclusion.

8.

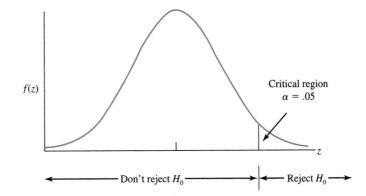

$f(z)$

Critical region
$\alpha = .05$

z

⟵ Don't reject H_0 ⟶ | ⟵ Reject H_0 ⟶

9. a. $H_0: \mu \le 15$ b. $H_1: \mu > 15$

10. Similarities: the sampling distributions of t and z have a mean of zero, are symmetrical, and are unimodal. Differences: the sampling distribution of t is more leptokurtic and has a larger variance than that for z when ν is less than ∞.

11. H_1 determines the location of the critical region and α determines its size.

12. a. $t_{.05, 11} = 1.796$ b. $t_{.01, 11} = 2.718$ c. $t_{.05, 24} = 1.711$
    d. $t_{.05, 16} = 1.746$

13. a. $-t_{.05, 11} = -1.796$ b. $-t_{.01, 11} = -2.718$ c. $-t_{.05, 30} = -1.697$
    d. $-t_{.05, 60} = -1.671$

14. See Section 10.2 for the meaning of the terms.

15. a. State the null and alternative hypotheses: $H_0: \mu \le 50, H_1: \mu > 50$.
       Specify the test statistic: $t = (\overline{X} - \mu_0)/(\hat{\sigma}/\sqrt{n})$ because the researcher wants to test $\mu \le 50$, σ is unknown, and the researcher assumes the population distribution of X is approximately normal.

       Specify the sample size: $n = 30$,
       and the sampling distribution: t distribution with $\nu = n - 1 = 29$ because σ is unknown and must be estimated and the researcher assumes the population distribution of X is approximately normal.

       Specify the level of significance: $\alpha = .05$.
       Obtain a random sample of size n,
       compute t, and make a decision.

   b. Reject the null hypothesis if t falls in the upper 5% of the sampling distribution of t; otherwise do not reject the null hypothesis. If the null hypothesis is rejected, conclude that habitual criminals have higher Pd scores than noncriminals; if the null hypothesis is not rejected, do not draw this conclusion.

16. a. $t = (55.1667 - 50)/(11.3353/\sqrt{30}) = 2.497$

    b. Because $t = 2.497 > t_{.05,\ 29} = 1.699$, the null hypothesis is rejected. Conclude that habitual criminals have higher Pd scores than noncriminals.

17. The null hypothesis would not have been rejected because $t = 2.497 < t_{.005,\ 29} = 2.756$. Do not conclude that habitual criminals have higher Pd scores than noncriminals.

18. a. $t = (54.8276 - 50)/(11.3800/\sqrt{29}) = 2.284$

    b. Because $t = 2.284 < t_{.005,\ 28} = 1.701$, the null hypothesis is rejected. Conclude that habitual criminals have higher Pd scores than noncriminals.

19. See Section 10.3 for the meaning of the terms.

20.

a.

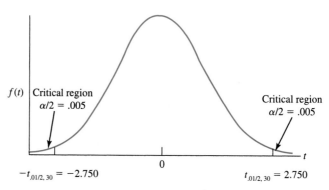

b.

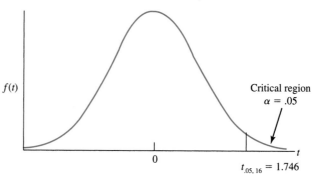

c.

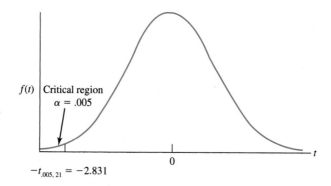

21. a. nondirectional   b. directional
    c. directional
22. a. Type I error   b. Type II error
    c. correct rejection   d. correct acceptance
    e. correct rejection   f. Type I error
23. $t = (3.001 - 2.93)/(0.3013/\sqrt{27}) = 1.224$; power is equal to $1 - \hat{\beta} = 1 - .116 = .884$.
24.

True Situation

Researcher's Decision		True Situation $\mu = 3.10$	$\mu' = 2.93$
	$\mu \geq 3.10$	Correct acceptance $1 - \alpha = .95$	Type II error $\hat{\beta} = .12$
	$\mu < 3.10$	Type I error $\alpha = .05$	Correct rejection $1 - \hat{\beta} = .88$

25. a. $n = 156$ b. $n = 43$ c. $n = 19$ d. $n = 27$
26. Statistical significance is concerned with whether a result is due to chance or sampling variability; practical significance is concerned with whether the result is useful in the real world.
27. a. (i) $p < .05$ (ii) $p < .0403$
    b. (i) $p < .01$ (ii) $p < .0092$
    c. (i) $p < .05$ (ii) $p < .0412$
    d. (i) $p < .01$ (ii) $p < .0089$
28. See Section 10.4 for the meaning of the terms.

CHAPTER 11

1. The assumptions are random sampling, normal population, and the population standard deviation is unknown.
2. A confidence interval specifies an estimate of the population parameter and the error variation qualifying that estimate. Any null hypothesis can be tested by examining the confidence interval.
3. a. $7.2 - 2.763(0.42)/\sqrt{29} < \mu < 7.2 + 2.763(0.42)/\sqrt{29}$
$$7.0 < \mu < 7.4$$

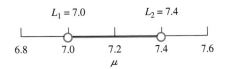

b. Yes
c. $g = (7.2 - 8.0)/0.42 = 1.9$. According to Cohen's guidelines, the effect is large.
4. a. I   b. C   c. I   d. C   e. C   f. I
5. a. The larger σ, the larger the interval.
    b. The larger n, the smaller the interval.
    c. The larger $1 - \alpha$, the larger the interval.

6. $g = 2.86/\sqrt{28} = 0.38$. According to Cohen's guidelines, the effect is small.

7. See Sections 11.2 and 11.3 for the meaning of the terms.

CHAPTER 12

1. The n should be at least 75 because then both $n(.20)$ and $n(1 - .20)$ are equal to or greater than 15.

2. a. State the statistical hypotheses—$H_0: p = .50$, $H_1: p \neq .50$. Specify the test statistic—$z = (\hat{p} - p_0)/\sqrt{p_0(1 - p_0)/n}$ because you want to test $p = .50$, the sample is random, and both np_0 and $n(1 - p_0)$ are greater than 15. Specify the sample size—$n = 1,000$—and the sampling distribution—z distribution. Specify the significance level—$\alpha = .01$. Obtain a random sample of size 1,000, compute z, and make a decision. Reject the null hypothesis if z falls in the lower 0.5% or the upper 0.5% of the sampling distribution of z; otherwise do not reject the null hypothesis. If the null hypothesis is rejected, conclude that the population proportion is not equal to .50; if the null hypothesis is not rejected, do not draw this conclusion.

   b. $z = (.55 - .50)/\sqrt{(.50)(.50)/1000} = 3.16$. Reject the null hypothesis because $z = 3.16 > z_{.01/2} = 2.576$.

   c. Mr. Mander wanted to avoid making a Type I error.

   d. $p = .0016$.

   e. $.55 - 2.576\sqrt{(.55)(.45)/1000} < p < .55 + 2.576\sqrt{(.55)(.45)/1000}$
   $$.51 < p < .59$$

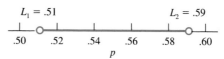

   Mr. Mander's decision to forego the Hawaii vacation was not a good one.

   f. $H_0: p \leq .51$ or $p \geq .59$

   g. $m = 2.576\sqrt{(.55)(.45)/1000} = .041$

   h. $n = (.50)(.50)(2.576)^2/(.02)^2 = 4,148$

3. a. State the statistical hypotheses—$H_0: p = .50$, $H_1: p \neq .50$. Specify the test statistic—$z = (\hat{p} - p_0)/\sqrt{p_0(1 - p_0)/n}$ because you want to test $p = .50$, the sample is random, and both np_0 and $n(1 - p_0)$ are equal to 15. Specify the sample size—$n = 30$—and the sampling distribution—z distribution. Specify the significance level—$\alpha = .05$. Obtain a random sample of size 30, compute z, and make a decision. Reject the null hypothesis if z falls in the lower 2.5% or the upper 2.5% of the sampling distribution of z; otherwise do not reject the null hypothesis. If the null hypothesis is rejected, conclude that babies have a color preference; if the null hypothesis is not rejected, do not draw this conclusion.

   b. $z = (.60 - .50)/\sqrt{(.50)(.50)/30} = 1.095$. Do not reject the null hypothesis because $z = 1.095 < z_{.05/2} = 1.96$. There is no reason to believe that the babies have a color preference.

   c. $p = .2735$.

d. $.60 - 1.96\sqrt{(.60)(.40)/30} < p < .60 + 1.96\sqrt{(.60)(.40)/30}$

$$.42 < p < .78$$

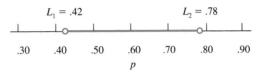

e. $H_0: p \leq .42$ or $p \geq .78$

f. $m = 1.96\sqrt{(.60)(.40)/30} = .18$

g. $n = (.50)(.50)(1.96)^2/(.04)^2 = 601$

4. a. State the statistical hypotheses—$H_0: p = .37$, $H_1: p \neq .37$. Specify the test statistic—$z = (\hat{p} - p_0)/\sqrt{p_0(1 - p_0)/n}$ because we want to test $p = .37$, the sample is random, and both np_0 and $n(1 - p_0)$ are greater than 15. Specify the sample size—$n = 300$—and the sampling distribution—z distribution. Specify the significance level—$\alpha = .01$. Obtain a random sample of size 300, compute z, and make a decision. Reject the null hypothesis if z falls in the lower 0.5% or the upper 0.5% of the sampling distribution of z; otherwise do not reject the null hypothesis. If the null hypothesis is rejected, conclude that the population proportion is not equal to .37; if the null hypothesis is not rejected, do not draw this conclusion.

b. $z = (.46 - .37)/\sqrt{(.37)(.63)/300} = 3.23$. Reject the null hypothesis because $z = 3.23 > z_{.01/2} = 2.576$.

c. $p = .0012$.

d. $.46 - 2.576\sqrt{(.46)(.54)/300} < p < .46 + 2.576\sqrt{(.46)(.54)/300}$

$$.39 < p < .53$$

e. $H_0: p \leq .39$ or $p \geq .53$

f. $m = 2.576\sqrt{(.46)(.54)/300} = .074$

g. $n = (.37)(.63)(2.576)^2/(.04)^2 = 967$

h. On the basis of a national survey of 300 unmarried old women between the ages of 15 and 19, it appears that the population proportion of 19-year-old women who had experienced sexual intercourse was higher than that for an earlier survey. The proportion who had experienced sexual intercourse in the more recent survey was .49; the proportion in the earlier survey was .37. The z test was statistically significant, $z = 3.23$, $p = 0012$. A 99% confidence interval for the population proportion in the recent survey was $.39 < p < .53$.

5. a. State the statistical hypotheses—$H_0: p = .10$, $H_1: p \neq .10$. Specify the test statistic—$z = (\hat{p} - p_0)/\sqrt{p_0(1 - p_0)/n}$ because we want to test $p = .10$, the sample is random, and both np_0 and $n(1 - p_0)$ are greater than 15. Specify the sample size—$n = 200$—and the sampling distribution—z distribution. Specify the significance level—$\alpha = .05$. Obtain a random sample of size 200,

compute z, and make a decision. Reject the null hypothesis if z falls in the lower 2.5% or the upper 2.5% of the sampling distribution of z; otherwise do not reject the null hypothesis. If the null hypothesis is rejected, conclude that the proportion of men who had a second heart attack after participating in the supervised physical fitness program is not equal to that for men who did not participate; if the null hypothesis is not rejected, do not draw this conclusion.

b. $z = (.08 - .10)/\sqrt{(.10)(.90)/200} = -0.943$. Do not reject the null hypothesis because $|z| = 0.943 < z_{.05/2} = 1.96$. There is no reason to believe that the supervised physical fitness program affected the chances of a man having a second heart attack.

c. $p = .346$.

d. $.08 - 1.96\sqrt{(.08)(.92)/200} < p < .08 + 1.96\sqrt{(.08)(.92)/150}$

$$.042 < p < .118$$

e. $H_0: p \leq .042$ or $p \geq .118$

f. $m = 1.96\sqrt{(.08)(.92)/200} = .038$

g. $n = (.10)(.90)(1.96)^2/(.04)^2 = 217$

6. See Section 12.2 for the meaning of the term.

7. a. 0.497   b. -0.234

   c. -1.946 d. .151

8. a. .500   b. $-.190$

   c. .240   d. $-.850$

9. a. According to Appendix Table D.6, a correlation of .374 is required to reject the null hypothesis that $\rho = 0$.

b. $.09 - 1.96\sqrt{1/(26-3)} < Z'_{Pop} < .09 + 1.96\sqrt{1/(26-3)}$

$$-.319 < Z'_{Pop} < .499$$

$$-.31 < \rho < .46$$

c. $H_0: \rho \leq -.31$ or $\rho \geq .46$

d. The effect size, $r = .09$, is just below Cohen's criterion of a small effect.

10.

   a. $.604 - 1.96\sqrt{1/(100-3)} < Z'_{Pop} < .604 + 1.96\sqrt{1/(100-3)}$

$$.405 < Z'_{Pop} < .803$$

$$.38 < \rho < .67$$

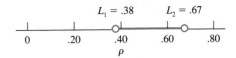

b. H_0: $\rho \leq .38$ or $\rho \geq .67$

c. No. Based on the confidence interval, there is no reason to believe that the correlation for this year's freshmen differs from the correlation for last year's freshmen.

d. The effect size, $r = .54$, is a large effect.

11. See Section 12.3 for the meaning of the term.

CHAPTER 13

1. When the null hypothesis is stated as $\mu_1 = \mu_2$, it indicates that $\delta_0 = 0$.

2. Pooling $\hat{\sigma}_1^2$ and $\hat{\sigma}_2^2$ is appropriate when it is reasonable to believe that the population variances are equal.

3. State the statistical hypotheses—H_0: $\mu_1 - \mu_2 \leq 0$, H_1: $\mu_1 - \mu_2 > 0$. Specify the test statistic—$t = (\overline{X}_1 - \overline{X}_2)/\hat{\sigma}_{\overline{X}_1 - \overline{X}_2}$ because the researcher wants to test $\mu_1 - \mu_2 \leq 0$, σ_1^2 and σ_2^2 are unknown, the samples are random, and the researcher assumes that the population distributions of X_1 and X_2 are normally distributed. Specify the sample sizes—$n_1 = 50$ and $n_2 = 52$—and the sampling distribution—t distribution. Specify the level of significance—$\alpha = .05$. Obtain random samples of size $n_1 = 50$ and $n_2 = 52$, compute t, and make a decision. Reject the null hypothesis if t falls in the upper 5% of the sampling distribution of t; otherwise do not reject the null hypothesis. If the null hypothesis is rejected, conclude that fraternity members have higher GPAs than nonmembers; if the null hypothesis is not rejected, do not draw this conclusion.

4. a. $t = (2.91 - 2.72)/\sqrt{0.2019\left(\dfrac{1}{50} + \dfrac{1}{52}\right)} = 2.135$ $t(100) = 2.135 > t_{.05,100} = $

1.660. Reject the null hypothesis.

b. $p < .025$; $p = .018$.

c. $g = |2.91 - 2.72|/0.4493 = 0.42$; the effect is small.

d. The sample size is adequate. The minimum sample size is $21 + 21 = 42$.

e. $0.042 < \mu_1 - \mu_2$

f. H_0: $\mu_1 - \mu_2 \leq 0.042$

5. a.

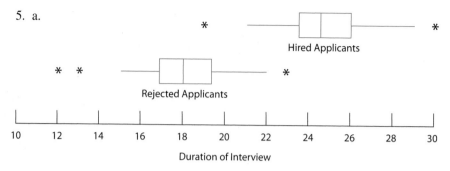

The data for the hired and rejected applicants contain outliers. The sample distributions appear to be relatively symmetrical.

b. State the statistical hypotheses—H_0: $\mu_1 - \mu_2 \leq 0$, H_1: $\mu_1 - \mu_2 > 0$. Specify the test statistic—$t = (\overline{X}_1 - \overline{X}_2)/\hat{\sigma}_{\overline{X}_1 - \overline{X}_2}$ because the researcher wants to test $\mu_1 - \mu_2 \leq 0$, σ_1^2 and σ_2^2 are unknown, the samples are random, and the researcher assumes that the population distributions of X_1 and X_2 are normally distributed. Specify the sample sizes—$n_1 = 26$ and $n_2 = 23$—and the sampling distribution—t distribution. Specify the level of significance—$\alpha = .05$. Obtain random samples of size $n_1 = 26$ and $n_2 = 23$, compute t, and make a decision. Reject the null hypothesis if t falls in the upper 5% of the sampling distribution of t; otherwise do not reject the null hypothesis. If the null hypothesis is rejected, conclude that employment interviewers spend more time talking to applicants who are hired than to applicants who are rejected; if the null hypothesis is not rejected, do not draw this conclusion.

c. $t' = (24.731 - 18.000)/0.7172 = 9.335$; $t'(22) = 9.335 > t_{.05,22} = 1.717$. The data support the researcher's scientific hypothesis. Because t' was significant using the smaller of $n_1 - 1$ and $n_2 - 1$, you know that it would be significant using the larger correct value of v' that is equal to 44.

d. $g = |24.7308 - 18.000|/2.3589 = 2.9$; the effect is large.

e. The sample size is adequate. The minimum sample size is $21 + 21 = 42$.

f. $5.53 < \mu_1 - \mu_2$

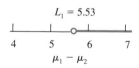

$L_1 = 5.53$

$\mu_1 - \mu_2$

g. H_0: $\mu_1 - \mu_2 \leq 5.53$

6. a.

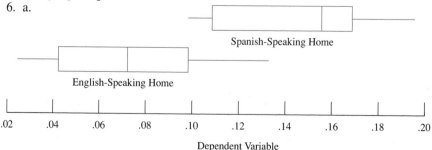

Neither distribution contains outliers. The sample distribution for infants raised in the Spanish-speaking homes is negatively skewed, the distribution for English-speaking homes is relatively symmetrical.

b. State the statistical hypotheses—H_0: $\mu_1 - \mu_2 = 0$, H_1: $\mu_1 - \mu_2 \neq 0$. Specify the test statistic—$t = (\overline{X}_1 - \overline{X}_2)/\hat{\sigma}_{\overline{X}_1 - \overline{X}_2}$ because the researcher wants to test $\mu_1 - \mu_2 = 0$, σ_1^2 and σ_2^2 are unknown, the samples are random, and the researcher assumes that the population distributions of X_1 and X_2 are normally distributed. Specify the sample sizes—$n_1 = 14$ and $n_2 = 14$—and the sampling distribution—t distribution. Specify the level of significance—$\alpha = .001$. Obtain random samples of size $n_1 = 14$ and $n_2 = 14$, compute t, and make a decision. Reject the null hypothesis if t falls in the upper or lower 0.1% of the sampling distribution of t; otherwise do not reject the null hypothesis. If the null hypothesis is rejected, conclude that early language experience affected the discrimination of speech sounds; if the null hypothesis is not rejected, do not draw this conclusion.

c. $t = (0.0728 - 0.1482)/0.0133 = -5.669$; $|t(26)| = |-5.669| > t_{.001/2,26} = 3.707$. Reject the null hypothesis and conclude that early language experience in Spanish-speaking homes resulted in better discrimination of the Spanish contrasts.

d. $p < .0001$; $p = .000006$.

e. $g = |0.0728 - 0.1482|/0.0352 = 2.1$; the effect is large.

f. $-0.125 < \mu_1 - \mu_2 < -0.026$

$$L_1 = -0.125 \qquad\qquad L_2 = -0.026$$

$$
\begin{array}{ccccc}
\;\;|\;\;\circ\;\;|\;\;\;\;\;\;\;|\;\;\;\;\;\;\;|\;\;\circ\;\;|\;\; \\
-0.15 \quad -0.10 \quad -0.05 \quad\;\; 0 \\
\mu_1 - \mu_2
\end{array}
$$

g. H_0: $\mu_1 - \mu_2 \leq -0.125$ or H_0: $\mu_1 - \mu_2 \geq -0.026$

7. b. State the statistical hypotheses—H_0: $\mu_1 - \mu_2 = 0$, H_1: $\mu_1 - \mu_2 \neq 0$. Specify the test statistic—$t = (\overline{X}_1 - \overline{X}_2)/\hat{\sigma}_{\overline{X}_1 - \overline{X}_2}$ because the researcher wants to test $\mu_1 - \mu_2 = 0$, σ_1^2 and σ_2^2 are unknown, the samples are random, and the researcher assumes that the population distributions of X_1 and X_2 are normally distributed. Specify the sample sizes—$n_1 = 25$ and $n_2 = 25$—and the sampling distribution—t distribution. Specify the level of significance—$\alpha = .05$. Obtain random samples of size $n_1 = 25$ and $n_2 = 25$, compute t, and make a decision. Reject the null hypothesis if t falls in the upper or lower 2.5% of the sampling distribution of t; otherwise do not reject the null hypothesis. If the null hypothesis is rejected, conclude that population mean of men's and women's stat grades are not equal; if the null hypothesis is not rejected, do not draw this conclusion.

8. See Section 13.2 for the meaning of the term.

9. a. The researchers' recommendation is not appropriate.

b. The researchers did not randomly assign the workers to the two conditions. It is possible that the workers who opted to use the iPod player would have had higher scores on the dependent measures if they had not used the player. Also, it is possible that the attention associated with receiving the player created a positive attitude toward the company. As a result, the workers were motivated to perform better and the improvement was not related to listening to the music. It also is possible that the workers who did not receive the players felt shortchanged and expressed these feelings by lowering their performance level.

10. You know nothing about the size of the difference, only that chance is an unlikely explanation for the difference.

11. All conditions except the independent variable must be held constant.

12. a. random assignment   b. random sampling
    c. random sampling   d. random assignment

13. See Section 13.3 for the meaning of the terms.

14. The order of presentation of the conditions should be randomized independently for each participant.

15. a. The larger the positive correlation between samples, the smaller is the standard error of the difference between means.
    b. The larger the positive correlation, the higher is the probability of rejecting a false null hypothesis.

16. a.

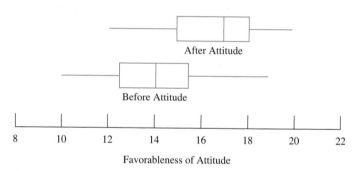

The data do not contain outliers. The "before attitudes" appear to be negatively skewed. The "after attitudes" are fairly symmetrical.

b. State the statistical hypotheses—$H_0: \mu_1 - \mu_2 \geq 0$, $H_1: \mu_1 - \mu_2 < 0$. Specify the test statistic—$t = (\overline{X}_1 - \overline{X}_2)/\hat{\sigma}_{\overline{X}_1 - \overline{X}_2}$ because the researcher wants to test $\mu_1 - \mu_2 \geq 0$, σ_1^2 and σ_2^2 are unknown, the samples are random, and the researcher assumes that the population distributions of X_1 and X_2 are normally distributed. Specify the sample size—$n = 16$—and the sampling distribution—t distribution. Specify the level of significance—$\alpha = .05$. Obtain a random sample of size $n = 16$, compute t, and make a decision. Reject the null hypothesis if t falls in the lower 5% of the sampling distribution of t; otherwise do not reject the null hypothesis. If the null hypothesis is rejected, conclude that attitudes toward legalization of the drug were more favorable after seeing the film; if the null hypothesis is not rejected, do not draw this conclusion.

c. $t = -2.1875/0.2772 = -7.891$; $t(15) = -7.891 < -t_{.05,15} = -1.753$. Reject the null hypothesis; viewing the film does result in more favorable attitudes toward legalization of marijuana.

d. $p < .0005$; $p < .0000006$

e. $g = | 14.1875 - 16.3750 | /2.5046 = 0\ 87$; the effect is large.

f. The sample size is adequate. The minimum sample size is 11.

g. $\mu_1 - \mu_2 < -1.70$

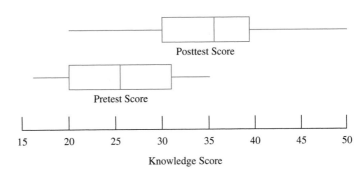

$L_2 = -1.70$

$\mu_1 - \mu_2$

h. $H_0: \mu_1 - \mu_2 \geq -1.70$

17. a.

Posttest Score

Pretest Score

Knowledge Score

The data do not contain outliers. The pretest scores are relatively symmetrical; the posttest scores are negatively skewed.

b. State the statistical hypotheses—$H_0: \mu_1 - \mu_2 = 0$, $H_1: \mu_1 - \mu_2 \neq 0$. Specify the test statistic—$t = (\overline{X}_1 - \overline{X}_2)/\hat{\sigma}_{\overline{X}_1 - \overline{X}_2}$ because the researcher wants to test $\mu_1 - \mu_2 = 0$, σ_1^2 and σ_2^2 are unknown, the samples are random, and the researcher assumes that the population distributions of X_1 and X_2 are normally distributed. Specify the sample size—$n = 22$—and the sampling distribution—t distribution. Specify the level of significance—$\alpha = .01$. Obtain a random sample of size $n = 22$, compute t, and make a decision. Reject the null hypothesis if t falls in the upper or lower 0.5% of the sampling distribution of t; otherwise do not reject the null hypothesis. If the null hypothesis is rejected, conclude that the mean pretest and posttest cognitive knowledge scores are not equal; if the null hypothesis is not rejected, do not draw this conclusion.

c. $t = -9.3182/1.2916 = -7.214$; $|t(21)| = |-7.214| > t_{.01/2,21} = 2.831$. Reject the null hypothesis.

d. $p < .001$; $p < .0000005$

e. $g = | 25.6818 - 35.0000 | /6.3710 = 1.5$; the effect is large.

f. The sample size is adequate. The minimum sample size is 20.

g. $-12.97 < \mu_1 - \mu_2 < -5.66$

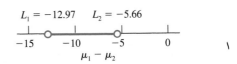

$L_1 = -12.97$ $L_2 = -5.66$

$\mu_1 - \mu_2$

h. $H_0: \mu_1 - \mu_2 \leq -12.97$ or $H_0: \mu_1 - \mu_2 \geq -5.66$
i. For independent samples, $t = -9.3182/1.9209 = -4.851$; $|t(42)| = |-4.851| > t_{.01/2,42} = 2.698$. Reject the null hypothesis. The use of repeated measures was an effective experimental design strategy because the absolute value of the dependent samples t statistic is approximately 2.5 times larger than the critical value; the independent samples t statistic is only 1.8 times larger than the critical value.
j. In the present experiment the difference $\overline{X}_1 - \overline{X}_2$ reflects the effects of the 10-day workshop as well as other effects, such as (1) improved test-taking skills due to taking the pretest, (2) increased sensitivity during the workshop to the kinds of material on the test due to taking the pretest, and (3) acquisition of cancer knowledge from sources other than the workshop such as professional journals and colleagues. The following design, with participants randomly divided into experimental and control groups, would enable the researcher to measure the effects of the workshop and acquisition of course knowledge from other sources.

	Pretest	Workshop	Posttest
Experimental group	X	W	X
Control group	X		X

The use of two experimental and two control groups as follows would enable the researcher to measure the effects of the workshop and the effects 1, 2, and 3 described earlier.

	Pretest	Workshop	Posttest
Experimental group 1	X	W	X
Experimental group 2		W	X
Control group 1	X		X
Control group 2			X

18. a. $n_1 + n_2 = 100$ b. $n_1 + n_2 = 1492$ c. $n_1 + n_2 = 84$
    d. $n = 21$ e. $n = 225$ f. $n = 22$
19. See Section 13.4 for the meaning of the terms.

CHAPTER 14

1. No, the form of the test statistic is a ratio that does not provide for values other than 1.
2. Because you want to detect situations in which the t test is not appropriate, the use of $\alpha = .15$ or $.20$ provides greater power for the F test. In such situations, a Type II error is considered to be more serious than a Type I error.

3. a.

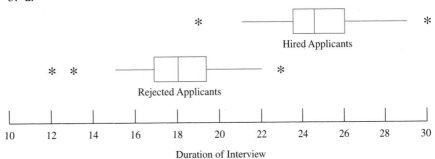

The data for the hired and rejected applicants contain outliers. The sample distributions appear to be relatively symmetrical.

b. $F(22, 25) = 1.11 < F_{.05/2; 22, 25} = 2.269$. Do not reject the null hypothesis.

c. $p < .40$

d. $0.49 < \sigma_2^2/\sigma_1^2 < 2.58$

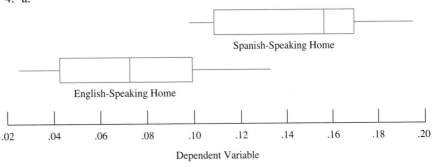

e. Because the confidence interval includes 1, it is consistent with the null hypothesis significance test.

4. a.

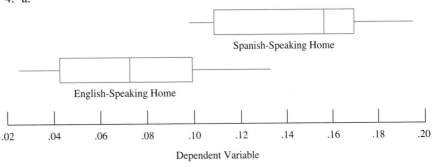

Neither distribution contains outliers. The sample distribution for infants raised in the Spanish-speaking homes is negatively skewed, the distribution for English-speaking homes is relatively symmetrical.

b. $F(13, 13) = 1.02 > F_{.05; 13, 13} = 2.577$. Do not reject the null hypothesis.

c. $p = 1 - .49 = .51$.

d. $\sigma_1^2/\sigma_2^2 < 2.63$

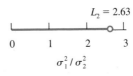

e. Because the confidence interval includes 1, it is consistent with the null hypothesis significance test.

5. a. $F(37, 34) = 2.172 > F_{.05/2; 37, 34} = 1.962$. Reject the null hypothesis.
   b. $p < .02$
   c. $1.11 < \sigma_1^2/\sigma_2^2 < 4.22$

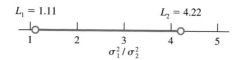

d. Because the confidence interval does not include 1, it is consistent with the null hypothesis significance test.
   e. $H_0: \sigma_1^2/\sigma_2^2 \leq 1.11$ and $H_0: \sigma_1^2/\sigma_2^2 \geq 4.22$

6. a.

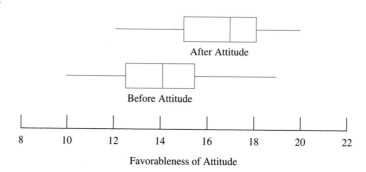

The data do not contain outliers. The before attitudes appear to be negatively skewed. The after attitudes are fairly symmetrical.

b. $t(14) = -0.718$; $|t(14)| = 0.718 < t_{.05/2, 14} = 2.145$. Do not reject the null hypothesis.
   c. $p < .50$; $p < .49$.
   d. $-4.071 < \sigma_1^2 - \sigma_2^2 < 2.029$

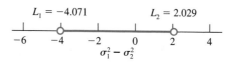

e. Because the confidence interval includes 0, it is consistent with the null hypothesis significance test.

7. a.

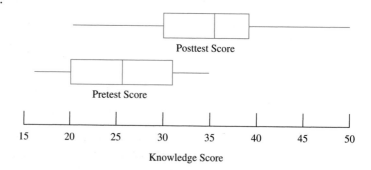

The data do not contain outliers. Both sample distributions are fairly symmetrical.

b. $t(20) = -1.109 < -t_{.05, 20} = -1.725$. Do not reject the null hypothesis.

c. $p < .15; p < .15$.

d. $\sigma_1^2 - \sigma_2^2 < 9.082$

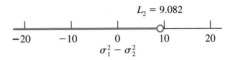

e. Because the confidence interval includes 0, it is consistent with the null hypothesis significance test.

8. a. $z = -2.66; |z| = 2.66 > z_{.05/2} = 1.96$. Reject the null hypothesis.

b. $p = 2(.0039) = .0076$

c. $-.122 < p_1 - p_2 < -.018$

L₁ = −.122 diagram

d. Because the confidence interval does not include 0, it is consistent with the null hypothesis significance test.

e. $H_0: p_1 - p_2 \leq -.122$ and $H_0: p_1 - p_2 \geq -.018$

9. a. $z = 3.33 > z_{.05/2} = 1.96$. Reject the null hypothesis.

b. $p = 2(.00043) = .0009$

c. $.033 < p_1 - p_2 < .127$

L₁ = .033 diagram

d. Because the confidence interval does not include 0, it is consistent with the null hypothesis significance test.

e. $H_0: p_1 - p_2 \leq .033$ and $H_0: p_1 - p_2 \geq .127$

10. a. $z = -1.105; |z| = 1.105 < z_{.05/2} = 1.96$. Do not reject the null hypothesis.

b. $p = 2(.1346) = .27$

c. $-.026 < p_1 - p_2 < .086$

L₁ = −.026 diagram

d. Because the confidence interval includes 0, it is consistent with the null hypothesis significance test.

11. See Section 14.4 for the meaning of the term.
12. a. $p_1 = .446$, $p_2 = .614$
    b. $z = -2.21$; $|z| = 2.21 > z_{.05/2} = 1.96$. Reject the null hypothesis.
    c. $p = 2(.0136) = .0272$
    d. $-.314 < p_1 - p_2 < -.024$

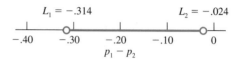

e. Because the confidence interval does not include 0, it is consistent with the null hypothesis significance test.
f. $H_0: p_1 - p_2 \le -.314$ and $H_0: p_1 - p_2 \ge -.024$

CHAPTER 15

1. a. $H_0: \mu_1 = \mu_2 = \mu_3 = \mu_4$
   b. $p(p - 1)/2 = 4(4 - 1)/2 = 6$
   c. Probability of a Type I error using ANOVA is .01; probability using multiple t tests is less than $1 - (1 - .01)^6 = .06$.
   d. The researcher knows that at least two population means are not equal.
2. The advantage of ANOVA is that it controls the probability of a Type I error at α for the omnibus null hypothesis. The multiple t approach allows the probability of a Type I error to exceed α for the collection of tests.
3. Factors that might affect the score include the effectiveness of the a_2 exercise program, diet during the preceding month, time of day that the measurement was made, and variation in the measurement procedures.
4. a. treatment level 2
   b. score for participant 2 in treatment level 4
   c. score for participant 16 in treatment level 1
   d. mean of treatment level 4
   e. grand mean
   f. sample model equation for participant 7 in treatment level 3
   g. a_2 treatment effect
   h. error effect for participant 1 in treatment level 3
5. a. subtract $\overline{X}..$ from both sides of the equation
   b. square both sides of the equation
   c. sum the squared deviations for $j = 1, \ldots, p$ and $i = i, \ldots, n$
   d. perform the square of the term on the right side of the equation
   e. distribute the summation operators
   f. delete the middle term on the right because $\sum_{i=1}^{n} (X_{ij} - \overline{X}_{\cdot j}) = 0$ (see Section 3.8)
6. a. correct   b. incorrect
   c. incorrect   d. incorrect
   e. correct

7. a. $X_{83} = \mu + (\mu_3 - \mu) + (X_{83} - \mu_3)$
   b. $X_{52} = \mu + (\mu_2 - \mu) + (X_{52} - \mu_2)$
   c. $X_{24} = \mu + (\mu_4 - \mu) + (X_{24} - \mu_4)$

8. a. $df_{TO} = 83$, $df_{BG} = 3$, $df_{WG} = 80$ b. $df_{TO} = 54$, $df_{BG} = 4$, $df_{WG} = 50$
   c. $df_{TO} = 31$, $df_{BG} = 3$, $df_{WG} = 28$ d. $df_{TO} = 16$, $df_{BG} = 2$, $df_{WG} = 14$

9. a. Both $MSBG$ and $MSWG$ estimate σ_ε^2 when random samples are drawn from normally distributed populations having equal means and equal variances.
   b. $MSBG$ should be bigger than $MSWG$ when any of the treatment effects, $\mu_j - \mu$, are not equal to 0.

10. See Section 15.3 for the meaning of the terms.

11. a.

Source	SS	df	MS	F
Between groups	168.000	3	56.000	3.50
Within groups	1216.000	76	16.000	
Total	1384.000	79		

   b. $p < .02$

12. a.

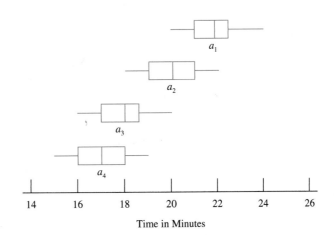

The sample distributions are relatively symmetrical. The data do not contain outliers.

   b. **Descriptive Statistics for Time Required to Learn Nonsense Syllables**

| | Association Value of Nonsense Syllables | | | |
| | 25% | 50% | 75% | 100% |
	a_1	a_2	a_3	a_4
$\overline{X}_{\cdot j}$	21.875	20.000	17.875	17.000
$\hat{\sigma}_j$	1.246	1.309	1.246	1.309

c. Yes
d. **Analysis of Variance Table for Time Required to Learn Nonsense Syllables**

Source	SS	df	MS	F
1 Between groups (association value)	115.1250	3	38.3750	$[\frac{1}{2}]$ 23.49*
2 Within groups	45.7500	28	1.6339	
3 Total	160.8750	31		

*$p < .0000001$.
Reject the null hypothesis.

e. According to the ANOVA and descriptive statistics, the learning-time population means for the four levels of association value are not all equal, $F(3, 28) = 23.49$, $p < .0000001$. It appears that there is an inverse relationship between association value and time required to learn nonsense syllables.

13. State the statistical hypotheses—$H_0: \mu_1 = \mu_2 = \mu_3 = \mu_4$, $H_1: \mu_j \neq \mu_{j'}$, for some j and j'. Specify the test statistic—$F = MSBG/MSWG$ because the researcher wants to test $\mu_1 = \mu_2 = \mu_3 = \mu_4$, random assignment was used, and the researcher assumed that the four populations are approximately normally distributed with equal variances. Specify the sample size—$np = 32$—and the sampling distribution—F distribution with $\nu_1 = 3$ and $\nu_2 = 28$ because the researcher assumes that the three populations are approximately normally distributed. Specify the level of significance—$\alpha = .05$. Obtain a sample of 32 participants, randomly assign the participants to the p treatment levels with the restriction that n participants are assigned to each level, compute F, and make a decision. Reject the null hypothesis if $F \geq 2.95$. If the null hypothesis is rejected, conclude that the time to learn the lists of nonsense syllables is not the same for the four association values; if the null hypothesis is not rejected, do not draw this conclusion.

14. a.

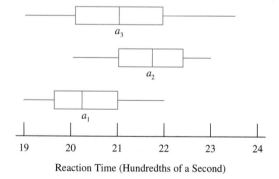

The sample distributions are relatively symmetrical. The data do not contain outliers.

b. **Descriptive Statistics for Reaction Time in Hundredths of a Seconds to Three Colors of Warning Lights**

	Color of Warning Light		
	Yellow a_1	Red a_2	Green a_3
$\overline{X}_{\cdot j}$	20.300	21.700	21.000
$\hat{\sigma}_j$	0.949	0.949	1.183

c. yes
d. **Analysis of Variance Table for Reaction Time to Warning Lights**

Source	SS	df	MS	F
Between groups (color of light)	9.8000	2	4.9000	$[\frac{1}{2}]$ 4.54*
Within groups	30.2000	28	1.0786	
Total	40.0000	30		

*$p < .02$
Reject the null hypothesis.

e. According to the ANOVA, the reaction-time population means for the three colors of instrument panel warning lights are not equal, $F(2, 28) = 4.54$, $p < .02$.

15. State the statistical hypotheses—H_0: $\mu_1 = \mu_2 = \mu_3$, H_1: $\mu_j \neq \mu_{j'}$, for some j and j'. Specify the test statistic—$F = MSBG/MSWG$ because the researcher wants to test $\mu_1 = \mu_2 = \mu_3$, random assignment was used, and the researcher assumes that the three populations are approximately normally distributed with equal variances. Specify the sample size—$n_1 + n_2 + n_3 = 31$—and the sampling distribution—F distribution with $v_1 = 2$ and $v_2 = 28$ because the researcher assumes that the three populations are approximately normally distributed. Specify the level of significance—$\alpha = .05$. Obtain a sample of 31 participants, randomly assign the participants to the p treatment levels with the restriction that approximately the same number of participants receives each level, compute F, and make a decision. Reject the null hypothesis if $F \geq 3.34$. If the null hypothesis is rejected, conclude that reaction time is not the same for the three colors of instrument-panel warning lights; if the null hypothesis is not rejected, do not draw this conclusion.
16. The F test is robust if the treatment populations all have the same shape, for example all positively skewed or all leptokurtic.

17. a. _____

	a_1	a_2	a_3	a_4
	f	f	f	f
24	|			
23	|			
22	|||	|		
21	||	||		
20	|	||	|	
19		||	|	|
18		|	|||	||
17			||	||
16			|	||
15				|

The distributions are relatively symmetrical. There is no reason to believe that the populations are not symmetrical.

b. _____

	a_1	a_2	a_3
X	f	f	f
23		||	|
22	|	||||	|||
21	|||	|||	|||
20	|||	|	|||
19	||		|

The distributions are relatively symmetrical. There is no reason to believe that the populations are not symmetrical.

18. This assumption states that the $j = 1, \ldots, p$ population variances are equal to σ_e^2.

19. See Section 15.5 for the meaning of the term.

20. a. $1, -1, 0, 0$ b. $0, 1, 0, -1$ c. $1, -\dfrac{1}{2}, -\dfrac{1}{2}, 0$

d. $1, -\dfrac{1}{3}, -\dfrac{1}{3}, -\dfrac{1}{3}$ e. $\dfrac{1}{2}, \dfrac{1}{2}, -\dfrac{1}{2}, -\dfrac{1}{2}$ f. $1, -\dfrac{2}{3}, -\dfrac{1}{3}, 0$

21. a. contrast   b. contrast   c. not a contrast
    d. contrast   e. contrast   f. contrast

22. a. satisfies   b. does not satisfy c. does not satisfy
    d. does not satisfy e. does not satisfy f. satisfies

23. a. $q_{.01;\ 4-1,\ 40} = 4.45$ b. $q_{.05;\ 5-1,\ 60} = 3.74$ c. $q_{.05;\ 3-1,\ 15} = 3.01$

24. a. $(4 - 1)F_{.01;\ 3,\ 40} = (4 - 1)4.31 = 12.93$

b. $(5 - 1)F_{.05;\ 4,\ 60} = (5 - 1)2.53 = 10.12$

c. $(3 - 1)F_{.05;\ 2,\ 18} = (3 - 1)3.55 = 7.10$

25. a. $qFH = -0.02/0.02 = -1.00$, $qFH = -0.10/0.02 = -5.00^*$, $qFH = -0.08/0.02 = -4.00^*$; $q_{.05;\ 3-1,\ 12} = 3.08$. Reject the null hypothesis for $\psi_2 = \mu_1 - \mu_3$ and $\psi_3 = \mu_2 - \mu_3$.

b. For $\hat{\psi}_1$, $g = 0.45$ For $\hat{\psi}_2$, $g = 2.24$ For $\hat{\psi}_3$, $g = 1.79$
The effect sizes for $\hat{\psi}_2$ and $\hat{\psi}_3$ are large.

26. a. $FS = 0.49/0.80 = 0.61$, $FS = 12.96/0.80 = 16.20^*$, $FS = 8.41/0.80 = 10.51^*$,
$FS = 10.56/0.60 = 17.60^*$; $(3 - 1)\,F_{.01;\,2,\,120} = 9.58$. Reject the null hypothesis for $\psi_2 = \mu_1 - \mu_3$, $\psi_3 = \mu_2 - \mu_3$, and $\psi_4 = (\mu_1 + \mu_2)/2 - \mu_3$.

b. $-3.47 < \psi_1 < 2.07$
$-6.37 < \psi_2 < -0.83$
$-5.67 < \psi_3 < -0.13$
$-5.65 < \psi_4 < -0.85$

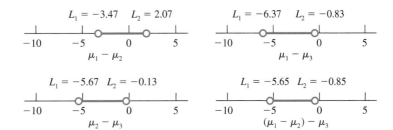

c. For $\hat{\psi}_1$, $g = 0.17$ For $\hat{\psi}_2$, $g = 0.89$ For $\hat{\psi}_3$, $g = 0.72$ For $\hat{\psi}_4$, $g = 0.80$
The effect sizes for $\hat{\psi}_2$, $\hat{\psi}_3$, and $\hat{\psi}_4$ are large.

27. a. $\hat{\omega}^2 = \dfrac{110.223}{162.509} = 0.68$

The strength of association is large; the independent variable accounts for
68% of the variance in the dependent variable.

b. For $\psi_1 = \mu_1 - \mu_2$, $qFH = 4.15^*$ For $\psi_2 = \mu_1 - \mu_3$, $qFH = 8.85^*$
For $\psi_3 = \mu_1 - \mu_4$, $qFH = 10.79^*$ For $\psi_4 = \mu_2 - \mu_3$, $qFH = 4.70^*$
For $\psi_5 = \mu_2 - \mu_4$, $qFH = 6.63^*$ For $\psi_6 = \mu_3 - \mu_4$, $qFH = 1.94$
$qFH_{.05;\,4-1,\,28} = 3.50$; reject the null hypothesis for all contrasts except ψ_6.

c. For $\hat{\psi}_1$, $g = 1.47$ For $\hat{\psi}_2$, $g = 3.13$ For $\hat{\psi}_3$, $g = 3.81$
For $\hat{\psi}_4$, $g = 1.66$ For $\hat{\psi}_5$, $g = 2.35$ For $\hat{\psi}_6$, $g = 0.68$
The effect sizes for $\hat{\psi}_1$, $\hat{\psi}_2$, $\hat{\psi}_3$, $\hat{\psi}_4$, and $\hat{\psi}_5$ are large.

28. See Sections 15.6 and 15.7 for the meaning of the terms.

CHAPTER 16

1. Nuisance variables are undesired sources of variation that increase the variance
of the error effects. They can be controlled or minimized by holding them constant, assigning experimental units randomly to the treatment levels, and including the nuisance variable as one of the factors in the experiment.
2. Any variable that is positively correlated with the dependent variable is a potential blocking variable.
3. a. The independent variable is a kind of instruction; the dependent variable is a
rating of the amount of help offered.

b. Nuisance variables that were held constant included the student's grade (first grade) and the student's gender (boy).
c. Idiosyncratic characteristics of the boys such as shyness, aggressiveness, and so forth.
d. The test scores could be used to form 16 blocks of three boys each, such that the boys in a block are matched with respect to their conforming-compulsive scores.
4. See Section 16.2 for the meaning of the terms.
5. **Analysis of Variance Table**

Source	SS	df	MS	F
1. Treatment A	51.765	3	17.255	$[\frac{1}{3}]$ 3.81**
2. Blocks	161.500	20	8.075	$[\frac{2}{3}]$ 1.78*
3. Residual	271.500	60	4.525	
4. Total	484.765	83		

$*p < .05$

$** p < .02$

6. a.

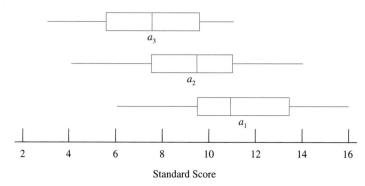

The a_2 and a_3 sample distributions are relatively symmetrical; the a_1 distribution is slightly positively skewed. The data do not contain outliers.

b. **Means and Standard Deviations for Three Psychological Tests**

	a_1 WAIS	a_2 WUMV	a_3 WSA
$\overline{X}_{.j}$	11.17	9.25	7.33
$\hat{\sigma}_j$	3.04	2.73	2.50

c. The means are consistent with the researcher's expectations—that is, the means for the *WUMV* and *WSA* tests are lower than the mean for the *WAIS* test. The *WAIS* standard deviation is close to the national norm value of 3;

the *WUMV* and *WSA* standard deviations are smaller than the national norm values. The standard deviations are quite homogeneous.

d. **Analysis of Variance Table for Psychological Test Data**

Source	SS	df	MS	F
1. Treatment A (tests)	88.1667	2	44.0834	$[\frac{1}{3}]\,31.80^*$
2. Blocks	222.0833	11	20.1894	$[\frac{2}{3}]\,14.56^{**}$
3. Residual	30.5000	22	1.3864^*	
4. Total	340.7500	35		

$^*p < .0000004$ $^{**}p < .0000002$

Reject the null hypothesis that the population means for the three tests are equal.

e. $\hat{\omega}^2_{X|A \cdot BL} = 0.63$. The strength of association is large. Treatment A accounts for 63% of the variance in the dependent variable.

f. $qFH = 1.9167/0.3399 = 5.64^*$ for μ_1 versus μ_2, $qFH = 3.8334/0.3399 = 11.28^*$ for μ_1 versus μ_3, and $qFH = 1.9167/0.3399 = 5.64^*$ for μ_2 versus μ_3; $q_{.05; 3 - 1, 22} = 2.94$. Reject the null hypothesis for all pairwise contrasts among the three population means.

g. $g = 0.69$ The effect size for μ_1 versus μ_2 is a medium size effect.
   $g = 1.39$ The effect size for μ_1 versus μ_3 is a large size effect.
   $g = 0.69$ The effect size for μ_2 versus μ_3 is a medium size effect.

h. According to the ANOVA, the population means for the *WUMV*, *WSA*, and *WAIS* tests are not equal, $F = 31.80$ (2, 22), $p < .0000004$.

i.

The blocking procedure was effective. When the block source of variation is removed from *SSWG*, a much smaller mean square (*MS RESIDUAL*) results.

The F statistic for the CR-3 design is $(88.1667/2)/(252.5833/33) = 5.81$; the F statistic for the RB-3 design is $(88.1667/2)/(30.5000/22) = 31.80$.

7. See Section 16.3 for the meaning of the terms.

8. a. $a_1b_1, a_1b_2, a_2b_1, a_2b_2$
   b. $a_1b_1, a_1b_2, a_2b_1, a_2b_2, a_3b_1, a_3b_2$
   c. $a_1b_1, a_1b_2, a_1b_3, a_2b_1, a_2b_2, a_2b_3, a_3b_1, a_3b_2, a_3b_3$

9. a. $N = 32$ b. $N = 48$ c. $N = 36$

10. **Analysis of Variance Table**

Source	SS	df	MS	F
1. Treatment A	273.000	4	68 250	$[\frac{1}{4}]$ 2.60**
2. Treatment B	263.550	2	131.775	$[\frac{2}{4}]$ 5.02***
3. AB interaction	302.400	8	37.800	$[\frac{3}{4}]$ 1.44*
4. Within cell	1575.000	60	26.250	
5. Total	2413.950	74		

$^*p < .20$ $^{**}p < .05$ $^{***}p < .01$

11. a.

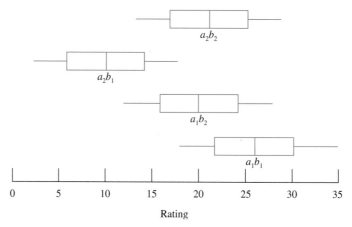

The sample distributions are symmetrical. The data do not contain outliers.

b. **Means and Standard Deviations for Ratings Data**

		Race of Confederate b_1 = black	Race of Confederate b_2 = white	$\overline{X}_{.j.}$	$\hat{\sigma}_{j.}$
a_1 = mild shock	$\overline{X}_{.1k} =$	26.00	20.00	23.00	6.75
	$\hat{\sigma}_{1k} =$	6.32	6.32		
a_2 = strong shock	$\overline{X}_{.2k} =$	10.0	21.00	15.50	8.32
	$\hat{\sigma}_{2k} =$	6.32	6.32		
	$\overline{X}_{..k} =$	18.00	20.50		
	$\hat{\sigma}_{.k} =$	10.33	5.99		

c. The participants assigned to the mild shock condition rated the confederate higher in likability, intelligence, and personal adjustment than did the participants assigned to the strong shock condition. The cell means are such as to suggest that shock level interacts with the race of the confederate. The cell standard deviations are homogeneous.

d. **Analysis of Variance Table for Ratings Data**

Source	SS	df	MS	F
1. Treatment A (shock level)	281.250	1	281.250	$[\tfrac{1}{4}]$ 7.03*
2. Treatment B (race of confederate)	31.250	1	31.250	$[\tfrac{2}{4}]$ 0.78
3. AB Interaction	361.250	1	361.250	$[\tfrac{3}{4}]$ 9.03**
4. Within cell	640.000	16	40.000	
5. Total	1313.750	19		

*$p < .02$ **$p < .009$

Reject the null hypothesis for treatment A and the AB interaction.

e.

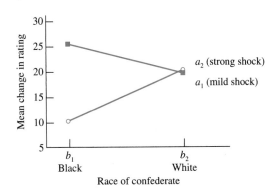

The graph is consistent with the AB interaction test.

f. $\hat{\omega}^2_{Y|AB \cdot A, B} = 0.29$. The strength of association is large. The AB interaction accounts for 29% of the variance in the dependent variable.

g. **Analysis of Variance Table for Treatment A and Treatment B**

Source	SS	df	MS	F
		Treatment A		
1. Treatment A (shock level)	281.2500	1	281.250	$[\tfrac{1}{2}]$ 4.90*
2. Within cell	1,032.5000	18	57.3611	
3. Total	1,313.7500	19		

(continued)

Source	SS	df	MS	F
Treatment B				
4. Treatment *B* (race of confederate)	31.2500	1	31.2500	$[\frac{4}{5}]$ 0.44
5. Within cell	1,282.5000	18	71.2500	
6. Total	1,313.7500	19		

$^{*}p < .05$

The CRF-22 design is preferable because it provides more powerful tests of treatments A and B than do the separate CR-2 designs. This occurs because sources of variation not specifically identified and isolated in the analysis are included in the denominator of the F statistic. For example, the error sum of squares for testing treatment A, $SSWG = 1,032.5000$, is equal to $SSB + SSAB + SSWCELL = 31.250 + 361.250 + 640.000 = 1,032.500$ from the ANOVA table in part (d). The CRF-22 design also is preferable because it enables a researcher to determine if the two treatments interact.

12. Advantages: the design permits a researcher to test hypotheses about interactions and makes efficient use of participants. Disadvantages: if numerous treatments are included in an experiment, the number of participants required may be prohibitive, the interpretation of the analysis is not straightforward if the test of the interaction is significant, and the use of a factorial design commits a researcher to a relatively large experiment. Small one-treatment exploratory experiments may indicate much more promising lines of investigation than those originally envisioned.
13. See Section 16.4 for the meaning of the terms.

CHAPTER 17

1. The tests for goodness of fit and independence both use one random sample. However, the test for goodness of fit classifies the elements of the sample into k mutually exclusive categories. The test for independence classifies each elements in terms of two variables. The test for equality uses c random samples and classifies each element in term of one of two mutually exclusive categories.
2. Seven mutually exclusive socioeconomic categories were used.
3. a. State the statistical hypotheses—H_0: $p_1 = .50$, H_1: $p_1 \neq .50$. Specify the test statistic—$\chi^2 = \Sigma(O_j - E_j)^2/E_j$. Specify the sample size—$n = 50$—and the sampling distribution—chi-square distribution. Specify the level of significance—$\alpha = .05$. Obtain a random sample of size 50, compute χ^2, and make a decision.
   b. $\chi^2 = (33 - 25)^2/25 + (17 - 25)^2/25 = 5.12$; $\chi^2(1, n = 50) = 5.12 > \chi^2_{.05, 1} = 3.841$. Reject the null hypothesis; the data suggest that opinion is not equally divided on the issue.
   c. $p < .03$
   d. $\hat{w} = \sqrt{5.12/50} = 0.32$. The effect size is medium.

4. a. $\chi^2 = (71 - 69.3333)^2/69.3333 + (52 - 52)^2/52 + (33 - 34.6667)^2/34.6667$
   $= 0.120$; $\chi^2(2, n = 156) = 0.120 < \chi^2_{.05,\,2} = 5.991$. The data do not suggest that there has been a change in party affiliation.
   b. $p < .95$
   c. $\hat{w} = \sqrt{0.120/156} = 0.03$. The effect size is negligible.

5. a. $\chi^2 = (53 - 50)^2/50 + (41 - 50)^2/50 + \cdots + (61 - 50)^2/50 = 9.280$; $\chi^2(5, n = 300) = 9.280 < \chi^2_{.05,\,5} = 11.070$. The data do not suggest that the die is not fair.
   b. $p < .10$
   c. $\hat{w} = \sqrt{9.280/300} = 0.18$. The effect size is small, and the nonsignificant test statistic suggests that it may be a chance effect.

6. See Sections 17.2 and 17.3 for the meaning of the terms.

7. Both r and $\hat{V}$ are measures of association, but, unlike r, $\hat{V}$ is appropriate for unordered qualitative variables and ranges over the values 0 to 1. Furthermore, $\hat{V}$ does not have a simple interpretation in terms of proportion of explained variance.

8. a. State the statistical hypotheses—H_0: $p(A \text{ and } B) = p(A)p(B)$, H_1: $p(A \text{ and } B) \neq p(A)p(B)$. Specify the test statistic—$\chi^2 = \Sigma\Sigma(O_{ij} - E_{ij})^2/E_{ij}$. Specify the sample size—$n = 200$—and the sampling distribution—chi-square distribution. Specify the level of significance—$\alpha = .001$. Obtain a random sample of size 200, compute χ^2 and make a decision.
   b. $\chi^2 = (58 - 44.08)^2/44.08 + (30 - 39.44)^2/39.44 + \cdots + (23 - 13.44)^2/13.44 = 32.28$; $\chi^2(4, n = 200) = 32.28 > \chi^2_{.001,\,4} = 18.467$. Reject the null hypothesis; the variables are not independent.
   c. $p < .000002$
   d. $\hat{V} = \sqrt{32.28/[200(3-1)]} = .284$
   e. $\hat{w} = \sqrt{32.28/200} = 0.40$. The effect size is medium.

9. a. $\chi^2 = (38 - 25.740)^2/25.740 + \cdots + (21 - 10.455)^2/10.455 = 44.574$; $\chi^2(6, n = 200) = 44.574 > \chi^2_{.05,\,6} = 12.592$. Reject the null hypothesis; the variables are not independent.
   b. $p < .00000006$
   c. $\hat{V} = \sqrt{44.574/[200(3-1)]} = .334$
   d. $\hat{w} = \sqrt{44.574/200} = 0.47$. The effect size is large.

11. See Section 17.4 for the meaning of the term.

12. a. H_0: $p_1 = p_2$, H_1: $p_1 \neq p_2$
    b. $\chi^2 = (16 - 10.5)^2/10.5 + \cdots + (25 - 19.5)^2/19.5 = 8.864$; $\chi^2(1, n = 60) = 8.864 > \chi^2_{.01,\,1} = 6.635$. Reject the null hypothesis.
    c. $p < .003$
    d. $\hat{w} = \sqrt{8.864/60} = 0.38$. The effect size is medium.

13. The population proportions in the three categories of variable A (.30, .60, .10) are equal across the three categories of variable B.

14. a.
$$H_0: \begin{bmatrix} p_{a_1|b_1} = p_{a_1|b_2} = p_{a_1|b_3} = p_{a_1|b_4} \\ p_{a_2|b_1} = p_{a_2|b_2} = p_{a_2|b_3} = p_{a_2|b_4} \\ p_{a_3|b_1} = p_{a_3|b_2} = p_{a_3|b_3} = p_{a_3|b_4} \\ p_{a_4|b_1} = p_{a_4|b_2} = p_{a_4|b_3} = p_{a_4|b_4} \end{bmatrix}$$

H_1: $p_{a_i|b_j} \neq p_{a_i|b_{j'}}$ in at least one row for some j and j'

b. $\chi^2 = (4 - 5)^2/5 + \cdots + (0 - 5)^2/5 = 17.560$; $\chi^2(9, n = 100) = 17.560 > \chi^2_{.05, 9} = 16.919$. Reject the null hypothesis.

c. $p < .05$

d. $\hat{w} = \sqrt{17.560/100} = 0.42$. The effect size is medium.

15. a.
$$H_0: \begin{bmatrix} p_{a_1|b_1} = p_{a_1|b_2} = p_{a_1|b_3} \\ p_{a_2|b_1} = p_{a_2|b_2} = p_{a_2|b_3} \\ p_{a_3|b_1} = p_{a_3|b_2} = p_{a_3|b_3} \end{bmatrix}$$

$H_1: p_{a_j|b_j} \neq p_{a_j|b_{j'}}$ in at least one row for some j and j'

b. $\chi^2 = (26 - 68.295918)^2/68.295918 + \ldots + (97 - 166.683674)^2/166.683674 = 120.219$; $\chi^2(2, n = 784) = 120.219 > \chi^2_{.05, 2} = 5.991$. Reject the null hypothesis.

c. $p = 7.8483 \times 10^{-27}$

d. $\hat{w} = \sqrt{120.219/784} = 0.39$. The effect size is medium.

16. c.
$$H_0: \begin{bmatrix} p_{a_1|b_1} = p_{a_1|b_2} \\ p_{a_2|b_1} = p_{a_2|b_2} \\ p_{a_3|b_1} = p_{a_3|b_2} \\ p_{a_4|b_1} = p_{a_4|b_2} \\ p_{a_5|b_1} = p_{a_5|b_2} \\ p_{a_6|b_1} = p_{a_6|b_2} \\ p_{a_7|b_1} = p_{a_7|b_2} \end{bmatrix}$$

$H_1: p_{a_i|b_1} \neq p_{a_i|b_2}$ in at least one row

CHAPTER 18

1. The Mann-Whitney U test assumes that the populations are continuous, the samples are independent, and either random sampling or random assignment has been used. The t test assumes random sampling or random assignment, normality, equal variances, and independent samples. The Mann-Whitney U test can be used with rank data and is almost as efficient as the t test.

2. $U(7, 6) = 42 + 28 - 64.5 = 5.5$; $U(7, 6) = 5.5 < U_{.05/2; 7, 6} = 6$. Reject the null hypothesis that the populations are identical.

3. Without the correction for ties,

$$z = \frac{(148.5 + 0.5) - 200}{\sqrt{\dfrac{400}{12}(41)}} = \frac{-51}{36.9685} = -1.3796$$

$|z| = 1.3796 < z_{.01/2} = 2.576$. Do not reject the null hypothesis. With the correction,

$$z = \frac{(148.5 + 0.5) - 200}{\sqrt{\dfrac{400}{12}(41)(1 - 0.0044)}} = \frac{-51}{36.8869} = -1.3826$$

$|z| = 1.3826 < z_{.01/2} = 2.576$. Do not reject the null hypothesis.

4. The value of PE is dependent on α, $1 - \beta$, H_0, and H_1, and the sample size of the more efficient comparison test statistic.
5. The approximate z test can be used when either n_1 or n_2 is greater that 20. The test is satisfactory if both n's are greater than 10.
6. a. 95%
   b. $\alpha = .01$, $1 - \beta = .80$, H_0 and H_1 are nondirectional, and $n_S = 82$.
7. See Sections 17.1 and 17.2 for the meaning of the terms.
8. $T(13) = 17.5 > T_{.05/2,\ 13} = 17$; do not reject the null hypothesis.
9. $T(16) = 30.5 < T_{.05,\ 16} = 35$; reject the null hypothesis.
10. $z = \dfrac{(175 + 0.5) - 35(35 + 1)/4}{\sqrt{\dfrac{35(35 + 1)[2(35) + 1]}{24}}} = -2.285;$

   $|z| = 2.285 > z_{.05} = 1.645$. Reject the null hypothesis.

11. $z = \dfrac{(30.5 + 0.5) - 16(16 + 1)/4}{\sqrt{\dfrac{16(16 + 1)[2(16) + 1]}{24} - \dfrac{(6^3 - 6) + (7^3 - 7) + (2^3 - 2)}{48}}}$

   $= \dfrac{-37.0000}{19.0394} = -1.943;$

   $|z| = 1.943 > z_{.05} = 1.645$. Reject the null hypothesis.
12. a. 95%
    b. $\alpha = .01$, $1 - \beta = .95$, H_0 and H_1 are nondirectional, and $n_S = 122$.
13. The differences between assumption-freer tests and parametric tests involve (a) their assumptions, (b) the level of mathematics necessary to understand their rationale, (c) their computational simplicity, and (d) the nature of the hypothesis they test.
14. Most assumption-freer procedures assume that (a) the population elements are randomly sampled or that the elements are randomly assigned to experimental conditions, (b) the sampled population is continuous, which implies that no two population elements have the same value (that is, no tied values), and (c) the null hypothesis is true. Most parametric test statistics assume that (a) the population elements are randomly sampled or that the elements are randomly assigned to experimental conditions, (b) the population is normally distributed, and (c) the null hypothesis is true. A fourth assumption is required by some test statistics if the null hypothesis concerns two or more populations—that the population variances are equal.

APPENDIX D

Tables

D.1   **Random Numbers**

D.2   **Areas under the Standard Normal Distribution**

D.3   **Percentage Points of Student's *t* Distribution**

D.4   **Upper Percentage Points of the Chi-Square Distribution**

D.5   **Upper Percentage Points of the *F* Distribution**

D.6   **Critical Values of the Pearson *r***

D.7   **Transformation of *r* to *Z'***

D.8   **Approximate *n* Required for Testing Hypotheses about Means**

D.9   **Percentage Points of the Studentized Range Distribution**

D.10   **Critical Values of the Mann-Whitney *U* Statistic**

D.11   **Critical Values of the Wilcoxon *T* Statistic**

TABLE D.1 Random Numbers[a]

	1	2	3	4	5	6	7	8	9	10	11	12	13	14	15	16	17	18	19	20	21	22	23	24	25
1	10	27	53	96	23	71	50	54	36	23	54	31	04	82	98	04	14	12	15	09	26	78	25	47	47
2	28	41	50	61	88	64	85	27	20	18	83	36	36	05	56	39	71	65	09	62	94	76	62	11	89
3	34	21	42	57	02	59	19	18	97	48	80	30	03	30	98	05	24	67	70	07	84	97	50	87	46
4	61	81	77	23	23	82	82	11	54	08	53	28	70	58	96	44	07	39	55	43	42	34	43	39	28
5	61	15	18	13	54	16	86	20	26	88	90	74	80	55	09	14	53	90	51	17	52	01	63	01	59
6	91	76	21	64	64	44	91	13	32	97	75	31	62	66	54	84	80	32	75	77	56	08	25	70	29
7	00	97	79	08	06	37	30	28	59	85	53	56	68	53	40	01	74	39	59	73	30	19	99	85	48
8	36	46	18	34	94	75	20	80	27	77	78	91	69	16	00	08	43	18	73	68	67	69	61	34	25
9	88	98	99	60	50	65	95	79	42	94	93	62	40	89	96	43	56	47	71	66	46	76	29	67	02
10	04	37	59	87	21	05	02	03	24	17	47	97	81	56	51	92	34	86	01	82	55	51	33	12	91
11	63	62	06	34	41	94	21	78	55	09	72	76	45	16	94	29	95	81	83	83	79	88	01	97	30
12	78	47	23	53	90	34	41	92	45	71	09	23	70	70	07	12	38	92	79	43	14	85	11	47	23
13	87	68	62	15	43	53	14	36	59	25	54	47	33	70	15	59	24	48	40	35	50	03	42	99	36
14	47	60	92	10	77	88	59	53	11	52	66	25	69	07	04	48	68	64	71	06	61	65	70	22	12
15	56	88	87	59	41	65	28	04	67	53	95	79	88	37	31	50	41	06	94	76	81	83	17	16	33
16	02	57	45	86	67	73	43	07	34	48	44	26	87	93	29	77	09	61	67	84	06	69	44	77	75
17	31	54	14	13	17	48	62	11	90	60	68	12	93	64	28	46	24	79	16	76	14	60	25	51	01
18	28	50	16	43	36	28	97	85	58	99	67	22	52	76	23	24	70	36	54	54	59	28	61	71	96
19	63	29	62	66	50	02	63	45	52	38	67	63	47	54	75	83	24	78	43	20	92	63	13	47	48
20	45	65	58	26	51	76	96	59	38	72	86	57	45	71	46	44	67	76	14	55	44	88	01	62	12
21	39	65	36	63	70	77	45	85	50	51	74	13	39	35	22	30	53	36	02	95	49	34	88	73	61
22	73	71	98	16	04	29	18	94	51	23	76	51	94	84	86	79	93	96	38	63	08	58	25	58	94
23	72	20	56	20	11	72	65	71	08	86	79	57	95	13	91	97	48	72	66	48	09	71	17	24	89
24	75	17	26	99	76	89	37	20	70	01	77	31	61	95	46	26	97	05	73	51	53	33	18	72	87
25	37	48	60	82	29	81	30	15	39	14	48	38	75	93	29	06	87	37	78	48	45	56	00	84	47
26	68	08	02	80	72	83	71	46	30	49	89	17	95	88	29	02	39	56	03	46	97	74	06	56	17
27	14	23	98	61	67	70	52	85	01	50	01	84	02	78	43	10	62	98	19	41	18	83	99	47	99
28	49	08	96	21	44	25	27	99	41	28	07	41	08	34	66	19	42	74	39	91	41	96	53	78	72
29	78	37	06	08	43	63	61	62	42	29	39	68	95	10	96	09	24	23	00	62	56	12	80	73	16
30	37	21	34	17	68	68	96	83	23	56	32	84	60	15	31	44	73	67	34	77	91	15	79	74	58
31	14	29	09	34	04	87	83	07	55	07	76	58	30	83	64	87	29	25	58	84	86	50	60	00	25
32	58	43	28	06	36	49	52	83	51	14	47	56	91	29	34	05	87	31	06	95	12	45	57	09	09
33	10	43	67	29	70	80	62	80	03	42	10	80	21	38	84	90	56	35	03	09	43	12	74	49	14
34	44	38	88	39	54	86	97	37	44	22	00	95	01	31	76	17	16	29	56	63	38	78	94	49	81
35	90	69	59	19	51	85	39	52	85	13	07	28	37	07	61	11	16	36	27	03	78	86	72	04	95
36	47	47	10	25	62	97	05	31	03	61	20	26	36	31	62	68	69	86	95	44	84	95	48	46	45
37	91	94	14	63	19	75	89	11	47	11	31	56	34	19	09	79	57	92	36	59	14	93	87	81	40
38	80	06	54	18	66	09	18	94	06	19	98	40	07	17	81	22	45	44	84	11	24	62	20	42	31
39	67	72	77	63	48	84	08	31	55	58	24	33	45	77	58	80	45	67	93	82	75	70	16	08	24
40	59	40	24	13	27	79	26	88	86	30	01	31	60	10	39	53	58	47	70	93	85	81	56	39	38
41	05	90	35	89	95	01	61	16	96	94	50	78	13	69	36	37	68	53	37	31	71	26	35	03	71
42	44	43	80	69	98	46	68	05	14	82	90	78	50	05	62	77	79	13	57	44	59	60	10	39	66
43	61	81	31	96	82	00	57	25	60	59	46	72	60	18	77	55	66	12	62	11	08	99	55	64	57
44	42	88	07	10	05	24	98	65	63	21	47	21	61	88	32	27	80	30	21	60	10	92	35	36	12
45	77	94	30	05	39	28	10	99	00	27	12	73	73	99	12	49	99	57	94	82	96	88	57	17	91
46	78	83	19	76	16	94	11	68	84	26	23	54	20	86	85	23	86	66	99	07	36	37	34	92	09
47	87	76	59	61	81	43	63	64	61	61	65	76	36	95	90	18	48	27	45	68	27	23	65	30	72
48	91	43	05	96	47	55	78	99	95	24	37	55	85	78	78	01	48	41	19	10	35	19	54	07	73
49	84	97	77	72	73	09	62	06	65	72	87	12	49	03	60	41	15	20	76	27	50	47	02	29	16
50	87	41	60	76	83	44	88	96	07	80	83	05	83	38	96	73	70	66	81	90	30	56	10	48	59

From Table XXXIII of *Statistical Tables for Biological, Agricultural and Medical Research* 6e, by R.A. Fisher and F. Yates, Pearson Education Limited. Reproduced by permission of Pearson Education Limited.
[a] Discussed in Section 8.2.

TABLE D.1   *(continued)*

	1	2	3	4	5	6	7	8	9	10	11	12	13	14	15	16	17	18	19	20	21	22	23	24	25
1	22	17	68	65	84	68	95	23	92	35	87	02	22	57	51	61	09	43	95	06	58	24	82	03	47
2	19	36	27	59	46	13	79	93	37	55	39	77	32	77	09	85	52	05	30	62	47	83	51	62	74
3	16	77	23	02	77	09	61	87	25	21	28	06	24	25	93	16	71	13	59	78	23	05	47	47	25
4	78	43	76	71	61	20	44	90	32	64	97	67	63	99	61	46	38	03	93	22	69	81	21	99	21
5	03	28	28	26	08	73	37	32	04	05	69	30	16	09	05	88	69	58	28	99	35	07	44	75	47
6	93	22	53	64	39	07	10	63	76	35	87	03	04	79	88	08	13	13	85	51	55	34	57	72	69
7	78	76	58	54	74	92	38	70	96	92	52	06	79	79	45	82	63	18	27	44	49	66	92	19	09
8	23	68	35	26	00	99	53	93	61	28	52	70	05	48	34	56	63	05	61	86	90	92	10	70	80
9	15	39	25	70	99	93	86	52	77	65	15	33	59	05	28	22	87	26	07	47	86	96	98	29	06
10	58	71	96	30	24	18	46	23	34	27	85	13	99	24	44	49	18	09	79	49	74	16	32	23	02
11	57	35	27	33	72	24	53	63	94	09	41	10	76	47	91	44	04	95	49	66	39	60	04	59	81
12	48	50	86	54	48	22	06	34	72	52	82	21	15	65	20	33	29	94	71	11	15	91	29	12	03
13	61	96	48	95	03	07	16	39	33	66	98	56	10	56	79	77	21	30	27	12	90	49	22	23	62
14	36	93	89	41	26	29	70	83	63	51	99	74	20	52	36	87	09	41	15	09	98	60	16	03	03
15	18	87	00	42	31	57	90	12	02	07	23	47	37	17	31	54	08	01	88	63	39	41	88	92	10
16	88	56	53	27	59	33	35	72	67	47	77	34	55	45	70	08	18	27	38	90	16	95	86	70	75
17	09	72	95	84	29	49	41	31	06	70	42	38	06	45	18	64	84	73	31	65	52	53	37	97	15
18	12	96	88	17	31	65	19	69	02	83	60	75	86	90	68	24	64	19	35	51	56	61	87	39	12
19	85	94	57	24	16	92	09	84	38	76	22	00	27	69	85	29	81	94	78	70	21	94	47	90	12
20	38	64	43	59	98	98	77	87	68	07	91	51	67	62	44	40	98	05	93	78	23	32	65	41	18
21	53	44	09	42	72	00	41	86	79	79	68	47	22	00	20	35	55	31	51	51	00	83	63	22	55
22	40	76	66	26	84	57	99	99	90	37	36	63	32	08	58	37	40	13	68	97	87	64	81	07	83
23	02	17	79	18	05	12	59	52	57	02	22	07	90	47	03	28	14	11	30	79	20	69	22	40	98
24	95	17	82	06	53	31	51	10	96	46	92	06	88	07	77	56	11	50	81	69	40	23	72	51	39
25	35	76	22	42	92	96	11	83	44	80	34	68	35	48	77	33	42	40	90	60	73	96	53	97	86
26	26	29	13	56	41	85	47	04	66	08	34	72	57	59	13	82	43	80	46	15	38	26	61	70	04
27	77	80	20	75	82	72	82	32	99	90	63	95	73	76	63	89	73	44	99	05	48	67	26	43	18
28	46	40	66	44	52	91	36	74	43	53	30	82	13	54	00	78	45	63	98	35	55	03	36	67	68
29	37	56	08	18	09	77	53	84	46	47	31	91	18	95	58	24	16	74	11	53	44	10	13	85	57
30	61	65	61	68	66	37	27	47	39	19	84	83	70	07	48	53	21	40	06	71	95	06	79	88	54
31	93	43	69	64	07	34	18	04	52	35	56	27	09	24	86	61	85	53	83	45	19	90	70	99	00
32	21	96	60	12	99	11	20	99	45	18	48	13	93	55	34	18	37	79	49	90	65	97	38	20	46
33	95	20	47	97	97	27	37	83	28	71	00	06	41	41	74	45	89	09	39	84	51	67	11	52	49
34	97	86	21	78	73	10	65	81	92	59	58	76	17	14	97	04	76	62	16	17	17	95	70	45	80
35	69	92	06	34	13	59	71	74	17	32	27	55	10	24	19	23	71	82	13	74	63	52	52	01	41
36	04	31	17	21	56	33	73	99	19	87	26	72	39	27	67	53	77	57	68	93	60	61	97	22	61
37	61	06	98	03	91	87	14	77	43	96	43	00	65	98	50	45	60	33	01	07	98	99	46	50	47
38	85	93	85	86	88	72	87	08	62	40	16	06	10	89	20	23	21	34	74	97	76	38	03	29	63
39	21	74	32	47	45	73	96	07	94	52	09	65	90	77	47	25	76	16	19	33	53	05	70	53	30
40	15	69	53	82	80	79	96	23	53	10	65	39	07	16	29	45	33	02	43	70	02	87	40	41	45
41	02	89	08	04	49	20	21	14	68	86	87	63	93	95	17	11	29	01	95	80	35	14	97	35	33
42	87	18	15	89	79	85	43	01	72	73	08	61	74	51	69	89	74	39	82	15	94	51	33	41	67
43	98	83	71	94	22	59	97	50	99	52	08	52	85	08	40	87	80	61	65	31	91	51	80	32	44
44	10	08	58	21	66	72	68	49	29	31	89	85	84	46	06	59	73	19	85	23	65	09	29	75	63
45	47	90	56	10	08	88	02	84	27	83	42	29	72	23	19	66	56	45	65	79	20	71	53	20	25
46	22	85	61	68	90	49	64	92	85	44	16	40	12	89	88	50	14	49	81	06	01	82	77	45	12
47	67	80	43	79	33	12	83	11	41	16	25	58	19	68	70	77	02	54	00	52	53	43	37	15	26
48	27	62	50	96	72	79	44	61	40	15	14	53	40	65	39	27	31	58	50	28	11	39	03	34	23
49	33	78	80	87	15	38	30	06	38	21	14	47	47	07	26	54	96	87	53	32	40	36	40	96	76
50	13	13	92	66	99	47	24	49	57	74	32	25	43	62	17	10	97	11	69	84	99	63	22	32	98

TABLE D.2   Areas under the Standard Normal Distribution[a]

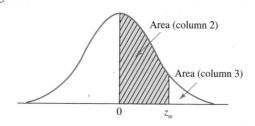

(1)	(2) Area Between Mean and	(3) Area Above	(1)	(2) Area Between Mean and	(3) Area Above	(1)	(2) Area Between Mean and	(3) Area Above
z_α	z_α	z_α	z_α	z_α	z_α	z_α	z_α	z_α
0.00	0.0000	0.5000	0.30	0.1179	0.3821	0.60	0.2257	0.2743
0.01	0.0040	0.4960	0.31	0.1217	0.3783	0.61	0.2291	0.2709
0.02	0.0080	0.4920	0.32	0.1255	0.3745	0.62	0.2324	0.2676
0.03	0.0120	0.4880	0.33	0.1293	0.3707	0.63	0.2357	0.2643
0.04	0.0160	0.4840	0.34	0.1331	0.3669	0.64	0.2389	0.2611
0.05	0.0199	0.4801	0.35	0.1368	0.3632	0.65	0.2422	0.2578
0.06	0.0239	0.4761	0.36	0.1406	0.3594	0.66	0.2454	0.2546
0.07	0.0279	0.4721	0.37	0.1443	0.3557	0.67	0.2486	0.2514
0.08	0.0319	0.4681	0.38	0.1480	0.3520	0.68	0.2517	0.2483
0.09	0.0359	0.4641	0.39	0.1517	0.3483	0.69	0.2549	0.2451
0.10	0.0398	0.4602	0.40	0.1554	0.3446	0.70	0.2580	0.2420
0.11	0.0438	0.4562	0.41	0.1591	0.3409	0.71	0.2611	0.2389
0.12	0.0478	0.4522	0.42	0.1628	0.3372	0.72	0.2642	0.2358
0.13	0.0517	0.4483	0.43	0.1664	0.3336	0.73	0.2673	0.2327
0.14	0.0557	0.4443	0.44	0.1700	0.3300	0.74	0.2704	0.2296
0.15	0.0596	0.4404	0.45	0.1736	0.3264	0.75	0.2734	0.2266
0.16	0.0636	0.4364	0.46	0.1772	0.3228	0.76	0.2764	0.2236
0.17	0.0675	0.4325	0.47	0.1808	0.3192	0.77	0.2794	0.2206
0.18	0.0714	0.4286	0.48	0.1844	0.3156	0.78	0.2823	0.2177
0.19	0.0753	0.4247	0.49	0.1879	0.3121	0.79	0.2852	0.2148
0.20	0.0793	0.4207	0.50	0.1915	0.3085	0.80	0.2881	0.2119
0.21	0.0832	0.4168	0.51	0.1950	0.3050	0.81	0.2910	0.2090
0.22	0.0871	0.4129	0.52	0.1985	0.3015	0.82	0.2939	0.2061
0.23	0.0910	0.4090	0.53	0.2019	0.2981	0.83	0.2967	0.2033
0.24	0.0948	0.4052	0.54	0.2054	0.2946	0.84	0.2995	0.2005
0.25	0.0987	0.4013	0.55	0.2088	0.2912	0.85	0.3023	0.1977
0.26	0.1026	0.3974	0.56	0.2123	0.2877	0.86	0.3051	0.1949
0.27	0.1064	0.3936	0.57	0.2157	0.2843	0.87	0.3078	0.1922
0.28	0.1103	0.3897	0.58	0.2190	0.2810	0.88	0.3106	0.1894
0.29	0.1141	0.3859	0.59	0.2224	0.2776	0.89	0.3133	0.1867

From Table IIi of *Statistical Tables for Biological, Agricultural and Medical Research* 6e, by R.A. Fisher and F. Yates, Pearson Education Limited. Reproduced by permission of Pearson Education Limited.
[a] Discussed in Section 9.2.

TABLE D.2   *(continued)*

(1)	*(2)* Area Between Mean and	*(3)* Area Above	*(1)*	*(2)* Area Between Mean and	*(3)* Area Above	*(1)*	*(2)* Area Between Mean and	*(3)* Area Above
z_α	z_α	z_α	z_α	z_α	z_α	z_α	z_α	z_α
0.90	0.3159	0.1841	1.30	0.4032	0.0968	1.70	0.4554	0.0446
0.91	0.3186	0.1814	1.31	0.4049	0.0951	1.71	0.4564	0.0436
0.92	0.3212	0.1788	1.32	0.4066	0.0934	1.72	0.4573	0.0427
0.93	0.3238	0.1762	1.33	0.4082	0.0918	1.73	0.4582	0.0418
0.94	0.3264	0.1736	1.34	0.4099	0.0901	1.74	0.4591	0.0409
0.95	0.3289	0.1711	1.35	0.4115	0.0885	1.75	0.4599	0.0401
0.96	0.3315	0.1685	1.36	0.4131	0.0869	1.76	0.4608	0.0392
0.97	0.3340	0.1660	1.37	0.4147	0.0853	1.77	0.4616	0.0384
0.98	0.3365	0.1635	1.38	0.4162	0.0838	1.78	0.4625	0.0375
0.99	0.3389	0.1611	1.39	0.4177	0.0823	1.79	0.4633	0.0367
1.00	0.3413	0.1587	1.40	0.4192	0.0808	1.80	0.4641	0.0359
1.01	0.3438	0.1562	1.41	0.4207	0.0793	1.81	0.4649	0.0351
1.02	0.3461	0.1539	1.42	0.4222	0.0778	1.82	0.4656	0.0344
1.03	0.3485	0.1515	1.43	0.4236	0.0764	1.83	0.4664	0.0336
1.04	0.3508	0.1492	1.44	0.4251	0.0749	1.84	0.4671	0.0329
1.05	0.3531	0.1469	1.45	0.4265	0.0735	1.85	0.4678	0.0322
1.06	0.3554	0.1446	1.46	0.4279	0.0721	1.86	0.4686	0.0314
1.07	0.3577	0.1423	1.47	0.4292	0.0708	1.87	0.4693	0.0307
1.08	0.3599	0.1401	1.48	0.4306	0.0694	1.88	0.4699	0.0301
1.09	0.3621	0.1379	1.49	0.4319	0.0681	1.89	0.4706	0.0294
1.10	0.3643	0.1357	1.50	0.4332	0.0668	1.90	0.4713	0.0287
1.11	0.3665	0.1335	1.51	0.4345	0.0655	1.91	0.4719	0.0281
1.12	0.3686	0.1314	1.52	0.4357	0.0643	1.92	0.4726	0.0274
1.13	0.3708	0.1292	1.53	0.4370	0.0630	1.93	0.4732	0.0268
1.14	0.3729	0.1271	1.54	0.4382	0.0618	1.94	0.4738	0.0262
1.15	0.3749	0.1251	1.55	0.4394	0.0606	1.95	0.4744	0.0256
1.16	0.3770	0.1230	1.56	0.4406	0.0594	1.96	0.4750	0.0250
1.17	0.3790	0.1210	1.57	0.4418	0.0582	1.97	0.4756	0.0244
1.18	0.3810	0.1190	1.58	0.4429	0.0571	1.98	0.4761	0.0239
1.19	0.3830	0.1170	1.59	0.4441	0.0559	1.99	0.4767	0.0233
1.20	0.3849	0.1151	1.60	0.4452	0.0548	2.00	0.4772	0.0228
1.21	0.3869	0.1131	1.61	0.4463	0.0537	2.01	0.4778	0.0222
1.22	0.3888	0.1112	1.62	0.4474	0.0526	2.02	0.4783	0.0217
1.23	0.3907	0.1093	1.63	0.4484	0.0516	2.03	0.4788	0.0212
1.24	0.3925	0.1075	1.64	0.4495	0.0505	2.04	0.4793	0.0207
			1.645	0.4500	0.0500			
1.25	0.3944	0.1056	1.65	0.4505	0.0495	2.05	0.4798	0.0202
1.26	0.3962	0.1038	1.66	0.4515	0.0485	2.06	0.4803	0.0197
1.27	0.3980	0.1020	1.67	0.4525	0.0475	2.07	0.4808	0.0192
1.28	0.3997	0.1003	1.68	0.4535	0.0465	2.08	0.4812	0.0188
1.29	0.4015	0.0985	1.69	0.4545	0.0455	2.09	0.4817	0.0183

TABLE D.2   *(continued)*

(1) z_α	(2) Area Between Mean and z_α	(3) Area Above z_α	(1) z_α	(2) Area Between Mean and z_α	(3) Area Above z_α	(1) z_α	(2) Area Between Mean and z_α	(3) Area Above z_α
2.10	0.4821	0.0179	2.45	0.4929	0.0071	2.80	0.4974	0.0026
2.11	0.4826	0.0174	2.46	0.4931	0.0069	2.81	0.4975	0.0025
2.12	0.4830	0.0170	2.47	0.4932	0.0068	2.82	0.4976	0.0024
2.13	0.4834	0.0166	2.48	0.4934	0.0066	2.83	0.4977	0.0023
2.14	0.4838	0.0162	2.49	0.4936	0.0064	2.84	0.4977	0.0023
2.15	0.4842	0.0158	2.50	0.4938	0.0062	2.85	0.4978	0.0022
2.16	0.4846	0.0154	2.51	0.4940	0.0060	2.86	0.4979	0.0021
2.17	0.4850	0.0150	2.52	0.4941	0.0059	2.87	0.4979	0.0021
2.18	0.4854	0.0146	2.53	0.4943	0.0057	2.88	0.4980	0.0020
2.19	0.4857	0.0143	2.54	0.4945	0.0055	2.89	0.4981	0.0019
2.20	0.4861	0.0139	2.55	0.4946	0.0054	2.90	0.4981	0.0019
2.21	0.4864	0.0136	2.56	0.4948	0.0052	2.91	0.4982	0.0018
2.22	0.4868	0.0132	2.57	0.4949	0.0051	2.92	0.4982	0.0018
2.23	0.4871	0.0129	2.576	0.4950	0.0050	2.93	0.4983	0.0017
2.24	0.4875	0.0125	2.58	0.4951	0.0049	2.94	0.4984	0.0016
			2.59	0.4952	0.0048			
2.25	0.4878	0.0122	2.60	0.4953	0.0047	2.95	0.4984	0.0016
2.26	0.4881	0.0119	2.61	0.4955	0.0045	2.96	0.4985	0.0015
2.27	0.4884	0.0116	2.62	0.4956	0.0044	2.97	0.4985	0.0015
2.28	0.4887	0.0113	2.63	0.4957	0.0043	2.98	0.4986	0.0014
2.29	0.4890	0.0110	2.64	0.4959	0.0041	2.99	0.4986	0.0014
2.30	0.4893	0.0107	2.65	0.4960	0.0040	3.00	0.4987	0.0013
2.31	0.4896	0.0104	2.66	0.4961	0.0039	3.01	0.4987	0.0013
2.32	0.4898	0.0102	2.67	0.4962	0.0038	3.02	0.4987	0.0013
2.33	0.4901	0.0099	2.68	0.4963	0.0037	3.03	0.4988	0.0012
2.34	0.4904	0.0096	2.69	0.4964	0.0036	3.04	0.4988	0.0012
2.35	0.4906	0.0094	2.70	0.4965	0.0035	3.05	0.4989	0.0011
2.36	0.4909	0.0091	2.71	0.4966	0.0034	3.06	0.4989	0.0011
2.37	0.4911	0.0089	2.72	0.4967	0.0033	3.07	0.4989	0.0011
2.38	0.4913	0.0087	2.73	0.4968	0.0032	3.08	0.4990	0.0010
2.39	0.4916	0.0084	2.74	0.4969	0.0031	3.09	0.4990	0.0010
2.40	0.4918	0.0082	2.75	0.4970	0.0030	3.10	0.4990	0.0010
2.41	0.4920	0.0080	2.76	0.4971	0.0029	3.11	0.4991	0.0009
2.42	0.4922	0.0078	2.77	0.4972	0.0028	3.12	0.4991	0.0009
2.43	0.4925	0.0075	2.78	0.4973	0.0027	3.13	0.4991	0.0009
2.44	0.4927	0.0073	2.79	0.4974	0.0026	3.14	0.4992	0.0008

TABLE D.2   *(continued)*

(1) z_α	*(2)* Area Between Mean and z_α	*(3)* Area Above z_α	*(1)* z_α	*(2)* Area Between Mean and z_α	*(3)* Area Above z_α
3.15	0.4992	0.0008	3.25	0.4994	0.0006
3.16	0.4992	0.0008	3.30	0.4995	0.0005
3.17	0.4992	0.0008	3.35	0.4996	0.0004
3.18	0.4993	0.0007	3.40	0.4997	0.0003
3.19	0.4993	0.0007	3.45	0.4997	0.0003
3.20	0.4993	0.0007	3.50	0.4998	0.0002
3.21	0.4993	0.0007	3.60	0.4998	0.0002
3.22	0.4994	0.0006	3.70	0.4999	0.0001
3.23	0.4994	0.0006	3.80	0.4999	0.0001
3.24	0.4994	0.0006	3.90	0.49995	0.00005
			4.00	0.49997	0.00003

TABLE D.3   Percentage Points of Student's *t* Distribution[a]

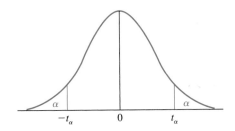

Degrees of Freedom, v	Level of Significance for a One-Tailed Test								
	.25	.20	.15	.10	.05	.025	.01	.005	.0005
	Level of Significance for a Two-Tailed Test								
	.50	.40	.30	.20	.10	.05	.02	.01	.001
1	1.000	1.376	1.963	3.078	6.314	12.706	31.821	63.657	636.619
2	.816	1.061	1.386	1.886	2.920	4.303	6.965	9.925	31.598
3	.765	.978	1.250	1.638	2.353	3.182	4.541	5.841	12.924
4	.741	.941	1.190	1.533	2.132	2.776	3.747	4.604	8.610
5	.727	.920	1.156	1.476	2.015	2.571	3.365	4.032	6.869
6	.718	.906	1.134	1.440	1.943	2.447	3.143	3.707	5.959
7	.711	.896	1.119	1.415	1.895	2.365	2.998	3.499	5.408
8	.706	.889	1.108	1.397	1.860	2.306	2.896	3.355	5.041
9	.703	.883	1.100	1.383	1.833	2.262	2.821	3.250	4.781
10	.700	.879	1.093	1.372	1.812	2.228	2.764	3.169	4.587
11	.697	.876	1.088	1.363	1.796	2.201	2.718	3.106	4.437
12	.695	.873	1.083	1.356	1.782	2.179	2.681	3.055	4.318
13	.694	.870	1.079	1.350	1.771	2.160.	2.650	3.012	4.221
14	.692	.868	1.076	1.345	1.761	2.145	2.624	2.977	4.140
15	.691	.866	1.074	1.341	1.753	2.131	2.602	2.947	4.073
16	.690	.865	1.071	1.337	1.746	2.120	2.583	2.921	4.015
17	.689	.863	1.069	1.333	1.740	2.110	2.567	2.898	3.965
18	.688	.862	1.067	1.330	1.734	2.101	2.552	2.878	3.922
19	.688	.861	1.066	1.328	1.729	2.093	2.539	2.861	3.883
20	.687	.860	1.064	1.325	1.725	2.086	2.528	2.845	3.850
21	.686	.859	1.063	1.323	1.721	2.080	2.518	2.831	3.819
22	.686	.858	1.061	1.321	1.717	2.074	2.508	2.819	3.792
23	.685	.858	1.060	1.319	1.714	2.069	2.500	2.807	3.767
24	.685	.857	1.059	1.318	1.711	2.064	2.492	2.797	3.745
25	.684	.856	1.058	1.316	1.708	2.060	2.485	2.787	3.725
26	.684	.856	1.058	1.315	1.706	2.056	2.479	2.779	3.707
27	.684	.855	1.057	1.314	1.703	2.052	2.473	2.771	3.690
28	.683	.855	1.056	1.313	1.701	2.048	2.467	2.763	3.674
29	.683	.854	1.055	1.311	1.699	2.045	2.462	2.756	3.659
30	.683	.854	1.055	1.310	1.697	2.042	2.457	2.750	3.646
40	.681	.851	1.050	1.303	1.684	2.021	2.423	2.704	3.551
60	.679	.848	1.046	1.296	1.671	2.000	2.390	2.660	3.460
120	.677	.845	1.041	1.289	1.658	1.980	2.358	2.617	3.373
∞	.674	.842	1.036	1.282	1.645	1.960	2.326	2.576	3.291

From Table III of *Statistical Tables for Biological, Agricultural and Medical Research* 6e, by R.A. Fisher and F. Yates, Pearson Education Limited. Reproduced by permission of Pearson Education Limited.

[a] Discussed in Section 10.2.

TABLE D.4   Upper Percentage Points of the Chi-Square Distribution[a]

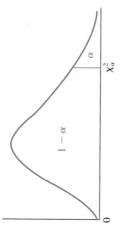

ν	99	.975	.95	.90	.80	.70	.50	.30	.20	.10	.05	.025	.01	.005
1	.0³157	.0²982	.00393	.0158	.0642	.148	.455	1.074	1.642	2.706	3.841	5.024	6.635	7.879
2	.0201	.0506	.103	.211	.446	.713	1.386	2.408	3.219	4.605	5.991	7.378	9.210	10.597
3	.115	.216	.352	.584	1.005	1.424	2.366	3.665	4.642	6.251	7.815	9.348	11.345	12.838
4	.297	.484	.711	1.064	1.649	2.195	3.357	4.878	5.989	7.779	9.488	11.143	13.277	14.860
5	.554	.831	1.145	1.610	2.343	3.000	4.351	6.064	7.289	9.236	11.070	12.832	15.086	16.750
6	.872	1.237	1.635	2.204	3.070	3.828	5.348	7.231	8.558	10.645	12.592	14.449	16.812	18.548
7	1.239	1.690	2.167	2.833	3.822	4.671	6.346	8.383	9.803	12.017	14.067	16.013	18.475	20.278
8	1.646	2.180	2.733	3.490	4.594	5.527	7.344	9.524	11.030	13.362	15.507	17.535	20.090	21.955
9	2.088	2.700	3.325	4.168	5.380	6.393	8.343	10.656	12.242	14.684	16.919	19.023	21.666	23.589
10	2.558	3.247	3.940	4.865	6.179	7.267	9.342	11.781	13.442	15.987	18.307	20.483	23.209	25.188
11	3.053	3.816	4.575	5.578	6.989	8.148	10.341	12.899	14.631	17.275	19.675	21.920	24.725	26.757
12	3.571	4.404	5.226	6.304	7.807	9.034	11.340	14.011	15.812	18.549	21.026	23.337	26.217	28.300
13	4.107	5.009	5.892	7.042	8.634	9.926	12.340	15.119	16.985	19.812	22.362	24.736	27.688	29.819
14	4.660	5.629	6.571	7.790	9.467	10.821	13.339	16.222	18.151	21.064	23.685	26.119	29.141	31.319
15	5.229	6.262	7.261	8.547	10.307	11.721	14.339	17.322	19.311	22.307	24.996	27.488	30.578	32.801
16	5.812	6.908	7.962	9.312	11.152	12.624	15.338	18.418	20.465	23.542	26.296	28.845	32.000	34.267
17	6.408	7.564	8.672	10.085	12.002	13.531	16.338	19.511	21.615	24.769	27.587	30.191	33.409	35.718
18	7.015	8.231	9.390	10.865	12.857	14.440	17.338	20.601	22.760	25.989	28.869	31.526	34.805	37.156
19	7.633	8.907	10.117	11.651	13.716	15.352	18.338	21.689	23.900	27.204	30.144	32.852	36.191	38.582
20	8.260	9.591	10.851	12.443	14.578	16.266	19.337	22.775	25.038	28.412	31.410	34.170	37.566	39.997

21	8.897	10.283	11.591	13.240	15.445	17.182	20.337	23.858	26.171	29.615	32.671	35.479	38.932	41.401
22	9.542	10.982	12.338	14.041	16.314	18.101	21.337	24.939	27.301	30.813	33.924	36.781	40.289	42.796
23	10.196	11.689	13.091	14.848	17.187	19.021	22.337	26.018	28.429	32.007	35.172	38.076	41.638	44.181
24	10.856	12.401	13.848	15.659	18.062	19.943	23.337	27.096	29.553	33.196	36.415	39.364	42.980	45.558
25	11.524	13.120	14.611	16.473	18.940	20.867	24.337	28.172	30.675	34.382	37.652	40.646	44.314	46.928
26	12.198	13.844	15.379	17.292	19.820	21.792	25.336	29.246	31.795	35.563	38.885	41.923	45.642	48.290
27	12.879	14.573	16.151	18.114	20.703	22.719	26.336	30.319	32.912	36.741	40.113	43.195	46.963	49.645
28	13.565	15.308	16.928	18.939	21.588	23.647	27.336	31.391	34.027	37.916	41.337	44.461	43.278	50.994
29	14.256	16.047	17.708	19.768	22.475	24.577	28.336	32.461	35.139	39.087	42.557	45.722	49.588	52.335
30	14.953	16.791	18.493	20.599	23.364	25.508	29.336	33.530	36.250	40.256	43.773	46.979	50.892	53.672
31	15.655	17.539	19.281	21.434	24.255	26.440	30.336	34.598	37.359	41.422	44.985	48.232	52.191	55.002
32	16.362	18.291	20.072	22.271	25.148	27.373	31.336	35.665	38.466	42.585	46.194	49.480	53.486	56.328
34	17.789	19.806	21.664	23.952	26.938	29.242	33.336	37.795	40.676	44.903	48.602	51.966	56.061	58.964
36	19.233	21.336	23.269	25.643	28.735	31.115	35.336	39.922	42.879	47.212	50.998	54.437	58.619	61.581
38	20.691	22.878	24.884	27.343	30.537	32.992	37.335	42.045	45.076	49.513	53.384	56.895	61.162	64.181
40	22.164	24.433	26.509	29.051	32.345	34.872	39.335	44.165	47.269	51.805	55.758	59.342	63.691	66.766
42	23.650	25.999	28.144	30.765	34.157	36.755	41.335	46.282	49.456	54.090	58.124	61.777	66.206	69.336
44	25.148	27.575	29.787	32.487	35.974	38.641	43.335	48.396	51.639	56.369	60.481	64.201	68.710	71.892
47	27.416	29.956	32.268	35.081	38.708	41.474	46.335	51.562	54.906	59.774	64.001	67.821	72.443	75.704
50	29.707	32.357	34.764	37.689	41.449	44.313	49.335	54.723	58.164	63.167	67.505	71.420	76.154	79.490

[a] Discussed in Section 17.3.

TABLE D.5 Upper Percentage Points of the *F* Distribution[a]

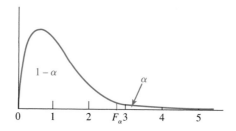

Degrees of Freedom for Denominator, ν_2	α	Degrees of Freedom for Numerator, ν_1											
		1	2	3	4	5	6	7	8	9	10	11	12
1	.25	5.83	7.50	8.20	8.58	8.82	8.98	9.10	9.19	9.26	9.32	9.36	9.41
	.10	39.9	49.5	53.6	55.8	57.2	58.2	58.9	59.4	59.9	60.2	60.5	60.7
	.05	161	200	216	225	230	234	237	239	241	242	243	244
2	.25	2.57	3.00	3.15	3.23	3.28	3.31	3.34	3.35	3.37	3.38	3.39	3.39
	.10	8.53	9.00	9.16	9.24	9.29	9.33	9.35	9.37	9.38	9.39	9.40	9.41
	.05	18.5	19.0	19.2	19.2	19.3	19.3	19.4	19.4	19.4	19.4	19.4	19.4
	.01	98.5	99.0	99.2	99.2	99.3	99.3	99.4	99.4	99.4	99.4	99.4	99.4
3	.25	2.02	2.28	2.36	2.39	2.41	2.42	2.43	2.44	2.44	2.44	2.45	2.45
	.10	5.54	5.46	5.39	5.34	5.31	5.28	5.27	5.25	5.24	5.23	5.22	5.22
	.05	10.1	9.55	9.28	9.12	9.01	8.94	8.89	8.85	8.81	8.79	8.76	8.74
	.01	34.1	30.8	29.5	28.7	28.2	27.9	27.7	27.5	27.3	27.2	27.1	27.1
4	.25	1.81	2.00	2.05	2.06	2.07	2.08	2.08	2.08	2.08	2.08	2.08	2.08
	.10	4.54	4.32	4.19	4.11	4.05	4.01	3.98	3.95	3.94	3.92	3.91	3.90
	.05	7.71	6.94	6.59	6.39	6.26	6.16	6.09	6.04	6.00	5.96	5.94	5.91
	.01	21.2	18.0	16.7	16.0	15.5	15.2	15.0	14.8	14.7	14.5	14.4	14.4
5	.25	1.69	1.85	1.88	1.89	1.89	1.89	1.89	1.89	1.89	1.89	1.89	1.89
	.10	4.06	3.78	3.62	3.52	3.45	3.40	3.37	3.34	3.32	3.30	3.28	3.27
	.05	6.61	5.79	5.41	5.19	5.05	4.95	4.88	4.82	4.77	4.74	4.71	4.68
	.01	16.3	13.3	12.1	11.4	11.0	10.7	10.5	10.3	10.2	10.1	9.96	9.89
6	.25	1.62	1.76	1.78	1.79	1.79	1.78	1.78	1.78	1.77	1.77	1.77	1.77
	.10	3.78	3.46	3.29	3.18	3.11	3.05	3.01	2.98	2.96	2.94	2.92	2.90
	.05	5.99	5.14	4.76	4.53	4.39	4.28	4.21	4.15	4.10	4.06	4.03	4.00
	.01	13.7	10.9	9.78	9.15	8.75	8.47	8.26	8.10	7.98	7.87	7.79	7.72
7	.25	1.57	1.70	1.72	1.72	1.71	1.71	1.70	1.70	1.69	1.69	1.69	1.68
	.10	3.59	3.26	3.07	2.96	2.88	2.83	2.78	2.75	2.72	2.70	2.68	2.67
	.05	5.59	4.74	4.35	4.12	3.97	3.87	3.79	3.73	3.68	3.64	3.60	3.57
	.01	12.2	9.55	8.45	7.85	7.46	7.19	6.99	6.84	6.72	6.62	6.54	6.47

Abridged from Table 19 in *Biometrika Tables for Statisticians*, Vol. 1 (3rd ed.), Oxford University Press, 1966. Edited by E.S. Pearson and H.O. Hartley. Copyright © 1966 by Biometrika Trust. Reproduced with permission by Biometrika Trust.
[a] Discussed in Section 14.2.

15	20	24	30	40	50	60	100	120	200	500	∞	α	ν_2
				Degrees of Freedom for Numerator, ν_1									Degrees of Freedom for Denominator,
9.49	9.58	9.63	9.67	9.71	9.74	9.76	9.78	9.80	9.82	9.84	9.85	.25	
61.2	61.7	62.0	62.3	62.5	62.7	62.8	63.0	63.1	63.2	63.3	63.3	.10	1
246	248	249	250	251	252	252	253	253	254	254	254	.05	
3.41	3.43	3.43	3.44	3.45	3.45	3.46	3.47	3.47	3.48	3.48	3.48	.25	
9.42	9.44	9.45	9.46	9.47	9.47	9.47	9.48	9.48	9.49	9.49	9.49	.10	2
19.4	19.4	19.5	19.5	19.5	19.5	19.5	19.5	19.5	19.5	19.5	19.5	.05	
99.4	99.4	99.5	99.5	99.5	99.5	99.5	99.5	99.5	99.5	99.5	99.5	.01	
2.46	2.46	2.46	2.47	2.47	2.47	2.47	2.47	2.47	2.47	2.47	2.47	.25	
5.20	5.18	5.18	5.17	5.16	5.15	5.15	5.14	5.14	5.14	5.14	5.13	.10	3
8.70	8.66	8.64	8.62	8.59	8.58	8.57	8.55	8.55	8.54	8.53	8.53	.05	
26.9	26.7	26.6	26.5	26.4	26.4	26.3	26.2	26.2	26.2	26.1	26.1	.01	
2.08	2.08	2.08	2.08	2.08	2.08	2.08	2.08	2.08	2.08	2.08	2.08	.25	
3.87	3.84	3.83	3.82	3.80	3.80	3.79	3.78	3.78	3.77	3.76	3.76	.10	4
5.86	5.80	5.77	5.75	5.72	5.70	5.69	5.66	5.66	5.65	5.64	5.63	.05	
14.2	14.0	13.9	13.8	13.7	13.7	13.7	13.6	13.6	13.5	13.5	13.5	.01	
1.89	1.88	1.88	1.88	1.88	1.88	1.87	1.87	1.87	1.87	1.87	1.87	.25	
3.24	3.21	3.19	3.17	3.16	3.15	3.14	3.13	3.12	3.12	3.11	3.10	.10	5
4.62	4.56	4.53	4.50	4.46	4.44	4.43	4.41	4.40	4.39	4.37	4.36	.05	
9.72	9.55	9.47	9.38	9.29	9.24	9.20	9.13	9.11	9.08	9.04	9.02	.01	
1.76	1.76	1.75	1.75	1.75	1.75	1.74	1.74	1.74	1.74	1.74	1.74	.25	
2.87	2.84	2.82	2.80	2.78	2.77	2.76	2.75	2.74	2.73	2.73	2.72	.10	6
3.94	3.87	3.84	3.81	3.77	3.75	3.74	3.71	3.70	3.69	3.68	3.67	.05	
7.56	7.40	7.31	7.23	7.14	7.09	7.06	6.99	6.97	6.93	6.90	6.88	.01	
1.68	1.67	1.67	1.66	1.66	1.66	1.65	1.65	1.65	1.65	1.65	1.65	.25	
2.63	2.59	2.58	2.56	2.54	2.52	2.51	2.50	2.49	2.48	2.48	2.47	.10	7
3.51	3.44	3.41	3.38	3.34	3.32	3.30	3.27	3.27	3.25	3.24	3.23	.05	
6.31	6.16	6.07	5.99	5.91	5.86	5.82	5.75	5.74	5.70	5.67	5.65	.01	

TABLE D.5   *(continued)*

Degrees of Freedom for Denominator, v_2	α	Degrees of Freedom for Numerator, v_1											
		1	2	3	4	5	6	7	8	9	10	11	12
8	.25	1.54	1.66	1.67	1.66	1.66	1.65	1.64	1.64	1.63	1.63	1.63	1.62
	.10	3.46	3.11	2.92	2.81	2.73	2.67	2.62	2.59	2.56	2.54	2.52	2.50
	.05	5.32	4.46	4.07	3.84	3.69	3.58	3.50	3.44	3.39	3.35	3.31	3.28
	.01	11.3	8.65	7.59	7.01	6.63	6.37	6.18	6.03	5.91	5.81	5.73	5.67
9	.25	1.51	1.62	1.63	1.63	1.62	1.61	1.60	1.60	1.59	1.59	1.58	1.58
	.10	3.36	3.01	2.81	2.69	2.61	2.55	2.51	2.47	2.44	2.42	2.40	2.38
	.05	5.12	4.26	3.86	3.63	3.48	3.37	3.29	3.23	3.18	3.14	3.10	3.07
	.01	10.6	8.02	6.99	6.42	6.06	5.80	5.61	5.47	5.35	5.26	5.18	5.11
10	.25	1.49	1.60	1.60	1.59	1.59	1.58	1.57	1.56	1.56	1.55	1.55	1.54
	.10	3.29	2.92	2.73	2.61	2.52	2.46	2.41	2.38	2.35	2.32	2.30	2.28
	.05	4.96	4.10	3.71	3.48	3.33	3.22	3.14	3.07	3.02	2.98	2.94	2.91
	.01	10.0	7.56	6.55	5.99	5.64	5.39	5.20	5.06	4.94	4.85	4.77	4.71
11	.25	1.47	1.58	1.58	1.57	1.56	1.55	1.54	1.53	1.53	1.52	1.52	1.51
	.10	3.23	2.86	2.66	2.54	2.45	2.39	2.34	2.30	2.27	2.25	2.23	2.21
	.05	4.84	3.98	3.59	3.36	3.20	3.09	3.01	2.95	2.90	2.85	2.82	2.79
	.01	9.65	7.21	6.22	5.67	5.32	5.07	4.89	4.74	4.63	4.54	4.46	4.40
12	.25	1.46	1.56	1.56	1.55	1.54	1.53	1.52	1.51	1.51	1.50	1.50	1.49
	.10	3.18	2.81	2.61	2.48	2.39	2.33	2.28	2.24	2.21	2.19	2.17	2.15
	.05	4.75	3.89	3.49	3.26	3.11	3.00	2.91	2.85	2.80	2.75	2.72	2.69
	.01	9.33	6.93	5.95	5.41	5.06	4.82	4.64	4.50	4.39	4.30	4.22	4.16
13	.25	1.45	1.55	1.55	1.53	1.52	1.51	1.50	1.49	1.49	1.48	1.47	1.47
	.10	3.14	2.76	2.56	2.43	2.35	2.28	2.23	2.20	2.16	2.14	2.12	2.10
	.05	4.67	3.81	3.41	3.18	3.03	2.92	2.83	2.77	2.71	2.67	2.63	2.60
	.01	9.07	6.70	5.74	5.21	4.86	4.62	4.44	4.30	4.19	4.10	4.02	3.96
14	.25	1.44	1.53	1.53	1.52	1.51	1.50	1.49	1.48	1.47	1.46	1.46	1.45
	.10	3.10	2.73	2.52	2.39	2.31	2.24	2.19	2.15	2.12	2.10	2.08	2.05
	.05	4.60	3.74	3.34	3.11	2.96	2.85	2.76	2.70	2.65	2.60	2.57	2.53
	.01	8.86	6.51	5.56	5.04	4.69	4.46	4.28	4.14	4.03	3.94	3.86	3.80
15	.25	1.43	1.52	1.52	1.51	1.49	1.48	1.47	1.46	1.46	1.45	1.44	1.44
	.10	3.07	2.70	2.49	2.36	2.27	2.21	2.16	2.12	2.09	2.06	2.04	2.02
	.05	4.54	3.68	3.29	3.06	2.90	2.79	2.71	2.64	2.59	2.54	2.51	2.48
	.01	8.68	6.36	5.42	4.89	4.56	4.32	4.14	4.00	3.89	3.80	3.73	3.67
16	.25	1.42	1.51	1.51	1.50	1.48	1.47	1.46	1.45	1.44	1.44	1.44	1.43
	.10	3.05	2.67	2.46	2.33	2.24	2.18	2.13	2.09	2.06	2.03	2.01	1.99
	.05	4.49	3.63	3.24	3.01	2.85	2.74	2.66	2.59	2.54	2.49	2.46	2.42
	.01	8.53	6.23	5.29	4.77	4.44	4.20	4.03	3.89	3.78	3.69	3.62	3.55

					Degrees of Freedom for Numerator, v_1								α	Degrees of Freedom for Denominator, v_2
15	20	24	30	40	50	60	100	120	200	500	∞			
1.62	1.61	1.60	1.60	1.59	1.59	1.59	1.58	1.58	1.58	1.58	1.58	.25	
2.46	2.42	2.40	2.38	2.36	2.35	2.34	2.32	2.32	2.31	2.30	2.29	.10	8
3.22	3.15	3.12	3.08	3.04	3.02	3.01	2.97	2.97	2.95	2.94	2.93	.05	
5.52	5.36	5.28	5.20	5.12	5.07	5.03	4.96	4.95	4.91	4.88	4.86	.01	
1.57	1.56	1.56	1.55	1.55	1.54	1.54	1.53	1.53	1.53	1.53	1.53	.25	
2.34	2.30	2.28	2.25	2.23	2.22	2.21	2.19	2.18	2.17	2.17	2.16	.10	9
3.01	2.94	2.90	2.86	2.83	2.80	2.79	2.76	2.75	2.73	2.72	2.71	.05	
4.96	4.81	4.73	4.65	4.57	4.52	4.48	4.42	4.40	4.36	4.33	4.31	.01	
1.53	1.52	1.52	1.51	1.51	1.50	1.50	1.49	1.49	1.49	1.48	1.48	.25	
2.24	2.20	2.18	2.16	2.13	2.12	2.11	2.09	2.08	2.07	2.06	2.06	.10	10
2.85	2.77	2.74	2.70	2.66	2.64	2.62	2.59	2.58	2.56	2.55	2.54	.05	
4.56	4.41	4.33	4.25	4.17	4.12	4.08	4.01	4.00	3.96	3.93	3.91	.01	
1.50	1.49	1.49	1.48	1.47	1.47	1.47	1.46	1.46	1.46	1.45	1.45	.25	
2.17	2.12	2.10	2.08	2.05	2.04	2.03	2.00	2.00	1.99	1.98	1.97	.10	11
2.72	2.65	2.61	2.57	2.53	2.51	2.49	2.46	2.45	2.43	2.42	2.40	.05	
4.25	4.10	4.02	3.94	3.86	3.81	3.78	3.71	3.69	3.66	3.62	3.60	.01	
1.48	1.47	1.46	1.45	1.45	1.44	1.44	1.43	1.43	1.43	1.42	1.42	.25	
2.10	2.06	2.04	2.01	1.99	1.97	1.96	1.94	1.93	1.92	1.91	1.90	.10	12
2.62	2.54	2.51	2.47	2.43	2.40	2.38	2.35	2.34	2.32	2.31	2.30	.05	
4.01	3.86	3.78	3.70	3.62	3.57	3.54	3.47	3.45	3.41	3.38	3.36	.01	
1.46	1.45	1.44	1.43	1.42	1.42	1.42	1.41	1.41	1.40	1.40	1.40	.25	
2.05	2.01	1.98	1.96	1.93	1.92	1.90	1.88	1.88	1.86	1.85	1.85	.10	13
2.53	2.46	2.42	2.38	2.34	2.31	2.30	2.26	2.25	2.23	2.22	2.21	.05	
3.82	3.66	3.59	3.51	3.43	3.38	3.34	3.27	3.25	3.22	3.19	3.17	.01	
1.44	1.43	1.42	1.41	1.41	1.40	1.40	1.39	1.39	1.39	1.38	1.38	.25	
2.01	1.96	1.94	1.91	1.89	1.87	1.86	1.83	1.83	1.82	1.80	1.80	.10	14
2.46	2.39	2.35	2.31	2.27	2.24	2.22	2.19	2.18	2.16	2.14	2.13	.05	
3.66	3.51	3.43	3.35	3.27	3.22	3.18	3.11	3.09	3.06	3.03	3.00	.01	
1.43	1.41	1.41	1.40	1.39	1.39	1.38	1.38	1.37	1.37	1.36	1.36	.25	
1.97	1.92	1.90	1.87	1.85	1.83	1.82	1.79	1.79	1.77	1.76	1.76	.10	15
2.40	2.33	2.29	2.25	2.20	2.18	2.16	2.12	2.11	2.10	2.08	2.07	.05	
3.52	3.37	3.29	3.21	3.13	3.08	3.05	2.98	2.96	2.92	2.89	2.87	.01	
1.41	1.40	1.39	1.38	1.37	1.37	1.36	1.36	1.35	1.35	1.34	1.34	.25	
1.94	1.89	1.87	1.84	1.81	1.79	1.78	1.76	1.75	1.74	1.73	1.72	.10	16
2.35	2.28	2.24	2.19	2.15	2.12	2.11	2.07	2.06	2.04	2.02	2.01	.05	
3.41	3.26	3.18	3.10	3.02	2.97	2.93	2.86	2.84	2.81	2.78	2.75	.01	

TABLE D.5   *(continued)*

Degrees of Freedom for Denominator, ν_2	α	Degrees of Freedom for Numerator, ν_1											
		1	2	3	4	5	6	7	8	9	10	11	12
17	.25	1.42	1.51	1.50	1.49	1.47	1.46	1.45	1.44	1.43	1.43	1.42	1.41
	.10	3.03	2.64	2.44	2.31	2.22	2.15	2.10	2.06	2.03	2.00	1.98	1.96
	.05	4.45	3.59	3.20	2.96	2.81	2.70	2.61	2.55	2.49	2.45	2.41	2.38
	.01	8.40	6.11	5.18	4.67	4.34	4.10	3.93	3.79	3.68	3.59	3.52	3.46
18	.25	1.41	1.50	1.49	1.48	1.46	1.45	1.44	1.43	1.42	1.42	1.41	1.40
	.10	3.01	2.62	2.42	2.29	2.20	2.13	2.08	2.04	2.00	1.98	1.96	1.93
	.05	4.41	3.55	3.16	2.93	2.77	2.66	2.58	2.51	2.46	2.41	2.37	2.34
	.01	8.29	6.01	5.09	4.58	4.25	4.01	3.84	3.71	3.60	3.51	3.43	3.37
19	.25	1.41	1.49	1.49	1.47	1.46	1.44	1.43	1.42	1.41	1.41	1.40	1.40
	.10	2.99	2.61	2.40	2.27	2.18	2.11	2.06	2.02	1.98	1.96	1.94	1.91
	.05	4.38	3.52	3.13	2.90	2.74	2.63	2.54	2.48	2.42	2.38	2.34	2.31
	.01	8.18	5.93	5.01	4.50	4.17	3.94	3.77	3.63	3.52	3.43	3.36	3.30
20	.25	1.40	1.49	1.48	1.46	1.45	1.44	1.43	1.42	1.41	1.40	1.39	1.39
	.10	2.97	2.59	2.38	2.25	2.16	2.09	2.04	2.00	1.96	1.94	1.92	1.89
	.05	4.35	3.49	3.10	2.87	2.71	2.60	2.51	2.45	2.39	2.35	2.31	2.28
	.01	8.10	5.85	4.94	4.43	4.10	3.87	3.70	3.56	3.46	3.37	3.29	3.23
22	.25	1.40	1.48	1.47	1.45	1.44	1.42	1.41	1.40	1.39	1.39	1.38	1.37
	.10	2.95	2.56	2.35	2.22	2.13	2.06	2.01	1.97	1.93	1.90	1.88	1.86
	.05	4.30	3.44	3.05	2.82	2.66	2.55	2.46	2.40	2.34	2.30	2.26	2.23
	.01	7.95	5.72	4.82	4.31	3.99	3.76	3.59	3.45	3.35	3.26	3.18	3.12
24	.25	1.39	1.47	1.46	1.44	1.43	1.41	1.40	1.39	1.38	1.38	1.37	1.36
	.10	2.93	2.54	2.33	2.19	2.10	2.04	1.98	1.94	1.91	1.88	1.85	1.83
	.05	4.26	3.40	3.01	2.78	2.62	2.51	2.42	2.36	2.30	2.25	2.21	2.18
	.01	7.82	5.61	4.72	4.22	3.90	3.67	3.50	3.36	3.26	3.17	3.09	3.03
26	.25	1.38	1.46	1.45	1.44	1.42	1.41	1.39	1.38	1.37	1.37	1.36	1.35
	.10	2.91	2.52	2.31	2.17	2.08	2.01	1.96	1.92	1.88	1.86	1.84	1.81
	.05	4.23	3.37	2.98	2.74	2.59	2.47	2.39	2.32	2.27	2.22	2.18	2.15
	.01	7.72	5.53	4.64	4.14	3.82	3.59	3.42	3.29	3.18	3.09	3.02	2.96
28	.25	1.38	1.46	1.45	1.43	1.41	1.40	1.39	1.38	1.37	1.36	1.35	1.34
	.10	2.89	2.50	2.29	2.16	2.06	2.00	1.94	1.90	1.87	1.84	1.81	1.79
	.05	4.20	3.34	2.95	2.71	2.56	2.45	2.36	2.29	2.24	2.19	2.15	2.12
	.01	7.64	5.45	4.57	4.07	3.75	3.53	3.36	3.23	3.12	3.03	2.96	2.90
30	.25	1.38	1.45	1.44	1.42	1.41	1.39	1.38	1.37	1.36	1.35	1.35	1.34
	.10	2.88	2.49	2.28	2.14	2.05	1.98	1.93	1.88	1.85	1.82	1.79	1.77
	.05	4.17	3.32	2.92	2.69	2.53	2.42	2.33	2.27	2.21	2.16	2.13	2.09
	.01	7.56	5.39	4.51	4.02	3.70	3.47	3.30	3.17	3.07	2.98	2.91	2.84

| | | | | Degrees of Freedom for Numerator, ν_1 | | | | | | | | | Degrees of Freedom for Denominator, |
15	20	24	30	40	50	60	100	120	200	500	∞	α	ν_2
1.40	1.39	1.38	1.37	1.36	1.35	1.35	1.34	1.34	1.34	1.33	1.33	.25	
1.91	1.86	1.84	1.81	1.78	1.76	1.75	1.73	1.72	1.71	1.69	1.69	.10	17
2.31	2.23	2.19	2.15	2.10	2.08	2.06	2.02	2.01	1.99	1.97	1.96	.05	
3.31	3.16	3.08	3.00	2.92	2.87	2.83	2.76	2.75	2.71	2.68	2.65	.01	
1.39	1.38	1.37	1.36	1.35	1.34	1.34	1.33	1.33	1.32	1.32	1.32	.25	
1.89	1.84	1.81	1.78	1.75	1.74	1.72	1.70	1.69	1.68	1.67	1.66	.10	18
2.27	2.19	2.15	2.11	2.06	2.04	2.02	1.98	1.97	1.95	1.93	1.92	.05	
3.23	3.08	3.00	2.92	2.84	2.78	2.75	2.68	2.66	2.62	2.59	2.57	.01	
1.38	1.37	1.36	1.35	1.34	1.33	1.33	1.32	1.32	1.31	1.31	1.30	.25	
1.86	1.81	1.79	1.76	1.73	1.71	1.70	1.67	1.67	1.65	1.64	1.63	.10	19
2.23	2.16	2.11	2.07	2.03	2.00	1.98	1.94	1.93	1.91	1.89	1.88	.05	
3.15	3.00	2.92	2.84	2.76	2.71	2.67	2.60	2.58	2.55	2.51	2.49	.01	
1.37	1.36	1.35	1.34	1.33	1.33	1.32	1.31	1.31	1.30	1.30	1.29	.25	
1.84	1.79	1.77	1.74	1.71	1.69	1.68	1.65	1.64	1.63	1.62	1.61	.10	20
2.20	2.12	2.08	2.04	1.99	1.97	1.95	1.91	1.90	1.88	1.86	1.84	.05	
3.09	2.94	2.86	2.78	2.69	2.64	2.61	2.54	2.52	2.48	2.44	2.42	.01	
1.36	1.34	1.33	1.32	1.31	1.31	1.30	1.30	1.30	1.29	1.29	1.28	.25	
1.81	1.76	1.73	1.70	1.67	1.65	1.64	1.61	1.60	1.59	1.58	1.57	.10	22
2.15	2.07	2.03	1.98	1.94	1.91	1.89	1.85	1.84	1.82	1.80	1.78	.05	
2.98	2.83	2.75	2.67	2.58	2.53	2.50	2.42	2.40	2.36	2.33	2.31	.01	
1.35	1.33	1.32	1.31	1.30	1.29	1.29	1.28	1.28	1.27	1.27	1.26	.25	
1.78	1.73	1.70	1.67	1.64	1.62	1.61	1.58	1.57	1.56	1.54	1.53	.10	24
2.11	2.03	1.98	1.94	1.89	1.86	1.84	1.80	1.79	1.77	1.75	1.73	.05	
2.89	2.74	2.66	2.58	2.49	2.44	2.40	2.33	2.31	2.27	2.24	2.21	.01	
1.34	1.32	1.31	1.30	1.29	1.28	1.28	1.26	1.26	1.26	1.25	1.25	.25	
1.76	1.71	1.68	1.65	1.61	1.59	1.58	1.55	1.54	1.53	1.51	1.50	.10	26
2.07	1.99	1.95	1.90	1.85	1.82	1.80	1.76	1.75	1.73	1.71	1.69	.05	
2.81	2.66	2.58	2.50	2.42	2.36	2.33	2.25	2.23	2.19	2.16	2.13	.01	
1.33	1.31	1.30	1.29	1.28	1.27	1.27	1.26	1.25	1.25	1.24	1.24	.25	
1.74	1.69	1.66	1.63	1.59	1.57	1.56	1.53	1.52	1.50	1.49	1.48	.10	28
2.04	1.96	1.91	1.87	1.82	1.79	1.77	1.73	1.71	1.69	1.67	1.65	.05	
2.75	2.60	2.52	2.44	2.35	2.30	2.26	2.19	2.17	2.13	2.09	2.06	.01	
1.32	1.30	1.29	1.28	1.27	1.26	1.26	1.25	1.24	1.24	1.23	1.23	.25	
1.72	1.67	1.64	1.61	1.57	1.55	1.54	1.51	1.50	1.48	1.47	1.46	.10	30
2.01	1.93	1.89	1.84	1.79	1.76	1.74	1.70	1.68	1.66	1.64	1.62	.05	
2.70	2.55	2.47	2.39	2.30	2.25	2.21	2.13	2.11	2.07	2.03	2.01	.01	

TABLE D.5 *(continued)*

Degrees of Freedom for Denominator, ν_2	α	Degrees of Freedom for Numerator, ν_1											
		1	2	3	4	5	6	7	8	9	10	11	12
40	.25	1.36	1.44	1.42	1.40	1.39	1.37	1.36	1.35	1.34	1.33	1.32	1.31
	.10	2.84	2.44	2.23	2.09	2.00	1.93	1.87	1.83	1.79	1.76	1.73	1.71
	.05	4.08	3.23	2.84	2.61	2.45	2.34	2.25	2.18	2.12	2.08	2.04	2.00
	.01	7.31	5.18	4.31	3.83	3.51	3.29	3.12	2.99	2.89	2.80	2.73	2.66
60	.25	1.35	1.42	1.41	1.38	1.37	1.35	1.33	1.32	1.31	1.30	1.29	1.29
	.10	2.79	2.39	2.18	2.04	1.95	1.87	1.82	1.77	1.74	1.71	1.68	1.66
	.05	4.00	3.15	2.76	2.53	2.37	2.25	2.17	2.10	2.04	1.99	1.95	1.92
	.01	7.08	4.98	4.13	3.65	3.34	3.12	2.95	2.82	2.72	2.63	2.56	2.50
120	.25	1.34	1.40	1.39	1.37	1.35	1.33	1.31	1.30	1.29	1.28	1.27	1.26
	.10	2.75	2.35	2.13	1.99	1.90	1.82	1.77	1.72	1.68	1.65	1.62	1.60
	.05	3.92	3.07	2.68	2.45	2.29	2.17	2.09	2.02	1.96	1.91	1.87	1.83
	.01	6.85	4.79	3.95	3.48	3.17	2.96	2.79	2.66	2.56	2.47	2.40	2.34
200	.25	1.33	1.39	1.38	1.36	1.34	1.32	1.31	1.29	1.28	1.27	1.26	1.25
	.10	2.73	2.33	2.11	1.97	1.88	1.80	1.75	1.70	1.66	1.63	1.60	1.57
	.05	3.89	3.04	2.65	2.42	2.26	2.14	2.06	1.98	1.93	1.88	1.84	1.80
	.01	6.76	4.71	3.88	3.41	3.11	2.89	2.73	2.60	2.50	2.41	2.34	2.27
∞	.25	1.32	1.39	1.37	1.35	1.33	1.31	1.29	1.28	1.27	1.25	1.24	1.24
	.10	2.71	2.30	2.08	1.94	1.85	1.77	1.72	1.67	1.63	1.60	1.57	1.55
	.05	3.84	3.00	2.60	2.37	2.21	2.10	2.01	1.94	1.88	1.83	1.79	1.75
	.01	6.63	4.61	3.78	3.32	3.02	2.80	2.64	2.51	2.41	2.32	2.25	2.18

				Degrees of Freedom for Numerator, ν_1								α	Degrees of Freedom for Denominator, ν_2
15	20	24	30	40	50	60	100	120	200	500	∞		
1.30	1.28	1.26	1.25	1.24	1.23	1.22	1.21	1.21	1.20	1.19	1.19	.25	
1.66	1.61	1.57	1.54	1.51	1.48	1.47	1.43	1.42	1.41	1.39	1.38	.10	40
1.92	1.84	1.79	1.74	1.69	1.66	1.64	1.59	1.58	1.55	1.53	1.51	.05	
2.52	2.37	2.29	2.20	2.11	2.06	2.02	1.94	1.92	1.87	1.83	1.80	.01	
1.27	1.25	1.24	1.22	1.21	1.20	1.19	1.17	1.17	1.16	1.15	1.15	.25	
1.60	1.54	1.51	1.48	1.44	1.41	1.40	1.36	1.35	1.33	1.31	1.29	.10	60
1.84	1.75	1.70	1.65	1.59	1.56	1.53	1.48	1.47	1.44	1.41	1.39	.05	
2.35	2.20	2.12	2.03	1.94	1.88	1.84	1.75	1.73	1.68	1.63	1.60	.01	
1.24	1.22	1.21	1.19	1.18	1.17	1.16	1.14	1.13	1.12	1.11	1.10	.25	
1.55	1.48	1.45	1.41	1.37	1.34	1.32	1.27	1.26	1.24	1.21	1.19	.10	120
1.75	1.66	1.61	1.55	1.50	1.46	1.43	1.37	1.35	1.32	1.28	1.25	.05	
2.19	2.03	1.95	1.86	1.76	1.70	1.66	1.56	1.53	1.48	1.42	1.38	.01	
1.23	1.21	1.20	1.18	1.16	1.14	1.12	1.11	1.10	1.09	1.08	1.06	.25	
1.52	1.46	1.42	1.38	1.34	1.31	1.28	1.24	1.22	1.20	1.17	1.14	.10	200
1.72	1.62	1.57	1.52	1.46	1.41	1.39	1.32	1.29	1.26	1.22	1.19	.05	
2.13	1.97	1.89	1.79	1.69	1.63	1.58	1.48	1.44	1.39	1.33	1.28	.01	
1.22	1.19	1.18	1.16	1.14	1.13	1.12	1.09	1.08	1.07	1.04	1.00	.25	
1.49	1.42	1.38	1.34	1.30	1.26	1.24	1.18	1.17	1.13	1.08	1.00	.10	∞
1.67	1.57	1.52	1.46	1.39	1.35	1.32	1.24	1.22	1.17	1.11	1.00	.05	
2.04	1.88	1.79	1.70	1.59	1.52	1.47	1.36	1.32	1.25	1.15	1.00	.01	

TABLE D.6   Critical Values of the Pearson r [a]

Degrees of Freedom, $\nu = n - 2$ [b]	Level of Significance for a One-Tailed Test			
	.05	.025	.01	.005
	Level of Significance for a Two-Tailed Test			
	.10	.05	.02	.01
1	0.988	0.997	0.9995	0.9999
2	0.900	0.950	0.980	0.990
3	0.805	0.878	0.934	0.959
4	0.729	0.811	0.882	0.917
5	0.669	0.754	0.833	0.874
6	0.622	0.707	0.789	0.834
7	0.582	0.666	0.750	0.798
8	0.549	0.632	0.716	0.765
9	0.521	0.602	0.685	0.735
10	0.497	0.576	0.658	0.708
11	0.476	0.553	0.634	0.684
12	0.458	0.532	0.612	0.661
13	0.441	0.514	0.592	0.641
14	0.426	0.497	0.574	0.623
15	0.412	0.482	0.558	0.606
16	0.400	0.468	0.542	0.590
17	0.389	0.456	0.528	0.575
18	0.378	0.444	0.516	0.561
19	0.369	0.433	0.503	0.549
20	0.360	0.423	0.492	0.537
21	0.352	0.413	0.482	0.526
22	0.344	0.404	0.472	0.515
23	0.337	0.396	0.462	0.505
24	0.330	0.388	0.453	0.496
25	0.323	0.381	0.445	0.487
26	0.317	0.374	0.437	0.479
27	0.311	0.367	0.430	0.471
28	0.306	0.361	0.423	0.463
29	0.301	0.355	0.416	0.456
30	0.296	0.349	0.409	0.449
35	0.275	0.325	0.381	0.418
40	0.257	0.304	0.358	0.393
45	0.243	0.288	0.338	0.372
50	0.231	0.273	0.322	0.354
60	0.211	0.250	0.295	0.325
70	0.195	0.232	0.274	0.302
80	0.183	0.217	0.256	0.283
90	0.173	0.205	0.242	0.267
100	0.164	0.195	0.230	0.254
120	0.150	0.178	0.210	0.232
150	0.134	0.159	0.189	0.208
200	0.116	0.138	0.164	0.181
300	0.095	0.113	0.134	0.148
400	0.082	0.098	0.116	0.128
500	0.073	0.088	0.104	0.115

From Table VII of *Statistical Tables for Biological, Agricultural and Medical Research* 6e, by R.A. Fisher and F. Yates, Pearson Education Limited. Reproduced by permission of Pearson Education Limited.

[a] Discussed in Section 12.3.

[b] n is the number of paired X and Y scores.

TABLE D.7 Transformation of r to Z' [a]

r	Z'	r	Z'	r	Z'	r	Z'	r	Z'
0.000	0.000	0.200	0.203	0.400	0.424	0.600	0.693	0.800	1.099
0.005	0.005	0.205	0.208	0.405	0.430	0.605	0.701	0.805	1.113
0.010	0.010	0.210	0.213	0.410	0.436	0.610	0.709	0.810	1.127
0.015	0.015	0.215	0.218	0.415	0.442	0.615	0.717	0.815	1.142
0.020	0.020	0.220	0.224	0.420	0.448	0.620	0.725	0.820	1.157
0.025	0.025	0.225	0.229	0.425	0.454	0.625	0.733	0.825	1.172
0.030	0.030	0.230	0.234	0.430	0.460	0.630	0.741	0.830	1.188
0.035	0.035	0.235	0.239	0.435	0.466	0.635	0.750	0.835	1.204
0.040	0.040	0.240	0.245	0.440	0.472	0.640	0.758	0.840	1.221
0.045	0.045	0.245	0.250	0.445	0.478	0.645	0.767	0.845	1.238
0.050	0.050	0.250	0.255	0.450	0.485	0.650	0.775	0.850	1.256
0.055	0.055	0.255	0.261	0.455	0.491	0.655	0.784	0.855	1.274
0.060	0.060	0.260	0.266	0.460	0.497	0.660	0.793	0.860	1.293
0.065	0.065	0.265	0.271	0.465	0.504	0.665	0.802	0.865	1.313
0.070	0.070	0.270	0.277	0.470	0.510	0.670	0.811	0.870	1.333
0.075	0.075	0.275	0.282	0.475	0.517	0.675	0.820	0.875	1.354
0.080	0.080	0.280	0.288	0.480	0.523	0.680	0.829	0.880	1.376
0.085	0.085	0.285	0.293	0.485	0.530	0.685	0.838	0.885	1.398
0.090	0.090	0.290	0.299	0.490	0.536	0.690	0.848	0.890	1.422
0.095	0.095	0.295	0.304	0.495	0.543	0.695	0.858	0.895	1.447
0.100	0.100	0.300	0.310	0.500	0.549	0.700	0.867	0.900	1.472
0.105	0.105	0.305	0.315	0.505	0.556	0.705	0.877	0.905	1.499
0.110	0.110	0.310	0.321	0.510	0.563	0.710	0.887	0.910	1.528
0.115	0.116	0.315	0.326	0.515	0.570	0.715	0.897	0.915	1.557
0.120	0.121	0.320	0.332	0.520	0.576	0.720	0.908	0.920	1.589
0.125	0.126	0.325	0.337	0.525	0.583	0.725	0.918	0.925	1.623
0.130	0.131	0.330	0.343	0.530	0.590	0.730	0.929	0.930	1.658
0.135	0.136	0.335	0.348	0.535	0.597	0.735	0.940	0.935	1.697
0.140	0.141	0.340	0.354	0.540	0.604	0.740	0.950	0.940	1.738
0.145	0.146	0.345	0.360	0.545	0.611	0.745	0.962	0.945	1.783
0.150	0.151	0.350	0.365	0.550	0.618	0.750	0.973	0.950	1.832
0.155	0.156	0.355	0.371	0.555	0.626	0.755	0.984	0.955	1.886
0.160	0.161	0.360	0.377	0.560	0.633	0.760	0.996	0.960	1.946
0.165	0.167	0.365	0.383	0.565	0.640	0.765	1.008	0.965	2.014
0.170	0.172	0.370	0.388	0.570	0.648	0.770	1.020	0.970	2.092
0.175	0.177	0.375	0.394	0.575	0.655	0.775	1.033	0.975	2.185
0.180	0.182	0.380	0.400	0.580	0.662	0.780	1.045	0.980	2.298
0.185	0.187	0.385	0.406	0.585	0.670	0.785	1.058	0.985	2.443
0.190	0.192	0.390	0.412	0.590	0.678	0.790	1.071	0.990	2.647
0.195	0.198	0.395	0.418	0.595	0.685	0.795	1.085	0.995	2.994

From Table VIIi of *Statistical Tables for Biological, Agricultural and Medical Research* 6e, by R.A. Fisher and F. Yates, Pearson Education Limited. Reproduced by permission of Pearson Education Limited.
[a]Discussed in Section 12.3.

TABLE D.8   Approximate *n* Required for Testing Hypotheses about Means[a]

<table>
<tr><th colspan="8" align="center">One-Sample Test</th></tr>
<tr><th rowspan="2">Effect Size,
d</th><th rowspan="2">α</th><th colspan="3" align="center">One-Sided
Hypothesis,
$1 - \beta$</th><th colspan="3" align="center">Two-Sided
Hypothesis,
$1 - \beta$</th></tr>
<tr><th>.80</th><th>.90</th><th>.95</th><th>.80</th><th>.90</th><th>.95</th></tr>
<tr><td>0.2</td><td>.05</td><td>156</td><td>215</td><td>272</td><td>198</td><td>264</td><td>326</td></tr>
<tr><td></td><td>.01</td><td>253</td><td>328</td><td>396</td><td>294</td><td>374</td><td>447</td></tr>
<tr><td>0.5</td><td>.05</td><td>27</td><td>36</td><td>45</td><td>34</td><td>44</td><td>54</td></tr>
<tr><td></td><td>.01</td><td>43</td><td>55</td><td>66</td><td>51</td><td>63</td><td>75</td></tr>
<tr><td>0.8</td><td>.05</td><td>12</td><td>15</td><td>19</td><td>15</td><td>19</td><td>22</td></tr>
<tr><td></td><td>.01</td><td>19</td><td>24</td><td>28</td><td>22</td><td>27</td><td>32</td></tr>
</table>

<table>
<tr><th>Effect Size,
d</th><th>α</th><th colspan="6" align="center">Two-Sample Test (Independent Samples)</th></tr>
<tr><td>0.2</td><td>.05</td><td>310</td><td>429</td><td>542</td><td>393</td><td>526</td><td>651</td></tr>
<tr><td></td><td>.01</td><td>503</td><td>652</td><td>790</td><td>586</td><td>746</td><td>892</td></tr>
<tr><td>0.5</td><td>.05</td><td>50</td><td>69</td><td>87</td><td>64</td><td>85</td><td>105</td></tr>
<tr><td></td><td>.01</td><td>82</td><td>105</td><td>128</td><td>95</td><td>120</td><td>144</td></tr>
<tr><td>0.8</td><td>.05</td><td>21</td><td>27</td><td>35</td><td>26</td><td>34</td><td>42</td></tr>
<tr><td></td><td>.01</td><td>33</td><td>42</td><td>51</td><td>38</td><td>48</td><td>57</td></tr>
</table>

<table>
<tr><th>Effect Size,
d</th><th>α</th><th colspan="7" align="center">Two-Sample Test (Dependent Samples)</th></tr>
<tr><td></td><td></td><td>ρ</td><td></td><td></td><td></td><td></td><td></td><td></td></tr>
<tr><td>0.2</td><td>.05</td><td>0.4</td><td>187</td><td>258</td><td>326</td><td>237</td><td>317</td><td>391</td></tr>
<tr><td></td><td></td><td>0.5</td><td>156</td><td>215</td><td>272</td><td>198</td><td>264</td><td>326</td></tr>
<tr><td></td><td></td><td>0.6</td><td>125</td><td>172</td><td>218</td><td>159</td><td>212</td><td>261</td></tr>
<tr><td></td><td></td><td>0.7</td><td>94</td><td>130</td><td>164</td><td>119</td><td>159</td><td>197</td></tr>
<tr><td></td><td></td><td>0.8</td><td>63</td><td>87</td><td>109</td><td>80</td><td>107</td><td>131</td></tr>
<tr><td></td><td></td><td>0.9</td><td>32</td><td>44</td><td>55</td><td>41</td><td>54</td><td>66</td></tr>
</table>

[a]Discussed in Sections 10.4, 13.2, and 13.4. Table D. 8 was prepared by Roger E. Kirk. For the two-sample test (independent samples), it is assumed that $\sigma_1^2 = \sigma_2^2$ and $n_1 = n_2$; the values in the table are for each of the samples. If dependent samples are used, the values in the table are for the number of pairs of dependent elements.

			Two-Sample Test (Dependent Samples)					
			One-Sided Hypothesis, $1-\beta$			Two-Sided Hypothesis, $1-\beta$		
Effect Size, d	α		.80	.90	.95	.80	.90	.95
		ρ						
0.2	.01	0.4	303	393	475	353	449	537
		0.5	253	328	396	294	374	447
		0.6	203	262	317	236	300	358
		0.7	153	197	239	177	225	269
		0.8	102	132	160	119	151	180
		0.9	52	67	81	60	76	91
0.5	.05	0.4	31	42	53	39	52	63
		0.5	26	35	44	33	44	53
		0.6	21	29	36	27	35	43
		0.7	16	22	27	20	27	33
		0.8	11	15	19	14	18	22
		0.9	6	8	10	8	10	12
	.01	0.4	50	65	78	58	73	88
		0.5	42	54	65	49	62	73
		0.6	34	44	52	39	50	59
		0.7	26	33	40	30	38	45
		0.8	18	23	27	21	26	31
		0.9	10	12	15	11	14	16
0.8	.05	0.4	13	17	21	16	21	26
		0.5	11	15	18	13	18	22
		0.6	9	12	15	11	15	18
		0.7	7	9	11	9	11	14
		0.8	5	7	8	6	8	10
		0.9	3	4	5	4	5	6
	.01	0.4	21	26	32	24	30	35
		0.5	18	22	27	20	25	30
		0.6	15	18	22	17	21	24
		0.7	11	14	17	13	16	19
		0.8	8	10	12	9	11	13
		0.9	5	6	7	6	7	8

TABLE D.9 Percentage Points of the Studentized Range Distribution[a]

Error df	α	Number of Means (p)									
		2	3	4	5	6	7	8	9	10	11
2	.05	6.08	8.33	9.80	10.9	11.7	12.4	13.0	13.5	14.0	14.4
	.01	14.0	19.0	22.3	24.7	26.6	28.2	29.5	30.7	31.7	32.6
3	.05	4.50	5.91	6.82	7.50	8.04	8.48	8.85	9.18	9.46	9.72
	.01	8.26	10.6	12.2	13.3	14.2	15.0	15.6	16.2	16.7	17.8
4	.05	3.93	5.04	5.76	6.29	6.71	7.05	7.35	7.60	7.83	8.03
	.01	6.51	8.12	9.17	9.96	10.6	11.1	11.5	11.9	12.3	12.6
5	.05	3.64	4.60	5.22	5.67	6.03	6.33	6.58	6.80	6.99	7.17
	.01	5.70	6.98	7.80	8.42	8.91	9.32	9.67	9.97	10.24	10.48
6	.05	3.46	4.34	4.90	5.30	5.63	5.90	6.12	6.32	6.49	6.65
	.01	5.24	6.33	7.03	7.56	7.97	8.32	8.61	8.87	9.10	9.30
7	.05	3.34	4.16	4.68	5.06	5.36	5.61	5.82	6.00	6.16	6.30
	.01	4.95	5.92	6.54	7.01	7.37	7.68	7.94	8.17	8.37	8.55
8	.05	3.26	4.04	4.53	4.89	5.17	5.40	5.60	5.77	5.92	6.05
	.01	4.75	5.64	6.20	6.62	6.96	7.24	7.47	7.68	7.86	8.03
9	.05	3.20	3.95	4.41	4.76	5.02	5.24	5.43	5.59	5.74	5.87
	.01	4.60	5.43	5.96	6.35	6.66	6.91	7.13	7.33	7.49	7.65
10	.05	3.15	3.88	4.33	4.65	4.91	5.12	5.30	5.46	5.60	5.72
	.01	4.48	5.27	5.77	6.14	6.43	6.67	6.87	7.05	7.21	7.36
11	.05	3.11	3.82	4.26	4.57	4.82	5.03	5.20	5.35	5.49	5.61
	.01	4.39	5.15	5.62	5.97	6.25	6.48	6.67	6.84	6.99	7.13
12	.05	3.08	3.77	4.20	4.51	4.75	4.95	5.12	5.27	5.39	5.51
	.01	4.32	5.05	5.50	5.84	6.10	6.32	6.51	6.67	6.81	6.94
13	.05	3.06	3.73	4.15	4.45	4.69	4.88	5.05	5.19	5.32	5.43
	.01	4.26	4.96	5.40	5.73	5.98	6.19	6.37	6.53	6.67	6.79
14	.05	3.03	3.70	4.11	4.41	4.64	4.83	4.99	5.13	5.25	5.36
	.01	4.21	4.89	5.32	5.63	5.88	6.08	6.26	6.41	6.54	6.66
15	.05	3.01	3.67	4.08	4.37	4.59	4.78	4.94	5.08	5.20	5.31
	.01	4.17	4.84	5.25	5.56	5.80	5.99	6.16	6.31	6.44	6.55
16	.05	3.00	3.65	4.05	4.33	4.56	4.74	4.90	5.03	5.15	5.26
	.01	4.13	4.79	5.19	5.49	5.72	5.92	6.08	6.22	6.35	6.46
17	.05	2.98	3.63	4.02	4.30	4.52	4.70	4.86	4.99	5.11	5.21
	.01	4.10	4.74	5.14	5.43	5.66	5.85	6.01	6.15	6.27	6.38
18	.05	2.97	3.61	4.00	4.28	4.49	4.67	4.82	4.96	5.07	5.17
	.01	4.07	4.70	5.09	5.38	5.60	5.79	5.94	6.08	6.20	6.31
19	.05	2.96	3.59	3.98	4.25	4.47	4.65	4.79	4.92	5.04	5.14
	.01	4.05	4.67	5.05	5.33	5.55	5.73	5.89	6.02	6.14	6.25
20	.05	2.95	3.58	3.96	4.23	4.45	4.62	4.77	4.90	5.01	5.11
	.01	4.02	4.64	5.02	5.29	5.51	5.69	5.84	5.97	6.09	6.19
24	.05	2.92	3.53	3.90	4.17	4.37	4.54	4.68	4.81	4.92	5.01
	.01	3.96	4.55	4.91	5.17	5.37	5.54	5.69	5.81	5.92	6.02
30	.05	2.89	3.49	3.85	4.10	4.30	4.46	4.60	4.72	4.82	4.92
	.01	3.89	4.45	4.80	5.05	5.24	5.40	5.54	5.65	5.76	5.85
40	.05	2.86	3.44	3.79	4.04	4.23	4.39	4.52	4.63	4.73	4.82
	.01	3.82	4.37	4.70	4.93	5.11	5.26	5.39	5.50	5.60	5.69
60	.05	2.83	3.40	3.74	3.98	4.16	4.31	4.44	4.55	4.65	4.73
	.01	3.76	4.28	4.59	4.82	4.99	5.13	5.25	5.36	5.45	5.53
120	.05	2.80	3.36	3.68	3.92	4.10	4.24	4.36	4.47	4.56	4.64
	.01	3.70	4.20	4.50	4.71	4.87	5.01	5.12	5.21	5.30	5.37
∞	.05	2.77	3.31	3.63	3.86	4.03	4.17	4.29	4.39	4.47	4.55
	.01	3.64	4.12	4.40	4.60	4.76	4.88	4.99	5.08	5.16	5.23

[a] Discussed in Section 15.6.

				Number of Means (p)						Error
12	13	14	15	16	17	18	19	20	α	df
14.7	15.1	15.4	15.7	15.9	16.1	16.4	16.6	16.8	.05	2
33.4	34.1	34.8	35.4	36.0	36.5	37.0	37.5	37.9	.01	
9.72	10.2	10.3	10.5	10.7	10.8	11.0	11.1	11.2	.05	3
17.5	17.9	18.2	18.5	18.8	19.1	19.3	19.5	19.8	.01	
8.21	8.37	8.52	8.66	8.79	8.91	9.03	9.13	9.23	.05	4
12.8	13.1	13.3	13.5	13.7	13.9	14.1	14.2	14.4	.01	
7.32	7.47	7.60	7.72	7.83	7.93	8.03	8.12	8.21	.05	5
10.70	10.89	11.08	11.24	11.40	11.55	11.68	11.81	11.93	.01	
6.79	6.92	7.03	7.14	7.24	7.34	7.43	7.51	7.59	.05	6
9.48	9.65	9.81	9.95	10.08	10.21	10.32	10.43	10.54	.01	
6.43	6.55	6.66	6.76	6.85	6.94	7.02	7.10	7.17	.05	7
8.71	8.86	9.00	9.12	9.24	9.35	9.46	9.55	9.65	.01	
6.18	6.29	6.39	6.48	6.57	6.65	6.73	6.80	6.87	.05	8
8.18	8.31	8.44	8.55	8.66	8.76	8.85	8.94	9.03	.01	
5.98	6.09	6.19	6.28	6.36	6.44	6.51	6.58	6.64	.05	9
7.78	7.91	8.03	8.13	8.23	8.33	8.41	8.49	8.57	.01	
5.83	5.93	6.03	6.11	6.19	6.27	6.34	6.40	6.47	.05	10
7.49	7.60	7.71	7.81	7.91	7.99	8.08	8.15	8.23	.01	
5.71	5.81	5.90	5.98	6.06	6.13	6.20	6.27	6.33	.05	11
7.25	7.36	7.46	7.56	7.65	7.73	7.81	7.88	7.95	.01	
5.61	5.71	5.80	5.88	5.95	6.02	6.09	6.15	6.21	.05	12
7.06	7.17	7.26	7.36	7.44	7.52	7.59	7.66	7.73	.01	
5.53	5.63	5.71	5.79	5.86	5.93	5.99	6.05	6.11	.05	13
6.90	7.01	7.10	7.19	7.27	7.35	7.42	7.48	7.55	.01	
5.46	5.55	5.64	5.71	5.79	5.85	5.91	5.97	6.03	.05	14
6.77	6.87	6.96	7.05	7.13	7.20	7.27	7.33	7.39	.01	
5.40	5.49	5.57	5.65	5.72	5.78	5.85	5.90	5.96	.05	15
6.66	6.76	6.84	6.93	7.00	7.07	7.14	7.20	7.26	.01	
5.35	5.44	5.52	5.59	5.66	5.73	5.79	5.84	5.90	.05	16
6.56	6.66	6.74	6.82	6.90	6.97	7.03	7.09	7.15	.01	
5.31	5.39	5.47	5.54	5.61	5.67	5.73	5.79	5.84	.05	17
6.48	6.57	6.66	6.73	6.81	6.87	6.94	7.00	7.05	.01	
5.27	5.35	5.43	5.50	5.57	5.63	5.69	5.74	5.79	.05	18
6.41	6.50	6.58	6.65	6.73	6.79	6.85	6.91	6.97	.01	
5.23	5.31	5.39	5.46	5.53	5.59	5.65	5.70	5.75	.05	19
6.34	6.43	6.51	6.58	6.65	6.72	6.78	6.84	6.89	.01	
5.20	5.28	5.36	5.43	5.49	5.55	5.61	5.66	5.71	.05	20
6.28	6.37	6.45	6.52	6.59	6.65	6.71	6.77	6.82	.01	
5.10	5.18	5.25	5.32	5.38	5.44	5.49	5.55	5.59	.05	24
6.11	6.19	6.26	6.33	6.39	6.45	6.51	6.56	6.61	.01	
5.00	5.08	5.15	5.21	5.27	5.33	5.38	5.43	5.47	.05	30
5.93	6.01	6.08	6.14	6.20	6.26	6.31	6.36	6.41	.01	
4.90	4.98	5.04	5.11	5.16	5.22	5.27	5.31	5.36	.05	40
5.76	5.83	5.90	5.96	6.02	6.07	6.12	6.16	6.21	.01	
4.81	4.88	4.94	5.00	5.06	5.11	5.15	5.20	5.24	.05	60
5.60	5.67	5.73	5.78	5.84	5.89	5.93	5.97	6.01	.01	
4.71	4.78	4.84	4.90	4.95	5.00	5.04	5.09	5.13	.05	120
5.44	5.50	5.56	5.61	5.66	5.71	5.75	5.79	5.83	.01	
4.62	4.68	4.74	4.80	4.85	4.89	4.93	4.97	5.01	.05	∞
5.29	5.35	5.40	5.45	5.49	5.54	5.57	5.61	5.65	.01	

TABLE D.10   Critical Values of the Mann-Whitney U Statistic[a]

For a one-tailed test at $\alpha = .01$ (roman type) and $\alpha = .005$ (boldface type) and for a two-tailed test at $\alpha = .02$ (roman type) and $\alpha = .01$ (boldface type)

n_2 \ n_1	1	2	3	4	5	6	7	8	9	10	11	12	13	14	15	16	17	18	19	20
1	—[b]	—	—	—	—	—	—	—	—	—	—	—	—	—	—	—	—	—	—	—
	—	—	—	—	—	—	—	—	—	—	—	—	—	—	—	—	—	—	—	—
2	—	—	—	—	—	—	—	—	—	—	—	—	0	0	0	0	0	0	1	1
	—	—	—	—	—	—	—	—	—	—	—	—	—	—	—	—	—	—	**0**	**0**
3	—	—	—	—	—	—	0	0	1	1	1	2	2	2	3	3	4	4	4	5
	—	—	—	—	—	—	—	—	**0**	**0**	**0**	**1**	**1**	**1**	**2**	**2**	**2**	**2**	**3**	**3**
4	—	—	—	—	0	1	1	2	3	3	4	5	5	6	7	7	8	9	9	10
	—	—	—	—	—	**0**	**0**	**1**	**1**	**2**	**2**	**3**	**3**	**4**	**5**	**5**	**6**	**6**	**7**	**8**
5	—	—	—	0	1	2	3	4	5	6	7	8	9	10	11	12	13	14	15	16
	—	—	—	—	**0**	**1**	**1**	**2**	**3**	**4**	**5**	**6**	**7**	**7**	**8**	**9**	**10**	**11**	**12**	**13**
6	—	—	—	1	2	3	4	6	7	8	9	11	12	13	15	16	18	19	20	22
	—	—	—	**0**	**1**	**2**	**3**	**4**	**5**	**6**	**7**	**9**	**10**	**11**	**12**	**13**	**15**	**16**	**17**	**18**
7	—	—	0	1	3	4	6	7	9	11	12	14	16	17	19	21	23	24	26	28
	—	—	—	**0**	**1**	**3**	**4**	**6**	**7**	**9**	**10**	**12**	**13**	**15**	**16**	**18**	**19**	**21**	**22**	**24**
8	—	—	0	2	4	6	7	9	11	13	15	17	20	22	24	26	28	30	32	34
	—	—	—	**1**	**2**	**4**	**6**	**7**	**9**	**11**	**13**	**15**	**17**	**18**	**20**	**22**	**24**	**26**	**28**	**30**
9	—	—	1	3	5	7	9	11	14	16	18	21	23	26	28	31	33	36	38	40
	—	—	**0**	**1**	**3**	**5**	**7**	**9**	**11**	**13**	**16**	**18**	**20**	**22**	**24**	**27**	**29**	**31**	**33**	**36**
10	—	—	1	3	6	8	11	13	16	19	22	24	27	30	33	36	38	41	44	47
	—	—	**0**	**2**	**4**	**6**	**9**	**11**	**13**	**16**	**18**	**21**	**24**	**26**	**29**	**31**	**34**	**37**	**39**	**42**
11	—	—	1	4	7	9	12	15	18	22	25	28	31	34	37	41	44	47	50	53
	—	—	**0**	**2**	**5**	**7**	**10**	**13**	**16**	**18**	**21**	**24**	**27**	**30**	**33**	**36**	**39**	**42**	**45**	**48**
12	—	—	2	5	8	11	14	17	21	24	28	31	35	38	42	46	49	53	56	60
	—	—	**1**	**3**	**6**	**9**	**12**	**15**	**18**	**21**	**24**	**27**	**31**	**34**	**37**	**41**	**44**	**47**	**51**	**54**
13	—	0	2	5	9	12	16	20	23	27	31	35	39	43	47	51	55	59	63	67
	—	—	**1**	**3**	**7**	**10**	**13**	**17**	**20**	**24**	**27**	**31**	**34**	**38**	**42**	**45**	**49**	**53**	**56**	**60**
14	—	0	2	6	10	13	17	22	26	30	34	38	43	47	51	56	60	65	69	73
	—	—	**1**	**4**	**7**	**11**	**15**	**18**	**22**	**26**	**30**	**34**	**38**	**42**	**46**	**50**	**54**	**58**	**63**	**67**
15	—	0	3	7	11	15	19	24	28	33	37	42	47	51	56	61	66	70	75	80
	—	—	**2**	**5**	**8**	**12**	**16**	**20**	**24**	**29**	**33**	**37**	**42**	**46**	**51**	**55**	**60**	**64**	**69**	**73**
16	—	0	3	7	12	16	21	26	31	36	41	46	51	56	61	66	71	76	82	87
	—	—	**2**	**5**	**9**	**13**	**18**	**22**	**27**	**31**	**36**	**41**	**45**	**50**	**55**	**60**	**65**	**70**	**74**	**79**
17	—	0	4	8	13	18	23	28	33	38	44	49	55	60	66	71	77	82	88	93
	—	—	**2**	**6**	**10**	**15**	**19**	**24**	**29**	**34**	**39**	**44**	**49**	**54**	**60**	**65**	**70**	**75**	**81**	**86**
18	—	0	4	9	14	19	24	30	36	41	47	53	59	65	70	76	82	88	94	100
	—	—	**2**	**6**	**11**	**16**	**21**	**26**	**31**	**37**	**42**	**47**	**53**	**58**	**64**	**70**	**75**	**81**	**87**	**92**
19	—	1	4	9	15	20	26	32	38	44	50	56	63	69	75	82	88	94	101	107
	—	**0**	**3**	**7**	**12**	**17**	**22**	**28**	**33**	**39**	**45**	**51**	**56**	**63**	**69**	**74**	**81**	**87**	**93**	**99**
20	—	1	5	10	16	22	28	34	40	47	53	60	67	73	80	87	93	100	107	114
	—	**0**	**3**	**8**	**13**	**18**	**24**	**30**	**36**	**42**	**48**	**54**	**60**	**67**	**73**	**79**	**86**	**92**	**99**	**105**

[a] Discussed in Section 18.3. Table D.10 was prepared by Roger E. Kirk. To be significant for any given n_1 and n_2, the observed U must be *equal to* or *less than* the value shown in the table.

[b] Dashes in the body of the table indicate that no decision is possible at the stated level of significance.

Critical values for a one-tailed test at $\alpha = .05$ (roman type) and $\alpha = .025$ (boldface type) and for a two-tailed test at $\alpha = .10$ (roman type) and $\alpha = .05$ (boldface type)

n_2	n_1=1	2	3	4	5	6	7	8	9	10	11	12	13	14	15	16	17	18	19	20
1	—	—	—	—	—	—	—	—	—	—	—	—	—	—	—	—	—	—	0	0
	—	—	—	—	—	—	—	—	—	—	—	—	—	—	—	—	—	—	—	—
2	—	—	—	—	0	0	0	1	1	1	1	2	2	2	3	3	3	4	4	4
	—	—	—	—	—	—	—	**0**	**0**	**0**	**0**	**1**	**1**	**1**	**1**	**1**	**2**	**2**	**2**	**2**
3	—	—	0	0	1	2	2	3	3	4	5	5	6	7	7	8	9	9	10	11
	—	—	—	**0**	**1**	**1**	**2**	**2**	**3**	**3**	**4**	**4**	**5**	**5**	**6**	**6**	**7**	**7**	**7**	**8**
4	—	—	0	1	2	3	4	5	6	7	8	9	10	11	12	14	15	16	17	18
	—	—	—	**0**	**1**	**2**	**3**	**4**	**4**	**5**	**6**	**7**	**8**	**9**	**10**	**11**	**11**	**12**	**13**	**13**
5	—	0	1	2	4	5	6	8	9	11	12	13	15	16	18	19	20	22	23	25
	—	—	**0**	**1**	**2**	**3**	**5**	**6**	**7**	**8**	**9**	**11**	**12**	**13**	**14**	**15**	**17**	**18**	**19**	**20**
6	—	0	2	3	5	7	8	10	12	14	16	17	19	21	23	25	26	28	30	32
	—	—	**1**	**2**	**3**	**5**	**6**	**8**	**10**	**11**	**13**	**14**	**16**	**17**	**19**	**21**	**22**	**24**	**25**	**27**
7	—	0	2	4	6	8	11	13	15	17	19	21	24	26	28	30	33	35	37	39
	—	—	**1**	**3**	**5**	**6**	**8**	**10**	**12**	**14**	**16**	**18**	**20**	**22**	**24**	**26**	**28**	**30**	**32**	**34**
8	—	1	3	5	8	10	13	15	18	20	23	26	28	31	33	36	39	41	44	47
	—	**0**	**2**	**4**	**6**	**8**	**10**	**13**	**15**	**17**	**19**	**22**	**24**	**26**	**29**	**31**	**34**	**36**	**38**	**41**
9	—	1	3	6	9	12	15	18	21	24	27	30	33	36	39	42	45	48	51	54
	—	**0**	**2**	**4**	**7**	**10**	**12**	**15**	**17**	**20**	**23**	**26**	**28**	**31**	**34**	**37**	**39**	**42**	**45**	**48**
10	—	1	4	7	11	14	17	20	24	27	31	34	37	41	44	48	51	55	58	62
	—	**0**	**3**	**5**	**8**	**11**	**14**	**17**	**20**	**23**	**26**	**29**	**33**	**36**	**39**	**42**	**45**	**48**	**52**	**55**
11	—	1	5	8	12	16	19	23	27	31	34	38	42	46	50	54	57	61	65	69
	—	**0**	**3**	**6**	**9**	**13**	**16**	**19**	**23**	**26**	**30**	**33**	**37**	**40**	**44**	**47**	**51**	**55**	**58**	**62**
12	—	2	5	9	13	17	21	26	30	34	38	42	47	51	55	60	64	68	72	77
	—	**1**	**4**	**7**	**11**	**14**	**18**	**22**	**26**	**29**	**33**	**37**	**41**	**45**	**49**	**53**	**57**	**61**	**65**	**69**
13	—	2	6	10	15	19	24	28	33	37	42	47	51	56	61	65	70	75	80	84
	—	**1**	**4**	**8**	**12**	**16**	**20**	**24**	**28**	**33**	**37**	**41**	**45**	**50**	**54**	**59**	**63**	**67**	**72**	**76**
14	—	2	7	11	16	21	26	31	36	41	46	51	56	61	66	71	77	82	87	92
	—	**1**	**5**	**9**	**13**	**17**	**22**	**26**	**31**	**36**	**40**	**45**	**50**	**55**	**59**	**64**	**67**	**74**	**78**	**83**
15	—	3	7	12	18	23	28	33	39	44	50	55	61	66	72	77	83	88	94	100
	—	**1**	**5**	**10**	**14**	**19**	**24**	**29**	**34**	**39**	**44**	**49**	**54**	**59**	**64**	**70**	**75**	**80**	**85**	**90**
16	—	3	8	14	19	25	30	36	42	48	54	60	65	71	77	83	89	95	101	107
	—	**1**	**6**	**11**	**15**	**21**	**26**	**31**	**37**	**42**	**47**	**53**	**59**	**64**	**70**	**75**	**81**	**86**	**92**	**98**
17	—	3	9	15	20	26	33	39	45	51	57	64	70	77	83	89	96	102	109	115
	—	**2**	**6**	**11**	**17**	**22**	**28**	**34**	**39**	**45**	**51**	**57**	**63**	**67**	**75**	**81**	**87**	**93**	**99**	**105**
18	—	4	9	16	22	28	35	41	48	55	61	68	75	82	88	95	102	109	116	123
	—	**2**	**7**	**12**	**18**	**24**	**30**	**36**	**42**	**48**	**55**	**61**	**67**	**74**	**80**	**86**	**93**	**99**	**106**	**112**
19	0	4	10	17	23	30	37	44	51	58	65	72	80	87	94	101	109	116	123	130
	—	**2**	**7**	**13**	**19**	**25**	**32**	**38**	**45**	**52**	**58**	**65**	**72**	**78**	**85**	**92**	**99**	**106**	**113**	**119**
20	0	4	11	18	25	32	39	47	54	62	69	77	84	92	100	107	115	123	130	138
	—	**2**	**8**	**13**	**20**	**27**	**34**	**41**	**48**	**55**	**62**	**69**	**76**	**83**	**90**	**98**	**105**	**112**	**119**	**127**

TABLE D.11 Critical Values of the Wilcoxon *T* Statistic[a]

	Level of Significance for a One-Tailed Test					Level of Significance for a One-Tailed Test			
	.05	*.025*	*.01*	*.005*		*.05*	*.025*	*.01*	*.005*
	Level of Significance for a Two-Tailed Test					Level of Significance for a Two-Tailed Test			
n	*.10*	*.05*	*.02*	*.01*	*n*	*.10*	*.05*	*.02*	*.01*
5	0	—	—	—	28	130	116	101	91
6	2	0	—	—	29	140	126	110	100
7	3	2	0	—	30	151	137	120	109
8	5	3	1	0	31	163	147	130	118
9	8	5	3	1	32	175	159	140	128
10	10	8	5	3	33	187	170	151	138
11	13	10	7	5	34	200	182	162	148
12	17	13	9	7	35	213	195	173	159
13	21	17	12	9	36	227	208	185	171
14	25	21	15	12	37	241	221	198	182
15	30	25	19	15	38	256	235	211	194
16	35	29	23	19	39	271	249	224	207
17	41	34	27	23	40	286	264	238	220
18	47	40	32	27	41	302	279	252	233
19	53	46	37	32	42	319	294	266	247
20	60	52	43	37	43	336	310	281	261
21	67	58	49	42	44	353	327	296	276
22	75	65	55	48	45	371	343	312	291
23	83	73	62	54	46	389	361	328	307
24	91	81	69	61	47	407	378	345	322
25	100	89	76	68	48	426	396	362	339
26	110	98	84	75	49	446	415	379	355
27	119	107	92	83	50	466	434	397	373

[a] Discussed in Section 18.4. The symbol *T* denotes the smaller of the sums of ranks associated with differences that are all of the same sign. For any given *n* (number of ranked differences), the obtained *T* is significant at a given level if it is *equal to* or *less than* the value shown in the table.

Student Database

DESCRIPTION OF DATABASE

Over the years I have collected data about students who enroll in my introductory statistics course. These data have been organized so that they can be updated from semester to semester and analyzed in a variety of ways. Such an organization of data is called a *database*. A portion of this database is reproduced in Table E.1. The following information is contained in the table:

Column 1: Student identification number (ID No.)
Range = 1–461

Column 2: Student identification number by gender (ID No. by Gen)
Men = 1–180   Women=181–461

Column 3: Student's gender (Gender)
M =Man   W =Woman

Column 4: Major in college (Major)
BIO = Biology   CHE = Chemistry
CSI = Computer science   ENG = English
HIS = History   LAW = Prelaw
MATH = Mathematics   MED = Premedicine
NURS = Nursing   OPT = Preoptometry
PSY = Psychology   PT = Physical therapy
REL = Religion   SPATH = Speech pathology
UNDE = Undecided

Column 5: Number of previous psychology courses (No. Psy)
Range = 0–13

Column 6: Number of previous mathematics courses (No. Math)
Range = 0–6

Column 7: Overall grade point average (GPA)

Column 8: Score on the Test of Mathematical Skills in Appendix A (Math Test)

Column 9: Grade in introductory statistics course (Stat Grade)
4 = A   3.5 = B+   3 = B
2.5 = C+   2 = C   1=D
0 = F   I = Incomplete   W = Withdrew

Missing information is indicated by a period.

TABLE E.1 Student Database

(1) ID No.	(2) ID No. by Gen	(3) Gender	(4) Major	(5) No. Psy	(6) No. Math	(7) GPA	(8) Math Test	(9) Stat Grade
1	1	M	PSY	3	2	2.84	29	2
2	2	M	PSY	6	1	3.30	17	2
3	3	M	PSY	1	2	3.46	37	4
4	4	M	PSY	3	3	3.34	45	2
5	5	M	PSY	2	1	3.22	25	3
6	6	M	PSY	4	3	2.35	16	2
7	7	M	PSY	3	3	2.04	34	W
8	8	M	PSY	8	2	3.38	39	3
9	9	M	PSY	1	1	3.33	20	3.5
10	10	M	PSY	4	2	2.41	31	2
11	11	M	MED	1	3	3.42	39	3
12	12	M	MATH	1	4	2.66	38	3
13	13	M	PSY	4	1	2.01	25	1
14	14	M	PSY	3	3	2.42	38	2
15	15	M	PSY	3	2	3.22	36	2.5
16	16	M	PSY	2	2	2.29	41	I
17	17	M	PSY	4	3	3.32	38	4
18	18	M	PSY	1	2	2.72	41	3
19	19	M	MED	2	2	3.76	37	4
20	20	M	PT	3	1	3.23	34	2.5
21	21	M	PSY	11	1	3.40	30	0
22	22	M	PSY	1	1	3.75	37	4
23	23	M	MED	1	2	3.26	35	3.5
24	24	M	PSY	4	1	3.76	40	4
25	25	M	PSY	4	1	3.23	26	2.5
26	26	M	PSY	1	3	3.87	39	4
27	27	M	PSY	5	1	2.32	26	2
28	28	M	PSY	7	3	2.79	41	2
29	29	M	PSY	8	1	3.13	37	3
30	30	M	PT	2	2	3.68	30	4
31	31	M	PSY	4	1	2.65	26	1
32	32	M	PSY	1	1	2.91	42	3
33	33	M	PSY	4	2	2.27	17	I
34	34	M	PSY	8	1	2.53	35	I
35	35	M	PSY	5	4	2.72	40	2
36	36	M	PSY	3	1	3.32	29	3.5
37	37	M	PSY	3	2	3.73	43	4
38	38	M	PSY	5	2	3.24	26	3
39	39	M	MED	2	4	3.72	41	3.5
40	40	M	PSY	2	2	3.01	34	3

TABLE E.1   *(continued)*

(1) ID No.	(2) ID No. by Gen	(3) Gender	(4) Major	(5) No. Psy	(6) No. Math	(7) GPA	(8) Math Test	(9) Stat Grade
41	41	M	.	2	5	3.74	44	4
42	42	M	PSY	4	1	3.27	31	4
43	43	M	PSY	.	.	2.82	22	2
44	44	M	PSY	1	2	3.52	29	3
45	45	M	PSY	1	2	3.79	40	4
46	46	M	PSY	.	.	3.71	32	3.5
47	47	M	PSY	3	1	2.31	28	2
48	48	M	PSY	5	1	2.25	16	1
49	49	M	PSY	4	1	3.06	27	3
50	50	M	MED	2	4	3.79	43	4
51	51	M	PSY	4	1	3.65	18	4
52	52	M	PSY	2	1	3.04	35	2.5
53	53	M	PSY	6	1	2.16	31	1
54	54	M	PSY	1	2	3.01	25	4
55	55	M	PSY	5	1	2.70	17	2
56	56	M	PSY	3	.	2.91	31	2
57	57	M	PSY	8	3	3.35	39	3
58	58	M	PSY	7	2	3.23	37	4
59	59	M	MED	1	1	2.94	35	3
60	60	M	PSY	1	5	3.79	40	4
61	61	M	PSY	5	4	2.32	34	2
62	62	M	PSY	2	1	2.96	29	2
63	63	M	PSY	.	1	2.51	37	3
64	64	M	.	2	2	2.42	43	2
65	65	M	PSY	1	1	4.00	40	4
66	66	M	PSY	4	2	1.01	17	0
67	67	M	PSY	1	4	2.71	45	W
68	68	M	.	1	2	2.86	37	3
69	69	M	BIO	2	2	3.71	39	3.5
70	70	M	PSY	2	3	2.94	35	I
71	71	M	PSY	3	1	2.80	18	2
72	72	M	PSY	1	1	2.55	25	2
73	73	M	LAW	3	1	2.29	39	2
74	74	M	PSY	2	2	3.44	40	3
75	75	M	PSY	4	2	2.26	37	2
76	76	M	PSY	2	2	2.89	33	2
77	77	M	PSY	2	0	2.95	14	2
78	78	M	PSY	2	2	3.31	39	3
79	79	M	PSY	2	2	2.32	31	3
80	80	M	PSY	3	2	3.11	45	2

TABLE E.1 *(continued)*

(1) ID No.	(2) ID No. by Gen	(3) Gender	(4) Major	(5) No. Psy	(6) No. Math	(7) GPA	(8) Math Test	(9) Stat Grade
81	81	M	PSY	1	2	3.02	37	4
82	82	M	PSY	2	0	2.16	25	0
83	83	M	PSY	4	4	3.87	43	4
84	84	M	PSY	2	3	3.03	34	3
85	85	M	PSY	3	3	3.21	36	4
86	86	M	CSI	1	1	1.00	37	I
87	87	M	PSY	4	2	3.39	29	3
88	88	M	PSY	3	1	3.42	18	4
89	89	M	PSY	8	0	3.21	20	2
90	90	M	PSY	1	3	3.24	31	3.5
91	91	M	PSY	4	2	3.60	38	4
92	92	M	PT	7	2	2.13	34	1
93	93	M	PSY	5	0	2.22	14	1
94	94	M	PSY	7	2	2.81	23	2
95	95	M	PSY	4	1	3.25	28	4
96	96	M	PSY	5	2	2.32	24	1
97	97	M	MED	2	4	2.82	42	2.5
98	98	M	MED	1	4	2.93	40	3.5
99	99	M	PSY	6	2	3.36	24	4
100	100	M	PSY	3	1	3.45	40	4
101	101	M	PT	3	1	2.51	25	2
102	102	M	PSY	6	3	2.65	45	1
103	103	M	PSY	2	1	3.24	19	4
104	104	M	PSY	8	1	2.60	19	1
105	105	M	PSY	6	0	2.37	19	0
106	106	M	PSY	0	1	2.24	25	2
107	107	M	PSY	2	2	2.72	38	3
108	108	M	PSY	.	1	2.24	25	W
109	109	M	PSY	2	2	3.14	44	3
110	110	M	PSY	4	2	2.43	33	1
111	111	M	PSY	2	2	3.35	30	3
112	112	M	PSY	5	1	2.90	41	2
113	113	M	PSY	3	3	3.95	43	4
114	114	M	BIO	2	3	3.71	42	3
115	115	M	PSY	4	1	2.65	41	2
116	116	M	PSY	3	3	3.00	35	4
117	117	M	PSY	2	1	2.51	23	2
118	118	M	OPT	.	1	3.32	39	4
119	119	M	PSY	2	1	2.62	31	1
120	120	M	PSY	3	2	2.97	38	3

TABLE E.1 *(continued)*

(1) ID No.	(2) ID No. by Gen	(3) Gender	(4) Major	(5) No. Psy	(6) No. Math	(7) GPA	(8) Math Test	(9) Stat Grade
121	121	M	PSY	3	2	2.83	41	3
122	122	M	PSY	1	2	2.99	25	3
123	123	M	PSY	1	3	3.21	39	4
124	124	M	PSY	2	1	2.32	26	2
125	125	M	PSY	7	3	2.79	41	2
126	126	M	PT	1	1	2.85	24	2
127	127	M	PSY	3	1	2.65	45	1
128	128	M	PSY	3	1	3.24	19	2
129	129	M	PSY	8	1	2.60	19	1
130	130	M	PSY	6	0	2.36	19	0
131	131	M	PSY	0	1	2.24	25	2
132	132	M	PSY	1	3	2.73	37	3
133	133	M	PSY	8	1	3.13	37	3
134	134	M	PT	1	2	3.87	31	4
135	135	M	PSY	1	2	2.29	41	I
136	136	M	PSY	4	3	3.32	38	4
137	137	M	PSY	1	3	2.72	43	3
138	138	M	MED	2	2	3.76	37	4
139	139	M	PT	3	1	2.76	34	2.5
140	140	M	PSY	1	3	2.37	15	2
141	141	M	PSY	4	2	2.04	34	W
142	142	M	PSY	8	2	3.38	39	3
143	143	M	PSY	3	2	3.31	23	3.5
144	144	M	PSY	1	1	2.51	30	2
145	145	M	PSY	1	1	2.09	28	2
146	146	M	PSY	1	3	2.30	41	2
147	147	M	PSY	4	1	3.31	28	2
148	148	M	PSY	8	2	2.90	44	.
149	149	M	MED	6	3	1.93	24	2
150	150	M	PSY	6	4	2.08	33	2
151	151	M	PSY	3	0	2.66	16	2
152	152	M	PSY	3	1	2.78	34	3
153	153	M	PSY	4	0	2.42	23	2
154	154	M	PSY	4	2	2.13	42	2
155	155	M	PSY	4	1	2.51	24	2
156	156	M	LAW	3	2	3.07	39	3
157	157	M	MED	2	2	3.90	46	4
158	158	M	PSY	3	0	2.55	27	2
159	159	M	MED	2	1	2.44	34	2
160	160	M	PSY	2	0	2.81	24	1

TABLE E.1 *(continued)*

(1) ID No.	(2) ID No. by Gen	(3) Gender	(4) Major	(5) No. Psy	(6) No. Math	(7) GPA	(8) Math Test	(9) Stat Grade
161	161	M	PSY	5	1	2.39	30	2
162	162	M	PSY	7	3	3.39	43	4
163	163	M	PSY	4	1	2.17	27	0
164	164	M	PSY	3	1	3.77	37	4
165	165	M	PSY	3	4	3.42	29	3
166	166	M	PSY	2	1	3.11	32	3.5
167	167	M	PSY	4	2	2.92	34	2.5
168	168	M	PSY	1	3	2.14	41	3
169	169	M	PSY	6	2	3.46	38	W
170	170	M	PSY	7	2	2.59	21	2
171	171	M	PSY	2	2	3.36	42	3.5
172	172	M	PSY	2	1	3.69	39	3.5
173	173	M	PSY	2	1	2.26	25	W
174	174	M	PSY	1	3	3.24	36	2.5
175	175	M	PSY	4	3	3.45	39	3
176	176	M	PSY	2	0	2.56	16	2
177	177	M	PSY	4	2	3.44	36	4
178	178	M	MED	5	2	3.00	33	4
179	179	M	PSY	2	1	3.47	31	3
180	180	M	CHE	1	3	3.10	44	3.5
181	1	W	PSY	2	1	3.23	26	2
182	2	W	PSY	1	4	2.85	39	4
183	3	W	PT	2	1	3.02	40	3
184	4	W	BIO	2	3	3.66	41	3
185	5	W	PSY	5	2	3.16	42	3
186	6	W	PT	1	2	3.46	34	2.5
187	7	W	BIO	1	2	3.51	45	4
188	8	W	PSY	1	1	2.83	17	3
189	9	W	PSY	3	4	3.31	45	4
190	10	W	PT	2	2	2.67	38	3
191	11	W	NURS	1	0	2.75	10	2
192	12	W	PSY	2	1	2.96	35	2.5
193	13	W	MED	3	2	3.07	33	W
194	14	W	PSY	3	2	3.84	42	4
195	15	W	PSY	4	3	2.97	30	3
196	16	W	PSY	6	2	3.18	37	3.5
197	17	W	MED	3	1	2.44	38	2
198	18	W	PSY	2	4	3.40	38	3
199	19	W	PSY	4	2	2.11	33	2
200	20	W	PSY	2	1	2.97	10	2

TABLE E.1   *(continued)*

(1) ID No.	(2) ID No. by Gen	(3) Gender	(4) Major	(5) No. Psy	(6) No. Math	(7) GPA	(8) Math Test	(9) Stat Grade
201	21	W	PSY	4	0	2.02	23	0
202	22	W	ENG	2	1	3.44	24	3
203	23	W	MED	2	3	3.16	38	3.5
204	24	W	PSY	2	0	3.93	10	4
205	25	W	PT	2	2	3.07	34	2
206	26	W	PSY	.	.	2.82	29	2
207	27	W	PSY	5	0	2.67	18	2
208	28	W	PSY	10	1	2.82	20	2
209	29	W	PSY	4	3	3.31	40	3
210	30	W	PSY	4	1	3.10	33	2
211	31	W	PSY	3	2	3.26	43	4
212	32	W	PSY	3	1	2.64	21	2
213	33	W	PSY	2	2	2.93	43	4
214	34	W	PSY	3	6	2.81	39	3
215	35	W	NURS	2	1	3.19	27	2
216	36	W	PSY	3	3	3.37	30	4
217	37	W	PT	3	2	3.31	28	1
218	38	W	PT	4	2	2.90	28	2
219	39	W	PSY	4	0	1.90	19	0
220	40	W	PSY	4	4	3.10	34	3
221	41	W	PSY	.	.	3.19	42	2.5
222	42	W	PSY	2	.	3.58	38	3.5
223	43	W	PSY	2	4	3.66	38	4
224	44	W	PSY	4	1	2.61	30	2
225	45	W	PT	1	1	3.09	37	2
226	46	W	PSY	6	1	2.48	18	2
227	47	W	PT	3	1	3.57	44	4
228	48	W	PSY	4	1	3.33	35	4
229	49	W	PSY	7	1	3.78	42	4
230	50	W	PSY	.	1	3.40	21	3
231	51	W	PT	1	1	2.64	43	2.5
232	52	W	PSY	3	1	3.09	38	3
233	53	W	PSY	.	1	2.93	39	2
234	54	W	PT	4	2	2.92	29	2
235	55	W	.	2	3	3.47	43	4
236	56	W	PSY	10	0	3.47	8	3
237	57	W	PSY	4	0	1.88	17	0
238	58	W	PSY	3	0	2.01	.	1
239	59	W	PSY	2	3	3.67	32	4
240	60	W	PSY	3	3	3.75	39	4

TABLE E.1   *(continued)*

(1) ID No.	(2) ID No. by Gen	(3) Gender	(4) Major	(5) No. Psy	(6) No. Math	(7) GPA	(8) Math Test	(9) Stat Grade
241	61	W	PSY	4	1	2.90	35	2
242	62	W	PSY	6	0	3.38	32	4
243	63	W	BIO	2	2	3.42	41	2
244	64	W	PSY	2	1	3.40	34	3
245	65	W	PSY	3	1	2.35	20	2
246	66	W	PSY	4	1	2.68	12	I
247	67	W	SPATH	2	1	3.89	26	4
248	68	W	PSY	2	1	2.33	30	W
249	69	W	PT	2	3	2.95	44	4
250	70	W	PSY	7	0	2.69	35	2
251	71	W	PSY	2	1	3.26	27	2
252	72	W	.	4	2	3.39	40	2
253	73	W	BIO	2	2	3.39	42	2
254	74	W	PSY	5	1	2.39	35	2
255	75	W	PSY	3	1	3.71	35	4
256	76	W	PSY	2	4	3.81	41	3.5
257	77	W	PSY	4	0	2.77	16	2
258	78	W	MED	3	2	3.65	41	4
259	79	W	PSY	10	1	2.47	36	4
260	80	W	PSY	3	3	3.32	40	4
261	81	W	PSY	2	3	3.68	31	4
262	82	W	PSY	4	2	3.41	23	3
263	83	W	PSY	2	1	2.90	8	3
264	84	W	PSY	8	1	3.72	32	4
265	85	W	UNDE	2	2	2.34	23	2.5
266	86	W	HIS	3	2	2.87	30	4
267	87	W	BIO	2	3	3.01	40	2
268	88	W	PT	1	1	2.75	39	3
269	89	W	PSY	2	3	3.58	33	3
270	90	W	PT	2	1	3.54	34	3
271	91	W	PT	1	1	3.64	39	4
272	92	W	PSY	2	3	3.33	42	3.5
273	93	W	PSY	2	2	2.83	41	2.5
274	94	W	MED	3	3	3.30	35	4
275	95	W	PSY	2	4	3.71	35	3
276	96	W	PSY	5	1	2.66	31	1
277	97	W	PSY	2	3	3.63	31	4
278	98	W	SPATH	4	2	3.45	20	2
279	99	W	PSY	4	1	2.31	37	2
280	100	W	PSY	4	2	3.54	35	4

TABLE E.1   *(continued)*

(1) ID No.	*(2)* ID No. by Gen	*(3)* Gender	*(4)* Major	*(5)* No. Psy	*(6)* No. Math	*(7)* GPA	*(8)* Math Test	*(9)* Stat Grade
281	101	W	PSY	3	2	3.38	44	4
282	102	W	PSY	5	2	2.70	45	3
283	103	W	PSY	3	3	3.62	39	4
284	104	W	PSY	2	2	2.42	25	2
285	105	W	PSY	5	3	2.53	37	2
286	106	W	PT	1	1	2.74	31	2
287	107	W	PSY	3	0	3.58	41	4
288	108	W	PSY	4	2	2.63	25	2
289	109	W	.	3	4	4.00	43	4
290	110	W	PSY	3	1	2.54	30	1
291	111	W	PSY	3	1	3.86	30	4
292	112	W	PT	4	1	3.75	37	4
293	113	W	PSY	7	1	2.28	21	1
294	114	W	BIO	3	3	2.91	42	3
295	115	W	PSY	5	1	2.43	28	2
296	116	W	NURS	4	2	2.16	36	2.5
297	117	W	PSY	2	4	3.22	43	4
298	118	W	PSY	2	**1**	3.89	34	3.5
299	119	W	PSY	1	1	2.62	42	2
300	120	W	PSY	2	2	2.95	27	I
301	121	W	PT	2	1	3.54	37	3.5
302	122	W	PSY	4	2	3.71	38	3
303	123	W	NURS	2	0	2.95	34	2
304	124	W	PSY	2	3	2.89	34	3
305	125	W	PT	.	.	3.84	40	4
306	126	W	PT	1	2	3.48	39	3.5
307	127	W	PSY	.	.	2.13	18	.
308	128	W	PSY	3	3	3.66	43	4
309	129	W	MED	3	1	2.55	33	2.5
310	130	W	PSY	5	2	2.01	30	2
311	131	W	PT	1	1	2.35	43	2
312	132	W	PSY	4	1	2.28	20	2
313	133	W	.	4	1	3.18	29	2
314	134	W	PSY	3	1	3.01	33	2
315	135	W	PSY	4	0	3.83	43	4
316	136	W	PSY	2	4	3.87	36	4
317	137	W	PSY	4	1	3.21	17	3
318	138	W	NURS	2	2	3.10	20	4
319	139	W	PSY	2	4	2.96	40	3
320	140	W	PSY	3	2	3.49	27	4

TABLE E.1   *(continued)*

(1) ID No.	*(2)* ID No. by Gen	*(3)* Gender	*(4)* Major	*(5)* No. Psy	*(6)* No. Math	*(7)* GPA	*(8)* Math Test	*(9)* Stat Grade
321	141	W	PSY	4	3	3.21	41	2.5
322	142	W	PT	2	2	3.75	43	4
323	143	W	PSY	2	5	3.60	41	4
324	144	W	PSY	6	1	3.08	43	2.5
325	145	W	PT	1	1	3.49	30	4
326	146	W	PSY	1	1	2.64	37	4
327	147	W	PSY	6	4	3.08	39	3
328	148	W	PSY	4	1	3.54	42	4
329	149	W	PSY	5	1	3.23	41	3
330	150	W	MED	3	3	3.65	39	4
331	151	W	PSY	4	3	3.44	45	4
332	152	W	PT	4	1	3.43	41	4
333	153	W	PSY	4	0	4.00	16	4
334	154	W	.	4	0	2.54	21	2
335	155	W	PT	2	4	3.82	33	4
336	156	W	PSY	3	1	3.58	30	4
337	157	W	PSY	6	1	3.32	27	3
338	158	W	PSY	1	.	2.88	31	2.5
339	159	W	PSY	3	3	3.38	40	2
340	160	W	PSY	4	1	2.91	23	2
341	161	W	PSY	3	2	2.51	36	2
342	162	W	PSY	4	1	3.48	28	W
343	163	W	PSY	2	1	3.43	33	3
344	164	W	PSY	1	0	2.38	22	3
345	165	W	PSY	2	0	3.84	35	4
346	166	W	PSY	1	1	2.73	30	2
347	167	W	PSY	4	2	2.29	21	1
348	168	W	PSY	1	3	3.98	38	4
349	169	W	PSY	5	1	2.63	28	3
350	170	W	PT	3	2	2.61	40	3
351	171	W	PSY	2	1	3.23	26	2
352	172	W	PSY	2	3	2.85	39	4
353	173	W	PT	2	1	3.02	40	3
354	174	W	BIO	2	2	3.66	41	3
355	175	W	PSY	5	2	3.16	42	3
356	176	W	PT	1	2	3.46	34	2.5
357	177	W	PSY	5	0	2.02	23	0
358	178	W	ENG	1	2	3.44	24	3
359	179	W	MED	2	3	3.16	38	3.5
360	180	W	PSY	2	0	3.93	10	4

TABLE E.1   *(continued)*

(1) ID No.	(2) ID No. by Gen	(3) Gender	(4) Major	(5) No. Psy	(6) No. Math	(7) GPA	(8) Math Test	(9) Stat Grade
361	181	W	PSY	3	1	3.19	42	2.5
362	182	W	PSY	1	.	3.58	38	3.5
363	183	W	PSY	2	3	3.75	39	4
364	184	W	PSY	4	2	2.90	35	2
365	185	W	PSY	6	0	3.38	32	4
366	186	W	MED	3	3	3.65	39	4
367	187	W	PSY	4	3	3.44	45	4
368	188	W	PT	4	1	3.43	41	4
369	189	W	PSY	5	0	4.00	16	4
370	190	W	PSY	4	2	2.54	21	.
371	191	W	PSY	4	2	2.40	26	2
372	192	W	PSY	3	1	3.40	34	3
373	193	W	PSY	5	3	3.66	38	4
374	194	W	PSY	4	1	2.91	23	2
375	195	W	PSY	4	2	2.51	36	2
376	196	W	PSY	3	1	3.48	28	W
377	197	W	PSY	4	2	3.43	33	3
378	198	W	PSY	1	0	2.38	22	3
379	199	W	PSY	5	1	2.61	30	2
380	200	W	MED	2	2	2.34	38	2
381	201	W	PT	2	2	3.50	46	3
382	202	W	PSY	5	1	2.58	21	2
383	203	W	PSY	2	2	2.79	40	2
384	204	W	MED	2	2	2.03	26	2
385	205	W	PT	1	1	3.80	36	4
386	206	W	PSY	3	2	3.51	41	3.5
387	207	W	MED	2	2	3.04	38	3
388	208	W	PSY	3	2	2.48	34	2
389	209	W	PSY	3	3	3.55	42	4
390	210	W	PSY	2	1	2.45	33	2
391	211	W	PSY	3	0	.	28	W
392	212	W	PSY	2	2	2.71	43	2
393	213	W	PSY	1	0	2.03	34	W
394	214	W	PSY	3	1	3.18	38	2
395	215	W	PSY	3	3	3.50	39	3.5
396	216	W	PSY	2	0	2.40	14	0
397	217	W	PSY	2	1	3.52	39	3
398	218	W	PSY	3	1	3.46	27	W
399	219	W	LAW	2	2	2.31	40	2.5
400	220	W	PSY	2	1	2.42	29	2

TABLE E.1 *(continued)*

(1) ID No.	(2) ID No. by Gen	(3) Gender	(4) Major	(5) No. Psy	(6) No. Math	(7) GPA	(8) Math Test	(9) Stat Grade
401	221	W	REL	3	1	2.92	21	2
402	222	W	PSY	3	1	2.88	36	2
403	223	W	PSY	2	0	3.26	26	2
404	224	W	PSY	1	1	3.13	34	2
405	225	W	PSY	6	0	1.81	15	0
406	226	W	PSY	2	1	3.62	43	4
407	227	W	PSY	8	1	3.04	30	4
408	228	W	PSY	2	0	2.36	13	1
409	229	W	PT	2	2	3.37	39	4
410	230	W	MATH	1	1	3.91	47	4
411	231	W	PSY	2	1	2.44	40	1
412	232	W	PSY	2	1	2.64	36	2
413	233	W	PSY	2	1	2.49	33	2
414	234	W	LAW	2	1	3.75	41	4
415	235	W	PSY	3	1	3.33	35	2
416	236	W	MED	2	2	2.51	30	2
417	237	W	BIO	1	1	3.68	47	4
418	238	W	PSY	1	2	3.40	23	4
419	239	W	PSY	3	2	3.21	28	2
420	240	W	PSY	2	0	3.06	22	2.5
421	241	W	PSY	3	1	3.49	28	3
422	242	W	PSY	1	1	2.96	16	2
423	243	W	PSY	1	0	3.25	27	2
424	244	W	PSY	2	5	2.19	37	2
425	245	W	PT	1	1	3.56	44	4
426	246	W	PSY	4	0	2.98	20	2
427	247	W	BIO	1	4	3.38	45	4
428	248	W	PSY	1	0	3.23	45	3.5
429	249	W	PSY	1	1	1.20	30	1
430	250	W	PSY	5	2	3.78	38	4
431	251	W	PSY	1	3	2.80	38	3
432	252	W	PSY	6	1	3.10	22	2
433	253	W	PSY	1	0	3.44	44	2
434	254	W	PSY	2	1	2.64	40	2
435	255	W	PSY	2	1	1.83	32	0
436	256	W	PSY	4	1	3.68	27	3.5
437	257	W	PSY	2	1	2.87	33	3.5
438	258	W	MED	2	2	2.99	33	2.5
439	259	W	PSY	3	2	3.50	38	4
440	260	W	PSY	2	1	2.73	32	2

TABLE E.1   *(continued)*

(1) ID No.	(2) ID No. by Gen	(3) Gender	(4) Major	(5) No. Psy	(6) No. Math	(7) GPA	(8) Math Test	(9) Stat Grade
441	261	W	PSY	2	2	2.12	38	I
442	262	W	PSY	3	0	2.27	18	1
443	263	W	PSY	5	1	3.45	22	2
444	264	W	PSY	6	1	2.98	32	4
445	265	W	PSY	5	1	2.96	30	2
446	266	W	PSY	3	1	1.82	15	0
447	267	W	PSY	2	1	2.89	30	3
448	268	W	PSY	3	2	3.66	46	4
449	269	W	PSY	2	0	3.49	45	3.5
450	270	W	PSY	2	1	2.62	35	2
451	271	W	MED	4	2	3.78	40	3
452	272	W	PSY	3	1	2.88	34	2
453	273	W	PSY	1	1	3.30	40	2
454	274	W	PSY	2	1	3.01	40	2
455	275	W	PSY	2	1	3.14	36	2
456	276	W	PSY	2	0	3.52	22	3.5
457	277	W	PSY	4	1	2.61	30	2
458	278	W	PSY	1	0	2.70	27	I
459	279	W	PSY	13	1	3.63	34	3.5
460	280	W	PSY	4	2	2.66	35	I
461	281	W	PSY	3	2	2.83	33	2

References

American Psychological Association. (2001). *Publication manual* (5th ed.). Washington, DC: Author. [*64, 292, 299, 473]

Arken, A., & Colton, R. (1938). *Graphs: How to make and use them* (2nd ed.). New York: Harper. [41]

Box, G. E. P. (1954). Some theorems on quadratic forms applied in the study of analysis of variance problems, I. Effect of inequality of variance in the one-way classification. *Annals of Mathematical Statistics, 25,* 290–302. [411]

Brown, L. D., Cai, T. T., & DasGupta, A. (2001). Interval estimation for a binomial proportion. *Statistical Science, 16,* 101–133. [308]

Cleveland, W. S. (1985). *The elements of graphing data.* Monterey, CA: Wadsworth. [41]

Clinch, J. J., & Keselman, H. J. (1982). Parametric alternatives to the analysis of variance. *Journal of Educational Statistics, 7,* 207–214. [411, 412]

Cohen, J. (1988). *Statistical power analysis for the behavioral sciences* (2nd ed.). Hillsdale, NJ: Lawrence Erlbaum. [281, 299, 317, 405, 419, 474]

Cohen, J. (1992). A power primer. *Psychological Bulletin, 112,* 155–159. [282]

Conover, W. J. (1974a). Rejoinder on "Some reasons for not using the Yates continuity correction on 2 × 2 contingency tables" by W. J. Conover. *Journal of the American Statistical Association, 69,* 382. [478]

Conover, W. J. (1974b). Some reasons for not using the Yates continuity correction on 2 × 2 contingency tables. *Journal of the American Statistical Association, 69,* 374–376. [478]

Cook, T. D., and Campbell, D. T. (1979). *Quasi-experimentation: Design and analysis issues for field settings.* Chicago: Rand McNally. [411]

Fisher, R. A., & Yates, F. (1974). *Statistical tables for biological, agricultural and medical research.* London: Longman. Previously, Edinburgh: Oliver & Boyd, 1963. [600, 602, 607, 618, 619]

Galton, F. (1889). *Natural inheritance.* London and New York: Macmillan. [126]

Grizzle, J. E. (1967). Continuity correction in the χ^2 test for 2 × 2 tables. *American Statistician, 21,* 28–32. [478]

Halperin, M., Hartley, H. O., & Hoel, P. G. (1965). Recommended standards for statistical symbols and notation. *American Statistician, 19,* 12–14. [64]

Hays, W. L. (1994). *Statistics* (5th ed.). New York: Holt, Rinehart and Winston. [141, 216, 458, 475, 482, 483]

Hooke, R., & Liles, J. M. (1983). *How to tell the liars from the statisticians.* New York: Marcel Dekker. [2]

Howell, D. C. (2002). *Statistical methods for psychology* (5th ed.). Boston: Duxbury Press. [445, 458]

---

*Page on which reference is cited.

Huff, D. (1954). *How to lie with statistics*. New York: Norton. [52]

Jaffe, A. J., & Spirer, H. F. (1986). *Misused statistics: Straight talk for twisted numbers*. New York: Marcel Dekker. [2]

Kirk, R. E. (1978). *Introductory statistics*. Monterey, CA: Brooks/Cole. [101, 149]

Kirk, R. E. (1994). Choosing a multiple comparison procedure. In B. Thompson (Ed.), *Advances in social science methodology* (pp. 77–121). Greenwich, CN: JAI Press. [414]

Kirk, R. E. (1995). *Experimental design: Procedures for the behavioral sciences* (3rd ed.). Monterey, CA: Brooks/Cole. [127, 281, 405, 418, 445, 454, 458]

Kirk, R. E. (1996). Practical significance: A concept whose time has come. *Educational and Psychological Measurement, 56,* 746–759. [299]

Kirk, R. E. (2005a). Analysis of variance: Classification. In B. Everitt & D. Howell (Eds.), *Encyclopedia of Statistics in Behavioral Science* (Vol. 1, pp. 66–83). New York: Wiley. [447]

Kirk, R. E. (2005b). Effect size measures. In B. Everitt & D. Howell (Eds.), *Encyclopedia of Statistics in Behavioral Science* (Vol. 2, pp. 532–542). New York: Wiley. [299]

Mantel, N. (1974). Comment and suggestion. *Journal of the American Statistical Association, 69,* 378–380. [478]

Marascuilo, L. A., & McSweeney, M. (1977). *Nonparametric and distribution-free methods for the social sciences*. Monterey, CA: Brooks/Cole. [486]

Mauro, J. (1992). *Statistical deception at work*. Hillsdale, NJ: Lawrence Erlbaum. [2]

Maxwell, S. E., & Delaney, H. D. (2004). *Designing experiments and analyzing data*. Belmont, CA: Wadsworth. [458]

McNemar, Q. (1947). Note on the sampling error of the difference between correlated proportions or percentages. *Psychometrika, 12,* 153–157. [379]

Micceri, T. (1989). The unicorn, the normal curve, and other improbable creatures. *Psychological Bulletin, 105,* 156–166. [265]

Miettinen, O. S. (1974). Comment on "Some reasons for not using the Yates continuity correction on 2×2 contingency tables" by W. J. Conover. *Journal of the American Statistical Association, 69,* 380–382. [478]

Pearson, E. S., & Hartley, H. O. (1966). *Biometrika tables for statisticians* (Vol. 1, 3rd ed.). New York: Cambridge. [610, 622]

Plackett, R. L. (1964). The continuity correction in 2×2 tables. *Biometrika, 51,* 327–337. [478]

Robinson, F. P. (1946). *Effective study*. New York: Harper & Brothers. [4]

Rosnow, R., &, Rosenthal, R. (1989). Statistical procedures and the justification of knowledge in psychological science. *American Psychologists, 44,* 1276–1284. [293]

Senders, V. L. (1958). *Measurement and statistics*. New York: Oxford. [19]

Siegel, S. (1956). *Nonparametric statistics for the behavioral sciences*. New York: McGraw-Hill. [19]

Siegel, S., & Castellan, N. J. (1988). *Nonparametric statistics* (2nd ed.). New York: McGraw-Hill. [501]

Starmer, C. J., Grizzle, J. E., & Sen, P. K. (1974). Comment on "Some reasons for not using the Yates continuity correction on 2×2 contingency tables" by W. J. Conover. *Journal of the American Statistical Association, 69,* 376–378. [478]

Stevens, S. S. (1946). On the theory of scales of measurement. *Science, 103,* 667–680. [1–24, 14, 19]

Stevens, S. S. (1951). Mathematics, measurement, and psychophysics. In S. S. Stevens (Ed.), *Handbook of experimental psychology* (pp. 1–49). New York: Wiley. [19]

Thompson, B. (1998). In praise of brilliance: Where the praise really belongs. *American Psychologist, 53,* 799–800. [292]

Tan, W. Y. (1982). Sampling distributions and robustness of *t, F* and variance-ratio in two samples and ANOVA models with respect to departure from normality. *Communications in*

Statistics—Theory and Methods, 11, 486–511. [411]

Tufte, E. R. (1983). *The visual display of quantitative information.* Cheshire, CT: Graphics Press. [41, 52]

Tukey, J. W. (1977). *Exploratory data analysis.* Reading, MA: Addison-Wesley. [46, 110]

Tukey, J. W. (1991). The philosophy of multiple comparison. *Statistical Science, 6*, 100–116. [292]

Ury, H. (1967). In response to Noether's letter, "Needed—a new name." *American Statistician, 21*, 53. [501]

Wilcox, R. R. (1996). *Statistics for the social sciences.* San Diego, CA: Academic Press. [265, 412, 462]

Index

A posteriori tests, 412
Abscissa, 41
Absolute value, 524
Addition rule of probability, 190
Alpha, specifying, 268–269, 280–281
Alternative hypothesis (*see* Hypothesis)
Analysis of variance:
  assumptions of completely
    randomized design, 410–412
  assumptions of completely
    randomized factorial design, 459
  assumptions of randomized block
    design, 444–445
  basic concepts, 394–402
  completely randomized design,
    403–408
  completely randomized factorial design,
    446–452
  degrees of freedom, 398–399
  expectations of mean squares, 400–402
  factorial design, 446–447
  interaction in, 452–454
  model equation, 396–397
  partition of total sum of squares,
    397–398
  purpose, 392–393
  randomized block design, 435–440
ANOVA, 392 (*see also* Analysis of
  variance)
Arithmetic mean (*see* Mean)
Association, measures of (*see* Correlation)
Associative law, 528
Assumption-freer tests:
  comparison with parametric tests,
    512–514
  introduction to, 500–501
Asymptotic relative efficiency, 506

Bar graph, 41–42
Bayesian inference, 185
Bernoulli, J., 22, 219
Bernoulli trial, 219
Bimodal distribution, 50
Binomial distribution, 220–222
  expected value, 222–223
  standard deviation, 223
Bivariate frequency distribution, 125
Blocking, 433–434
Box plot, 110–111

Casual relationship, 139, 339–340
Centile, 94
Central limit theorem, 247
Central tendency, measures of (*see* Mean;
  Median; Mode)
Chi-square distribution, 470
Chi-square test for frequency data
  (*see* Pearson's chi-square statistic)
Class interval, 31
  midpoint, 45
  nominal limits, 32
  open-ended, 74
  preferred number, 34
  preferred size, 34
  real limits, 32–33
  size, 33
Coefficient of determination, 135–137
Coefficient of multiple determination,
  176–177
Coefficient of nondetermination,
  135–137
Cohen's d, 281–282, 300
Cohen's $\hat{w}$, 474–475, 483
Combination ($_nC_r$), 201
Commutative law, 528
Comparison among means (*see* Multiple
  comparisons among means)
Complement of events, 191
Completely randomized design, 403–408
Completely randomized factorial design,
  446–454
Concomitant relationship, 139, 339–340
Conditional probability, 193
Confidence coefficient, 293
Confidence interval, 243, 293–295
  comparison with hypothesis testing,
    298–299
  interpretation, 296–297
  one-sided, 297–298
  for p, 310–311
  for $p_1 - p_2$, 376–377, 380–382
  for μ, 293–295
  for $\mu_1 - \mu_2$, 332–334, 347–348
  for ρ, 316–317
  for σ_1^2/σ_2^2, 366–367, 371–372
Confidence limits, 295
Constant, 11
Contingency table, 477
Continuity, correction for, 476, 504, 510

normal approximation for
  Mann-Whitney U, 504
normal approximation for Wilcoxon T,
  510
Pearson's chi-square test, 476,
  478–479, 497
Contrast (*see* Multiple comparisons among
  means)
Control group, 273
Correlation:
  and causality, 139
  coefficient, 127
  Cramér's measure of association, 151,
    482
  cross product, information in,
    131–133
  distinguished from regression,
    124–125
  eta squared, 140
  multiple, 176–177
  Pearson product-moment correlation
    coefficient, 127, 129–131
    interpretation, 135–137
    errors in interpreting, 138–139
    factors that affect size, 140–146
    and truncated range, 141–142
  phi coefficient, 482
  ratio, 140
  Spearman rank correlation coefficient,
    147–149
    and tied ranks, 149
Correlation matrix, 176
Covariance, 132
Cramér's measure of association,
  151, 482
Critical region, 269
Critical value, 270
Cross product, 131
Cumulative polygon, 45–46

Data snooping, 412
Database, 627
Datum, 7
Decision rule, 269
Degrees of freedom, 266 (*see also*
  specific test, such as Pearson's
  Chi-square, F, and t)
Denominator, 525
Dependent samples, 341–342

Descriptive statistics, nature of, 7
Dispersion, measures of (*see* Index of
    dispersion; Range; Semi-
    interquartile range; Standard
    deviation)
Distribution:
    asymmetrical, 50
    bell-shaped, 49–50
    bimodal, 50
    binomial, 220–222
    bivariate, 125
    chi-square sampling, 470
    cumulative frequency, 37–38
    discontinuous, 144
    F sampling, 363
    frequency (*see* Frequency distribution)
    hypergeometric, 223
    J, 50–51
    leptokurtic, 49, 114
    mesokurtic, 49, 114
    multimodal, 50
    multinomial, 223
    negatively skewed, 50
    normal, 231–232
        history of, 22, 231
        inflection points, 109, 232
    open-ended, 74
    platykurtic, 49, 114
    positively skewed, 50
    probability, 213
    rectangular, 51
    relative frequency, 36–37
    sampling, 220, 243
    skewed, 50
    standard normal, 232
    symmetrical, 50
    t sampling, 266–268
    U, 50–51
    uniform, 51
Distribution-free tests, 501
Distributive law, 529
Double-blind study, 375

Effect magnitude, 299–301
Effect size, 281–282, 299–301
Equation:
    algebraic, 529
    arithmetic, 529
    conditional, 530
    identity, 529
    permissible operations, 530–531
    roots of, 530
Equivalence class, 14, 30
Error effect, 396–397
Error variance, 400
Estimate:
    interval, 242
    point, 242
Estimation, 242
Estimator, 242
    minimum variance, 248
    properties of good estimators, 248
    unbiased, 248

Eta squared, 140
Euler, Leonhard, 187
Euler diagram, 187–188
Events:
    complement of, 191
    compound, 187
    disjoint, 192
    exhaustive, 192
    intersection of, 190
    mutually exclusive, 192
    simple, 187
        graph of, 187–189
    statistically independent, 195
    union of, 190
Expected value:
    binomial distribution, 222–223
    continuous random variable, 216–217
    discrete random variable, 215–216
Experiment, 187
Experimental design, 430
    controlling nuisance variables, 430–433
Exponents, operation with, 526–527
Ex post facto experiment, 348

F distribution, 363–364
F test for $\sigma_1^2 = \sigma_2^2$, 362–364
    assumptions, 363
    degrees of freedom, 363
Factorial design, 446
    advantages and disadvantages, 458–459
Factoring, 528
Fermat, P. de, 22
Fisher, R. A., 23, 363, 392
Fisher-Hayter test, 412–414
Fisher's r-to-Z' transformation, 316
Formula:
    deviation, 97
    raw score, 97
Fractions, operations with, 525–526
Frequency distribution, 31
    bivariate, 125
    cumulative, 37–38
    grouped, 31, 32–35
        advantages and disadvantages, 36
    for qualitative variables, 38–39
    for quantitative variables, 31–34
    relative, 36–37
    rules for constructing, 34
    ungrouped, 31–32
Frequency polygon, 45
function, 212
Fundamental counting rule, 198

g statistic:
    for contrasts in completely randomized
        design, 420
    for contrasts in completely randomized
        factorial design, 457–458
    for contrasts in randomized block de-
        sign, 443
    for one-sample t statistic, 300
    for two-sample t statistic, 331–332, 346
Galton, F., 23, 125–126

Gauss, C. F., 22
Goodness of fit, test for, 470–473
    (*see also* Pearson's chi-square
        statistic)
Gosset, W. S., 23, 266
Graph:
    bar, 41–42
    cumulative polygon, 45–46
    frequency polygon, 45
    histogram, 44–45
    misleading, 52–53
    pictogram, 53
    pie chart, 42–43
    for qualitative variables, 41–43
    for quantitative variables, 44–48
    stem-and-leaf display, 46–48
Graunt, J., 22
Group matching, 348–349

Hedges's g statistic (*see* g statistic)
Helmert, F. R., 470
Heteroscedasticity, 145
Histogram, 44–45
History of statistics, 22–24, 125–127,
    230–231
Homogeneity of variance, 326, 411
Homoscedasticity, 145, 172
Huygens, C., 22
Hypergeometric distribution, 223
Hypothesis:
    alternative, 260
    directional, 275
    nondirectional, 275–276
    null, 260
    omnibus, 392
    one-sided, 275
    scientific, 258
    statistical, 260
    two-sided, 275–276
Hypothesis testing, 243, 260
    comparison with confidence interval,
        298–299
    criticisms of, 292–293
    and method of indirect proof, 260–261
    role of logic in, 262–263
    steps, 263–270
    types of errors in, 277, 280–281

Identity, 529
Independence, statistical, 195
    Pearson's chi-square test for, 477–482
        (*see also* Pearson's chi-square
            statistic)
Independent samples, 325
Index of dispersion, 99–101
    properties, 108
    relative merits, 106–107
Index of summation, 65
Inequality:
    defined, 531
    permissible operations, 531–532
Inferential statistics, nature of, 8
Interaction, 452–454

Intercept, 41
Intersection of events, 190
Interval estimate, 242
Interval measurement, 16

J distribution, 50–51
John Henry effect, 273

Kurtosis, 49, 114

Laplace, P. S. de, 22
Law of large numbers, 247
Least squares, principle of, 162
Leptokurtic distribution, 49, 114
Levels of measurement (*see* Measurement)
Linear relationship, 125, 140

Mann-Whitney U test, 502–505
    assumptions, 502
    efficiency, 506
    normal distribution approximation,
        504–505
Margin of error, 312
Marginal probability, 194
Mathematics, review of, 519–532
Mean, 64–67
    grand, 396
    merits, 73–74
    properties, 76
    of several means, 78–79
    weighted, 78–79
Mean square, 399
Measurement, 14
    interval, 16
    levels, 18
    metric (numeric), 18
    nominal, 14
    ordinal, 15
    ratio, 17
Median, 68–72
    merits, 75
    properties, 76
Mesokurtic distribution, 49, 114
Midpoint of class interval, 45
Mode, 62–63
    merits, 75–76
    properties, 76
Model equation:
    completely randomized design,
        396–397
    completely randomized factorial design,
        448
    randomized block design, 435
Moivre, A. de, 22, 231
Monotonic relationship, 149
Multicollinearity, 177
Multimodal distribution, 50
Multinomial distribution, 223
Multiple comparisons among means:
    a posteriori tests, 412
    in completely randomized factorial
        design, 454–456
    contrast (comparison), 412–416

Fisher-Hayter test, 414–416
    pairwise, 414
    in randomized block design, 440–442
    Scheffé's test and confidence interval,
        416–418
Multiple correlation, 176–177
Multiple regression, 173–176
Multiplication principle, 198
Multiplication rule of probability, 194

Neyman, J., 23
n factorial, 199, 528
Nominal measurement, 14
Nonparametric test, 501
Nonrandom sample, 9
Nonrandom sampling, 9, 208
Normal distribution, 231–232 (*see also*
        Distribution, normal)
    approximation to binomial distribution,
        236–237
    finding area under, 233–235
    history of, 22, 231
Nuisance variable, 430–433
Null hypothesis (*see* Hypothesis)
Numerator, 525

Observation, 7
Ogive, 47
Omega squared, 419,
One-sided hypothesis, 275
One-tailed test, 275
Ordinal measurement, 15
Ordinate, 41
Outlier, 109–111

Parameter, 64
Parametric tests, comparison with
        assumption-freer tests, 512–514
Partial omega squared, 442–443, 456–457
Participant matching, 341
Pascal, B., 22
Pearson, E., 23
Pearson, K., 23, 129, 468
Pearson's chi-square statistic:
    applications, 468–470
    characteristics of test statistic, 473–474
    for equality of proportions, 485–488
        degrees of freedom, 486
        with more than two response cate-
            gories, 487–488
    for goodness of fit, 470–473
        assumptions, 475–476
        degrees of freedom, 470, 474
        Yates' correction, 476
    for independence, 477–482
        assumptions, 483
        Cramér's measure of association,
            482
        degrees of freedom, 479–480
Pearson's product-moment correlation
        coefficient, 127, 129–131
        (*see also* Correlation)
Percentage frequency, 36–37

Percentile point, 94
Percentile rank, 94
    interpreting scores in terms of, 238–239
Permutation:
    $_nP_n$, 199
    $_nP_r$, 199–200
Pictogram, 53
Pie chart, 42–43
Placebo, 8
Platykurtic distribution, 49, 114
Point estimate, 242
Population, 6, 209
    conceptual, 7
    concrete, 6
    element, 6, 209
    finite, 6, 209
    identifying the, 209
    infinite, 6, 209
    intact, 340
Power, 277, 278
    calculation, 278–280
Power efficiency, 505–506
Practical significance, 282, 299–301
    completely randomized design,
        419–420
    completely randomized factorial design,
        456–457
    for $\overline{X}$, 299–301
    for $\overline{X}_1 - \overline{X}_2$, 331–332
    Pearson correlation, 317–318
    randomized block design, 442–443
    test of goodness of fit, 474–475
    test of independence, 482–483
Prediction error, 162
    and standard error of estimate, 169–170
Probability:
    addition rule, 190
    classical, or logical, view, 185
    of combined events, 190–196
    common errors in applying, 196
    conditional, 193
    empirical relative-frequency view, 186
    history of, 22–23
    marginal, 194
    multiplication rule, 194
    properties of, 189
    subjective-personalistic view, 184–185
    value, 282
Probability distribution, 213
Product of two numbers, 524
Proportionate frequency, 36–37
Proportions, test for equality, 485–488
    (*see also* z test for $p_1 = p_2$;
        Pearson's chi-square statistic)
p-value, 282–284

Qualitative variable, 12
Quantitative variable, 12
Quartile point:
    first, 92
    third, 92
Quetelet, L. A. J., 23
Quotient, 524

Radicals, operations with, 527–528
Random assignment, 337–339
Random numbers, 210
Random sample, 8, 208
Random sampling, 8, 208, 337–338
  procedures, 210–211
  versus random assignment, 337–340
Random variable, 212–213
  continuous, 213
  discrete, 213
  expected value, 215–217
  probability distribution, 213
Randomized block design, 435–440
Range, 91–92
  inclusive, 91
  noninclusive, 91
  properties, 107
  relative merits, 106
Rank correlation, 147–149
Ratio measurement, 17
Rectangular distribution, 51
Regression, 160–167
  distinguished from correlation, 124–125
  line, 162
    assumptions, 172
    of best fit, 162
    predicting X from Y, 166–167
    predicting Y from X, 161–165
    slope of, 163, 165
  multiple, 173–176
  plane, 174
Regression toward the mean, 125–126
Relationship:
  causal, 139, 339–340
  concomitant, 139, 339–340
  linear, 125, 140
  monotonic, 149
  nonlinear, 140–141
Relative efficiency, 505–506
Reliability, test-retest, 138
Residual, 162
Reversion, 126
Robustness:
  of ANOVA, 410–412
  of F test for σ_1^2/σ_2^2, 363
  of t test for μ, 265, 267–268
  of t test for $\mu_1 - \mu_2$, 326
Roots of equation, 530
Rounding numbers, 522–523
r to Z' transformation (*see* Fisher's r-to-Z'
  transformation)

Sample, 7
  nonrandom, 9, 208
  point, 188
  random, 8, 208
  space, 188
Sample size, determining:
  for one-sample t statistic for μ,
    281–282
  for one-sample z statistic for p,
    312–313

  for two-sample t statistic for $\mu_1 - \mu_2$,
    332, 346–347
Sampling:
  distribution, 220, 243
    of the mean, 244–247
    under H_0 and under H_1,
      278–280
    of t test statistic, 266–268
  fluctuation, 9
  stability, 74
  systematic, 211
  with replacement, 209
  without replacement, 209
Scale of measurement:
  interval, 16
  nominal, 14
  ordinal, 15
  ratio, 17
Scatterplot (Scatter diagram), 125
Scheffé's test and confidence interval,
  416–418
Scientific hypothesis (*see* Hypothesis)
Semi-interquartile range, 92–94
  properties, 107
  relative merits, 106
Significance level, 269
Skewness, 50, 112–113
Slope of regression line, 163–165
Snedecor, G. W., 363
Spearman's rank correlation coefficient,
  147–149
SQ3R study method, 4
Standard deviation, 95–99
  of binomial distribution, 223
  deviation formula, 97
  of discrete random variable,
    217–218
  population, 95–96
  properties, 107
  raw score formula, 97
  relative merits, 105
  sample, 95
Standard error:
  defined, 247
  of the difference between two
    means, 325
  of one-sample t statistic, 265
  of a proportion, 311
  of two-sample t statistic, 325,
    342–343
Standard error of estimate, 169–172
  assumptions in, 172
Standard normal distribution, 232
Standard score, 232–233, 238
  advantages over percentile rank,
    239–240
  kinds, 240
Statistic, 64
Statistical hypothesis (*see* Hypothesis)
Statistical independence (*see* Independence, statistical)
Statistical inference, 259

Statistical significance versus practical
  significance, 282
Statistical test, 262
Statisticians, types, 3–4
Statistics, 3
  descriptive, 7
  experimental, 23–24
  history of, 22–24, 125–127, 231
  how to study, 4–6
  inferential, 8
  national, 22
  terminal, 83
Stem-and-leaf display, 46–48
Student, 23, 266
Summation, 64–65
  index, 65
  rules, 79–81
Sum of squares, 397–398
Symmetrical distribution, 50

t test for μ, 271–273
  assumptions, 265, 267–268
  comparison with z, 265–266
  degrees of freedom, 266–267
  estimating sample size, 281–282
  sampling distribution, 266–268
t test for $\mu_1 - \mu_2$:
  dependent samples, 342–344
    degrees of freedom, 343
    estimating sample sizes,
      346–347
  independent samples, 324–326
    degrees of freedom, 325
    estimating sample sizes, 332
t test for ρ, 315
  assumptions, 315
  degrees of freedom, 315
t test for $\sigma_1^2 = \sigma_2^2$, 370–371
t' test for $\mu_1 - \mu_2$, 330
Test statistic, 248–249
  specifying the, 265–266
Transformation:
  Fisher's r-to-Z', 316
  monotonic, 15
  multiplication by positive constant,
    17
  one-to-one, 14
  percentage frequency, 36–37
  positive linear, 17
  proportionate frequency, 36–37
  z score, 232–233
Treatment, 394
  combination, 446
  effect, 396
  level, 394
Truncated range, 141–142
Two-sided hypothesis, 275–276
Two-tailed test, 275
Type I and II errors, 277, 280–281

U distribution, 50–51
Unbiased estimator, 248

Uniform distribution, 51
Union of events, 190

Validity, 138
Variable, 11
  continuous, 13
  dependent, 124
  discrete, 13
  independent, 124
  nuisance, 430–433
  qualitative, 12
    ordered, 12
    unordered, 121
  quantitative, 12
    continuous, 13
    discrete, 13
  random, 212–213 (*see also* Random
    variable)

range of, 11
value of, 11
Variance, 96
  error, 400
  of chi-square distribution, 470
  homogeneity of, 326, 411
  of t distribution, 267
Variability, chance, 9

$\hat{w}$ statistic, 474–475, 483
Wilcoxon rank-sum test, 502
Wilcoxon T test, 507–512
  assumptions, 507
  efficiency, 507
  normal distribution approximation,
    510–511

X axis, 41

Yates' correction for continuity, 476, 478
  (*see also* Continuity, correction
    for)
Y axis, 41

z score (*see* Standard score)
z test for p, 308–309
  assumptions, 309
  estimating sample size, 312–313
z test for $p_1 = p_2$:
  dependent samples, 379–380
  independent samples, 374–375
Zero, operations with, 525

Descriptive Statistics
Quick Reference

*2.2 Proportionate frequency, Prop $f = \dfrac{f}{n}$

. 2.2 Percentage frequency, $\%f = \dfrac{f}{n} \times 100$

3.3 Mean, $\overline{X} = \dfrac{\Sigma X_i}{n}$

3.4 Median, $Mdn = X_{ll} + i\left(\dfrac{n/2 - \Sigma f_b}{f_i}\right)$

3.7 Weighted mean, $\overline{X}_W = \dfrac{n_1\overline{X}_1 + n_2\overline{X}_2 + \cdots + n_n\overline{X}_n}{n_1 + n_2 + \cdots + n_n}$

4.2 Range, $R = X_{ul(\text{largest score})} - X_{ll(\text{smallest score})}$

4.2 Semi-interquartile range, $Q = \dfrac{Q_3 - Q_1}{2}$

4.2 Percentile point, $P_\% = X_{ll} + i\left(\dfrac{n(P_R/100) - \Sigma f_b}{f_i}\right)$

4.2 Percentile rank, $P_R = \dfrac{100}{n}\left[\Sigma f_b + \dfrac{f_i(P_\% - X_{ll})}{i}\right]$

4.2 Standard deviation, $S = \sqrt{\dfrac{\Sigma(X_i - \overline{X})^2}{n}}$

4.2 Index of dispersion, $D = \dfrac{DP}{DP_{max}}$

4.6 Skewness, $Sk = \dfrac{\dfrac{\Sigma(X_i - \overline{X})^3}{n}}{S^3}$

4.6 Kurtosis, $Kur = \dfrac{\dfrac{\Sigma(X_i - \overline{X})^4}{n}}{S^4} - 3$

5.3 Pearson correlation,

$$r = \dfrac{\dfrac{\Sigma(X_i - \overline{X})(Y_i - \overline{Y})}{n}}{\sqrt{\left[\dfrac{\Sigma(X_i - \overline{X})^2}{n}\right]\left[\dfrac{\Sigma(Y_i - \overline{Y})^2}{n}\right]}}$$

5.7 Spearman correlation, $r_s = 1 - \dfrac{6\Sigma(R_{X_i} - R_{Y_i})^2}{n(n^2 - 1)}$

6.2 Regression, $Y'_i = a_{Y \cdot X} + b_{Y \cdot X} X_i$

6.3 Standard error of estimate, $S_{X \cdot Y} = S_Y \sqrt{1 - r^2}$

6.5 Multiple correlation,

$$R_{Y \cdot X_1 X_2} = \sqrt{\dfrac{r_{YX_1}^2 + r_{YX_2}^2 - 2r_{YX_1}r_{YX_2}r_{X_1X_2}}{1 - r_{X_1X_2}^2}}$$

7.1 Probability of A, $p(A) = n_A/n_S$

7.3 Prob of A or B, $p(A \text{ or } B)$
$$= p(A) + p(B) - p(A \text{ and } B)$$

7.3 Prob of A and B, $p(A \text{ and } B) = p(A)p(B \mid A)$

7.4 Permutation, $_nP_n = n! = n(n - 1)(n - 2) \cdots (1)$

7.4 Permutation, $_nP_r = \dfrac{n!}{(n - r)!}$

7.4 Combination, $_nC_r = \dfrac{n!}{r!(n - r)!}$

8.3 Expected value, $E(X) = \Sigma p(X_i) X_i$

9.2 z score, $z = (X - \overline{X})/S$

10.4 Cohen's effect size, $d = \dfrac{|\overline{X} - \mu_0|}{\sigma}$

11.3 Hedges' effect size, $g = \dfrac{|\overline{X}_1 - \overline{X}_2|}{\hat{\sigma}_{Pooled}}$

15.7 Omega squared, $\hat{\omega}^2 = \dfrac{(p - 1)(F - 1)}{(p - 1)(F - 1) + np}$

17.3 Cohen's effect size, $\hat{w} = \sqrt{\dfrac{\chi^2}{n}}$

17.4 Cramér's correlation, $\hat{V} = \sqrt{\dfrac{\chi^2}{n(s - 1)}}$

*Section where statistic is described.